This book is due on the last date stamped below.
Failure to return books on the date due may result
in assessment of overdue fees.

FINES	.50 per day	

Guns

Who Should Have Them?

Guns

Who Should Have Them?

Edited by David B. Kopel

Prometheus Books
Amherst, New York

Published 1995 by Prometheus Books

99 98 97 96 95   5 4 3 2

A longer version of chapter 3 was first published in volume 80 of the *Georgetown Law Journal*. Chapter 4 contains material that first appeared in volume 20 of the *Journal of Contemporary Law*. Chapter 5, with various editorial revisions, appeared in volume 30 of the *Tennessee Law Review*. Portions of other chapters written by David Kopel have appeared in monographs published by the Independence Institute or the Cato Institute. In most cases, the chapters in this book represent substantial revisions of earlier publications.

Library of Congress Cataloging-in-Publication Data

Guns : who should have them? / edited by David B Kopel.
   p.   cm.
   Includes index.
   ISBN 0-87975-958-5 (alk. paper)
   1. Gun control—United States. I. Kopel, David B.
HV7436.G88   1995
363.3'3'0973—dc20   95-16635

CIP

Printed in the United States of America on acid-free paper

To my parents, Jerry and Dolores Kopel, who taught me the importance of the Bill of Rights, and who showed me the value of independent thinking.

Contents

7

8   Guns: Who Should Have Them?

Acknowledgments

I would like to thank Paul Blackman, Becky Dawson, Deron Dilger, Ted Harvey, Jerry and Dolores Kopel, Chris Little, Patty Price, and Edgar Suter for their assistance with this project. Errors are, of course, the authors' alone.

Finally, I am grateful to all the persons who were kind enough to supply quotes which appear on the bookjacket, but it should not be assumed that anyone who offered the quotes, or their organizations, necessarily endorses all the ideas contained in this volume.

Introduction

David B. Kopel

The great American gun-control debate shows no signs of cease-fire. In the last several years, the gun control issue has grown even more passionate. And, paradoxically, both sides of the controversy are stronger and more determined than ever.

Membership in the antigun lobbies has never been higher. With the enactment of the Brady Bill in 1993 and the federal "assault weapon" ban in 1994, Congress has gone further than ever in imposing national gun restrictions. Whereas only a few years ago enactment of the Brady Bill appeared almost impossible, by 1994 many gun control advocates were suggesting that a national handgun prohibition bill, or at least very restrictive handgun licensing, was a feasible goal within a few years. President Clinton, with the enthusiastic assistance of much of the executive branch, has put more political muscle behind gun control than any president in history.

And yet, the National Rifle Association (NRA) and other progun groups are also stronger than ever. Membership in the NRA has reached record levels. The first two years of the Clinton administration marked the best years ever for the American firearms industry, as all-time sales records set in 1993 were broken in 1994. The tremendous gun proliferation of 1993–94 was fueled in part by fears of crime, and also by fears that buying a gun in the future might become significantly more difficult.

The November 1994 elections were phenomenally successful for gun-rights forces, in large part because of record numbers of grassroots volunteers who participated. From President Clinton on down, political analysts have credited the NRA with delivering the U.S. House of Representatives into Republican hands after forty years of Democratic control. House Speaker Thomas Foley was only the most visible of nearly two dozen incumbents who were ousted in 1994 in part because of their support for gun control.

During the 1980s, media attention on gun control was focused on Washington, D.C., where the NRA succeeded in 1986 in significantly weakening the Gun Control Act of 1968. But the most important gun control action of the 1980s was at the state level, where many state legislatures enacted preemption laws which wiped out city and county gun controls. Today, only a handful of states lack preemption laws, and the NRA appears to be achieving success at rounding up the stragglers. Moreover, an idea that only a few years ago seemed absurdly radical—that citizens should be able not only to keep guns in their homes, but also to carry them on the streets for protection—is now the law in about half of the fifty states.

Perhaps the best indicator of the continuing importance of the gun issue is the tremendous proliferation of grassroots state and local progun and antigun groups. At every level, it seems, people are taking the gun issue more seriously, and getting personally involved.

The gun control debate continues to attract so much attention, from partisans on both sides of the issue, because of the fundamental values at stake. Is it legitimate to use deadly force? What is the proper relationship between the citizen and the government? Should groups which have often been considered unfit to possess firearms—namely women, blacks, and children—now be allowed to do so? Is owning a gun a basic human right, or a privilege to be carefully regulated by the government? And how can we protect children?

And, of course, the gun-control debate continues in part because America's violent crime rate, while stable over the last few years, persists at the unacceptably high level it rose to three decades ago.

For all the attention paid to the gun debate, most people are miserably informed about it, in large part because the media have done such a poor job making the public aware of relevant facts. Few people actually know what an "assault weapon" is or how often fatal gun accidents involving children actually occur. Much of what the public does know about guns is thirdhand information (or misinformation): newspaper summaries of press releases of poorly executed, misleading studies about gun crime that appear in medical journals. This book aims to raise the level of understanding about gun control by examining six controversies that have been leading elements of the control debate during the last decade.

In chapter 1, Mary Zeiss Stange looks at the issue of women and guns through a feminist lens, explaining the conflict between feminists who believe that owning a gun can be one path to empowerment and those who believe that gun ownership, as a male power device, must be rejected.

In chapter 2, I discuss the Brady Bill and other background check proposals for gun buyers. This chapter details the disparity between the extravagant statements sometimes made about background checks and the actual data. I also suggest a background check proposal that is better than both the Brady Bill and the National Rifle Association's "instant check" alternative.

Legal historians Robert Cottrol and Ray Diamond detail in chapter 3 the history of gun control as applied to blacks. They examine how, throughout most of American history, gun control has, either overtly or covertly, been used as a means of disarming black victims of white violence.

In chapter 4, I look at "assault weapons," a subject which, more than any other recent gun control issue, has been obscured by misinformation and disinformation.

A criminologist, a professor of biomathematics, a professor of medicine, and two professors of psychiatry team up in chapter 5 to analyze the "public health" literature regarding gun control. They show how ostensibly scientific research has been twisted to serve gun prohibition.

Finally, chapter 6 addresses the growing problem of children and guns. Although gun accidents involving children are growing more and more rare, violent crime perpetrated by armed juveniles is one of America's most serious problems. The chapter proposes a comprehensive agenda for fighting teenage violent crime.

In the conclusion, I set forth the policy recommendations that can be inferred from each of the previous discussions. I also propose changes in both drug and welfare policies that could lead to a long-term reduction in gun misuse.

Few readers will agree with every idea offered in this book, but I hope that every reader will come away with a deeper understanding of the gun-control question.

Some, but not all, of the authors belong to Second Amendment organizations, including the NRA. This should not disqualify them from contributing their knowledge, any more than the fact that some employees of Handgun Control, Inc., sometimes write articles on gun control should mandate that those articles be dismissed out of hand. Similarly, the fact that I am an active member of the American Civil Liberties Union (ACLU), and that my employer, the Independence Institute, has engaged in a number of projects in conjunction with the ACLU, should not prevent my arguments (in chapter 6), against censorship of media violence from being considered on their merits.

The method of this book is *not* an argument from authority. Indeed, one of the worst aspects of the gun debate is how much it depends on people who, on no basis other than their supposed authority, simply assert some fact without proving it. Just because a police chief says that "assault weapons" are commonly used in crime, it does not mean that they really are. Likewise, if the federal Centers for Disease Control and Prevention says that guns are like germs, that does not make the statement true. Thus, you should not, for example, uncritically accept the arguments in chapter 5 simply because the authors include Harvard professors and an eminent professor of medicine. Nor should you unquestioningly embrace the arguments in my own chapters simply because my previous book on gun control, *The Samurai, the Mountie, and the Cowboy: Should America Adopt the Gun Controls of Other Democracies?* was named book of the year by the American Society of Criminology's Division of International Criminology.

In contrast to the argument from authority, this book begins with substantiated facts, supported by extensive notes and references. Antigun organizations such as Handgun Control, Inc. (HCI), appear in various chapters; when authors disagree with HCI's arguments, they attempt to offer persuasive refutation, rather than simply to dismiss HCI's arguments out of hand because the arguments come from a source with a preconceived ideological position. I hope that readers will extend the same courtesy to the authors in this volume; our analysis should be criticized, when appropriate, on the basis of logic and facts, rather than dismissed on the basis of its political incorrectness.

1

Arms and the Woman: A Feminist Reappraisal*

Mary Zeiss Stange

This above all, to refuse to be a victim. Unless I can do that I can do nothing. I have to recant, give up the old belief that I am powerless and because of it nothing I can do will ever hurt anyone. A lie which was always more disastrous than the truth would have been.

Margaret Atwood, *Surfacing* (1972)

I. THE "GREAT EQUALIZER," OR TOOL OF MALE OPPRESSION?

The premise that women are helpless victims, unable to defend themselves, was entirely ignored by twelve million women who did something highly unvictimlike throughout the 1980s: they bought handguns. As violence against women reached epidemic proportions, women were not just sitting around. Quietly, carefully, with thorough training . . . while they looked after their families and tended their marriages, they were also teaching themselves to blow away potential assailants.[1]

A Lou Harris poll published in 1993 predicted that gun control might well become "the next great women's issue in the country."[2] That prediction seems to be

*The author wishes to thank, for their generous assistance, Kitty Beuchert, Professor Frances Haga, Professor Fran Hoffmann, and especially Don B. Kates, Jr.

15

coming true, though in ways perhaps not entirely foreseen by Harris. Millions of women are purchasing and using firearms in huge numbers, for recreational shooting and hunting, as well as for self-defense.[3] Women also comprise "one half of purely precautionary gun owners,"[4] i.e., those who own firearms solely for the purpose of self-protection. Of the approximately sixty-five to eighty million gun owners in America today, by conservative estimate seventeen million are female, and a far greater number than that have access to firearms owned by other members of their households.[5] Given current trends, there is no reason (other than severely restricting women's legal access to guns) why these numbers should not continue to grow. Guns and gun control are, indeed, women's issues of ever-increasing importance.

The above facts are liable to be unsettling to the majority of feminists who have tended to adhere to the conventional wisdom that to be feminist is to be antiviolence, and to be antiviolence is *ipso facto* to be antigun. Their argument surely has some merit; in the best of all possible worlds, women would not feel the need for lethal force to protect themselves or their children from abusers, known and unknown. However, in our violence-ridden society, most women have a legitimate reason to fear for their safety and the well-being of their loved ones.[6]

That a procontrol, or an antigun, position can be a valid component of feminist analysis surely goes without saying, given feminism's overriding concerns for values of peace and nonaggression. Yet it is equally reasonable to suggest that in a society where violence against women is so common, responsible gun use and ownership (and even, in some recreational contexts, enjoyment) among women ought to come under the purview of feminist theory as one valid option among many. Constructive dialogue is effectively blocked as long as women who argue for armed self-defense, for example, are branded as "right-wingers" or traitors to the cause of feminism.

The late poet Audre Lorde's statement that the Master's house will never be dismantled using the Master's tools[7] is often cited in feminist arguments against resorting to male-identified instruments of power, guns chief among them. There is a certain historical irony in this. In the last century, masters knew only too well the potential consequences of giving slaves access to firearms, which might become the means to their liberation. It is surely not an exaggeration to say that the antifeminist (and largely male) backlash precipitated by the film *Thelma and Louise* (1991) resonated with the same sense of nervousness at the prospect of armed and dangerous women as did the reaction of slaveholders faced with the potential of armed rebellion a hundred and fifty years earlier. It is perhaps with a sense of this historical irony that Naomi Wolf used Lorde's statement as an epigraph for her *Fire With Fire,* one of the very few feminist texts that view women arming themselves in a serious and positive light .

Yet Wolf paid for this apparent lapse in ideological consistency in the popular and feminist press. Laura Shapiro, in a *Newsweek* review of the book, castigated Wolf at some length for suggesting that women opting to arm themselves in self-defense might be a positive development.[8] Ann Jones, in *Ms.* magazine, summed up the sorry state of American society today by saying we live in "a world where popular, state-of-the-art, so-called feminist Naomi Wolf cites pistol-packin' mamas in NRA publications as splendid examples of 'pioneer feminism.' " A mere three issues earlier, Wolf had shared the cover of *Ms.* with three other noted feminists, for a major feature on diversity in feminist thought.[10] That one might fall so quickly, and decisively, from grace over breaking rank on the issue of women and guns suggests that, at least as far as what may be considered "mainstream" feminism is concerned, there are some areas of theory where diversity of opinion does not apply.

It also helps to illustrate the extent of controversy with which the issue of women and guns is symbolically fraught; indeed, it is such a sensitive one in feminist circles precisely because, as we shall see below, it engages so many culturally rooted ideas and assumptions about the nature of power in the hands of women and men.

In American culture, the gun is a symbol of power—*male* power—par excellence. As David Kopel writes:

> The historical reality and the lurid mythology of the gun in America continue their struggle today. Extremists on each side are drawn to the same myth. The mythology attracts some "pro-gun" types into a swaggering world of combat fatigues and hypermasculinity. The mythology convinces other Americans that the gun is horrible and evil and even demonic. While the historical reality is more complex than either extreme will admit, America's view of the history of the gun is shaped as much by the myth as by the reality.[11]

This mythologizing of the gun as cultural symbol, owing in large part to the popular arts and news media, is further complicated by the association of firearms with sexual potency. In a *New York Times* article about Hollywood's long-standing love affair with firearms (dating back to *The Great Train Robbery* [1903]), cultural critic Jeff Silverman observed in 1993 that guns have "become sex symbols—for both men and women. . . . Guns have become increasingly eroticized and increasingly prominent."[12] Noting the flurry of "bad girl" films that followed on the heels of *Thelma and Louise,* Silverman suggests that Hollywood has finally discovered the power of a big gun (like the Remington 870 shotgun wielded both by Linda Hamilton in *Terminator 2* and Michael Douglas in *Falling Down*) to "be the new Great Equalizer." He quotes Tamra Davis, director of 1992's *Guncrazy* (which he characterizes as "a triangle involving a Lolita [Drew Barrymore], a man and a gun"): "In films like 'Point of No Return' [the American remake of *La Femme Nikita*], what I hope we see is not just women with guns but women in control. We need more cinematic images of women in control."

Of course, the woman "in control" in the above instance happened to be a hired assassin. It is the appropriation of this sort of "male power" (sexual or otherwise) which rightly concerns feminists when it is posited as a goal of some sort for women.

Yet *Thelma and Louise,* the pivotal scenes of which involve shooting a rapist in cold blood and blowing away a lecherous truckdriver's semi, received widespread feminist approbation. In the year following the film's release, "Graduate of the Thelma and Louise Finishing School" T-shirts, and "Thelma and Louise Live!" buttons were prominently displayed at women's studies conferences, and at such feminist events as the April 1992 March on Washington for reproductive rights. Something about *Thelma and Louise*'s message of fighting back against abuse struck a clear and positive feminist chord.[13]

Callie Khouri, who wrote the screenplay, told *Glamour* magazine that "Every time you see a strong female character on-screen, it's helpful because it's a validation of strength." Khouri went on to remark, however, that such screen images work precisely to the extent that audiences are able to distinguish between fantasy and reality:

> People tell me Thelma and Louise are terrible role models. . . . I say, "I know. Don't try this at home!" Movies are meant to take you places that you can't go physically, but you can go emotionally. You are not supposed to give up your identity because you see something on-screen.[14]

The notion of giving up one's sexual identity seems to lie at the heart of the opposition many women have to gun use, whether in fantasy or in fact. For example, when interviewed by the *New York Times* regarding the National Rifle Association's "Refuse To Be A Victim" women's self-defense program, Handgun Control, Inc., chairwoman Sarah Brady declared: "They prey on fear, they prey on guilt. The newest twist is 'Be assertive; do what the men are doing.' Well, no, thank you, very much, those kind of men are not men in my estimation."[15]

If guns are cultural symbols of male power, and women who take up arms in self-defense (or for whatever reason) are trying to "do what the men are doing," then these women are crossing a very treacherous line, in terms of gender roles. The fact that feminists have, for the last generation or more, been on the receiving end of charges that they are "just trying to act like men" may account, at least in part, for an uneasiness with the idea of espousing guns as symbols of female empowerment.

Any aversion to firearms founded in cultural gender stereotypes is amply supported by the advice meted out in the popular media. "Should you own a gun?" asks a typical item in *Glamour.* "The answer is probably no . . ." the piece begins, and it continues by enumerating several implicit disincentives to gun ownership, among them "Are you willing to kill someone?" and "Have you considered the likelihood of a tragic accident—for example, suppose you shot a so-called intruder who turned out to be a family member come home unexpectedly?"[16] A *Vogue* article titled "What You Know About Guns Can Kill You" even more flatly rules out firearms possession as a reasonable option for women: "The familiar argument says guns don't kill, people do. But scientists now see violence as a disease, guns as *dangerous in themselves*—and women as *especially vulnerable.*"[17]

In her negative review of Wolf's *Fire With Fire,* Shapiro sarcastically strikes a warning note about Wolf's assertion that women arming themselves against abuse is a sign of so-called power feminism: "No victim feminists here by golly. (At least, not until they become victims. Studies show that having a gun at home is dangerous chiefly to the people who live there.)" An editorial in *USA Today* puts the case even more boldly. It reads, in part:

> Women of America: Watch out. The National Rifle Association is increasing its focus on you as gun owners. More of you and your children are going to die. . . . According to *The New England Journal of Medicine,* a house with a firearm is three times more likely to be the scene of a homicide, usually of a family member or friend. Those same people are 43 times more likely than an intruder to be shot. . . . Women are five times more likely to be shot dead by a spouse, boyfriend, family member or acquaintance than an unknown assailant. . . . [A]n accessible, loaded firearm in the home is a prescription for tragedy that is regularly filled. . . . They [the NRA, in its "Refuse To Be a Victim" self-defense program] merely encourage women to add to their daily peril. That's a sure path to more gun violence, more spattered blood, and more pointless death.[18]

That these and similar messages, directed at women in the popular media, reflect a virulent antigun bias is no accident. Most of the scientific studies[19] cited again and again in the press are those championed by the antigun lobby. Indeed, until relatively recently, antigun polemicists have had a "virtual monopoly of the scholarly literature" in medicine about guns and gun use.[20]

These medical studies provide grist for the mill of antigun fundraising, much of it targeted specifically at women. A good example is an elaborate fund-solicitation mailing used by the Coalition to Stop Gun Violence in 1993. The cover letter this author received began as follows:

> Like most people, Pam thought gun violence always happened to someone else.
> So she was caught off guard when she was held up at gunpoint.
> And even when she gave up her purse and ran to her car, the gunmen followed and shot her dead.
> Dear Mary Stange,
> You could be next. . . .[21]

Sarah Brady notwithstanding, the gun lobbies are not the only ones capable of preying on women's fears. The mailing went on to cite, under the heading "Frightening Gun Facts," several statistics already familiar from antigun literature, including the widely discredited finding from the *New England Journal of Medicine* that a handgun "purchased for home protection" is "forty-three times more likely to be used to kill the owner, family member or friend than it is to be fired in self-defense."[22]

Of course, as feminists have tirelessly, and rightly, insisted, women's fears are legitimate enough in a society in which, according to FBI statistics one in three women will be sexually assaulted at least once during her lifetime, and a woman is beaten every sixteen seconds. What is, frankly, odd about antigun feminism in this regard is that the same analysts who routinely, and often angrily, question the factual accuracy of the way other economic and social issues pertaining to women[23] are portrayed in popular print and the electronic media, accept uncritically the incessant warnings about the inherent dangers guns pose to women. They are also, in regard to gun regulation, willing to tolerate precisely the kind of government intrusion into individual behavior that they abhor, on sound feminist grounds, when it comes to such issues as sexual orientation or reproductive rights.

A curious picture thus emerges in antigun feminism. In rejecting firearms as symbols of male power (the "Master's tools"), those who posit an antigun position as a sine qua non of feminism run the risk of reinforcing precisely those age-old stereotypes of female weakness and vulnerability which feminist theory seeks to dismantle. That those stereotypes are powerful—indeed, powerful enough effectively to block constructive dialogue about alternative views on women and guns—is amply borne out by a consideration of the following three cases. In each instance, an "orthodox" feminist antigun position has been maintained only at the expense of rationality and an objective consideration of the facts.

II. Feminist Opposition to Firearms: Three Case Studies

A. The Rapist in the Wilderness

An unfortunate consequence of antigun feminism is the alienation of a number of women who might otherwise identify themselves as feminists, but who have become convinced by the rhetoric that feminism is indeed reducible to "politically correct" stereotypes about it. For example, Karen McNutt, an attorney specializing in Second Amendment issues who writes for *Women & Guns* magazine, appeared to have antigun feminism in mind in a column titled "Swapping Freedom For Illusion":

> We are told that guns are an evil talisman that causes crime, accidents, and even suicides. If we can only get rid of or reduce the number of guns in our society, they preach, we will have a better community. These same self-appointed determiners of "politically correct thinking" are appalled to think that women might want to have guns.[24]

Indeed, the editors of *Ms.* magazine found the mere suggestion that gun ownership and use might be appropriate for women so ludicrous that they relegated the very existence of a publication devoted to "Women and Guns" to the level of a sick joke in *Ms.*'s "The Good, the Bad, and the Absurd" roundup of 1991 events.[25] They thereby wrote off not only *Women & Guns,* but its preponderantly female readership as well, lending a good deal of credence to McNutt's criticism.

Such wholesale dismissal of an entire group, in this case women gun owners and enthusiasts, can only arise from stereotyping. An excellent example of the process at work was provided a few years ago, in an exchange of viewpoints that appeared in the *Yale Law Journal.* In an article titled "The Embarrassing Second Amendment," University of Texas law professor Sanford Levinson cogently argued the case that both in terms of the original intent of its framers and of the best insights of constitutional interpretation, the Second Amendment must be construed as guaranteeing the individual right of private gun ownership.[26] He did this to some extent against his own will, since as a self-proclaimed ACLU liberal Levinson was inclined toward strict prohibitory gun regulation. Noting a relative dearth of legal literature on the Second Amendment, Levinson ventured the suggestion that the only logical way to account for the legal academy's near-silence on what had become an explosive social issue was to acknowledge that "the Amendment may be profoundly embarrassing to many who both support . . . regulation and view themselves as committed to zealous adherence to the Bill of Rights." He concluded that it appeared easier for gun-control advocates to leave the Second Amendment to stereotypical right-wing "gun nuts" and retreat to the moralistic high ground, than to confront the fact that "what it means to take rights seriously is that one will honor them even when there is significant social cost in doing so."[27] In the name of spurring "serious, engaged discussion," Levinson urged a sort of truce in which proponents of gun regulation would cease referring to their opponents as gun nuts, while gun-control opponents for their part would refrain from dismissing him and his colleagues as "bleeding heart liberals."

In a counterpoint essay, Women's Studies professor Wendy Brown, of the University of California, Santa Cruz, castigated Levinson for upholding—in the name of Constitutional law—a macho-sexist line of reasoning that "depicts man, collectively or individually, securing his autonomy, his woman and his territory with a gun."[28] Brown admitted that she was to some extent attracted by Levinson's contention that people may, for the sake of reasoned discourse, leave their prejudices about apparent differences aside. But she contended that her own social experience, as defined by feminist analysis, flew in the face of such placid acceptance of difference. To bring this point home, Brown illustrated her objection to Levinson's defense of the right to keep and bear arms with a story about her own experience.[29]

Brown recounted the dismay she and some friends felt when they returned from a week of backpacking in the High Sierras to find that her car would not start. Stranded at a remote trailhead, they were understandably relieved to discover another vehicle parked nearby. Seeking assistance, Brown encountered in it "a California sportsman making his way through a case of beer, flipping through the pages of a porn magazine and preparing to survey the area for his hunting club in anticipation of the opening of deer season." He was wearing an "NRA freedom" cap that told her that he and she were "at opposite ends of the political and cultural universe." But, "Not feeling particularly discriminating, I enlisted his aid." After two hours of concentrated labor, the man managed to get Brown's auto running, and she and her friends were on their way.

Afterward, Brown reflected that her rescuer and she were indeed opposite numbers. He had come to the high country "preparing to shoot the wildlife I came to revere, he living out of his satellite-dished Winnebago and me out of my dusty backpack, he sustained by his guns and beer, me by my Nietzsche and trail mix." His gun (or, rather, his NRA cap, since there is no evidence that he was in fact armed on this occasion) was, however, the decisive factor separating them.

> It occurred to me then, and now, that if I had run into him in those woods with-
> out my friends or a common project for us to work on, I would have been seized
> with one great and appropriate fear: rape. During the hours I spent with him, I
> had no reason to conclude that his respect for women's personhood ran any
> deeper than his respect for the lives of Sierra deer, and his gun could well have
> made the difference between an assault that my hard-won skills in self-defense
> could have fended off and one against which they were useless.[30]

Nothing in Brown's own tale suggests that the man had in any way threatened her. Unwittingly, she therein provided an illustration of precisely the point Levinson had been making about the futility of combating one stereotype (in this case, the beer-drinking lecherous gun nut) with another (the nonviolent nature devotee). That the former is male, the latter female, is not accidental. Quite the contrary, for Brown this fact is the heart of the matter, because of the way it points to "the differences between the social positioning and experiences of men and women in our culture." Men (especially gun-wielding sportsmen) are potential rapists, women (especially left-leaning feminists?) potential victims. Feminist analysis is in this case reduced to the facile application of an unflattering stereotype, without concern for any factual evidence which might challenge its legitimacy.

Noting that another interpreter might well have seen in Brown's experience "a wonderful story about the best of America: two strangers who disagree on practically everything, ignoring differences of politics, sex, and social and economic class, cooperating in the wilderness to solve a serious problem faced by only one of them," legal scholar Douglas Laycock supplies some of the factual information which Brown had blithely overlooked:

> There is no evidence that hunters or gun enthusiasts are disproportionately prone
> to rape. One study found no correlation between reported incidents of rape and
> the number of hunting licenses issued in a jurisdiction; another study found sta-
> tistically significant negative correlations after controlling for population. A

third study found no correlation between rape and the number of subscriptions to gun and hunting magazines. A fourth study found no correlation between gun ownership and attitudes toward feminism. Guns are used in only 9 percent of all rapes and attempts, and it is a reasonable guess that nearly all of these are hand-guns.[31]

Laycock also observes that it is instructive to consider how differently this story would have been told, had Brown's car broken down in Harlem and her Good Samaritan been a young black male carrying "a gun, a beer, a porn magazine, and a boombox."

> Either her fear of rape would not have appeared in a respectable journal, or it would have appeared in a confessional tone and emphasized a very different moral. The point would have been: "He came only to help me, and I was afraid to let him; see how fear and racism distorts our whole society." The point would not have been: "I was forced to ask him for help, and it is a good thing I was not alone or he might have raped me."[32]

At a time when feminist literature on rape and sexual assault is coming increasingly under attack by interpreters who would like to write it off as simply so much antimale hysteria,[33] Brown's ungracious characterization of the man in the NRA cap is particularly unfortunate. Not only does she sound like a "victim feminist" who at heart thinks all (or most) men are rapists, she also seems utterly blind to the class snobbery implied in her anecdote. Brown also appears to be unaccountably unaware of the fact—well established in the rape literature—that the majority of rapes are committed by husbands, boyfriends, or acquaintances. Not only would rape have been unlikely in the situation she describes, her closing suggestion that the man's very assertion of his right to keep and bear arms amounts to a form of "violation" for her suggests that she is incapable of conceiving this man to be anything other than a walking embodiment of a stereotype. This is an extraordinary amount of symbolic baggage for an NRA cap to carry.

As we shall see in the next case, the antigun lobby counts upon the NRA to evoke precisely this response in people.

B. *"The Most Powerful and Evil Lobby in the World"*

According to the Coalition to Stop Gun Violence, the National Rifle Association—"the most powerful and evil lobby in the world"—is Public Enemy No. 1. "For years the NRA has terrorized, bullied and intimidated our representatives in Washington."[34] In 1993, a group of twenty-six U.S. Congresswomen decided to take on the evil lobby. The issue was women's self-defense.

The congresswomen's charge was that the NRA was exploiting women for political and financial gain. Whatever these representatives' original objective may have been, they wound up accomplishing two things. First, they helped attract far more national media attention to the NRA's newly launched "Refuse To Be A Victim" program than it otherwise would have gotten. And, second, they put themselves on record as opposing the distribution of free information, and the offering of low-cost seminars, about women's self-defense options.

While unlikely to be confused with an aggressively profeminist organization, the NRA has paid steadily increasing attention to women's concerns in the 1990s. In January 1990, a Women's Issues and Information (WI&I) Office was established. In April of 1992 both NRA magazines (*American Hunter* and *American Rifleman*) began running a bimonthly "NRA Women's Voice" column, authored by WI&I director Liz Swasey. While the stated objectives of the WI&I office include, "to promote and publicize the association and its programs to women and to increase women's participation in hunting and shooting sports,"[35] Swasey's column regularly focused on various aspects of women's gun ownership for self-protection. The NRA's official stance relative to women and guns, emphasized in one way or another in each of Swasey's columns, is summed up as follows:

> Whether for self-protection, competitive or recreational shooting, hunting or a variety of other reasons, the decision to own a firearm is a highly personal one. And while the NRA doesn't *advocate* gun ownership for everyone, it does stand completely committed to the right of the individual to *choose*—a right guaranteed by the Constitution and reaffirmed through safe, responsible and effective firearms use.[36]

With Swasey's departure from WI&I in 1994 to head the NRA's "Crime Strike" anticrime program, and the appointment of Sonny Jones (founding editor of *Women & Guns*) to head the new Women's Personal Safety office, the NRA appeared to be consolidating its efforts to make women's issues—especially those relating to self-defense, armed or otherwise—more prominent features of the organization's overall political and social agenda.

The reasons for this move were obviously complex, and fundraising—via attracting new female members—cannot be discounted as an important motivation. However, the oft-repeated charge that this amounts to crass manipulation and exploitation of women does not necessarily follow: the NRA, after all, is an advocacy organization, and it is consistent with its mission to attract like-minded members, perhaps especially from among traditionally underrepresented constituencies. Given the marked increase in female gun ownership and use over the last decade, the NRA's vigorous interest in appealing to women makes a certain amount of practical sense.[37]

Indeed, the NRA would have to be extraordinarily sexist and stupid to ignore the significant portion of the female population that appears to be in complete agreement with the NRA's agenda. An article in *Campaigns and Elections* magazine in early 1995 analyzed exit polling results from seven different states; the pollsters had listed various organizations and asked respondents, "I'd like to know for each individual organization if that group speaks for you all of the time, most of the time or some of the time." In Idaho, Oklahoma, Tennessee, and South Carolina, the percentage of female voters who said that the NRA speaks for them "all the time" was higher than the number who said that the Democratic party or the Republican party spoke for them "all of the time."[38] In Michigan, Minnesota, and Pennsylvania, the NRA finished behind the Democrats but ahead of the Republican party for "all the time" support from female voters.[39]

In terms of outreach to women who are not necessarily in complete agreement with the NRA, the centerpiece in the NRA's women's initiative is the "Refuse To Be A Victim" program, an ambitious public information effort comprised of two major parts: a national toll-free number that provides callers with information in the form of a brochure about women's self-defense strategies, and an economically priced ($20.00) three-hour self-defense seminar taught by women. In both the brochure and the seminar, firearms are briefly mentioned as among the options available to women for self-protection. The emphasis is on women's responsibly choosing from among various alternatives, and their taking positive steps to develop a "personal safety strategy."[40]

The idea of choice at the heart of the "Refuse To Be A Victim" promotional campaign ("How to choose to refuse to be a victim") has led some critics to accuse the NRA of cynically appropriating the feminist language of reproductive rights.[41] The NRA is in something of a double-bind in this regard: it either ignores the changing roles of women and draws the charge of being insensitive to women's needs and interests, or it seeks to speak to the legitimate concerns of contemporary American women, thus risking the accusation of employing exploitative tactics. Hence, the NRA's promotional literature about the program takes pains to stress that "You won't be encouraged to own a firearm. You won't be asked to join the NRA."[42]

Rep. Nita Lowey (D-NY) and twenty-five of her House colleagues,[43] however, were not inclined to take the NRA at its word. In October 1993, shortly after the NRA had launched the "Refuse To Be A Victim" seminar program in three test cities (Miami, Houston, and Washington, D.C.), the congresswomen sent a letter to NRA president Robert Corbin demanding that NRA "immediately cease your advertising campaign aimed at the women of America." The letter read, in part:

> Under the guise of providing information about ways to increase personal safety, your four-page magazine ad[44] invites women to call an NRA hotline and join the "NRA's grassroots movement," and learn about firearms.
>
> While we enthusiastically support legitimate efforts to increase personal safety awareness, your commitment to women's safety is undermined by your continued opposition to gun control legislation that would make America safer.

This ad campaign is a thinly veiled attempt by NRA to add new members and promote gun ownership by preying on women's legitimate fears of violence. Women who fear crime must not be cynically exploited as an untapped market.[45]

The letter went on to cite several bits of statistical data from "a study recently released by the *New England Journal of Medicine*"[46] and urged NRA support for the Brady Bill then pending congressional approval. It concluded, "Removing guns from our streets would certainly provide American women with more protection than the NRA."[47]

To coincide with the delivery of the letter to Corbin, Rep. Lowey announced to the press that there would be a demonstration in front of NRA's Washington headquarters. Only five of the letter's signers showed up, to be confronted by a substantial media corps, one of whom asked whether any of the demonstrators had any firsthand experience of a "Refuse To Be A Victim" seminar. None had.

Meanwhile, Tanya Metaksa, head of NRA's lobbying arm Institute for Legislative Action (ILA) also arrived, accompanied by several progun spokeswomen,[48] to hold an impromptu press conference. This quickly led to appearances by Metaksa on CNN news and Larry King's radio program, as well as the "Good Morning, America" and "Today" shows. In the first three weeks of the "Refuse To Be A Victim" program's existence, and no doubt largely owing to this national exposure, the NRA received close to five thousand requests for more information about the program.

On October 25, Metaksa, who also chairs the NRA's Women's Policy Committee, wrote a letter to the twenty-six Congresswomen. Quoting their statement of "enthusiastic" support for "legitimate efforts to increase personal safety awareness," she invited them to attend the next "Refuse To Be A Victim" seminar, scheduled for October 30. The letters were hand-delivered to Capitol Hill. None of the twenty-six women replied, or attended the seminar.

The congresswomen's response would seem to be a case of the devil you don't know being better than the one you do. It was apparently easier to demonize the NRA's effort on behalf of women's self-defense than to take any substantial steps to learn about it. Those who did, such as *Washington Post* columnist Judy Mann, reported that the NRA was indeed true to its advertising when it came to not pushing guns or NRA membership at the seminars. Mann noted that she had approached the "Refuse To Be A Victim" program as a skeptic, but had retained an open mind:

One cannot help but be somewhat skeptical about a campaign that is obviously good public relations. But the NRA didn't become the most feared lobby in the country by being out of touch with public sentiment, so it is possible that the revulsion sweeping the country over mass murder by firearms has finally gotten through to its 75-member board.

Mann came away from her investigation with an altered view of "the most evil lobby in the world"; she concluded,

> What is particularly appealing about the NRA campaign is its emphasis on the idea that there are other things women can do to ensure their safety besides getting a gun. They can refuse to be victims. This is an empowering idea. If the campaign also signals a move toward more responsible civic behavior on the part of NRA, then that should be welcomed too.[49]

Whatever one's views regarding the "deeply personal choice" of firearms ownership, an informed perspective like Mann's is clearly a more adequate response to the NRA's women's self-defense campaign than the congresswomen's knee-jerk antigun hyperbole. The same tendency toward blanket condemnation, rather than objectively reasoned investigation of the issues, characterizes the next case of feminist stereotyping as well.

C. *"Is This Power Feminism?"*

In the May 1992 issue of *Women & Guns,* Sonny Jones wrote an editorial in which she blasted feminists as "progressively militant" and hypocritically out of touch with the real-life concerns of "women like you and me." Stating (inaccurately) that groups like the National Organization for Women (NOW) did not take personal safety seriously as an issue of primary importance for women, Jones (with somewhat more accuracy) castigated feminist groups for their "categorical" opposition to "gun ownership as a viable self-defense option." She concluded that the feminist movement, in essence, had nothing to offer her or her readers, who inhabit "the land of reality."[50]

Reader response to the editorial must have come as something of a shock to Jones. A significant number of *Women & Guns* readers turned out to be self-identified feminists, who reprimanded her for selling feminism short. Jones subsequently wrote, "Reaction to the May commentary on feminism just goes to show how diverse a group gun owners really are. And despite the official positions of NOW and like organizations, we all agree that self-defense is among the most important rights of all."[51] More recently, Peggy Tartaro (Jones's successor as *Women & Guns* executive editor) commented that "Women gun owners, and our readers in particular, probably skew a whole lot more liberal than either the general gun-owning population, or than the popular conception of what a gun owner is like."[52]

That this might be the case apparently never occurred to the editors of *Ms.* magazine when, relying on the popular conception of gun owners (the stereotype created largely by the media and the antigun lobby), they set out to do a special issue on women and guns. The cover of the May/June 1994 issue featured a photo of a Smith and Wesson semi-automatic pistol (casting a hot-pink shadow), with the words "Is This Power Feminism? The Push To Get Women Hooked on Guns."

Inside were two articles, one by Ann Jones, author of *Women Who Kill,* titled "Living With Guns, Playing With Fire," the other by *USA Today* reporter Ellen Neuborne, under the title "Cashing In on Fear: The NRA Targets Women." That the "most evil lobby in the world" was the *bête noire* behind the *Ms.* articles was clear in the editorial comment preceding them:

> Just when we thought we were beginning to turn the tide in favor of gun control, along comes the NRA with a campaign that encourages women to exercise our right to "choose to refuse to be a victim." The new focus on women comes not because this organization supports our right to be free from rape and battery, harassment and discrimination, but because these sharpshooters are trying to seduce women into becoming dues-paying, gun-toting members with promises of power from the barrel of a gun.[53]

We have already seen that an objective consideration of the "Refuse To Be A Victim" campaign shows this not to be the case. Yet the power of a stereotype lies precisely in its ability to blind an already biased observer to what is before her very eyes. How else can one account for Neuborne's reiterating in her article every charge about the NRA's cynical manipulation of women and its progun ulterior motives, notwithstanding her own admission that in the seminar she in fact attended guns only "came up at the very end."[54] Neuborne does mount a valid, and important, criticism of NRA's approach in the campaign. The "Refuse To Be A Victim" materials all focus on what one instructor called " 'garden variety bad guys'—strangers who commit acts of violence. Stalking, domestic violence, and workplace violence—all major crime problems for women—were ignored."[55] Her criticism would have been more pointed, and carried more argumentative weight, had it not been accompanied by what has by now become the standard array of antigun statistics derived from the Kellermann studies, bolstered by an equally familiar conspiracy theory about the NRA's hidden agenda "to frighten women into buying guns."[56]

While Neuborne settles for rehashing antigun propaganda in the name of investigative journalism, Ann Jones's article presents a more problematic take on feminist opposition to women's gun ownership. Jones also questions the NRA's motives and its use of the rhetoric of choice, but she acknowledges that the question of armed self-defense might indeed occur to a reasonable woman faced with life in a violently antifeminist society.

> Women are fearful, yes. With good reason. But we're also beyond fear. We're fed up. . . . Women's interest in guns—such as it is—isn't just about fear. It's about fighting back.[57]

She goes on to disclose that "I know something about fighting back myself—and about the consolations of a gun." Jones had grown up hunting with her father, but gave it up at eighteen, when she shot her first deer and "the deadly and irrevocable consequence of what I was doing came home to me." However, she kept the shotgun her father had given her as a memento. Years later, on the day Martin Luther King, Jr., was assassinated, Jones borrowed a canoe and paddled into the center of a lake, where she dropped the shotgun into the water.

> I wanted to rid the world of guns and all the violence and death they seem to represent; at least I could get rid of mine. The nonviolent path of Dr. King would be my own.

Jones's symbolic resolve was to weaken twice in later life: once when, hounded by racists in the Southern town where she was teaching at an African-American college, she acquired a .38 special for self-protection, and later, when that same handgun gave her a feeling of security after she was made a victim of harassment while investigating a murder for a book she was working on. However, she eventually decided, "The threat of violence, if it makes you play by its rules, is just as deadly to the spirit as violence itself. It wasn't a gun I needed. It was courage." She disposed of the pistol.

Remarking that it saddens her now to read stories of women purchasing guns "to gain a sense of power and control . . . for I imagine them afflicted with the same incapacitating fear and the same profound anger at being made to feel afraid," Jones next recounts the story of April LaSalata. In 1988, this Long Island woman was viciously assaulted by her ex-husband, Anthony, who was charged with attempted murder as a result. When he was released on bond and the judge refused the prosecutor's request to increase bail to keep the man in jail, April LaSalata applied for a permit to carry a gun for self-protection. Her permit was denied, and within a year she was dead at thirty-four, shot twice in the head on her own doorstep, by her ex-husband.

This is an all-too-familiar scenario in American society; indeed, it is precisely the sort of data the NRA might use to build its case for women's right to armed self-defense.[58] Jones's use of it, however, defies logic. "If April LaSalata had been granted that gun permit, could she have saved herself? Maybe so. Maybe not." Jones immediately follows this equivocation by remarking, "As a practical matter, leaving the human drama aside and looking at the studies and the numbers, it doesn't make much sense to own a gun." With this cavalier dismissal of LaSalata's "human drama" (perhaps it wasn't a gun she lacked, it was courage?), Jones proceeds to recite the standard litany of "facts" derived from antigun studies.

As is the case in the Neuborne article, Jones's retreat into antigun rhetoric blunts the effect of one very solid criticism she has to make of the way gun violence is handled in our society: the fact that women who shoot men in self-defense in domestic violence situations too often receive unusually harsh prison sentences.[59] For Jones, however, it is up to the law to protect women from domestic abuse, and achieving women's safety through legal means is a job for women and men collectively. It is not, in her view, "a job to be done piecemeal by lone women, armed with pearl-handled pistols, picking off batterers and rapists one by one."

Significantly, Jones sees individual women's decisions to arm themselves as attributable, at least in part, to a widespread "mother lode of anger" among women, "a vast buildup of unrequited insults and injuries."

> Women exchange high fives in the street when Lorena Bobbitt is acquitted. Women cheer in the movie theater when Louise pulls the trigger on that scumbag wanna-be rapist in the parking lot. It's like living on an emotional fault-line; we go along calmly and then one day, boom, some little incident sets us quaking with laughter that smacks of sweet revenge.[60]

Who knows just how much anger lurks in the heart that beats beneath the "Thelma and Louise Finishing School" T-shirt, and how that anger might reasonably translate into some women's resolve to take charge of their own self-protection through responsible gun ownership? Unfortunately, Jones leaves the latter question unresolved, owing to her conviction that gun ownership inevitably represents a capitulation to male-defined institutionalized violence.

A measure of the diversity of opinion among feminists on the issue of armed self-defense did, however, emerge in the reader response to the *Ms.* antigun issue. Of the nine letters published in the September/October issue, five argued a far more balanced view of the issue of women and guns than the Jones and Neuborne articles had offered. One writer commented, "How uncharacteristically sexist for *Ms.* to treat women as a homogenous group and to portray women gun owners as in a 'panic' and as dupes of the NRA!" This self-identified gun owner (who also proclaimed her respect for women who choose not to own guns) went on to observe:

> It is ironic that on page 16 of this same issue, *Ms.* gave the armed women of the Zapatista Army of National Liberation unqualified respect and support. . . . *Ms.* apparently finds no need for an antigun stance when a worthy uprising is sanctioned and led by men.[61]

Another reader, who identified herself as an advocate of nonlethal forms of self-defense, asked:

> Instead of condescending to women with guns by viewing them as dupes of male domination, why not simply acknowledge that not all women agree on how to challenge the rape culture? Why not address gun-toting women as a competent, committed, articulate group of people with whom you disagree and then dialogue?[62]

This last question captures the essence of the problem raised by reductive feminist stereotyping of gun owners, and the general denial within feminist literature of the complexity of the issues of gun ownership and gun control. As Sanford Levinson noted, constructive dialogue can begin only when opposing sides agree to disagree with a sense of respect and mutual regard.

The most reliable factual evidence currently available in fact provides the foundation for a feminist argument in favor of women's armed self-defense. The construction of this argument, however, entails confronting and dismantling several traditional ideas about the nature of power and aggression as women and men experience them in our culture. It is to this topic we now turn in our effort toward creating the ground for constructive debate of the gun-control issue within feminism.

III. WOMEN, AGGRESSION, AND THE QUESTION OF SELF-DEFENSE

> "When I get out of here," said Ruth Childers, whose shotgun went off by accident, "I'll never have a gun around the house again." "If I ever get out of here," countered Joyce DeVillez, "I'll never have a man around the house again."[63]

The question of women's armed self-defense is clearly more complex than what the conventional feminist reductionism of "male power" versus "female nonviolence" allows. Indeed, at issue is the very nature of women's relation to violence. D. A. Clarke, a lesbian feminist, throws considerable light on the contours of the problem in an essay titled "A Woman with a Sword: Some Thoughts on Women, Feminism and Violence." Clarke wants to call radically into question feminism's too-ready reliance upon strategies of nonviolence, especially in response to male sexual assault and battery. She acknowledges that nonviolence can indeed be a powerful form of resistance to oppression. But, she shrewdly observes, nonviolence is powerful and effective only when practiced by people who clearly *could* resort to violent force should they so choose. Women's advocacy of nonviolence tends to be ineffective, she observes,

> because women are traditionally considered incapable of violence, particularly of violence against men. . . . One of our great myths is that a "real lady" can and shall handle any difficulty, defuse any assault, without ever raising her voice or losing her manners. Female rudeness or violence in resistance to male aggression has often been taken to prove that the woman was not a lady in the first place, and therefore deserved no respect from the aggressor or sympathy from others.[64]

It may seem, at first blush, as if feminist theory would be the last place one would look to find conventional images of "femininity" or ladylike behavior. Yet, as we saw in the cases of Wendy Brown and Ann Jones above, cultural stereotypes of female vulnerability and nonaggression can all too easily slip into the guise of feminist analysis. Feminist psychologist Naomi Goldenberg sees in this tendency a real pitfall for feminism:

> For a long time, an important part of feminist ideology has been the relative innocence of women in comparison with men. As so many fine theorists argue, because women have not been the direct architects of violent institutions, they are more likely to dismantle those institutions. . . . However, if we women are to be successful at creating more humane institutions, we must not become too enamoured with a rhetoric of female purity.[65]

She cites Melanie Klein's observation that attempts to focus solely on the "positive, well-wishing efforts" of persons (male or female), without acknowledging aggression as a nasty fact of human psychology, are "doomed to failure from the beginning."[66]

Studies show that women are clearly as capable of aggression as men; gender differences in aggressive behavior arise from cultural stereotypes that are internalized at a very early age, with the result not only that girls grow up seeming "naturally" less inclined toward aggression, but also feeling more anxiety about their aggressive tendencies.[67] Girls learn very early on that aggressive behavior is not an appropriate or effective option for them.

> By the age of two, girls' aggression is much more likely to be ignored by playmates than is boys', and this lack of response is very effective in stopping behavior. Boys are overwhelmingly more successful than girls in using aggression to gain compliance from another child. So the little girl learns not only that aggression is emotionally dangerous but that it doesn't get her what she wants.[68]

Aggression comes to be identified with masculinity and male power. For a man, to be aggressive is to be in control; for a woman, it is to be out of control. Thus, the image of a woman "armed and dangerous"—the woman who can fight back when attacked—is extremely problematic, for both men and women.[69] According to psychologist and criminologist Anne Campbell:

> The very use of violence clearly casts a woman in the role of villain. Boys recognize bad guys by their refusal to follow the rules of fighting. Girls recognize bad women by their use of aggression at all. Good girls don't fight.[70]

And they certainly don't fight back.[71]

While feminist psychology has in the last generation or so made great strides in laying bare the sexist underpinnings of gender-role socialization, it has tended to do an end-run around the issue of female aggression, seeking in general to celebrate women's skills for "affiliation" and peacemaking.[72] Yet, as Campbell notes,

> By the 1970s and 1980s, women's aggression had become harder and harder to ignore. Female criminologists began to write about this taboo subject, and national surveys revealed women's high level of aggression in the home. Instead

of putting a spotlight on the new findings, however, these uncomfortable events triggered the minimization phase. Men preferred not to dwell on women's aggression because it was an ugly sign of potential resistance. Women's groups colluded with them; to recognize its existence would draw attention away from men's far more lethal aggression as well as highlighting undesirably assertive qualities in a group they wanted to depict as victims. Most violent offenders were men, so women's aggression was not a serious social problem. It could be studied as a curiosity, an aberration, characteristic of very few women but not weighty enough to join the mainstream social agenda.[73]

To the extent to which female aggression remains viewed as essentially pathological, feminist arguments grounded in an ethic of nonviolent resistance are fundamentally meaningless. This is the irony that Clarke points to when she argues that nonviolence would only really make sense as a political and ethical position were more women willing to engage in violent resistance against aggression:

> If the risk involved in attacking a woman were greater, there might be fewer attacks. If women defended themselves violently, the amount of damage they were willing to do to would-be assailants would be the measure of their seriousness about the limits beyond which they would not be pushed. If more women killed husbands and boyfriends who abused them or their children, perhaps there would be less abuse. A large number of women refusing to be pushed any further would erode, however slowly, the myth of the masochistic female which threatens all our lives.[74]

Naomi Wolf strikes a similar note when she suggests that one effective strategy for rape prevention might well be publicizing the growing number of women who are armed and potentially dangerous to attackers. She writes:

> I don't want to carry a gun or endorse gun proliferation. But I am happy to benefit from publicizing the fact that an attacker's prospective victim has a good chance of being armed. . . . Our cities and towns can be plastered with announcements that read, "A hundred women in this town are trained in combat. They may be nurses, students, housewives, prostitutes, mothers. The next women to be assaulted might be one of these."[75]

Antigun feminism, of course, would argue that this is not an effective strategy for women, appealing to the conventional wisdom that it tends to be more dangerous to resist an attacker, especially to use armed resistance,[76] than it is to try to flee, to talk him out of it, or ultimately to submit. However, the commonplace idea that aggressive resistance spurs more violent attack is increasingly being called into question by empirical data.

In one major rape study conducted by Sarah Ullman and Raymond Knight of

Brandeis University, two facts emerge with startling clarity. One is that women who employ forceful resistance stand a higher chance of avoiding rape than do those who attempt such nonforceful strategies as fleeing, pushing the offender away, pleading, or reasoning. The other is that nonforceful verbal strategies actually exacerbate the situation:

> Research on rapist motivation suggests that some offenders seek to feel power and control over a weaker person. . . . Such nonforceful verbal, sex-stereotypical responses (e.g., begging, pleading, and reasoning) following violent physical attacks might thus coincide with how many rapists want a woman to act.[77]

They conclude, therefore, that "women should be encouraged to scream and fight when physically attacked,"[78] rather than conform to behavior dictated by gender stereotypes.

Overall, the more violent the initial attack, the higher the chance of a woman's being raped, no matter what she does. However, Ullman and Knight argue, along with other researchers, "resistance must be at an equal level to the offender's attack to avoid rape."[79] There is simply no empirical evidence that a woman's forceful resistance makes her more likely to be raped; indeed, the evidence implies quite the opposite. Ullman and Knight focused their research on stranger rape, but suggest that there is good reason to infer that forceful self-defense strategies may work equally well in situations of acquaintance and marital rape.

Their suggestions are borne out by another study, conducted by Frances Haga and a team of researchers from North Carolina State and Virginia Commonwealth Universities. Driving their research was a question "of central concern to all women":

> What's a woman to do to defend herself, and why does whatever she actually does in her own physical defense upset people enough to seem to be always telling her she should have done something else?[80]

Utilizing a telephone survey of nearly ten thousand respondents, the researchers verified what will come as no surprise to any woman: the perception of what constitutes violent crime against a person, and that person's appropriate level of response, depends very much upon whether the perpetrator of the violence is a stranger or an acquaintance. When the attacker is a stranger, "we can envision ourselves responding with sufficient unmitigated violence to end the attack." Hence, notwithstanding the conventional prescription of nonviolent resistance, there tends to be fairly unified social support for a woman who does manage to exercise lethal force against an unknown assailant (the so-called dark stranger in sociological literature).

But, as we know, the great majority of attacks against women are not stranger rapes or random predatory violence. The woman who seeks to use forceful self-defense at home finds lacking the public approbation that would come her way, were she to have exerted the same level of resistance against a stranger. Haga and her associates locate the problem in patriarchal domestic arrangements:

> Women will continue to fear assault from strangers, but it turns out that the people actually attacking them are people known to them, where all the dynamics of ending the attack are fraught with the constraints of civilized hierarchical arangements, second-guessing and one-ups-personship.

Haga's study amply demonstrates that the "blame the victim" reflex is alive and well in the popular mind, though in the wake of the women's movement it now takes the form less of saying the woman "brought on" the attack than of asking what she could have done (nonforcefully) to avoid it. Haga concludes:

> Intuitively, women appear to understand that half the battle of surviving physical/sexual assault is to have conducted themselves "with common sense" for so long, with so many public witnesses and personal friends of irreproachable character that if any criminal predator crashes through the fences of common sense everyone will know that she always locked every door and it wasn't her fault. If as much energy were directed into repelling assailants as is expended in avoiding blame for being in the wrong place at the wrong time, women could be even more successful in defending themselves against predatory attack.

Prior to the telephone survey, Haga had conducted another study which she called the "Images of Fear" project, in which she sought to gauge men's and women's responses to pictorial images of gun-armed women, many of them in clear situations of danger. Noting the "unusually emotional" reactions of her respondents, Haga reports:

> People seemed to have already developed intensely held answers to the question of *whether or not women should be defending themselves at all,* and nobody seemed to be wondering who women might be arming themselves against, and with what?[81]

Ambivalence about women's armed self-defense arises both from men's and women's subjective impressions about what is appropriate female behavior, and from commonly held cultural views about women's relationship to violence. Haga and her associates concluded that:

> the growth in female gun ownership may be in response to perceived risk from predatory crime [i.e., the "dark stranger" against whom, if anyone, it is arguably all right for a woman to arm herself], while resistance to female gun-handling may be due to male perception of being at increased risk in domestic violence.

This, of course, recalls the oft-cited argument, derived from the Kellermann studies, that the presence of a gun in the home makes spousal homicide more likely. And indeed, women who kill their husbands most often use a firearm to do it.[82] Yet, submerged in the statistics is the large number of domestic violence cases in which the killing was in self-defense. As to the legitimacy of men's fears of female retaliation, Edgar Suter says of Arthur Kellermann's study of "Men, Women and Murder":

> Almost all the "spouses and domestic partners" killed by women each year are the very same men, well known to the police, often with substance abuse histories, who have been brutalizing their wives, girlfriends and children. . . . The most meaningful conclusion from this study, the conclusion missed by Kellermann and Mercy, is the tremendous restraint shown by women, that they kill so few of their contemptible abusers.[83]

That more women do not resort to killing in self-defense probably has less to do with any incapacity (real or perceived) for aggression, than with the structure of the law. Whether in situations of domestic battery or predatory violence, lethal-force self-defense is only a right under the law when the victim is threatened with death or grievous bodily harm. Recently, feminist legal theory has begun to question the role of sex-bias in self-defense law, especially with regard to when the "reasonable woman" is justified in believing she is under threat of great or lethal bodily injury.[84] However, the law has a difficult time deciding whether rape and other forms of sexual assault constitute, in themselves, grievous bodily harm.[85] University of Maryland law professor Robin West observes:

> Sexual invasion through rape is understood to be a harm, and is criminalized as such, only when it involves some other harm: today, when it is accompanied by violence that appears in a form men understand (meaning plausible threat of annihilation); in earlier times, when it was understood as theft of another man's property.[86]

As Wendy Williams of Georgetown Law School points out, thanks to gender-role stereotypes that are literally millennia old, the law continues to define rape as a sexual act (rather than an act of violence), and sex as something a man does to a woman. The male is the sexual aggressor, so the problem for police and the courts revolves around whether the woman consents, submits, or declines.[87]

This fact helps shed light on the question that emerged from Haga's "Images of Fear" study, i.e., *whether or not women should be defending themselves at all.* According to the conventional wisdom, women should look elsewhere for protection: to the men in their lives (though too many of these are the source, not the solution, of the problem), or to the police and courts. Yet the police often cannot be counted upon to provide protection for private citizens, and restraining orders against abusers and stalkers are notoriously ineffective.[88] This leads Don Kates to ask:

> How does society benefit if, instead of shooting the ex-husband who breaks into her house, a woman allows herself to be strangled because the civilized thing to do is to wait for him to be arrested for her murder? Far from advancing the cause of rational gun control, such attitudes actually retard it by creating "straw men" which aid the gun lobby in diverting attention from serious arguments for control. Unfortunately, such extreme attitudes seem to have played a major part in shaping the ideology and rhetoric of the gun control movement and have particularly influenced its analysis of defensive gun use.[89]

The same attitudes led to an astonishing arrogance on the part of some apologists for the antigun movement. Arthur Kellermann told an interviewer for *Health* magazine that "I don't think, in good conscience, I could advise a woman to get a handgun. Dial 911. Get an alarm instead."[90] This in itself is hardly a surprising comment, coming from the lead author of the several studies that drive the antigun lobby's campaign. What is rather more surprising is his admission, in the same article, that, "If you've got to resist, your chances of being hurt are less the more lethal your weapon. . . . If that were my wife, would I want her to have a thirty-eight special in her hand? . . . Yeah."[91]

Kellermann appears to be assuming here that the only sort of violence that could possibly befall his wife is random, predatory violence; hence, his reaction may be consistent with the findings of Haga's study about the sort of violent resistance permitted women in polite society.[92] The *Health* article reiterates the commonplace that "most" violent crimes occur away from home. However, random predatory violence is statistically less likely to happen to a woman than to a man.[93] As Kates has pointed out, most of the arguments typically employed by those who want to severely restrict or ban handgun use and ownership arise from middle-class, Caucasian, male experience.[94] The same is true for most of the crime reported on the evening news. Robbery, mugging, and assault—random violence for the most part, and for most individuals once-in-a-lifetime occurrences—are legitimate fears primarily for white men; thus it is only from a white male perspective that the argument that most violence occurs outside the home could make much sense as an argument against gun ownership in the home.

The claim that violence overwhelmingly occurs outside the home smacks of middle-class elitism, and—despite all protestations to the contrary—is inherently antifeminist. It erases domestic battery and acquaintance rape as crimes committed against women, cutting across all ethnic and economic categories and most usually in the home.[95] It also ignores the everyday reality of criminal violence in poor, generally nonwhite, neighborhoods and housing projects, violence which impacts nonwhite men and especially nonwhite women in disproportionate numbers.[96]

One can only marvel at the inconsistency implicit in Kellermann's allowing his wife a gun (in the abstract), while doing all he can to deprive women of the option of arming themselves against attack.[97] A kindred sort of middle-class tunnel vision is reflected in Ann Jones's reply to a question from *Ms.* regarding readers' responses to her antigun article. When asked, "What do we tell women who feel the police won't help them?" Jones responded:

> That's a good question. The alternative may be to go underground, and many women do that. . . . I got letters, too, from women who said that they managed to save themselves with a gun, and I think it's a terrible commentary on how we live now. I would suggest that women go underground, but I understand why many women don't.[98]

Exactly what kind of feminism sees the best alternative responses to male violence being either going "underground" or engaging in hand-wringing about the terrible state of things? The desire Jones shares with her colleagues at *Ms.* to imagine a better world, a world in which women could live in freedom from fear, is laudable. But what are women at risk to do in the meantime, while she and women of like persuasion debate nonviolent strategies for building that world? As Carol Ruth Silver and Don Kates remark, "musings about better solutions are of very little aid to a woman who is being strangled or beaten to death."[99] Regarding all those potential dangers of gun ownership and use repeated over and over by the antigun lobby, they go on to say:

> We find the dangers of individual choice considerably more acceptable than the arrogation of decision-making to a callous bureaucracy which sees to its own protection (and that of an influential, elite few others) while it cannot and will not provide protection to the ordinary individual to whom it denies a permit.[100]

Indeed, the gun issue for women seems to come down to the matter of choice, in the best feminist sense of that term. There is inevitably some risk involved in any choice as consequential as gun ownership; but ought not that risk be weighed by the individual woman herself, rather than by a paternalistic system that may not really understand her best interests, let alone share them? Thus, Ann Japenga summed up her investigative report on women's defensive gun ownership:

> For a woman considering this decision, the final call, in part, has to do with whether you believe people are basically reliable or unreliable. . . . This is where Kleck [Kellermann's opponent in the gun-control debate] and Kellermann really part ways. Kleck gives women credit for being able to make sound judgments. "A woman considering whether to get a gun is in a better position than any conceivable researcher to judge the likelihood that there's someone in her household—her or anyone else—who's likely to slaughter someone," he says.[101]

As we saw at the outset, growing numbers of women are discounting conventional wisdom about female passivity, and are making informed decisions to purchase firearms today. It remains to consider who these women are, what packing a firearm means to them, and what it may mean more broadly in the context of a rapidly changing society.

IV. WOMEN, FIREARMS, AND EMPOWERMENT

> The real issue has to do with the use of lethal force, not with the means . . . the real issue is not the polemics of guns versus no guns; rather, for some women it is the choice of being victor or victim.[102]

Feminism is surely in some ways responsible for the large number of women who say they are arming themselves out of a deep sense that their self-protection is worth fighting for. Are these women, then, capitulating to male violence, or are they—as Wolf suggests—fighting fire with fire? Gun owner Leslita Williams, a forty-four-year-old librarian, responds this way:

> So much of nonviolent philosophy was dreamed up by men who didn't have to worry about the kinds of violence women face today. . . . Everyone has to decide for herself. . . . In some ways I feel buying a gun is selling out. But the bottom line is, there is a war going on out there. You've got to do what it takes to stay alive.[103]

Williams decided to purchase a handgun ten years ago, when she and her women friends were terrorized by a rapist on the loose in their city (Athens, Georgia). Eight women, all of them "weaned on sixties-style nonviolence," enrolled in an armed self-defense course, meeting together in a consciousness-raising discussion over pizza after each class session. Ultimately, four of the women decided against arming themselves, arguing "We'd be stooping to the level of the enemy." Williams and three others judged a pacifist approach to be incongruent with the fact of a rapist at large.

Two things stand out about this anecdote. One is that it clearly exemplifies that the choice to arm oneself may certainly arise from a commitment to feminist politics and practice: that is, from the conviction that women's lives, safety, and peace of mind matter, and that it is up to women themselves to take responsibility for their own well-being. The other is that these women, in deciding either for or against gun ownership, had made an informed choice; they had not relied upon press reports or propaganda to make up their minds. As it turns out, both these facts are characteristic of women who own guns.

Hard data about women gun owners are not easy to come by. One reasonably reliable source of information is a reader survey published by *Women & Guns* magazine in 1994.[104] In light of this survey, Leslita Williams appears to be a fairly typical woman gun owner. The majority of women responding to the survey (52 percent) were middle-aged, between thirty-six and forty-nine years old, and 70 percent were married. Two-thirds had college or advanced degrees (34 percent had graduated from college, and an additional 32 percent had completed some form of postgraduate degree work);[105] by occupation they ranged from housewives' to professionals. An impressive 87 percent had taken some form of firearms instruction. Among reasons for gun ownership, 68 percent listed self-defense,[106] and the firearms of choice tended to be larger-caliber handguns. While only one-third of respondents had themselves been victims of serious crime, a significant 82 percent believed crime was on the increase in their locality (which tended to be rural and small town/city, probably reflecting among other things the relative difficulty of procuring firearms permits and instruction in many major population centers). Ninety-six percent were registered voters, as compared to 75 percent of the eligible voting population, indicative of a high level of political interest and engagement.

Interestingly, and no doubt reflecting the fact that *Women & Guns* counts among its readers a fairly large proportion of persons who might be classed not merely as gun owners, but as gun-enthusiasts,[107] the average length of time respondents had owned firearms was eleven and a half years, and on the average the women owned two or more firearms (long guns included).

In 1991, *Women & Guns* had published other survey data, collected by Fran Haga, reflecting the experience of women newer to gun ownership. Haga's survey was based upon data collected during a series of women-only firearms instruction clinics offered during the summer of 1990 in Raleigh, North Carolina.[108] All participants in the clinics were novice shooters. They had come for instruction primarily out of concern for firearm safety and proficiency. As one woman phrased it (summarizing, Haga says, the "reasons given by the majority"), "I desire to become proficient in the use of my handgun. I've had little experience/exposure to handguns but have decided to consider it as an option for my personal safety."

In other key respects, however, their demographics looked much like those of the more experienced gun owners in the 1994 survey.[109] Sixty-five percent were over thirty years of age; half were heads of households. Over half (56 percent) had a college or advanced degree, and an additional 35 percent had "some college." Fifty-three percent listed their occupation as "professional", and 75 percent were registered voters.

Given the information yielded by these two surveys, it strains credulity to regard women gun owners as merely the unwitting dupes of the gun lobby. No one appears to be coercing them into considering gun ownership, and in fact their response to the prospect of firearms possession and use shows far more responsibility than that typically shown by novice, and even some experienced, male gun owners. Owing largely to ingrained cultural stereotypes, many teenage boys and adult men seem to believe that gun use should be natural, even instinctual, for them. Women tend to approach firearms—whether for self-protection, hunting, or recreational shooting—with far more respect, and more willingness to learn, and abide by, rules of safe handling and operation.[110]

Women also approach gun use with a somewhat greater sense of urgency than men typically do. In light not only of the violence of American society, but also of the social and cultural proscriptions against women's armed self-defense, gun ownership for women is necessarily serious business. This is particularly borne out by one hypothetical question that was included in the 1994 survey. *Women & Guns* asked its readers, "If it were illegal for you to carry a handgun for personal protection, and you felt threatened, would you carry [a gun] anyway, or obey the law?" Ninety-one percent of respondents said they would carry one anyway.[111]

What does it take to induce nine out of ten individuals in a sample of highly educated, socially responsible, and politically active women to readily imagine defying the law?[112] Tanya Metaksa has commented, relative to women's right to gun ownership, "There is a closet sisterhood of women who believe [in gun ownership] no matter what the law is."[113] Might this "closet sisterhood" be a counterpart to Ann Jones's women who opt to go "underground"? And should not all these women, who share so many fundamental concerns and experiences, be able to dialogue openly with one another?

Surely, the same sense of urgency is at work in both cases. Self-defense expert Paxton Quigley writes:

> As a former campus Vietnam War peace demonstrator and an early staff member of the first national gun-control organization, I have always championed the causes of peace and nonviolent behavior. But as a mother of two sons, I have always recognized in me a deeper, almost animal-like rage capable of causing me to do anything within my power, even kill, to protect my children. Every mother knows this undercurrent; we would die for our children, and most of us would kill to protect them. In a way, a person must know this warrior spirit is there, and can be called upon in a life-or-death crisis, even to think it would be possible to shoot someone in self-defense. If you recognize this kind of instinct in yourself, then I would say you should continue with your plans to learn self-defense skills with a gun.
>
> If, on the other hand, you have never been in touch with a feeling like that, and believe completely that you could not possibly fight back in a life-threatening crisis, do not buy a gun, whatever you do.[114]

Gun ownership is obviously not the best choice for every woman (nor for every man). But for those who approach it responsibly, it can be an empowering choice, both on the practical and on the symbolic level.

We saw early on that the gun is a potent cultural symbol of power; to a broader extent this is true of all arms. D. A. Clarke recognizes this with reference to the sword:

> A woman with a sword . . . is a powerful emblem. She is no one's property. A crime against her will be answered by her own hand. She is armed with the traditional weapon of honor and vengeance, implying both that she has a sense of personal dignity and worth, and that efforts against that dignity will be hazardous to the offending party.[115]

There is historical precedent for Clarke's assertion here. Don Kates remarks on the ancient symbolic significance of arms as signaling the status of free person: "From Anglo-Saxon times 'the ceremony of freeing a slave included the placing in his hands of' arms 'as a symbol of new rank.' "[116] In this contextual setting, the sword or gun is no longer the "Master's tool" of oppression, but rather a sign of equality among persons.

In 1792, in the heat of the French Revolution, three hundred Parisian women presented the first of several petitions to the Legislative Assembly arguing their "natural right" to organize themselves into a unit of the National Guard. According to feminist historian Dominique Godineau:

> To be part of the armed organization of the sovereign people was one of the fundamental elements of citizenship . . . . With this demand, which would be repeated several times by 1793, these militant women laid claim to one of the rights of citizenship and thus to a place for themselves in the political sphere. Their wish to bear arms was not simply a matter of patriotic sentiment . . . it transcended sentiment to become a matter of power, of citizenship, and of equal rights for women.[117]

Then, as too frequently still, the women's request for equality on both the experiential and symbolic planes was met by the political and intellectual establishment with gasps of admonishment over the hazards inherent in inverting the "order of nature," as well as fears of the prospect that "a society destabilized by confusion of the sexes leads inevitably to chaos."[118]

Similar fears have apparently ruled gender politics in Switzerland, where "since 1291, when the people's assemblies formed circles in the village squares, and only men carrying a sword could vote, weapons have been synonymous with citizenship." David Kopel observes that "this tradition helps explain why the political and social emancipation of women has taken so much longer in Switzerland than in the rest of the Western world."[119]

The equation—actual as well as symbolic—of arms and citizenship may seem too politically charged for some tastes. Yet since the dawn of human time, men have in various ways sought to keep arms out of the hands of women. The discrete political and psychological reasons for the disarming of women fall outside the purview of this chapter. But the social consequences, in terms of women's lives and livelihoods, are all too apparent in contemporary America. So, too, as a result of the women's movement, are women's expanded options for confronting their history of disempowerment.

The traditional figure of Justice—an armed woman—is blind. When it comes to women's right to self-protection and freedom from fear, it is time to take the blindfold off that woman with a sword. Those millions of women who are taking charge of their own security, through firearms and other nonpassive means, present a forceful model of social and psychological empowerment. In the evolution of society toward genuine equality of the sexes, the "great equalizer" surely has a place.

NOTES

1. Naomi Wolf, *Fire With Fire: The New Female Power and How It Will Change the 21st Century* (New York: Random House, 1993), p. 216.

2. Associated Press report, "Support Grows for Plugging Handgun Sales," *Billings* (Montana) *Gazette,* June 4, 1993, p. 1. Harris likened the galvanizing of public opinion on the gun control issue to the earlier "crystallization of public support for abortion rights."

3. In fact, the National Sporting Goods Association reports that in the three years from 1989 to 1992, proportionally more women bought long guns for hunting or target shooting than purchased handguns. Grits Gresham, "Women Take the Field," *Sports Afield,* May 1994, p. 50. However, among women who own guns for multiple purposes, 68 percent cite self-defense as one of their reasons for arming themselves. Peggy Tartaro, "A Picture of Women Gun Owners," *Women & Guns,* March, 1994, p. 31.

In the 1980s and 1990s, the growing attention being paid to armed women has often been accompanied by the suggestion that women are arming themselves in record numbers. The precise number of armed women is not the focus of this chapter; instead, the chapter evaluates, from a feminist viewpoint, the decisions of the millions of women who have chosen to arm for protection, and the criticisms of those women by some feminists.

One recent study, conducted by the National Opinion Research Center, is widely cited for the proposition that there has not been an increase in female gun ownership. See Tom W. Smith and Robert J. Smith, "Changes in Firearms Ownership Among Women, 1980–1994," paper presented at the annual meeting of the American Society of Criminology, Miami, November 1994. This paper should, perhaps, not be considered the final word on the subject. The percentage of women owning guns fluctuates wildly according to the paper's data: The percentage starts at 10.5 in 1980, increases by nearly half, to 14.5 in 1982, falls by over a third to 9.3 in 1989, again rises by half to 13.8 in 1993, and then settles off at 12.7 in 1994. Whatever the trends of female gun ownership in the last fifteen years, it seems unlikely that the period has seen two separate, major booms punctuated by one major bust that have eluded the attention of other observers and social scientists. The data do show an increase in the percentage of women owning firearms from 10.5 percent in the first year (1980) to 12.7 percent in the final year (1994). Ibid., p. 12, Table 1. Many women who may not report that they "own" a gun may use a gun formally owned by someone else in their household, such as a husband.

4. See Don Kates, *Guns, Murders and the Constitution: A Realistic Assessment of Gun Control* (S.F., Pacific Research Institute for Public Policy, 1990), p. 31.

5. Liz Swasey, then director of Women's Issues at the National Rifle Association, in an

interview reported by Bryan Miller in "Guns and Women," *Chicago READER,* February 4, 1994, p. 11. Swasey explained that the NRA estimates there are between fifteen and twenty million women gun owners. She also noted that the National Opinion Research Center, in a recent annual survey, had reckoned that thirty-four million American women have "access to firearms."

6. See, e.g., Margaret Gordon and Stephanie Rigor, *The Female Fear: The Social Cost of Rape* (Chicago: University of Illinois Press, 1989).

7. See Audre Lorde in Cherrie Moraga and Gloria Anzaldua, eds., *This Bridge Called My Back: Writings of Radical Women of Color* (Latham, N.Y.: Kitchen Table Press, 1983).

8. Laura Shapiro, "She Enjoys Being a Girl," *Newsweek,* November 15, 1993, p. 82. It is worth noting that Wolf's discussion of women and guns occupies a total of six pages in a 353-page book, infinitesimal in comparison to the relative page-space Shapiro devoted to critiquing it.

9. Ann Jones, "Living With Guns, Playing With Fire," *Ms.,* May/June 1994, p. 44.

10. "No, Feminists Don't All Think Alike (Who Says We Have To?)," *Ms.,* September/October 1993. The other analysts featured in the round-table discussion were Gloria Steinem, bell hooks, and Urvashi Vaid; see pp. 34–43.

11. David B. Kopel, *The Samurai, The Mountie, and The Cowboy: Should America Adopt the Gun Controls of Other Democracies?* (Amherst, N.Y.: Prometheus Books, 1992), p. 346.

12. Jeff Silverman, "Romancing the Gun," *New York Times,* June 20, 1993.

13. Naomi Wolf remarks about the film's popularity among female audiences: "They were cheering the public affirmation of the part of themselves that was no longer content to just take it, whatever 'it' might be, in silence any longer." Wolf, *Fire With Fire,* p. 38.

14. "Women As Action Heroes," *Glamour,* March 1994, p 153. Original italics.

15. Melinda Henneberger, "The Small Arms Industry Comes On to Women," *New York Times,* October 24, 1993.

16. "Should You Own a Gun?" *Glamour,* January 1994, p. 44.

17. Steve Fishman, "What You Know About Guns Can Kill You," *Vogue,* October 1993, p. 142. Italics added.

18. "Targeting Women," *USA Today,* May 24, 1994, p. 12A.

19. Chief among them: A. Kellermann et al., "Gun Ownership as a Risk Factor for Homicide in the Home," *New England Journal of Medicine* 329, no. 15 (1993): 1084–91; A. Kellermann and D. Reay, "Protection or Peril? An Analysis of Firearms-Related Deaths in the Home," *New England Journal of Medicine* 314 (1986): 1557–60; A. Kellermann et al., "Suicide in the Home in Relationship to Gun Ownership," *New England Journal of Medicine* 327 (1992): 467–72; A. Kellermann and J. Mercy, "Men, Women and Murder: Gender-Specific Differences in Rates of Fatal Violence and Victimization," *Journal of Trauma* 33 (1992): 1–5; J. Sloan, A. Kellermann, et al., "Handgun Regulations, Crime, Assaults and Homicide: A Tale of Two Cities," *New England Journal of Medicine* 319 (1988): 1256–62.

For critiques of the methodological problems raised by these and other poorly reasoned antigun articles in the medical literature, see Edgar A. Suter, "Guns in the Medical Literature—A Failure of Peer Review," *Journal of the Medical Association of Georgia* 83 (March 1994): 133–48; Miguel A. Faria, "Second Opinion: Women, Guns and the Medical Literature—A Raging Debate," *Women & Guns,* October 1994, pp. 14-17, 52-53. See chapter 5 of this book.

20. Don Kates, "The Value of Civilian Handgun Possession as a Deterrent to Crime or a Defense against Crime," *American Journal of Criminal Law* 18 (Winter 1991): 115, 130–31. Elsewhere, Kates notes some "remarkable aspects" of the firearms-related medical literature: "One is that firearms and their ownership are invariably discussed as social pathology rather than as a value-neutral phenomenon. . . . The only admissible firearms article topics in medico-public health journals are problematic: gun accidents, gun violence, gun ownership among extremist groups. . . . These things are seen as fairly representing the 50 percent of American households that contain guns. It never seems to have occurred to the gatekeepers of the medico-public health literature that gun ownership could present any issue worthy of nonproblematic or

neutral study." Don Kates, "A Controlled Look At Gun Control: A White Paper on Firearms and Crime in Connection with the Author's Oral Presentation before the Select Committee of the Pennsylvania Legislature to Investigate the Use of Automatic and Semi-automatic Firearms," Harrisburg, September 20, 1994, p. 21. In the same White Paper, Kates discusses Kellermann's "adamant refusal" to share his data with other scholars who wish to evaluate it themselves (p. 47). Along similar lines, Suter, who chairs Doctors for Integrity in Research and Public Policy, criticizes the *New England Journal of Medicine*'s "no-data-are-needed" policy: "For matters of 'fact,' it is not unusual to find third-hand citations of editorials rather than citations of primary data." See Suter, "Guns in the Medical Literature," p. 133.

21. Coalition to Stop Gun Violence, packet of promotional materials with the cover "America is bleeding to death from gun violence," mailed in the spring of 1993.

22. "Clouding the public debate, this fallacy is one of the most misused slogans of the anti-self-defense lobby." Suter, "Guns in the Medical Literature," p. 136. On this "43 percent fallacy," see also the "Doctors and Guns" chapter in this book; and David Kopel, "Peril or Protection? The Risks and Benefits of Handgun Prohibition," *Saint Louis University Public Law Review* 12 (1993): 285–359. In the latter article, Kopel points out that the 43 times figure "is mostly a factoid, since thirty-seven of the forty-three deaths were suicides," (p. 341). Kellermann also ignored, among other things, the facts that most gun-related accidents and homicides occur in violent households, and that most often the defensive use of a firearm does not entail firing it. On the latter point, see especially Gary Kleck, *Point Blank: Guns and Violence in America* (Hawthorne, N.Y.: Aldine de Gruyter, 1991), pp. 120–45.

23. For example, the feminization of poverty, the "glass ceiling" encountered by women in the workforce, womens' health issues, women in politics, antifeminist backlash, sexual harassment, and date rape.

24. Karen McNutt, "Legally Speaking: Swapping Freedom For Illusion," *Women & Guns,* March 1992, p. 33. On the idea that many women are reluctant to self-identify as feminists, even though they share many basic viewpoints with ideological feminism, because they are deterred by its stridency or narrow-mindedness on some issues, see also Wolf, *Fire With Fire,* pp. 57–132. Paula Kamen argues a similar point in *Feminist Fatale: Voices From the "Twentysomething" Generation Explore the Future of the "Women's Movement"* (New York: Donald I. Fine, 1991).

25. *Ms.,* January/February 1992, p. 19.

26. See Sanford Levinson, "The Embarrassing Second Amendment," *Yale Law Journal* 99 (December 1989): 637–59.

27. Ibid., p. 658.

28. Wendy Brown, "Guns, Cowboys, Philadelphia Mayors, and Civic Republicanism: On Sanford Levinson's 'The Embarrassing Second Amendment,'" *Yale Law Journal* 99 (December 1989): 661–67.

29. Ibid., pp. 666–67.

30. Brown is of course probably correct about the uselessness of her self-defense training; numerous studies have shown that for aggressive resistance to succeed against sexual assault, the level of resistance must be equivalent to the level of force employed by the attacker. See Section III below. Significantly, the option of arming herself to forestall the sort of assault in the circumstances she imagines here does not seem to have occurred to her.

31. Douglas Laycock, "Vicious Stereotypes in Polite Society," *Constitutional Commentary* 8 (Summer 1991): 399, 406; original italics. For another critique of Brown's response to Levinson, see Mary Zeiss Stange, "Feminism and the Second Amendment," *Guns & Ammo Annual 1992,* pp. 6-9.

32. "Laycock, "Vicious Stereotypes in Polite Society," p. 401.

33. See, for example, Camille Paglia, *Sex, Art, and American Culture* (New York: Vintage Books, 1992); Katie Roiphe, *The Morning After: Sex, Fear and Feminism on Campus*

(Boston: Little, Brown and Company, 1993); Christina Hoff Sommers, *Who Stole Feminism?* (New York: Simon and Shuster, 1994)

34. From the same fundraising literature cited above.

35. "NRA Blazes Trail For New Hunters," sidebar to Kathy Etling's "Women Afield," *American Hunter,* January 1992, p. 67.

36. NRA Fact Sheet, "Women and Firearms: The Responsibilities of Choice," no date; original italics.

37. According to Kitty Beuchert, director of WI&I, as of August 1994, the NRA recorded a female membership of 116,404, up from 102,000 in December 1993, and 85,000 in December 1992. While this would appear to be a fairly small percentage of the NRA's total membership of 3.5 million, Beuchert stresses that fully one third of the NRA's membership is signed up by initials only. There is no reliable way to "genderize" these million individuals, but—especially since women are known frequently to use initials only—it is fair to assume that many of them are female. (Telephone conversation, October 19, 1994).

38. In Tennessee, two different pollsters (Mason-Dixon and Luntz Research) asked the same question. The NRA won the Mason-Dixon poll; in the Luntz Research poll, the NRA and Democrats both received 6.2 percent "all the time" support, while Republicans received 3.5 percent.

39. Brad O'Leary, "Fire Power," *Campaigns & Elections,* December 1994/January 1995, p. 34.

40. The NRA is adamant in its insistence that this is not a "gun program." Seminar participants who do express an interest in pursuing the option of arming themselves in self-defense are directed to other NRA programs, or other training opportunities in their locality.

41. To put this accusation in perspective, it is probably fair to say that many major advertising campaigns mounted by advocacy groups in the last two or three years have also cashed in on feminist rhetoric regarding choice The fur, tobacco, and beef industries have all promoted consumers' "right to choose" their products, and even anti-abortion groups have rallied around such mottos as "Choose Life" and "Life: What a Beautiful Choice." Both sides of the health care debate have focused on choice (of physicians and services) as a key issue, and the Libertarian party proclaims itself "pro-choice on everything."

42. Cover letter, signed by NRA Board member Susan Howard, mailed with the brochure "Refuse To Be A Victim: 42 Strategies for Personal Safety."

43. All, as it happens, Democrats: Eleanor Holmes Norton (delegate-DC), Patricia Schroeder (CO), Nancy Pelosi (CA), Lynn Woolsey (CA), Carrie Meek (FL), Nydia Velazquez (NY), Anna Eshoo (CA), Leslie Byrne (VA), Rosa DeLauro (CT), Lucille Roybal-Allard (CA), Corrine Brown (FL), Marjorie Margolies-Mezvinski (CA), Patsy Mink (HI), Louise Slaughter (NY), Lynn Schenk (CA), Barbara Kennelly (CT), Elizabeth Furse (OR), Eva Clayton (NC), Maxine Waters (CA), Eddie Bernice Johnson (TX), Cynthia McKinney (GA), Maria Cantwell (WA), Carolyn Maloney (NY), Cardiss Collins (IL), and Karen Shepherd (UT) (listed in the order in which their signatures appear on the letter). Not all members of the Congressional Women's Caucus signed the letter, of course. Those who refused included Jolene Unsoeld (WA), a progun liberal Democrat.

44. Run in regional editions of such national magazines as *People, Ladies Home Journal,* and *Woman's Day.*

45. Letter dated October 15, 1993, over the signatures of the twenty-six congresswomen. According to *Women & Guns,* the letter was originally intended to be on Congressional Women's Caucus letterhead, but owing to objections by some members of the women's caucus was typed on standard House letterhead instead. See "New NRA 'Refuse To Be A Victim' Launched into Nationwide Orbit," *Women & Guns,* January 1994, pp. 8–9.

46. Presumably, Kellermann et al., "Gun Ownership as a Risk Factor for Homicide in the Home." The letter specified that the presence of a handgun in the home triples the chance some-

one will be killed there; that three-quarters of homicide victims are killed by a family member, spouse or acquaintance; and that battered women were more likely than others to be involved in a fatal shooting; all these findings that have been discredited by knowledgeable critics; see discussion in endnotes above, and in chapter 5.

47. This conclusion is a blatant non sequitur, considering that all the Kellermann data cited in the preceding paragraph of the letter related to violence in the home.

48. They included Susan Brewster (wife of Bill Brewster, Democratic Congressman from Oklahoma and NRA board member), Dr. Suzanna Gratia (a survivor of the Luby's Cafeteria mass murder in Killeen, Texas), and Amy Fleming (a New Jersey woman stalked by her abusive ex-husband).

49. Judy Mann, "Annie Doesn't Have to Get a Gun," *Washington Post,* October 1, 1993, p. E3.

50. "From the Editor," *Women & Guns,* May 1992, pp. 6–7.

51. *Women & Guns,* September 1992, p. 6.

52. Telephone conversation with Peggy Tartaro, October 13, 1994. Tartaro's perception is based on a series of reader surveys, as well as the letters she receives from readers.

53. *Ms.,* May/June 1994, p. 37.

54. "Cashing In On Fear," p. 49.

55. Ibid., p. 48.

56. Ibid., p. 47. To put it bluntly, the NRA's political agenda has been anything but "hidden"; indeed, few advocacy groups are more transparent in stating their goals and objectives. It remains open to question why critics who recognize NRA's tendency toward an "all or nothing" approach to gun rights and regulation in every other area would suddenly discern a lapse into subtlety and subterfuge when it comes to women's issues.

57. Jones, "Living With Guns, Playing With Fire," p. 43.

58. In fact, the "The Armed Citizen" feature that appears in each issue of the NRA's two national magazines regularly features stories about women who used firearms successfully to defend themselves against abusive ex-husbands or ex-boyfriends, frequently in stalking situations. "The Armed Citizen" is comprised of press accounts drawn from newspapers around the country.

59. Jones, "Living With Guns, Playing With Fire," p. 44. Jones does aver that spending time in prison is, at any rate, "better than being dead."

60. Jones, "Living With Guns, Playing With Fire," p. 42. It is unclear whether the "little incident" referred to here is the cutting off of part of a man's penis or the shooting to death of a would-be rapist.

61. Letter by Adriene Sere, *Ms.,* September/October 1994, p. 5.

62. Letter by Martha McCaughey, *Ms.,* September/October 1994, p. 7.

63. From Ann Jones, *Women Who Kill* (New York: Fawcett Columbine, 1980), pp. 323–24, original italics. The conversation is between two women convicted of murdering their abusers. Childers claimed her shotgun had misfired, fatally wounding her former husband; DiVillez admitted to having hired a hit man to kill her husband.

64. D. A. Clarke, "A Woman With a Sword: Some Thoughts on Women, Feminism and Violence," in Emilie Buchwald, Paula R. Fletcher & Martha Roth, eds., *Transforming a Rape Culture* (New York: Milkweed Editions, 1993), pp. 396–97.

65. Naomi Goldenberg, *Returning Words to Flesh: Feminism, Psychology and Religion* (Boston: Beacon Press, 1990), p. 171.

66. Ibid., p. 170.

67. See, for example, Bernice Lott, *Women's Lives: Themes and Variations in Gender Learning* (Belmont, Calif.: Brooks/Cole Publishing Company, 1987), pp. 254–55; Margaret W. Matlin, *The Psychology of Women* (Fort Worth, Tex.: Harcourt Brace Jovanovich, 1983, 1987), pp. 218–23; Jean Stockard and Miriam M. Johnson, *Sex and Gender in Society* (Englewood Cliffs, N.J.: Prentice-Hall, 1992), pp. 143–45.

68. Anne Campbell, *Men, Women, and Aggression* (New York: Basic Books, 1993), pp. 34–35.

69. See Mary Zeiss Stange, "Disarmed By Fear," *American Rifleman,* March 1992, pp. 34–37, 92.

70. Campbell, *Men, Women, and Aggression,* pp. 37–38. The bulk of Campbell's research has dealt with girls and women who deviate from the behavioral norm; her other books include *Girl Delinquents* (1981) and *The Girls in the Gang* (1984).

71. Meanwhile, violence is sometimes viewed as normative male behavior. For example, British journalist Joan Smith quotes the London judge who in 1985 sentenced a man to six years in prison after he admitted to killing his wife, chopping her body up into pieces, and scattering them around London, his defense being that she was a nag and impossible to live with: "You stand convicted of manslaughter. I will deal with you on the basis you were provoked, you lost your self-control, and that a man of reasonable self-control might have been similarly provoked and might have done what you did." See Joan Smith, *Misogynies: Reflections on Myths and Malice* (New York: Fawcett Columbine, 1989), pp. 7–9.

72. Some theorists strike a pragmatic note, observing that since aggression does not serve women's interests all that well anyway, they ought more profitably to focus their energies elsewhere; see, for example, Carol Gilligan, *In A Different Voice: Psychological Theory and Women's Development* (Cambridge, Mass.: Harvard University Press, 1982), pp. 43–47, and Jean Baker Miller, *Toward a New Psychology of Women* (Boston: Beacon Press, 1986), pp. 86–87. Others retreat into language suggesting a more transcendent essentialist perspective, in which women are viewed as literally less capable of aggression and more passive and peaceful by nature than are men; see, for example, Susan Griffin, *Woman and Nature* (New York: Harper Colophon, 1978); Mary Daly, *Gyn/Ecology: The Meta-Ethics of Radical Feminism* (Boston: Beacon Press, rev. ed. 1990); Carol Adams, *The Sexual Politics of Meat: A Feminist-Vegetarian Critical Theory* (New York: Continuum, 1990); and Andree Collard with Joyce Contrucci, *Rape of the Wild: Man's Violence Against Animals and the Earth* (Bloomington: Indiana University Press, 1989). It should be noted that those theorists who have mounted the most radical arguments about the essentially pacifistic nature of female psychology are not, by training, psychologists.

73. Campbell, *Men, Women, and Aggression,* p. 143.

74. Clarke, "A Woman with a Sword," p. 401. Not surprisingly, Clarke's essay—and this particular passage—were singled out by Judith Viorst in her review of the book for the *New York Times Book Review,* November 28, 1993, as being "quite at odds with the anti-violence agenda of the book."

75. Wolf, *Fire With Fire,* p. 315. This is, among other things, a clever inversion of the antigun "you could be next" scare tactic.

76. One of the most frequently invoked arguments against women's use of guns for self-protection is that it is easy for an attacker to wrest a gun away from a victim and use it against her. Gary Kleck notes that in actuality, this is an extremely rare occurrence: at best, 1 percent of defensive uses of firearms result in the victim's loss of the firearm, and "even these few cases did not necessarily involve the offender snatching a gun out of the victim's hands." Kleck's data relate to burglaries; however, he remarks elsewhere that data regarding gun-armed resistance against rape would probably yield similar findings. See *Point Blank,* pp. 122, 126. Self-defense expert Paxton Quigley stresses the superiority of handguns over long guns in this regard; while rifles and shotguns are both more lethal than handguns, long guns are potentially easier to take away. See Paxton Quigley, *Armed and Female* (New York: St. Martin's, 1989), p. 170.

77. Sarah E. Ullman and Raymond A. Knight, "Fighting Back: Women's Resistance to Rape," *Journal of Interpersonal Violence* 7 (March 1992): 33.

78. Ibid., p. 41. See also Sarah E. Ullman and Raymond A. Knight, "The Efficacy of Women's Resistance Strategies in Rape Situations," *Psychology of Women Quarterly* 17 (1993): 23–38; P. B. Bart et al., "The Effects of Sexual Assault on Rape and Attempted Rape Victims,"

Victimology 7 (1982): 106–13; B. S. Griffin and C. T. Griffin, "Victims in Rape Confrontation," *Victimology* 6 (1981): 59–75; P. B. Bart and P. B. O'Brien, *Stopping Rape: Successful Survival Strategies* (Elmsford, N.Y.: Pergamon Press, 1985).

79. Ullman and Knight, "The Efficacy of Women's Resistance Strategies in Rape Situations," p. 35.

80. Frances O. F. Haga, Michael L. Vasu, and William V. Pelfrey, "Domestic Violence versus Predatory Assault," a paper presented in the Division on Family Violence, 1993 Annual Meeting of the American Society of Criminology, Phoenix, Arizona. All subsequent citations are to this study, the copy of which the author received from Professor Haga via electronic transmission which was not paginated.

81. From "Domestic Violence versus Predatory Assault," original emphasis. Haga presented her findings from the "Images of Fear" study at the 1992 annual meeting of the American Society of Criminology in New Orleans, and published a portion of it, "Can Pretty Girls Be Strong?" in *Women & Guns,* March 1992, pp. 10–16. Significantly, with regard to how deeply embedded are cultural ideas about the inappropriateness of women's taking aggressive action, the men and women in this study were all either gun-owners or martial-arts self-defense specialists.

82. By contrast, men who kill their girlfriends and wives tend to stab, strangle, or bludgeon them to death. See James D. Wright, "Second Thoughts about Gun Control," *The Public Interest* 91 (1988): 32.

The various studies from antigun organizations and their medical allies about the supposed inutility of women owning guns for protection tend to suffer from a common set of flaws: First, they consider a defensive gun use successful only if the criminal is shot dead, rather than merely frightened away. Second, they pretend that the only criminals who attack women are complete strangers; if a woman shoots an ex-boyfriend who is stalking her, the stalker's death is labeled a "tragic domestic homicide" that took place during "an argument," rather than lawful self-defense against a violent predator. Third, the studies undercount justifiable homicide because they look only at arrest reports, rather than final case disposition. Finally, the studies deliberately ignore the distinction between households that are at high risk for gun misuse (households containing criminals, alcoholics, and drug abusers) and all other households, for which the risks of gun misuse are quite low.

83. Suter, "Guns in the Medical Literature," p. 140, original italics.

84. See, e.g., Elizabeth M. Schneider, "The Dialectic of Rights and Politics: Perspectives from the Women's Movement," in D. Kelly Weisberg, ed., *Feminist Legal Theory: Foundations* (Philadelphia: Temple University Press, 1993), pp. 512–14, on the Wanrow case, for which Schneider was a co-counsel on appeal. (In *State* v. *Wanrow,* a Native American woman was convicted of second-degree murder in the shooting death of a white man she believed posed an immediate threat to one of her children; the jury rejected the defense's argument of self-defense—5'4" Yvonne Wanrow was on crutches with a broken leg, her child's assailant was 6'2" and intoxicated—because of the judge's instruction that an "equal force" standard be applied. The Washington State Supreme Court reversed the conviction on appeal in a landmark decision, ruling that "care must be taken to assure that our self-defense instructions afford women the right to have their conduct judged in light of the individual physical handicaps which are the product of sex-discrimination. To fail to do so is to deny the right of the individual woman involved to trial by the same rules which are applicable to male defendants.") Don Kates and Nancy Jean Engberg summarize the implications of *Wanrow* for rethinking gender-bias in self-defense law in "Deadly Force Self-Defense against Rape," *University of California-Davis Law Review* 15 (1983): 890–94. See also Sayoko Blodgett-Ford, "Do Battered Women Have a Right to Bear Arms?" *Yale Law and Policy Review* 11 (1993): 547–53, on jury instructions regarding women's right to bear arms for self-protection; and Cynthia K. Gillespie, *Justifiable Homicide: Battered Women, Self-Defense, and the Law* (Columbus: Ohio State University Press, 1989), pp. 116–18, on the limits of the applicability of the subjective standard established by *Wanrow.*

85. See Kates and Engberg, on *People* v. *Caudillo* (1978), in which the "defendant . . . was convicted of raping his victim in addition to kidnapping and robbing her. The [California Supreme Court] found that the victim suffered serious psychological and emotional trauma but only 'insubstantial' physical injuries." Kates and Engberg, "Deadly Force Self-Defense against Rape," p. 901. Ullman and Knight note that bodily injury in most sexual assaults is confined to the rape itself, not to additional "serious injury"; see "The Efficacy of Women's Resistance Strategies In Rape Situations."

86. Robin West, "Jurisprudence and Gender," in Katharine T. Bartlett and Rosanne Kennedy, eds., *Feminist Legal Theory: Readings in Law and Gender* (Boulder, Colo.: Westview Press, 1991), p. 230.

87. Wendy W. Williams, "The Equality Crisis: Some Reflections on Culture, Courts, and Feminism," in Bartlett and Kennedy, *Feminist Legal Theory,* pp. 15–34.

88. See Kleck, *Point Blank,* p. 121; also, Carol Ruth Silver and Don Kates, "Self-Defense, Handgun Ownership, and the Independence of Women in a Violent, Sexist Society," in Don Kates, ed., *Restricting Handguns: The Liberal Skeptics Speak Out* (Croton-on-Hudson, N.Y.: North River Press, 1979), pp.144–46; and Kates, *Guns, Murders and the Constitution,* pp. 19–21. In *Warren* v. *District of Columbia* (1981), a case involving the sexual assault of three women who were held hostage for fourteen hours when the police failed to respond to their call for help, the appellate court ruled that the "government and its agents are under no general duty to provide public services, such as police protection, to any individual citizen." See Don Kates, "The Value of Civilian Handgun Possession as a Deterrent to Crime or a Defense against Crime," *American Journal of Criminal Law* 18 (Winter 1991): 123–25. In 1989, the U.S. Supreme Court applied similar logic in the *DeShaney* case, ruling that the due process clause of the Fourteenth Amendment exists to protect people from the state, not from each other. Police and other authorities are not, according to this reasoning, required to intervene in domestic disputes, or even in crimes in progress; their responsibility is to apprehend the offender after the crime has been committed. Ann Jones addresses this problem in *Next Time She'll Be Dead: Battering and How to Stop It* (Boston: Beacon Press, 1993), but sees the solution in near-utopian reform of the legal system.

89. Kates, "The Value of Civilian Handgun Possession as a Deterrent to Crime or a Defense against Crime," pp. 126–27. Illustrating the sort of "straw men" he has in mind, Kates explains: "It is, of course, tragic when, for instance, an abused woman has to shoot to stop a current or former boyfriend or husband from beating her to death. Still, it is highly misleading to count such incidents as costs of gun ownership by misclassifying them with the very thing they prevent: murder between 'family and friends' " (p. 128). In a similar vein, Suter asks "Would it be more 'politically correct' if women or children were killed by their attackers—the common outcome when women do not defend themselves and their children with guns?" See Suter, "Guns in the Medical Literature," p. 140.

90. Ann Japenga, "Would I Be Safer With a Gun?" *Health,* March/April 1994, p. 57.

91. Ibid., pp. 59, 61.

92. It also ironically reflects the kind of violence featured in antigun fundraising literature, which thrives on images of the gun-armed "dark stranger."

93. According to Bureau of Justice statistics, women are one-third less likely to be victims of robbery or assault (rape excepted) than are men. Those women who do fall prey to random violent crime tend to belong to one or more of the following risk groups: aged 20–24 years, African-American; divorced, separated, or single; urban dwellers; never graduated from high school; and earning less than $10,000 a year.

94. Kates, *Guns, Murders and the Constitution,* pp. 34–36.

95. Alternatively, this point of view implicitly regards rape and battery as noncriminal behaviors, a fact amply borne out by the tendency for the law to regard male-on-male violence as a matter for the criminal courts, male-on-female violence being often regarded as a civil matter.

96. See Robert Cottrol and Ray Diamond (chapter 3 of this volume).

97. To his credit, for the sake of ideological consistency this apparently remains an abstract question for Kellermann. The same cannot be said for those prominent proponents of strict gun regulation who have possessed firearms for their own protection, even as they have argued against extending that privilege to other people; among gun-owning gun-prohibitionists are Dianne Feinstein (when mayor of San Francisco), journalist Carl Rowan, and *New York Times* publisher Arthur Sulzberger. See Kates, "A Controlled Look at Gun Control," p. 16; also "Elite in NYC Are Packing Heat," *Boston Globe,* January 8, 1993, p. 3.

98. "Where Do We Go from Here? An Interview with Ann Jones," *Ms.,* September/October 1994, p. 60.

99. Silver and Kates, "Self-Defense, Handgun Ownership, and the Independence of Women in a Violent, Sexist Society," p. 139.

100. Ibid., p. 143. This is a problem of particular poignancy for women, who typically have a harder time getting gun-carry permits than do men. In addition, especially for a woman in a domestic abuse situation, the imposition of a waiting period to purchase a handgun can create undue hardship, or even result in her death; see Blodgett-Ford, "Do Battered Women Have a Right to Bear Arms?" pp. 541–47.

101. Japenga, "Would I Be Safer With a Gun?" p. 61.

102. Quigley, *Armed and Female,* p. 108. Quigley had begun as a vociferous supporter of strict gun regulation, only to become disillusioned with the inefficacy of the gun-control legislation she had worked to get passed in the 1960s.

103. Japenga, "Would I Be Safer With a Gun?" p. 61.

104. Peggy Tartaro, "A Picture of Women Gun Owners," *Women & Guns,* March 1994, pp. 30–32. Based upon readers' mailing in a questionnaire, this survey was not scientific. However, because of its voluntary nature, and the fact the survey results are borne out by reader mail, Tartaro thinks the responses provide not only reliable information but information derived from the most committed women gun-owners—those who, with nothing to gain, took the time to respond. Over 400 persons responded, which provided a reasonably large sample. Eighteen percent of the responses were from men (Tartaro estimates that 16 percent of *Women & Guns'* approximately 18,000 readers are men); their responses were factored out of the figures finally reported in the magazine, so that the survey report would "show a clearer picture of women gunowners."

105. This compares quite interestingly to statistics available about male gun-owners, specifically hunters. A 1991 survey carried out by Gallup for the National Shooting Sports Foundation (NSSF) found 21 percent had had "some college", 19 percent were college graduates, and 14 percent had either some graduate work or a graduate degree. Women comprised only 7 percent of the NSSF survey sample.

106. The other reasons being recreation (21 percent), hunting (6 percent), and competition (5 percent); Tartaro notes that "in all cases where multiple reasons were checked, self-defense was one of the responses."

107. The two categories of precautionary and recreational gun use are, of course, not mutually exclusive. In fact one California woman responded, "My first gun was for defense— I found target practice so much fun that I wish I had gotten a gun years ago" ("A Picture of Women Gunowners," p. 31); hers is probably not an uncommon experience.

108. See Fran Haga, "Evolution of a Successful Handgun Clinic," *Women & Guns,* February 1991, pp. 7–12. Information is based on exit surveys collected from the seventy participants.

109. The women in Haga's sample did seem to report a rather higher incidence of victimization: 17 percent had experienced assault, burglary, abuse, or theft themselves; 28 percent had not only been victimized themselves, but also had close friends/family who were crime victims, while 19 percent had not been victimized but were close to someone who had been. Haga's survey, however, posed the question in less restrictive fashion than the 1994 survey, so the differences may be largely artificial.

110. This is corroborated by the testimony of firearms safety instructors nationwide, who consistently report that they find women and girls far more teachable than males. See the remarks by psychologist Robert Jackson of the University of Wisconsin-LaCrosse, in the conference proceedings from "Breaking Down the Barriers to Participation of Women in Angling and Hunting," University of Wisconsin-Stevens Point (August 1990), edited by and available from Professor Christine L. Thomas, College of Natural Resources, University of Wisconsin-Stevens Point.

111. Tartaro, "A Picture of Women Gunowners," p. 31. Tartaro noted regarding this question, "We have asked it in past years, with an eye toward gauging the reader's view of the entire self-defense issue. In years past, results on a similarly worded question were strikingly close" to the 1994 percentages.

112. Assuming that some of the respondents live in jurisdictions where handgun ownership itself may be prohibited, or permits to carry impossible or virtually so to obtain, this question was anything but hypothetical for them.

113. See Peggy Tartaro, "Tanya Metaksa Has Grassroots Lessons To Teach Washington," *Women & Guns,* June 1994, p. 54.

114. Quigley, *Armed and Female,* p. 117. Don Kates has persuasively argued that, far from it being the case that people will in the "heat of the moment" unthinkingly pick up and fire a gun wounding or killing someone irresponsibly, it is reasonable to assume that serious precautionary gun-owners in fact have a heightened sense of awareness about the power of firearms, and the ethical responsibilities attaching to their use. See Kates, "The Value of Civilian Handgun Possession As A Deterrent to Crime," pp. 149–50.

115. D. A. Clarke, "A Woman With A Sword," in *Transforming A Rape Culture,* p. 395.

116. Don Kates, "The Second Amendment and the Ideology of Self-Protection," *Constitutional Commentary* 9 (Winter 1992): 94. Kates is quoting A. V. B. Norman, *The Medieval Soldier* (Thomas Crowell, 1971), p. 73.

117. Dominique Godineau, "Daughters of Liberty and Revolutionary Citizens," translated by Arthur Goldhammer, in Genevieve Fraisse and Michelle Perrot, eds., *A History of Women in the West, Volume IV: Emerging Feminism from Revolution to World War* (Cambridge, Mass.: The Belknap Press of Harvard University Press, 1993), p. 25.

118. Godineau, "Daughters of Liberty and Revolutionary Citizens," pp. 26–27. Along with the right to bear arms, French *citoyennes* also demanded, and won, the right to wear the tricolor cockade (a small ribbon, worn usually on one's hat) as an emblem of their full citizenship. The response, on the part of many men (and no doubt some women as well) was to conjure up "apocalyptic visions of women arming to murder men in a sort of Saint Bartholomew's Day Massacre." Ibid.

119. Kopel, *The Samurai, the Mountie, and the Cowboy,* p. 285. Kopel notes that today women have the same rights to purchase firearms as do men, though their participation in the national militia is still limited to noncombat roles and, although optional premilitia training is open to both sexes in high school, women are not required to undergo militia training. Ibid., pp. 282, 285, 299, n. 62.

2

Background Checks and Waiting Periods

David B. Kopel

INTRODUCTION

Since 1988, the American gun control debate has been primarily over "the Brady Bill." This bill, championed by Sarah Brady, the chair of Handgun Control, Inc., has became synonymous with gun control.

After years of struggle, the Brady Bill was enacted by Congress in November 1993, and became effective the following February.[1] Handgun sales, already heavy after President Clinton's election the year before, surged to record levels in the interim before the Brady Bill went into effect, as prospective gun owners feared (incorrectly) that the Brady Bill would make purchase of a handgun much more difficult.

As finally enacted by Congress, the Brady Act reflected major changes from the original Brady Bill. A copy of the Brady Act is appended to the end of this chapter. The most visible, and irrelevant, change was to redefine the Brady Bill's "seven-day waiting period" as a "five-day waiting period" (for which only government working days would count). In the culture of Washington, D.C., a change in the waiting period from seven normal days to five government working days was presented as a "compromise" that would supposedly make the bill more palatable to gun owners. The cynicism of such a cosmetic switch says much about the culture of Washington and that culture's contempt for the intelligence of the average American.

Other changes, which received virtually no attention in the national press, were far more important. A provision requiring handgun buyers to provide the serial number of the gun they wanted to buy was removed, since the main utility of the provision would be to facilitate gun registration. A tax-exempt affiliate of Handgun Control, Inc., had begun boasting about its success at suing police departments that performed allegedly insufficient background checks; accordingly, a provision immunizing government agencies from Brady-related lawsuits was added.[2] Technical changes were made which prevented a police department from stopping all handgun purchases simply refusing to acknowledge or process background check requests.

The most significant change, however, is that the Brady Bill will, for all practical purposes, vanish before the end of this century. Under the current Brady Act, whenever a person wishes to buy a handgun at retail, the gun dealer sends a form to the local police.[3] The police have five government working days during which they are required to perform a background check of the gun buyer. At the end of the five government working days, the handgun sale may proceed, unless the police have vetoed the sale.

The Brady Act does not apply in states that already have their own background check or gun licensing systems. Among those exempted from the Brady Act are states such as Virginia, which have an instant background check performed at the point of purchase. The instant check is similar to a credit card verification; the gun dealer calls a state government telephone number and within a few minutes (ideally) receives authorization to proceed with the handgun sale, or is ordered not to make the sale. Before the Brady Act went into effect, Colorado and South Carolina set up their own instant check systems, thereby exempting themselves from the Brady Act. Since then, several other states have enacted instant check laws, and more states are expected to do so over the next several years.

Under the Brady Act, the United States Department of Justice is directed to begin setting up a nationwide instant check to be used for handguns and for long guns. When the attorney general certifies that the national instant check is ready for use, the Brady Act's five government working day waiting period disappears. As an incentive for the Department of Justice to move expeditiously to create the national instant check, the Brady waiting period automatically expires in November 1998 even if the national instant check has not been put into place.

Throughout the waiting period debate of 1988–93, the National Rifle Association had always argued for the instant check as the proper alternative to Brady. The NRA had claimed that an instant check could be useable in the near future, while Handgun Control, Inc., had countered that an instant check would not be viable for many years. Congress essentially split the difference, by making the Brady Bill into a transitional law, to last no longer than five years, before implementation of the NRA's instant check.

One other provision of the Brady Act is undergoing significant change, although the change is being made by courts, not by Congress. The Act orders that local police and sheriff's departments "shall make a reasonable effort" to conduct a background check on handgun buyers. In six states, police chiefs or sheriffs have sued to have this provision declared unconstitutional under the Tenth Amendment. (The Tenth Amendment reserves to the states all powers not specifically granted to the federal government; the Amendment has been interpreted to prevent Congress from ordering state and local governments to perform any tasks.) Courts have agreed that Congress has no authority to compel local police and sheriffs to perform a background check.[4]

Although in practice the Brady Act amounts to a transitional law on the way to the NRA's preferred law, the Act nevertheless represented a significant victory on the part of Handgun Control, Inc. First of all, the very fact that the NRA and Handgun Control, Inc., were debating what kind of national background check should be enacted reflects the latter's success at defining the terms of the gun debate.

Moreover, the Brady Bill was always intended to be the "first step" or the "cornerstone" of a new national gun policy. One way the Brady Bill was to serve as a first step was by breaking the NRA's "stranglehold" on Congress. If Congresspersons were convinced that it was safe to vote against the NRA on a relatively mild gun control measure, the Congress could eventually be convinced that voting for gun control was not only politically harmless but actually advantageous. In an August 15, 1993, interview in the *New York Times,* Mrs. Brady set forth the agenda for the controls which she expected passage of the Brady Bill would make "easier and easier" to enact.[5]

The strategy worked brilliantly. In the 1988, 1990, and 1992 congressional elections, hundreds of representatives and senators who had voted for versions of the Brady Bill went before the electorate. Hardly any of them were defeated as a direct result of their pro-Brady vote. True, there were some exceptions (such as Rep. Peter Smith, ousted from his Vermont House seat in 1990, and Rep. Beryl Anthony, defeated in the Arkansas Democratic primary in 1992), but in elections in which almost all sitting Congresspersons who chose to run were reelected, most candidates had reason to conclude that the NRA was not going to take their seat away. As Handgun Control, Inc., had hoped, the softening effect of pro-Brady votes led many Congresspersons to feel comfortable taking "the next step" by voting for a ban on "assault weapons." Although the "assault weapon" ban passed the 103rd Congress by the narrowest of margins (one vote in each house), it is doubtful that the ban would have passed at all but for the political groundwork laid by the Brady Bill. (As we will discuss in chapter 4, the Brady Bill's political groundwork was undone by the 1994 elections and the backlash against gun control, prompted mainly by the "assault weapon" ban.)

The Brady Bill was, and is, intended to be a first step as well as a matter of substantive policy. Having used the Brady Bill to establish the principle that the federal government should carefully control firearms purchases in all fifty states,

Handgun Control, Inc., is now working to layer more restrictive standards on top of the Brady Bill. For example, the lobby's new flagship proposal, "Brady II," makes permanent the handgun purchase waiting period which is set to expire by 1998, and limits handgun purchases to one per month. The bill also requires all states to set up handgun licensing systems, with possession of a handgun permitted only to persons who pass federally mandated safety training. The mandatory state licensing provision would probably be found to have the same Tenth Amendment problems as the current Brady Bill's order that local police perform background checks. All handgun transfers would be registered with the government.

Brady II also bans small handguns, outlaws ammunition clips holding more than six rounds (such clips are used in over half of all handguns), and requires that many gun owners obtain an "arsenal" license that would subject their home to unannounced police inspections.[6]

Brady II, in turn, appears to be a transitional law to what Mrs. Brady calls a "needs-based-licensing" system, with what the *New York Times,* after an August 1993 interview with Mrs. Brady, summarized as "different requirements for hunters, target shooters and security guards." A system where a prospective gun owner must prove to the police her "need" for a particular gun is much stricter than even the gun controls in effect in countries such as Canada and New Zealand. In Great Britain, a country that does have a "needs" system, police abuse of discretion has driven the percentage of lawful gun owners down to 4 percent of the population.[7] In American jurisdictions where police currently have discretion over "need" (such as New York City for handgun licensing), Handgun Control, Inc., has supported limitless police discretion, even when such discretion has been used to create a near-prohibition on handgun purchases by citizens.

Absent from Mrs. Brady's list of persons who might "need" a gun is someone who needs a handgun or long gun for home protection. As she puts it, "To me, the only reason for guns in civilian hands is for sporting purposes."[8] Mrs. Brady and her organization recognize that the abolition of the right to possess guns for home protection could not take place overnight. In countries such as Great Britain, the elimination of the right proceeded in gradual stages; as successive layers of "reasonable" controls were added to previous layers, what was once an unquestionable right became a privilege dependent on police discretion. And when police discretion became nearly absolute, the privilege was eliminated.

Thus, even though the Brady Bill was, as an actual gun control, of only passing significance, the law is of much greater significance as a "first step" toward much stricter gun laws.

Thanks to Brady II, the issue of waiting periods and background checks will continue to be an important part of the gun-control debate. The waiting period/background debate directly confronts the question of who should have guns. The issue arises first of all as a question of how to keep guns away from people who plainly should not have them (violent criminals); and as particular gun controls to disarm violent criminals are discussed, other questions arise about who should have guns, such as persons who think they need a gun immediately, or those who think they need to own a gun for protection.

This chapter discusses the following issues: Would a waiting period have stopped John Hinckley? Would a waiting period have made a difference in some other individual cases? What are the results, so far, of the Brady Bill, and what have been the results of similar laws in states where waiting periods have been in effect for years? What do the polls of police and of citizens say about waiting periods, and what implications should be drawn from the results? If a waiting period could save at least one life (and it certainly could), isn't it a good idea? What are the disadvantages and risks of waiting periods and other police permission systems like the instant telephone check? Finally, I analyze a driver's license identification system as a possible alternative to the Brady Bill and to the instant check.

JOHN HINCKLEY

Without John Hinckley, there would be no Brady Bill. Hinckley's March 1981 attempt to assassinate President Ronald Reagan resulted in Jim Brady, President Reagan's press secretary, being shot in the head and permanently paralyzed. The shooting helped galvanize Mrs. Brady into becoming the most effective gun-control lobbyist in American history.

The Bradys and Hinckley himself agree that a waiting period would have prevented the crime. Currently under indefinite commitment to St. Elizabeth's mental hospital in Washington, Hinckley petitioned to be allowed access to reporters so that he could speak out for handgun control and for a waiting period. Hinckley explained that he was in "a Valium depression" when he acted, and a waiting period might have given his better self time to reassert control. But in fact, Hinckley bought his gun in October 1980, months before the assassination attempt. A seven-day wait would obviously have had no impact.

Legislators usually pay little attention to the policy suggestions of the criminally insane. The more persuasive spokesperson for the waiting period was Sarah Brady. "Had a waiting period been in effect seven years ago, John Hinckley would not have not have had the opportunity to buy the gun he used," said Mrs. Brady in 1988.[9] Although many supporters of the Brady Bill conceded that it would have a minimal impact on criminal gun acquisition, the fact that the law could have helped the Bradys (a popular couple in Washington) seemed one good reason to enact it. But would the Brady Bill have really helped the Bradys?

Mrs. Brady pointed out that Hinckley was able to buy his gun with no waiting period to determine whether he had a criminal or mental illness record.[10] But Hinckley had no public record of mental illness; hence a mental records check would have done no good.[11]

As for a criminal records check, a police background check was run on Hinckley a few days before he bought the guns, and nothing turned up. Hinckley was caught trying to smuggle a gun aboard a plane on October 9, 1980, in Nashville. His name was run through the National Crime Information Center, which reported, correctly, that he had no felony convictions in any jurisdiction. He was promptly released after paying a fine of $62.50 and pleading guilty to a misdemeanor.[12]

Although Mrs. Brady bemoaned the lack of a criminal/mental check on Hinckley, she did not explicitly claim that such checks would have stopped him. Instead, Mrs. Brady's detailed theorizing involves Hinckley's residence status.

On October 13, 1980, John Hinckley walked into Rocky's Pawn Shop in Dallas, Texas, and walked out shortly thereafter with two .22 caliber RG revolvers. As with the retail purchase of any firearm, the gun dealer was required to complete a federal form that listed Hinckley's address. Because Hinckley was buying two handguns in the same five-day period (in fact, at the same moment), the dealer also filled out another federal form. That form was sent to the local office of the Bureau of Alcohol, Tobacco, and Firearms (BATF).

By federal law, the dealer was required to verify that Hinckley was a resident of Texas, the state in which he was buying the handgun. When asked for identification, Hinckley offered his Texas driver's license.[13]

Mrs. Brady detailed how a background check might have helped: "He lied about his address and used an old Texas driver's license to purchase that revolver. He was not a Texas resident. A police check would have stopped him from buying a handgun in Texas."[14] As she put it, "He lied on his purchase application. Given time, the police could have caught the lie and put him in jail."[15]

Accordingly, Mrs. Brady stated: "A simple check would have stopped him. . . . John Hinckley might well have been in jail instead of on his way to Washington."[16] Indeed, her assurance that the waiting period would have stopped Hinckley was often unequivocal: "There's no doubt that he would not have been able to purchase that gun."[17] Or, "John Hinckley would never have walked out of that Texas pawnshop with the handgun that came within an inch of killing Ronald Reagan."[18]

But Hinckley's situation may not be so clear-cut.

Hinckley moved around a great deal, from one Texas address to another. The Lubbock address he listed on his federal gun form (the address of a rooming house) was different from both his driver's license address and his address in the then-current Lubbock phone book.[19] Of course, moving frequently is not a federal crime. Because the only use of the driver's license (on a gun purchase) is to prove identity and residence in the state, there is no federal requirement that a handgun purchaser reside at the street address shown on his license, as long as the address is in the same state. Even if Hinckley had deliberately made a false statement about his address, the act would not have been illegal; a false statement on the federal form is illegal only if it relates to the purchaser's eligibility.[20] While a person's state of residence does relate to eligibility, address within that state does not.

In other words, Hinckley's purchase would have been illegal under federal law only if he was not a resident of Texas. Merely offering a Texas driver's license with a street address that was no longer current and was different from the address put on the federal form was not in itself illegal.

Was Hinckley a Texas resident? Contrary to what Handgun Control, Inc., implies, it has never been determined that he was not. During the previous summer, he had attended both summer sessions at Texas Tech in Lubbock. According to federal gun regulations, a university student is considered a resident of the area where he attends school, and may purchase firearms there.[21] When Hinckley was arrested in Nashville (a few days before he bought the handguns), he identified himself as a Texas resident.

Significantly, Hinckley, after the assassination attempt, was the subject of an intensive federal investigation. The federal government used every resource possible to convict Hinckley. Yet, he was not charged with illegally purchasing the handguns in Texas. Had the prosecutors believed that Hinckley was guilty of an illegal gun purchase, the charges would likely have been brought. The case could have been prosecuted before a conservative Dallas jury, rather than a liberal Washington one. Further, Hinckley would then have had to convince the Texas jury that he was insane not just on the day of the assassination attempt, but six months beforehand.

If the full resources of the Department of Justice did not find enough evidence even to charge Hinckley with an illegal gun purchase, it is not realistic to claim that a five government working-day background check would have found the same transaction illegal.

On the other hand, it is possible that the entire team of federal prosecutors simply overlooked a major felony for which they almost certainly could have convicted Hinckley. If a team of federal prosecutors investigating a presidential assassination attempt missed Hinckley's alleged offense, it seems unlikely that a lone Dallas police officer, wading through a mountain of paperwork and background checks for hundreds of gun buyers, would find it.

In any case, law enforcement authorities already had an opportunity to run a check on Hinckley. Because Hinckley bought two handguns on the same day, his purchase was immediately reported to BATF, as required by federal law. At the time, the bureau reportedly ran name checks as standard procedure, but did not run detailed background checks on multiple handgun purchasers (such as Hinckley) even though it had the legal authority to do so. Perhaps BATF concluded that the expense of running the checks exceeded the likely benefits.

Hypothesize as true Handgun Control, Inc.'s, assumption (which the Justice Department apparently had no evidence of) that Hinckley was no longer a Texas resident. Would the assassination have been prevented by a background check? Almost certainly not.

How would the police have found Hinckley's "lie"? If they had looked in the phone book, they would have seen him listed as a Lubbock resident. To ascertain that Hinckley did not reside in Texas, the police would have had to visit or telephone his purported residence at least once. Since many police departments do not have the time to visit the scene of residential burglaries, it may not be realistic to assume that they would have had time to verify the address listed as Hinckley's residence.

Most importantly, the police never would have found the "lie" about Hinckley's address, because they would not be checking addresses. Under the Brady Bill, the police do not verify anyone's address within a state. The Brady Bill does not discuss any kind of address/residence check. As one of Handgun Control, Inc.'s, key congressional supporters explained, "The 'investigation' is limited to the review of police and court records."[22]

Assume that, despite the evidence to the contrary, Hinckley actually was not a Texas resident, and further assume that the Texas police would have found it worthwhile to do what the federal Bureau of Alcohol, Tobacco and Firearms did not, and run a background check; and further assume that although the background check was intended to be run according to Handgun Control, Inc.'s, description, and to apply only to criminal/mental records, the Texas police would have expanded the background check and tried to verify Hinckley's address; and additionally assume that the police would have committed the manpower necessary to verify that Hinckley was not a Texas resident. If all these assumptions are valid (and if any one of the assumptions were incorrect, Hinckley clearly would not have been halted), would Hinckley have been stopped? Perhaps.

Assuming the police found that Hinckley was trying to make a purchase without the proper residency status, would they have arrested him for that offense? Would he have been imprisoned for more than a few days, if that long? Only a few days before Hinckley bought the Texas guns, he had been caught attempting to smuggle a gun onto a plane and had been released from custody almost immediately, having pleaded guilty to a misdemeanor. Unless Hinckley were imprisoned for a term of years for the out-of-state gun purchase, he would have speedily been back on the streets. He could have taken any of the other handguns which he already owned, and gone on to Washington for the assassination with one of them. (Among the guns he could have used was the .38 special he bought in Colorado, in full compliance with the law. Had he used that gun, rather than the .22 from Texas, President Reagan and Mr. Brady would likely have been killed.)[23]

Handgun Control, Inc.'s, version of the attempted assassination seems incorrect in other details as well. For example, one Handgun Control, Inc., advertisement depicted Mrs. Brady saying "A $29 dollar handgun shattered my family's life."[24] Hinckley's gun cost $47.[25] The difference is of no real importance, except that it shows Handgun Control, Inc., to be loose with basic facts of the case.[26]

Handgun Control, Inc., and Mrs. Brady garnered substantial press support by claiming that the "Brady Bill" would have stopped John Hinckley.[27] Since Sarah Brady heads Handgun Control, Inc., the group's fund-raising letters rely heavily on personal testimonies by Mrs. Brady and her husband.[28] The image of a man disabled by an assassin, but who could have been saved by "The Brady Bill," is compelling to press and politicians alike.

To say the least, the evidence suggesting that a waiting period would have stopped John Hinckley is not strong. Long after the facts of the Hinckley case have been detailed, antigun advocates continue to maintain that the Brady Bill could have made a difference for Jim Brady. As *USA Today* wrote, after the Brady Bill had become law, "Despite these problems, the people behind the Brady law remain convinced background checks are the first step to controlling handguns. They argue that background checks might have prevented the 1981 assassination attempt against President Reagan, when John Hinckley also shot Reagan's press secretary, James Brady, in the head and left him disabled for life."[29] Actually, only a very unlikely set of events would have enabled police armed with a "Brady Bill" to stop John Hinckley. Quite apart from Hinckley himself, there were many other plausible rationales for the Brady Bill. As the misuse of John Hinckley's crime illustrates, however, one should be careful in using anecdotal evidence as the basis for changing the law.[30]

SOME PREVENTABLE SHOOTINGS

The success of the gun control movement in defining the terms of debate over the Brady Bill was illustrated one evening on the CNN "Crossfire" television program. Host Michael Kinsley supported the Brady Bill, and co-host Pat Buchanan opposed it. Buchanan argued forcefully that the Brady Bill would do nothing to disarm criminals. Kinsley pressed Buchanan to explain what harm the Brady Bill could do, and Buchanan had no answer. In other words, the Brady Bill was discussed as something that might accomplish some good, or might accomplish nothing. Given these two alternatives, enactment of the Brady Bill would be logical. Since there would be no negative consequences, it would be worth taking a chance that the Brady Bill might do at least a little good.

The flaw with Kinsley's reasoning, though, is that the Brady Bill could do serious harm to some people. It is possible, of course, that the greater good accomplished by the Brady Bill could far outweigh scattered instances of harm. Later, I will detail the criminological data regarding the Brady Bill and similar laws. But for now, it is important to realize that the Brady Bill and its offspring will prevent some shootings and other uses of a gun, and that such prevention might result in innocent people being harmed. Consider the following cases:

Bonnie Elmasri

On March 5, 1991, Bonnie Elmasri called a firearms instructor, worried that her husband—who was subject to a restraining order to stay away from her—had been threatening her and her children. When she asked the instructor about getting a handgun, the instructor explained that Wisconsin has a 48-hour waiting period. Ms. Elmasri and her two children were murdered by her husband twenty-four hours later.

Rayna Ross

On June 29, 1993, at three o'clock in the morning, a 21-year-old woman named Rayna Ross was awakened by the sound of a burglar who had broken into her apartment and entered her bedroom. The burglar was her ex-boyfriend, a man who had previously assaulted her. This time, having smashed his way into her apartment, he was armed with a bayonet. Miss Ross took aim with a .380 semi-automatic pistol and shot him twice. The burglar's death was classified as a "justifiable homicide" by the Prince William County commonwealth's attorney, which determined that Miss Ross had acted lawfully in shooting the attacker.

Miss Ross had bought her handgun one full business day before the attack, thanks to Virginia's "instant background check." Virginia's 1993 Democratic candidate for governor, Mary Sue Terry (endorsed by Handgun Control, Inc.), proposed that—although the Virginia instant check already checks all handgun buyers—Virginia handgun purchasers should undergo a "cooling-off period" of five business days. Had the proposal been law in Virginia in 1993, Rayna Ross would now be undergoing a permanent "cooling-off period."[31]

Sonya Miller

Armed with a knife, Charles A. Grant, Jr., sexually assaulted a 33-year-old woman on a Virginia beach one Tuesday in 1991. The assault was videotaped by a tourist who (not having a permit to carry a concealed handgun for protection) apparently could do nothing to help except record the crime.

The following day, Wednesday, Charles Grant raped a 12-year-old girl. News broadcasts of the videotape of Grant's Tuesday assault frightened many people in the nearby Nags Head community.

A young woman named Sonya Miller had been wanting a handgun for a while, and on that Wednesday, her father bought her a .38 Special revolver. He gave her the revolver that evening.

At about 9 P.M., Miss Miller went to the post office to pick up her mail. As she stepped into the dimly lit parking lot near the post office, Charles Grant saw her, and she saw Charles Grant. They both screamed. Grant told the young woman he would not hurt her, but when she attempted to get into her car, Grant lunged at the door. He stuck a .25 caliber pistol in her face, began climbing into the car's back seat, and said, "I'm going to kill you."

"No," she replied, "I'm going to kill you." Sonya Miller picked up the revolver she had acquired less than fifteen minutes before. When she pulled the hammer back (a step preparatory to firing), he dropped his gun and fled. Miss

Miller drove home; her father called the sheriff's offices, and Charles Grant was apprehended.

Regarding the handgun Miss Miller had just acquired, "It's the only thing that saved her life," her father observed.[32]

An Unnamed Victim

Peter Kasler, a self-defense instructor in California, wrote in the *New York Times*:

> I know a woman whose once pretty face is now disfigured by a steel-plated jaw; it was shattered by her 6-foot 3-inch 200-pound husband. He inflicted the beating while she shielded her infant in her arms. . . . I've seen the blood-stained imprint her head made as it smashed against the wall, complete with rivulets running nearly to the floor. . . .
>
> The woman tried to press charges after she left the hospital, but sheriff's deputies and county medical health workers persuaded her not to because her husband had promised to attend counseling sessions. After two sessions, his mental health counselor refused to see him again out of terror; he threatened to kill her, and the counselor believes he meant it.
>
> When his wife tried to reinstitute charges, the deputies told her it was too late to do so. This was untrue. . . . While the police refused to arrest him, he entered her property daily, prowled around the outside of her house, slept on her lawn at night and telephoned persistently, often thirty times a day. He stole her mail repeatedly, once removing her telephone bill and calling every number on it to slander her and threaten those who answered the phone.
>
> The police wouldn't arrest him for violating the restraining order because information that we had served it had not been entered in their computer. They weren't swayed by the fact that service was acknowledged by the county clerk's office and that we showed them county certified documentation of service.
>
> Nor would they arrest him unless the district attorney issued a warrant. But the D.A. wouldn't do that because the county file on the case was "temporarily mislaid."
>
> . . . [T]he threatened woman knew that the only person who could be relied upon to protect her life was herself. She studied the laws and techniques of self-defense, trained to defend herself, and tried to buy a good pistol. But because of the California waiting period, she couldn't have it for fifteen days.
>
> During the waiting period, her life was a living hell. He broke into her house while she and her two children were asleep. Awakened by the barking of the dog, she sneaked outside with the kids and hid in the bushes till he left the next morning. Employed as a housekeeper, she was vacuuming in a client's house one day when he appeared and once again assaulted her. Another time, he hid in her garage as she returned and tried to close her inside with the electric garage door. She managed to drive out of the trap, but not without damage to the car, the garage door, and her psyche.

She survived to receive the handgun, and he was told of its presence. Although he continues to telephone her and steal her mail, he has not tried to assault her again, and she feels safe enough to have filed for divorce. . . .[33]

Virgen Blanca

At the age of seventeen, Virgen Blanca emigrated to the United States from Spain. By the time she was twenty-three, she had three children and was divorced. To make ends meet for her family, she had to work two or three jobs, as long as eighteen hours a day. In 1993, Ms. Blanca and her three teenage children moved from Mesquite, Texas, to Dallas, in order to be closer to her job as a house painter. The family moved into a seven-unit apartment building, where they were the sole tenants.

During the night of Saturday, July 24, 1993, a prowler twice attempted to break into the apartment. The second time, Ms. Blanca's 15-year-old son Reel jumped out a second-story window to call the police. By the time they arrived, the prowler was gone, having left behind a message scrawled on a light switch next to the Blanca apartment, "I'll be back."

On Sunday, Mrs. Blanca purchased a Bryco semi-automatic pistol. On Monday night, Mrs. Blanca left the apartment to buy food. Moments later, 15-year-old Reel, 14-year-old Alexandra, and 10-year-old John Paul heard a door creaking outside the apartment house. Recognizing the man to be the same man who had twice attempted to break in Saturday night, Reel took the Bryco pistol from his mother's room, and aimed it out the window at the man in the courtyard below. Reel yelled "Freeze!" but the man began to open the door to the apartment building. Reel shot the gun three times, wounding the man in the groin.

The man limped two blocks, asked someone to call an ambulance, and claimed that he had merely been looking for a place to urinate. Because Mrs. Blanca could not make a positive identification of the man, police dropped burglary charges.[34]

What a Difference a Day Makes

In 1985 in San Leandro, California, a woman and her daughter were threatened by a neighbor. Instead of being able immediately to obtain a handgun for self-defense, the woman had to wait fifteen days. The day after she finally was allowed to pick up her gun, the neighbor attacked them, and she shot him in self-defense. Had the man attacked fourteen rather than sixteen days after his initial threat, the woman and her daughter might have been raped.

Catherine Latta

In September 1990, a mail carrier named Catherine Latta of Charlotte, North Carolina, went to the police to obtain permission to buy a handgun. Her ex-boyfriend had previously robbed her, assaulted her several times, and raped her. The clerk at the sheriff's office informed her the gun permit would take two to four weeks. "I told her I'd be dead by then," Ms. Latta later recalled. That afternoon, she went to a bad part of town, and bought an illegal $20 semi-automatic pistol on the street. Five hours later, her ex-boyfriend attacked her outside her house, and she shot him dead. The county prosecutor decided not to prosecute Ms. Latta for either the self-defense homicide, or the illegal gun.[35]

It is theoretically possible, of course, that some of these cases would have turned out no differently without a waiting period. Perhaps Bonnie Elmasri would not have been able to use the gun successfully when she was attacked. Perhaps Sonya Miller and Catherine Latta would have survived the homicidal criminal attacks even without a gun. But it seems hard to deny that any waiting period law will inevitably disarm some people who need a firearm for immediate protection, thus causing their rape, injury, or death.

In contrast to most state waiting periods, the Brady Act does allow a waiver of the wait if the locality's chief law enforcement official (or his designee) issues a written order stating that immediate purchase is necessary to protect the life of the gun purchaser or someone in his or her household. In practical terms, it is doubtful that a potential crime victim (particularly the poor and minorities who are the victims of most violent crime) will be able to obtain a rapid appointment with the police administrator who will issue a gun authorization. If the administrator is out of town, or busy, or uninterested, the victim is out of luck. And if the potential victim is receiving threatening phone calls that deal only with rape, aggravated assault, or mayhem, even a sympathetic police chief cannot issue an exemption, since there is no direct threat to the victim's life.

At least some police administrators will not be sympathetic. In an Oklahoma case that arose shortly after the Brady Act became law, a woman asked the local police chief for immediate authorization to purchase a handgun, since her ex-husband (the subject of a court restraining order) was stalking her. The chief turned her down, not because the ex-husband was not a threat, but because the woman had not taken a firearms class, and the chief thought that the woman therefore could not use the gun successfully. The Brady Act, of course, does not specifically authorize a police chief to deny a request for a self-defense exemption on the basis of allegedly insufficient training. (And given a homicidal attack, an untrained gun user is still better off with a gun than unarmed.) But the more that gun purchases become subject to the discretion of government administrators, the fewer people who will be able to obtain guns based on their own perception of their needs, rather than the government's perception. In the long run, that is the objective of the gun control lobbies.

Again, I am not suggesting that these incidents prove that the Brady Bill or Brady II or "needs-based gun licensing" are not a net benefit to society. The cases do show that, at least sometimes, restrictive gun laws cause harm, and are therefore only a good idea to the extent that their benefits outweigh their harm.

PUBLIC AND POLICE OPINION

Before turning to the data regarding the benefits and costs of the Brady Bill and similar laws, I would like to briefly address two particularly unpersuasive reasons that were offered in support of the law: the police wanted it, and the public wanted it.

Neither claim was necessarily true, and, even if it were, it should not have mattered. Because misleading claims about police and public opinion are made with regard to many other gun control issues, it is appropriate to examine how reliable those claims were in regard to the Brady Bill.

Police

Handgun Control, Inc., and its congressional allies claimed that a waiting period was supported by "every major police organization" in the country.[36] Most media reports of the Brady Bill debate assumed that the police almost unanimously supported the law. But the American Federation of Police (AFP) which, with its 103,000 members, is the second-largest rank-and-file police organization in the United States, opposed a waiting period. Apparently being merely the second-largest in its field, AFP did not qualify as a "major police organization."[37]

Many important police organizations did endorse a waiting period.[38] Yet some of these police organizations did not bother to ask the police what they think. One group that did ask was the Police Executive Research Forum (PERF), a Washington think tank with a membership of about five hundred present and former big-city police executives. A 1989 PERF membership poll (Table 2.1) found 92 percent in favor of a national seven-day waiting period for handguns, and 6 percent opposed.[39] Thus, among big-city police chiefs, support for a waiting period was nearly unanimous.

In 1993, the Southern States Police Benevolent Association (PBA) surveyed its 10,614 members about gun control (Tables 2.3 and 2.4). Association President Jack Roberts explained that the survey was conducted because, "We simply had enough of every special interest group, including a number of national police organizations, claiming they spoke for rank and file officers on the subject of gun control . . . .What our members told us may be quite an eye-opener for some people, but it won't be to anyone who is in touch with rank-and-file cops." Asked about the Brady Bill, 86.5 percent of the Southern officers said it would affect only law-abiding citizens, and would not prevent criminals from getting guns. An instant check on gun buyers at the point of sale was supported by 63.8 percent, while only 23.1 percent supported a waiting period for handgun purchases. In addition, 96.4 percent strongly supported firearms ownership for self-protection, and 90.1 percent thought the United States Constitution guaranteed the right of law-abiding citizens to own guns. Strict gun control laws as a way to cut violent crime were considered effective by 34.7 percent.[40]

BIG-CITY CHIEFS ON GUN CONTROL

Table 2.1

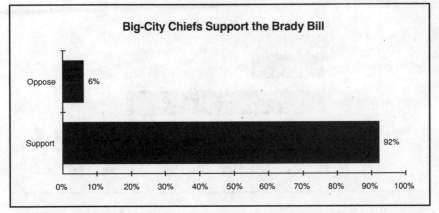

The Police Executive Research Forum found that big-city chiefs, if asked to choose between no new gun laws and the Brady Bill, overwhelmingly support the Brady Bill.

Table 2.2

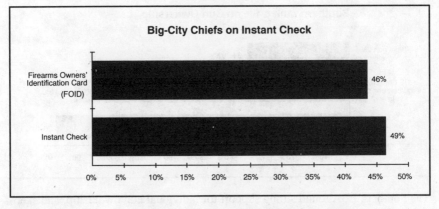

Big-city chiefs narrowly prefer an instant check to a firearms owners identification card.

SOUTHERN RANK AND FILE ON GUN CONTROL

Table 2.3

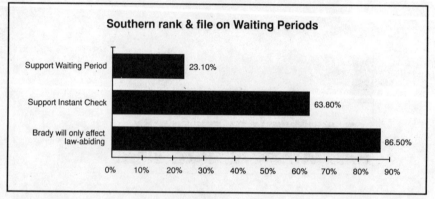

The Southern States Police Benevolent Association (PBA) found that most members thought the Brady Bill would not work, and that an instant check would be preferable.

Table 2.4

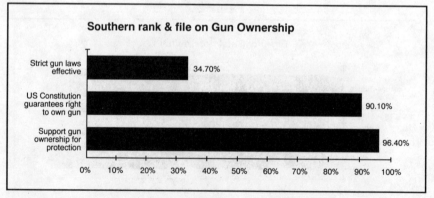

The Southern PBA found strong support for individual gun ownership, and skepticism about the efficacy of strict gun controls.

Table 2.5

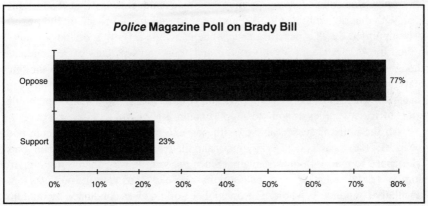

Police magazine found its readers strongly opposed to the Brady Bill.

Table 2.6

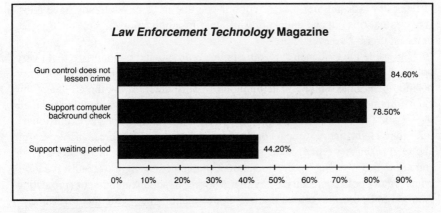

Law Enforcement Technology magazine's polling was consistent with other police polls.

Police magazine, the largest-circulation magazine for police officers, conducted its own poll of police attitudes in 1993 (Table 2.5). Asked "Do you support the Brady Bill, including a waiting period and background check before a handgun can be sold?" Twenty-three percent of *Police* readers said yes, and 77 percent said no. Eighty-five percent thought that gun ownership by civilians increased public safety. Ninety percent thought that gun ownership by citizens did not negatively affect their job.[41]

Law Enforcement Technology magazine also conducted a poll in 1991 (Table 2.6), with the following results: A computerized background check of gun buyers was supported by 78.5 percent of respondents, while a waiting period was supported by 44.2 percent. Seventy-seven and four-tenths percent of respondents thought that gun control infringed on the right to bear arms; 84.6 percent thought that gun control did not lessen crime. Overall, police chiefs, sheriffs, and top managers were more likely to support gun control than middle managers, while street officers were least likely to support controls.[42]

All the polls discussed above, with one exception, suffer from a common weakness: they were conducted by mail, and the results are based on respondents who chose to mail in a questionnaire. Since the sample was, therefore, nonrandom, it is not certain that the population that chose to respond to the poll was representative of police as whole. The one police poll that was conducted by random sample, using the professional polling firm Spectrum Resources of Tallahassee, Florida, was the Southern States Police Benevolent Association poll. (That poll found Southern rank-and-file police strongly opposed to gun control in general, and the Brady Bill in particular.)

A large number of working officers seem to agree with Willis Booth, a former police chief and executive director of the Florida Police Chiefs Association: "I think any working policeman will tell you that the crooks already have guns. If a criminal fills out an application and sends his application . . . he's the biggest, dumbest crook I've ever seen."

Put aside the evidence regarding police opinion, and hypothesize that every police chief in the United States supported a national waiting period. Should their position determine the law? The opinion of police chiefs is not the arbiter of our Constitutional rights. Police chiefs are, after all, not generally renowned for their regard for the Constitution. Some police executives criticize the exclusionary rule; they claim that a strong Fourth Amendment (barring unreasonable search and seizure) causes crime. Some police executives criticize the *Miranda* decision and argue that a strong Sixth Amendment (guaranteeing right to counsel) causes crime. Many police executives say that a strong Second Amendment (protecting the right to bear arms) causes crime.[43] Police administrators are the government, and the Bill of Rights is designed to control the government. So when government officials claim that any part of the Bill of Rights should be curtailed, the claims, while entitled to serious attention, should not be taken as the final word on the issue.

Why did the Brady Bill have nearly unanimous support among big-city police executives? While it is true that some big-city chiefs strongly oppose the right to bear arms, not all are so inclined. One reason for supporting the waiting period is its intuitive appeal; at first glance, it seems like a way to interdict at least some criminals without interfering with legitimate gun owners.

Perhaps another reason that some police chiefs favor the waiting period is that police chiefs, like any other administrators of large government offices, often seek to expand their official power. From the perspective of a police administrator, more power may mean more officers performing administrative tasks and supervising more transactions by the citizenry.

Public Opinion Polls

The Gallup poll reported: "91 percent of Americans Favor Brady Amendment."[44] If the polls are for it, who can be against it?

One reason to be cautious about polls is that the bias of the pollster can skew the poll. By modifying the wording of a question, "You can come up with any result you want," says Peter Hart, pollster for the 1988 Dukakis presidential campaign.

The Gallup poll about waiting periods posed the question in a way that assumed the waiting period really would help the police keep guns away from those who should not have them: "Would you favor or oppose a national law requiring a seven-day waiting period before a handgun could be purchased, in order to determine whether the prospective buyer has been convicted of a felony or is mentally ill?"[45] As discussed below, the criminological and real-world evidence on waiting periods suggests that they do little good in keeping illegitimate users from getting guns; criminals do not buy guns in gun stores.

Most people are for something that works. If the question assumes that a waiting period would be effective, it is bound to receive nearly unanimous support.

Similarly, a 1993 Lou Harris poll warmed up the respondents with a long parade of "questions" designed to illustrate the horrors of gun ownership. Respondents were presented with facts such as, "In 1988, one in every six pediatricians treated a young person who was the victim of a gunshot wound." The respondents were then asked if such facts made them feel more urgently about the problems of guns and children. After the battery of advocacy, respondents were then asked if they supported the Brady Bill, and 89 percent said yes.[46]

Lou Harris's 1993 claim to have found a "sea-change in public attitudes" in favor of gun control was rendered somewhat less credible by the fact that Harris claimed to have found the same thing in 1975, when he told a Senate committee that, "There is as clear a national mandate for this committee, for the House, and for the Senate as any you have ever had . . . I think we will see in 1976, if someone takes national leadership on the gun control issue, you will see some casualties on the other side, that those who dared to oppose gun control will be casualties as opposed to those who dared to stand up for gun control being casualties. That is how radically, I think, the American people are changing."[47]

Notably, pollsters such as Gallup and Harris, who use their organizations to promote whatever happens to be the current agenda of the gun control lobbies, studiously avoided asking respondents about the actual issue before Congress: which is better, a mandatory instant check or the Brady Bill? In May 1991, Lawrence Research asked Americans whether they preferred a waiting period with an optional check (the spring 1991 version of the Brady Bill) or a mandatory instant telephone check, with no waiting period (the NRA alternative). By 78 percent to 14 percent, the public chose the instant check, a margin which, at least, suggests that support for the Brady Bill was far from unanimous.[48]

In 1993, Luntz Weber Research & Strategic Services, the firm that had conducted candidate Ross Perot's polling, asked the same question; 93 percent of the public chose the instant check. The Luntz Weber firm also asked respondents what they knew about the Brady Bill. Twenty-seven percent knew nothing about it; 30 percent could only identify it as a "gun control" bill.[49] Quite plainly, a large majority of Americans want a background check on handgun buyers. Just as plainly, they prefer a mandatory instant check (the NRA proposal) to the waiting period (the Brady Bill).

Even if the Brady Bill did enjoy the huge public support which the skewed polling questions suggested, opinion poll results are not always an appropriate guide to public policy because the Constitution does not depend on polls. Violating the Constitution can be a popular thing. By huge majorities, Americans would favor all of the following:

- banning use of civic auditoriums by atheists, by people denouncing the government, or by patriotic groups advocating war against a foreign enemy;
- using a federal censorship board to decide which television shows are permissible;
- infiltrating nonviolent dissident groups with FBI agents.[50]

Every one of those popular ideas would violate the Constitution. The precise reason for putting certain fundamental rights in the Constitution is to protect them from transient majorities.[51] No measure could have been more unconstitutional than herding American citizens of Japanese descent into concentration camps during WWII. Public opinion and the press heavily favored this repression, despite the total lack of evidence that these Americans were disloyal.

Even though they sometimes back unconstitutional measures, the public may still know that the Constitution is more important. One survey asked: "Suppose the President and Congress have to violate a Constitutional principle to pass an important law the people wanted. Would you support them in this action?" Twenty-eight percent said yes, "because the Constitution shouldn't be allowed to stand in the way of what the people need and want." Forty-nine percent said no, "because protecting the Constitution is more important to the national welfare than any law could possibly be."[52]

While the majority of the public does favor some kind of background check (although probably by less than the 91 percent majority found by Gallup's biased questioning), the public opposes "a law giving police the power to decide who may or may not own firearms" by a 68 percent to 29 percent margin.[53] Accordingly, if a waiting period were conducted within the limits implied in the Gallup poll (every legitimate owner got the gun in no more than seven days), the public might well support a waiting period. But if waiting periods turned out to give police the opportunity to interfere with citizens' right to buy firearms, the vast majority of the public would oppose a waiting period. As detailed below, waiting periods in practice often lead to the kinds of police abuses which the public overwhelmingly opposes.

The Brady Bill may or not have been a good idea, but the incorrect claims that the police and the public nearly unanimously wanted the bill would not, even if the claims had been accurate, have made it any better as a matter of public policy.

HOW WELL DO WAITING PERIODS WORK?

As of this writing, the Brady Act has been in effect for about a year. Before discussing the data regarding the Brady Act, it makes sense to review the research regarding the state-level waiting periods that have been law for many years.

Criminological Studies

"Virtually every study ever conducted proves that where there are local or state laws requiring a waiting period and background check, handguns are harder to obtain by those who are prone to misuse them," claims Handgun Control, Inc.[54] Actually, there is not a single study published in any academic journal which concludes that waiting periods are effective.

Professor Matthew DeZee, formerly a criminologist at Florida State University, wrote: "I firmly believe that more restrictive legislation is necessary to reduce the volume of gun crime." Yet his comparative study of state laws, including waiting periods, found that "The results indicate that not a single gun control law, and not all the gun control laws added together, had a significant impact . . . in determining gun violence. It appears, then, that present legislation created to reduce the level of violence in society falls short of its goals. . . . Gun laws do not appear to affect gun crimes."[55]

Professors Joseph P. Magadinno and Marshall H. Medoff, both of California State University, Long Beach, conducted two studies of waiting periods at the state level. The first study, using data from 1979 and previous years, compared the 1979 robbery and homicide rates in states that had waiting periods with states that did not.

The study also looked at changes in the robbery and homicide rates in states that had recently changed their laws regarding firearms sales. Both aspects of the study found no correlation between waiting periods and lower homicide or robbery rates.[56]

A second Magadinno-Medoff study analyzed state gun laws and rates of homicide, robbery, and aggravated assault in 1960 and 1970. The results were consistent with the hypothesis that stricter state gun control laws have no impact on crime.[57]

When the United States Senate Judiciary Committee investigated the issue, the committee found no evidence that waiting periods affect crime. Nor was there any correlation between a waiting period and lower crime rates.[58]

Duke University's Philip Cook, who is generally supportive of gun control, explains why there is no apparent statistical impact:

> [W]e suspect that most felons and other ineligibles who obtain guns do so not because the state's screening system fails to discover their criminal record, but rather because these people find ways of circumventing the screening system entirely. . . . Under these circumstances, developing a more intensive and reliable screening process is probably not worth the additional cost. . . . It is known that such screening systems are widely circumvented and, furthermore, that state criminal record files are sufficiently incomplete that a felon who did choose to submit to the required police check before buying a handgun would have a sporting chance of having his application accepted.[59]

As former Assistant Attorney General John Bolton observed, "Those persons with a criminal record who are prohibited from purchasing a handgun are the ones most likely to obtain false identification documents to support a new name."[60]

University of Maryland criminologist David McDowall, generally a supporter of gun control, performed before-and-after analyses of the effects of new or extended waiting periods in Cincinnati, St. Louis, Los Angeles, and San Francisco on intentional deaths in those cities. McDowall concluded that "waiting periods have no influence on either gun homicides or gun suicides."[61]

The most thorough study of waiting periods was performed by Florida State University Professor of Criminology Gary Kleck. Analyzing data from every U.S. city with a population over one hundred thousand, and controlling for social variables such as race, income, and religion, Kleck found no statistically significant effect from waiting periods.[62]

Of course the Kleck, McDowall, Magadinno-Medoff, and DeZee studies do not completely destroy the case for a waiting period. It might be that state or city waiting periods have a small impact on crime, even if that impact is too small to be statistically significant. Moreover, even if state waiting periods were acknowledged as demonstrable failures, it might be that a federal wait would be effective.

Under the Carter administration, the National Institute of Justice (NIJ) offered a grant to the former president of the American Sociological Association and two colleagues to survey the field of research on gun control. Peter Rossi and his co-authors, Jim Wright and Kathleen Daly, began their work convinced of the importance of strict national gun control. Indeed, Wright had already written about the need for more control. After looking at the data, however, the three researchers found no convincing evidence that gun control curbs crime.[63]

A few years later, Wright and Rossi conducted another NIJ study, this time on the gun use patterns of criminals. They interviewed prisoners in ten state systems. The study confirmed that many criminals are frightened of armed citizens.[64] Notably, the second NIJ study discovered that felons in states with strict laws found obtaining a gun no more difficult than in those with more moderate laws. Almost all felons, regardless of the severity of their state's laws, reported that they would have little or no difficulty obtaining a gun soon after release.

When Wright and Rossi asked the prisoners where they obtained their last handgun, 21 percent replied at a gun store.[65] Hence, Handgun Control, Inc., argues that a waiting period and background check would affect a significant number of gun crimes. But Wright and Rossi disagree with the group's interpretation of the data. According to Wright and Rossi:

> One might as a matter of federal policy require that every firearms transaction be reported to the cognizant authorities, and the appropriate criminal records check undertaken; but one quickly senses that this measure would have little or no effect on the criminal users whom we are trying to interdict and a considerable effect on legitimate users. . . . The ideal gun crime policy is one that impacts directly on the illicit user but leaves the legitimate user pretty much alone.[66]

Analysis of the Wright-Rossi data suggests that far less than 21 percent of criminal gun users would be affected by a background check. The 21 percent who obtained their last crime handgun at a gun store included 5 percent who had obtained the gun by theft rather than by purchase. Of the 16 percent who had obtained the gun by purchase, at least some likely did not have a disqualifying criminal record at the time of purchase.

Further, not all the guns obtained by criminals are acquired for crime. Many criminals live in neighborhoods with other criminals, and hence own guns for defense. The more likely a felon was to be a serious gun criminal, the less likely he was to have acquired a retail gun. For example, of the criminals who specialized in unarmed crime, 30 percent obtained their most recent handgun at a store, by purchase or by theft. Of the "handgun predators" who specialize in handgun crime, only 7 percent had gotten a handgun from a store. For criminals as a whole, of the guns that had been obtained "to use in a crime," 12 percent came from a store.[67]

Since about one-fourth of the handguns from stores were stolen from stores, only about 9 percent of handguns obtained to use in a crime (and about 5 to 6 percent of handguns obtained by handgun predators) came from a retail purchase. Nine percent or even 5 percent is still a significant number of criminals buying guns in gun stores. But Wright and Rossi explain that their data

[do] not imply that the men in question themselves simply walked into a gun shop and bought themselves a gun, in direct defiance of the Gun Control Act of 1968. In many cases, these purchases would have been made in the felon's behalf by friends or associates with "clean" records, which is, to be sure, still quite illegal. Although we asked these men where and how they had obtained their most recent guns, we did not ask who, exactly, had obtained them.[68]

Assuming that only half the purchases were made by legal surrogates, the background check is entirely irrelevant to 95 to 98 percent of crime gun acquisitions.

The large majority of all gun acquisitions are by people who already own a gun.[69] If the pattern also holds true for criminals, then the background check would impact less than half of the already tiny percentage of criminals who personally buy guns at retail. In other words, of all guns acquired for crime, only about one-half of 1 percent to 2 or 3 percent are personally bought at a retail outlet by a person with an existing criminal record who does not already have another gun.[70] This estimate is consistent with a 1970s Bureau of Alcohol, Tobacco, and Firearms study of gun dealer sales in Des Moines and Greenville, which found that about 1 to 2 percent of sales were to dangerous criminals.[71] In short, waiting periods have no statistically noticeable impact on any type of crime because only a tiny fraction of crime guns are purchased at retail by ineligible buyers. And no matter how intense the checking process on gun buyers, almost every criminal will still know one person with a clean record who could make a purchase for the criminal.

Three percent (as a high) or one-half of 1 percent (as a low) is still a large number of crime guns coming from retail stores, in a purchase that could be prevented by a background check of gun buyers. Indeed, any law that could make the American gun crime problem 1 percent less severe would be quite a successful and important piece of legislation. The difficulty, however, in attempting to stop criminals from buying guns in stores is that there are so many other methods available for them to obtain firearms, as will be discussed below. Of course disarming a single violent criminal is still forward progress, but the criminological data help show why the public should not be surprised or disappointed that the Brady Act has not apparently led to a major drop in armed crime.

In this conclusion, the criminologists appear to be in agreement with the criminals. For example, after the Brady Bill passed the House of Representatives in 1991, Reilly Johnson, a prisoner serving a life sentence in New Mexico, asked some of his fellow convicts what they thought:

- "Where do I get a gun? That's easy. I steal it or I buy one from someone who stole it."
- "Once I'm outta' the joint, it'll take me maybe an hour to get a gun. If you know a junkie, you know where to buy one. Junkies are the residential burglars."

- (When told that California's waiting period law had caught felons trying to buy guns in gun stores) "You gotta be kiddin'! Somebody that tried to buy a gun from a place where you have to give your real name has taken one too many pulls on the Krylon silver. Can you picture me goin' in some Straight John's gun shop with all these tattoos? Hey, the guy runnin' the shop is gonna' bust himself callin' the cops. He takes one look at me and he won't think I'm there to buy. He'll think I'm there to rob him."
- "You know what my worst nightmare is? I bust into someone's living room and I find Joe Citizen in his lazy boy with his gun."
- "This is just more magic from Washington. Just like no more taxes was supposed to cure poverty, no more guns is supposed to cure crime. Guns are only the tip of the iceberg. Gun control is cosmetics, a band-aid on a broken leg."[72]

The statements by these New Mexico prisoners are consistent with the polling data of felony prisoners in other states, where the prisoners reported that gun control laws would pose essentially no impediment to their obtaining a gun upon release.

State Data

Although the academics have never found any statistically significant effect from waiting periods, it would be incorrect to conclude that waiting periods accomplish nothing. The following section reports results in several jurisdictions that had waiting periods before the Brady Bill.

California

California's fifteen-day waiting period, applicable to long guns as well as handguns, and private transfers as well as retail sales, has a "hit" rate of one to one-and-a-half percent.[73] An analysis by researcher Clayton Cramer of California handgun murders ratès from 1952 until the present shows no discernible impact from the waiting periods, even as they grew from one day for handguns to fifteen days for all guns.[74] As discussed below, the California waiting period forms have been used to build a government data base of gun owners.

About 10 percent of California's three hundred thousand "assault weapon" owners have registered their weapons, as required by California law. The group that complied with the retroactive registration law surely qualifies as a highly law-abiding set of people. Yet this group of highly law-abiding gun owners, when they attempt to buy a new rifle or pistol following California's fifteen-day waiting period, sometimes find that the California Department of Justice has put a hold on their application because they are registered "assault weapon" owners.[75]

A Los Angeles City councilman, noting the thriving market in stolen Rolex watches, suggested that all Rolex watches be registered, and a five-day waiting period be imposed on transfers of second-hand Rolexes. The Rolex waiting period was ridiculed by most other Los Angeles politicians and written up in the national press as another instance of California silliness. It might be asked why so many people who dismiss the idea that registration and a waiting period would affect the criminal sale of Rolex watches think that similar action would affect the criminal sale of firearms.

Illinois

Prospective gun purchasers must obtain a Firearms Owners Identification Card (FOID), which is valid for five years. There are about five thousand applications every week for the card. Over the weekend, a list of applicants is run through the state Department of Mental Health, revealing about ten applicants who are ineligible to buy because of mental disability.[76] Illinois's automated licensing system often takes sixty days to authorize a clearance.[77]

In 1993, out of about 250,000 FOID applications, there were 3,382 denials for felony convictions, and 715 for mental hospitalization. While the FOID system has been in place since the 1960s, an instant-check system was layered on top of the FOID system in 1992, to verify a gun buyer's continued eligibility. In 1993, there were 203,936 instant checks conducted, which resulted in 157 denials to persons whose FOID cards had been revoked; 96 denials for outstanding criminal warrants; 343 denials for warrants on other offenses, such as traffic tickets; and 63 denials for felony convictions.[78]

The most thorough study of the Illinois system was conducted by Professor David Bordua. Happily, "the system was run with real attention to due process protections for firearms owners." Unfortunately, "even its administrators were not convinced it was effective." The system, which costs over a million dollars a year to administer, was summarized as "inherently weak."[79]

Maryland

About 700 to 800 of every 20,000 gun purchase applicants are denied in a given year. (The waiting period/police permission applies to all handguns and to long guns labeled "assault weapons.") According to state police testimony before a congressional subcommittee, the hundreds of denials typically lead to only a handful of prosecutions.[80]

Notably, 78 percent of appeals by denied applicants result in a reversal of the initial denial by the police.[81] The success rate on appeals likely understates the police error rate in initial denials. Many people who have been improperly denied may have neither the finances nor the energy to pursue an appeal. (Similarly, the American Civil Liberties Union points out that only a minority of people improperly denied welfare benefits attempt to appeal.)

Although the waiting period is by statute supposed to last only one week, the check police often take much longer; although not legally required to wait more than a week, many gun shops will not release the firearm until the police have completed their review.[82]

New Jersey

Firearms laws in New Jersey are the strictest of any American state. Handgun Control, Inc., states that "10,000 convicted felons have been caught trying to buy handguns."[83] The number of New Jersey citizens arbitrarily denied the right to possess arms under the New Jersey law is almost as large as that of persons with criminal records identified by the system. About one-quarter of the rejections in New Jersey are based on the hunch of police that it would not be a good idea for a particular person to own a gun, rather than on any specific disqualifying criterion.[84] Although New Jersey law requires that the authorities act on gun license applications within thirty days, delays of three to four months are standard; some applications are delayed for years for no valid reason.[85]

The cost to the New Jersey taxpayers has not been small. The New Jersey licensing system is so expensive that it costs $4,442.13 (more than the salary of a state trooper for one month) for each denial based on criminal, mental, or alcohol abuse records. (The figure is based on the average four-hour processing time for an application, the number of applications and denials, and the average state trooper salary.)[86] It might be that the resources diverted into the licensing system would have saved far more lives if they had been spent on putting state troopers on patrol, instead of putting workers behind a desk.

The overall crime rate and the gun crime rate in New Jersey have remained consistent with those in other states in the region, even though none of them imposes gun controls as strict as New Jersey's.

Pennsylvania

In Pennsylvania, handgun buyers face a forty-eight hour waiting period (seventy-two hours in practice), during which the local police or sheriff may conduct a check.[87] After the buyer picks up the handgun, the transaction record is sent to the state police firearms unit, which checks the name against a list of violent felons. Data for the first check by local police are kept at the county level, so there are no comprehensive figures available.

In addition to checking the approximately 130,000 to 150,000 handgun transfers that occur in a year, the state police are also automating their old records of firearms transfers (which date back to 1931) and checking the old names against the same list of violent felons. In 1988, the state police performed about 230,000 total records checks, resulting in about eighty "hits."

When a "hit" occurs, state troopers are sent to confiscate the gun, and the local district attorney may bring charges for unlawful gun possession by a felon. Ms. Sharon Crawford, head of the state police firearms unit, recalled only one case in her memory where a person had committed a crime in the two to three week interval between taking possession of the gun and the arrival of the state trooper, or had refused to hand the gun over to the trooper. In the one case, the person had shot (not fatally) someone else during an argument.

The explanation for the generally peaceful behavior of the persons caught with illegal guns is that the purchases were not with the intention of use in a crime, but rather were self-defense or sporting purchases by persons who did not realize they were ineligible, or who hoped to slip through the system.[88]

Indeed, it should be recognized that many of the felons who are "caught" by background checks are persons who have never committed any act of violence. Their felony conviction may stem from having cheated on their income taxes or having been convicted of possessing a small quantity of drugs a decade before in college. The attempted purchase of a firearm by such persons is hardly a serious threat to public safety. Yet some gun control advocates trumpet the number of "felons caught attempting to purchase guns" as if every person caught were a bank robber procuring the tools of his trade.

The Pennsylvania data validate the findings by Wright and Rossi: there are many attempted and/or completed firearms acquisitions by ex-felons that are unrelated to any effort to use the gun in a crime. Accordingly, the number of crimes prevented by a system that keeps ex-felons from buying guns in stores is likely to be significantly less than the number of ex-felons who are caught buying guns. All this is not to say that the "felon-in-possession" cases should not be prosecuted or taken seriously; the point is simply that most attempted acquisitions were not for a criminal purpose.

It would not be correct to use the Pennsylvania state data to conclude that background checks are pointless. The data above refer only to the state police check of names against violent felony convictions. The data do not show what impact the first check, by the local police had. It might be that most violent felons buying guns for crime are stopped at the local level, and hence are never checked by the state system.

Virginia

In 1989, Virginia enacted an instant telephone check, with the consent of both Handgun Control, Inc., and the NRA. The next year, the instant check was expanded to apply to long guns as well as handguns. The Virginia law is the model for the national instant check that should replace the waiting period sometime before late 1998. About 16 to 20 percent of phone applications result in a "hit," requiring the rejected applicant to submit fingerprints to the police to prove his noncriminal identity.[89] The ultimate denial rate is about 1 percent.[90] The Virginia system requires twenty-eight full-time state employees and $696,341 in annual operating costs.[91] All applicants over eighty years old are automatically rejected by the Virginia instant check, since the federal database of felonies and arrests automatically purges all persons of that age.[92]

In sum, the evidence from around the country shows that a permission system does result in some denials, at least half of which turn out to be incorrect. Even in the case of denials that are correctly applied to ineligible purchasers, it is erroneous to assume that the denial has thereby prevented a crime. Virtually no one who intends to commit a gun crime buys from a gun store. Ineligible people do sometimes attempt retail transactions, but that act is hardly proof that they intended a crime.

Of the people who are rejected by permission systems, a mere 1 percent are arrested.[93] In other words, where a permission system is in effect, about one in ten thousand applicants turns out to be a criminal who is arrested. A success rate of one true "hit" for every ten thousand searches is literally not much better than the odds of finding a needle in a haystack—and not a cost-effective method of catching criminals.

The Brady Bill

On the Brady Act's first anniversary, the Treasury Department sampled 441,545 handgun purchase applications. Those applications had resulted in 15,506 denials, a rate of 3.5 percent. Of the denials, 4,365 (slightly under 1 percent of total purchase attempts) were for felony convictions, 945 were for failure to appear in court, 97 were because of a pending but unresolved indictment, and 649 were for drug use. In Ohio, the Brady Act found 16,499 applications leading to 129 denials.[94]

In states that rejected the Brady waiting period and instead set up their own instant check program, the number of felons caught trying to buy guns has been at least equal to that in states implementing Brady. In Nevada, for example, an instant check allows about 70 percent of gun buyers to receive approval within two to three minutes, and most of the rest within a few hours. Of 25,171 handgun purchase applications made from February 28, 1994, to September 30, 1994, there were 333 denials, twelve of which led to the arrest of fugitives.[95] In the first six months of Colorado's instant check, the denial rate was 8 percent—2,750 denials out of 34,000 applications. (Colorado's disqualification criteria for gun possession were broader than the federal criteria, since Colorado disqualifies all subjects of a restraining order related to domestic conflict.) The Colorado instant check located 356 fugitives, although many of these were people who had failed to appear in court for traffic offenses and similar petty crimes.[96]

In the discussion of state background checks, it was suggested that most of the people denied as a result of background checks are not professional criminals, but rather those who failed to realize that a distant felony (such as for tax evasion or a fight in a bar) disqualified them from gun ownership. The generally harmless nature of the vast majority of people denied under Brady is demonstrated by the tiny number of prosecutions that have resulted. (Any person with a felony conviction who attempts to purchase a gun commits a federal felony and, in almost all states, a state felony.) As of December 1994, BATF had pursued less than two dozen prosecutions of felons stemming from Brady Act denials.[97] As of

September 1994 (when Brady review hearings where held in Congress), not a single prosecution had been commenced for violating the Brady Act itself.[98] On the Brady Act's first anniversary, the Treasury Department reported only four prosecutions under the Brady Act, although the Department did not know how many, if any, state prosecutions might have resulted.[99]

Upon closer examination, the large number of denials may indicate a large number not of violent felons denied guns but of lawful citizens denied, at least temporarily, their right to purchase a handgun. For example, according to the police in Austin, Texas, 85 percent of denials resulted in a later approval. The wrongful denials were the result primarily of applicants with a name similar to someone with a felony conviction. In some cases, the applicant was correctly identified, but national criminal history files recorded only the fact of the person's prior arrest for a felony and not the subsequent dismissal of charges, plea to a misdemeanor, or acquittal.[100]

According to the Brady Act, the police are allowed to deny permission to purchase a handgun only when, under federal or state law, the applicant is legally ineligible to do so. But as in every other country where the police have been given power to approve gun sales, the power has been used for ends beyond those intended. For example, in response to a request from a city councilman, the Phoenix, Arizona, police department produced a report detailing the reason for every Brady denial in the week of March 28 to April 3, 1994. During that period, there were thirty-five denials, all of them arising from a criminal warrant for failure to appear in court for various charges. Of the thirty-five failure-to-appear warrants, thirty-one related to misdemeanors; even a misdemeanor conviction is not a bar under federal law to the purchase of firearms.[101] Of the four outstanding felony warrants, two were for "dangerous drugs" and two were for larceny. None was for a violent felony. Some people were denied the ability to purchase a handgun because they had failed to make a court date for charges stemming from failure to obtain a dog license, fishing without a license, or speeding.[102] In Texas, a domestic temporary restraining order was not a legal bar to gun possession; however, the police began using Brady to reject handgun purchase applications from persons subjected to a restraining order.[103]

Incidentally, unlawful governmental implementation of handgun permission-to-purchase laws did not begin in February 1993. For example, in the 1980s, Broward County, Florida, had a ten-day handgun waiting period (which was later preempted by state law). Nearly half of Broward's rejections were for unpaid traffic tickets or similar offenses which do not legally disqualify Floridians from gun ownership.[104]

PARTICULAR TARGETS OF WAITING PERIODS

Although waiting periods might have little impact on the average street criminal, it is sometimes suggested that they might deter particular kinds of gun misusers.

Drug Dealers

In 1988, Handgun Control, Inc., attempted to hang its national waiting period on a comprehensive drug bill, under the theory that the waiting period would disarm narcotics distributors. Handgun Control, Inc., continued to promise that a waiting period would help take guns away from drug dealers.[105]

It taxes credulity to assume that any kind of gun legislation, including a waiting period, would impact drug dealers. Dealers, being expert in the black market, would have the readiest access to false identification and to underground supplies. They are the last people gun control could affect.

Drug dealers obviously cannot count on the police or the courts for protection from violence. Because of this, and because dealers are a valuable robbery target, it would be virtual suicide for them not to carry a gun.[106] In addition, drug dealers cannot use normal legal and social commercial dispute resolution mechanisms. Like the gangsters of alcohol prohibition days, today's drug dealers need guns to protect their business's income and territory. Thus, many must own a gun for their lives and their livelihoods.

No matter how scarce guns become for civilians, there will always be one for a criminal who can pay enough. If the price of street handguns went up to $2,000, dealers would still buy them, simply because they have to.[107] Spending a few hours' or days' profits on self-protection is the only logical decision for a dealer. Can anyone really believe that an individual who buys pure heroin by the ounce, who transacts in the highly illegal chemicals used to produce amphetamines, or who sells cocaine on the toughest streetcorners in the worst neighborhoods will not know where to buy an illegal gun?

Homicidal Maniacs

Background checks may do more good with regard to mentally deranged murderers than with any other particular class of criminal. First of all, mentally ill mass murderers are rarely sophisticated criminals (or even competent career criminals). Denied a gun at a retail store, they may be too inept to acquire firearms any other way.

Francesco Duran, who fired bullets at the White House in October 1994, used a rifle (which he bought with no background check), but he had been turned down in a separate attempt to purchase a handgun. (Duran had a felony conviction dating back to an assault while he had been in the army a few years before.)

It is important, though, to recognize that background checks will not necessarily disarm all, or most psychopaths. For example, Patrick Purdy, who killed five children in Stockton, California, in 1989, bought five guns over the counter in California, despite the state's strict fifteen-day waiting period. Laurie Dann bought a handgun and shot up a second-grade classroom in Illinois, killing one child, wounding five, and then killing herself, despite that state's requirement that all gun owners be licensed and undergo a waiting period.[108] Mark David Chapman, John

Lennon's assassin, bought a handgun in Hawaii, a state with one of the strictest waiting periods in the nation. Canada has a nationwide licensing system, yet a deranged man was able to buy a rifle with which he shot and killed fourteen women at a Montreal university in December 1989.[109]

Moreover, some psychopaths are professional criminals, such as Eugene Thompson, a felon and a cocaine addict who shot up a Denver suburb in March 1989. (Thompson should have been in prison but apparently had been released as part of a deal by which he would provide undercover information to the police.)

One should be cautious in evaluating the assertions of gun control advocates that a waiting period or background check would have stopped a particular murderer. In 1990, a mental patient who bought a gun in an Atlanta suburb without a waiting period, opened fire on shoppers at Atlanta's Perimeter Mall, killing one and wounding four others. Responding to gun control lobbyists' claims that a waiting period would have prevented the killing, DeKalb County promptly approved a fifteen-day waiting period.[110] Actually, the killer's record of mental disorder was entirely private, and he had never been adjudicated mentally incompetent or involuntarily committed.

Although a background check might disarm at least a few of the least competent mass murderers, it would not be realistic to expect that a waiting period would have an additional beneficial effect. The criminally insane are, case histories show, criminally insane day after day for years and years, not just for the days or weeks covered by a waiting period.

Domestic Homicides

Many handgun control advocates assume that a waiting period would prevent domestic "impulse killings."[111] But most domestic killings occur at night, when gun stores are closed. Most perpetrators are intoxicated with drugs or alcohol, and thus legally forbidden to buy a gun anyway. The image of a murderously enraged person leaving home, driving to a gun store, finding one open after ten P.M. (when most crimes of passion occur), buying a weapon, and driving home to kill is implausible.[112]

In any case, husbands who kill wives rarely use guns. Wives who kill husbands often do use guns, and are often defending themselves or their children against felonious attacks.[113] Imposing a waiting period which prevents people in domestic turmoil from obtaining guns immediately will not lessen the ability of men to kill women, although it will reduce the ability of wives to defend themselves against ex-husbands, ex-boyfriends, and other predators.

The issue of guns as a "risk factor" for domestic homicide is discussed in chapter 5.

People in Need of "Cooling Off"

As the Brady Bill was moving through Congress, one of the key issues of contention was the purpose of the five government working-days waiting period. Handgun Control, Inc., argued that the waiting period was a good thing in itself, since it would impose a "cooling-off period" on gun buyers and thereby prevent them from committing hotheaded crimes. Congress, though, apparently disagreed; the waiting period applies only until the national instant check becomes operational. Accordingly, Congress apparently conceived of the waiting period solely as a facilitator of the police background check. Once the local police check can be replaced by a national instant check, the waiting period disappears, according to the Brady Act as currently enacted.

To Handgun Control, Inc., this is not a satisfactory result; as noted above, the group's Brady II proposal would set up a permanent waiting/cooling-off period.

Criminologist Gary Kleck (whose gun policy book *Point Blank* won the American Society of Criminology's Hindelang Prize as the most significant contribution to criminology in a three-year period) points out that for a "cooling-off" period to prevent homicide, a number of conditions must be fulfilled: (1) The gun the killer uses is the only one he owns, or the only one he could have used in the crime; (2) the killer acquires the gun from a source that would be expected to obey gun control laws (i.e., a licensed dealer); (3) the gun was purchased and used in the homicide in a time period shorter than the "cooling-off" period. Reviewing an analysis of 1982 Florida homicides, Kleck found that 0.9 percent of homicides fit all three criteria. He estimated that nationally about 0.5 percent would fit all three criteria.

Nevertheless, Kleck suggested that a waiting period would not prevent even one in two hundred homicides. For the homicide actually to be prevented, several other conditions would all have to be fulfilled: (1) the killer is the kind of person who would not be willing to kill even after waiting; in other words, the killing is an isolated act rather than the culmination of a long history of assaults by the killer; (2) the killer could not acquire and successfully use a gun that does not require a cooling-off period (such as a long gun, in most states); (3) the killer would not be able to complete the homicide with any weapon other than a gun; (4) the killer would not be able or willing to obtain a gun from a nonretail source.

Considering all the necessary criteria, Kleck did not find any Florida homicides which a cooling-off period clearly would have prevented.[114] While supporting a background check, Kleck concluded that a cooling-off period would in itself do no good. Hence, he thought the waiting period offered no advantage over the instant check.

What Benefits Can Be Expected from the Brady Bill?

Few legislative acts have been accompanied by as much overpromising as the Brady Bill. Former New York City Mayor David Dinkins asserted that "The

Brady Bill could save thousands of lives in its first year."[115] Although many credulous New Yorkers believed their mayor and flooded then House of Representatives Speaker Tom Foley's office with phone calls demanding passage of the waiting period, there was not a serious criminologist in the United States who thought the mayor's assertion had any basis in reality. One year after the Brady Bill's enactment, no one would claim that thousands of lives have been saved.

Even a perfect waiting period or other permission system would not stop criminals from obtaining retail guns. False identification is not hard to procure. And although a fingerprint or other biometric check (possible within a decade, perhaps) would defeat false identification, most criminals would still likely know someone without a felony record. The surrogate buyer could still buy a gun for a criminal at retail.

Without preventing criminals from getting guns, the Brady Bill might perhaps make them go to more trouble to do so. When pressed for whether the waiting period will deprive criminals of guns, Handgun Control, Inc., expressed confidence that a waiting period would make gun acquisition more troublesome for criminals.[116] Likewise, the Bush administration federal task force which studied background checks acknowledged that "[E]ven a perfect felon identification system would not keep most felons from acquiring firearms."[117] The task force nonetheless supported a background check system, hoping that forcing some criminal buyers onto the black market would leave them less able to obtain high-quality firearms.[118]

But would a waiting period or other permission even inconvenience criminals, considering that few of them obtain crime guns through dealers anyway? Moreover, the current black market supplies even fully automatic firearms, which have been under a strict federal licensing system since 1934, and illegal to manufacture for civilians since 1986. If the black market can (and does) supply machine guns, it is doubtful that it cannot supply other high-quality weapons.

Still, as Professors Cook and Blose point out, there must be at least a few inexperienced or impecunious criminals for whom even a porous permission system would delay gun acquisition for at least some period. Moreover, the waiting period, simply because it will reduce gun sales to legal purchasers (discussed below), could reduce the number of guns in circulation. It seems likely that one of those unbought guns might one day have been part of a suicide, homicide, or accident that might not otherwise have occurred.

Proponents of the Brady Bill have said that waiting periods would be successful if they saved even a single life.[119] It seems clear that a waiting period or other permission-to-purchase system would, inevitably, prevent at least one firearms fatality. Even if a waiting period had no discernable impact on crime in general, it would save at least one life.

PROBLEMS CAUSED BY A WAITING PERIOD

The anecdotal evidence, presented earlier in this chapter, of crime victims who would have been disarmed at just the wrong time as a result of the Brady Bill suggests that the "save one life" argument for the Brady Bill is not persuasive. At least occasionally, the Brady Bill may cost lives, too. Accordingly, an argument in favor of the Brady Bill must depend on more than the hope that somehow, somewhere, a life will be saved. Moreover, the Brady Bill does not come free. It imposes substantial costs.

The Drain on Police Resources

Police resources are finite. The question is not whether a waiting period would save one life, but whether the police resources spent administering a waiting period might save more lives if used elsewhere. The sheriffs who have sued the federal government to have the Brady Bill's unfunded mandate on local government declared unconstitutional are making precisely this point. The point is also made by other police chiefs and sheriffs who, while not suing the federal government, have seen the results of the Brady suits, and have decided to stop performing background checks and to put their time into more productive endeavors.

Under Brady II's proposed new national waiting period, along with a comprehensive handgun registration and handgun owner licensing system, the drain on police resources would be staggering. In California, Handgun Control, Inc., convinced the legislature to make the background check apply to long guns and handguns, and to private transfers, as well as retail sales. Nationally, there are about 7.5 million gun transfers per year.[120] If a waiting period were to be rigorous enough to stop future Hinckleys, it would have to include address verification. How many hours would it take for a policeman to run a national criminal records check, and to visit or telephone the home of every person who applied? An average of one hour, at the very least, considering that many phone calls would be unanswered, and followup visits would be required. That would be 7.5 million police hours spent checking up on gun transactions rather than being engaged in other investigations. In the haystack of applications by honest citizens, police would search for a few needles left by the nation's stupidest criminals. Looking for crime, police officers would be directed into a paperwork enterprise particularly unlikely to lead to criminals. Would not all those millions of police hours be better spent patrolling, the streets instead of sitting behind a desk?[121]

The NRA's ideal, the national mandatory instant background check, will also impose huge costs. As the state experience regarding instant checks shows, about half of all denials are caused by identity confusion—the prospective gun buyer has the same name as a convicted felon. These gun buyers will be denied by the instant check, and must obtain permission to purchase by being fingerprinted, so that they can prove that they are not the same person as the convicted felon with the same name. According to the federal task force which studied background checks, implementing a national comprehensive permission system would require the FBI to hire 395 additional clerical employees to process the requests for fingerprint card readings for the (approximately) 725,000 citizens who would be denied permission to purchase because they have the same name as a criminal, or because police records noted an arrest but not a subsequent acquittal.[122]

To reduce these costs, one useful modification to the Brady Act (and to state counterparts) would be to exempt persons who already have a gun. Proof of lawful purchase of another gun would suffice for the exemption. After all, the biggest danger of gun purchases is an unarmed person who acquires a gun for malign purposes; someone who already owns one gun does not become significantly more dangerous when he buys another. Partly because gun collectors buy a disproportionate number of guns, requiring the background check only for first-time gun buyers would create major cost savings.

Besides draining police resources, the Brady Bill has impeded effective law enforcement in a more subtle way: Local politicians who are failing to take effective steps to control crime have used the campaign for a national waiting period as a tool to divert the attention to the national scene and away from local law enforcement. For example, after Utah tourist Brian Watkins was stabbed to death in a New York City subway in the summer of 1990, then New York Mayor Dinkins announced that what was needed to stop New York City crime was a national gun waiting period, or even gun prohibition. The mayor made the call for the national Brady Bill the centerpiece of his response to other publicized shootings in New York, regardless of whether evidence indicated that a waiting period would have any effect on a particular shooting.

Covert Registration

Many gun owners, including those who supported the Brady Bill, intensely oppose gun registration. They fear that if the government has a list of who owns which guns, such a list could one day be used to facilitate gun confiscation. Registration lists have been used for confiscation in some foreign countries, and in New York City and some other American jurisdictions.[124] On a more philosophical level, many persons believe the government has no authority to register people merely for exercising their Constitutional rights.[125]

Waiting periods and other permission systems can operate as de facto gun registration. Once the police are told who is applying to buy a gun, they may simply add that person's name to their list of gun owners, as is already the practice in New Jersey, New York, and other states. The California Justice Department has used the waiting period, without statutory authorization, to compile a list of handgun owners.[126] In Oregon, the police are allowed to retain handgun purchase records for up to five years.

The Brady Act attempts to solve the problem of covert registration by requiring the police to destroy the purchase application records. But Congress has no authority to compel an act by a state or local officer which is not required by the U.S. Constitution.[127] (For the same reason, the Brady Act's mandate that local police departments perform a background check has been declared unconstitutional by several federal courts.)

Even without the Constitutional problem, the Brady Act's promise of required records destruction is not backed up by meaningful enforcement. Police who keep illegal records are subject to no penalties or civil liability. Significantly, the practice of making daily computer backup tapes means that even if original records are destroyed, backup records may still exist.

One partial solution to the registration problem would be for Congress (and state legislatures) to specify liquidated damages against officials who illegally compile registration lists. In cases of intentional wrongdoing, criminal prosecutions, similar to existing criminal prosecutions for federal Privacy Act violations, should be allowed.[128]

Privacy of Medical Records

The vast majority of people with mental illnesses, such as John Hinckley, never enter state treatment systems. As background checks become more entrenched, pressure will inevitably build to end the confidentiality of private medical records, so the police can check those records as well. In California, legislators broadening the waiting period law were told that mental health records would be kept fully confidential. But the same year the law was enacted, the California Department of Justice began ordering public and private mental health clinics to report their clients to the state; the state puts them in a database (along with felons) that is accessible by the police. Included in the database are nonviolent persons who have voluntarily checked themselves into private facilities for problems such as anxiety or stress.[129]

Under state laws that preceded the Brady Bill, a number of jurisdictions already required purchasers to waive the confidentiality of their medical or mental health records.[130] Illinois queries, "Are you mentally retarded?"[131] New Jersey asks the McCarthy-style question "Have your ever been attended, treated or observed by any doctor or psychiatrist, or at any hospital or mental institution on an inpatient or outpatient basis for any mental or psychiatric condition?" The state also inquires, "Do you suffer from a physical defect or sickness?"[132] The mother who consulted a psychiatrist on one occasion because her son had died must confess herself to the New Jersey police, upon pain of criminal prosecution.[133]

And it is not only the government that can use firearms background checks to uncover private medical information. An employer can conduct inexpensive inquiries into the mental health records and criminal background of prospective or current employees by ordering them to produce proof that they are eligible to buy a gun, and hence have no mental or criminal record. Some employers in Illinois use this tactic. Presently, society has not granted to employers the right to access mental health databases in order to check up on their employees. While arguments in favor of changing the law could be made, such arguments have not yet been adopted by legislatures. Unless a legislature decides to open mental health records to employers, gun background checks should not be used as a way to evade existing privacy laws. Criminal and civil penalties should be allowed against employers who misuse gun background checks.

Denial of Ability to Obtain a Gun

As discussed above, a waiting period can sometimes prevent persons in peril by preventing them from obtaining a firearm when they need it most. Moreover, as the data regarding the Brady Act's effect show, once the government is given the opportunity to say yes or no to gun sales, the government may issue denials for wholly illegal reasons (such as unpaid traffic tickets).

If a particular police administrator simply opposes citizens owning guns for any reason, a permission-to-purchase law can provide an easy opportunity for abuse. In New Jersey, as noted above, some police have simply refused to process gun purchase applications.[134] In cases of budgetary constraint, firearms applications may be permanently ignored.[135]

Although a statute may specifically limit the reasons for disqualifying a buyer, police may disqualify for other, illegal reasons. As noted before, in Maryland, where an appeals process exists, the police are overruled in 78 percent of appeals.[136]

Indeed, many of the police departments which most vociferously champion "reasonable" gun controls routinely abuse those controls once enacted. The St. Louis police have denied handgun possession permits to homosexuals, nonvoters, and wives who lack their husband's permission.[137] Mayor Richard Hatcher of Gary, Indiana, ordered his police department not to give license application forms to anyone.[138] The police department in New York City has refused to issue legally required licenses, even when twice commanded by appeals courts to do so. The department has also refused even to hand out blank application forms.[139]

Most police, fortunately, are law-abiding and would not engage in the abuses typical in New York City and New Jersey. Nevertheless, even in law-abiding jurisdictions, the waiting period, by definition, delays for a number of days a citizen's acquisition of a firearm. For a hunter planning a trip next month, the delay is inconsequential. For a young woman such as Rayna Ross or Catherine Latta being threatened by an ex-boyfriend, the delay may be fatal. As the Fifth Circuit Court of Appeals has held, "the right to defend oneself from deadly attack is fundamental."[140] A waiting period puts that fundamental right on hold.[141]

A person who is falsely imprisoned by the state can get out of jail a week later, with perhaps no permanent harm done. Newspapers that libel someone by mistake can always publish corrective stories the next week. A person who is denied the right to bear arms for a week may, at the end of that week, be dead. A deprivation of the means to self-defense for even twenty-four hours may mean a deprivation of life itself.

Of course the number of persons who will be killed or injured because of the Brady Act will be small, so small as to be statistically unnoticeable. But so will the number of persons saved by a waiting period. Proponents of the Brady Act have not carried the burden of demonstrating that a waiting period would be a net saving of lives, taking into account the people who die because they cannot defend themselves as well as the diversion of police resources.

To reduce the abuses and injuries that waiting periods could cause, a number of preventative measures make sense: First, any waiting period should have an explicit appeals process. (The Brady Act does not, other than suing the police.) At the appeal, the government should have the burden of proving that the citizen is not entitled to possess a firearm. Normal rules of evidence should apply, and citizens should not be victimized by anonymous rumors and other sorts of hearsay evidence. Citizens who are victorious in their appeal should be entitled to recoup attorney's fees.

Moreover, any person injured by the failure of police to properly and promptly approve an application should have a right to sue for damages. When a person is killed because the police failed to act, the survivors should have the right to sue.

Under the legal doctrine of sovereign immunity, the police (like all other government agencies) are generally immune to lawsuit, except when the government allows a suit. As a result, the police have no enforceable legal duty to protect any individual citizen from crime, even if that citizen has received death threats and the police have negligently failed to provide protection.[142] In situations where the government affirmatively interferes with a person's ability to protect herself (the interval between an application to purchase a firearm and approval), the doctrine of sovereign immunity should not apply. The government should not be able to strip a person of her right to defend herself, and then assert that it has no responsibility for the consequences.

Financial Hardships

Many waiting period/permission systems require the firearms purchaser to pay the entire cost of the system. The national Brady Act and the national instant check do not impose fees, but many of their state counterparts do. It is Constitutionally questionable to make people pay the government so the government can satisfy itself that they are fit to exercise their Constitutional rights. The young woman in a rough neighborhood who needs an inexpensive handgun for self-defense or the young man in Appalachia who wishes to hunt squirrel with a .22 rifle are not the cause of the crime problem. Even a twelve-dollar fee may drive the cost of their fifty-dollar gun out of reach.

For all firearms purchasers, not just poor people who need a gun for defense, a waiting period requires an additional trip to the firearms store, more time spent by the clerk at the store, lost sales due to people who do not have the time to make repeated trips, and a host of other transaction costs. For a person who lives in a small town and needs to make a long trip to get to a store with a good selection of merchandise, the inconvenience can be substantial.

The Data Quality Problem

Any kind of background check, as part either of a waiting period or of an instant check, requires better criminal records than are available in many jurisdictions. The FBI "estimates that approximately one-half of the arrest charges in their records do not show a final disposition."[143]

For citizens regarding whom false information has been incorrectly recorded on a rap sheet, there is no remedy. Courts have held that even after an acquittal or dismissal of charges, a person has no Constitutional right to have an arrest purged from his record.[144] It should be noted that racial minorities are disproportionately victimized by arrests that do not prove worthy of a conviction.

Because of the problems with existing data quality, the Department of Justice task force on background checks concluded: "approximately 50 percent of the cases where persons appear to have a criminal history record based on an initial name search are eventually found to be false hits. . . . Indeed, in many (perhaps most) cases an initial indication of a criminal record would eventually be shown to be untrue because it resulted from misidentification with someone else with a common name and date of birth." As a result, only 84 to 88 percent of gun purchasers would be able to pass an initial check, predicted the task force.[145] The task force's prediction is generally consistent with the high number of denials and the low number of criminal prosecutions resulting from the Brady Act. Fortunately, the 1994 federal crime bill included a one hundred million dollar appropriation to improve data quality in the Interstate Identification Index, the federal database of arrests and convictions throughout the nation.

A Step toward More Restrictive Laws

Why waiting periods? The Coalition to Stop Gun Violence (CSGV [formerly the National Coalition to Ban Handguns]) candidly admits that gun controls do little to prevent criminals from obtaining guns.[146] CSGV believes that criminals are not the issue; handguns have no place in civilian hands. Moderate controls over handguns are a step toward a ban. Policy statements distributed by the CSGV forthrightly say so.[147]

Even in the most academic settings, the question may come down to whether a person is "for" guns or "against" them. At a debate at the American Society of Criminology conference in November 1989, the participants were asked what number of lives saved would be necessary for them to consider a waiting period worthwhile. Both sides of the debate agreed that the number of lives saved was not determinative of their positions. Dr. Paul Blackman, the NRA representative, replied that he thought the waiting period might end up with a net cost of lives. He also stated that the prohibition of alcohol had saved lives, but still was not a good idea. Darrel Stephens, Executive Director of the Police Executive Research Forum, replied that he would still favor a waiting period even if it were proven not to save any lives. He reasoned that the extra effort required to purchase a gun would convince some people not to buy a firearm, and fewer guns in civilian hands would be good in itself.[148]

What about Handgun Control, Inc., the more powerful of the two major antigun lobbies? Its stated motto is "Keeping handguns out of the wrong hands." But the organization's founder stated that he favored intermediate control as a way station to near-total handgun prohibition.[149] The organization supports Washington, D.C.'s, handgun prohibition.[150] Although Handgun Control, Inc., does not currently promote complete handgun prohibition, the introduction to this chapter detailed the group's apparent use of the Brady Bill as a steppingstone to a national gun licensing policy which would prevent people from owning handguns or long guns for self-defense.

As enacted, the Brady Act did not go as far as it could have in setting the stage for further controls. The Brady Bill (which at first had mandated gun buyers to provide the serial number and model of their gun) was changed to prohibit (in theory at least) the police from receiving or retaining gun registration data.

The 1991 version of the Brady Bill included a subtle provision that could have facilitated prohibition: an antigun police chief could indefinitely delay a purchase application by refusing to mail back acknowledgment of receipt of the application.[151] This, too, was changed.

Most importantly, from the long-term gun-control viewpoint, the waiting period is social conditioning. It sends the message that citizens do not possess a right to bear arms, but merely a privilege dependent on police permission. Once the idea of a right to bear arms is replaced with a government-granted privilege, a broad range of prohibitions and restrictions become politically viable.

ALTERNATIVES

In the years preceding the Brady Bill's enactment, several alternatives were proposed. At least one of them is clearly superior to the Brady Bill at keeping felons from buying guns in gun stores, while not infringing the right to keep and bear arms.

Instant Checks

As stated, a mandatory, national point-of-sale instant check for all retail gun purchases is scheduled to replace the Brady Bill waiting period by 1998. In terms of sorting out ineligible buyers, the instant check is just as effective as a seven-day waiting period, according to the Department of Justice task force, and for that reason was supported by Attorneys General Barr and Thornburgh.[152]

Of course criminals can evade an instant check just as easily as they can evade any other check. All they need is a fake driver's license with another name. Since false social security and alien registration cards may sometimes be bought for as little as thirty-five dollars,[153] and since those cards are usually sufficient to obtain a driver's license, the instant check is likely to be just as porous as longer checks. The instant check, therefore, like a check tied to a waiting period, could be evaded by anyone with false identification.[154]

The instant check is subject to the same problem of creating a gun and gun-owner registration system as is a waiting period. As the Department of Justice task force observed, "Any system that requires a criminal history record check prior to purchase of a firearm creates the potential for the automated tracking of individuals who seek to purchase firearms."[155] The instant check in Brady does bar gun-owner record retention, although the practical enforceability of the provision is hard to determine.

Despite the name, instant checks are often not instant, even for persons who are not mistaken for a felon with the same name. In Florida, gun buyers frequently have to wait ten to fifteen minutes for an approval from the state system. The system may go down for periods of three or four hours or an entire day. Sometimes the phone will ring and ring without being answered; other times, the instant check phone may be answered and the gun dealer put on hold indefinitely.[156]

The instant check, however, is clearly preferable to a waiting period.[157] It uses the same criminal/mental data base as would a waiting period, and would therefore be equally effective in denying ineligible buyers. Because the large majority of sales would be approved on the spot, abusive administrators would have much less of an opportunity to interfere with the right to bear arms. It is true that an instant check eliminates the cooling off feature of a waiting period; but as discussed above, the number of crimes that could be prevented by cooling off is very, very small. The small loss to public safety from the elimination of the cooling off period is more than offset by allowing persons who need a gun for immediate self-defense to get one, and by substantially reducing the numbers of arbitrary denials of firearms purchases. Accordingly, within the parameters of the Brady Act, it would be sensible to accelerate the waiting period's replacement with the instant check.

Firearms Owners Identification Cards

One suggested alternative to waiting periods for each firearm purchase is the creation of a Firearm Owners Identification (FOID) card. A person applies once for a FOID and submits her fingerprints to the authorities; after a four-to-six-week review process, the applicant is granted a card that allows her to make unlimited purchases, with no further approval needed, as long as the card remains valid. The card might expire after one or three years, or be valid for life. Massachusetts and Illinois are among the states currently using a FOID system.

At a national level, the Department of Justice task force suggests that each FOID would cost thirty dollars. Approximately 1,700 new FBI employees would be required to process the necessary fingerprint checks of FBI files. According to the task force, the FOID, taking up to six weeks to process, would be substantially more accurate than an instant check or a short waiting period.

As with the instant check or the waiting period, the list of FOID owners would be a *de facto* registration list of gun owners. The more serious civil liberties problem, however, involves massive fingerprinting.

The National Association of Police Organizations favors the collection of fingerprints of gun owners as the first step toward a comprehensive fingerprint system: "the development of such an integrated national fingerprint system should be considered not merely for its benefits in connection with felon identification concerning firearms purchases but also in connection with improving law enforcement in general."[158]

The American Civil Liberties Union states that "limited criminal history record checks, with fingerprint cards, are justified in certain licensing and employment situations. However, we oppose routine fingerprinting of all individuals who seek to buy firearms as an intrusion into privacy that cannot be justified by the minuscule benefit that may be achieved. . . ."[159] Of course the ACLU's principle should also apply not only to proposed national fingerprint proposals, but also to the current practice in states such as New York and Illinois which routinely fingerprint the large fraction of the population that exercises its right to bear arms.

The same arguments that led to rejection of a national identity card apply to federal gun licensing through a FOID. A national licensing system would require the collection of dossiers on half the households in the United States (or a quarter, for handgun-only record keeping).

Implementing national gun licensing would make introduction of a national identity card more likely. Assuming that a large proportion of American families would become accustomed to the government collecting extensive data about them, they would probably not oppose making everyone else go through the same procedures for a national identity card.

Instant Fingerprint Check

In a few years, an instant fingerprint check in gun stores will be technologically feasible, using either an in-store fingerprint reader or a fingerprint that is part of a driver's license.[160] An instant fingerprint scan should not replace the present instant check system. As the NRA notes, "Exercise of a constitutional right cannot be conditioned on making fingerprints available to the police."[161] Indeed, the

Supreme Court has held that the Constitution forbids states to collect fingerprints of people merely because they exercise their Constitutional rights.[162]

An instant driver's license fingerprint scan offers few anticrime advantages over the instant telephone check. Both can be evaded with false identification. (In the case of the fingerprint scan, the criminal just makes sure to have someone else's print placed on his fake driver's license.)[163] The instant fingerprint scan proposal would result in every state having a fingerprint of many of its adult citizens. It is questionable whether states currently ought to be fingerprinting citizens who obtain drivers' licenses.

Driver's License Magnetic Coding

Of all the proposals for identifying persons with felony convictions who attempt to purchase guns at retail outlets, the best proposal is for magnetic coding of drivers' licenses. When a person applied for a driver's license, the state department of motor vehicles would run a background check. If the applicant had a felony conviction, the driver's license would be embedded with a magnetic code indicating the existence of the conviction. If the applicant had no felony convictions, a different magnetic code would be inserted. The Department of Motor Vehicles would send, along with the actual license, a letter informing the applicant of the information contained in the magnetic code (felon or nonfelon). When that person went to a gun store to make a purchase, the store would run the driver's license through a magnetic card reader. If the "not a felon" code appeared on the license, the sale could proceed.

Unlike the instant check and the waiting period, the driver's license check does not result in the police being supplied with the names of gun buyers. The check would be at least as fast as the "instant check" and, on days when the state central computer breaks down, would be faster.

Unlike the instant check, there would be no problem of buyers being denied their right to buy a gun because they had the same name as someone else with a felony conviction. Any mistaken identification of the person as a felon would be noticed by that person when he received his driver's license, and a correction process could begin at that point. Indeed, the driver's license application process would allow many innocent people to discover that the government has records incorrectly identifying them as felons; the innocent would then have the opportunity to have their police records corrected.

To keep driver's licenses up to date, persons indicted for or convicted of a felony would be required to surrender their current (nonfelon) driver's license. (Persons under indictment are barred by federal law from buying guns.) If the newly indicted/convicted individual was not being incarcerated, he would be required to obtain a new (felon-coded) license. For persons who do not drive, the state would issue state identification cards, just as they currently do to nondrivers.

The coding program could have other uses as well. In states that prohibit felons from voting and that already require voters to provide identification, code readers at the polling place would identify felons attempting to vote. (A code-reading program at a polling place would have to be implemented carefully, to avoid making long lines for voting even longer.)

The driver's license coding program is not perfect, however. First of all, it is a step in the direction of turning drivers' licenses into universal smart cards, which might contain all sorts of personal information.

Second, the coding program interferes to some degree with the privacy interests of persons who have felony convictions. Even if the licenses used special types of coding designed to be recognizable only to government-made magnetic code readers, it seems possible that someone would design private code readers capable of deciphering the licenses. Thus, employers might use the private code readers to inquire into the background of prospective employees.

But balanced against the potential privacy infringements on the small fraction of the population with a felony conviction must be the certainty of privacy infringements for half the population (gun owners) that would result from all the alternatives discussed above. Having the government compile a list of those who exercise their right to keep and bear arms is a much more widespread privacy violation than having the fact of someone's felony conviction become discoverable by private persons who own magnetic card readers and can cajole or coerce a felon into handing over his driver's license.

One way to reduce the privacy invasions for persons with felony convictions would be for states and the federal government to reexamine the list of those prohibited from owning guns. It certainly makes sense to bar persons with recent violent felony convictions from owning firearms. It is doubtful that public safety is much enhanced by prohibiting gun possession to persons who took too many deductions on their income tax fifteen years ago or got caught with a small quantity of psychedelic mushrooms in college. Likewise, a dishonorable discharge from the military (which can be on the basis of simply having a homosexual orientation) should not be a lifetime bar to gun ownership.

More fundamentally, the federal government should not be in the business of creating laws about who can and cannot own a firearm. The Constitution grants the federal government no general power over criminal law. While Congress has the authority to legislate on firearms when using the powers granted to Congress (such as the interstate commerce power to control interstate gun-running, or the federal property power to control gun possession in national parks), Congress has no legitimate Constitutional authority to control the simple possession of firearms. Such control properly belongs to state governments (provided of course, that they comply with the minimum standards of the federal Constitution).

In the long run, the best approach to avoid civil liberties violations in government policing of retail gun sales is for politicians and the gun control lobbies to stop pretending that control of retail gun sales has something to do with crime control. Instead of controlling retail gun buyers, the government should instead focus on controlling criminals.

Anticrime Strategies

If the goal is really to keep felons from obtaining guns (rather than imposing gun control for its own sake), then the focus on retail sales is misplaced. Hardly any felons buy crime guns in stores; almost all of the guns come from the underground market. A system aimed at disarming criminals should aim primarily at the black market.

The NIJ authors James D. Wright and Peter Rossi suggest "stiff penalties for firearms transfers to felons whenever these were detected and, in the same framework, stiff penalties for the crime of gun theft."[164] Enhanced penalties for gun transfers to felons were added to federal law in 1986, and should be added to state laws as well. To assist prosecutions of gun theft, states should follow Virginia's lead, and make sale of a stolen firearm a special, serious offense.[165] In many states, the theft and sale of a $75 gun amounts to only petty larceny. Selling a "hot" $75 pistol should be a more serious offense than selling a "hot" $75 toaster-oven.

Other ways to keep criminals away from guns include closer monitoring of parolees and probationers, and more intensive crackdowns on fencing operations for stolen firearms. State or federal strike forces aimed directly at gun-runners might be introduced or augmented.

Funding for any of the above programs should come from the same general revenues that support all law enforcement.[166] Persons exercising their Constitutional right to bear arms should not be forced to pay a special tax to support enforcement efforts against gun criminals, any more than camera owners or magazine readers should be taxed to pay for enforcement of child pornography laws.

CONCLUSION

Especially when a legislature is considering laws that impact fundamental rights, it is improper to pass legislation simply because "it might help a little" or "it won't do much harm." Proponents of a new law have the burden of proving that their new law will accomplish a significant positive good. The burden is all the greater when proposed legislation affects a significant number of people, and the Brady Act regulates the 50 percent of American households that choose to possess firearms. Proponents of a waiting period have failed to carry their burden of persuasion, although they have carried the day in Congress.

The premise of the waiting period—and of most suggested alternatives—is that citizens can be required to ask police permission before exercising their rights. The waiting period forces us to consider whether we want gradually to change the traditional right to keep and bear arms for protection into a privilege to possess "sporting" guns.

THE BRADY BILL

H.R.1025

One Hundred-Third Congress of the United States of America

AT THE FIRST SESSION

Begun and held at the City of Washington on Tuesday, the fifth day of January, one thousand nine hundred and ninety-three

AN ACT

To provide for a waiting period before the purchase of a handgun, and for the establishment of a national instant criminal background check system to be contacted by firearms dealers before the transfer of any firearm.

Be it enacted by the Senate and House of Representatives of the United States of America in Congress assembled,

TITLE I—BRADY HANDGUN CONTROL

SEC. 101. SHORT TITLE.

This title may be cited as the "Brady Handgun Violence Prevention Act."

SEC. 102. FEDERAL FIREARMS LICENSEE REQUIRED TO CONDUCT CRIMINAL BACKGROUND CHECK BEFORE TRANSFER OF FIREARM TO NON-LICENSEE.

(a) INTERIM PROVISION.—

    (1) IN GENERAL.—Section 922 of title 18, United States Code, is amended by adding at the end the following:

    (s)(1) Beginning on the date that is ninety days after the date of enactment of this subsection and ending on the day before the date that is sixty months after such date of enactment, it shall be unlawful for any licensed importer, licensed manufacturer, or licensed dealer to sell, deliver, or transfer a handgun to an individual who is not licensed under section 923, unless—

    (A) after the most recent proposal of such transfer by the transferee—

        (i) the transferor has—

            (I) received from the transferee a statement of the transferee containing the information described in paragraph (3);

            (II) verified the identity of the transferee by examining the identification document presented;

            (III) within 1 day after the transferee furnishes the statement, provided notice of the contents of the statement to the chief law enforcement officer of the place of residence of the transferee; and

            (IV) within 1 day after the transferee furnishes the statement, transmitted a copy of the statement to the chief law enforcement officer of the place of residence of the transferee; and

(ii)(I)   five business days (meaning days on which State offices are open) have elapsed from the date the transferor furnished notice of the contents of the statement to the chief law enforcement officer, during which period the transferor has not received information from the chief law enforcement officer that receipt or possession of the handgun by the transferee would be in violation of Federal, State, or local law; or

(II)   the transferor has received notice from the chief law enforcement officer that the officer has no information indicating that receipt or possession of the handgun by the transferee would violate Federal, State, or local law;

(B)   the transferee has presented to the transferor a written statement, issued by the chief law enforcement officer of the place of residence of the transferee during the 10-day period ending on the date of the most recent proposal of such transfer by the transferee, stating that the transferee requires access to a handgun because of a threat to the life of the transferee or of any member of the household of the transferee;

(C) (i) he transferee has presented to the transferor a permit that—

(I)   allows the transferee to possess or acquire a handgun; and

(II)   was issued not more than 5 years earlier by the State in which the transfer is to take place; and

(ii) the law of the State provides that such a permit is to be issued only after an authorized government official has verified that the information available to such official does not indicate that possession of a handgun by the transferee would be in violation of the law;

(D)   the law of the State requires that, before any licensed importer, licensed manufacturer, or licensed dealer completes the transfer of a handgun to an individual who is not licensed under section 923, an authorized government official verify that the information available to such official does not indicate that possession of a handgun by the transferee would be in violation of law;

(E)   the Secretary has approved the transfer under section 5812 of the Internal Revenue Code of 1986; or

(F)   on application of the transferor, the Secretary has certified that compliance with subparagraph (A)(i)(III) is impracticable because—

    (i) the ratio of the number of law enforcement officers of the State in which the transfer is to occur to the number of square miles of land area of the State does not exceed 0.0025;

    (ii) the business premises of the transferor at which the transfer is to occur are extremely remote in relation to the chief law enforcement officer; and

    (iii) here is an absence of telecommunications facilities in the geographical area in which the business premises are located.

(2) A chief law enforcement officer to whom a transferor has provided notice pursuant to paragraph (1)(A)(i)(III) shall make a reasonable effort to ascertain within 5 business days whether receipt or possession would be in violation of the law, including research in whatever State and local recordkeeping systems are available and in a national system designated by the Attorney General.

(3) The statement referred to in paragraph (1)(A)(i)(I) shall contain only—

    (A) the name, address, and date of birth appearing on a valid identification document (as defined in section 1028(d)(1)) of the transferee containing a photograph of the transferee and a description of the identification used;

    (B) a statement that the transferee—

        (i) is not under indictment for, and has not been convicted in any court of, a crime punishable by imprisonment for a term exceeding 1 year;

        (ii) is not a fugitive from justice;

        (iii) is not an unlawful user of or addicted to any controlled substance (as defined in section 102 of the Controlled Substances Act);

        (iv) has not been adjudicated as a mental defective or been committed to a mental institution;

        (v) is not an alien who is illegally or unlawfully in the United States;

        (vi) has not been discharged from the Armed Forces under dishonorable conditions; and

        (vii) is not a person who, having been a citizen of the United States, has renounced such citizenship;

    (C) the date the statement is made; and

    (D) notice that the transferee intends to obtain a handgun from the transferor.

(4) Any transferor of a handgun who, after such transfer, receives a report from a chief law enforcement officer containing information

that receipt or possession of the handgun by the transferee violates
Federal, State, or local law shall, within 1 business day after receipt
of such request, communicate any information related to the transfer
that the transferor has about the transfer and the transferee to—
  (A) the chief law enforcement officer of the place of business of
      the transferor; and
  (B) the chief law enforcement officer of the place of residence of
      the transferee.

(5) Any transferor who receives information, not otherwise available
    to the public, in a report under this subsection shall not disclose
    such information except to the transferee, to law enforcement
    authorities, or pursuant to the direction of a court of law.

(6) (A) Any transferor who sells, delivers, or otherwise transfers a hand-
        gun to a transferee shall retain the copy of the statement of the
        transferee with respect to the handgun transaction, and shall retain
        evidence that the transferor has complied with subclauses (III) and
        (IV) of paragraph (1)(A)(i) with respect to the statement.

   (B) Unless the chief law enforcement officer to whom a statement
       is transmitted under paragraph (1)(A)(i)(IV) determines that a
       transaction would violate Federal, State, or local law—
       (i)   the officer shall, within 20 business days after the date
             the transferee made the statement on the basis of which
             the notice was provided, destroy the statement, any
             record containing information derived from the state-
             ment, and any record created as a result of the notice
             required by paragraph (1)(A)(i)(III);
       (ii) the information contained in the statement shall not be
             conveyed to any person except a person who has a need
             to know in order to carry out this subsection; and
       (iii) the information contained in the statement shall not be used
             for any purpose other than to carry out this subsection.

   (C) If a chief law enforcement officer determines that an individ-
       ual is ineligible to receive a handgun and the individual
       requests the officer to provide the reason for such determina-
       tion, the officer shall provide such reasons to the individual in
       writing within 20 business days after receipt of the request.

(7) A chief law enforcement officer or other person responsible for
    providing criminal history background information pursuant to this
    subsection shall not be liable in an action at law for damages—
    (A) for failure to prevent the sale or transfer of a handgun to a per-

son whose receipt or possession of the handgun is unlawful under this section; or

(B) for preventing such a sale or transfer to a person who may lawfully receive or possess a handgun.

(8) For purposes of this subsection, the term 'chief law enforcement officer' means the chief of police, the sheriff, or an equivalent officer or the designee of any such individual.

(9) The Secretary shall take necessary actions to ensure that the provisions of this subsection are published and disseminated to licensed dealers, law enforcement officials, and the public.

(2) HANDGUN DEFINED.—Section 921(a) of title 18, United States Code, is amended by adding at the end the following:

(29) The term 'handgun' means—
   (A) a firearm which has a short stock and is designed to be held and fired by the use of a single hand; and
   (B) any combination of parts from which a firearm described in subparagraph (A) can be assembled.

(b) PERMANENT PROVISION.—Section 922 of title 18, United States Code, as amended by subsection (a)(1), is amended by adding at the end the following:

(t)(1) Beginning on the date that is 30 days after the Attorney General notifies licensees under section 103(d) of the Brady Handgun Violence Prevention Act that the national instant criminal background check system is established, a licensed importer, licensed manufacturer, or licensed dealer shall not transfer a firearm to any other person who is not licensed under this chapter, unless—

   (A) before the completion of the transfer, the licensee contacts the national instant criminal background check system established under section 103 of that Act;
   (B) (i) the system provides the licensee with a unique identification number; or
       (ii) 3 business days (meaning a day on which State offices are open) have elapsed since the licensee contacted the system, and the system has not notified the licensee that the receipt of a firearm by such other person would violate subsection (g) or (n) of this section; and
   (C) the transferor has verified the identity of the transferee by examining a valid identification document (as defined in section 1028(d)(1) of this title) of the transferee containing a photograph of the transferee.

(2) If receipt of a firearm would not violate section 922 (g) or (n) or State law, the system shall—
(A) assign a unique identification number to the transfer;
(B) provide the licensee with the number; and
(C) destroy all records of the system with respect to the call (other than the identifying number and the date the number was assigned) and all records of the system relating to the person or the transfer.

(3) Paragraph (1) shall not apply to a firearm transfer between a licensee and another person if—
(A) (i)   such other person has presented to the licensee a permit that—
    (I)   allows such other person to possess or acquire a firearm; and
    (II) was issued not more than 5 years earlier by the State in which the transfer is to take place; and
    (ii) the law of the State provides that such a permit is to be issued only after an authorized government official has verified that the information available to such official does not indicate that possession of a firearm by such other person would be in violation of law;
(B) the Secretary has approved the transfer under section 5812 of the Internal Revenue Code of 1986; or
(C) on application of the transferor, the Secretary has certified that compliance with paragraph (1)(A) is impracticable because—
    (i)   the ratio of the number of law enforcement officers of the State in which the transfer is to occur to the number of square miles of land area of the State does not exceed 0.0025;
    (ii) the business premises of the licensee at which the transfer is to occur are extremely remote in relation to the chief law enforcement officer (as defined in subsection (s)(8)); and
    (iii) there is an absence of telecommunications facilities in the geographical area in which the business premises are located.

(4) If the national instant criminal background check system notifies the licensee that the information available to the system does not demonstrate that the receipt of a firearm by such other person would violate subsection (g) or (n) or State law, and the licensee transfers a firearm to such other person, the licensee shall include in the record of the transfer the unique identification number provided by the system with respect to the transfer.

(5) If the licensee knowingly transfers a firearm to such other person and knowingly fails to comply with paragraph (1) of this subsection

with respect to the transfer and, at the time such other person most recently proposed the transfer, the national instant criminal background check system was operating and information was available to the system demonstrating that receipt of a firearm by such other person would violate subsection (g) or (n) of this section or State law, the Secretary may, after notice and opportunity for a hearing, suspend for not more than six months or revoke any license issued to the licensee under section 923, and may impose on the licensee a civil fine of not more than $5,000.

(6) Neither a local government nor an employee of the Federal Government or of any State or local government, responsible for providing information to the national instant criminal background check system shall be liable in an action at law for damages—

(A) for failure to prevent the sale or transfer of a firearm to a person whose receipt or possession of the firearm is unlawful under this section; or

(B) for preventing such a sale or transfer to a person who may lawfully receive or possess a firearm.

(c) PENALTY.—Section 924(a) of title 18, United States Code, is amended—

(1) in paragraph (1), by striking "paragraph (2) or (3) of"; and

(2) by adding at the end the following:

(5) Whoever knowingly violates subsection (s) or (t) of section 922 shall be fined not more than $1,000, imprisoned for not more than 1 year, or both.

SEC. 103. NATIONAL INSTANT CRIMINAL BACKGROUND CHECK SYSTEM.

(a) DETERMINATION OF TIMETABLES.—Not later than 6 months after the date of enactment of this Act, the Attorney General shall—

(1) determine the type of computer hardware and software that will be used to operate the national instant criminal background check system and the means by which State criminal records systems and the telephone or electronic device of licensees will communicate with the national system;

(2) investigate the criminal records system of each State and determine for each State a timetable by which the State should be able to provide criminal records on an online capacity basis to the national system; and

(3) notify each State of the determinations made pursuant to paragraphs (1) and (2).

(b) ESTABLISHMENT OF SYSTEM.—Not later than 60 months after the date of the enactment of this Act, the Attorney General shall establish a national instant criminal background check system that any licensee may contact, by telephone or by other electronic means in addition to the telephone, for information, to be supplied immediately, on whether receipt of a firearm by a prospective transferee would violate section 922 of title 18, United States Code, or State law.

(c) EXPEDITED ACTION BY THE ATTORNEY GENERAL.—The Attorney General shall expedite—

(1) the upgrading and indexing of State criminal history records in the Federal criminal records system maintained by the Federal Bureau of Investigation;
(2) the development of hardware and software systems to link State criminal history check systems into the national instant criminal background check system established by the Attorney General pursuant to this section; and
(3) the current revitalization initiatives by the Federal Bureau of Investigation for technologically advanced fingerprint and criminal records identification.

(d) NOTIFICATION OF LICENSEES.—On establishment of the system under this section, the Attorney General shall notify each licensee and the chief law enforcement officer of each State of the existence and purpose of the system and the means to be used to contact the system.

(e) ADMINISTRATIVE PROVISIONS.—

(1) AUTHORITY TO OBTAIN OFFICIAL INFORMATION.—Notwithstanding any other law, the Attorney General may secure directly from any department or agency of the United States such information on persons for whom receipt of a firearm would violate subsection (g) or (n) of section 922 of title 18, United States Code or State law, as is necessary to enable the system to operate in accordance with this section. On request of the Attorney General, the head of such department or agency shall furnish such information to the system.
(2) OTHER AUTHORITY.—The Attorney General shall develop such computer software, design and obtain such telecommunications and computer hardware, and employ such personnel, as are necessary to establish and operate the system in accordance with this section.

(f) WRITTEN REASONS PROVIDED ON REQUEST.—If the national instant criminal background check system determines that an individual is ineligible to receive a firearm and the individual requests the system to provide the reasons for the determination, the system shall provide such reasons to the individual, in writing, within 5 business days after the date of the request.

(g) CORRECTION OF ERRONEOUS SYSTEM INFORMATION.—If the system established under this section informs an individual contacting the system that receipt of a firearm by a prospective transferee would violate subsection (g) or (n) of section 922 of title 18, United States Code or State law, the prospective transferee may request the Attorney General to provide the prospective transferee with the reasons therefor. Upon receipt of such a request, the Attorney General shall immediately comply with the request. The prospective transferee may submit to the Attorney General information to correct, clarify, or supplement records of the system with respect to the prospective transferee. After receipt of such information, the Attorney General shall immediately consider the information, investigate the matter further, and correct all erroneous Federal records relating to the prospective transferee and give notice of the error to any Federal department or agency or any State that was the source of such erroneous records.

(h) REGULATIONS.—After 90 days' notice to the public and an opportunity for hearing by interested parties, the Attorney General shall prescribe regulations to ensure the privacy and security of the information of the system established under this section.

(i) PROHIBITION RELATING TO ESTABLISHMENT OF REGISTRATION SYSTEMS WITH RESPECT TO FIREARMS.—No department, agency, officer, or employee of the United States may—

   (1) require that any record or portion thereof generated by the system established under this section be recorded at or transferred to a facility owned, managed, or controlled by the United States or any State or political subdivision thereof; or

   (2) use the system established under this section to establish any system for the registration of firearms, firearm owners, or firearm transactions or dispositions, except with respect to persons, prohibited by section 922 (g) or (n) of title 18, United States Code or State law, from receiving a firearm.

(j) DEFINITIONS.—As used in this section:

   (1) LICENSEE.—The term "licensee" means a licensed importer (as defined in section 921(a)(9) of title 18, United States Code), a licensed manufacturer (as defined in section 921(a)(10) of that title), or a licensed dealer (as defined in section 921(a)(11) of that title).

   (2) OTHER TERMS.—The terms "firearm", "handgun", "licensed importer", "licensed manufacturer", and "licensed dealer" have the meanings stated in section 921(a) of title 18, United States Code, as amended by subsection (a)(2).

(k) AUTHORIZATION OF APPROPRIATIONS.—There are authorized to be appropriated, which may be appropriated from the Violent Crime Reduction Trust Fund established by section 1115 of title 31, United States Code, such sums as are necessary to enable the Attorney General to carry out this section.

SEC. 104. REMEDY FOR ERRONEOUS DENIAL OF FIREARM.

(a) IN GENERAL.—Chapter 44 of title 18, United States Code, is amended by inserting after section 925 the following new section:

S 925A. Remedy for erroneous denial of firearm

Any person denied a firearm pursuant to subsection (s) or(t) of section 922—

(1) due to the provision of erroneous information relating to the person by any State or political subdivision thereof, or by the national instant criminal background check system established under section 103 of the Brady Handgun Violence Prevention Act; or

(2) who was not prohibited from receipt of a firearm pursuant to subsection (g) or (n) of section 922, may bring an action against the State or political subdivision responsible for providing the erroneous information, or responsible for denying the transfer, or against the United States, as the case may be, for an order directing that the erroneous information be corrected or that the transfer be approved, as the case may be. In any action under this section, the court, in its discretion, may allow the prevailing party a reasonable attorney's fee as part of the costs.

(b) TECHNICAL AMENDMENT.—The chapter analysis for chapter 44 of title 18, United States Code, is amended by inserting after the item relating to section 925 the following new item:

925A. Remedy for erroneous denial of firearm.

SEC. 105. RULE OF CONSTRUCTION.

This Act and the amendments made by this Act shall not be construed to alter or impair any right or remedy under section 552a of title 5, United States Code.

SEC. 106. FUNDING FOR IMPROVEMENT OF CRIMINAL RECORDS.

(a) USE OF FORMULA GRANTS.—Section 509(b) of title I of the Omnibus Crime Control and Safe Streets Act of 1968 (42 U.S.C. 3759(b)) is amended—

(1) in paragraph (2) by striking "and" after the semicolon;

(2) in paragraph (3) by striking the period and inserting "; and"; and

(3) by adding at the end the following new paragraph:

(4) the improvement of State record systems and the sharing with the Attorney General of all of the records described in paragraphs (1), (2), and (3) of this subsection and the records required by the Attorney General under section 103 of the Brady Handgun Violence Prevention Act, for the purpose of implementing that Act.

(b) ADDITIONAL FUNDING.—

(1) GRANTS FOR THE IMPROVEMENT OF CRIMINAL RECORDS.—The Attorney General, through the Bureau of Justice Statistics, shall, subject to appropriations and with preference to States that as of the date of enactment of this Act have the lowest percent currency of case dispositions in computerized criminal history files, make a grant to each State to be used—

(A) for the creation of a computerized criminal history record system or improvement of an existing system;

    (B) to improve accessibility to the national instant criminal background system; and

    (C) upon establishment of the national system, to assist the State in the transmittal of criminal records to the national system.

  (2) AUTHORIZATION OF APPROPRIATIONS.—There are authorized to be appropriated for grants under paragraph (1), which may be appropriated from the Violent Crime Reduction Trust Fund established by section 1115 of title 31, United States Code, a total of $200,000,000 for fiscal year 1994 and all fiscal years thereafter.

TITLE II—MULTIPLE FIREARM PURCHASES TO STATE AND LOCAL POLICE

SEC. 201. REPORTING REQUIREMENT.

Section 923(g)(3) of title 18, United States Code, is amended—

  (1) in the second sentence by inserting after "thereon," the following: "and to the department of State police or State law enforcement agency of the State or local law enforcement agency of the local jurisdiction in which the sale or other disposition took place";

  (2) by inserting "(A)" after "(3)"; and

  (3) by adding at the end thereof the following:

    (B) Except in the case of forms and contents thereof regarding a purchaser who is prohibited by subsection (g) or (n) of section 922 of this title from receipt of a firearm, the department of State police or State law enforcement agency or local law enforcement agency of the local jurisdiction shall not disclose any such form or the contents thereof to any person or entity, and shall destroy each such form and any record of the contents thereof no more than 20 days from the date such form is received. No later than the date that is 6 months after the effective date of this subparagraph, and at the end of each 6-month period thereafter, the department of State police or State law enforcement agency or local law enforcement agency of the local jurisdiction shall certify to the Attorney General of the United States that no disclosure contrary to this subparagraph has been made and that all forms and any record of the contents thereof have been destroyed as provided in this subparagraph.

TITLE III—FEDERAL FIREARMS LICENSE REFORM

SEC. 301. SHORT TITLE.

This title may be cited as the "Federal Firearms License Reform Act of 1993."

SEC. 302. PREVENTION OF THEFT OF FIREARMS.

(a) COMMON CARRIERS.—Section 922(e) of title 18, United States Code, is amended by adding at the end the following: "No common or contract carrier shall require or cause any label, tag, or other written notice to be placed on the outside of any package, luggage, or other container that such package, luggage, or other container contains a firearm."

(b) RECEIPT REQUIREMENT.—Section 922(f) of title 18, United States Code, is amended—
   (1) by inserting "(1)" after "(f)"; and
   (2) by adding at the end the following new paragraph:

> (2) It shall be unlawful for any common or contract carrier to deliver in interstate or foreign commerce any firearm without obtaining written acknowledgement of receipt from the recipient of the package or other container in which there is a firearm.

(c) UNLAWFUL ACTS.—Section 922 of title 18, United States Code, as amended by section 102, is amended by adding at the end the following new subsection:

> (u) It shall be unlawful for a person to steal or unlawfully take or carry away from the person or the premises of a person who is licensed to engage in the business of importing, manufacturing, or dealing in firearms, any firearm in the licensee's business inventory that has been shipped or transported in interstate or foreign commerce.

(d) PENALTIES.—Section 924 of title 18, United States Code, is amended by adding at the end the following new subsection:

> (i)(1) A person who knowingly violates section 922(u) shall be fined not more than $10,000, imprisoned not more than 10 years, or both.

> (2) Nothing contained in this subsection shall be construed as indicating an intent on the part of Congress to occupy the field in which provisions of this subsection operate to the exclusion of State laws on the same subject matter, nor shall any provision of this subsection be construed as invalidating any provision of State law unless such provision is inconsistent with any of the purposes of this subsection.

SEC. 303. LICENSE APPLICATION FEES FOR DEALERS IN FIREARMS.

Section 923(a)(3) of title 18, United States Code, is amended—
   (1) in subparagraph (A), by adding "or" at the end;
   (2) in subparagraph (B) by striking "a pawnbroker dealing in firearms other than" and inserting "not a dealer in";
   (3) in subparagraph (B) by striking "$25 per year; or" and inserting "$200 for three years, except that the fee for renewal of a valid license shall be $90 for 3 years"; and
   (4) by striking subparagraph (C).

NOTES

1. A few provisions, not relevant to this chapter, became effective earlier. For example, at the request of the National Rifle Association, the Brady Act changed the law regarding the use of tags for checked airline luggage containing an unloaded firearm; now, the special firearms tag that must be attached to the luggage must be placed inside the luggage, rather than outside, so as not to make the luggage a target for theft. The luggage tagging change went into effect upon enactment.

The Brady Bill was originally named for Sarah Brady. Later, it was said to have been named for James Brady. Handgun Control, Inc., *What You Should Know about the Brady Bill* (brochure, 1987)("Handgun Control's flagship bill the Handgun Violence Prevention Act known as the 'Brady Bill' for Sarah Brady, requires a seven-day waiting period for handgun purchases from both dealers and individuals."); "Handguns: Foes Waging Battle," *Denver Post,* June 26, 1988 ("The Brady Law is named for gun-control activist Sarah Brady").

2. N.T. "Pete" Shields, fund-raising letter for Handgun Legal Action Fund, "confidential, Wednesday morning" (1988), pp. 2–3. The group noted that a woman won $350,000 from the city of Philadelphia for not conducting a thorough enough background check of a woman who killed her husband. Eileen Welsome, "Killing Spree Leads to Talk of Gun Control," *Albuquerque Tribune,* n.d.; Shields, fund-raising letter (1988), p. 3.

Perhaps in a few years, aggressive lawyers and their lobbyists will seek to repeal the police liability exclusion, or avoid it through creative litigation.

3. As a result of a clarification added in the omnibus crime bill that became law in September 1994, reclaiming one's own gun at a pawn shop is not considered a retail purchase.

4. *Romero* v. *United States,* No. 94-0419, W.D. Louisiana, December 8, 1994)(mandatory background check is unconstitutional "unfunded mandata on the states"); *Frank* v. *United States,* No.2:94–CV–135 (D.Vt., August 2, 1994); *Mack* v. *United States,* No. 2:94-CV–113 TCUC JMR (D. Ariz., June 29, 1994); *McGee* v. *United States,* No. 2:94–CV–67PS (S.D. Miss., June 2, 1994). *Printz* v. *United States,* No.CV 94–35–M–CCL (D. Mont., May 16, 1994). But see *Koog* v. *United States,* No.DR–94–CA-8 (W.D. Tex., June 1, 1994) ("minimal duties" of Brady Act are not unconstitutional). See also "More NM Sheriffs Join Suit against Brady Bill," *The Courier,* December 22, 1994 (five New Mexico sheriffs joining another sheriff's suit); "Louisiana Federal Judge Strikes Down Part of Brady Law," Associated Press, December 12, 1994; "Ruling Means Police Won't Be Required to Do Gun Checks," Associated Press, August 4, 1994 (Montpelier, Vt.); "Judge Strikes Down Police-Check Part of Brady Gun Law," *Washington Times,* June 29, 1994, p. A9 (A.P., Ariz.); Joyce Price, "Sheriffs Take Shots at Brady Laws as Judge Bars Mandate for Checks," *Washington Times,* May 18, 1993, p. A3.

5. Erik Eckholm, "A Little Gun Control, a Lot of Guns," *New York Times,* August 15, 1993, p. B1. Likewise, Handgun Control, Inc., President Richard Aborn, before the Brady Bill's passage, illustrated how the Brady Bill would be used as a springboard for further controls: "It [Brady] is by no means sufficient. . . . Brady becomes a referendum on whether we're going to have gun control in this country." Larry Bivens, "Preventive Medicine," *Detroit News,* October 17, 1993 (in other words, passage of a relatively mild gun control bill would be promoted as proof of national desire for a much stricter law).

6. The current federal ban on magazines holding more than ten rounds imposes no restrictions on current owners of magazines. A woman who owns a fifteen-round clip for a Glock pistol does not need to register the clip. And she can sell the clip without any need for government record-keeping.

Brady II would require every owner of a "large" ammunition clip to be licensed the same way that the federal government licenses machine gun owners. Simply to retain the magazines currently owned, a person would have to be fingerprinted, and pay heavy federal taxes. Brady II would also lower the ten-round limit to six rounds. As a result, the owner of a Colt .45 pistol and the standard seven-round magazine for the gun would need to go through the federal machine gun licensing system.

Under Brady II, anyone who owned at least twenty guns or 1,000 rounds of ammunition would be required to obtain a federal "arsenal" license. Licensees would be subjected to three unannounced police inspections per year. Persons who were required to have a license but did not obtain one would of course be subject to whatever enforcement action the Bureau of Alcohol, Tobacco, and Firearms deemed appropriate.

For purposes of defining an "arsenal," firearms, firearms parts, and ammunition clips would all count as a "firearm." In other words, if a person owned three rifles, three handguns, two ammunition clips for each gun, and a set of disassembled spare parts for the rifles and the handguns, he would have an "arsenal" consisting of at least twenty "guns."

A thousand rounds of ammunition also count as an arsenal. So the hundreds of thousands of target shooters who pick up a pair of bricks of rimfire ammunition for fifteen dollars every few months would also become the owners of "arsenals."

7. For more, see David B. Kopel, *The Samurai, the Mountie, and the Cowboy: Should America Adopt the Gun Controls of Other Democracies?* (Amherst, N.Y.: Prometheus Books, 1992).

8. Tom Jackson, "Keeping the Battle Alive," *Tampa Tribune,* October 21, 1993.

9. Mrs. Brady quoted in Sam Meddis, "Petitioners Taking Aim at Gun Laws," *USA Today,* July 20, 1988.

10. Sarah Brady, Testimony before House of Representative Judiciary Committee, October 28, 1985, quoted in *Congressional Record,* February 5, 1987, p. S792.

11. For another plea based on Hinckley's private medical records, James Brady, fund-raising letter for Handgun Control, Inc., "Wednesday morning" (summer 1990), p. 1: "John Hinckley—a man with a history of mental problems—purchased an easily concealed handgun." Most recipients of the fund-raising letter were not aware, as Mr. Brady surely must be, that no background check could have discovered Hinckley's entirely private record of consultation with mental therapists.

The fund-raising letter, which includes substantial portions of Mr. Brady's testimony before congressional committees, is hereinafter cited as "James Brady fund-raising letter."

12. Hinckley trial transcript, pp. 1489–1559; Opposition to Defendant's Motion for Bail. He also forfeited the guns he had been attempting to carry onto the plane.

13. Texas driver's license #9457099, issued to John W. Hinckley, Jr., 1612 Avenue Y, Lubbock, Texas, in Hinckley trial transcript, pp. 1751–52.

14. Sarah Brady, "How to Deter Future Hinckleys," *New York Times,* November 8, 1985. Also: Barbara Lautman, Handgun Control, Inc., Communications Director, "Only the Criminals Are Hurt By Waiting," *USA Today,* May 26, 1987, p. 12A; Handgun Control, Inc., "Briefing Paper on the Brady Amendment" (1988): "Had a waiting period been in effect and a background check undertaken, it could have been determined that Hinckley committed a felony by lying about his address on the federal forms and he could have been stopped."

Ohio Senator Metzenbaum (the lead Senate sponsor of the waiting period) claimed that Hinckley submitted "a defective driver's license." Sen. Metzenbaum, *Congressional Record,* February 4, 1987, p. S792.

15. Advertisement, "A $29 handgun shattered my family's life." *The New Republic,* July 18, 1988, inside front cover. Also, same advertisement, *New York Times,* August 1, 1988, p. 1.

Former Rep. Edward Feighan (House sponsor of waiting period), "Feighan Introduces Bill to Deter Criminals and Save Lives," Press Release, February 4, 1987: "One check would have told a Texas dealer that John Hinckley was using a false address and could have prevented him from purchasing a handgun."

16. Sarah Brady, Congressional testimony, quoted in "Flagship Bill Introduced," *Washington Report* (Handgun Control, Inc., newsletter), Spring 1987, pp. 1–2.

17. "Brady Backs a Wait on Handgun Sales," *USA Today,* June 17, 1987, p. 2A.

18. Advertisement, "A $29 handgun shattered my family's life," *The New Republic,* July 18, 1988, inside front cover. Also, same advertisement, *New York Times,* August 1, 1988, p. 1.

19. Southwestern Bell, *Lubbock-Slaton Telephone Directory* (November 1979) (listing "John W. Hinckley . . . 409 University Av.")

20. 18 United States Code § 922(a)(6).

21. ATF Rul. 80–21, reprinted in Department of the Treasury, Bureau of Alcohol, Tobacco, and Firearms, *(Your Guide to) Federal Firearms Regulation 1988–89,* ATF P 5300,4 (6–88), p. 73.

22. Rep. James Sensenbrenner, Jr. (R-Wisc.), "Fact versus Fiction on the Brady Amendment," August 11, 1988 (part of "Dear Colleague" letter titled "NRA Shoots Self in Foot"), p. 2.

Thus, at the same time that Handgun Control, Inc.'s, congressional forces were reassuring Congress that the "Brady bill" involved solely a criminal/mental records check, and not an address or other check, Mrs. Brady was imploring the public to support her bill because an address check would have stopped John Hinckley.

23. Shots from a .38 caliber handgun are almost twice as likely to kill as .22 caliber attacks. Franklin Zimring, "The Medium Is the Message: Firearms Caliber as a Determinant of Death from Assault," *Journal of Legal Studies* 97 (1972): 1.

24. Advertisement, "A $29 handgun shattered my family's life," p. 1. See also James Brady fund-raising letter, p. 1: "That shot—from a $29 Saturday Night Special—changed my life. . . ." Also, Sarah Brady: "Nine years ago, I got thrown into the issue when John Hinckley bought a $29 handgun in Dallas," in Peter Nye, "National Gun-Control Position," *The National Voter* (League of Women Voters), October/November 1990, p. 5.

25. "Gun Used to Shoot Reagan called a $47 'Saturday Night Special,' " *Baltimore Sun,* March 31, 1981 (reporting testimony of federal agents based on their examination of the purchase record for the transaction involving Hinckley). See also Pete Earley, "The Gun: A Saturday Night Special From Miami," *Washington Post,* March 31, 1981: "[W]hen model RG14 finally reaches the public, its price tag is about $47.50—one of the cheapest pistols available" (article about model of gun used by Hinckley).

26. Mrs. Brady also offers diverse stories about her own involvement in the antigun crusade. In a November 1985 *New York Times* op-ed, she explained her involvement as directly triggered by the NRA's attempt to repeal federal gun control through the McClure-Volkmer bill:

> *Last July,* the Senate passed the McClure-Volkmer bill, which would make it even easier for the kind of tragedy that struck down my husband to happen again. This bill would severely undermine federal gun laws by allowing anyone to buy a handgun across state lines, by limiting Government inspections of gun dealers' records and by repealing certain handgun record-keeping requirements. *I decided I had to do more than think about the problem.*

Sarah Brady, "How to Deter Future Hinckleys," *New York Times,* November 8, 1985 (emphasis added).

As a *New York Times* reporter described it:

> Mrs. Brady first enlisted in the fight for gun control in the summer of 1985 when it appeared that the Senate was about to adopt a measure backed by the NRA that was designed to weaken the 1968 Gun Control Act.
>
> "It just enraged me," she recalled of the effort to alter the comprehensive law.

Barbara Bamarekian, "Fighting the Fight on Gun Control," *New York Times,* February 10, 1987, p. B10.

But another newspaper states that Mrs. Brady has been an antigun activist since 1973, not 1985, as she twice stated in the *New York Times.* According to a *USA Today* profile, "Sarah

Brady has spent nearly a third of her life arguing for tougher gun laws. . . . Brady, daughter of an FBI agent, *began her fight for stronger gun laws in 1973,* when she tried to ban Saturday Night Specials. . . ." "Brady Backs a Wait on Handgun Sales," *USA Today,* June 17, 1987, p. 2A (emphasis added).

Mrs. Brady congratulates herself: "I have tried very hard not to make it an emotional issue because I think that is what the gun lobby has done." *New York Times,* February 10, 1987. A reader of Handgun Control's late 1990 fund-raising letter might find the rhetoric somewhat emotional:

> *[Y]ou* are at risk. *You* are in danger of also becoming a victim of the senseless handgun violence. . . . [S]top our insane national handgun war. . . . Frankly, what makes me livid is that the NRA opposes the Brady Bill because they claim it's an inconvenience. . . . For their convenience, I experience pain—sometimes so intense I cry . . . I need help getting out of bed, help taking a shower, help getting dressed and, damn it, even help going to the bathroom. . . . *The NRA lobbyists can go to hell!* . . . [T]he NRA lobbyists scream FOUL! . . . But the mighty NRA roars NO! And the cowards in Congress cringe! . . . I desperately need your help.

James Brady fund-raising letter (emphasis in original).

27. For example, Hank Johnson, Executive Editor, "Making a Case for Gun Control," *Athens Daily News* (Georgia), September 16, 1990 ("Had such a waiting period been in effect when John Hinckley walked into a Dallas pawn shop . . . he could have been stopped.")

28. Mrs. Brady insisted: "[T]his shooting could have been prevented if legislation such as that proposed here had been in force in 1981." Sarah Brady, Vice Chair, Handgun Control, Inc., Statement (press release), February 4, 1987, p. 1. Presumably she meant to say "1980."

29. Debbie Howlett, "Jury Still Out on Success of the Brady Law," *USA Today,* December 28, 1994.

30. While the John Hinckley story had some weaknesses as an argument for the Brady Bill, the Hinckley story was much closer to reality than the one that President Clinton told when signing the Brady Bill into law. At the signing ceremony, President Clinton emotionally recounted how a friend of his, an Arkansas gun dealer, sold a firearm to an escaped mental patient, who then murdered six people.

"My friend is not over it to this day," said the president, as the crowd applauded. "Don't tell me this bill will not make a difference. That is not true. That is not true."

"Not true" turns out to be a pretty good summation of the president's story, which he told not only in November 1993 but throughout the 1992 campaign.

The *Arkansas Democrat-Gazette* (Little Rock) tried to track down the origin of the tale. Back in 1984, an Arkansas man named Wayne Lee Crossley used a .45 pistol and a shotgun to murder four people in a bar. Contrary to the Clinton story, Crossley did not buy the guns himself; he convinced a woman friend to buy the guns for him. The Brady Act does nothing to prevent people with clean records from buying guns for anyone they want.

When the media started asking for substantiation of Clinton's story, the White House stonewalled. But before the no-answers rule was put in force, one White House staffer admitted that the man might just have been treated at a mental institution, rather than having "escaped from a mental hospital." Simply having undergone mental therapy does not legally disqualify a person from owning a gun under the Brady Act. Moreover, there is no central registry of persons who have been involuntarily committed to state mental hospitals, and the Brady Act does nothing to create such a registry.

And while the president spoke movingly about how his "friend is not over it to this day," the dealer/"friend" who sold the guns died several years before Clinton spoke. Timothy Clifford, "Clinton's Gun Story Is a Murder Mystery," (New York) *Daily News,* December 3, 1993.

31. "No Duty to Protect," *Washington Times,* July 13, 1993.

32. Elizabeth Thiel, "Gift of a Gun Warded Off Attack, Father Says," *Virginian-Pilot,* April 12, 1991, p. D1.

33. Peter Alan Kasler, "A Victim of Gun Control," *New York Times,* July 13, 1991.

34. Todd J. Gilman, Olive Talley, "Violent Reactions: Citizens' Growing Use of Force to Fight Crime Stirs Societal Questions," *Dallas Mornings News,* August 1, 1993, p. 1A.

35. Gary L. Wright, "Woman Won't Be Charged: Boyfriend's Slaying Ruled Self-Defense," *Charlotte Observer,* October 3, 1990.

36. Handgun Control, Inc., "Briefing Paper on the Brady Amendment" (1988); Rep. Feighan (sponsor of waiting period), remarks, *Congressional Record,* September 15, 1988, p. H7636.

37. The National Sheriffs Association (NSA), which eventually supported the waiting period, certainly qualifies as a major law enforcement organization, since it is the largest group of sheriffs in the United States. Interestingly, Handgun Control, Inc., claimed in 1988 to have the support of "every major law enforcement organization," even though in 1988 the NSA had not voted to support a waiting period. Apparently when the NSA later changed its mind and supported Handgun Control, it then qualified as a "major police organization."

The American Federation of Police is a for-profit organization, associated with retired police chief Gerald Arenberg, who is also associated with other for-profit organizations. Handgun Control, Inc., sometimes announces this fact as if it somehow delegitimizes the AFP—although the more than 100,000 law enforcement officers who have joined these organizations apparently do not agree. Perhaps no major law enforcement organization has been more tainted by financial impropriety than has the International Association of Chiefs of Police (IACP), a strong supporter of the waiting period; the questionable financial practices of IACP's former leadership should certainly not disqualify it as a voice for its members. *A fortiori,* the for-profit status of AFP, untainted by any hint of scandal, should not disqualify the group as a police voice.

38. The Federal Law Enforcement Officers Association, Fraternal Order of Police, International Brotherhood of Police Officers, International Association of Chiefs of Police, Major Cities Chief Administrators, National Association of Police Organizations, National Organization of Black Law Enforcement Executives, National Sheriffs Association, National Troopers Coalition, Police Executive Research Forum, Police Foundation, and Police Management Association. *Congressional Record,* September. 15, 1988, p. H 7639; Handgun Control, Inc., "Briefing Paper on the Brady Bill," p. 2.

39. "What PERF Members Think about Police Education, Assault Weapons, Toy Guns, Etc.," *Subject to Debate* (PERF newsletter) March/April 1989, p. 1.

40. Steve Glasser, "Southern Police Survey Shows Little Gun Control Support," UPI, July 9, 1993 (Atlanta Bureau); Scott Marshall, "Poll: South's Police Leery of Strict Gun Control," *Atlanta Constitution,* July 13, 1993.

41. "Funny You Should Ask," *Police,* April 1993, p. 56.

42. "The Law Enforcement Technology Gun Control Survey," *Law Enforcement Technology,* July/August 1991, pp. 14–15.

43. Regarding the criminal procedure amendments to the Constitution, only a small percentage of cases are not prosecuted or are reduced to lesser charges because of the rules against illegally seized physical evidence and coerced confessions. Peter F. Nardulli, "The Societal Cost of the Exclusionary Rule: An Empirical Assessment," 1983 *American Bar Foundation Research Journal* (1983): 585–610; Thomas Y. Davies, "A Hard Look at What We Know (and Still Need to Learn) about the 'Costs' of the Exclusionary Rule: The NIJ Study and Other Studies of 'Lost' Arrests," 1983 *American Bar Foundation Research Journal* (1983): 611–90; "Legal Safeguards Don't Hamper Crime-Fighting," *National Law Journal,* December 12, 1988, p. 5: Six-tenths of one percent to 2.35 percent of cases are dismissed because of bad searches; in a survey of prosecutors, 87 percent said that 5 percent or less of their cases were dismissed because of *Miranda* problems.

44. "91 percent of Americans Favor Brady Amendment," *Subject to Debate,* November/December 1988, p. 10.

45. Ibid.

46. The Joyce Foundation, *News Release,* June 3, 1993; LH Research, *A Survey of the American People on Guns as a Children's Health Issue,* prepared for the Harvard School of Public Health under a grant from the Joyce Foundation, study 930018.

47. Testimony of Louis Harris, Public Opinion Pollster, Before the U.S. Senate Committee on Government Operations at Hearings on Presidential Protection, October 24, 1975, reprinted in "Handgun Crime Control—1975–1976," Hearings Before the Subcommittee to Investigate Juvenile Delinquency of the Comm. on the Judiciary of the Senate, 94th Cong., 1st Sess., Vol. I, pp. 800, 803.

48. Gary W. Lawrence, "Results of a National Telephone Survey of Registered Voters on Waiting Period and Immediate Check Legislation," May 1991. The final question had been preceded with a number of questions which, while accurate, all served to highlight weaknesses of the Brady Bill. Accordingly, the public opinion in favor of the instant check was probably not as strong as Lawrence reported.

49. Luntz Weber Research and Strategic Services, "A National Survey on Crime, Violence, and Guns," June 1993.

50. Polling data from Herbert McClosky and Alida Brill, *Dimensions of Tolerance: What Americans Believe about Civil Liberties* (New York: Russell Sage Foundation, 1988).

51. "It established some rights of the individual as unalienable and which consequently, no majority has a right to deprive them of." Albert Gallatin, Congressman and Cabinet officer of the early American Republic, quoted in Richard E. Gardiner, " 'To Preserve Liberty': A Look at the Right to Keep and Bear Arms," *Northern Kentucky Law Review* 10 (1982): 63, 79n.

52. McCloskey and Brill, *Dimensions of Tolerance.*

53. James D. Wright, Peter Rossi, and Kathleen Daly, *Under the Gun: Weapons, Crime, and Violence in America* (Hawthorne, N.Y.: Aldine, 1983), pp. 223–35.

54. Sarah Brady, fund-raising letter for Handgun Control, Inc., "Wednesday," (no month or day), 1988.

55. Matthew DeZee, "Gun Control Legislation: Impact and Ideology," *Law & Policy Quarterly* 5 (July 1983): 363–79. Although DeZee stated that he supported stricter gun laws, he did not offer any proposals.

56. "Homicides, Robberies and State 'Cooling-Off' Schemes," in Don Kates, ed., *Why Handgun Bans Can't Work* (Bellevue, Wash.: Second Amendment Foundation, 1982), pp. 101–12.

57. "An Empirical Analysis of Federal and State Firearms Control Laws," in Don Kates, ed., *Firearms and Violence: Issues of Public Policy* (Cambridge, Mass.: Ballinger, 1984): 225–58. (The study also found no perceptible impact on crime or gun acquisition from the federal Gun Control Act of 1968.)

58. *Report on the Federal Firearm Owners Protection Act,* S. Rep. no 3476, 97th Cong., 2d sess. (1982), pp. 51–52.

59. Philip. J. Cook and James Blose, "State Programs for Screening Handgun Buyers," *Annals of the American Academy of Political Science* 455 (May 1981): 88–90. Although skeptical about screening systems as a panacea, Cook and Blose still favor screening since it might increase the marginal price or time needed to obtain a gun for inexperienced criminals (such as teenagers), and might keep weakly motivated criminals from obtaining guns at all. Ibid., pp. 90–91.

60. Assistant Attorney General John R. Bolton, letter to House Judiciary Chairman Peter Rodino, March 19, 1986.

61. David McDowall, "Preventive Effects of Firearms Regulations on Injury Mortality," paper presented at the annual meeting of the American Society of Criminology, Phoenix, Arizona, November 1993.

62. Gary Kleck, *Point Blank: Guns and Violence in America* (Hawthorne, N.Y.: Aldine, 1991), Table 10.5.

63. James Wright, Peter Rossi, and Kathleen Daly, *Under the Gun: Weapons, Crime and Violence in America* (Hawthorne, N.Y.: Aldine, 1983).

64. James Wright and Peter Rossi, *Armed and Considered Dangerous: A Survey of Felons and Their Firearms* (New York: Aldine, 1986). Three-fifths of the prisoners studied said that a criminal would not attack a potential victim who was known to be armed. Two-fifths of them had decided not to commit a crime because they thought the victim might have a gun. Criminals in states with higher civilian gun ownership rates worried the most about armed victims.

65. Generally consistent with the Wright-Rossi study, an NIJ prisoner study published in 1993 found that 27 percent of state prison inmates reported a purchase from a store as the source of their guns, and another 9 percent reported theft (including theft from a store) as their source. Allen Beck et al., *Survey of State Prison Inmates, 1991,* NCJ–136949 (Washington, D.C.: Bureau of Justice Statistics, 1993), p. 19.

66. *The Armed Criminal in America,* p. 46 (report to National Institute of Justice; later republished as *Armed and Considered Dangerous*).

67. Wright and Rossi, *Armed and Considered Dangerous,* pp. 181–87.

68. Ibid., p. 188, n. 3.

69. James D. Wright, "Ten Essential Observations on Guns in America," *Society,* March–April 1995, pp. 62–67.

70. There is of course some value in keeping a criminal from obtaining a second gun or a better gun, but the process would be unlikely to stop a criminal from perpetrating a given armed crime.

71. Bureau of Alcohol, Tobacco, and Firearms, Assistant Director of Criminal Enforcement, Memorandum to Director, July 10, 1975 (Greenville survey. Of 20,047 names submitted to the FBI for record checks, sixty-eight had felony convictions; of those, forty-one had not been represented by counsel at their conviction or had committed crimes in the distant past; twenty-seven buyers were prosecuted. Of the 1.3 percent of buyers selected for prosecution, .9 percent had nonviolent felony convictions, and .4 percent had violent convictions); Bureau of Alcohol, Tobacco, and Firearms, Assistant Director for Criminal Enforcement, memorandum to Director, May 8, 1975 (of 374 records checked, thirty-nine were purchasers with felony records who were not appropriate for prosecution because of age or nonviolent nature of felony; six purchasers were prosecuted).

72. Reilly Johnson, "'Brady Bill' Gets Guffaws from Guys behind Bars," *Sante Fe New Mexican,* June 30, 1991.

73. Edward J. Scheidegger, "The California System: Access to Other Databases, Name Searches and the Waiting Period," in *National Conference on Criminal Justice Records: Brady and Beyond,* NCJ–151263 (Washington, D.C.: Department of Justice, Bureau of Justice Statistics, 1995)(papers presented at a February 1994 conference), p. 51.

74. Clayton E. Cramer, "Waiting for a Gun," *San Jose Mercury News,* June 20, 1993.

75. William Davis, "Gun Law Backfires," *Los Angeles Daily News,* March 4, 1991 (letter to the editor from law enforcement officer and licensed federal firearms dealer whose application was put on hold).

There are also reports that all "assault weapon" registrants have been placed in police computer lists of persons who pose a special hazard. California's practice of enforcing its laws with special severity against persons who are especially law-abiding makes the registrants seem naïve, and seems to vindicate the intuitive distrust of gun registration felt by most gun owners.

76. Bureau of Justice Statistics, *Identifying Persons, Other Than Felons, Ineligible to Purchase Firearms: A Feasibility Study* (May 1990) (report performed under contract by Enforth Corporation, Cambridge, Mass.), p. 25.

77. Pete Shields, *Guns Don't Die—People Do* (New York: Arbor House, 1981), p. 83.

78. Gary D. McAlvey, "The Illinois Experience: 25 Years of Firearms Control through Comprehensive Background Checks," in *National Conference on Criminal Justice Records: Brady and Beyond,* p. 38.

79. David Bordua, "Operation and Effects of Firearms Owners Identification and Waiting Period Legislation in Illinois" (University of Illinois, unpublished paper, 1985).

80. Sgt. R. G. Pepersack, Sr., Maryland State Police, Commander, Firearms License Section, written testimony and oral questioning before United States Senate Committee on the Judiciary, Subcommittee on the Constitution, regarding S. 466, "Handgun Violence Prevention Act," June 16, 1987. (In 1986, there were 20,704 applications, 1,102 initial disapprovals, 370 approvals granted upon appeal, and fourteen currently active cases involving an applicant who had a conviction of a crime of violence, of whom five or six had been selected for prosecution for attempting an illegal purchase.)

81. Ibid., p. 2 (of 471 appellants in 1986, 370 [78 percent] were ultimately approved).

82. Todd Spangler, "Gun-Sale Delays Draw Fire," *Washington Times,* May 3, 1993.

83. "The Case for a Waiting Period"; also, "Flagship Bill Introduced," *Washington Report* (Handgun Control, Inc., newsletter), Spring 1987, p. 1.

84. From 1966 (when current controls were enacted) until June 1988, there were 1,153,400 applications for either a permit to purchase a handgun or a firearms identification card. Of those applications, 28,850 (2.5 percent) were denied. According to reporter Eugene Kiley of the *Bergen Record,* the state police conducted a random survey of 507 applicants in 1985. Applying the percentages from the 1985 survey to the data as a whole leads to the following breakdowns for the denials:

Reason	Percent	Number
Criminal Record	29	8,366
Falsifying Application	35	10,097
Public Health, Safety, and Welfare	20	5,770
Mental or Alcoholic	7	2,020
Insufficient Reason to Issue	6	1,731

In other words, the total denials for actual danger (8,366 criminal records plus 2,020 mental or alcoholic cases = 10,386) comes uncomfortably close to the number of denials for patently arbitrary reasons (5,770 public health plus 1,731 insufficient reason = 7,501). If the denials based on falsifying applications (10,097) are also considered arbitrary (since the category may not include falsifications relating to criminal, mental, or alcoholic ineligibility), the number of arbitrary denials significantly exceeds the number of legitimate denials.

85. Ron Marsico, "Senator Pushes for U.S. to Follow Virginia's Lead in Handgun Control," (Newark) *Star-Ledger,* July 8, 1993 (according to Sgt. 1st Class Robert Zupko, head of the state police firearms unit, the application process generally takes three to four months); statement of Robert F. Mackinnon, on behalf of the Coalition of New Jersey Sportsmen, before the House Committee on the Judiciary, *Legislation to Modify the 1968 Gun Control Act,* part 2, serial no. 131, 99th Congress, 1st and 2d sess., February 27, 1986 (Washington, D.C.: Government Printing Office, 1987), p. 1418. According to the Department of Justice Task Force, the typical delay in New Jersey is six to ten weeks. Task Force, p. 84.

For an example of the New Jersey law in operation, see W. Peter Haas, Chairman, Public Safety Committee, Borough of Mountain Lakes, letter to Police Chief Joseph Spinozzi, July 29, 1968 ("it is my opinion that you as Chief of Police of our Borough deny any applications for any type for weapons permits. You may accept the application and fully process that application to the point of approval or disapproval, then disapprove and notify the applicant of your decision and their recourse through the County Court . . . Article 4 Section 2A: 151–33 [d] . . .

authorizes the disapproval of any person where the issuance would not be in the public interest or welfare. It is my belief that it is not in the public interest to issue permits . . .").

86. Each application takes about four hours to process. Colonel Clinton Pagano, testimony before the New Jersey Assembly Law and Public Safety Committee, hearing on A. 594, February 1988. If one assumes that each man-hour costs the state of New Jersey ten dollars, the licensing system has cost New Jersey $46,136,000. (The figure is in 1988 dollars, and based on the figure of 1,153,400 total applications in 1966–88, cited in the previous note.) There have been 10,386 denials based on criminal, mental, or alcohol records (see note 84), and dividing that number into the total dollar cost yields the cost per denial of $4,442.13.

87. The dealer must report the sale to local police within six hours. The police have forty-eight hours to veto the sale, but in practice dealers generally wait seventy-two hours to be sure to avoid liability for a sale to an ineligible person. Weekends and holidays do not count for purposes of the forty-eight hour computation.

All above information regarding Pennsylvania comes from the author's August 28, 1990, telephone conversation with Ms. Sharon H. Crawford, head of the state police firearms unit in Harrisburg.

Police believe that the law requires all private transfers to be routed through retail dealers so that police can perform the check, but the requirement, if it exists, is widely ignored.

88. A good number of "hits" are based on felony convictions from many years before, or on a conviction of aggravated assault, which some people (negligently) do not realize is a disqualifying felony. Task Force on Felon Identification System, *Report to the Attorney General on Systems for Identifying Felons Who Attempt to Purchase Firearms* (Washington, D.C.: Department of Justice, October 1989), p. 24 (hereinafter, "Task Force").

89. Task Force, p. 87.

90. In 1992, Virginia processed 191,540 instant check requests. Of these, final denials resulted for 1,287 persons with felony convictions, 295 persons with outstanding felony charges, and seventy-three persons listed as "fugitives" (including those who failed to make court appearances but were not hiding from the law). "Virginia Firearms Transaction Program Performance 1990 and 1992," in *A Final Report: Governor's Commission on Violent Crime in Virginia* (Richmond: Dept. of Public Safety, January 1994), p. 72.

91. R. Lewis Vass, "The Virginia Point-of-Sale Firearms Transaction Program," in *National Conference on Criminal Justice Records: Brady and Beyond,* p. 41 (1993 costs; the costs also include some other firearms regulations, such as maintaining the statewide list of permits to carry a concealed weapon).

92. Terry D. Miller, "Letters: Virginia Not so Instant," *Government Technology,* May 1994, p. 22.

93. In Virginia in the instant check's first year, eight of 673 ineligibles (1.2 percent) were arrested. Handgun Control, Inc., "The Case for a Waiting Period" (1990). See also the Maryland data discussed above.

94. Judy Keen and Robert Davis, "Brady's Law Scorecard: 1 Year Later," *USA Today,* February 28, 1995. See also, Debbie Howlett, "Jury Still Out on Success of the Brady Law," *USA Today,* December 28, 1994 (2 percent estimated denial rate). A BATF source suggested the Treasury Secretary Lloyd Bentsen's September 1994 estimate of a 5 percent denial rate was too high. Ibid. Even further off the mark was a press release from BATF the month after the Brady Bill went into effect. The press release claimed that "up to" 23,610 felons (out of 375,000 handgun buyers) had been stopped by the Brady Act. Bureau of Alcohol, Tobacco and Firearms, "Brady Law Success," press release (Washington, D.C.: BATF: March 31, 1994). Actually (as BATF well knew), the 23,610 figure was merely the number for second-level inquiries into the federal database of felons (the FBI Interstate Identification Index). Most second-level inquiries were eventually determined not to relate to actual felons but to law-abiding persons who had a similar name, or to other cases in which the buyer was eventually approved.

95. "333 Felons Kept from Buying Guns in Nevada," *Reno Gazette-Journal*, December 12, 1994 (Associated Press).

96. Marilyn Robinson, "Background Check Disqualifies 8% of Gun Buyers," *Denver Post*, September 1, 1994, p. 6B; "New Way to Find Fugitives: Run Check on Gun Buyers," *Denver Post*, September 6, 1994.

97. Howlett, "Jury Still Out on Success of the Brady Law."

98. BATF explained that it did not have sufficient agents to arrest felons who lied on Brady handgun application forms. "Brady Law," *Washington Times*, April 4, 1994, p. A–6.

The Bureau of Alcohol, Tobacco and Firearms prosecutions that did take place were apparently for violating the federal felon-in-possession (or attempted possession) statutes, which were enacted in 1968, and strengthened in 1986.

99. Pierre Thomas, "Brady Law Halts Gun Buys, But Prosecutions Are Lagging," *Washington Post*, February 24, 1995, p. A2.

100. "Clintonites Spin Brady Act 'Success,' " *American Rifleman*, September 1994, p. 24.

101. Later in 1994, the federal crime bill made domestic violence restraining order a disqualification under certain circumstances.

102. Dennis A. Garrett, Police Chief, memorandum to Assistant City Manager, "Brady Bill Turndowns for Warrants," April 9, 1994.

103. "Austin Expands Brady Check," *Firearms Business*, July 15, 1994, p. 7.

104. "Gun Control: It Threatens the Right People," *Tallahassee Democrat*, February 1, 1985. (In the six months since the waiting period went into effect, thirty-seven of 1,425 applicants were denied; of these thirty-seven, fourteen were denied for outstanding arrest records for traffic offenses or misdemeanors.)

105. James Brady, fund-raising letter for Handgun Control, Inc., "Wednesday morning" (summer 1990), p. 3: "Seven days to help police thwart a purchase by a drug dealer."

106. As Sterling Johnson, New York City's former special narcotics prosecutor, acknowledged, "You either have to protect yourself with a gun or get out of the [drug] business." Anthony M. DeStefano, "City Teens: Armed and Dangerous," *New York Newsday*, September 24, 1990, p. 30.

107. An article that applied standard economic concepts of price elasticity to the demand for guns concluded that recreational firearms users would be the most likely to reduce gun buying as a result, while persons "within the subculture of violence" would change their gun buying habits the least. Gary Kleck and David J. Bordua, "The Assumptions of Gun Control," in *Firearms and Violence*, ch. 2.

108. Douglas A. Blackmon, "Gun Sale Limits Don't Cut Crime, Experts Say," *Atlanta Journal & Constitution*, May 29, 1990, p. A–9.

109. "Killer Fraternized with Men in Army Fatigues," *The Globe and Mail*, December 9, 1989; "Killer's Letter Blames Feminists," *The Globe and Mail*, December 8, 1989.

In 1978, Canada implemented a national law requiring police permission for every handgun purchase and a one-time license (good for five years) for long gun purchases. The license application requirement served, in effect, as a waiting period for most first-time gun purchasers.

110. Blackmon, "Gun Sale Limits"; James Brady fund-raising letter.

111. "Legislature: Pass Handgun Law," *Denver Post*, January 24, 1975.

112. David Hardy, "Legal Restrictions on Firearms Ownership as an Answer to Violent Crime: What Was the Question?" *Hamline Law Review* 6 (July 1983): 404. It might be wondered if lives would be saved if homicidally enraged husbands "cooled off" while driving around at night to look for open firearms dealers willing to sell to drunken and agitated customers, rather than staying home and finding alternative weapons.

113. In a Detroit study, 75 percent of wives who shot and killed their husbands were legally defending themselves or their children against illegal attacks. The figure for Miami was 60 percent, and for Houston, 85.7 percent. "[W]hen women kill, their victims are . . . most typi-

cally men who have assaulted them." Martin Daly and Margo Wilson, *Homicide* (New York: Aldine, 1988), pp. 15, 200.

Also: Saunders, "When Battered Women Use Violence: Husband Abuse or Self-Defense," *Violence and Victims* 1 (1986), p. 49; Barnard et al., "Till Death Do Us Part: A Study of Spouse Murder," *Bulletin of the American Academy of Psych. and the Law* 10 (1982): 271; Donald T. Lunde, *Murder and Madness* (San Francisco: San Francisco Book Co., 1976), p. 10 (in 85 percent of decedent-precipitated interspousal homicides, the wife kills an abusing husband); E. Benedek, "Women and Homicide," in Bruce Danto, ed., *The Human Side of Homicide* (New York: Columbia, 1982); Don Kates, *Guns, Murders, and the Constitution* (San Francisco: Pacific Research Institute, 1990), p. 25.

It is sometimes suggested that the abused woman is to blame for not leaving the relationship. Many women do leave, only to be followed and killed by their former mate. See generally Cynthia K. Gillespie, *Justifiable Homicide: Battered Women, Self-Defense, and the Law* (Columbus: Ohio State University Press, 1989).

114. Gary Kleck, *Point Blank* (Hawthorne, N.Y.: Aldine, 1991), chapter 8. The study of 1982 data Kleck reviewed is Ted Mannelli, "Handgun Control," unpublished report to the Executive Office of the Governor, State of Florida (Tallahassee: University of Florida, 1982).

115. "Excerpts from Dinkins's Address: Mobilizing to Fight Crime," *New York Times,* October 3, 1990, p. B2.

116. Eric Stenson, "Laws Limiting Access to Guns Putting Dent in NRA's Clout," *Asbury Park Press,* August 5, 1990.

117. 54 Fed. Reg. 43532.

118. Task Force, p. 24.

119. For example, the Lakewood, Colorado, police chief defended a proposed twenty-one day wait: "If we can save one life, it's worth it." Also, Richard Boyd, President of Fraternal Order of Police, quoted in "Two Sides Spiritedly Debate Bill on Gun-purchase Waiting Period," *The Capital Times* (Madison, Wisc.), June 18, 1987; Rep. Edward Feighan (House sponsor of waiting period), "Feighan Introduces Bill to Deter Criminals and Save Lives," Press Release, February 4, 1987 ("If this bill can save even one life, which I know it can, Congress should act on it now."); Fraternal Order of Police: "If the seven-day waiting period will save just one life— the life of a law enforcement officer or a citizen—then [Congress's] work will be successful." quoted in Handgun Control, Inc., "Waiting Periods Work."

If the criterion for legislation is whether it will save a single life, legislatures would also want to consider a ban on new private swimming pools and on cigarette lighters, as well as a reduction of the speed limit to fifteen m.p.h.

120. BATF estimate cited in Task Force, p. 34.

121. One way to reduce the number of required checks by the police would be to exempt low-volume firearms dealers (fifty or fewer sales per year) from the required check. Most such dealers sell only to persons they already know (such as members of their shooting club) and therefore perform, in effect, their own background check prior to sales.

122. Task Force on Felon Identification System, *Report to the Attorney General on Systems for Identifying Felons Who Attempt to Purchase Firearms* (Washington, D.C.: Department of Justice, October 1989).

123. For example, David Seifman, "City's Latest Crime Shocker Fails to Stir Mayor's Anger," *New York Post,* September 5, 1990, p. 4; Donatella Lorch, "Girl Is Killed by Stray Bullet in Brooklyn," *New York Times,* September 24, 1990, p. A1 (the Mayor stated: "Her death leaves me griefstricken and outraged . . . at the failure of our state and federal governments to bring an end to the manufacture and distribution of these tools of death"); "Excerpts from Dinkins's Address: Mobilizing to Fight Crime," *New York Times,* October 5, 1990, p. B2 (the speech concluded, "We ache for the protection that only a federal law can give us—the Brady Bill." Dinkins implored New Yorkers to call U.S. House Speaker Foley to demand passage of the Brady Bill, "which could save thousands of lives in its first year, including yours").

124. Registration lists facilitated gun confiscation in Greece, Ireland, Jamaica, and Bermuda. B. Bruce-Briggs, "The Great American Gun War," *The Public Interest,* Fall 1976, p. 59; Kates, *Why Handguns Bans Can't Work,* p. 16.

The Washington, D.C., city council considered (but did not enact) a proposal to use registration lists to confiscate all handguns in the city. When reminded that the registration plan had been enacted with the explicit promise to gun owners that it would not be used for confiscation, the confiscation's sponsor retorted, "Well, I never promised them anything!" "Wilson's Gun Proposal," *Washington Star,* February 15, 1975, p. A12; Lawrence Francis, "Washington Report," *Guns & Ammo,* December 1976, p. 86.

The Evanston, Illinois, police department also attempted to use state registration lists to enforce a gun ban. Paul Blackman, "Civil Liberties and Gun-Law Enforcement: Some Implications of Expanding the Power of the Police to Enforce a 'Liberal' Victimless Crime," paper presented at the annual meeting of the American Society of Criminology, Cincinnati, 1984, p. 14. In 1989, the Illinois Legislature considered a proposal to confiscate semi-automatics, using the existing gun registration forms to find out where to round up the guns.

When Illinois Firearms Owners Identification Cards were first issued, persons with a felony conviction were eligible to possess a firearm if the conviction was more than five years in the past. Later, the Illinois legislature retroactively changed the bar date to twenty years. Registered owners who had a felony conviction more than five years old and less than twenty had their guns confiscated. Since there are always proposals to expand the class of prohibited persons (such as barring all persons with even single misdemeanor drug or violent offense, no matter how long ago), and always proposals to confiscate various lawfully acquired types of weapons, many gun owners are leery of being placed on any kind of government list—even if they are in full compliance with the (current) law.

New York City has used registration lists to confiscate lawfully purchased firearms, such as M1 carbine, which the City retroactively classified as "assault weapons." *Daily News,* September 5, 1992.

125. The Supreme Court has ruled that the Constitution prohibits the government from registering purchasers of newspapers and magazines, even of foreign Communist propaganda. *Lamont, DBA Basic Pamphlets* v. *Postmaster General,* 381 U.S. 301 (1965). The U.S. Post Office was intercepting "foreign Communist propaganda" before delivery, and requiring addressees to sign a form before receiving the items. The Court's narrow holding was based on the principle that addressees should not have to go to the trouble of filling out a form to receive particular items of politically oriented mail. Since the Post Office had stopped maintaining lists of propaganda recipients before the case was heard, the Court did not specifically rule on the list-keeping practices. One may infer that the Post Office threw away its lists because it expected the Court would find them unconstitutional. See also *Thomas* v. *Collins,* 323 U.S. 516 (1944) (registration of labor organizers).

126. "Background Checks Done Strictly by the Book," *San Diego Union,* February 21, 1990 ("'We have an archive where we keep all those records, alphabetized by the gun owners' names,' said Entricon" [Justice Department official]).

127. *Puerto Rico* v. *Branstad,* 483 U.S. 219 (1987).

Of course Congress could compel destruction of registration records if it made a finding that gun registration violates the Second Amendment. Congress has the power under section five of the Fourteenth Amendment to outlaw state violations of Constitutional rights.

128. 5 United States Code § 552a(I)(1).

129. Carl Ingram, "Gun Law Forces Mental Hospitals to Name Patients," *Los Angeles Times,* February 7, 1991.

130. For example, Arlington, Virginia, requires handgun applicants to "authorize a review and full disclosure of all arrest and medical psychiatric records." Form 2020–63 (Form 4/88).

131. State of Illinois, Department of Public Safety, Firearm Owners Identification Application, question 9, FOID–1.

132. State of New Jersey,"Application for Firearms Purchaser Identification Card," form STS-3 (rev. 9-1-79).

133. Some studies have concluded that former mental patients are no more prone to commit violent crimes than is the public as a whole. U.S. Senate Subcommittee on the Constitution, Judiciary Committee, "Hearings on the Constitutional Rights of the Mentally Ill," 91st Congress, 1st & 2d sessions (Washington: 1977), p. 277; B. Ennis, *Prisoners of Psychiatry* (1970), pp. vi, 225; G. Morris, "Criminality and the Right to Treatment," in *The Mentally Ill and the Right to Treatment* (1970), pp. 121-24; Livermore, Malmquist, and Meehl, "On the Justifications for Civil Commitment," *University of Pennsylvania Law Review* 117 (1969): 75, 83 n.22.

Some studies suggest that committal decisions are often unfair and incorrect. A. Wiley, "Rights of the Mentally Ill," p. 11; Ennis, *Prisoners of Psychiatry*, p. vii.

134. Rep. Marlenee, *Congressional Record*, September 15, 1988, pp. H7643-44.

135. For several months in 1970, the FBI ran out of funds to process state requests for fingerprint checks. Some New Jersey chiefs of police stopped processing firearms permit applications, and told gun applicants to sue in court to obtain a license. J. Edgar Hoover, Director, Federal Bureau of Investigation, Letter to All Fingerprint Contributors, May 21, 1970; Joseph Santiago, "Chief Balks On Permits For Guns," *The Record*, July 10, 1970; John Spencer, "Registration of Guns Becomes Prohibition of Guns," (letter to the editor), *The Record*, n.d. (written August 27, 1970).

136. Testimony of Sergeant R. G. Pepersack, Md. St. Police Commander, Firearms Lic. Sect., before Subcomm. on the Const., June 16, 1987.

137. Don Kates, "On Reducing Violence or Liberty," *Civil Liberties Review* (American Civil Liberties Union), August/September 1976, p. 56.

138. For a variety of cases of lawless enforcement of the gun laws, see *Motley* v. *Kellogg*, 409 N.E.2d 1207 (Ind. App. 1980) (police chief "denied members of the community the opportunity to obtain a gun permit and bear arms for their self-defense"); *Schubert* v. *DeBard*, 398 N.E.2d 1339 (Ind. App. 1980) (police determination that self-defense did not constitute "good reason" for gun permit voided by court); *Buffa* v. *Police Dept. of Suffolk County*, 47 A.D.2d 841, 366 N.Y.S.2d 162 (2d Dept. 1975) (mere "withdrawal of police approval" was insufficient grounds to revoke license); *Storace* v. *Mariano* , 35 Conn. Sup. 28, 391 A.2d 1347, 1349 (1978) ("in my opinion, he is an unsuitable person to carry a gun" was not a suitable reason for denying a permit); *Salute* v. *Pitchess*, 61 Cal. App. 3d 557, 132 Cal. Rptr. 345, 347 (2d Dist. 1976) (sheriff's unilateral determination "that only selected public officials can show good cause for a permit" was illegal); *Schwanda* v. *Bonney*, 418 A.2d 163, 165 (Me. 1980) (voiding police effort to impose criteria not based on statute); *Iley* v. *Harris*, 345 So.2d 336, 337 (Fla. 1977).

139. For some examples of the New York City Police Department's flagrant abuse of the statutory licensing procedure, see: *Shapiro* v. *Cawley*, 46 A.D.2d 633, 634, 360 N.Y.S.2d 7, 8 (1st Dept. 1974) (ordering N.Y.C. Police Department to abandon illegal policy of requiring applicants for on-premises pistol license to demonstrate unique "need"); *Turner* v. *Codd*, 85 Misc. 2d 483, 484, 378 N.Y.S.2d 888, 889 (Special Term Part 1, N.Y. County, 1975) (ordering N.Y.C. Police Department to obey Shapiro decision); *Echtman* v. *Codd*, no. 4062-76 (N.Y. County) (class action lawsuit which finally forced Police Department to obey *Shapiro* decision). Also: *Bomer* v. *Murphy*, no. 14606-71 (N.Y. County) (to compel Department to issue blank application forms for target shooting licenses); *Klapper* v. *Codd*, 78 Misc.2d 377, 356 N.Y.S.2d 431 (Sup. Ct., Spec. Term, N.Y. Cty.) (overturning refusal to issue license because applicant had changed jobs several times); *Castelli* v. *Cawley*, *New York Law Journal*, March 19, 1974, p. 2, col. 2 (Applicant suffered from post-nasal drip, and repeatedly cleared his throat during interview. His interviewer "diagnosed" a "nervous condition" and rejected the application. An appeals court overturned the decision, noting that the applicant's employment as a diamond cutter indicated "steady nerves.")

140. *United States* v. *Panter*, 688 F.2d 268, 271 (5th Cir. 1982).

141. Notably, many gun control activists do not consider self-defense legitimate. The United Methodist Church, which founded the National Coalition to Ban Handguns (NCBH) (now named the Coalition to Stop Gun Violence), and whose Washington office building also houses the NCBH, declares that people should submit to rape and robbery rather than endanger the criminal's life by shooting him. Methodist Board of Church and Society, "Handguns in the United States" (pamphlet); same statement in Rev. Brockway, "But the Bible Doesn't Mention Pistols," *Engage-Social Action Forum,* May 1977, pp. 39–40. The Presbyterian Church, another affiliate of the coalition, supports a complete ban on handguns because it opposes "the killing of anyone, anywhere, for any reason," including defense of others against a life-threatening attack. Rev. Young, Director of Criminal Justice Program for Presbyterian Church, testifying in 1985–86 Hearings on Legislation to Modify the 1968 Gun Control Act, House Judiciary Committee, Subcommittee on Crime, 1: 128. The *Washington Post* condemned "the need that some homeowners and shopkeepers believe they have for weapons to defend themselves" as representing "the worst instincts in the human character." Editorial, "Guns and the Civilizing Process," *Washington Post,* September 26, 1972.

142. See, for example, *Bowers* v. *DeVito* 686 F.2d 616 (7th Cir. 1982) (no federal Constitutional requirement that police provide protection); *Calogrides* v. *Mobile,* 475 So. 2d 560 (Ala. 1985); Cal. Govt. Code §§ 845 (no liability for failure to provide police protection) and 846 (no liability for failure to arrest or to retain arrested person in custody); *Davidson* v. *Westminster,* 32 Cal.3d 197, 185 Cal. Rep. 252; 649 P.2d 894 (1982); *Stone* v. *State* 106 Cal.App.3d 924, 165 Cal. Rep. 339 (1980); *Morgan* v. *District of Columbia,* 468 A.2d 1306 (D.C.App. 1983); *Warren* v. *District of Columbia,* 444 A.2d 1 (D.C. App 1981); *Sapp* v. *Tallahassee,* 348 So.2d 363 (Fla. App. 1st Dist.), *cert. denied* 354 So.2d 985 (Fla. 1977); Ill. Rev. Stat. 4–102; *Keane* v. *Chicago,* 98 Ill. App.2d 460, 240 N.E.2d 321 (1st Dist. 1968); *Jamison* v. *Chicago,* 48 Ill. App. 3d 567 (1st Dist. 1977); *Simpson's Food Fair* v. *Evansville,* 272 N.E.2d 871 (Ind. App.); *Silver* v. *Minneapolis* 170 N.W.2d 206 (Minn. 1969); *Wuetrich* v. *Delia,* 155 N.J. Super. 324, 326, 382 A.2d 929, 930, *cert. denied* 77 N.J. 486, 391 A.2d 500 (1978); *Chapman* v. *Philadelphia,* 290 Pa. Super. 281, 434 A.2d 753 (Penn. 1981); *Morris* v. *Musser,* 84 Pa. Cmwth. 170, 478 A.2d 937 (1984).

The law in New York remains as decided by the Court of Appeals in the 1959 case *Riss* v. *New York:* the government is not liable even for a grossly negligent failure to protect a crime victim. In the *Riss* case, a young woman telephoned the police and begged for help because her ex-boyfriend had repeatedly threatened, "If I can't have you no one else will have you, and when I get through with you, no one else will want you." The day after she had pleaded for police protection, the ex-boyfriend threw lye in her face, blinding her in one eye, severely damaging the other, and permanently scarring her features. "What makes the City's position particularly difficult to understand," wrote a dissenting opinion, "is that, in conformity to the dictates of the law, Linda did not carry any weapon for self-defense. Thus, by a rather bitter irony she was required to rely for protection on the City of New York which now denies all responsibility to her." *Riss* v. *New York,* 22 N.Y.2d 579, 293 N.Y.S.2d 897, 240 N.E.2d 806 (1958).

Ruth Brunell called the police on twenty different occasions to beg for protection from her husband. He was arrested only one time. One evening Mr. Brunell telephoned his wife and told her he was coming over to kill her. When she called the police, they refused her request that they come to protect her. They told Mrs. Brunell to call back when her husband got there. Mr. Brunell stabbed his wife to death before she could call the police. The court held that the San Jose police were not liable for ignoring Mrs. Brunell's pleas for help. *Hartzler* v. *City of San Jose,* 46 Cal. App. 3d 6 (1st Dist. 1975).

143. Task Force Draft, 54 Federal Register 43528, October 25, 1989.

144. *Hammons* v. *Scott,* 423 F. Supp. 618 (N.D. Cal. 1976); *Rowlett* v. *Fairfax,* 446 F. Supp. 186 (W.D. Mo. 1978).

145. 54 Fed. Reg. 43545.

146. As Josh Sugarmann, former communications director for the CSGV, wrote: "Handgun controls do little to stop criminals from obtaining handguns." Josh Sugarmann, "The NRA Is Right: But We Still Need to Ban Handguns," *Washington Monthly,* June 1987, pp. 11–15.

147. National Coalition to Ban Handguns, "Twenty Questions and Answers" (n.d.), question 8 ("Banning 'Saturday Night Specials' would be a useful first step towards an ultimate solution").

148. The author was a member of the panel that questioned the two debaters.

149. Founding Chair Pete Shields explained his strategy for prohibition: "The first problem is to slow down the number of handguns being produced and sold in this country. The second problem is to get handguns registered. The final problem is to make possession of all handguns and all handgun ammunition—except for the military, police, licensed security guards, licensed sporting clubs, and licensed gun collectors—totally illegal." Richard Harris, "A Reporter at Large: Handguns," *The New Yorker,* July 26, 1976, p. 58.

150. Handgun Control, Inc., also supports the Chicago law, which prohibits the lawful acquisition of handguns. Handgun Control, Inc., "Fact Card." District of Columbia Code §§ 6–2132(4) and 6–2372.

151. H.R. 7, §§ (a)(1)(A)(ii)(I) (a sale may proceed only if "the transferor has received written verification that the chief law enforcement officer has received the statement"); (a)(2) ("Paragraph (1) shall not be interpreted to require any action by a chief law enforcement officer which is not otherwise required.")

152. Former Attorney General Thornburgh believed that any verification system for firearms purchasers should be at the point of sale without further delays; he reasoned that any check that would be significantly more accurate would take a month, and "Such a delay would impose an unreasonable burden on legitimate gun purchasers." Richard Thornburgh, Attorney General, letter to Dan Quayle, November 20, 1989, p. 2; Bureau of Justice Statistics, *Identifying Persons, Other Than Felons,* p. 91.

153. "U.S.'s Barriers to Employment Are Not Stopping the Influx," *New York Times,* October 9, 1989, p. A13 (quoting I.N.S. assistant district director for investigation for Los Angeles. Several illegal workers said that a good set of papers cost three hundred dollars.)

154. 54 Fed. Reg. 43537.

155. 54 Fed. Reg. 43546.

156. "Screwed Up System," *American Firearms Industry,* August 1993, p. 43.

157. To keep the instant check at least somewhat "instant," the law should be changed to specify that if computer or other failure prevents the police from approving the sale, it should be delayed no more than twenty-four hours.

158. Comments to the Task Force.

159. Ibid.

160. William S. Sessions, FBI Director, "The FBI and the Challenges of the 21st Century," *FBI Law Enforcement Bulletin,* January 1989, p. 3 (near-term feasibility of instant fingerprint readers in police cars).

161. National Rifle Association, "Comments of the National Rifle Association of America, Inc., on Draft Report for Identifying Felons Who Attempt to Purchase Firearms" (July 26 1989), p. 30.

162. In *Schneider* v. *State,* 308 U.S. 147, 164 (1939), the Court voided a New Jersey law requiring pamphleteers to undergo a "burdensome and inquisitorial examination, including photographing and fingerprinting." Despite the plain language of *Schneider,* a New Jersey township enacted a law requiring political canvassers to be fingerprinted. A federal appeals court found the fingerprinting "stigmatizing, and an inappropriate burden on their right to do political work." *New Jersey Citizen Action* v. *Edison Township,* 797 F.2d 1250, 1262–65 (3d Cir. 1986), *cert. denied,* 479 U.S. 1103 (1987).

163. As the Task Force explained, "the biometric card does not solve the problem of individuals using fraudulent 'breeder' documents, such as birth certificates, to obtain the biometric ID card."

164. Wright and Rossi, *Armed and Considered Dangerous,* p. 191.

The "McClure-Volkmer" firearms law reform in 1986 enhanced penalties for gun transfers to felons. 18 United States Code § 922(d).

165. Virginia Code § 18.2.-108.1 (1988).

166. 18 United States Code § 3013.

3

...d Amendment:
...ericanist Reconsideration

...nd Raymond T. Diamond

...ould give to persons of the Negro race, who ... one State of the Union, the right to enter every other State whenever they pleased, . . . and it would give them the full liberty of speech in public and in private upon all subjects upon which its own citizens might speak; to hold public meetings upon political affairs, and to keep and carry arms wherever they went.[1]

INTRODUCTION

Many of the issues surrounding the Second Amendment debate are raised in particularly sharp relief from the perspective of African-American history. With the exception of Native Americans, no people in American history have been more influenced by violence than blacks. Private and public violence maintained slavery.[2] The Civil War, the nation's most destructive conflict, ended this "peculiar institution."[3] That all too brief experiment in racial egalitarianism, Reconstruction, was ended by private violence[4] and abetted by Supreme Court sanction. Jim Crow was sustained by private violence, often with public assistance.

If today the memories of past interracial struggles are beginning to fade, they are being quickly replaced by the frightening phenomenon of black-on-black violence, making life all too precarious for poor blacks in inner city neighborhoods.

127

Questions raised by the Second Amendment, particularly those concerning self-defense, crime, participation in the security of the community, and the wisdom or utility of relying exclusively on the state for protection, thus take on a peculiar urgency in light of the modern Afro-American experience. in this chapter we explore the connection in American history between gun control and race control.

I. ARMED CITIZENS, FREEMEN, AND WELL-REGULATED MILITIAS: THE BEGINNINGS OF AN AFRO-AMERICAN EXPERIENCE WITH AN ANGLO-AMERICAN RIGHT

Any discussion of the Second Amendment should begin with the commonplace observation that the framers of the Bill of Rights did not believe they were creating new rights. Instead, they believed that they were simply recognizing rights already part of their English constitutional heritage and implicit in natural law.[5] In fact, many of the framers cautioned against a bill of rights, arguing that the suggested rights were inherent to a free people, and that a specific detailing of rights would suggest that the new constitution empowered the federal government to violate other traditional rights not enumerated.[6]

Thus, an analysis of the framers' intentions with respect to the Second Amendment should begin with an examination of their perception of the right to bear arms as one of the traditional rights of Englishmen, a right necessary to perform the duty of militia service. Such an analysis is in part an exercise in examining the history of arms regulation and militia service in English legal history. But a simple examination of the right to own weapons in English law combined with an analysis of the history of the militia in English society is inadequate to a full understanding of the framers' understanding of what they meant by "the right to keep and bear arms." By the time the Bill of Rights was adopted, nearly two centuries of settlement in North America had given Americans constitutional sensibilities similar to, but nonetheless distinguishable from, those of their English counterparts.[7] American settlement had created its own history with respect to the right to bear arms, a history based on English tradition, and modified by the American experience—a history deeply influenced by the racial climate in the American colonies.

English Law and Tradition

The English settlers who populated North America in the seventeenth century were heirs to a tradition over five centuries old concerning both the right and duty to be armed. In English law, the idea of an armed citizenry responsible for the security of the community had long co-existed, perhaps somewhat uneasily, with regulation of the ownership of arms, particularly along class lines. The Assize of Arms of 1181 required the arming of all free men, and obligated free men to possess armor suitable to their condition.[8] By the thirteenth century, villeins (freemen, though bound in service to a lord) possessing sufficient property were also expected to be armed and contribute to the security of the community.[9] Lacking both professional police forces and a standing army,[10] English law and custom dictated that the citizenry as a whole, privately equipped, assist in both law enforcement and military matters. By law, all men between sixteen and sixty were liable to be summoned into the sheriff's posse comitatus. All subjects were expected to participate in the hot pursuit of criminal suspects, supplying their own arms for the occasion. There were legal penalties for failure to participate.[11]

Moreover, able-bodied men were considered part of the militia, although by the sixteenth century the general practice was to rely on select groups intensively trained for militia duty rather than on the armed male population as a whole. This move toward a selectively trained militia was an attempt to remedy the often indifferent proficiency and motivation that occurred when relying on the entire population.[12]

Although English law recognized a duty to be armed, it was a duty and a right highly circumscribed by English class structure. The law often regarded the common people as a dangerous class, useful perhaps in defending shire and realm, but also capable of mischief with their weapons—toward each other, toward their betters, and toward their betters' game. Restrictions on the type of arms deemed suitable for common people had long been part of English law and custom. A sixteenth-century statute designed as a crime control measure prohibited the carrying of handguns and crossbows by those with incomes of less than one hundred pounds a year.[13] Catholics were also often subject to being disarmed as potential subversives after the English reformation.[14]

It took the religious and political turmoil of seventeenth-century England to bring about large-scale attempts to disarm the English public and to bring the right to keep arms under English constitutional protection. Post-Restoration attempts by Charles II to disarm large portions of the population known or believed to be political opponents, and James II's efforts to disarm his Protestant opponents led, in 1689, to the adoption of the Seventh provision of the English Bill of Rights: "That the Subjects which are Protestants may have Arms for their Defence suitable to their Conditions, and as allowed by Law."[15]

By the eighteenth century, the right to possess arms, both for personal protection and as a counterbalance against state power, had come to be viewed as part of the rights of Englishmen by many on both sides of the Atlantic. Sir William Blackstone listed the right to possess arms as one of the five auxiliary rights of English subjects without which their primary rights could not be maintained.[16] He discussed it in traditional English terms:

> The fifth and last auxiliary right of the subject, that I shall at present mention, is that of having arms for their defence, suitable to their condition and degree, and such as are allowed by law, which is also declared by the same statute 1 W. &

M. st. 2 c. 2* and is indeed a public allowance, under due restrictions, of the natural right of resistance and self- preservation, when the sanctions of society and laws are found insufficient to restrain the violence of oppression.[17]

Arms and Race in Colonial America

If the English tradition involved a right and duty to bear arms qualified by class and later religion, both the right and the duty were strengthened in the earliest American settlements. From the beginning, English settlement in North America had a quasi-military character, an obvious response to harsh frontier conditions. Governors of settlements often also held the title of militia captain, reflecting both the civil and military nature of their office. Special effort was made to ensure that white men capable of bearing arms were imported into the colonies.[18] Far from the security of Britain, often bordering on the colonies of other frequently hostile European powers, colonial governments viewed the arming of able-bodied white men and the requirement that they perform militia service as essential to a colony's survival.

There was another reason for the renewed emphasis on the right and duty to be armed in America: race. Britain's American colonies were home to three often antagonistic races: red, white, and black. For the settlers of British North America, an armed and universally deputized white population was necessary to ward off not only dangers from the armies of other European powers, but also attacks from the indigenous population who feared the encroachment of English settlers on their lands. An armed white population was also essential to maintain social control over blacks and Indians who toiled unwillingly as slaves and servants in English settlements.[19]

This need for racial control helped transform the traditional English right into a much broader American one. If English law had qualified the right to possess arms by class and religion, American law was much less concerned with such distinctions. Initially all Englishmen, and later all white men, were expected to possess and bear arms to defend their commonwealths, both from external threats and from the internal ones posed by blacks and Indians. The statutes of many colonies specified that white men be armed at public expense.[20] In most colonies, all white men between the ages of sixteen and sixty, usually with the exception of clergy and religious objectors, were considered part of the militia and required to be armed.[21] Not only were white men compelled to perform traditional militia and posse duties, they also had to serve as patrollers, a specialized posse dedicated to keeping order among the slaves, in those colonies with large slave populations.[22] This broadening of the right to keep and bear arms reflected a more general lessening of class, religious, and ethnic distinctions among whites in colonial America. The right to possess arms was, therefore, extended to classes traditionally viewed with suspicion in England, including indentured servants.[23]

---

*The English Bill of Rights, enacted during the reign of William and Mary.

If there was virtually universal agreement concerning the need to arm the white population,[24] the law was much more ambivalent with respect to blacks. The progress of slavery in colonial America reflected English lack of familiarity with the institution, in both law and custom.[25] In some colonies, kidnapped Africans initially were treated like other indentured servants, held for a term of years, and then released from forced labor and allowed to live as free people.[26] In other colonies, the social control of slaves was one of the law's major concerns; in still others, the issue was largely of private concern to the slave owner.[27]

These differences were reflected in statutes concerned with the right to possess arms and the duty to perform militia service. One colony—Virginia—provides a striking example of how social changes were reflected, over time, in restrictions concerning the right to be armed. A Virginia statute enacted in 1639 required the arming of white men at public expense.[28] While the statute did not specify the arming of black men, it also did not prohibit black men from arming themselves.[29] By 1680 a Virginia statute prohibited Negroes, slave and free, from carrying weapons, including clubs.[30] Yet, by the early eighteenth century, free Negroes who were house owners were permitted to keep one gun in their house, and blacks, slave and free, who lived on frontier plantations were able to keep guns.[31] Virginia's experience reflected three sets of concerns: the greater need to maintain social control over the black population as caste lines sharpened;[32] the need to use slaves and free blacks to help defend frontier plantations against attacks by hostile Indians; and the recognition on the part of Virginia authorities of the necessity of gun ownership for those living alone.

These concerns were mirrored in the legislation of other colonies. Massachusetts did not have general legislation prohibiting blacks from carrying arms,[33] but free Negroes in that colony were not permitted to participate in militia drills; instead they were required to perform substitute service on public works projects.[34] New Jersey exempted blacks and Indians from militia service, though the colony permitted free Negroes to possess firearms.[35] Ironically, South Carolina, which had the harshest slave codes of this period, may have been the colony most enthusiastic about extending the right to bear arms to free Negroes. With its majority black population, that state's need to control the slave population was especially acute. To secure free black assistance in controlling the slaves, South Carolina in the early eighteenth century permitted free blacks the rights to vote, to keep firearms, and to undertake militia service.[36] As the century unfolded, however, those rights were curtailed.[37]

Overall, these laws reflected the desire to maintain white supremacy and control. With respect to the right to possess arms, the colonial experience had largely eliminated class, religious, and ethnic distinctions among the white population. Those who had been part of the suspect classes in England—the poor, religious dissenters, and others who had traditionally only enjoyed a qualified right to possess arms—found the right to be considerably more robust in the American context. But blacks had come to occupy the social and legal space of the suspect classes in England. Their right to possess arms was highly dependent on white opinion of black loyalty and reliability. Their inclusion in the militia of freemen was frequently confined to times of crisis. Often, there were significant differences between the way northern and southern colonies approached this question, a reflection of the very different roles that slavery played in the two regions. These differences would become sharper after the Revolution, when the northern states began to move toward the abolition of slavery even as the southern states, some of which had also considered abolition, began to strengthen the institution.

Ironically, while the black presence in colonial America introduced a new set of restrictions concerning the English law of arms and the militia, it helped strengthen the view that the security of the state was best achieved through the arming of all free citizens. It was this new view that was part of the cultural heritage Americans brought to the framing of the Constitution.

The Right of Which People?

1. Revolutionary Ideals

The colonial experience helped strengthen the appreciation of early Americans for the merits of an armed citizenry. That appreciation was strengthened yet further by the American Revolution. If necessity forced the early colonists to arm, the Revolution and the friction with Britain's standing army that preceded it— and in many ways precipitated it—served to revitalize Whiggish notions that standing armies were dangerous to liberty, and that militias, composed of the whole of the people, best protected both liberty and security.[38]

These notions soon found their way into the debates over the new constitution, debates which help place the language and meaning of the Second Amendment in context. Like other provisions of the proposed constitution, the clause that gave Congress the power to provide for the organizing, arming, and disciplining of the militia excited fears among those who believed that the new constitution could be used to destroy both state power and individual rights.[39]

Indeed, it was the very universality of the militia that was the source of some of the objections. A number of critics of the proposed constitution feared that congressional power could subject the whole population to military discipline and therefore pose a clear threat to individual liberty. Others complained that the Militia Clause provided no exemptions for those with religious scruples against bearing arms.[40]

But others feared that the Militia Clause could be used to disarm the population as well as do away with the states' control of the militia. Some critics expressed fear that Congress would use its power to establish a select militia, a group of men specially trained and armed for duty, similar to the earlier English experience. Richard Henry Lee of Virginia argued that a select militia might be used to disarm the population and that, in any event, it would pose more of a danger to individual liberty than one composed of the whole population. He charged that a select militia "commits the many to the mercy and the prudence of the few." A number of critics objected to giving Congress the power to arm the militia, fearing that such power would likewise give Congress the power to withhold arms. The fear that this new congressional authority could be used to both destroy state power over the militia and to disarm the people led delegates to state ratifying conventions to urge measures that would preserve the traditional right. The Virginia convention proposed language that would provide protection for the right to keep and bear arms in the federal constitution.[41]

In their efforts to defend the proposed constitution, Alexander Hamilton and James Madison addressed these charges. Hamilton's responses are interesting because he wrote as someone openly skeptical of the value of the militia of the whole. The former Revolutionary War artillery officer expressed the view that, while the militia fought bravely during the Revolution, it had proven to be no match when pitted against regular troops. Hamilton, who Madison claimed initially wanted to forbid the states from controlling any land or naval forces, called for uniformity in organizing and disciplining the militia under national authority. He also urged the creation of a select militia that would be more amenable to the training and discipline he saw as necessary.[42]

If Hamilton gave only grudging support to the concept of the militia of the whole, Madison, author of the Second Amendment, was a much more vigorous defender of the concept. He answered critics of the Militia Clause provision allowing Congress to arm the militia by stating that the term "arming" meant that Congress's authority to arm extended only to prescribing the type of arms the militia would use, not furnishing them.[43] But Madison's views went further. He envisioned a militia consisting of virtually the entire white male population, writing that a militia of 500,000 citizens could prevent any excesses that might be perpetrated by the national government and its regular army. Madison left little doubt that he envisioned the militia of the whole as a potential counterweight to tyrannical excess on the part of the government.[44]

It is against this background that the meaning of the Second Amendment must be considered. For the revolutionary generation, the idea of the militia and an armed population were related. The principal reason for preferring a militia of the whole over either a standing army or a select militia was rooted in the idea that, whatever the inefficiency of the militia of the whole, the institution would better protect the newly won freedoms than a reliance on security provided by some more select body.

2. Racial Limitations

One year after the ratification of the Second Amendment and the Bill of Rights, Congress passed legislation that reaffirmed the notion of the militia of the whole and explicitly introduced a racial component into the national deliberations on the subject of the militia. The Uniform Militia Act[45] called for the enrollment of every free, able-bodied white male citizen between the ages of eighteen and forty-five. The act further specified that every militia member was to provide himself with a musket or firelock, a bayonet, and ammunition.

This specification of a racial qualification for militia membership was somewhat at odds with general practice in the late eighteenth century. Despite its recognition and sanctioning of slavery, the Constitution had no racial definition of citizenship.[46] Free Negroes voted in a majority of states. A number of states had militia provisions that allowed free Negroes to participate.[47] Particularly in the Northern states, many were well aware that free Negroes and former slaves had served with their state forces during the Revolution. Despite the prejudices of the day, lawmakers in late eighteenth-century America were significantly less willing to write racial restrictions into constitutions and other laws guaranteeing fundamental rights than were their counterparts a generation or so later in the nineteenth century.[48] The 1792 statute restricting militia enrollment to white men was one of the earliest federal statutes to make a racial distinction.

The significance of this restriction is not altogether clear. For the South, there was a clear desire to have a militia that was reliable and could be used to suppress potential slave insurrections. But despite the fear that free Negroes might make common cause with slaves, and despite federal law, some southern states in the antebellum period enrolled free blacks as militia members. Northern states at various times also enrolled free Negroes in the militia despite federal law and often strident prejudice. States both north and south employed free Negroes in state forces during times of invasion. While southern states often prohibited slaves from carrying weapons and strictly regulated access to firearms by free Negroes, those in the North generally made no racial distinction with respect to the right to own firearms,[49] and federal law was silent on the subject.

The racial restriction in the 1792 statute indicates the unrest the revolutionary generation felt toward arming blacks and perhaps the recognition that one of the functions of the militia would indeed be to put down slave revolts. Yet, the widespread use of blacks as soldiers in time of crisis and the absence of restrictions concerning the arming of blacks in the northern states may provide another clue concerning how to read the Second Amendment. The 1792 act specified militia enrollment for white men between the ages of eighteen and forty-five. Yet, while it specifically included only this limited portion of the population, the statute excluded no one from militia service.

The authors of the statute had experience, in the Revolution, with a militia and Continental Army considerably broader in membership. Older and younger men had served with the Revolutionary forces. Blacks had served, though their service had been an object of considerable controversy. Even women had served, though, given the attitudes of the day, this was far more controversial than black service. Given this experience and the fact that the Constitutional debates over the militia had constantly assumed an enrollment of the male population between sixteen and sixty, it is likely that the framers of the 1792 statute envisioned a militia even broader than the one they specified. This suggests to us how broad the term "people" in the Second Amendment was meant to be.

The 1792 statute also suggests to us how crucial race has been in our history. If the racial distinction made in that statute was somewhat anomalous in the late eighteenth century, it was the kind of distinction that would become more common in the nineteenth. The story of blacks and arms would continue in the nineteenth century as racial distinctions became sharper and the defense of slavery more militant.

II. ARMS AND THE ANTEBELLUM EXPERIENCE

If, as presaged by the Uniform Militia Act of 1792, racial distinctions became sharper in the nineteenth century, that development was at odds with the rhetoric of the Revolution as well as with developments of the immediate postrevolutionary era. Flush with the precepts of egalitarian democracy, America had entered a time of recognition and expansion of rights. Eleven of the thirteen original states, as well as Vermont, passed new constitutions in the period between 1776 and 1777. Five of these states rewrote their constitutions by the time of the ratification of the Bill of Rights in 1791. A twelfth original state, Massachusetts, passed a new constitution in 1780. Many of the new constitutions recognized the status of citizens as "free and equal" or "free and independent." In Massachusetts and Vermont, these clauses were interpreted as outlawing the institution of slavery. Many of the new constitutions guaranteed the right to vote regardless of race to all men who otherwise qualified,[50] and guaranteed many of the rights that would later be recognized in the Bill of Rights. In no instance were any of these rights limited only to the white population; several states explicitly extended rights to the entire population irrespective of race.[51]

The right to vote, perhaps the most fundamental of rights, was limited in almost all instances to men who met property restrictions, but in most states was not limited according to race. Ironically, only in the nineteenth century would black voting rights be curtailed, as Jacksonian democracy expanded voting rights for whites. In its constitution of 1821, New York eliminated a one hundred dollar property requirement for white males, and concomitantly increased the requirement to two hundred fifty dollars for blacks. Other states would eliminate black voting rights altogether. Other than Maine, no state admitted to the union in the nineteenth century's antebellum period allowed blacks to vote.[52]

This curtailment of black voting rights was part and parcel of a certain hostility toward free blacks, which ran throughout the union of states. In Northern states, where slavery had been abandoned or was not a serious factor in social or economic relations, such hostility was the result of simple racism. In Southern states, where slavery was an integral part of the social and economic framework, it was occasioned by the threat that free blacks posed to the system of Negro slavery.[53]

The Southern Antebellum Experience: Control of Arms as a Means of Racial Oppression

The threat that free blacks posed to Southern slavery was twofold. First, free blacks were a bad example to slaves. For a slave to see free blacks enjoy the trappings of white persons—freedom of movement, expression, and association, relative freedom from fear for one's person and one's family, and freedom to own the fruits of one's labor—was to offer hope and raise desire for that which the system could not produce. A slave with horizons limited only to a continued existence in slavery was one who did not threaten the system, whereas a slave with visions of freedom nursed rebellion.

This threat of rebellion is intimately related to the second threat that free blacks posed to the system of Negro slavery, namely, that free blacks might instigate or participate in a rebellion by their slave brethren. To forestall this threat of rebellion, Southern legislatures undertook to limit the freedom of movement and decision of free blacks. States limited the number of free blacks who might congregate at one time; they curtailed the ability of free blacks to choose their own employment, and to trade and socialize with slaves. Free blacks were subject to questioning, to search, and to summary punishment by patrols established to keep the black population, slave and free, in order.[54] To forestall the possibility that free blacks would rebel either on their own or with slaves, the Southern states limited not only the right of slaves, but also that of free blacks, to bear arms.[55]

The idea was to restrict the availability of arms to blacks, both slave and free, to the extent consistent with local conceptions of safety. At one extreme was Texas, which, between 1842 and 1850, prohibited slaves from using firearms altogether. Also at this extreme was Mississippi, which forbade firearms to both free blacks and slaves after 1852. At the other extreme was Kentucky, which merely provided that, should slaves or free blacks "wilfully and maliciously" shoot at a white, or otherwise wound a free white person while attempting to kill another, the slave or free black would suffer the death penalty.[56]

More often than not, slave state statutes restricting black access to firearms were aimed primarily at free blacks, as opposed to slaves, perhaps because the vigilant master was presumed capable of denying arms to all but the most trustworthy slaves and would give proper supervision to the latter. Thus, Louisiana provided that a slave was denied the use of firearms and all other offensive weapons, unless the slave carried written permission to hunt within the boundaries of the owner's plantation. South Carolina prohibited slaves outside the company of whites or without written permission from their master from using or carrying firearms unless they were hunting or guarding the master's plantation. Georgia, Maryland, and Virginia did not statutorily address the question of slaves' access to firearms, perhaps because controls already inherent in the system made such laws unnecessary in these states' eyes.

By contrast, free blacks not under the close scrutiny of whites were generally subject to tight regulation with respect to firearms. The State of Florida, which had in 1824 provided for a weekly renewable license for slaves to use firearms to hunt and for "any other necessary and lawful purpose,"[57] turned its attention to the question of free blacks in 1825. Section 8 of "An Act to Govern Patrols"[58] provided that white citizen patrols "shall enter into all negro houses and suspected places, and search for arms and other offensive or improper weapons, and may lawfully seize and take away all such arms, weapons, and ammunition. . . ." By contrast, the following section of that same statute expanded the conditions under which a slave might carry a firearm: a slave might do so either by means of the weekly renewable license or if "in the presence of some white person."[59]

Florida had gone back and forth on the question of licenses for free blacks, but in February 1831 repealed all provision for firearm licenses for free blacks.[60] This development predated by six months the Nat Turner slave revolt in Virginia, which was responsible for the deaths of at least fifty-seven white people[61] and which caused the legislatures of the Southern states to reinvigorate their repression of free blacks.[62] Among the measures that slave states took was to further restrict the right to carry and use firearms. In its December 1831 legislative session, Delaware for the first time required free blacks desiring to carry firearms to obtain a license from a justice of the peace.[63] In December 1831 legislative sessions, both Maryland[64] and Virginia[65] entirely prohibited free blacks from carrying arms; Georgia followed suit in 1833, declaring that "it shall not be lawful for any free person of colour in this state, to own, use, or carry fire arms of any description whatever."[66]

Perhaps as a response to the Nat Turner rebellion, Florida in 1833 enacted another statute authorizing white citizen patrols to seize arms found in the homes of slaves and free blacks, and provided that blacks without a proper explanation for the presence of the firearms be summarily punished, without benefit of a judicial tribunal.[67] In 1846 and 1861, the Florida legislature provided once again that white citizen patrols might search the homes of blacks, both free and slave, and confiscate arms held therein.[68] Yet, searching out arms was not the only role of the white citizen patrols: they were intended to enforce pass systems for both slaves and free blacks, to be sure that blacks did not possess liquor and other contraband items, and generally to terrorize blacks into accepting their subordination.[69] The patrols would meet no resistance from those who were simply unable to offer any.

The Northern Antebellum Experience: Use of Firearms to Combat Racially Motivated Deprivations of Liberty

Even as Northern racism defined itself in part by the curtailment of black voting rights,[70] it cumulatively amounted to what some have called a widespread

"Negrophobia."[71] With notable exceptions, public schooling, if available to blacks at all, was segregated.[72] Statutory and constitutional limitations on the freedom of blacks to emigrate into Northern states were a further measure of Northern racism.[73] While the level of enforcement and the ultimate effect of these constitutional and statutory provisions may not have been great,[74] the very existence of these laws speaks to the level of hostility Northern whites had for blacks during this period. It is against this background—if not poisonous, then racist and hostile—that the black antebellum experience with the right to bear arms must be measured.

Perhaps nothing makes this point better than the race riots and mob violence against blacks that occurred in many Northern cities in the antebellum period. These episodes also illustrate the uses to which firearms might be put in pursuit of self-defense and individual liberty.

A good deal of racial tension was generated by economic competition between whites and blacks during this period, which accounted in part for violent attacks against blacks.[75] Moreover, whites were able to focus their attacks because blacks were segregated into distinct neighborhoods in northern states, rendering it easy for white mobs to find the objects of their hostility.[76]

Quite often, racial violence made for bloody, destructive confrontations. Awareness of racial hostility generally, and of particular violent incidents, made blacks desirous of forming militia units.

Though the Uniform Militia Act of 1792 had not specifically barred blacks from participation in the state-organized militia,[77] the Northern states had treated the act as if it had, and so the state-organized militia was not an option.[78] Blacks could nonetheless form private militia groups that might serve to protect against racial violence, and did so. Free blacks in Providence formed the African Greys in 1821.[79] Oscar Handlin recounts of an attempt by black Bostonians in the 1850s to form a private militia company.[80] Black members of the Pittsburgh community had no private militia but nonetheless took action against a mob expected to riot in April 1839. Instead of acting on their own, they joined an interracial peacekeeping force proposed by the city's mayor, and were able to put a stop to the riot.[81]

It is not clear whether private black militia groups ever marched on a white mob. But that they may never have been called on to do so may be a measure of their success. The story of the July 1835 Philadelphia riot is illustrative. Precipitated when a young black man assaulted a white one, the two-day riot ended without resort to military intervention when a rumor reached the streets that "fifty to sixty armed and determined black men had barricaded themselves in a building beyond the police lines."[82]

Undoubtedly, the most striking examples of the salutary use of firearms by blacks in defense of their liberty, and concurrently the disastrous results from the denial of the right to carry firearms in self-defense, lie in the same incident. In Cincinnati, in September 1841, racial hostility erupted in two nights of assaults by white mobs of up to 1,500 people. On the first evening, after destroying property owned by blacks in the business district, the mobs descended upon the black residential section, there to be repulsed by blacks who fired into the crowd, forcing it out of the area. The crowd returned, however, bringing with it a six-pound cannon, and the battle ensued. Two whites and two blacks were killed, and more than a dozen of both races were wounded. Eventually, the militia took control; but on the next day the blacks were disarmed at the insistence of whites, and all adult black males were taken into protective custody. On the following evening, white rioters again assaulted the black residential district, resulting in more personal injury and property damage.[83]

This history shows that if racism in the antebellum period was not limited to the Southern states, neither was racial violence. Competition with and hostility toward blacks accounted for this violence in Northern states, whereas the need to uphold slavery and maintain security for the white population accounted for racial violence in the South. Another difference between the two regions is that in the Southern states blacks did not have the means to protect themselves, while in the North, blacks by and large had access to firearms and were willing to use them.

The 1841 Cincinnati riot represents the tragic, misguided irony of the city's authorities who, concerned with the safety of the black population, chose to disarm and imprison them—in effect, to leave the black citizens of Cincinnati as Southern authorities left the black population in slave states, exposed to whatever indignities private parties might heap upon them, and dependent on a government either unable or unwilling to protect their rights. As a symbol for the experience of Northern blacks protecting themselves against deprivations of liberty, the 1841 riot holds a vital lesson for those who would shape the content and meaning of the Fourteenth Amendment.

III. Arms and the Postbellum Southern Order

The end of the Civil War did more than simply bring about the end of slavery; it gave birth to a heightened conflict between two contrasting constitutional visions. One vision, largely held by Northern Republicans, saw the former slaves as citizens[84] entitled to those rights long deemed as natural rights in Anglo-American society. Theirs was a vision of national citizenship and national rights, rights that the federal government had the responsibility to secure for the freedmen and, indeed, for all citizens. This vision, developed during the antislavery struggle and heightened by the Civil War, caused Republicans of the Civil War and postwar generations to view the question of federalism and individual rights in a way significantly different from that of the original framers of the Constitution and Bill of Rights. If many who debated the original Constitution feared that the newly created national government could violate long-established rights, those who changed the Constitution in the aftermath of war and slavery had firsthand experience with states violating fundamental rights. The history of the right to bear arms is, thus, inextricably linked with the efforts to reconstruct the nation and bring about a new racial order.

If the Northern Republican vision was to bring the former slaves into the ranks of citizens, the concern of the defeated white South was to preserve as much of the antebellum social order as could survive Northern victory and national law. The Emancipation Proclamation and the Thirteenth Amendment[85] abolished slavery; chattel slavery as it had existed before the war could not survive these developments. Still, in the war's immediate aftermath, the South was not prepared to accord to the newly emancipated black population the general liberties that Northern states had allowed free blacks.[86] Instead, while recognizing emancipation, Southern states imposed on the freedmen the legal disabilities of the antebellum free Negro population.

In 1865 and 1866, Southern states passed a series of statutes known as the black codes. These statutes, which one historian described as "a twilight zone between slavery and freedom,"[87] were an expression of the South's determination to maintain control over the former slaves. Designed in part to ensure that traditional Southern labor arrangements would be preserved, these codes attempted "to put the state much in the place of the former master."[88] They often required blacks to sign labor contracts that bound black agricultural workers to their employers for one year.[89] Blacks were forbidden to serve on juries, and could not testify or act as parties against whites.[90] Vagrancy laws were used to force blacks into labor contracts and to limit freedom of movement.[91]

As further indication that the former slaves had not yet joined the ranks of free citizens, Southern states passed legislation prohibiting blacks from carrying firearms without licenses, a requirement to which whites were not subjected. The Louisiana[92] and Mississippi[93] statutes were typical of the restrictions found in the codes. Alabama's was even harsher.[94]

The restrictions in the black codes caused strong concerns among Northern Republicans. The charge that the South was trying to reinstitute slavery was frequently made, both in and out of Congress.[95] The news that the freedmen were being deprived of the right to bear arms was of particular concern to the champions of Negro citizenship. For them, the right of the black population to possess weapons was not merely of symbolic and theoretical importance; it was vital as a means both of maintaining the recently reunited Union and of preventing virtual reenslavement of those formerly held in bondage. Faced with a hostile and recalcitrant white South determined to preserve the antebellum social order by legal and extralegal means,[96] Northern Republicans were particularly alarmed at provisions of the black codes that effectively preserved the right to keep and bear arms for former Confederates while disarming blacks, the one group in the South with clear unionist sympathies.[97] This fed the determination of Northern Republicans to provide national enforcement of the Bill of Rights.[98]

The efforts to disarm the freedmen were in the background when the 39th

Congress debated the Fourteenth Amendment, and played an important part in convincing the 39th Congress that traditional notions concerning federalism and individual rights needed to change. While a full exploration of the incorporation controversy[99] is beyond the scope of this chapter, it should be noted that Jonathan Bingham, author of the Fourteenth Amendment's Privileges or Immunities Clause,[100] clearly stated that it applied the Bill of Rights to the states.[101] Others shared that same understanding.[102]

Although the history of the black codes persuaded the 39th Congress that Congress and the federal courts must be given the authority to protect citizens against state deprivations of the Bill of Rights, the Supreme Court in its earliest decisions on the Fourteenth Amendment moved to maintain much of the structure of prewar federalism. A good deal of the Court's decision making that weakened the effectiveness of the Second Amendment was part of its overall process of eviscerating the Fourteenth Amendment soon after its enactment.

That process began with the Slaughterhouse Cases,[103] which dealt a severe blow to the Fourteenth Amendment's Privileges or Immunities Clause, a blow from which it has yet to recover. It was also within its early examination of the Fourteenth Amendment that the Court first heard a claim directly based on the Second Amendment. Ironically, the party first bringing an allegation before the Court concerning a Second Amendment violation was the federal government. In *United States* v. *Cruikshank,*[104] federal officials brought charges against William Cruikshank and others under the Enforcement Act of 1870.[105] Cruikshank had been charged with violating the rights of two black men to peaceably assemble and to bear arms. The Supreme Court held that the federal government had no power to protect citizens against private action that deprived them of their Constitutional rights. The Court held that the First and Second Amendments were limitations on Congress, not on private individuals and that, for protection against private criminal action, the individual was required to look to state governments.[106]

The Cruikshank decision, which dealt a serious blow to Congress's ability to enforce the Fourteenth Amendment, was part of a larger campaign of the Court to ignore the original purpose of the Fourteenth Amendment—to bring about a revolution in federalism as well as race relations.[107] While the Court in the late 1870s and 1880s was reasonably willing to strike down instances of state-sponsored racial discrimination,[108] it also showed a strong concern for maintaining state prerogative and a disinclination to carry out the intent of the framers of the Fourteenth Amendment to make states respect national rights.

This trend was demonstrated in *Presser* v. *Illinois,*[109] the second case in which the Court examined the Second Amendment. *Presser* involved an Illinois statute which prohibited individuals who were not members of the militia from parading with arms.[110] Although Justice William Woods, author of the majority opinion, noted that the Illinois statute did not infringe upon the right to keep and bear arms,[111] he nonetheless went on to declare that the Second Amendment was a limitation on the federal and not the state governments. Woods's opinion also contended that, despite the nonapplicability of the Second Amendment to state action, states were forbidden from disarming their populations because such action would interfere with the federal government's ability to maintain the federal militia.[112] With its view both that the statute restricting armed parading did not interfere with the right to keep and bear arms, and that Congress's militia power prevented the states from disarming its citizens, the *Presser* Court had gone out of its way in dicta to reaffirm the old federalism and to reject the framers' view of the Fourteenth Amendment that the Bill of Rights applied to the states.

The rest of the story is all too well known. The Court's denial of an expanded role for the federal government in enforcing civil rights played a crucial role in redeeming white rule. The doctrine in *Cruikshank,* that blacks would have to look to state government for protection against criminal conspiracies, gave the green light to private forces, often with the assistance of state and local governments, that sought to subjugate the former slaves and their descendants. Private violence was instrumental in driving blacks from the ranks of voters.[113] It helped force many blacks into peonage, a virtual return to slavery,[114] and was used to reduce many blacks to a state of ritualized subservience.[115] With the protective arm of the federal government withdrawn, protection of black lives and property was left to largely hostile state governments. In the Jim Crow era that would follow, the right to possess arms would take on critical importance for many blacks. This right, seen in the eighteenth century as a mechanism that enabled a majority to check the excesses of a potentially tyrannical national government, would for many blacks in the twentieth century become a means of survival in the face of private violence and state indifference.

IV. ARMS AND AFRICAN-AMERICAN SELF-DEFENSE IN THE TWENTIETH CENTURY: A HISTORY IGNORED

For much of the twentieth century, the black experience in this country has been one of repression. This repression has not been limited to the Southern part of the country, nor is it a development divorced from the past. Born perhaps of cultural predisposition against blacks,[116] and nurtured by economic competition between blacks and whites, particularly immigrant groups and those whites at the lower rungs of the economic ladder,[117] racism in the North continued after the Civil War, abated but not eliminated in its effects.[118] In the South, defeat in the Civil War and the loss of slaves as property confirmed white Southerners in their determination to degrade and dominate their black brethren.[119]

Immediately after the Civil War and the emancipation it brought, white Southerners adopted measures to keep the black population in its place.[120] Southerners saw how Northerners had utilized segregation as a means to avoid the black presence in their lives,[121] and they already had had experience with segregation in Southern cities before the war.[122] Southerners extended this experience of segregation to the whole of Southern life through the mechanism of "Jim Crow." Jim Crow was established both by the operation of law, including the black codes and other legislation, and by an elaborate etiquette of racially restrictive social practices. The Civil Rights Cases[123] and *Plessy* v. *Ferguson*[124] gave the South freedom to pursue the task of separating black from white. The Civil Rights Cases went beyond *Cruikshank,* restricting even more severely congressional power to provide for the equality of blacks under Section 5 of the Fourteenth Amendment,[125] and *Plessy* v. *Ferguson* declared separate facilities for blacks and whites to be consonant with the Fourteenth Amendment's mandate of "equal protection of the laws."[126] In effect, states and individuals were given full freedom to effect their "social prejudices"[127] and "racial instincts"[128] to the detriment of blacks throughout the South and elsewhere.[129]

This is not to say that blacks went quietly or tearfully to their deaths. Oftentimes they were able to use firearms to defend themselves, though usually without success: Jim McIlherron was lynched in Estell Springs, Tennessee, after having exchanged over one thousand rounds with his pursuers.[130] The attitude of individuals such as McIlherron is summed up by Ida B. Wells-Barnett, a black antilynching activist who wrote of her decision to carry a pistol: "I had bought a pistol the first thing after [the lynching], because I expected some cowardly retaliation from the lynchers. I felt that one had better die fighting against injustice than to die like a dog or a rat in a trap. I had already determined to sell my life as dearly as possible if attacked. I felt if I could take one lyncher with me, this would even up the score a little bit."[131]

Thus, when blacks used firearms to protect their rights, they were often partially successful but ultimately doomed. In 1920, two black men in Texas fired on and killed two whites in self-defense. The black men were arrested and soon lynched.[132] When the sheriff of Aiken, South Carolina, came with three deputies to a black household to attempt a warrantless search and struck one female family member, three other family members used a hatchet and firearms in self-defense, killing the sheriff. The three wounded survivors were taken into custody, and after one was acquitted of murdering the sheriff, with indications of a similar verdict for the other two, all three were lynched.[133]

Although individual efforts of blacks to halt violence to their persons or property were largely unsuccessful, there were times that blacks succeeded through concerted or group activity in halting lynchings. In her autobiography, Ida Wells-Barnett reported an incident in Memphis in 1891, in which a black militia unit guarded for two or three nights approximately one hundred jailed blacks deemed at risk of mob violence. When it seemed the crisis had passed, the militia unit ceased its work. It was only after the militia left that a white mob stormed the jail and lynched three black inmates.[134]

A. Philip Randolph, the longtime head of the Brotherhood of Sleeping Car Porters, and Walter White, onetime executive secretary of the National Association for the Advancement of Colored People (NAACP), vividly recalled incidents in which their fathers had participated in collective efforts to use firearms to successfully forestall lynchings and other mob violence. As a 13-year-old, White participated in his father's efforts,[135] which, he reported, left him "gripped by the knowledge of my own identity, and in the depths of my soul, I was vaguely aware that I was glad of it."[136] After his father stood armed at a jail all night to ward off lynchers,[137] Randolph was left with a vision, not "of powerlessness, but of the 'possibilities of salvation,' which resided in unity and organization."[138]

The willingness of blacks to use firearms to protect their rights, their lives, and their property, in conjunction with their ability to do so successfully when acting collectively, renders many gun control statutes, particularly of Southern origin, all the more worthy of condemnation. This is especially so in view of the purpose of these statutes, which, like that of the gun control statutes of the black codes, was to disarm blacks.

That the Southern states did not prohibit firearms ownership outright is fortuitous. During the 1960s, while many blacks and white civil rights workers were threatened and even murdered by whites with guns, firearms in the hands of blacks served a useful purpose, i.e., to protect civil rights workers and blacks from white mob and terrorist activity.[139]

It struck many, then, as the height of blindness, confidence, courage, or moral certainty for the civil rights movement to adopt nonviolence as its credo, and thus to leave its adherents open to attack by terrorist elements within the white South. Yet, while nonviolence had its adherents among the mainstream civil rights organizations, many ordinary black people in the South, who believed in resistance and in the necessity of maintaining firearms for personal protection, lent their assistance and their protection to the civil rights movement.[140]

Daisy Bates, the leader of the Little Rock NAACP during the desegregation crisis, wrote in her memoirs that armed volunteers stood guard over her home.[141] David Dennis, a worker for the Congress of Racial Equality (CORE), a frontline, mainstream civil rights group, who had been targeted for the fate that actually befell Goodman, Schwerner, and Chaney during the Freedom Summer of 1964,[142] has told of black Mississippi citizens with firearms who followed civil rights workers in order to keep them safe.[143]

Ad hoc efforts were not the sole means by which black Southern adherents of firearms protected workers in the civil rights movement. The Deacons for Defense and Justice were organized first in 1964 in Jonesboro, Louisiana, but achieved prominence in Bogalousa, Louisiana.[144] The Deacons organized in Jonesboro after their founder saw the Ku Klux Klan marching in the street and realized that the "fight against racial injustice include[d] not one but two foes: White reactionaries and police."[145] Jonesboro's Deacons obtained a charter and weapons, and vowed to shoot back if fired upon.[146] The word spread throughout the South, but most significantly to Bogalousa, where the Klan was rumored to have its largest per capita membership.[147] There, a local chapter of the Deacons would grow to include "about a tenth of the Negro adult male population," or about nine hundred members, although the organization was deliberately secretive about exact numbers.[148] What is known, however, is that in 1965 there were fifty to sixty chapters across Louisiana, Mississippi, and Alabama.[149] In Bogalousa, as elsewhere, the Deacons' job was to protect black people from violence, and they did so by threatening violence against anyone who attacked.[150] This capacity and willingness to use force to protect blacks provided a deterrent to white terrorist activity.

A prime example of how the Deacons accomplished their task lies in the experience of James Farmer, then head of CORE. Before Farmer left on a trip for Bogalousa, the Federal Bureau of Investigation informed him that he had received a death threat from the Klan. The FBI apparently also informed the state police, who met Farmer at the airport. But there were also representatives of the Bogalousa chapter of the Deacons, who escorted Farmer into town. Farmer stayed with the local head of the Deacons, and the Deacons provided close security throughout the rest of this stay and Farmer's next visit. Farmer later wrote in his autobiography that he was secure with the Deacons, "in the knowledge that unless a bomb were tossed . . . the Klan could only reach me if they were prepared to swap their lives for mine."[151]

Blacks in the South found the Deacons helpful because they were unable to rely upon police or other legal entities for racial justice. This provided a practical reason for a right to bear arms: In a world in which the legal system was not to be trusted, perhaps the ability of the system's victims to resist might convince the system to restrain itself.

CONCLUSION: SELF-DEFENSE AND THE GUN-CONTROL QUESTION TODAY

Throughout American history, black and white Americans have had radically different experiences with respect to violence and state protection. Perhaps one reason the Second Amendment has not been taken very seriously by the courts and the academy is that for many of those who shape or critique constitutional policy, the state's power and inclination to protect them is a given. But for all too many black Americans, that protection historically has not been available. Nor, for many, is it readily available today. If in the past the state refused to protect black people from the horrors of white lynch mobs, today the state seems powerless in the face of the tragic black-on-black violence that plagues the mean streets of our inner cities, and at times appears blind to instances of unnecessary police brutality against minority populations.[152]

The history of blacks, firearms regulations, and the right to bear arms should cause us to ask new questions regarding the Second Amendment. These questions will pose problems both for advocates of stricter gun controls and for those who argue against them. Since much of the contemporary crime that concerns Americans takes place in poor black neighborhoods, a case can be made that greater firearms restrictions might alleviate this tragedy. But another, perhaps stronger, case can be made that a society with a dismal record of protecting a people has a dubious claim to the authority to disarm them. Perhaps a reexamination of this history can lead us to a modern realization of what the framers of the Second Amendment understood: that it is unwise to place the means of protection totally in the hands of the state, and that self-defense is also a civil right.

NOTES

1. *Dred Scott* v. *Sanford,* 60 U.S. (19 How.) 393, 417 (1857).

2. See Kenneth M. Stampp, *The Peculiar Institution: Slavery in the Antebellum South* (1956), pp. 141–91.

3. The combined fatality figure for the Union and Confederate armies was 498,332. By comparison, World War II, the nation's second bloodiest conflict, cost the United States 407,316 fatalities. See *The World Almanac & Book of Facts,* Mark S. Hoffman, ed. (1991), p. 793.

4. See generally Eric Foner, *Reconstruction: America's Unfinished Revolution, 1863-1877* (1988), pp. 564–600; George C. Rable, *But There Was No Peace: The Role of Violence in the Politics of Reconstruction* (1984).

5. Especially pertinent is John Philip Reid's reminder: "There are other dimensions that the standing-army controversy, when studied from the perspective of law, adds to our knowledge of the American Revolution. One is the degree to which eighteenth-century Americans thought seventeenth-century English thoughts." John Phillip Reid, *In Defiance of the Law: The Standing-Army Controversy, The Two Constitutions, and the Coming of the American Revolution* (1981), p. 4 (emphasis added).

6. See, e.g., *The Federalist,* No. 84 (Alexander Hamilton).

7. This can be seen with reference to the right of trial by jury. A number of scholars have noted that Americans in the late eighteenth century regarded the right of trial by jury as including the right to have the jury decide issues of law as well as fact. This was, of course, a departure from traditional English practice. See Morton J. Horowitz, *The Transformation of American Law, 1780–1860* (1977), pp. 28–29; William Edward Nelson, *Americanization of the Common Law: The Impact of Legal Change on Massachusetts Society, 1760–1830* (1975), pp. 3–4, 8, 20–30.

8. 1 Frederick Pollock and Frederic W. Maitland, *The History of English Law before the Time of Edward I* (1968), pp. 421–42, 565.

9. Ibid.

10. Historian Joyce Lee Malcolm notes that England did not have a standing army until the late seventeenth century and no professional police force until the nineteenth. See Malcolm, "The Right of the People to Keep and Bear Arms: The Common Law Tradition," *Hastings Constitutional Law Quarterly* (1983); rpt. in Don Kates, ed., *Firearms and Violence: Issues of Public Policy* (1984), p. 391.

11. A. Harding, *A Social History of English Law* (1966), p. 59; Malcolm, "The Right of the People to Keep and Bear Arms," p. 391.

12. Malcolm, "The Right of the People to Keep and Bear Arms," pp. 391–92.

13. Ibid. p. 393.

14. Ibid. pp. 393–94.

15. Ibid. p. 408.

16. 1 William Blackstone, *Commentaries,* pp. *143–45. Blackstone listed three primary rights—personal security, personal liberty, and private property—all of which he regarded as

natural rights recognized and protected by the common law and statutes of England. He also argued that these would be "dead letters" without the five auxiliary rights which he listed as: (1) the constitution, powers and privileges of Parliament; (2) the limitation of the king's prerogative; (3) the right to apply to the courts of justice for redress of injuries; (4) the right to petition the king or either house of Parliament, and for the redress of grievances; and (5) the right of subjects to have arms for their defense. Ibid., pp. *121–45.

Some commentators have argued that Blackstone's remarks and other evidence of English common law and statutory rights to possess arms should be viewed in the light both of the extensive regulation of firearms that traditionally existed in England and of English strict gun control in the twentieth century. See, e.g., Franklin E. Zimring and Gordon Hawkins, *The Citizen's Guide to Gun Control* (1987), pp. 142–43; Keith A. Ehrman and Dennis A. Henigan, "The Second Amendment in the Twentieth Century: Have You Seen Your Military Lately?" *U. Dayton L. Rev.* 15 (1989): 5. Two points should be made in that regard. First, much of English firearms regulation had an explicit class base largely inapplicable in the American context. Second, neither a common law right to keep and bear arms nor a similar statutory right such as existed in the English Bill of Rights of 1689 would, in the light of parliamentary supremacy, be a bar to subsequent statutes repealing or modifying that right. Blackstone is cited here not as evidence that the English right, in precise form and content, became the American right; instead Blackstone is evidence that the idea of an individual right to keep and bear arms existed on both sides of the Atlantic in the eighteenth century.

Blackstone's importance to this discussion is twofold. His writings on the right to possess arms can be taken as partial evidence of what the framers of the Second Amendment regarded as among the rights of Englishmen that they sought to preserve. Blackstone's views greatly influenced late eighteenth-century American legal thought. But Blackstone's importance in this regard does not cease with the Second Amendment, since he also had a marked impact on nineteenth-century American legal thinking. One leading antebellum American jurist, Justice Joseph Story, was significantly influenced by his readings of Blackstone. See R. Kent Newmyer, *Supreme Court Justice Joseph Story: Statesman of the Old Republic* (1985), pp. 40–45, 137, 246. Story viewed the Second Amendment as vitally important in maintaining a free republic. In his *Commentaries on the Constitution,* he wrote:

> The right of the citizens to keep, and bear arms has justly been considered, as the palladium of the liberties of a republic; since it offers a strong moral check against the usurpation and arbitrary power of rulers; and will generally, even if they are successful in the first instance, enable the people to resist, and triumph over them.

Joseph Story, *Commentaries on the Constitution of the United States* (1833; Carolina Academic Press 1987), p. 708.

While it would be inaccurate to attribute Story's Second Amendment views solely to his reading of Blackstone, Blackstone doubtless helped influence Story and other early nineteenth-century lawyers and jurists to regard the right to keep and bear arms as an important prerogative of free citizens. All this is important for our discussion, not only with regard to antebellum opinion concerning the Second Amendment, but also in considering the cultural and legal climate that informed the framers of the Fourteenth Amendment who intended to extend what were commonly regarded as the rights of free men to the freedmen, and who also intended to extend the Bill of Rights to the states. See below Section III.

17. 1 Blackstone, *Commentaries,* pp. *143–44.

18. Abbott E. Smith, *Colonists in Bondage: White Servitude and Convict Labor in America, 1607–1776,* (1947; reprint W. W. Norton, 1971), pp. 30–34.

19. Daniel J. Boorstin, *The Americans: The Colonial Experience* (1958), pp. 355–56.

20. See A. Leon Higginbotham, Jr., *In the Matter of Color: Race and the American Legal Process: The Colonial Period* (1978), p. 32.

It should also be added that the abundant game found in North America during the colonial period eliminated the need for the kind of game laws that had traditionally disarmed the lower classes in England. Malcolm, "The Right of the People to Keep and Bear Arms," pp. 393–94.

21. See, e.g., 2 *Laws of the Royal Colony of New Jersey,* Bernard Bush, ed. (1977), pp. 15–21, 49, 96, 133, 289.

22. Higginbotham, *In the Matter of Color,* pp. 260–62.

23. For a good discussion of the elevation of the rights of white indentured servants as a means of maintaining social control over the black population, see generally Edmund S. Morgan, *American Slavery, American Freedom: The Ordeal of Colonial Virginia* (1975).

24. Stephen Halbrook notes that Virginia's royal government in the late seventeenth century became very concerned that the widespread practice of carrying arms would tend to foment rebellion and that, as a result, statutes were enacted to prevent armed groups of men from gathering. See Halbrook, *That Every Man Be Armed: The Evolution of a Constitutional Right* (1984), pp. 56–57. The sharpening of racial distinctions and the need for greater social control over slaves that occurred toward the end of the seventeenth and beginning of the eighteenth centuries lessened the concern authorities had over the armed white population. See Morgan, *American Slavery, American Freedom,* pp. 354–55.

25. See Raymond T. Diamond, "No Call to Glory: Thurgood Marshall's Thesis on the Intent of a Pro-Slavery Constitution," *Vanderbilt Law Review* 42 (1989): 93, 101–102 (colonies dealt with slavery in an unsystematic and piecemeal fashion). See generally Winthrop D. Jordan, *White over Black: American Attitudes towards the Negro, 1550–1812* (1968), pp. 48–52.

26. Higginbotham, *In the Matter of Color,* pp. 21–22.

27. See Herbert Aptheker, *American Negro Slave Revolts,* 5th ed. (1983); Diamond, "No Call to Glory," pp. 101–102, 104; Robert J. Cottrol and Raymond T. Diamond, "Review of A. Leon Higginbotham, Jr., *In the Matter of Color: Race and the American Legal Process: The Colonial Period,*" *Tulane Law Review* 56 (1982) : 1107, 1110–12.

28. 1 William W. Hening, *Statutes at Large of Virginia* (New York: R. & W. & G. Bartow 1823), p. 226; see also Higginbotham, *In the Matter of Color,* p. 32.

29. 1 Hening, *Statutes at Large of Virginia,* pp. 226; see Higginbotham, *In the Matter of Color,* p. 32.

30. Higginbotham, *In the Matter of Color,* p. 39.

31. Ibid., p. 58.

32. Ibid., pp. 38–40.

33. Higginbotham informs us that the Boston selectmen passed such an ordinance after some slaves had allegedly committed arson in 1724. See ibid., p. 76.

34. See Lorenzo J. Greene, *The Negro in Colonial New England* (1968), p. 127. Greene notes that blacks probably served in New England militias until the latter part of the seventeenth century. Ibid. It is interesting to note that, despite the prohibition on militia service, blacks served with New England forces during the French and Indian Wars. Ibid., pp. 188–89. Winthrop Jordan notes that in 1652 the Massachusetts General Court ordered Scotsmen, Indians, and Negroes to train with the Militia, but that, in 1656, Massachusetts and, in 1660, Connecticut excluded blacks from Militia service. See Jordan, *White over Black,* pp. 71.

35. See 2 *Laws of the Royal Colony of New Jersey,* pp. 49, 96, 289.

36. See Higginbotham, *In the Matter of Color,* pp. 201–15.

37. Ibid.

38. See generally John Phillip Reid, *In Defiance of the Law: The Standing-Army Controversy, the Two Constitutions, and the Coming of the American Revolution* (1981).

39. Elbridge Gerry of Massachusetts thought a national government which controlled

the militia would be potentially despotic. James Madison's "Notes on the Constitutional Convention of 1787" (August 21, 1787), in 1 *1787: Drafting the U.S. Constitution,* Wilbowin E. Benton, ed. (1986), p. 916. With this power, national government "may enslave the States." Ibid., p. 846. Oliver Ellsworth of Connecticut suggested that "[t]he whole authority over the Militia ought by no means to be taken away from the States whose consequence would pine away to nothing after such a sacrifice of power." Ibid., p. 909.

It is interesting, in light of the current debate, that both advocates and opponents of this increase in federal power assumed that the militia they were discussing would be one that enrolled almost all of the white male population between the ages of sixteen and sixty, and that that population would supply their own arms. George Mason of Virginia proposed "the idea of a select militia," but withdrew it. Ibid., p. 909.

40. *The Antifederalists,* Cecelia M. Kenyon, ed. (1966), p. 57. This concern was the reason for the original language of the Second Amendment.

41. The Virginia convention urged the adoption of the following language:

That the people have a right to keep and bear arms; that a well-regulated militia, composed of the body of the people trained to arms, is the proper, natural, and safe defence for a free state; that standing armies, in time of peace, are dangerous to liberty, and therefore ought to be avoided, as far as the circumstances and protection of the community will admit; and that in all cases, the military should be under strict subordination to, and governed by, the civil power.

3 *The Debates in the Several State Conventions on the Adoption of the Federal Constitution, as Recommended by the General Convention at Philadelphia, in 1787 Together with the Journal of the Federal Convention,* Jonathan Elliot, ed. (1907; reprint Ayer Co., 1987), pp. 657–59 (hereinafter *Elliot's Debates*).

42. *The Federalist,* No. 25 (Alexander Hamilton) (The Heritage Press, 1945), p. 161. For a modern study that supports Hamilton's views concerning the military ineffectiveness of the militia, see Boorstin, *The Americans,* pp. 352–72.

43. 5 *Elliot's Debates,* pp. 464–65.

44. *The Federalist,* No. 46, p. 319 (James Madison). The census of 1790 listed the white male population over age sixteen as 813,298. See *Bureau of the Census, U.S. Department of Commerce, Statistical History of the United States from Colonial Times to the Present* (1976), p. 16. The census did not list the number of men over sixty who would have been exempt from militia duty.

45. 1 Stat. 271.

46. U.S. Constitution, art I, § 2, cl. 3 (specifying congressional representation) is often cited for the proposition that blacks were not citizens because of the three-fifths clause. It should be noted that, under this clause, free Negroes were counted as whole persons for purposes of representation. The original wording of this provision specifically mentioned "white and other citizens," but that language was deleted by the committee on style as redundant. See 5 *Elliot's Debates,* p. 451.

47. Jordan, *White over Black,* pp. 125–26, 411–12.

48. Robert J. Cottrol, "The Thirteenth Amendment and the North's Overlooked Egalitarian Heritage," *National Black Law Journal* 11 (1989): 198; 202–203 (discussing racism in early nineteenth-century America).

49. Paul Finkelman, "Prelude to the Fourteenth Amendment: Black Legal Rights in the Antebellum North," *Rutgers Law Journal* 17 (1986): 415, 476.

50. See, e.g., Ga. Const. of 1779, art. IV, § 1, in 1 *Federal and State Constitutions, Colonial Charters, and Other Organic Laws of the United States,* Benjamin B. Poore, ed., 2d ed. (Washington, D.C.: Government Printing Office, 1878) (hereinafter *Federal and State Constitutions*), p. 386; Md. Const. of 1776, art. II, 1 *Federal and State Constitutions,* p. 821; Mass. Const. of 1776,

pt. I, declaration of rights, art. IX, in 1 *Federal and State Constitutions*, p. 958; N.H. Const. of 1784, pt. I, bill of rights, art. XI, in 2 *Federal and State Constitutions*, p. 1281; N.J. Const. of 1776, art. IV, in 2 *Federal and State Constitutions*, p. 1311; N.C. Const. of 1776, constitution or frame of government, art. IX, in 2 *Federal and State Constitutions*, pp. 1411–12; Pa. Const. of 1776, declaration of rights, art. VII, in 2 *Federal and State Constitutions*, p. 1541; Vt. Const. of 1777, ch. 1, declaration of rights, art. VIII, in 2 *Federal and State Constitutions*, pp. 1859.

Only Georgia, under its 1776 constitution, and South Carolina, in its 1790 constitution, provided explicit racial restrictions on the right to vote. See Ga. Const. of 1776, art. IX, in 1 *Federal and State Constitutions*, p. 379; S.C. Const. of 1790, art. I § 4, in 2 *Federal and State Constitutions*, p. 1628.

51. See Ga. Const. of 1776, art. LVI, in 1 *Federal and State Constitutions*, p. 283; Ga. Const. of 1789, art. IV, § 5, in 1 *Federal and State Constitutions*, p. 386; Md. Const. of 1776, art. XXXIII, in 1 *Federal and State Constitutions*, pp. 819–20 (freedom of religion for "all persons"); N.C. Const. of 1776, art. VIII (rights in criminal proceedings to be informed of charges, to confront witnesses, and to remain silent for "every man," and freedom of religion for "all men"), in 2 *Federal and State Constitutions*, p. 1409; N.Y. Const. of 1777, art. XIII (due process to be denied "no member of this state"), art. XXXVIII (freedom of religion "to all mankind"); Pa.Const. of 1776, art. II (freedom of religion for "all men"), art. VIII (due process for "every member of society"), in 2 *Federal and State Constitutions*, p. 1541; Pa. Const. of 1790, art. XI, § 3 (freedom of religion to be denied to "no person"), art. XI, § 7 (freedom of the press for "every person" and freedom of speech for "every citizen"), art. XI, § 10 (due process to be denied to "no person"), in 2 *Federal and State Constitutions*, pp. 1554–55; S.C. Const. of 1778, art. XXXVIII (freedom of religion), in 2 *Federal and State Constitutions*, pp. 1626–27; S.C. Const. of 1790, art. VIII (freedom of religion "to all mankind"), in 2 *Federal and State Constitutions*, pp. 1632.

52. Leon F. Litwack, *North of Slavery: The Negro in the Free States, 1790–1860* (1961), p. 79.

53. See Stampp, *The Peculiar Institution*, pp. 56–68.

54. Ibid., pp. 214–16.

55. See text accompanying notes 56–66.

56. Chapter 448, § 1, of the Kentucky Acts of 1818 was limited solely to slave offenders. Act of February 10, 1819, ch. 448, § 1, 1819 Acts of Ky. 787. The Kentucky Acts of 1850 extended these provisions to free blacks as well. Act of Mar. 24, 1851, ch. 617, art. VII, § 7, 1850 Acts of Ky. 291, 300–01.

57. An Act Concerning Slaves, § 11, Acts of Fla. 289, 291 (1824). In 1825, Florida had provided a penalty for slaves using firelight to hunt at night, but this seems to have been a police measure intended to preserve wooded land, for whites were also penalized, although less stringently, for this offense. Act of December 10, 1825, § 5, 1825 Laws of Fla. 78–80. Penalties for "firehunting" were reenacted in 1827, Act of January 1, 1828, 1828 Laws of Fla. 24–25, and the penalties for a slave firehunting were reenacted in 1828, Act of November 21, 1828, § 46, 1828 Laws of Fla. 174, 185.

58. 1825 Acts of Fla. 52, 55.

59. Ibid. § 9.

60. Act of January 31, 1831, 1831 Fla. Laws 30.

61. Herbert Aptheker, *American Negro Slave Revolts*, 5th ed. (1983), p. 298. For a full account of this revolt, the bloodiest in United States history, see ibid., pp. 293–324. For a compilation of documentary sources on the revolt, see also Henry I. Tragle, *The Southampton Slave Revolt of Eighteen Thirty-One: A Compilation of Source Material* (1971). An account of the revolt novelized from Turner's confession can be found in William Styron, *The Confessions of Nat Turner* (1967). Styron's novel has been criticized as failing to capture the power of religion for the nineteenth-century black, and thus failing to tell the truth of the revolt. See, e.g., William F. Cheek, *Black Resistance before the Civil War* (1970), pp. 116–17.

62. See Herbert Aptheker, *Nat Turner's Slave Rebellion* (1966), pp. 74–94.

63. Ibid., pp. 74–75.

64. Ibid., p. 75.

65. Ibid., p. 81.

66. Act of December 23, 1833, § 7, 1833 Ga. Laws 226, 228.

67. Act of February 17, 1833, ch. 671, §§ 15, 17, 1833 Fla. Laws 26, 29. The black person offending the statute was to be "severely punished," incongruously enough, "by moderate whipping," not to exceed thirty-nine strokes on the bare back. Ibid. § 17.

68. Act of January 6, 1847, ch. 87, § 11, 1846 Fla. Laws 42, 44; Act of December 17, 1861, ch. 1291, § 11, 1861 Fla. Laws 38, 40.

69. Stampp, *The Peculiar Institution,* pp. 214–15.

70. See text accompanying note 52.

71. See, e.g., Raoul Berger, *Government by Judiciary: The Transformation of the Fourteenth Amendment* (1977), p. 10.

72. After *Roberts* v. *Boston,* 59 Mass. (5 Cush.) 198 (1849), upheld the provision of segregated public education in the city of Boston, the Massachusetts legislature outlawed segregated education. Act of March 24, 1855, ch. 256, 1855 Mass. Acts 256; see Paul Finkelman, "Prelude to the Fourteenth Amendment: Black Legal Rights in the Antebellum North," *Rutgers Law Journal* 17 (1986): 465–67. In Connecticut, most schools were integrated before 1830; only in response to a request from the Hartford black community was a separate system established in that year. Ibid., p. 468. The Iowa constitution provided for integration in public schools. See *Clark* v. *Board of Directors,* 24 Iowa 266 (1868) (construing Iowa Const. of 1857, art. IX, § 12).

In Ohio, blacks were excluded entirely from public schools until 1834, when the state Supreme Court ruled that children of mixed black ancestry who were more than half white might attend; not until 1848 did the legislature provide for public education of any sort for other black children. *Williams* v. *Directors of Sch. Dist.,* Ohio 578 (1834); see also *Lane* v. *Baker,* 12 Ohio 237 (1843). In 1848, the state legislature allowed blacks to be serviced by the public schools unless whites in the community were opposed; in the alternative, the legislature provided for segregated education. Act of February 24, 1848, 1848 Ohio Laws 81. The following year, the legislature provided that the choice of segregated or integrated public education lie at the option of local school districts. Act of February 10, 1849, 1849 Ohio Laws 17.

73. From 1807 to 1849, Ohio required blacks entering the state to post a bond. Act of Jan. 25, 1807, ch. VIII, 1807 Ohio Gen. Assem. Laws 53, repealed by Act of February 10, 1849, 1849 Ohio Laws 17. Michigan Territory passed a similar law in 1827, though there was only one recorded attempt to enforce it. Act of April 13, 1827, 1827 Mich. Revised Laws 1–10 (1st & 2d Councils); David M. Katzman, *Before the Ghetto: Black Detroit in the Nineteenth Century* (1973), p. 7 n.6. Indiana required a bond from 1831 until 1851, when a new constitution forbade black immigration entirely. Act of February 10, 1831, 1831 Ind. Revised Laws 375, superseded by Ind. Const. of 1851, art. XIII, § 1 (amended 1881). Illinois went the same route by coupling the repeal of its 1829 bond provisions with a prohibition on black immigration in its 1848 constitution. Ill. Const. of 1848, art. XIV; Act of January 17, 1832–33, Ill. Revised Laws 463, amended by Act of February 1, 1831, 1832–33 Ill. Revised Laws 462, repealed by Act of February 12, 1853, 1853 Ill. Laws 57. Oregon's 1859 constitution forbade blacks to enter the state, Or. Const. of 1859, art. XVIII (repealed 1926), and Iowa provided for a fine of two dollars a day for any black remaining in the state for more than three days. Act of February 5, 1851, 1851 Iowa Laws 172.

74. From 1833 to 1838, Connecticut prohibited the establishment of schools for nonresident blacks. Act of May 24, 1833, ch. IX, 1833 Conn. Pub. Acts 425, repealed by Act of May 31, 1838, ch. XXXIV, 1838 Conn. Pub. Acts 30; see also *Crandall* v. *State,* 10 Conn. 339 (1834) (attempted prosecution under this statute failed due to an insufficient information). See

Finkelman, "Prelude to the Fourteenth Amendment," pp., 430–43 (discussing the lack of enforcement of statutes regulating black immigration).

75. See Litwack, *North of Slavery,* pp. 159, 165 (in fields where blacks were allowed to compete with whites, who were often the new Irish immigrants, violence often erupted).

76. Ibid., p. 153; see also Leonard P. Curry, *The Free Black in Urban America 1800– 1850: The Shadow of the Dream* (1981), pp. 96–111.

77. See above, p. 134.

78. Jack D. Foner, *Blacks and the Military in American History: A New Perspective* (1974), pp. 20–21.

79. See Robert J. Cottrol, *The Afro-Yankees: Providence's Black Community in the Antebellum Era* (1982), p. 63.

80. Oscar Handlin, *Boston's Immigrants: A Study in Acculturation* (1959), p. 175 and n.110.

81. Leonary P. Curry, *The Free Black in Urban America 1800 to 1850: The Shadow of the Dream* (1981), p. 100; Victor Ullman and Martin R. Delany, *The Beginnings of Black Nationalism* (1971), pp. 29–31.

82. Curry, *The Free Black in Urban America,* pp. 105–106.

83. Ibid., pp. 107–108; Wendell P. Dabney, *Cincinnati's Colored Citizens: Historical, Sociological and Biographical* (1926; reprint Dabney Publishing Co., 1970), pp. 48–55; "Cincinnati Riot," *Niles' Nat'l Reg.* (Baltimore), September 11, 1841, p. 32.

84. Even during the Civil War, the Lincoln administration and Congress acted on the legal assumption that free blacks were citizens. Despite Chief Justice Taney's opinion in *Dred Scott* that neither free blacks nor slaves could be citizens, *Dred Scott* v. *Sanford,* 60 U.S. (15 How.) 393, 417 (1856), Lincoln's attorney general, Edward Bates, issued an opinion in 1862 declaring that free blacks were citizens and entitled to be masters of an American vessel. See 10 Op. Atty. Gen. 382, 413 (1862). That same year, Congress amended the 1792 militia statute, striking out the restriction of militia membership to white men. See Act of July 17, 1862, ch. 36, § 12, 12 Stat. 597, 599. While it could be argued that these measures were in part motivated by military needs, it should be noted that the United States as a whole and various individual states had previously enlisted black troops during times of crisis despite the restrictions in the 1792 Act. See above, p. 134. Thus, these measures reflected long standing Republican and antislavery beliefs concerning the citizenship of free Negroes. See generally Robert J. Cottrol, "A Tale of Two Cultures: Or Making the Proper Connections between Law, Social History and the Political Economy of Despair," *San Diego Law Review* 25 (1988). For a good discussion of black citizenship rights in the antebellum North, see generally Finkelman, "Prelude to the Fourteenth Amendment."

85. Section 1. Neither slavery nor involuntary servitude, except as a punishment for crime whereof the party shall have been duly convicted, shall exist within the United States, or any place subject to their jurisdiction.

Section 2. Congress shall have power to enforce this article by appropriate legislation.

U.S. Const. amend. XIII.

86. See generally Finkelman, "Prelude to the Fourteenth Amendment,."

87. Kenneth Stampp, *The Era of Reconstruction 1865–1877* (1965), p. 80.

88. Foner, *Reconstruction,* p. 198 (quoting letter from William H. Trescot to James Law Orr, December 13, 1865, South Carolina's Governor's Papers).

89. Ibid., p. 200.

90. Stampp, *The Era of Reconstruction,* p. 80

91. Ibid.

92. "No Negro who is not in the military service shall be allowed to carry firearms, or any kind of weapons, within the parish, without the special permission of his employers, approved and indorsed by the nearest and most convenient chief of patrol. Anyone violating the provisions of this section shall forfeit his weapons and pay a fine of five dollars, or in default

of the payment of said fine, shall be forced to work five days on the public road, or suffer corporal punishment as hereinafter provided." Louisiana Statute of 1865, reprinted in Walter L. Fleming, ed., *Documentary History of Reconstruction: Political, Military, Social, Religious, Educational and Industrial, 1865 to the Present Time* (1960), p. 280.

93. "[N]o freedman, free negro or mulatto, not in the military service of the United States government, and not licensed so to do by the board of police of his or her county, shall keep or carry firearms of any kind, or any ammunition, dirk or bowie knife, and on conviction thereof in the county court shall be punished by fine, not exceeding ten dollars, and pay the cost of such proceedings, and all such arms or ammunition shall be forfeited to the informer; and it shall be the duty of every civil and military officer to arrest any freedman, free negro, or mulatto found with any such arms or ammunition, and cause him or her to be committed to trial in default of bail." Mississippi Statute of 1865, reprinted in *Documentary History of Reconstruction*, p. 290.

94. 1. That it shall not be lawful for any freedman, mulatto, or free person of color in this State, to own firearms, or carry about his person a pistol or other deadly weapon.

2. That after the 20th day of January, 1866, any person thus offending may be arrested upon the warrant of any acting justice of the peace, and upon conviction fined any sum not exceeding $100 or imprisoned in the county jail, or put to labor on the public works of any county, incorporated town, city, or village, for any term not exceeding three months.

3. That if any gun, pistol or other deadly weapon be found in the possession of any freedman, mulatto or free person of color, the same may by any justice of the peace, sheriff, or constable be taken from such freedman, mulatto, or free person of color; and if such person is proved to be the owner thereof, the same shall, upon an order of any justice of the peace, be sold, and the proceeds thereof paid over to such freedman, mulatto, or person of color owning the same.

4. That it shall not be lawful for any person to sell, give, or lend firearms or ammunition of any description whatever, to any freedman, free negro or mulatto; and any person so violating the provisions of this act shall be guilty of a misdemeanor, and upon conviction thereof, shall be fined in the sum of not less than fifty nor more than one hundred dollars, at the discretion of the jury trying the case.

See Alfred Avins, ed., *The Reconstruction Amendments' Debates* (1967), p. 209.

95. See Foner, *Reconstruction*, pp. 225–27; Stampp, *The Era of Reconstruction*, pp. 80–81.

96. The Ku Klux Klan was formed in 1866 and immediately launched its campaign of terror against blacks and Southern white unionists. See Foner, *Reconstruction*, p. 342.

97. During the debates over the Civil Rights Act of 1866, Republican Representative Sidney Clarke of Kansas expressed the fears of many Northern Republicans who saw the clear military implications of allowing the newly formed white militias in Southern states to disarm blacks:

Who, sir, were those men? Not the present militia; but the brave black soldiers of the Union, disarmed and robbed by this wicked and despotic order. Nearly every white man in [Mississippi] that could bear arms was in the rebel ranks. Nearly all of their able-bodied colored men who could reach our lines enlisted under the old flag. Many of these brave defenders of the nation paid for their arms with which they went to battle. And I regret, sir, that justice compels me to say, to the disgrace of the Federal Government, that the "reconstructed" state authorities of Mississippi were allowed to rob and disarm our veteran soldiers and arm the rebels fresh from the field of treasonable strife. Sir, the disarmed loyalists of Alabama, Mississippi, and Louisiana are powerless today, and oppressed by the pardoned and encouraged rebels of those States.

The Reconstruction Amendments' Debates, p. 209.

98. Representative Roswell Hart, Republican from New York, expressed the following sentiments during the debates over the Civil Rights Act of 1866:

The Constitution clearly describes that to be a republican form of government for which it was expressly framed. A government which shall "establish justice, insure domestic tranquillity, provide for the common defense, promote the general welfare, and secure the blessings of liberty"; a government whose "citizens shall be entitled to all privileges and immunities of other citizens"; where "no law shall be made prohibiting the free exercise of religion"; where "the right of the people to keep and bear arms shall not be infringed"; where "the right of the people to be secure in their persons, houses, papers and effects, against unreasonable searches and seizures, shall not be violated," and where "no person shall be deprived of life, liberty, or property without due process of law."

Have these rebellious States such a form of government? If they have not, it is the duty of the United States to guaranty that they have it speedily.

The Reconstruction Amendments' Debates, p. 193.

99. For a good general discussion of the incorporation question, see Michael K. Curtis, *No State Shall Abridge: The Fourteenth Amendment and the Bill of Rights* (1986). For a good discussion of the 39th Congress's views concerning the Second Amendment and its incorporation via the Fourteenth, see Halbrook, *That Every Man Be Armed*, pp. 107–23; Stephen Halbrook, "Personal Security, Personal Liberty, and 'The Constitutional Right to Bear Arms': Visions of the Framers of the Fourteenth Amendment," *Seton Hall Constitutional Law Journal* 5 (1995): 341–434.

100. "No state shall make or enforce any law which shall abridge the privileges or immunities of citizens of the United States. . . ." U.S. Const. amend. XIV, § 1.

101. *The Reconstruction Amendments' Debates*, pp. 156–60, 217–18.

102. Ibid., p. 219 (remarks by Republican Sen. Jacob Howard of Michigan on privileges and immunities of citizens).

103. *Butchers Benevolent Ass'n* v. *Crescent City Live-Stock Landing & Slaughter-House Co.*, 83 U.S. (16 Wall.) 36 (1872).

104. 92 U.S. 542 (1876)

105. 16 Stat. 140 (1870) (codified as amended at 18 U.S.C. §§ 241–42 [1988]). The relevant passage reads:

That if two or more persons shall band or conspire together, or go in disguise upon the public highway, or upon the premises of another, with intent to violate any provision of this act, or to injure, oppress, threaten, or intimidate any citizen with intent to prevent or hinder his free exercise and enjoyment of any right or privilege granted or secured to him by the Constitution or laws of the United States or because of his having exercised the same, such persons shall be held guilty of a felony. . . .

Ibid. at 141

106. 92 U.S. at 548–59.

107. This can also be seen in the Court's reaction to the federal government's first public accommodations statute, the Civil Rights Act of 1875. With much the same reasoning, the Court

held that Congress had no power to prohibit discrimination in public accommodations within states. See *The Civil Rights Cases,* 109 U.S. 3 (1883).

108. See, e.g., *Yick Wo* v. *Hopkins,* 118 U.S. 356, 373 (1886) (declaring the administration of a municipal ordinance discriminatory); *Strauder* v. *West Virginia,* 100 U.S. 303, 308 (1879) (striking down a statute prohibiting blacks from serving as jurors).

109. 116 U.S. 252 (1886).

110. Ibid., p. 253.

111. Ibid., p. 265.

112. Ibid.

113. Rable, *But There Was No Peace,* pp. 88–90; Stampp, *The Era of Reconstruction,* pp. 199–204.

114. Benno C. Schmidt, Jr., "Principle and Prejudice: The Supreme Court and Race in the Progressive Era. Part 2: The Peonage Cases," *Columbia Law Review* 82 (1982): 646, 653–55.

115. George M. Fredrickson, *White Supremacy: A Comparative Study in American and South African History* (1981), pp. 251–52; Charles E. Silberman, *Criminal Violence, Criminal Justice* (1978), p. 32; Joel Williamson, *A Rage for Order: Black/White Relations in the American South since Emancipation* (1986), p. 124.

116. See generally Jordan, *White over Black,* pp. 3–43.

117. Litwack, *North of Slavery,* pp. 153–86.

118. Cottrol, "A Tale of Two Cultures," pp. 1007–19.

119. C. Vann Woodward, *The Strange Career of Jim Crow,* 3d ed. (1974), pp. 22–23.

120. See notes 87–94. See generally Woodward, *The Strange Career of Jim Crow,* pp. 22–29.

121. See Woodward, pp. 18–21 (the Jim Crow system was born in the North where systematic segregation, with the backing of legal and extralegal codes, permeated black life in the free states by 1860); see also Litwack, *North of Slavery,* pp. 97–99 (in addition to statutes and customs that limited the political and judicial rights of blacks, extralegal codes enforced by public opinion perpetuated the North's systematic segregation of blacks from whites).

122. See Richard C. Wade, *Slavery in the Cities: The South 1820–1860* (1964), pp. 180–208 (although more contact between blacks and whites occurred in urban areas of the South, both social standards and a legal blueprint continued the subjugation of blacks to whites).

123. 109 U.S. 3 (1883).

124. 163 U.S. 537 (1896).

125. 109 U.S. 3.

126. 163 U.S. at 548.

127. Ibid., p. 551.

128. Ibid.

129. Jim Crow was not exclusively a southern experience after the Civil War. For example, at one point or another, antimiscegenation laws have been enacted by forty-one of the fifty states. Harvey M. Applebaum, "Miscegenation Statutes: A Constitutional and Social Problem," *Georgetown Law Journal* 53 (1964): 49, 50–51, and 50 n.9. The Adams case, in which the federal government challenged separate university facilities throughout the union, involved the state of Pennsylvania. See *Adams* v. *Richardson,* 356 F. Supp. 92, 100 (D.D.C. 1973); *Adams* v. *Richardson,* 351 F. Supp. 636, 637 (D.D.C. 1972). *Hansberry* v. *Lee,* 311 U.S. 32 (1940), involved a covenant restricting the sale of property in Illinois to blacks. The set of consolidated cases that outlawed the separate but equal doctrine would later be known as *Brown* v. *Board of Education,* 347 U.S. 483 (1954). The defendant board of education was located in Kansas, a Northern state.

130. "Blood-Curdling Lynching Witnessed by 2,000 Persons," *Chattanooga Times,* February 13, 1918; reprint in Ralph Ginzburg, *100 Years of Lynchings,* pp. 114–16.

131. Ida B. Wells-Barnett, *Crusade for Justice: The Autobiography of Ida B. Wells,* Alfreda M. Duster, ed. (1970), p. 62. Wells-Barnett's fears for her safety, fortunately, were never realized. Born a slave in 1862, she died of natural causes in 1931. Ibid., pp. xxx–xxxi, 7. Eli Cooper of Caldwell, Georgia was not so lucky, however. Cooper was alleged to have said that the "Negro has been run over for fifty years, but it must stop now, and pistols and shotguns are the only weapons to stop a mob." Cooper was dragged from his home by a mob of twenty men and killed as his wife looked on. "Church Burnings Follow Negro Agitator's Lynching," *Chicago Defender,* September 6, 1919; reprint in Ginzburg, *100 Years of Lynchings,* p. 124.

132. "Letter from Texas Reveals Lynching's Ironic Facts," *N.Y. Negro World,* August 22, 1920; rpt. in Ginzburg, *100 Years of Lynchings,* pp. 139–40.

133. "Lone Survivor of Atrocity Recounts Events of Lynching," *N.Y. Amsterdam News,* June 1, 1927, reprinted in Ginzburg, *100 Years of Lynchings,* pp. 175–78.

134. Wells-Barnett, *Crusade for Justice,* p. 50. To forestall the occurrence of future incidents of the same nature, a Tennessee court ordered the local sheriff to take charge of the arms of the black militia unit. Ibid.

135. Walter White, *A Man Called White* (1948), pp. 4–12; reprint in *The Negro and the City,* pp. 121–26.

136. Ibid., p. 126.

137. Jervis Anderson, *A. Phillip Randolph: A Biographical Portrait* (1973), pp. 41–42.

138. Ibid., p. 42.

139. See, e.g., John R. Salter, Jr., and Don Kates, "The Necessity of Access to Firearms by Dissenters and Minorities Whom Government is Unwilling or Unable to Protect," in Don Kates, ed., *Restricting Handguns: The Liberal Skeptics Speak Out* (1979), pp. 185, 189–93.

140. Don Kates recalls:

> As a civil rights worker in a Southern State during the early 1960s, I found that the possession of firearms for self-defense was almost universally endorsed by the black community, for it could not depend on police protection from the KKK. The leading civil rights lawyer in the state (then and now a nationally prominent figure) went nowhere without a revolver on his person or in his briefcase. The black lawyer for whom I worked principally did not carry a gun all the time, but he attributed the relative quiescence of the Klan to the fact that the black community was so heavily armed. Everyone remembered an incident several years before, in which the state's Klansmen attempted to break up a civil rights meeting and were routed by return gunfire. When one of our clients (a school-teacher who had been fired for her leadership in the Movement) was threatened by the Klan, I joined the group that stood armed vigil outside her house nightly. No attack ever came—though the Klan certainly knew that the police would have done nothing to hinder or punish them.

Restricting Handguns: The Liberal Skeptics Speak Out, p. 186.

141. Daisy Bates, *The Long Shadow of Little Rock, A Memoir* (1982), p. 94.

142. Howell Raines, *My Soul Is Rested: Movement Days in the Deep South Remembered* (1977), pp. 275–76.

143. Telephone interview with David Dennis (October 30, 1991).

144. Hamilton Bims, "Deacons for Defense," *Ebony,* September 1965, pp. 25, 26; see also Roy Reed, "The Deacons, Too, Ride by Night," *New York Times Magazine,* August 15, 1965, p. 10.

145. Bims, "Deacons for Defense," pp. 25–26.

146. Ibid., p. 26. Like the Deacons for Defense and Justice, the Monroe, North Carolina, chapter of the NAACP acquired firearms and used them to deal with the Ku Klux Klan. Robert F. Williams, *Negroes with Guns* (1962), pp. 42–49, 54–57. The Deacons for Defense and Justice

are to be contrasted with the Black Panther Party for Self-Defense. The Black Panther Program included the following statement:

> We believe we can end police brutality in our black community by organizing black self-defense groups that are dedicated to defending our black community from racist police oppression and brutality. The Second Amendment to the Constitution of the United States gives a right to bear arms. We therefore believe that all black people should arm themselves for self-defense.

"Black Panther Party—Platform and Program"; reprint in Reginald Major, *A Panther Is a Black Cat* (1971), p. 286. The Black Panthers, however, deteriorated into an ineffective group of revolutionaries, at times using arguably criminal means of effecting their agenda. See generally Gene Marine, *The Black Panthers* (1969); Bobby Seale, *Seize the Time: The Story of the Black Panther Party and Huey P. Newton* (1968).

147. James Farmer, *Lay Bare the Heart: An Autobiography of the Civil Rights Movement* (1985), p. 287.

148. See Bims, "Deacons for Defense," p. 26; see also Reed, "The Deacons, Too, Ride by Night," p. 10.

149. See Reed, "The Deacons, Too, Ride by Night," p. 10; see also Bims, "Deacons for Defense," p. 26.

150. Raines, *My Soul Is Rested,* p. 417 (interview with Charles R. Sims, leader of the Bogalousa Deacons); see Bims, "Deacons for Defense," p. 26; Reed, "The Deacons, Too, Ride by Night," pp. 10–11.

151. Farmer, *Lay Bare the Heart,* p. 288.

152. The beating of Rodney King on March 3, 1991, by members of the Los Angeles Police Department, captured on tape by an amateur photographer who happened to be nearby, has focused attention in recent years on the problem of police brutality, though the problem predates and presumably continues beyond this incident. See Tracey Wood and Faye Fiore, "Beating Victim Says He Obeyed Police," *Los Angeles Times,* March 7, 1991, p. A1.

4

"Assault Weapons"

David B. Kopel

It comes to pass that nothing is so firmly believed as that which we know least.
Montaigne, *Essays,* book 1, chap. 32

INTRODUCTION

The "assault weapon" issue has been, since it first burst into national consciousness in 1989, the most polarizing of all gun control issues. Many persons are repulsed by the fierce intensity of gun owners apparently defending the right to own weapons of mass destruction such as machine guns. Many "assault weapon" owners believe themselves and their guns to be the victim of a deliberate group libel. More than any other gun control topic, the "assault weapon" controversy has made more difficult the formation of any kind of unifying consensus on national gun policy.

For all the loathing that separates the progun and the antigun lobbies, the Brady Bill in its final form represented a consensus. Both sides agreed that the federal government should impose a national background check on handgun buyers. The disagreements were in the details of the check, and Congress chose a middle path, in which Handgun Control, Inc.'s, preferred method would be used until 1998, and the National Rifle Association's method used thereafter. In contrast, the "assault weapon" debate was perceived by both sides as involving not merely the mechanics of background checks but the very nature of gun ownership and the essence of the citizenry's relation to the government.

The Brady Bill was built on the foundation of twenty-two state laws that provided some kind of background check for handgun buyers (although many of the twenty-two states were not as strict at Brady). The proposal for a federal ban on "assault weapons" lacked a broad base of state law. Only three states—California,[1] New Jersey,[2] and Connecticut[3]—have enacted "assault weapon" prohibitions.[4] Two other states—Hawaii and Maryland—have enacted narrower bans on "assault pistols."[5] Thus, the passage (by a one-vote margin in the U.S. House and Senate) of a federal "assault weapons" ban was all the more impressive an accomplishment of the gun control lobbies.[6]

The federal "assault weapon" ban could not have become law without the substantial, energetic assistance of President Clinton. In April and May of 1994, the president ordered the executive branch into a full-court press to pass the "assault weapon" prohibition in the House of Representatives. The ban lost by a single vote, but House Speaker Tom Foley violated the rules of the House, and delayed declaring the vote ended until House leaders could cajole after-the-fact vote switches, thereby giving the ban a 216-to-214 victory. The "assault weapon" ban was incorporated into a comprehensive federal crime bill several weeks later.

When the crime bill came to the floor of the House of Representatives in August 1994, a combination of Republicans, gun rights advocates, and death penalty opponents appeared to have killed the bill on a procedural vote. Senate Majority Leader George Mitchell and House Speaker Foley went to the White House, and told President Clinton that the crime bill could not pass if the "assault weapon" ban was included. Moreover, they warned that voting for a crime bill containing an "assault weapon" ban would hurt Democrats all over the country.[7]

President Clinton's pollster Stanley Greenberg disagreed. He produced data which he said showed that not a single Democrat would lose his seat over the "assault weapon" ban. White House strategists suggested that because the "assault weapon" issue had such high public visibility, the president would appear indecisive if he did not insist on retaining the gun ban. The president did insist, and, after weeks of hard-fought insider politicking, the House and the Senate both passed the crime bill with the full-strength version of the "assault weapon" ban.

A few weeks after the November 1994 elections, President Clinton telephoned one of the leading Democratic supporters of the "assault weapon" ban. After congratulating the Congressman on his reelection, the president opined that the "assault weapon" ban had cost the Democrats twenty-one seats in the House of Representatives. Clinton later told the Cleveland *Plain-Dealer* that the "assault weapon" issue and the NRA's efforts had given the Republicans twenty additional seats.[9] If the President was correct, then the gun ban was a decisive factor in the Republicans' taking control of the House of Representatives. (The Republicans won a fourteen-seat majority, meaning that without the twenty or twenty-one "assault weapon" victories, they would have remained in the minority.)

The president's conclusion was consistent with the analysis in *Campaigns and Elections* magazine, which identified numerous congressional races in which the winning (progun) candidate's margin of victory was smaller (often much smaller) than the number of self-identified NRA supporters in the district (or state).[10] Washington pundits attributed the defeat of many prominent Democrats, such as House Speaker Foley and Pennsylvania Senator Harris Wofford, to a voter backlash against gun control in general, and the "assault weapon" ban in particular.

In the short term, the main political effect of the Brady Bill was to convince many Congresspeople that voting against the NRA was safe. This political effect led to the passage of the strict federal "assault weapon" ban. The "assault weapon" ban, in turn, played a crucial role in many congressional races and led to the defeat of many gun control supporters. As a political matter, the effect of the "assault weapon" ban was to erase the Brady Bill's message that voting for gun control was a smart electoral strategy. The conventional wisdom, which in 1993 had claimed that the NRA was politically impotent, concluded that the NRA was "back" and that voting against the NRA was still a risky political move.

As discussed in chapter 2, the Brady Bill will no longer be a contentious part of American political dialogue. The bill expires in 1998, to be replaced with a national instant check of purchasers of handguns and long guns. In contrast, the "assault weapon" ban will likely remain a major "gun control" issue, as efforts are made to repeal the law entirely or to soften it.

While the political impact of the "assault weapon" ban may be clear enough, the practical impact remains murky to many people. What exactly is an "assault weapon"? Why would anyone, other than a mass murderer, want to own one? To what extent are "assault weapons" the weapon of choice of criminals?

In answering these questions, we can better understand a topic which, more than any other in the contemporary gun debate, has been obscured by misunderstanding of the basic facts. We can also see how effectively the gun control lobbies frame the debate on issues involving the technical features of guns. And in studying that debate—with a real understanding of the characteristics of "assault weapons"—we can clarify answers to the question of who should have guns. The "assault weapon" controversy starkly raises the question about to what degree, if any, people should be allowed to own guns for purposes other than sports. The "assault weapon" debate goes to the core of the relation between the people and the government.

WHAT IS AN "ASSAULT WEAPON"?

"Assault weapons" are said to possess unique features which render them far more dangerous than other firearms. I shall first discuss the physical characteristics which make a gun an "assault weapon." In doing so, I will use the federal definition of "assault weapon" and also the California definition (which is the model for most state and local bans). A copy of the federal "assault weapon" law is printed at the end of this chapter.

The federal "assault weapon" law consists of four components. The first outlaws nineteen "types" of "assault weapon" by name. The second is a generic prohibition which outlaws all rifles, shotguns, or pistols that possess two or more characteristics from a list of "assault weapon" characteristics. The characteristic ban combined with the ban on nineteen "types" of guns results in a law that covers approximately two hundred firearms. (The media sometimes reported, incorrectly, that the ban involved "only" nineteen guns.)

Following the definition of guns that are banned, the legislation specifically lists 670 "recreational" rifles and shotguns that are not banned. Although the federal law was titled the "Public Safety and Recreational Firearms Use Protection Act," it provides no new legal protection for the 670 "sporting" guns; the law protects them only by not banning them.[11]

Lastly, the law bans detachable magazines (ammunition feeding devices) that hold more than ten rounds.

People who currently own "assault weapons" and large capacity magazines need not register them, and may sell them freely, subject to whatever other state or federal gun laws would apply. The removal of any registration requirement was one of only two significant concessions which prohibition advocates found necessary to win passage. (The other concession was to make the law automatically expire after ten years.)

So what is an "assault weapon"?

At this point, it should be stated that this chapter will have nothing to do with assault rifles. As the United States Defense Department's Defense Intelligence Agency book *Small Arms Identification and Operation Guide* explains, "assault rifles" are "short, compact, selective-fire weapons that fire a cartridge intermediate in power between submachine gun and rifle cartridges."[12] In other words, assault rifles are a type of battlefield rifle that can fire automatically.[13]

Weapons capable of fully automatic fire, including assault rifles, have been regulated heavily in the United States since the National Firearms Act of 1934.[14] Taking possession of such a gun requires a two hundred dollar federal transfer tax and an FBI background check, including ten-print fingerprints.[15] Today, ownership of automatic firearms remains lawful, subject to payment of the transfer tax and passing the FBI background check. Nothing in the recent "assault weapon" legislation changed the law relating to automatics.

This point should be restated: "assault weapon" legislation has nothing to do with machine guns.

Many firearms manufacturers have offered for civilian sale semi-automatic-only rifles that look like military assault rifles. These civilian rifles are, unlike actual assault rifles, incapable of automatic fire. For example, the AK-47 is an assault rifle formerly used by the Russian military (which now uses the AKM-

74). Only a few hundred AK-47 firearms have been imported into the United States. The AKS rifle is a Chinese semi-automatic rifle that looks like the AK-47, but cannot fire automatically. Tens of thousands of AKS firearms have been imported into the United States and sold to civilians.

Similarly, the semi-automatic Colt AR-15 Sporter rifle, of which many tens of thousands have been sold, looks like the automatic U.S. Army M16 assault rifle.[16] "Assault weapon" legislation involves semi-automatic firearms (like the AKS and the Colt Sporter) and not automatic firearms (like the AK-47 or the M16).

Other firearms manufacturers produce guns that do not look like any assault rifle, but do have a military appearance that some persons find repugnant. Such guns typically have black plastic components, in contrast to the brown wood components found on more familiar firearms. The Calico M-900 carbine is an example of a gun which, although related in design to no military firearm, has a military appearance. The TEC-9 handgun, while resembling no military guns, also has futuristic styling. Many guns with a science fiction look, such as the Calico and the TEC-9, are outlawed by "assault weapon" legislation.

No gun that is an assault rifle (by Defense Intelligence Agency definition) is an "assault weapon"—because all assault rifles are automatic and no "assault weapons" are automatic.[17] Assault rifles are used by the military, whereas no "assault weapon" is.[18] Assault rifles are all rifles, whereas "assault weapons" may include semi-automatic rifles, semi-automatic shotguns, revolver-action shotguns, semi-automatic handguns, and (under New Jersey's law) semi-automatic airguns.

Table 4.1 summarizes the difference between assault rifles and "assault weapons." The photo insert shows various assault rifles and "assault weapons."

Let us now examine the various characteristics which "assault weapons" are said to possess.[19]

Table 4.1

Assault Rifles vs. "Assault Weapons"

	Assault Rifles	"Assault Weapons"
Source of Definition?	Defense Intelligence Agency	Legislative
Squeezing the trigger once fires:	Every cartridge in the magazine	One cartridge
Military Use?	Military combat rifles	Not used by any military force
Type of action?	Automatic or semi-automatic depending on setting of selector switch	Semi-automatic only
To fire in automatic mode:	Flip the selector switch	Find a skilled gunsmith willing to spend hours performing a felonious conversion
Is the gun a machine gun?	Yes	In appearance but not in function
Type of ammunition?	Intermediate power	Intermediate power

Rate of Fire

Foremost among the features said to make "assault weapons" different from other firearms is their "high rate of fire."[20] If "assault weapons" were actually automatic firearms (such as machine guns), then the claim would clearly be true. With an automatic weapon, if the shooter squeezes and holds the trigger, bullets will fire automatically and rapidly until the trigger is released.

Semi-automatic firearms are by definition not automatic. In a semi-automatic, pressing the trigger fires one, and only one, bullet. To fire another, the shooter must release the trigger and then press it again. Thus, a semi-automatic can shoot only as fast as a person can repeatedly press the trigger. So although gun control advocates sometimes use the catch-phrase "spray-fire," a semi-automatic firearm cannot "spray fire," since the shooter must press the trigger for each shot.

The "semi" in "semi-automatic" comes from the fact that the energy created by the explosion of gunpowder (used to force the bullet down the barrel) is diverted away from the shooter. The energy is directed forward, and is used to reload the next cartridge into the firing chamber. Thus, with a semi-automatic action firearm, the shooter does not need to perform an additional step, such as cocking a lever ("lever action") or operating a slide ("slide action"), in order to load the next round.

While a semi-automatic firearm does not require a separate step to load the next round into the firing chamber, it is not unique in this regard. In a revolver or a double-barreled shotgun or rifle, the shooter does not need to perform a manual step to load the next shot.

How does the actual rate of fire of a semi-automatic compare to that of other guns? The Winchester Model 12 pump action shotgun (defined as a "recreational" firearm by the new federal "assault weapon" ban) can fire six 00 buckshot shells, each shell containing twelve .33 caliber pellets, in three seconds. Each of the pellets is about the same size as the bullet fired by an AKS (a semi-automatic look-alike of an AK-47 rifle). In other words, the Winchester Model 12 pump action shotgun can in three seconds unleash seventy-two separate projectiles, each one capable of causing injury or death. The Remington Model 1100 shotgun (a common semi-automatic duck-hunting gun, also defined as a "recreational" firearm) can unleash the same seventy-two projectiles in 2.5 seconds. In contrast, an AKS would take about a minute to fire forty aimed shots (or perhaps twice that many without aiming); the AKS rounds would be slightly smaller in diameter than pellets from the Winchester or Remington.[21] Similarly, an old-fashioned .357 revolver can fire six shots in as little as two seconds.

If one tests a firearm under highly artificial conditions—such as bolting the gun to a heavy platform and squeezing the trigger by jerking one's arm back and forth—a semi-automatic will "cycle" slightly faster than other firearms. But the only meaningful rate of fire for a weapon is how fast a person who is shooting at actual targets can hit those targets. In terms of actually hitting a target, a study conducted by the U.S. Navy Seals found that at close range, a bolt-action gun[22] cycles only one-tenth of a second slower than a semi-automatic; at longer ranges, the cyclic rate is the same for both types of guns.

The Navy studies also confirmed something that most gun owners under-stand—but those whose familiarity with weapons is limited to *Rambo* movies do not: shooters who fire without aiming virtually never hit their target. And it is nearly impossible for even trained shooters to fire on target at much faster than one shot per second.[23]

In other words, as a practical matter, most guns, including semi-automatics and other types, have an effective rate of fire of no more than one shot per sec-ond. Under real-world conditions, semi-automatics do not fire significantly faster.

In any case, there is no logical basis for banning some semi-automatics under the theory that they have a uniquely high rate of fire. American "assault weapon" legislation always bans some but not all semi-automatics. Yet all semi-automat-ics have one of three types of action design (recoil-operated, blowback, or gas operated[24]), and the guns typically selected for prohibition are not exclusively of one type or another. Thus, some semi-automatics are prohibited because of their alleged high rate of fire, while others, with an identical rate of fire, are not pro-hibited. Accordingly, "assault weapon" legislation does not single out guns that have uniquely high rate of fire. California Senator Diane Feinstein, the leading proponent of the federal ban, acknowledged that political considerations were the basis for the decision to ban some but not all semi-automatics.[25]

Persons who do not know much about guns may be forgiven for thinking that "assault weapons" are machine guns; these people are victims of what has been, in some cases, a quite deliberate fraud. For example, CBS's Chicago affiliate, WBBM-TV, showed a reporter buying a (then legal) semi-automatic Uzi carbine (small rifle); the report later showed an *automatic* Uzi being fired, and viewers were never informed that the guns had been switched.[26]

Magazine Capacity

A second feature said to be unique to "assault weapons" is their high ammunition capacity.[27] Most semi-automatic firearms (both banned and nonbanned) store their ammunition in detachable boxes called "magazines."[28] How many rounds a gun can fire without reloading depends on the size of the magazine—an inter-changeable, removable part that can be purchased separately. Thus, ammunition capacity has nothing to do with the gun itself; the magazine, not the gun, is the variable. Any gun that accepts detachable magazines can accept a magazine of any size.[29]

The rational way to ban guns based on potentially large ammunition capacity would be to outlaw all guns that can accept detachable magazines. Alternatively, a rational ban might apply only to guns in which large-capacity magazines (however "large" is defined) are actually inserted. Another approach would be to regulate or outlaw magazines that hold more than a certain number of rounds; the federal "assault weapon" law bans new magazines that hold more than ten rounds.[30]

How much of a difference the ban on ten-round magazines would actually make to a criminal is debatable. Changing a magazine takes only a second or two.[31] A person simply hits the magazine release button; the empty magazine falls to the ground and a new magazine is inserted.

The magazine ban would not have made any difference in the case that ignited the whole "assault weapons" controversy. In January 1989, at an elementary schoolyard in Stockton, California, Patrick Purdy killed five children and wounded twenty-nine. Using a Chinese semi-automatic rifle with large capacity magazines, Purdy fired about 110 rounds in four to six minutes; the rate of fire could be duplicated by virtually every gun currently manufactured. Even including time for reloading, a simple revolver or a bolt-action hunting rifle can easily fire that fast.[32]

Magazine capacity limitations do not usually matter in situations where a person is shooting at unarmed victims. Someone planning a mass murder can simply bring along a handy supply of ten-round magazines, taking only a second or two to remove an empty magazine and insert a fresh one. On the other hand, if the killer is clumsy or tremulous, and has not brought a spare loaded gun, he may take much longer to insert a new magazine in his weapon; victims would then have several seconds in which to attempt to incapacitate him.

Alternatively, if the mass murderer forgets to load the replacement magazines beforehand, it will take him a while to load cartridges one-by-one into an empty magazine; a potential victim might then have a chance to subdue the attacker. This is what happened in the December 1993 commuter train shooting perpetrated by Colin Ferguson in Long Island. Ferguson was stopped not because he had to switch magazines, but because he had failed to load his magazines beforehand.

Magazine limits may, however, have a major impact in other scenarios. If the situation involves not a single person shooting at unarmed victims but rather a gunfight, then the gunfighter with the smaller magazine is at a disadvantage.

Suppose, for example, that one person who has a handgun with a ten-round magazine also carries a spare magazine. Another person has a seventeen-round magazine. In the two seconds that the first person takes to replace an empty magazine, the second person may shoot him.

Whether or not this shooting is a "good" thing depends on who the two persons are. If the first person is a violent criminal, and the second person a police officer, it is a good thing that the magazine capacity limitation leads to the first person's losing the gunfight and getting shot. On the other hand, if the first person is a crime victim who obeys all the gun laws, and the second is a criminal who does not, then the fact that the magazine limitation leads to the crime victim's being shot is a bad thing.

Thus, the public safety benefits of the magazine limitation depend on whom we expect to be affected by the magazine law. Law-abiding gun owners will, by definition, be left only with the smaller-size magazines.[33] Police officers, by the terms of the federal law, are exempt. Criminals, by definition, will not obey the law, and at least some criminals will be able to buy large magazines on the black market.

Therefore, the effect of the large magazine ban (in terms of premature deaths) might fall most heavily on law-abiding gun owners. Those who have a permit to carry a concealed handgun usually do not carry spare magazines. Likewise, homeowners who pick up their handgun to investigate the sound of breaking glass in another part of their house generally do not bring a spare magazine with them. These people may find themselves outgunned by criminals with illegal large magazines.

Of course, most gunfights do not progress beyond two or three shots, let alone ten. But sometimes they do. One morning in August 1994, an armed robber entered a furniture store in Inglewood, California, and threatened to kill both the owner and an employee, who both grabbed their guns; the owner fired thirteen shots, and the employee seven, before the robber was finally stopped.[34] There are also special situations, such as those involving more than one attacker or a criminal under the influence of drugs, where the crime victim will be disadvantaged by the magazine limitation. (Such situations are discussed in more detail below.)

There is, however, an important assumption that one can make in order to find that the magazine limitation would be a net plus for public safety; the assumption is that armed defense by nongovernmental actors should not count. In other words, if we assume that citizens only possess guns for sports, then the magazine ban will be beneficial. The government will not be affected by the magazine limit (since it is exempt); at least a few criminals may be affected, since a total prohibition might make large black-market magazines too expensive for some criminals. Thus, the police might be better off in gunfights and certainly would be no worse off. The large magazine ban would save innocent lives.

But is it correct to assume that citizens do not use guns for self-defense? It is certainly possible to assume that citizens *should* not own guns for nonrecreational purposes. "To me, the only reason for guns in civilian hands is for sporting purposes," says Mrs. Sarah Brady, Chair of Handgun Control, Inc.[35] If ordinary people should not own guns for protection in the first place, then laws that impair defensive gun use by ordinary citizens are no danger to public safety. Whether owning guns for nonrecreational purposes is legitimate is the core question of the "assault weapon" debate.

The magazine ban is by far the most significant feature of the federal gun ban. The number of people who own outlawed guns is probably not more than a few million. The number of those who own magazines affected by the ban is much larger, since many handguns from major manufacturers such as Ruger, Glock, Beretta, Smith & Wesson, and Colt's include magazines holding eleven to seventeen rounds.

Conversion to Full Automatic

One of the most widely asserted, erroneous claims about semi-automatic "assault weapons" is that they can easily be converted to full automatic. According to the Bureau of Alcohol, Tobacco and Firearms (BATF), all "assault weapons" are "difficult to convert to automatic fire."[36] The conversion requires several hours' work by a skilled gunsmith willing to commit a major felony.[37] The gunsmith must also have access to expensive equipment, such as precision lathes.

The origin of the easy convertibility misinformation may lie with the semi-automatic M10 pistol. Versions of the pistol built during the early 1980s were easy to convert, with no technical skill and only five minutes of work required. BATF, using administrative authority, interpreted the law to treat those early M10s as machine guns (requiring a federal license for possession), since the guns seemed to BATF essentially to be machine guns.[38] Subsequent models of the M10 have been produced without the easy convertibility.

Lethality of Ammunition

"Assault weapons" are also said to fire "high-power" or "high-velocity" bullets which are unusually destructive. Elementary ballistics shows this claim to be incorrect.[39]

As noted above, ammunition for genuine assault rifles (battlefield weapons such as the AK-47 or M16) is classified as "intermediate" in power. The ammunition for semi-automatic rifles which look like (but do not fire like) automatic rifles is the same. This ammunition uses bullets that weigh the same or less than bullets used for big-game hunting.

For example, a 7.62 x 39 bullet (used in the AKS rifle, an "assault weapon") weighs 110 to 125 grains. In contrast, the bullet for the popular .30-06 hunting rifle (not an "assault weapon") ranges from 55 to 250 grains (with 21 of the 22 bullet types being 100 grains or above). Likewise, bullets for the .458 Winchester magnum (not an "assault weapon") weigh between 300 and 510 grains.[40]

One of the reasons that the ammunition for the military-style rifle is smaller, and hence less powerful, is that it was created for soldiers who would have to carry large quantities of ammunition over long distances; in contrast, standard hunting ammunition can be heavier, since a hunter will carry only a few rounds on a trip that is usually completed in a single day, or at most a few days.[41]

Besides weight, the second major factor in the force of a bullet's impact is its velocity. Other things being equal, a bullet traveling at high velocity will be more destructive than one traveling at lower velocity. The muzzle velocities for the ammunition types listed above are: for the 7.62 x 39 from 2,100 to 2,500 fps (feet per second); for the .30-06 from 2,100 to 4,080 fps; and for the .458 Winchester magnum from 2,100 to 2,500 fps.[42]

A bullet's power to damage its target depends mainly on the kinetic energy

Table 4.2

"Assault weapon" cartridges have less destructive energy than standard hunting rounds. Dark bar = muzzle velocity. Light bar = muzzle energy.

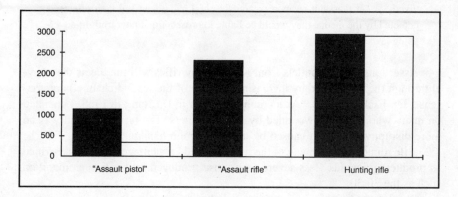

delivered by the bullet. Kinetic energy is produced by the combination of bullet weight and velocity.[43] A typical 7.62 x 39 bullet for the AKS rifle achieves 1,445 foot-pounds of kinetic energy. In contrast, the .30-06 hunting rifle bullet carries 2,820 foot-pounds of energy.[44] Table 4.2 shows muzzle velocity (feet per second) and muzzle energy (foot-pounds) for some typical "assault weapons" and for a typical hunting rifle.

The claim that the ammunition for semi-automatic pistols and shotguns is uniquely destructive is even less plausible than the claim regarding ammunition for semi-automatic rifles. Most "assault pistols" fire ammunition in the .45 or 9mm calibers, and have the same velocity as any other pistol in those common calibers.[45] The shotguns labeled "assault weapons" also fire the exact same shotgun shells (usually 12 gauge) as do all other shotguns.

The great irony of the claim that the rifles labeled semi-automatic "assault weapons" are uniquely destructive is that they are the only rifles that have ever been designed not to kill. The semi-automatic rifles use the same ammunition as battlefield weapons such as the M16, which deliberately use intermediate-power ammunition intended to wound rather than to kill. The theory is that wounding an enemy soldier uses up more of his side's resources (to haul him off the battlefield and then care for him) than does killing an enemy.[46]

Col. Martin L. Fackler, M.D., former Director of the United States Army Wound Ballistics Lab (the only research center in the world which studies wound ballistics), states:

Military bullets are designed to limit tissue disruption—to wound rather than kill. The full-metal-jacketed bullet is actually more effective for most warfare; it removes the one hit and those needed to care for him. . . . Newspaper descriptions comparing their effects with a grenade exploding in the abdomen . . . must cause the thinking individual to ask: . . . how is it possible that twenty-nine children and one teacher out of thirty-five hit in the Stockton schoolyard survived . . . ? If ["assault weapon" manufacturers] had advertised their effects as depicted by the media, they would be liable to prosecution under truth-in-advertising laws.[47]

Assertions that the bullets from Kalashnikov rifles will tumble as they travel through the body (thereby increasing the size of the wound channel) are nonsense, Dr. Fackler writes. "As a combat surgeon in Da Nang in 1968, I operated on many who had been wounded by AK-47 bullets. The typical wound was no more disruptive than that caused by many common handgun bullets. . . ."[48] The .223 rifle round, used in many of the rifles dubbed "assault weapons" is described as producing wounds "less severe than those produced by hunting ammunition such as the 30-30."[49]

People who get most of their knowledge about guns from television may have a different impression of the lethality of "assault weapons" as the result of bad reporting on the part of some stations. For example, in early 1989, when "assault weapons" had just become a major interest of the media, a Los Angeles television station arranged with the Los Angeles County Sheriff's Department for a demonstration of the "awesome power" of "assault weapons." Using a rifle like the one used by Patrick Purdy in the Stockton shootings, an officer shot a watermelon that had been set up on a target stand. The bullet punched a hole the size of a dime in the watermelon, leaving the large fruit otherwise intact. The television reporter complained that the result was "visually unimpressive." The officer obligingly unholstered his service gun (a Beretta pistol, not an "assault weapon"). Loaded in the officer's pistol were high-performance Winchester Silvertip STHP rounds. He fired once, and the watermelon exploded into tiny fragments. By the time the "demonstration" had been edited for broadcast, viewers saw only the officer holding the "assault weapon" and then the exploding watermelon. Viewers were deliberately misled into believing that the "assault weapon" had caused the explosion.[50]

Shortly thereafter, a San Francisco station built a story around the Emergency Room at Highland Hospital in Oakland. The story described the result of a person being shot with an "AK-47": a "terrible compound fracture with the leg bone shattered into twenty to thirty pieces." When Dr. Fackler later investigated the news story, he found that the patient had been shot by a .25 or .32 pistol (not an "AK-47" or any type of "assault weapon") and that the leg injury was a simple fracture.[51]

Accessories

The federal "characteristic" definition of "assault weapon" asks whether a firearm has two or more of a certain set of accessories. Unlike classifications based on the invalid premise that "assault weapons" fire faster, have more ammunition capacity, or use more destructive ammunition, the accessory-based definitions actually do define a discrete set of firearms. Likewise, a law prohibiting only pool tables with bumpers in the playing area ("bumper pool") would define a unique set of pool tables.

But do the accessory-based classifications create a distinction without a difference? If bumper pool is no more pernicious than regular pool, are guns with "assault weapon" accessories more pernicious than those without them? Let us examine the characteristics that make a gun an "assault weapon" under federal law.[52]

Pistol Grips

All pistols, obviously, have pistol grips. Only some rifles and shotguns have pistol grips; on a rifle or shotgun, a pistol grip is considered an "assault weapon" characteristic. The pictures in the photo insert show an automatic AK-47, an M16, and a semi-automatic Norinco AK-56s rifle, a Heckler & Koch HK91 rifle, and a Colt AR-15A2 rifle with pistol grips.

The major purpose of a pistol grip on a long gun is to stabilize the firearm while firing it from the shoulder. By holding the pistol grip, the shooter keeps the barrel from rising after the first shot, and thereby stays on target for a followup shot. The defensive application is obvious, as is the public safety advantage in preventing stray shots. Even if we assume that the only legitimate purpose of guns is hunting, hunters often need to take a second shot.

It is true that a pistol grip allows a rifle to be fired without resting it against the shoulder. Does this make the rifle illegitimate? Only if handguns were also being banned, for every handgun, because it has a pistol grip, can be fired without resting it against the shoulder.

Unless self-defense is considered illegitimate, a pistol grip is a legitimate defensive tool. With a pistol grip, a rifle can be held with one hand while the other hand dials 911 or opens a door.[53] The application in a home defense situation is obvious, since victims of a burglary will not always have time to draw their gun to the shoulder nor be in a position to take a shot from the shoulder.

Threaded Muzzles

A threaded muzzle that makes it easy to attach muzzle brakes or flash suppressors is another "assault weapon" characteristic. While a gunsmith can attach a muzzle brake to any gun, many semi-automatic rifles dubbed "assault weapons" have (like true military assault rifles) a threaded barrel for easy attachment of the brake. A muzzle brake reduces the gun's recoil and makes it easier to control.

Recoil vibrations look, if viewed mathematically, like a sine wave; as the recoil sine waves travel from the firing chamber toward the muzzle end of the barrel, the waves will whip the muzzle around slightly. As a result, accuracy is diminished; a bullet that exits the muzzle when the muzzle is being whipped in one direction (at the top of a sine wave) will travel in a different direction than a bullet that leaves when the muzzle is whipped in a different direction (at the bottom of the sine wave).[54] This whipping effect is diminished by muzzle brakes.

Clearly a gun with a muzzle brake is different: it is more accurate because the muzzle and the shooter are both less likely to move out of position, and it is more comfortable to shoot. Improved accuracy and shooting comfort would seem a dubious basis for classifying a firearm as uniquely suitable for prohibition.

Flash Suppressors

Another common accessory that can be attached to a barrel thread is a flash suppressor, which reduces the flash of light from a rifle shot. Reduced flash decreases shooter's blindness—the momentary blindness caused by the sudden flash of light from the explosion of gunpowder. The flash reduction is especially important for shooting at dawn or at dusk. Additionally, reduced flash means that a person shooting at an attacker at night will less markedly reveal his own position. The flash hider also adds about one to three inches to the barrel length, thus making the firearm more difficult to conceal.

In the summer of 1993, a Virginia Governor's Task Force held meetings on "assault weapons." Ed Owens, a senior official with the federal Bureau of Alcohol, Tobacco, and Firearms was asked "if the flash suppressor, the bayonet mount, and the grenade launcher are features that affect the fire power?" Owens replied "it doesn't have a thing to do with it." Owens was then asked "if you had to pick the characteristics that give these weapons their killing power, what would be the main features?" Owens replied, "killing power is the cartridge; the larger the cartridge, the more deadly the weapon."[55] (As noted above, "assault weapons" fire a *smaller* cartridge than standard hunting rifles.[56])

Folding Stocks

Guns with folding stocks are sometimes considered "assault weapons." For example, the New Jersey legislature's "assault weapon" ban outlaws the Ruger Mini-14 rifle, but only the model with a folding stock.[57] Likewise, the federal gun ban specifically lists the fixed-stock Ruger Mini-14 as a protected "recreational" gun. (The folding stock version is neither specifically banned nor specifically protected.)

A folding stock makes a gun shorter and easier to carry, thus making it useful to hunters. A folding stock also makes a gun more maneuverable in a confined setting such as a home, and hence harder for an attacker to take away.[58] The

reduced size makes the gun easier to conceal, for legitimate or illegitimate purposes. Unless it is argued that all handguns are also illegitimate (since they are
far more concealable than rifles in any configuration), it is hard to claim that a
rifle's folding stock makes it less legitimate than other firearms.

Bayonet Mounts

The federal "assault weapon" ban counts a bayonet mount as one of the illegitimate accessories that make a gun an "assault weapon." Under legislation sponsored by Representative William Hughes in 1990, any gun that could use a bayonet mount could be considered an illegal "assault weapon." Bayonets are obviously of no sporting utility, although they could be marginally useful in the personal and civil defense contexts. The major problem with the bayonet-ban, however, is that any rifle or shotgun can accept a bayonet. Moreover, it might be wondered how many, if any, crimes have ever been committed by criminals charging
their victim with a bayonet.[59]

Grenade Launchers

Like a bayonet mount, a grenade launcher mount is a defining "characteristic" for
an "assault weapon" under federal law. A gun that launches grenades is plainly
distinguishable from one that does not; the explosion from a grenade is much
more powerful than is a bullet from a firearm. Bullets can be aimed, but grenades
may kill everyone in the area.

Possession of grenades, as well as the components necessary to assemble
them, is already strictly regulated under federal law, in terms similar to those applicable to machine guns. Possession of grenade launchers is similarly regulated.[60]

Given the existing regulation of grenades, grenade components, and grenade
launchers, it must then be asked, whether the fact that, theoretically, a grenade
launcher could be attached to a particular gun has any genuine impact on public
safety.

When asked by a reporter from the *Wall Street Journal*, neither BATF nor the
Department of Justice was able to supply a single instance of a grenade launcher
(or a bayonet attached to a rifle) being used in a crime in the United States.[61]

Design History

The features discussed above all relate to the physical characteristics of a firearm.
Besides particular physical traits, having the wrong design history may also make
a gun into an "assault weapon." The federal law states that one of the characteristics of an "assault pistol" is that it is "a semi-automatic version of an automatic firearm." A common statutory definition in state and local "assault weapon"
bans is that "assault pistols" are the following:

All semi-automatic pistols that are modifications of rifles having the same make, caliber and action design but a shorter barrel and no rear stock or modifications of automatic weapons originally designed to accept magazines with a capacity of twenty-one (21) or more rounds.

Both the short and the long design history definitions raise serious problems of vagueness, because gun owners are required to know details of the design history of their gun, or of the guns that preceded the gun they own.[62]

Even assuming that details of firearms design history were common knowledge among ordinary gun owners, there is no rational basis for outlawing a gun based on its design history. To whatever extent guns with an allegedly pernicious design history have common physical traits making them more dangerous, legislation can be drafted on the basis of those traits. To hold that a firearm's design history creates a rational basis for prohibition would be the same as authorizing a prohibition on "CJ" Jeeps, which, although operationally similar to other civilian jeeps, have a military design history.[63]

POSITIVE OPERATIONAL CHARACTERISTICS

Given the above discussion, which has pointed out the ways in which so-called assault weapons are similar to other guns, it may be wondered why anyone would want to own such a gun. Although a person's choice of firearms model (like the choice of an automobile) may reflect emotional or aesthetic rather than pragmatic values, there are several practical reasons why many gun owners would choose an "assault weapon."

Reliability, Durability, and Simplicity

First, most of the rifles dubbed "assault weapons" have a greater immunity to weather conditions and abuse than more traditional hunting rifles.[64] A semi-automatic AKS can be dropped in the mud, dragged through brush, and can withstand extremely cold or hot climates. Although the guns are not military arms, they share the imperviousness to rough conditions and to lack of cleaning that the military weapons enjoy.

The ruggedness stems in part from the fact that these guns have fewer moving parts than specialized sports guns, and are hence easier for persons who are not firearms hobbyists to maintain in a safe condition.

In addition, many "assault weapons" have large trigger guards which are designed so that the shooter can press the trigger while wearing gloves. Plastic stocks (found on many "assault weapons") are superior because wood stocks, when cold and wet, may swell, thereby degrading the accuracy of the firearm. Plastic stocks are also less likely than wood stocks to break if the gun is dropped while being carried through the field.

The simplicity of design and ease of use (nothing except a revolver is easier to load and shoot) also makes the guns well suited for self-defense for persons who are not gun aficionados. The ease of use is, however, precisely the problem from the viewpoint of some gun prohibitionists. Councilwoman Cathy Reynolds, sponsor of Denver's "assault weapon" prohibition, complained that these guns "are very easy to use."[65] If guns are only for sports, not for protection, then a gun's ease of use might be considered an invitation to "misuse."

Accuracy

The firing of any gun produces recoil. Recoil makes it more difficult to aim and control a shot. Guns with lesser recoil are easier to fire safely, and better suited for self-defense. People without a great deal of upper body strength—such as some women, the elderly, or the frail—may find a low-recoil gun to be the only kind they can use successfully for self-defense.

As detailed above, in a semi-automatic, the energy from the gunpowder explosion is directed forward (rather than backward toward the shooter). The energy is used to load the next cartridge into the firing chamber, ready for a new trigger press. As a result, semi-automatics have lower recoil than other guns, and are therefore quite appropriate for use in situations where accuracy is crucial for safety, such as self-defense in an urban environment.

In addition, some rifles or shotguns labeled "assault weapons" have a pistol grip or a muzzle brake which (as discussed above) help control recoil and enhance accuracy.

Also enhancing the accuracy of a followup shot is the fact that in many "assault weapons," the stock is relatively level with the barrel—a configuration which helps the barrel stay on target after the first shot.

If people are to be allowed to own guns for protection, it would be irrational to ban a firearm because it was particularly accurate, and hence posed less of a danger of stray shots.[66] Public safety is enhanced if persons using guns for defense can hit the target. And, obviously, defensive uses of firearms sometimes involve more than a single shot. Of what benefit to public safety is a law that encourages citizens to use guns with high recoil that fire wildly, thereby endangering everyone in the vicinity?

Resistance to Gangs or Criminals under the Influence of Drugs

All the features described above make many "assault weapons" well suited for defense against many types of crime. Gulf Coast pleasure boaters have been stocking up on such guns, including Uzi pistols. Why? Because drug smugglers sometimes pull alongside pleasure boats, murder all the passengers, use the boat to transport a load of drugs to the mainland, and then abandon the boat. The drug runners do their killing with guns stolen from the military, or bought on the same international black market that supplies cocaine by the pound. Boat owners who hope to survive an encounter with the smugglers must arm themselves with reliable weapons capable of firing accurately at several attackers in succession.

Anyone who reasonably fears attack by a gang could conclude that a semi-automatic rifle or pistol is the most effective device to protect his or her family from murder. During the Los Angeles riots of May 1992, Korean merchants carrying "assault weapons" defended their families and their neighborhoods in a period of civil chaos.

In rural areas, farmers who may confront a bear attacking their livestock also carry semi-automatics. Bears do not fall down after being shot just once. In urban areas, criminals under the influence of drugs are often not stopped by one shot, and sometimes not stopped by several shots. The capacity to keep firing at an attacker until the attacker stops may determine if the victim lives or dies.

That the guns to be prohibited may sometimes be the best firearms for self-defense does not matter to some advocates of prohibition. As former New York City Mayor David Dinkins responded to self-defense arguments: "I'm telling you this nonsense that the Constitution entitles us to a weapon to defend ourselves is not an appropriate response to [gun prohibition] legislation."[67]

The Difference between Guns and Pornography

Then Attorney General Richard Thornburgh told the Senate Judiciary Committee in 1990 that the committee's "assault weapon" legislation had nothing to do with the function of the banned guns, but instead seemed to focus on whether the gun had a black plastic stock. How could legislatures expend so much energy on outlawing guns which, except for appearances, are no more dangerous than many other guns?

The answer is that most of the legislators who wrote and voted for the gun bans have never studied the functional characteristics of "assault weapons." Gun bans are not drafted by technical experts who compare guns at a firing range. Instead, the California gun list (which is the source of the list in most other gun-banning jurisdictions, and, with some modifications, is the basis of the federal list) was derived by flipping through a picture book of guns and picking out those that looked most menacing.[68] When one of the sponsors of the California gun ban was challenged about what an "assault weapon" really was, the senator replied that he knew one when he saw one.

The senator's reply echoed former Supreme Court Justice Potter Stewart's claim about pornography, "I know it when I see it." Pornography, however, *is* the picture; the social harm said to be caused by pornography depends on the nature of the picture and its effect on the viewer. Whether the picture is real or a computer simulation is irrelevant.

In contrast, "assault weapons" are not pictures of guns. A picture cannot convey the gun's rate of fire or many other features that make a particular gun unique.

Relying on pictures of weapons rather than on functional tests can lead to embarrassing results. California, for example, outlawed a "semi-automatic assault weapon" called the "Encom CM-55" shotgun. In a picture book, the CM-55 shotgun appears particularly "military," since it has a large pistol grip and a ventilated barrel. But despite appearances, the CM-55 is not an "assault weapon" or even a semi-automatic. The CM-55 is a single-shot weapon. After the one shot is fired, the CM-55 must be manually reloaded. But because of the CM-55's threatening appearance, the gun became an illegal "assault weapon" in California.[69]

The incoherence of a picture book-based firearms law was pointed out in a confidential memorandum from the California Attorney General's chief firearms expert, who observed that "Artificial distinctions were made between semi-automatic weapons. . . . We can effectively control *all* semi-automatic weapons or leave them all alone."[70]

Contrary to the imagery promoted by some gun control advocates, so-called assault weapons do not fire faster and do not have a greater ammunition capacity than many other firearms. Indeed, observes New York University law professor and criminologist James Jacobs, there is less of a rational basis for banning "assault weapons" than there is for almost any other firearm:

> Pistols are dangerous because they are easily carried and concealed; shotguns because they spray metal projectiles over a wide area; certain hunting rifles because they fire large caliber bullets, and certain "sniper rifles" because they are accurate over great distances. Assault rifles are not remarkable by any of these criteria.[71]

Because the federal "assault weapon" ban is based almost entirely on cosmetic features of firearms as well as nontechnical political considerations, the ban accomplishes nothing in terms of removing a class of dangerous weapons. For example, the ban specifically outlaws the Colt AR-15 rifle. First of all, the AR-15 is an automatic rifle; the sponsors meant to outlaw (but, technically, did not) semi-automatic derivatives of the AR-15, such as the Colt AR-15 Sporter. In any case, the Colt semi-automatic rifle is essentially identical to the Ruger Mini-14 rifle. Both the Colt and the Ruger have a military look; they use the same semi-automatic action, they can both use large detachable magazines, and they fire the same caliber ammunition. Yet while the Colt is banned, the Ruger Mini-14 is specifically protected from the ban, being classified as a "recreational" firearm. The difference between Colt and Ruger is political, not technical. For years, Colt's management and union lobbied intensively against "assault weapon" bans; in contrast, Ruger endorsed the prohibition of magazines holding more than fifteen rounds, refused to join the shooting industry lobbying organization (the American Shooting Sports Council), and did little to resist the gun control lobbies. Ruger was appropriately rewarded, and its guns remain legal. (The antigun lobbies had other reasons to avoid going after Ruger; the number of those who own the Ruger Mini-14 or Mini-30 is probably at least equal to the combined number of people who own all other types of "assault weapon.") Thus, anyone who wants to own a Colt "assault weapon" can buy a very similar gun from Ruger, secure in the knowledge that Congress has declared the Ruger to be a benign "recreational" firearm.

If instead of wanting an "assault weapon" that fires the NATO caliber (5.56mm), the buyer wants an "assault weapon" that fires the Warsaw Pact caliber (7.62mm), he can purchase a Ruger Mini-30. That gun, too, is a protected "recreational" firearm. Another example of the bill's capriciousness is that it outlaws detachable magazines which hold more than ten rounds (as supposedly not "recreational") yet classifies as "recreational" various firearms with magazines holding more than ten rounds.[72]

Because the definition of "assault weapon" depends on accessories such as bayonet lugs and muzzle threads, many gun manufacturers have already reconfigured their new gun production to meet the law. For example, Intratec, manufacturer of the TEC-9 "assault pistol," has simply removed a few accessories from the pistol (thus saving production costs) and brought out a new pistol, the AB-10 ("after ban"). The rate of fire of the AB-10 and the TEC-9 are identical; both guns can use detachable thirty-round magazines; and both fire the same caliber cartridge.

Likewise, Springfield Armory removed the bayonet lug from its M1A rifle, thus turning the gun from an "assault weapon" into a "recreational" firearm. The Springfield gun remains what it has always been: an expensive target rifle derivative of the rifle carried by U.S. forces in World War II. The new Colt Sport Rifle, with no flash suppressor and no bayonet lug, has shed its ancestor's status as an "assault weapon" and is now a "recreational firearm."

As a result of the 1989 import ban on "assault weapons," many foreign gun manufacturers had already made the same kinds of redesign in their products. By changing a stock and removing a pistol grip, an unimportable "assault weapon" was transformed into a "sporting" gun.

Gun control advocates will point out, quite correctly, that the new guns such as the Intratec AB-10 are only trivially different from their "assault weapon" predecessors. But it was the gun control advocates, after all, who insisted that features like bayonet mounts were the essence of differentiating a "bad" gun from a "good" gun.

As one gun control strategist admitted to me privately, the only logical line to draw in banning "assault weapons" would be to outlaw all semi-automatics that accept a detachable magazine. Efforts to distinguish "assault" semi-automatics from "recreational" semi-automatics have proved saleable in Congress, but they have no rational basis.

THE CRIMINAL WEAPON OF CHOICE?

In addition to the alleged special destructiveness of "assault weapons," a second rationale for their prohibition has been the frequency of their use in crime.

In Denver, for example, Chief of Police Ari Zavaras testified to the City Council that "assault weapons are becoming the weapons of choice for drug traffickers and other criminals."[73] But in a lawsuit resulting from the prohibition that the Chief had endorsed, the Colorado attorney general's office examined the chief's *ipse dixit.* The State of Colorado inventoried every single firearm in Denver police custody. Of the 232 shotguns held by the police, not a single one was covered by the ordinance. Of the 282 rifles in the police inventory, nine were covered by the ordinance (3.2 percent). Of the 1,248 handguns in the police inventory, a mere eight were "assault pistols" covered by the Denver "assault weapon" ordinance (0.6 percent).[74] And of the fourteen banned guns in Denver police custody, only one had been used in a crime of violence. Half had been seized from persons who were never charged with any offense.[75]

In every other jurisdiction where criminal gun use has been studied in detail, the results are similar to Denver.

One Percent of Gun Crime

The following statistics summarize the findings of official governmental statistical surveys. Since different governments reported data for different years, or reported different types of data (e.g., homicides or gun seizures), the raw figures reported from each jurisdiction are sometimes not directly comparable. But they all show that "assault weapons" constitute a very small percentage of guns used in crime.

Akron, Ohio. Of the 689 guns seized by the Akron police in 1992, fewer than 1 percent were "assault weapons."[76] The 1 percent figure represents a decline from 1988, when about 2 percent of seized guns were "assault weapons."[77]

Baltimore County. During the first nine months of 1990, out of 644 weapons logged in to the Baltimore County Police Property Room, only two were "assault weapons." Of 305 murders in the City of Baltimore in 1990, only seven (2.3 percent) involved rifles and shotguns of any kind, much less the subset of those firearms labeled "assault weapons."[78]

Bexar County, Texas (including San Antonio). From 1987 to 1992, "assault weapons" were used in 0.2 percent of homicides and 0.0 percent of suicides. From 1985 to 1992, they constituted 0.1 percent of guns seized by the police, according to Vincent DiMaio, the county's Chief Medical Examiner.[79]

California. In 1990, "assault weapons" comprised thirty-six of the 963 firearms involved in homicide or aggravated assault and analyzed by police crime laboratories, according to a report prepared by the California Department of Justice and based on data from police firearms laboratories throughout the state. The report concluded that "assault weapons play a very small role in assault and homicide firearm cases."[80] Of the 1,979 guns seized from California narcotics dealers in 1990, fifty-eight were "assault weapons."[81]

Chicago. From 1985 through 1989, only one homicide was perpetrated with a military caliber rifle.[82] Of the 17,144 guns seized by the Chicago police in 1988, 175 were "military-style weapons."[83]

Chicago suburbs. From 1980 to 1989, "assault weapons" totaled 1.6 percent of seized drug-related guns.[84]

Connecticut. "Assault weapons" constituted 198 of the 11,002 firearms confiscated by police in the years 1988 through 1992.[85]

Los Angeles. Of the more than 4,000 guns seized by police during 1988, 1 to 2 percent were "assault weapons."[86] A study by the *New England Journal of Medicine* investigated the 583 drive-by shootings in Los Angeles in 1991 in which a person under the age of eighteen was shot at. "Use of an assault weapon was documented in one incident." Handguns were used in 73 percent of the incidents, shotguns in 13 percent, rifles in 3 percent, multiple weapons in 4 percent, and the firearm type was unknown for 12 percent.[87]

Maryland. In 1989–90, there was only one death involving a "semi-automatic assault rifle" in all twenty-four counties of the State of Maryland.[88]

Massachusetts. Of 161 fatal shootings in Massachusetts in 1988, three involved "semi-automatic assault rifles."[89] From 1985 to 1991, the guns were involved in 0.7 percent of all shootings.[90]

Miami. The Miami police seized 18,702 firearms from January 1, 1989, to December 31, 1993. Of these, 3.13 percent were "assault weapons."[91]

Minneapolis. From April 1, 1987, to April 1, 1989, the Minneapolis police property room received 2,200 firearms, of which nine were "assault weapons."[92]

Nashville. Of the 190 homicides perpetrated in Nashville in 1991–92, none was committed with an "assault weapon."[93]

Newark. According to surgeons at the University Hospital in Newark, in the 1980s there was one wounding in the city in which the bullet removed was the type found in "semi-automatic assault rifles."[94]

New Jersey. According to the Deputy Chief Joseph Constance of the Trenton New Jersey Police Department, in 1989 there was not a single murder involving any rifle, much less a "semi-automatic assault rifle," in the State of New Jersey.[95] No one in New Jersey was killed with an "assault weapon" in 1988.[96] The New

Jersey legislature nevertheless enacted in 1990 an "assault weapon" ban that included low-power .22 rifles and even BB guns. Based on the legislature's broad definition of "assault weapons," such guns were used in five of 410 murders in New Jersey in 1991, in forty-seven of 22,728 armed robberies, and in twenty-three of 23,720 aggravated assaults.[97]

New York City. Of 16,378 crime guns seized by New York City police in 1988, eighty were "assault-type" firearms.[98]

New York State. Of the 2,394 murders in New York State in 1992, semi-automatic "assault rifles" were used in twenty.[99]

Oakland. "Assault weapons" were 3.9 percent of guns seized in 1990,[100] and were used in 3.7 percent of homicides in 1991.[101]

Orange County (Orlando), Florida. In 1993, the sheriff's office seized 1,238 firearms, of which twenty-three (1.9 percent) were "assault weapons."[102]

Philadelphia. A study of all firearms homicide victims in Philadelphia in 1985 and in 1990 (469 total) found not a single one was killed by "assault or military-style rifles."[103]

San Diego. Of the 3,000 firearms seized by the San Diego police in 1988–90, nine were "assault weapons" under the California definition.[104]

San Francisco. Only 2.2 percent of the firearms confiscated in 1988 were military-style semi-automatics.[105]

Virginia. Of the 1,171 weapons analyzed in state forensics laboratories in 1992, 3.3 percent were "assault weapons."[106]

Washington, D.C. The *Washington Post* reports: "law enforcement officials say that the guns have not been a factor in the area's murder epidemic."[107] "Assault weapons" were 3 percent of guns seized in 1990.[108]

National statistics. Less than 4 percent of all homicides in the United States involve rifles of any type.[109] No more than 0.8 percent of homicides are perpetrated with rifles using military calibers. And not all rifles using such calibers are usually considered "assault weapons."

Police Shootings

Although readers of popular magazines might infer that police officers by the score are being murdered by "assault weapons," police officer deaths in the line of duty are at the lowest level in decades, as Table 4.3 illustrates.[110] From 1975 to 1992, out of 1,534 police officers feloniously murdered in the United States, sixteen were killed with firearms defined as "assault weapons" by California law.[111] A police officer's own gun is far more likely to be used against him than is some-

Table 4.3

About 1 percent of police gun murders involve "assault weapons."

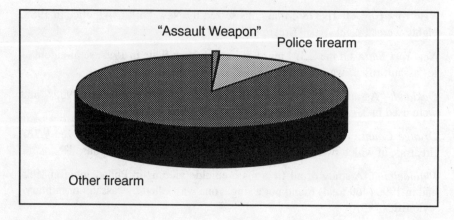

one else's "assault weapon."[112] The *Journal of California Law Enforcement* wrote: "It is interesting to note, in the current hysteria over semi-automatic and military look-alike weapons, that the most common weapon used to murder peace officers was that of the .38 Special and the .357 Magnum revolver." The *Journal* found that "Calibers which correspond to military-style shoulder weapons" accounted for 8 percent of firearms used to murder police officers in California.[113]

Despite the impression conveyed by some television programs that shootouts between police and criminals involve steadily escalating amounts of firepower, according to a New York City police department study of shootings at police, the average number of shots fired at the police per encounter was 2.55, which represented a decline from previous years.[114]

The Cox Newspapers Study

Against all the evidence discussed above, there is one report, from the Cox newspapers chain, which finds that "assault weapons" are disproportionately used in crime.[115]

At the request of local law enforcement, BATF will "trace" a gun used in a crime, using registration records to follow the gun's path from manufacturer to wholesaler to retailer to consumer. The Cox reporters examined records of gun traces conducted by BATF and found that for drug offenses, "assault weapons" were involved in approximately 12 percent of the traces. Since "assault weapons" are less than 12 percent of the firearms stock, if the guns amount to 12 percent of all drug guns, then "assault weapons" would be disproportionately involved in drug crime.[116]

Extrapolating from the trace data, the Cox newspaper reporters asserted that "assault weapons" were used in 10 percent of all firearms crime, and that since "assault weapons" were (by Cox's estimate) 0.5 percent of the total gun supply, "assault weapons" are "twenty times more likely to be used in a crime than a conventional firearm." Yet when asked about the figure, BATF wrote: "[C]oncluding that assault weapons are used in one of ten firearms related crimes is tenuous at best since our traces and/or the UCR [FBI Uniform Crime Reports] may not truly be representative of all crimes."[117] (Under the Clinton administration, BATF reversed field and began claiming that the disproportionate trace statistics did prove that "assault weapons" were common crime guns.)

As detailed above, the police statistics for the major cities report far less prevalence of "assault weapons" than the Cox report claimed. For example, the percentage of "assault weapons" reported by Cox newspapers, based on the BATF traces, was 10 percent for Chicago, 19 percent for Los Angeles, 11 percent for New York City, and 13 percent for Washington, D.C. In each of those cities, police departments conducted complete counts of all guns that had been seized from criminals (not just the guns for which the police department requested a BATF trace). According to the actual police department counts of crime guns in each city, the percentage of assault weapons was only 3 percent for Chicago, 1 percent for Los Angeles, 1 percent for New York City, and 0 percent for Washington, D.C.[118] Table 4.4 contrasts the Cox trace data with the actual police gun crime data.

Cox's problem may be that BATF traces are not an accurate indicator of which guns are used in crime. In an average year, about 360,000 violent crimes are committed with firearms. Of those 360,000 crimes, BATF is asked to trace about 5,600 crime guns, less than 2 percent of total crime guns.[119]

It was statistically likely that there would be a difference between the 2 percent of guns traced and crime guns as a whole. The 2 percent of guns selected for a trace request is not a random sample, but rather a select group chosen by local police departments. According to basic statistics theory, a nonrandom sample of 2 percent is unlikely accurately to represent the larger whole. A nonrandom sample becomes statistically valid only when 60 to 70 percent of the total relevant population is sampled. As the Congressional Research Service explains:

> the firearms selected for tracing do not constitute a random sample and cannot be considered representative of the larger universe of all firearms used by criminals, or any subset of that universe. As a result, data from the tracing system may not be appropriate for drawing inferences such as which makes or models of firearms are used for illicit purposes.[120]

Table 4.4

BATF Traces vs. Actual Crime Use. Dark bar = Traces. Light bar = Actual.

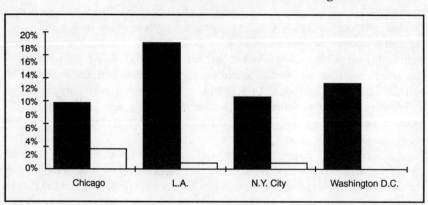

There are a number of possible reasons why "assault weapons" would be more likely be selected for a trace request than other guns. Most "assault weapons" were manufactured relatively recently, and newer guns are easier to trace. Moreover, many "assault weapons" have an unusual appearance, which might pique curiosity (and hence a trace request) more than an old-fashioned, common crime gun such as Smith & Wesson .38 Special. The vast publicity surrounding "assault weapons" may also have increased police interest in the guns, and hence the likelihood that traces would be requested.

A Future Problem?

Although the gun control lobbies sometimes made loose claims that "assault weapons" were the current criminal "weapon of choice," the lobbies, in their more careful statements, simply warned that "assault weapons" could become common crime guns unless precautionary bans were instituted.

Semi-automatics, though, are about a century old, and large-capacity magazines are older still.[121] If semi-automatics and large-capacity magazines, after a century of availability, remain rarely used in crime, it seems unlikely that they will one day turn into crime guns.[122]

Even if it were true that "assault weapons" were frequently used by criminals, the fact does not form a proper justification for prohibiting their possession by law-abiding citizens. As attorney Jeff Snyder writes: ". . . to ban guns because criminals use them is to tell the innocent and the law-abiding that their rights and liberties depend not on their own conduct, but on the conduct of the guilty and the lawless. . . . By criminalizing an act that is not wrong in itself—the purchase and sale of a firearm—the ban violates the presumption of innocence, the principle that ensures that government honors the liberty of its citizens until their deeds convict them."[123]

COUNTERPRODUCTIVE RESULTS

Many legislators will concede that gun prohibition may do little to affect criminals; still, some legislators support prohibition based on the need "to do something," and hope that the legislation might have a small positive impact. To the contrary, "assault weapon" prohibition may make the streets more dangerous by enriching organized crime, by disarming citizens, and by alienating citizens from the police.

Criminals and Guns

As discussed in chapter 2, lawful purchase is a small percentage of the supply line for crime guns. Tulane University's James Wright, author of the comprehensive National Institute of Justice (NIJ) study of gun acquisition patterns of criminals, warned that "assault weapon" prohibition was unlikely to be effective.[124] He predicted that gun controls aimed at ordinary citizens were less likely to reduce the pool of criminal guns than to provide organized crime with a lucrative new business.[125]

The supply of "assault weapons" in the United States is already more than sufficient to supply the market for stolen guns. Even if by some miracle the government managed to confiscate all the legally and illegally owned "assault weapons," criminal resupply would be easy. A good gunsmith can build a fully automatic rifle, especially if supplied with precision tools. (In fact, building an automatic from scratch is less complex than converting a semi-automatic.) Illegal home production of handguns is already common; a BATF study found that one-fifth of the guns seized by the police in Washington, D.C., were homemade.[126] If organized crime can perform the complex laboratory chemistry necessary to produce cocaine, there is little reason to believe that it cannot perform the simpler mechanical task of manufacturing illegal guns of any description.

When asked about the effects of the "assault weapon" ban, Crips Four Trey gang member Rick (Li'l Loc 2) Hardson stated, "Well, a gun is illegal. . . . So what? . . . Everything [gangs] do is illegal."[127] "Assault weapon" legislation may actually benefit gangs, partly by disarming their potential victims, and also by giving them another illegal commodity to deal.

The Persecution and Alienation of Law-Abiding Citizens

Perhaps no laws in American history have been more universally ignored than "assault weapon" prohibitions. Legislative orders that "assault weapon" owners register or surrender their guns have achieved approximately 10 percent compliance in California. In other jurisdictions, such as Denver, Boston, and Cleveland, the compliance rate has been about 1 percent.[128]

To some gun prohibition lobbyists, this disobedience is good reason for filling the jails with recalcitrant gun owners.

Not everyone agrees. As the late Stanford law professor John Kaplan observed, "When guns are outlawed, all those who have guns will be outlaws."[129] Professor Kaplan explained that when a law criminalizes behavior that its practitioners do not believe improper, the new outlaws lose respect for society and the law.

The "new criminals" created by the prohibition on guns which had been lawfully acquired are of course more fearful of the police, and less likely to get involved in reporting crime or assisting law officers. According to Chief Joseph Constance, of the Trenton, New Jersey, Police Department, the New Jersey laws criminalizing possession of "assault weapons" were "mistakes" which "created a wall of suspicion between police and the citizens." Chief Constance urged the Maryland legislature to avoid New Jersey's mistakes: "Please don't turn the citizens, your neighbors, into suspects, who understandably will become resentful and distrustful of law enforcement."[130]

The law enforcement community already has its hands full catching the existing criminals. Would it be a good social policy to create millions more by fiat? If a citizen decides to hold on to his $900 target rifle which a legislature has commanded him to register or surrender without compensation, will he continue to respect other laws? Will he be more or less likely to call 911, "get involved," and take the risk that a police officer may stop by his home to ask questions? Are the potential public safety gains (if any) of "assault weapon" prohibition worth depriving law enforcement of the cooperation of millions of previously law-abiding citizens and their families?

Although the retroactive registration requirements of the federal "assault weapon" law received almost no public attention during the debate over the law, the removal of the registration requirements during the bill's final passage was of immense importance. Otherwise, millions of gun owners and tens of millions of owners of "large" magazines would have been required to register with the government. History suggests that most of them would have refused and, overnight, millions of new criminals would have been created.

Even those who attempt to comply with the law may be turned into criminals by registration laws. Under the New Jersey "assault weapon" ban, people who owned "assault weapons" before the law was enacted could keep them only if they rendered them inoperable, and obtained a certificate of inoperability from the local police. Gun collector Daniel Elrose of Piscataway had three "assault weapons" which he deactivated (made inoperable). When he asked the local police for a certificate, the police told him, incorrectly, that he was not required to register inoperable guns. Months later, the police came to Elrose's house to investigate a domestic complaint (later dismissed) made by his wife. When the police asked him if he owned any guns, he showed the police his collection. Elrose was arrested, prosecuted for the felony of possessing "assault weapons" without a certificate of inoperability, and convicted. On appeal, the court noted that "There is no question here that the firearms in question were rendered inoperable within the meaning of the law," but upheld the felony conviction for failing to obtain the certificate. As a convicted felon, Elrose must dispose of his entire $80,000 gun collection.[131]

Whatever the benefits of reducing the supply of "assault weapons" and magazines holding more than ten rounds, state and federal legislation has been counterproductive. The rise of the "assault weapon" issue in January 1989 set off a massive surge of purchasing of those firearms threatened with prohibition. This surge continued until November 1993, when the Senate (by one vote) decided to keep the "assault weapon" ban in the draft omnibus crime bill. That vote (coupled with the contemporaneous enactment of the Brady Bill and intense press coverage of the gun debate) set off the fastest, largest mass armament in human history.

Firearms factories working round-the-clock had difficulty keeping up with consumer demand. The buying frenzy continued until September 1994, when President Clinton signed the crime bill; firearms sales (as of early 1995) remain high, but not as intense as the year before.

Now that *Guns and Ammo,* a magazine with a circulation of half a million, has begun publishing tips about how to bury guns for long-term storage, it is safe to assume that a rather large number of gun owners are putting away provisions for a rainy day. Of course the guns that are being buried are mostly "assault weapons."

Firearms manufacturers are allowed to sell "assault weapons" and large magazines which they manufactured before the crime bill was signed. Thanks in part to President Clinton (he went on vacation the day the crime bill passed Congress, and did not sign it until a month later), some "assault weapon" manufacturers now have a two-year supply of inventory. There is a ten-year supply of new magazines holding more than ten rounds. The federal "assault weapon" law expires by its own terms in September of 2004; it may be repealed even sooner. Unless the federal "assault weapon" law is reenacted before it expires, the major effect of the law will have been to stimulate a massive increase in ownership of precisely the items which the law sought to eliminate.

POLICE OPINION, PUBLIC OPINION, AND MISINFORMATION

Chapter 2 suggested that police opinion and public opinion polls should not be considered dispositive guides to civil liberties issues. The chapter also suggested that police opinion was far from unanimous in favor of the Brady Bill, and that public opinion favored the Brady Bill only to the extent that the public was less than fully informed. (The public preferred the instant check, once the option was presented.)

As with the Brady Bill, careful examination of police opinion finds a difference between police hierarchy and the rank-and-file.

Most major city police chiefs supported some kind of restrictive "assault weapon" legislation. So did the Washington lobbying branches of most police organizations. Police firearms examiners (who catalogue and study all crime guns seized by their department) often told a very different story from the chiefs and the lobbyists. For example, all seven of the firearms examiners in Dade County (Miami), Florida, have stated that the use of "assault weapons" in shootings in the county has been *declining* throughout the last decade.[132] According to George R. Wilson, the chief of the firearms section of the Washington, D.C., Metropolitan Police, drug dealers most commonly use sophisticated nine-millimeter pistols.[133] Lieutenant Reginald Smith, a spokesman for the District's police department, stated that "assault weapons" were seen by his department "occasionally, but it's rare. The vast majority of weapons we see are revolvers or pistols."[134] Detective Jimmy L. Trahin of the Los Angeles Police Department's Firearms/Forensics Ballistics Unit testified before Congress that "assault weapons" were definitely not the weapons of choice of Los Angeles criminals.[135] Lieutenant James Moran, the commander of the New York City Police Department Ballistics Unit, told reporters that NYPD experience was quite different from some press claims: "A rifle is not what is usually used by the criminals. They'll have handguns or sawed off shotguns. . . . These drug dealers are more inclined to use the 9 mm pistol than go to a cumbersome AK-47 rifle."[136]

One reason that the firearms examiners were often not heard in the prohibition debate is that some politicians deliberately avoided asking them for their opinion. An internal memorandum from the California attorney general's office revealed that as the Roberti-Roos "assault weapon" prohibition was being rushed through the California legislature, Senator Roberti and Attorney General Van de Kamp made a conscious decision: "Information on assault weapons would not be sought from forensic laboratories as it was unlikely to support the theses on which the legislation would be based."[137]

Some police chiefs attempted to suppress dissenting voices in their department. For example, in San Jose, then police chief Joseph McNamara wrote fundraising letters for Handgun Control, Inc., on official city stationery, and claimed to represent what "every police officer" believed. In 1989, one of McNamara's officers, a firearms instructor named Leroy Pyle, was subpoenaed by the California legislature and legally required to testify before that body. Officer Pyle did so, on his own time, and out of uniform. The next day, Pyle was suspended from duty, and McNamara attempted to fire him.[138] In Cincinnati, Lieutenant Harry Thomas was harassed for speaking out (on his own time and out of uniform) against the gun prohibition policies favored by the police hierarchy.

Carefully orchestrated images of police support for the gun ban were sometimes simple frauds. For example, shortly before the May 1994 House of Representatives vote on the gun ban, Treasury Secretary Lloyd Bentsen was photographed walking up the steps of the Capitol to lobby for the ban, while a phalanx of uniformed police officers lined the steps to shake his hand. The picture appeared on the CBS Evening News while a reporter explained how "cops came to hate assault guns and joined Treasury Secretary Lloyd Bentsen in a last-ditch bid to sway critical votes." *USA Today* ran the police photo, with the caption "Arlington County, Virginia, police officers greet Treasury Secretary Bentsen as he arrives at Capitol Hill on Thursday to lobby for a ban on assault-style weapons."

As it turned out, the officers had been ordered by the Arlington police chief to perform the "special detail" in Washington. When one officer objected that he did not support the "assault weapon" ban, he was ordered to attend anyway, and threatened with discipline if he refused. Several other officers, who also opposed the gun ban, had volunteered for the detail because a supervisor had told them that the detail was a photo opportunity for Police Week. At the Capitol, the officers were ordered not to speak with anyone.

The Capitol steps incident was not untypical. A few days after the omnibus crime bill (including the "assault weapon" ban) lost a key procedural vote in August 1994, President Clinton delivered a fiery speech in Minneapolis promoting the crime bill in general, and the gun ban in particular, and pointing to the overwhelming police support for the bill. He spoke against a backdrop of dozens of police officers who watched him attentively and respectfully. As it turned out, those officers had been ordered to serve as props for the Clinton speech, after event organizers had been unable to find enough off-duty police to volunteer to join the president on stage. Shortly before the speech, White House aides even ordered police working security at the event to abandon their posts and "get up on stage to fill up the holes."

As the House showdown approached nine days later, the Washington, D.C., police department ordered a dozen on-duty officers over to the capitol to lobby for the bill. When a police inspector overheard some of the officers expressing their opposition to the gun ban, the officers were ordered back to regular duty.[139]

What limited polling of law enforcement has been done does not support claims that all the police want "assault weapon" prohibition. The Florida chapter of the Fraternal Order of Police polled its membership, and found 75 percent opposed to an "assault weapon" ban. *Law Enforcement Technology* magazine polled its readership and found that "75 percent do not favor gun control legislation . . . with street officers opposing it by as much as 85 percent." In particular,

78.7 percent opposed a ban on "assault weapons." About 37 percent of top management supported a ban, and about 11 percent of street officers.[140]

Every spring the National Association of Chiefs of Police (NACOP) conducts a nationwide survey of command-rank police officers (not just top management or chiefs). The survey includes all command-rank officers, including those who do not belong to NACOP. Sixty-seven percent said that they believed a citizen should have the right to purchase any type of firearm for sport or self-defense.[141]

Neither the *Law Enforcement Technology* nor the NACOP surveys may be statistically precise, since the surveys were compiled from respondents who voluntarily mailed in a reply. But at the very least, the surveys indicate police support for "assault weapon" prohibition was far from unanimous.[142]

Public Opinion

Proponents of "assault weapon" prohibition justified the proposals by referring to the opinion polls. Public opinion polls do indicate that Americans favor restrictions on "assault weapons." In the weeks following the Stockton schoolyard shootings, a Gallup poll found that 72 percent believed that "assault weapons" should be outlawed. Public opinion on the subject has changed little since then, with most polls reporting about 70 percent of the population in favor of prohibition.[143]

It seems entirely possible, though, that many respondents thought that they were answering a question about rapid-fire military guns, which the semi-automatics are not. For example, Gallup asked about banning "assault guns, such as the AK-47."[144]

The Texas poll was cited by Handgun Control, Inc., to assert that even bedrock America wanted controls on "assault weapons." What the Texas poll actually showed was the pollsters' ignorance of the actual guns at issue. It asked if sale of "assault weapons remains legal, should there be a mandatory seven-day waiting period to purchase a high-caliber, fast-firing assault rifle."[145] Ever since 1934, there has been not a "seven-day waiting period," but a six-month transfer application period for all real assault rifles (and all other machine guns). Thus, the Texas poll found 89 percent of Texans in favor of something less strict than the federal law which had been in existence since 1934. Yet the Texas poll was used to promote control on semi-automatics—which the question had not even covered.

Further, the Texas poll described the guns as "high caliber." Most people's common sense would suggest that large calibers are more deadly, and some research supports this intuition.[146] Thus, it would be expected that those asked a question about controls on "high-caliber" guns in particular would be more supportive than they might be about gun control in general. The results from the "high-caliber" gun question were touted in legislatures to promote laws that did not regulate high caliber guns, but instead applied to intermediate-caliber weapons. Almost all polls dealing with "assault weapons" suffer from similar flaws.

The fact that the public would not understand the difference between automatic and semi-automatic was one of the reasons one antigun strategist suggested for starting the "assault weapon" issue in the first place. In September 1988, Josh Sugarmann, formerly of the National Coalition to Ban Handguns, and presently head of his own organization, the Violence Policy Center, authored a report for the antigun movement. Sugarmann observed that the handgun-ban issue was considered old news by the media, and there was little realistic possibility of enacting handgun bans in the immediate future. In contrast, suggested Sugarmann, the "assault weapon" issue could open a massive attack on a new front. Sugarmann noted that public misunderstanding over the nature of semi-automatics would play directly into the hands of the gun prohibition movement. The report explained:

> The semi-automatic weapons' menacing looks, coupled with the public's confusion over fully automatic machine guns versus semi-automatic assault weapons—anything that looks like a machine gun is assumed to be a machine gun—can only increase that chance of public support for restrictions on these weapons.[147]

Pollsters and respondents are not the only persons who have been confused. *Time* magazine's February 6, 1989, cover story included a chart titled "Street Favorites: Assault Weapons Available Over the Counter."[148] The first entry is the "AK-47" and readers are told that the AK-47 is "Soviet designed, adopted by armed forces in many nations."[149] The technical description of the AK-47 is accurate, but the gun is not "available over the counter." It is subject to the rigorous controls on machine guns that have been in place for decades.[150] If *Time* meant to refer to semi-automatics such as the AKS which look like the AK-47, those guns are not Soviet-designed, and have not been "adopted by armed forces in many nations" (or any nations) because they do not have full-automatic capability. While *Time*'s errors may have resulted from simple ignorance, in the summer of 1989 the magazine announced that the time had passed for neutral reporting of the gun control issue, and that *Time*'s mission was actively to promote gun control.[151]

Bill Peters, news correspondent for KABC-TV and KABC radio, Los Angeles, told the U.S. Senate: "Normally, this is a battle the media would stay out of—except to report the news. But this battle is too critical. . . . [T]oday it is our [the media's] responsibility—using all the powerful means we have at our disposal . . . both to inform the public of the dangers to society posed by military assault rifles and to help build support for getting rid of them." Mr. Peters explained how his ABC-owned stations promoted gun prohibition: "Every time there is an incident using a semi-automatic assault rifle in the city of Los Angeles, we report it on the news and we ask people to write to the State legislature to ban these weapons."[152] As the police data discussed above demonstrated, "assault weapons" constitute only 1 percent of Los Angeles crime guns; "semi-automatic assault rifles" would amount to an even smaller percentage. But with stations such as KABC putting every crime with an "assault rifle" on television, while ignoring much more frequent types of gun crime—such as shootings with old-fashioned revolvers—Mr. Peters and KABC helped generate public hysteria and created the false impression that "assault rifles" were commonly used in crime.[153]

Confused or not, much of the media actively promoted "assault weapon" prohibition. In January 1994, then Surgeon General Joycelyn Elders gave a speech at the National Press Club in Washington in which she said, "I'm counting on your help . . .for you all to do your part later this year on banning assault weapons." The crowd broke into enthusiastic applause.[154]

THE PURPOSES OF "ASSAULT WEAPONS"

Some supporters of "assault weapon" legislation assert that they are not impinging on the right to bear arms because "assault weapons" are not "sporting guns." In fact, many "assault weapons" are well suited for target shooting and other sports.

That this should be so, however, has little to do with why society should permit their ownership.

Hunting

Proponents of laws against semi-automatics often make the straw man argument that no one requires a thirty-round magazine to go big game or bird hunting. The fact that thirty-round magazines are not necessary for big game hunting, however, has nothing to do with whether guns that can use small or large magazines (e.g., most semi-automatics) are good for hunting.

It is true that most semi-automatic rifles are not as accurate at long distances as traditional bolt-action hunting guns. The longer barrel length and tighter chambering of the bolt action guns gives them greater long-range accuracy (especially for a single shot) than most semi-automatics. The semi-automatics' pistol grips and low recoil improve accuracy for repeated shots at shorter ranges, as discussed above; but the bolt action's advantages become more important for single shots at longer distances.

One other disadvantage of "assault weapons" as big-game hunting guns is that they fire intermediate-sized cartridges, and not the large cartridges necessary to kill large animals such as moose or elk from far away. Thus, it is not surprising that most hunting guides (who tend to specialize in big game) do not place semi-automatic "assault weapons" at the top of their recommendation list for hunting rifles.

Nevertheless, many hunters do prefer to use a Kalashnikov or Colt AR-15 Sporter rifle. First of all, the intermediate caliber cartridge used in most "assault

ASSAULT RIFLES VS. "ASSAULT WEAPONS"

1. ASSAULT RIFLES

The two rifles pictured below fit the Defense Intelligence Agency definition of assault rifle. The guns can fire automatically, and are used by military forces. These guns are not the subject of "assault weapon" legislation.

Soviet AK-47 Assault Rifle

U.S. Army M16 Assault Rifle

2. ASSAULT WEAPONS

The firearms below and on the following two pages are "assault weapons," as defined by legislation supported by the gun control lobbies. (The Norinco, the Heckler & Koch, and the Colt are "assault weapons" under the new federal law.) None of these firearms can fire automatically, and none of them is used by any military force anywhere in the world.

Crossman BB Gun

Remington 7400 Rifle

Colt .32 Pistol (1903)

Smith & Wesson Model 745

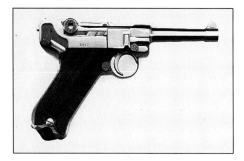

**Mitchell Arms
American Eagle P-'08**

**Colt AR-15A2
Rifle**

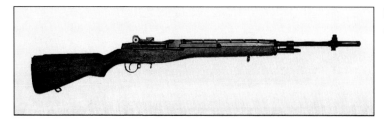

**Springfield
Armory M1A**

**Norinco
AK-56s Rifle**

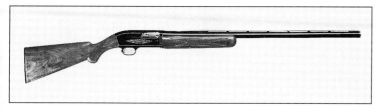

**Browning DA
Shotgun
("assault
weapon" if
folding stock
attached)**

M1 Carbine

**Ruger
10/22 Rifle**

**Heckler &
Koch HK91
Rifle**

**Ruger
Mini-14 Rifle**

Pictures courtesy National Rifle Association and *Gun World* magazine.

The NRA's Eddie Eagle gun safety program does not endorse gun use, but is still opposed by some persons who disagree with the NRA's stand on policy questions. A sample page from *Learn Gun Safety With Eddie Eagle* workbook ©1992, National Rifle Association. Reproduced courtesy of the National Rifle Association.

weapons" is adequate for game no larger than deer at medium distances.[155] Significantly, the ruggedness and durability of "assault weapons" makes them well suited for the rough outdoor conditions of hunting. Further, the low-recoil semi-automatic mechanism, muzzle brake, and pistol grip make an accurate second shot easier. That is why a Finnish company has designed a Kalashnikov especially for hunting, the Valmet Hunter, which is prized for its quick followup shots. Similarly, Rugers and Colts are particularly popular as ranch or varmint-control rifles.[156] The destructive power of a single cartridge is low enough for the guns to be usable on rodents, and the greater accuracy of the followup shots makes the guns more effective.

Competitive Target Shooting

Some "assault weapons," such as the Colt AR-15 Sporter and the Heckler & Koch HK91 (pictured in photo insert) are among the best-built rifles that a citizen can purchase. With sterling accuracy (at shorter distances), they are valuable target rifles.[157]

The apex of the world of target shooting is the national target matches held every year at Camp Perry, Ohio, under the supervision of the federal government's Civilian Marksmanship Program.[158] The Colt AR-15 Sporter and its ancestors, loaded with twenty or thirty round magazines, have long been required weapons in some Civilian Marksmanship competitions. Most of the other rifles outlawed by the gun bans are usable in other Civilian Marksmanship events and are highly prized competition target guns.[159] Before the "assault weapon" controversy erupted, firearms experts with the California Department of Justice had privately warned that "assault weapon" legislation would devastate the world of target competition.[160]

The Irrelevance of Sports

"Assault weapons" are said to be appropriate for prohibition because they are not suitable for sports—because they are, as the Denver City Council put it, "designed primarily for military or antipersonnel use."[161] Consistent with these findings, BATF exercised its authority to ban the import of certain "assault weapons" because the bureau found that they were not "particularly suitable" for sports; the bureau also noted that several of the nonimportable guns were well suited for defensive purposes.[162] Firearms expert Jack Lewis, whose two books on "assault weapons" are cited as authoritative by gun control advocates in their briefs defending "assault weapon" bans, writes that almost all the guns dubbed "assault weapons" are well-suited for defensive purposes, although some are too heavy and cumbersome for field sports.[163]

Yet virtually all guns (except for a few highly specialized models such as biathlon trainers) were designed for antipersonnel use. Indeed, the listing of nonbanned "recreational" guns in Appendix A of the federal "assault weapon" law includes three guns with the word "military" in their name.

Almost all guns are made for injuring and killing. It is irrational to ban particular guns based on a characteristic that they share with almost all guns. A law might as well assert that "assault weapons" are uniquely pernicious because they share the characteristic of using gunpowder.

Assuming that there is a real line between sporting guns and antipersonnel guns, and that the "assault weapon" bans draw the line correctly, drawing the line so as to prohibit defensive guns is illegitimate.

Even without reference to a right to keep and bear arms, use of deadly physical force for defense of self and others is lawful in every state; many state Constitutions guarantee a right of self-defense, and the common law recognizes a self-defense right of very long standing.[164] Because self-defense is a lawful activity everywhere, the prohibition of an object simply because it is useful for self-defense rather than for sport cannot be legitimate.[165]

Persons who claim that the Second Amendment protects only "sporting guns" implicitly assert that protection of recreational hunting and target shooting was seen by the authors of the Bill of Rights as some particularly important activity to a free society. The framers, as the "sporting gun" theory goes, apparently intended to exalt sports equipment used in recreational hunting to a level of protection not enjoyed by equipment for any other sport. It is difficult to believe that the Framers would follow an amendment guaranteeing speech, assembly, and the free exercise of religion with an amendment protecting sporting goods.

Moreover, to the extent that there is a real conflict between public safety and sports equipment, public safety should win. Except for shooting in Director of Civilian Marksmanship (DCM) programs, which have been created to enhance civil preparedness, recreational use of "assault weapons" does not directly enhance public safety.[166] Hence, if "assault weapons" posed a substantial threat to public safety, control would be in order because protecting many people from death is more important than enjoying sports. (As the government statistics discussed above indicate, "assault weapons" are rarely used in crime.)

The reason that "assault weapons" have a proper place in the hands of the people is that they are useful for defense—against lone criminals and against criminal governments.

"Assault weapons" are well suited for personal defense against criminals, suggested the technical analysis at the beginning of this chapter. In addition, the guns are suitable for community defense against dangers both internal and external.

Domestic Disorder

As noted above, when antigun police chief Daryl Gates spent the first night of the Los Angeles riots at a fund-raiser to oppose a referendum limiting the Los Angeles police chief's powers, tens of thousands of Los Angeles residents were learning the hard way that government cannot always protect citizens against crime. Many of them used "assault weapons" to protect themselves against rampaging mobs.

Were the Los Angeles riots a bizarre and rare event, in which Americans needed to use semi-automatic firearms to protect their neighborhoods when the police would or could not? Apparently not. In May 1988, the gang known as the Bloods attacked a Los Angeles housing project containing Cambodian-Americans. The Cambodians fought back with M1s and Kalashnikovs and drove away the Bloods.[167]

In 1977, a blizzard in Buffalo, New York, and a flood in Johnstown, Pennsylvania, both prompted local officials to call for citizens to arm themselves and restore the public order.[168] Armed citizens also helped preserve order after Hurricane Andrew hit southern Florida in 1992. In other situations, as in the aftermath of an earthquake or hurricane, there may not even be any public officials around to urge citizens to protect themselves. As recently as World War II, American citizens bearing their own firearms were called to coastal watch and other civil defense duties.[169] In the chaotic frontier circumstances of an area after a natural disaster—or the modern inner city under day-to-day conditions—a reliable, rugged, easy-to-operate firearm is the type of weapon often suitable for the protection of life.

Resistance to Tyranny

There is another purpose for which "assault weapons" are well suited, and that is resistance to tyrannical government. Over the last fifteen years, a vast body of scholarly literature has been produced regarding the original intent of the Second Amendment to the United States Constitution.

The literature has been unanimous in concluding that the main objective of the Second Amendment was to facilitate armed resistance to the federal government. The nearly unanimous conclusion is that armed resistance was to be facilitated by "the people" having a right to keep and bear arms.[170]

The same view has been espoused by many gun rights advocates in the twentieth century, including the late Vice President Hubert Humphrey, who explained: "The right of citizens to bear arms is just one more guarantee against arbitrary government, one more safeguard against the tyranny which now appears remote in America, but which historically has proved to be always possible."[171]

It could be contended, however, that the authors of the Constitution (and Vice President Humphrey) were just a bunch of paranoid gun nuts. There is no need to fear the federal government. "It can't happen here."

It *did* happen here. The conquest of North America by the European settlers of the future United States was accomplished by federal government troops assisting the extermination of many Indian tribes.[172] The forced march of the Cherokee people from the southeast United States into Oklahoma along the "Trail of Tears" resulted in the deaths of a large portion of the Cherokee population, and differs only quantitatively, rather than qualitatively from the twentieth-century genocides in countries such as the Soviet Union, Uganda, Ethiopia, and Guatemala. Hitler looked with admiration at how the United States government had cleared the continent of Indians, and he used this as a model for his own policies of clearing *Lebensraum* (living space) for the German people.

In the twentieth century, the United States government forced 100,000 United States citizens into concentration camps. In 1941, American citizens of Japanese descent were herded into concentration camps. Like the victims of other mass deportations, these Americans were allowed to retain only the property they could carry with them. Everything else—including family businesses built up over generations—had to be sold immediately at fire-sale prices or abandoned. The camps were "ringed with barbed wire-fences and guard towers."[173] During the war, the federal government pushed Central and South American governments to round up persons of Japanese ancestry in those nations and have them shipped to the U.S. concentration camps.[174]

The American concentration camps were not death camps. The Americans held prisoner were subject to strict discipline but not to mass murder.[175] After the American victory at Midway in June 1942, the threat of a Japanese landing on the mainland United States vanished, and the tide in the Pacific began to turn. Nevertheless, the incarceration of Japanese-Americans continued long after any plausible national security justification had vanished.

But what if the war had gone differently? What if a frustrated, angry America, continuing to lose a war in the Pacific, had been tempted to take revenge on the "enemy" that was, in the concentration camps, a safe target.[176] Would killing all the Japanese be a potential policy option? In 1944, by which time America's eventual victory in the war was assured, the Gallup Poll asked Americans, "What do you think we should do with Japan, as a country, after the war?" Thirteen percent of Americans chose the response "Kill all Japanese people."[177]

Sadly, Roger Daniels, the author of a recent study of the Japanese internment, concludes that a concentration camp episode could indeed happen again in America.[178] He points out that in 1950, by which time the oppressiveness and uselessness of the American concentration camps during World War II had been well established, Congress enacted the Emergency Detention Act, which gave the attorney general unilateral authority to imprison Americans at will, using the World War II concentration camps as a model. Fortunately, the law was repealed in 1971; but, as Daniels points out, the original detentions occurred even though they were not authorized by any law.[179]

Disarming citizens before killing or oppressing them is a time-honored American tradition. After the Civil War, the first act of Ku Klux Klan (like the Khmer Rouge), upon moving into a county, was to round up all the guns in the hands of ex-slaves. Only then did other oppressive measures begin.[180] From the middle of the nineteenth century to the first quarter of the twentieth, race riots in the United States usually took the forms of white mobs rampaging against innocent blacks. Black attempts to resist or to shoot back were often followed with governmental efforts to disarm them.[181]

Are modern Americans so dramatically different from their ancestors that concentration camps or mob violence are safely confined to the past? While mayor of New York City, Edward Koch (who is Jewish) proposed that the federal government set up concentration camps for drug users in such remote locations as Nevada and Alaska. Under Mayor David Dinkins, rampaging black mobs conducted a three-day pogrom against a Jewish section of Brooklyn, after a Jewish driver accidentally ran over a black child. They killed an Australian Jew who was visiting the United States, while the police passively refused to intervene.[182]

People such as Louis Farrakhan are now treated as important leaders by an increasingly large segment of the African-American community, including by the NAACP, which for decades before had been steadfastedly opposed to racial hatred and anti-Semitism. In an age of Farrakhan, Al Sharpton, and others is America immune from the influence of bigots, crackpots, hatemongers, or potential dictators? A Klansman and former Nazi named David Duke was elected to the State House of Representatives in Louisiana in 1989. He then won 44 percent of the vote against the incumbent U.S. senator in 1990. The next year, he won 39 percent of the vote in a race for governor, garnering over 60 percent of the vote from the white middle-class and from white Protestants.[183]

What other countries can be presumed forever safe from hatemongering rule? In August 1994, the labor minister of the Italian government (a nation which half a century before had been a Fascist ally of Hitler) blamed the fall of the lira on the "Jewish lobby" in the United States.[184] Virtually none of the world's democratic nations can boast an uninterrupted history of democracy, nor can they claim that racist or anti-Semitic elements are of no significance in their current political life.

Imagine the year is 1900. You are told that within fifty years, a nation in the world will kill over six million members of a religious minority. Which country would you pick? If you were well-informed about world affairs, it is unlikely that you would pick Germany. In 1900, Germany was a democratic, progressive nation. Jews living there enjoyed fuller acceptance in society than they did in Britain, France, or the United States. Thirty-five years later, circumstances had changed. In 1900, probably much less than 13 percent of the German population favored killing all Jews.

The prospect of a dictatorial American government thirty-five years from now seems almost impossible. What about a hundred years from today? Two hundred?

It is possible to say, with reasonable certainty, that "It can't happen here—in the near future." But for the long run, no one can say; the fact that it *did* happen here a century ago, and that American concentration camps were opened in our own century, ought to suggest that only someone willfully blind to American and world history would attempt to guarantee to future generations of potential American victims that "It can't happen here."

If the Second Amendment was intended to facilitate resistance to government, and if American history suggests that it is possible (but unlikely) that armed resistance to government might at some distant point become necessary, is there any chance that citizens could resist successfully? Recent history suggests that the answer is yes.

The most common argument against an armed population as an antidote to tyranny or genocide is that, in the late twentieth century, the balance of power between governments and the people has tipped decisively toward the government side. How can a ragtag collection of citizens with rifles, pistols, and shotguns hope to resist a modern standing army with artillery, helicopters, tanks, jets, and nuclear weapons? Such a question is most frequently posed by persons who have neither personal nor intellectual familiarity with the military or with guerrilla warfare. If we actually try to answer the question, rather than just presume the government will win, then the case for the uselessness of citizen resistance becomes weak indeed.

First of all, the purpose of civilian small arms in any kind of resistance scenario is not to defeat the federal army in a pitched battle, and then triumphantly march into Washington, D.C. Citizen militias and other popular forces, such as guerrilla cadres, have rarely been strong enough to defeat a professional army in a head-on battle. Guerrilla warfare aims to conduct quick surprise raids on the enemy, at a time and place of the guerrillas' choosing. Almost as soon as the first casualties have been inflicted, the guerrillas flee, before the army can bring its superior firepower to bear.

In the early years of a guerrilla war, as Mao Tse-tung explained, before guerrillas are strong enough to attack a professional army head on, heavy weapons would be a detriment, impeding the guerrillas' mobility. As a war progresses, the guerrillas use ordinary firearms to capture better small arms and eventually heavy equipment.[185]

The military history of the twentieth century shows rather clearly that, if guerrillas are willing to wage a prolonged war, they can be quite successful. As one author notes:

Far from proving invincible, in the vast majority of cases in this century in which they have confronted popular insurgencies, modern armies have been unable to suppress the insurgents. This is why the British no longer rule in Israel and Ireland, the French in Indo-China, Algeria, and Madagascar, the Portuguese in Angola, the whites in Rhodesia, or General Somoza, General Battista, or the Shah in Nicaragua, Cuba, and Iran respectively—not to mention the examples of the United States in Vietnam and the Soviet Union in Afghanistan.[186]

Moreover, guerrillas need not overthrow a government in order to accomplish their purposes. During World War II, Yugoslav partisans did not directly overthrow the occupying Nazi government; but they did tie down a large fraction of the German army, leaving the German armies in the Eastern, Western, and Mediterranean fronts that much weaker. As the war ended, the presence of a well-equipped popular fighting force ready to assume power helped convince the advancing Soviet armies not to move into Yugoslavia, and consequently set the foundation for a Yugoslavia that would, relative to the rest of Eastern Europe, be less subject to a Soviet sphere of influence.

A popular guerrilla resistance can also deprive an occupying government of much or all of the economic benefit that would normally be gained by occupation.

And perhaps most importantly, for purposes of this chapter, an armed populace can ensure that any efforts to kill people or to send them to prisons and concentration camps carry a price that must be paid by the government. If the Jews of Nazi-occupied Europe had shot the Nazi soldiers who came to herd them onto cattle cars, Jews would still have been killed, but so would have some of their oppressors. Would the Nazis have had such an easy time sending soldiers into the ghettos to collect the Jews if the soldiers knew that some of them would not come back alive? If the kinds of people who specialize in perpetrating genocide are bullies by nature, how many bullies are willing to take a chance of getting shot by the intended victim? If potential victims of massacre can plausibly threaten to harm at least a few of their attackers, then the calculus of the attackers may change dramatically. As University of Texas law professor Sanford Levinson notes, it is not implausible to argue:

> "[I]f all the Chinese citizens kept arms, their rulers would hardly have dared to massacre the [Tiananmen Square] demonstrators." . . . It is simply silly to respond that small arms are irrelevant against nuclear-armed states . . . a state facing a totally disarmed population is in a far better position, for good or ill, to suppress popular demonstrations and uprisings than one that must calculate the possibilities of its soldiers and officials being injured or killed.[187]

Although the American federal government is the best-armed and wealthiest in the world, so is the American populace. Approximately half of all American households possess a gun. In the United States, there is more than one gun for every adult American. Hundreds of thousands (or millions) of Americans practice "reloading" (the home manufacture of ammunition) as a hobby. As of early 1995, commercial American ammunition makers are producing *well over a million rounds of ammunition per day,* and yet cannot keep up with the immense consumer demand.[188] In response to the "gun control" laws being enacted and proposed in 1993 and 1994, the American gun-owning public has begun stockpiling weapons and ammunition in quantities that may be without historical precedent.

Everything else that a guerrilla army could want is also abundant in America:

binoculars, camouflage (owned by millions of hunters), ham radios and other sophisticated communications equipment, and abundant quantities of well-preserved food.[189]

There is also something else in abundance in America that guerrillas love: places to hide. The great swamps of the South; the thick forests of the Rocky Mountains and the Northwest; and the dense, crowded cities throughout the nation are only a few of the American locales which would be eminently suitable to providing havens for guerrilla fighters.

The American military is also powerful. But the police and military combined (assuming that every soldier and every police officer would assist a dictatorial government) comprise only about 1 percent of the U.S. population.[190] Many of the modern army's most effective weapons—tanks, artillery, and helicopters—are easy to deploy in a Kuwaiti desert but considerably less effective in an urban area. Indeed, a million-dollar tank can be incapacitated by a Molotov Cocktail (a glass bottle filled with gasoline, and topped with a wick that is lit just before the cocktail is thrown).[191] As a last resort, a dictatorial government could resort to nuclear warfare, but such a step would risk provoking the nonmilitant fraction of the population into full-scale rebellion; risk provoking a faction of the army into attempting a coup; and would, by bombing the area, certainly deprive the government of deriving any benefit from it.

Finally, the most important benefit of any defensive arms is their deterrent power. As long as a potential dictator (or a potentially genocidal dictator) must take into account very serious risks involved with taking action against the American people, then the prospect for such action being taken becomes markedly smaller.

No one can forecast exactly what would happen if the American people took up arms against a dictatorial government. But there is no evidence from the history of warfare, or from any other source, to support a simplistic assertion that resistance could not possibly achieve success in any form.

"Assault weapons" are not essential to resistance to tyranny. Freedom-fighters around the world have, with very low-quality weapons, fought effectively against powerful modern armies. But "assault weapons" use light ammunition that is easy to carry long distances. They are rugged, easy to maintain, and easy to shoot accurately. They would be the best guns with which to resist tyranny.

The possibility of a need for an uprising against federal tyranny one day in the distant future is very rare. However, the need for armed protection against criminals and criminal gangs is present in every American city and county. "Assault weapons" are well suited for protection against nongovernmental criminals; making it harder for Americans to own high-quality firearms or twelve-round magazines will reduce the success of lawful self-defense, and increase the number of criminal victimizations.

If it is legitimate to own firearms for protection—and American law clearly says so, even if the gun control lobbies do not agree—then all types of semi-automatic firearms and their magazines have a legitimate place in the hands of the American people.

Evolving Technology

Some proponents of "assault weapons" legislation have argued that even if one recognizes an individual right to bear arms, "assault weapons" are not the type of arms that individuals have a right to bear. While conceding that the framers might have intended that citizens have a right to possess the single-shot rifles, shotguns, and pistols of their day, the gun prohibitionists assert that the Second Amendment never intended to "give" citizens the right to own modern small arms such as semi-automatics.

It is self-evident that the authors of the Second Amendment never intended to protect the right to own semi-automatics specifically, just as they never intended to protect the right to talk privately on a telephone or to broadcast news on a television, since no such technology existed in their day. To assert that Constitutional protections only extend to the technology in existence in 1791 would be to claim that the First Amendment only protects the right to write with quill pens and not with computers, and that the Fourth Amendment only guarantees the right to freedom from unreasonable searches in log cabins and not in homes made from high-tech synthetics.

The Constitution does not protect particular physical objects, such as quill pens, muskets, or log cabins. Instead, it defines a relationship between individuals and the government that is applied to every new technology. For example, in *Katz* v. *United States,* the Court applied the privacy principle underlying the Fourth Amendment to prohibit unwarranted eavesdropping on telephone calls made from a public phone booth—even though telephones had not been invented at the time of the Fourth Amendment.[192] Likewise, the principle underlying freedom of the press—that an unfettered press is an important check on secretive and abusive governments—remains the same whether a publisher uses a Franklin press to produce a hundred copies of a pamphlet or laser printers to produce a hundred thousand.

It is true that an individual who misuses a semi-automatic today can shoot more people than could someone with a musket 150 years ago.[193] Yet if greater harm were sufficient cause to invalidate a right, there would be little left to the Bill of Rights, since modern technology has rendered the misuse of all Constitutional rights more destructive.

Virtually every freedom guaranteed in the Bill of Rights causes some damage to society, such as reputations ruined by libelous newspapers or criminals freed by procedural requirements. The authors of the Constitution knew that legislatures were inclined to focus too narrowly on short-term harms: to think only about society's loss of security from criminals not caught because of search restrictions, and to forget the security gained by privacy and freedom from arbitrary searches. That is precisely why the framers created a Bill of Rights—to put a check on the tendency of legislatures to erode essential rights for short-term gains.

TRUST THE PEOPLE OR TRUST THE GOVERNMENT?

The "assault weapon" controversy wears the mask of a crime control issue, but it is in reality a moral issue. Regardless of whether "assault weapons" are a serious crime problem and whether prohibitions will reduce criminal use of these guns, such weapons have no legitimate place in a civilized society—or so many gun prohibitionists feel. These prohibitionists do not trust their fellow citizens to possess "assault weapons"; but astonishingly, they do trust the government to possess such guns.

Every "assault weapon" prohibition ever enacted or proposed includes an exception for police possession of such weapons. Yet the only reason for police to possess firearms is for protection activities.

If "assault weapons" can legitimately be used for police protection of self and others, then a ban on those guns should not be applied to ordinary citizens, because they, too, have the moral right to bear arms for personal defense and, like the police, face a risk of being attacked by criminals. (And unlike police, ordinary citizens cannot make a radio call for backup that will bring assistance in seconds.) The lives of ordinary citizens are just as valuable as those of police officers, and they are just as entitled to use the best firearms available for protection.[194]

Conversely, are "assault weapons," as some police administrators insist, only made for slaughtering the innocent? If so, such killing machines have no place in the hands of domestic law enforcement. Unlike in less free countries, police in the United States do not need highly destructive weapons designed for murdering many innocent people at once.

"Government is the great teacher," wrote the late Justice Louis Brandeis. What lessons does government teach when police chiefs insist that "assault weapons" have no reasonable defensive use, and are evil machines for killing many innocent people quickly— but that prohibitions on these killing machines should not apply to the police? Are massacres acceptable if perpetrated by the public sector?[195]

In Maryland, the police staged an illegal warrantless raid on a gun rights group's office the night before a gun control referendum in 1988.[196] When pro-Second Amendment protestors picketed at the state capitol, Governor William Donald Schaefer's police photographed them.[197] The police-state tactics in Maryland led one newspaper (which favors gun control as a substantive matter) to note, "Just because you're paranoid doesn't mean they're not out to get you." The paper labeled the tactics of Governor Schaefer and his police a validation of the paranoid worldview allegedly held by proponents of the right to bear arms.[198] Is the Maryland police hierarchy the kind of government agency that should be trusted to disarm citizens, while it keeps "assault weapons" for itself?

After the Tiananmen Square massacre in June 1989, the response of the NRA was to purchase print advertisements suggesting that the core purpose of the Second Amendment is resistance to tyranny. The response of Chicago police superintendent LeRoy Martin—a vociferous advocate of gun prohibition—was to accept a paid trip to China from the Communist government. Upon returning, Chief Martin pronounced his admiration for the Chinese system of criminal justice, and suggested that in the United States zones should be created where the Constitution would be suspended. Is LeRoy Martin the kind of police chief who should be trusted to enforce an "assault weapon" ban, while he keeps such weapons for himself?

If, as the Declaration of Independence suggests, the government is the servant, and the people the master, why should it be assumed that the police are entitled to be better armed than the people? The political theory on which our nation is founded would suggest just the opposite.

SUMMARY

"Assault weapon" laws are not well grounded in fact. Semi-automatic "assault weapons" (which are distinct from actual automatic assault rifles) *do not* fire faster than many guns that are not banned. They *do not* have a larger ammunition capacity. All the other purported physical characteristics of "assault weapons" which form the basis for prohibition simply are either not true (such as claims about ammunition lethality), or are trivial (such as bayonet lugs), or are designed to make the gun more accurate (such as muzzle brakes). Police statistics prove that so-called assault weapons are only rarely involved in criminal activity. The ban on "assault weapons" because they are said to be better for protection than for recreation is illegitimate, because use of deadly force for protection is lawful in the United States.

The demand for "assault weapon" prohibition is often accompanied by a self-righteous insistence that only a criminal or a maniac would oppose prohibition of extremely dangerous firearms which are the criminal weapon of choice, and for which there is no legitimate use. But the closer one looks at "assault weapon" prohibition, the less there is. The cornerstone of a rational gun policy should be prompt repeal of such an irrational gun prohibition.

APPENDIX A

"Assault Weapon" ban signed into law in September 1994 by President Clinton. The law is reproduced as it appeared in the federal crime bill.

TITLE XI—FIREARMS

Subtitle A—Assault Weapons

SEC. 110101. SHORT TITLE. [Note: The six-digit section numbers refer to sections of the crime bill; the numbers are not part of the law as it appears in the United States Code.]

This subtitle may be cited as the "Public Safety and Recreational Firearms Use Protection Act".

SEC. 110102. RESTRICTION ON MANUFACTURE, TRANSFER, AND POSSESSION OF CERTAIN SEMI-AUTOMATIC ASSAULT WEAPONS.

(a) RESTRICTION. Section 922 of title 18, United States Code, is amended by adding at the end the following new subsection:

(v)(1) It shall be unlawful for a person to manufacture, transfer, or possess a semi-automatic assault weapon.

(2) Paragraph (1) shall not apply to the possession or transfer of any semi-automatic assault weapon otherwise lawfully possessed under Federal law on the date of the enactment of this subsection.

(3) Paragraph (1) shall not apply to—

(A) any of the firearms, or replicas or duplicates of the firearms, specified in Appendix A to this section, as such firearms were manufactured on October 1, 1993;

(B) any firearm that—
(i)   is manually operated by bolt, pump, lever, or slide action;
(ii) has been rendered permanently inoperable; or
(iii) is an antique firearm;

(C) any semi-automatic rifle that cannot accept a detachable magazine that holds more than five rounds of ammunition; or

(D) any semi-automatic shotgun that cannot hold more than five rounds of ammunition in a fixed or detachable magazine.

The fact that a firearm is not listed in Appendix A shall not be construed to mean that paragraph (1) applies to such firearm. No firearm exempted by this subsection may be deleted from Appendix A so long as this subsection is in effect.

(4) Paragraph (1) shall not apply to—

(A) the manufacture for, transfer to, or possession by the United States or a department or agency of the United States or a State or a department, agency, or political subdivision of a State, or a transfer to or possession by a law enforcement officer employed by such an entity for purposes of law enforcement (whether on or off duty);

(B) the transfer to a licensee under title I of the Atomic Energy Act of 1954 for purposes of establishing and maintaining an on-site physical protection system and security organization required by Federal law, or possession by an employee or contractor of such licensee on-site for such purposes or off-site for purposes of licensee-authorized training or transportation of nuclear materials;

(C) the possession, by an individual who is retired from service with a law enforcement agency and is not otherwise prohibited from receiving a firearm, of a semi-automatic assault weapon transferred to the individual by the agency upon such retirement; or

(D) the manufacture, transfer, or possession of a semi-automatic assault weapon by a licensed manufacturer or licensed importer for the purposes of testing or experimentation authorized by the Secretary."

(b) DEFINITION OF SEMI-AUTOMATIC ASSAULT WEAPON. Section 921(a) of title 18, United States Code, is amended by adding at the end the following new paragraph:

(30) The term 'semi-automatic assault weapon' means—

(A) any of the firearms, or copies or duplicates of the firearms in any caliber, known as—

    (i)   Norinco, Mitchell, and Poly Technologies Avtomat Kalashnikovs (all models);

    (ii)   Action Arms Israeli Military Industries UZI and Galil;

    (iii) Beretta Ar70 (SC-70);

    (iv) Colt AR-15;

    (v)   Fabrique National FN/FAL, FN/LAR, and FNC;

    (vi) SWD M-10, M-11, M-11/9, and M-12;

    (vii) Steyr AUG;

    (viii) INTRATEC TEC-9, TEC-DC9 and TEC-22; and

    (ix) revolving cylinder shotguns, such as (or similar to) the Street Sweeper and Striker 12;

(B) a semi-automatic rifle that has an ability to accept a detachable magazine and has at least two of—

    (i)   a folding or telescoping stock;

    (ii)   a pistol grip that protrudes conspicuously beneath the action of the weapon;

    (iii) a bayonet mount;

    (iv) a flash suppressor or threaded barrel designed to accommodate a flash suppressor; and

    (v)   a grenade launcher;

(C) a semi-automatic pistol that has an ability to accept a detachable magazine and has at least two of—

    (i)   an ammunition magazine that attaches to the pistol outside of the pistol grip;

    (ii)   a threaded barrel capable of accepting a barrel extender, flash suppressor, forward handgrip, or silencer;

    (iii) a shroud that is attached to, or partially or completely encircles, the barrel and that permits the shooter to hold the firearm with the nontrigger hand without being burned;

    (iv) a manufactured weight of fifty ounces or more when the pistol is unloaded; and

    (v)   a semi-automatic version of an automatic firearm; and

(D) a semi-automatic shotgun that has at least two of—

    (i)   a folding or telescoping stock;

    (ii)   a pistol grip that protrudes conspicuously beneath the action of the weapon;

    (iii) a fixed magazine capacity in excess of five rounds; and

    (iv) "an ability to accept a detachable magazine."

(c) PENALTIES.

(1) VIOLATION OF SECTION 922(v). Section 924(a)(1)(B) of such title is amended by striking "or (q) of section 922" and inserting "(r), or (v) of section 922".

(2) USE OR POSSESSION DURING CRIME OF VIOLENCE OR DRUG TRAFFICKING CRIME. Section 924(c)(1) of such title is amended in the first sentence by inserting ", or semi-automatic assault weapon," after "short-barreled shotgun,".

(d) IDENTIFICATION MARKINGS FOR SEMI-AUTOMATIC ASSAULT WEAPONS. Section 923(i) of such title is amended by adding at the end the following: "The serial number of any semi-automatic assault weapon manufactured after the date of the enactment of this sentence shall clearly show the date on which the weapon was manufactured."

SEC. 110103. BAN OF LARGE CAPACITY AMMUNITION FEEDING DEVICES.

(a) PROHIBITION. Section 922 of title 18, United States Code, as amended by section 110102(a), is amended by adding at the end the following new subsection:

(w)(1) Except as provided in paragraph (2), it shall be unlawful for a person to transfer or possess a large capacity ammunition feeding device.

(2) Paragraph (1) shall not apply to the possession or transfer of any large-capacity ammunition feeding device otherwise lawfully possessed on or before the date of the enactment of this subsection.

(3) This subsection shall not apply to—

(A) the manufacture for, transfer to, or possession by the United States or a department or agency of the United States or a State or a department, agency, or political subdivision of a State, or a transfer to or possession by a law enforcement officer employed by such an entity for purposes of law enforcement (whether on or off duty);

(B) the transfer to a licensee under title I of the Atomic Energy Act of 1954 for purposes of establishing and maintaining an on-site physical protection system and security organization required by Federal law, or possession by an employee or contractor of such licensee on-site for such purposes or off-site for purposes of licensee-authorized training or transportation of nuclear materials;

(C) the possession, by an individual who is retired from service with a law enforcement agency and is not otherwise prohibited from receiving ammunition, of a large capacity ammunition feeding device transferred to the individual by the agency upon such retirement; or

(D) the manufacture, transfer, or possession of any large capacity ammunition feeding device by a licensed manufacturer or licensed importer for the purposes of testing or experimentation authorized by the Secretary.

(4) If a person charged with violating paragraph (1) asserts that paragraph (1) does not apply to such person because of paragraph (2) or (3), the Government shall have the burden of proof to show that such paragraph (1) applies to such person. The lack of a serial number as described in section 923(i) of title 18, United States Code, shall be a

presumption that the large capacity ammunition feeding device is not subject to the prohibition of possession in paragraph (1).

(b) DEFINITION OF LARGE-CAPACITY AMMUNITION-FEEDING DEVICE. Section 921(a) of title 18, United States Code, as amended by section 110102(b), is amended by adding at the end the following new paragraph:

(31)   The term 'large-capacity ammunition-feeding device'—

(A)   means a magazine, belt, drum, feed strip, or similar device manufactured after the date of enactment of the Violent Crime Control and Law Enforcement Act of 1994 that has a capacity of, or that can be readily restored or converted to accept, more than ten rounds of ammunition; but

(B)   does not include an attached tubular device designed to accept, and capable of operating only with, .22 caliber rimfire ammunition.

(c) PENALTY. Section 924(a)(1)(B) of title 18, United States Code, as amended by section 110102(c)(1), is amended by striking "or (v)" and inserting "(v), or (w)".

(d) IDENTIFICATION MARKINGS FOR LARGE-CAPACITY AMMUNITION-FEEDING DEVICES. Section 923(i) of title 18, United States Code, as amended by section 110102(d) of this Act, is amended by adding at the end the following: "A large-capacity ammunition-feeding device manufactured after the date of the enactment of this sentence shall be identified by a serial number that clearly shows that the device was manufactured or imported after the effective date of this subsection, and such other identification as the Secretary may by regulation prescribe."

SEC. 110104. STUDY BY ATTORNEY GENERAL.

(a) STUDY. The Attorney General shall investigate and study the effect of this subtitle and the amendments made by this subtitle, and in particular shall determine their impact, if any, on violent and drug trafficking crime. The study shall be conducted over a period of eighteen months, commencing twelve months after the date of enactment of this Act.

(b) REPORT. Not later than thirty months after the date of enactment of this Act, the Attorney General shall prepare and submit to the Congress a report setting forth in detail the findings and determinations made in the study under subsection (a).

SEC. 110105. EFFECTIVE DATE.

This subtitle and the amendments made by this subtitle—

(1) shall take effect on the date of the enactment of this Act; and

(2) are repealed effective as of the date that is ten years after that date.

SEC. 110106. APPENDIX A TO SECTION 922 OF TITLE 18.

Section 922 of title 18, United States Code, is amended by adding at the end the following appendix:

APPENDIX B

Centerfire Rifles—Autoloaders

Browning BAR Mark II Safari Semi-Auto Rifle, Browning BAR Mark II Safari Magnum Rifle, Browning High-Power Rifle, Heckler & Koch Model 300 Rifle, Iver Johnson M-1 Carbine, Iver Johnson 50th Anniversary M-1 Carbine, Marlin Model 9 Camp, Carbine, Marlin Model 45 Carbine, Remington Nylon 66 Auto-Loading Rifle, Remington Model 7400 Auto Rifle, Remington Model 7400 Rifle, Remington Model 7400 Special Purpose Auto Rifle, Ruger Mini-14 Autoloading Rifle (w/o folding stock), Ruger Mini Thirty Rifle

Centerfire Rifles—Lever and Slide

Browning Model 81 BLR Lever-Action Rifle, Browning Model 81 Long Action BLR, Browning Model 1886 Lever-Action Carbine, Browning Model 1886 High Grade Carbine, Cimarron 1860 Henry Replica, Cimarron 1866 Winchester Replicas, Cimarron 1873 Short Rifle, Cimarron 1873 Sporting Rifle, Cimarron 1873 30" Express Rifle, Dixie Engraved 1873 Rifle, E.M.F. 1866 Yellowboy Lever Actions, E.M.F. 1860 Henry Rifle, E.M.F. Model 73 Lever-Action Rifle, Marlin Model 336CS Lever-Action Carbine, Marlin Model 30AS Lever-Action Carbine, Marlin Model 444SS Lever-Action Sporter, Marlin Model 1894S Lever-Action Carbine, Marlin Model 1894CS Carbine, Marlin Model 1894CL Classic, Marlin Model 1895SS Lever-Action Rifle, Mitchell 1858 Henry Replica, Mitchell 1866 Winchester Replica, Mitchell 1873 Winchester Replica, Navy Arms Military Henry Rifle, Navy Arms Henry Trapper, Navy Arms Iron Frame Henry, Navy Arms Henry Carbine, Navy Arms 1866 Yellowboy Rifle, Navy Arms 1873 Winchester-Style Rifle, Navy Arms 1873 Sporting Rifle, Remington 7600 Slide Action, Remington Model 7600 Special Purpose Slide Action, Rossi M92 SRC Saddle-Ring Carbine, Rossi M92 SRS Short Carbine Savage 99C Lever-Action Rifle, Uberti Henry Rifle, Uberti 1866 Sporting Rifle, Uberti 1873 Sporting Rifle, Winchester Model 94 Slide Eject Lever-Action Rifle, Winchester Model 94 Trapper Side Eject, Winchester Model 94 Big Bore Side Eject, Winchester Model 94 Ranger Side Eject Lever-Action Rifle, Winchester Model 94 Wrangler Side Eject

Centerfire Rifles—Bolt Action

Alpine Bolt-Action Rifle, A-Square Caesar Bolt-Action Rifle, A-Square Hannibal Bolt-Action Rifle, Anschutz 1700D Classic Rifles, Anschutz 1700D Custom Rifles, Anschutz 1700D Bavarian Bolt-Action Rifle, Anschutz 1733D Mannlicher Rifle, Barret Model 90 Bolt-Action Rifle, Beeman/HW 60J Bolt-Action Rifle, Blaser R84 Bolt-Action Rifle, BRNO 537 Sporter Bolt-Action Rifle, BRNO ZKB 527 Fox Bolt-Action Rifle, BRNO ZKK 600, 601, 602 Bolt-Action Rifles, Browning A-Bolt Rifle, Browning A-Bolt Stainless Stalker, Browning A-Bolt Left Hand, Browning A-Bolt Short Action, Browning Euro-Bolt Rifle, Browning A-Bolt Gold Medallion, Browning A-Bolt Micro Medallion, Century Centurion 14 Sporter, Century Enfield Sporter #4, Century Swedish Sporter #38, Century Mauser 98 Sporter, Cooper Model 38 Centerfire Sporter, Dakota 22 Sporter Bolt-Action Rifle, Dakota 76 Classic Bolt-Action Rifle, Dakota 76 Short Action Rifles, Dakota 76 Safari Bolt-Action Rifle, Dakota 416 Rigby African, E.A.A./Sabatti Rover 870 Bolt-Action Rifle, Auguste Francotte Bolt-Action Rifles, Carl Gustaf 2000 Bolt-Action Rifle, Heym Magnum Express Series Rifle, Howa Lightning Bolt-Action Rifle, Howa Realtree Camo Rifle, Interarms Mark X Viscount Bolt-Action Rifle, Interarms Mini-Mark X Rifle, Interarms Mark X Whitworth Bolt-Action Rifle, Interarms Whitworth Express Rifle, Iver Johnson Model 5100A1 Long-Range Rifle, KDF K15 American Bolt-Action Rifle, Krico Model 600 Bolt-Action Rifle, Krico Model 700 Bolt-Action Rifles, Mauser Model 66 Bolt-Action Rifle, Mauser Model 99 Bolt-Action Rifle, McMillan Signature Classic Sporter, McMillan Signature Super Varminter, McMillan Signature Alaskan, McMillan Signature Titanium Mountain Rifle, McMillan Classic Stainless Sporter, McMillan Talon Safari Rifle, McMillan Talon Sporter Rifle, Midland 1500S Survivor Rifle, Navy Arms TU-33/40 Carbine Parker-Hale Model 81 Classic Rifle, Parker-Hale Model 81 Classic African Rifle Parker-Hale Model 1000 Rifle, Parker-Hale Model 1100M African Magnum, Parker-Hale Model 1100 Lightweight Rifle, Parker-Hale Model 1200 Super Rifle, Parker-Hale Model 1200 Super Clip Rifle, Parker-Hale Model 1300C Scout Rifle, Parker-Hale Model 2100 Midland Rifle, Parker-Hale Model 2700 Lightweight Rifle, Parker-Hale Model 2800 Midland Rifle, Remington Model Seven Bolt-Action Rifle, Remington Model Seven Youth Rifle, Remington Model Seven Custom KS, Remington Model Seven Custom MS Rifle, Remington 700 ADL Bolt-Action Rifle, Remington 700 BDL Bolt-Action Rifle, Remington 700 BDL Varmint Special, Remington 700 BDL European Bolt-Action Rifle, Remington 700 Varmint Synthetic Rifle, Remington 700 BDL SS Rifle, Remington 700 Stainless Synthetic Rifle, Remington 700 MTRSS Rifle, Remington 700 BDL Left Hand, Remington 700 Camo Synthetic Rifle, Remington 700 Safari, Remington 700 Mountain Rifle, Remington 700 Custom KS Mountain Rifle, Remington 700 Classic Rifle, Ruger M77 Mark II Rifle, Ruger M77 Mark II Magnum Rifle, Ruger M77RL Ultra Light, Ruger M77 Mark II All-Weather Stainless

Rifle, Ruger M77 RSI International Carbine, Ruger M77 Mark II Express Rifle, Ruger M77VT Target Rifle, Sako Hunter Rifle, Sako Fiberglass Sporter, Sako Safari Grade Bolt Action, Sako Hunter Left-Hand Rifle, Sako Classic Bolt Action, Sako Hunter LS Rifle, Sako Deluxe Lightweight, Sako Super Deluxe Sporter, Sako Mannlicher-Style Carbine, Sako Varmint Heavy Barrel, Sako TRG-S Bolt-Action Rifle, Sauer 90 Bolt-Action Rifle, Savage 110G Bolt-Action Rifle, Savage 110CY Youth/Ladies Rifle, Savage 110WLE One of One Thousand Limited Edition Rifle, Savage 110GXP3 Bolt-Action Rifle, Savage 110F Bolt-Action Rifle, Savage 110FXP3 Bolt-Action Rifle, Savage 110GV Varmint Rifle, Savage 112FV Varmint Rifle, Savage Model 112FVS Varmint Rifle, Savage Model 112BV Heavy Barrel Varmint Rifle, Savage 116FSS Bolt-Action Rifle, Savage Model 116FSK Kodiak Rifle, Savage 110FP Police Rifle, Steyr-Mannlicher Sporter Models SL, L, M, S, S/T, Steyr-Mannlicher Luxus Model L, M, S, Steyr-Mannlicher Model M Professional Rifle, Tikka Bolt-Action Rifle, Tikka Premium Grade Rifles, Tikka Varmint/Continental Rifle, Tikka Whitetail/Battue Rifle, Ultra Light Arms Model 20 Rifle, Ultra Light Arms Model 28, Model 40 Rifles, Voere VEC 91 Lightning Bolt-Action Rifle, Voere Model 2165 Bolt-Action Rifle, Voere Model 2155, 2150 Bolt-Action Rifles, Weatherby Mark V Deluxe Bolt-Action Rifle, Weatherby Lasermark V Rifle, Weatherby Mark V Crown Custom Rifles, Weatherby Mark V Sporter Rifle, Weatherby Mark V Safari Grade Custom Rifles, Weatherby Weathermark Rifle, Weatherby Weathermark Alaskan Rifle, Weatherby Classicmark No. 1 Rifle, Weatherby Weatherguard Alaskan Rifle, Weatherby Vanguard VGX Deluxe Rifle, Weatherby Vanguard Classic Rifle, Weatherby Vanguard Classic No. 1 Rifle, Weatherby Vanguard Weatherguard Rifle, Wichita Classic Rifle, Wichita Varmint Rifle, Winchester Model 70 Sporter, Winchester Model 70 Sporter WinTuff, Winchester Model 70 SM Sporter, Winchester Model 70 Stainless Rifle, Winchester Model 70 Varmint, Winchester Model 70 Synthetic Heavy Varmint Rifle, Winchester Model 70 DBM Rifle, Winchester Model 70 DBM-S Rifle, Winchester Model 70 Featherweight, Winchester Model 70 Featherweight WinTuff, Winchester Model 70 Featherweight Classic, Winchester Model 70 Lightweight Rifle, Winchester Ranger Rifle, Winchester Model 70 Super Express Magnum, Winchester Model 70 Super Grade, Winchester Model 70 Custom Sharpshooter, Winchester Model 70 Custom Sporting Sharpshooter Rifle

Centerfire Rifles—Single Shot

Armsport 1866 Sharps Rifle, Carbine, Brown Model One Single Shot Rifle, Browning Model 1885 Single Shot Rifle, Dakota Single Shot Rifle, Desert Industries G-90 Single Shot Rifle, Harrington & Richardson Ultra Varmint Rifle, Model 1885 High Wall Rifle, Navy Arms Rolling Block Buffalo Rifle, Navy Arms #2 Creedmoor Rifle, Navy Arms Sharps Cavalry Carbine, Navy Arms Sharps Plains Rifle, New England Firearms Handi-Rifle, Red Willow Armory

Ballard No. 5 Pacific, Red Willow Armory Ballard No. 1.5 Hunting Rifle, Red Willow Armory Ballard No. 8 Union Hill Rifle, Red Willow Armory Ballard No. 4.5 Target Rifle, Remington-Style Rolling Block Carbine, Ruger No. 1B Single Shot, Ruger No. 1A Light Sporter, Ruger No. 1H Tropical Rifle, Ruger No. 1S Medium Sporter, Ruger No. 1 RSI International, Ruger No. 1V Special Varminter, C. Sharps Arms New Model 1874 Old Reliable, C. Sharps Arms New Model 1875 Rifle, C. Sharps Arms 1875 Classic Sharps, C. Sharps Arms New Model 1875 Target & Long Range, Shiloh Sharps 1874 Long Range Express, Shiloh Sharps 1874 Montana Roughrider, Shiloh Sharps 1874 Military Carbine, Shiloh Sharps 1874 Business Rifle, Shiloh Sharps 1874 Military Rifle, Sharps 1874 Old Reliable, Thompson/Center Contender Carbine, Thompson/Center Stainless Contender Carbine, Thompson/Center Contender Carbine Survival System, Thompson/Center Contender Carbine Youth Model, Thompson/Center TCR '87 Single Shot Rifle, Uberti Rolling Block Baby Carbine

Drillings, Combination Guns, Double Rifles

Beretta Express SSO O/U Double Rifles, Beretta Model 455 SxS Express Rifle, Chapuis RG Express Double Rifle, Auguste Francotte Sidelock Double Rifles, Auguste Francotte Boxlock Double Rifle, Heym Model 55B O/U Double Rifle, Heym Model 55FW O/U Combo Gun, Heym Model 88b Side-by-Side Double Rifle, Kodiak Mk. IV Double Rifle, Kreighoff Teck O/U Combination Gun, Kreighoff Trumpf Drilling, Merkel Over/Under Combination Guns, Merkel Drillings Merkel Model 160 Side-by-Side Double Rifles, Merkel Over/Under Double Rifles, Savage 24F O/U Combination Gun, Savage 24F-12T Turkey Gun, Springfield Inc. M6 Scout Rifle/Shotgun, Tikka Model 412s Combination Gun, Tikka Model 412S Double Fire, A. Zoli Rifle-Shotgun O/U Combo

Rimfire Rifles—Autoloaders

AMT Lightning 25/22 rifle, AMT Lightning Small-Game Hunting Rifle II, AMT Magnum Hunter Auto Rifle, Anschutz 525 Deluxe Auto, Armscor Model 20P Auto Rifle, Browning Auto-22 Rifle, Browning Auto-22 Grade VI, Krico Model 260 Auto Rifle, Lakefield Arms Model 64B Auto Rifle, Marlin Model 60 Self-Loading Rifle, Marlin Model 60ss Self-Loading Rifle, Marlin Model 70 HC Auto, Marlin Model 990l Self-Loading Rifle, Marlin Model 70P Papoose, Marlin Model 922 Magnum Self-Loading Rifle, Marlin Model 995 Self-Loading Rifle, Norinco Model 22 ATD Rifle, Remington Model 522 Viper Autoloading Rifle, Remington 552BDL Speedmaster Rifle, Ruger 10/22 Autoloading Carbine (w/o folding stock), Survival Arms AR-7 Explorer Rifle, Texas Remington Revolving Carbine, Voere Model 2115 Auto Rifle

Rimfire Rifles—Lever and Slide Action

Browning BL-22 Lever-Action Rifle, Marlin 39TDS Carbine, Marlin Model 39AS Golden Lever-Action Rifle, Remington 572BDL Fieldmaster Pump Rifle, Norinco EM-321 Pump Rifle, Rossi Model 62 SA Pump Rifle, Rossi Model 62 SAC Carbine, Winchester Model 9422 Lever-Action Rifle, Winchester Model 9422 Magnum Lever-Action Rifle

Rimfire Rifles—Bolt Actions and Single Shots

Anschutz Achiever Bolt-Action Rifle, Anschutz 1416D/1516D Classic Rifles, Anschutz 1418D/1518D Mannlicher Rifles, Anschutz 1700D Classic Rifles, Anschutz 1700D Custom Rifles, Anschutz 1700 FWT Bolt-Action Rifle, Anschutz 1700D Graphite Custom Rifle, Anschutz 1700D Bavarian Bolt-Action Rifle, Armscor Model 14P Bolt-Action Rifle, Armscor Model 1500 Rifle, BRNO ZKM-452 Deluxe Bolt-Action Rifle, BRNO ZKM 452 Deluxe, Beeman/HW 60-J-ST Bolt-Action Rifle, Browning A-Bolt 22 Bolt-Action Rifle, Browning A-Bolt Gold Medallion, Cabanas Phaser Rifle, Cabanas Master Bolt-Action Rifle, Cabanas Espronceda IV Bolt-Action Rifle, Cabanas Leyre Bolt-Action Rifle, Chipmunk Single Shot Rifle, Cooper Arms Model 36S Sporter Rifle, Dakota 22 Sporter Bolt-Action Rifle, Krico Model 300 Bolt-Action Rifles, Lakefield Arms Mark II Bolt-Action Rifle, Lakefield Arms Mark I Bolt-Action Rifle, Magtech Model MT-22C Bolt-Action Rifle, Marlin Model 880 Bolt-Action Rifle, Marlin Model 881 Bolt-Action Rifle, Marlin Model 882 Bolt-Action Rifle, Marlin Model 883 Bolt-Action Rifle, Marlin Model 883SS Bolt-Action Rifle, Marlin Model 25MN Bolt-Action Rifle, Marlin Model 25N Bolt-Action Repeater, Marlin Model 15YN "Little Buckaroo," Mauser Model 107 Bolt-Action Rifle, Mauser Model 201 Bolt-Action Rifle, Navy Arms TU-KKW Training Rifle, Navy Arms TU-33/40 Carbine, Navy Arms TU-KKW Sniper Trainer, Norinco JW-27 Bolt-Action Rifle, Norinco JW-15 Bolt-Action Rifle, Remington 541-T, Remington 40-XR Rimfire Custom Sporter, Remington 541-T HB Bolt-Action Rifle, Remington 581-S Sportsman Rifle, Ruger 77/22 Rimfire Bolt-Action Rifle, Ruger K77/22 Varmint Rifle, Ultra Light Arms Model 20 RF Bolt-Action Rifle, Winchester Model 52B Sporting Rifle

Competition Rifles—Centerfire and Rimfire

Anschutz 64-ms Left Silhouette, Anschutz 1808D RT Super Match 54 Target, Anschutz 1827B Biathlon Rifle, Anschutz 1903D Match Rifle, Anschutz 1803D Intermediate Match, Anschutz 1911 Match Rifle, Anschutz 54.18MS REP Deluxe Silhouette Rifle, Anschutz 1913 Super Match Rifle, Anschutz 1907 Match Rifle, Anschutz 1910 Super Match II, Anschutz 54.18MS Silhouette Rifle, Anschutz Super Match 54 Target Model 2013, Anschutz Super Match 54 Target Model

2007, Beeman/Feinwerkbau 2600 Target Rifle, Cooper Arms Model TRP-1 ISU Standard Rifle, E.A.A./Weihrauch HW 60 Target Rifle, E.A.A./HW 660 Match Rifle, Finnish Lion Standard Target Rifle, Krico Model 360 S2 Biathlon Rifle, Krico Model 400 Match Rifle, Krico Model 360S Biathlon Rifle, Krico Model 500 Kricotronic Match Rifle, Krico Model 600 Sniper Rifle, Krico Model 600 Match Rifle, Lakefield Arms Model 90B Target Rifle, Lakefield Arms Model 91T Target Rifle, Lakefield Arms Model 92S Silhouette Rifle, Marlin Model 2000 Target Rifle, Mauser Model 86-SR Specialty Rifle, McMillan M-86 Sniper Rifle, McMillan Combo M-87/M-88 50-Caliber Rifle, McMillan 300 Phoenix Long Range Rifle, McMillan M-89 Sniper Rifle, McMillan National Match Rifle, McMillan Long Range Rifle, Parker-Hale M-87 Target Rifle, Parker-Hale M-85 Sniper Rifle, Remington 40-XB Rangemaster Target Centerfire, Remington 40-XR KS Rimfire Position Rifle, Remington 40-XBBR KS, Remington 40-XC KS National Match Course Rifle, Sako TRG-21 Bolt-Action Rifle, Steyr-Mannlicher Match SPG-UIT Rifle, Steyr-Mannlicher SSG P-I Rifle, Steyr-Mannlicher SSG P-III Rifle, Steyr-Mannlicher SSG P-IV Rifle, Tanner Standard UIT Rifle, Tanner 50 Meter Free Rifle, Tanner 300 Meter Free Rifle, Wichita Silhouette Rifle

Shotguns—Autoloaders

American Arms/Franchi Black Magic 48/AL, Benelli Super Black Eagle Shotgun, Benelli Super Black Eagle Slug Gun, Benelli M1 Super 90 Field Auto Shotgun, Benelli Montefeltro Super 90 20-Gauge Shotgun, Benelli Montefeltro Super 90 Shotgun, Benelli M1 Sporting Special Auto Shotgun, Benelli Black Eagle Competition Auto Shotgun, Beretta A-303 Auto Shotgun, Beretta 390 Field Auto Shotgun, Beretta 390 Super Trap Super Skeet Shotguns, Beretta Vittoria Auto Shotgun, Beretta Model 1201F Auto Shotgun, Browning BSA 10 Auto Shotgun, Browning BSA 10 Stalker Auto Shotgun, Browning A-500R Auto Shotgun, Browning A-500G Auto Shotgun, Browning A-500G Sporting Clays, Browning Auto-5 Light 12 and 20, Browning Auto-5 Stalker, Browning Auto-5 Magnum 20, Browning Auto-5 Magnum 12 Churchill Turkey Automatic Shotgun, Cosmi Automatic Shotgun, Maverick Model 60 Auto Shotgun, Mossberg Model 5500 Shotgun, Mossberg Model 9200 Regal Semi-Auto Shotgun, Mossberg Model 9200 USST Auto Shotgun, Mossberg Model 9200 Camo Shotgun, Mossberg Model 6000 Auto Shotgun, Remington Model 1100 Shotgun, Remington 11-87 Premier Shotgun, Remington 11-87 Sporting Clays, Remington 11-87 Premier Skeet, Remington 11-87 Premier Trap, Remington 11-87 Special Purpose Magnum, Remington 11-87 SPS-T Camo Auto Shotgun, Remington 11-87 Special Purpose Deer Gun, Remington 11-87 SPS-BG-Camo Deer/Turkey Shotgun, Remington 11-87 SPS-Deer Shotgun, Remington 11-87 Special Purpose Synthetic Camo, Remington SP-10 Magnum-Camo Auto Shotgun, Remington SP-10 Magnum Auto Shotgun, Remington SP-10 Magnum

Turkey Combo, Remington 1100 LT-20 Auto, Remington 1100 Special Field, Remington 1100 20-Gauge Deer Gun, Remington 1100 LT-20 Tournament Skeet, Winchester Model 1400 Semi-Auto Shotgun

Shotguns—Slide Actions

Browning Model 42 pump Shotgun, Browning BPS Pump Shotgun, Browning BPS Stalker Pump Shotgun, Browning BPS Pigeon Grade Pump Shotgun, Browning BPS Pump Shotgun (Ladies and Youth Model), Browning BPS Game Gun Turkey Special, Browning BPS Game Gun Deer Special, Ithaca Model 87 Supreme Pump Shotgun, Ithaca Model 87 Deerslayer Shotgun, Ithaca Deerslayer II Rifled Shotgun, Ithaca Model 87 Turkey Gun, Ithaca Model 87 Deluxe Pump Shotgun, Magtech Model 586-VR Pump Shotgun, Maverick Models 88, 91 Pump Shotguns, Mossberg Model 500 Sporting Pump, Mossberg Model 500 Camo Pump, Mossberg Model 500 Muzzleloader Combo, Mossberg Model 500 Trophy Slugster, Mossberg Turkey Model 500 Pump, Mossberg Model 500 Bantam Pump, Mossberg Field Grade Model 835 Pump Shotgun, Mossberg Model 835 Regal Ulti-Mag Pump, Remington 870 Wingmaster, Remington 870 Special Purpose Deer Gun, Remington 870 SPS-BG-Camo Deer/Turkey Shotgun, Remington 870 SPS-Deer Shotgun, Remington 870 Marine Magnum, Remington 870 TC Trap, Remington 870 Special Purpose Synthetic Camo, Remington 870 Wingmaster Small Gauges, Remington 870 Express Rifle Sighted Deer Gun, Remington 879 SPS Special Purpose Magnum, Remington 870 SPS-T Camo Pump Shotgun, Remington 870 Special Field, Remington 870 Express Turkey, Remington 870 High Grades, Remington 870 Express, Remington Model 870 Express Youth Gun, Winchester Model 12 Pump Shotgun, Winchester Model 42 High Grade Shotgun, Winchester Model 1300 Walnut Pump, Winchester Model 1300 Slug Hunter Deer Gun, Winchester Model 1300 Ranger Pump Gun Combo & Deer Gun, Winchester Model 1300 Turkey Gun, Winchester Model 1300 Ranger Pump Gun

Shotguns—Over/Unders

American Arms/Franchi Falconet 2000 O/U, American Arms Silver I O/U, American Arms Silver II Shotgun, American Arms Silver Skeet O/U, American Arms/Franchi Sporting 2000 O/U, American Arms Silver Sporting O/U, American Arms Silver Trap O/U, American Arms WS/OU 12 TS/OU 12 Shotguns, American Arms WT/OU 10 Shotgun, Armsport 2700 O/U Goose Gun, Armsport 2700 Series O/U, Armsport 2900 Tri-Barrel Shotgun, Baby Bretton Over/Under Shotgun, Beretta Model 686 Ultralight O/U, Beretta ASE 90 Competition O/U Shotgun, Beretta Over/Under Field Shotguns, Beretta Onyx Hunter Sport O/U Shotgun, Beretta Model SO5, SO6, SO9 Shotguns, Beretta Sporting Clay Shotguns, Beretta 687EL Sporting O/U, Beretta 682 Super

Sporting O/U, Beretta Series 682 Competition Over/Unders, Browning Citori O/U Shotgun, Browning Superlight Citori Over/Under, Browning Lightning Sporting Clays, Browning Micro Citori Lightning, Browning Citori Plus Trap Combo, Browning Citori Plus Trap Gun, Browning Citori O/U Skeet Models, Browning Citori O/U Trap Models, Browning Special Sporting Clays, Browning Citori GTI Sporting Clays, Browning 325 Sporting Clays, Centurion Over/Under Shotgun, Chapuis Over/Under Shotgun, Connecticut Valley Classics Classic Sporter O/U, Connecticut Valley Classics Classic Field Waterfowler, Charles Daly Field Grade O/U, Charles Daly Lux Over/Under, E.A.A./Sabatti Sporting Clays Pro-Gold O/U, E.A.A/Sabatti Falcon-Mon Over/Under, Kassnar Grade I O/U Shotgun, Krieghoff K-80 Sporting Clays O/U, Krieghoff K-80 Skeet Shotgun, Krieghoff K-80 International Skeet, Krieghoff K-80 Four-Barrel Skeet Set, Krieghoff K-80/RT Shotguns, Krieghoff K-80 O/U Trap Shotgun, Laurona Silhouette 300 Sporting Clays, Laurona Silhouette 300 Trap, Laurona Super Model Over/Unders, Ljutic LM-6 Deluxe O/U Shotgun, Marocchi Conquista Over/Under Shotgun, Marocchi Avanza O/U Shotgun, Merkel Model 200E O/U Shotgun, Merkel Model 200E Skeet, Trap Over/Unders, Merkel Model 203E, 303E Over/Under Shotguns, Perazzi Mirage Special Sporting O/U, Perazzi Mirage Special Four-Gauge Skeet,Perazzi Sporting Classic O/U, Perazzi MX7 Over/Under Shotguns, Perazzi Mirage Special Skeet Over/Under, Perazzi MX8/MX8 Special Trap, Skeet, Perazzi MX8/20 Over/Under Shotgun, Perazzi MX9 Single Over/Under Shotguns, Perazzi MX12 Hunting Over/Under, Perazzi MX28, MX410 Game O/U Shotguns, Perazzi MX20 Hunting Over/Under, Piotti Boss Over/Under Shotgun, Remington Peerless Over/Under Shotgun, Ruger Red Label O/U Shotgun, Ruger Sporting Clays O/U Shotgun, San Marco 12-Ga. Wildflower Shotgun, San Marco Field Special O/U Shotgun, San Marco 10-Ga. O/U Shotgun, SKB Model 505 Deluxe Over/Under Shotgun, SKB Model 685 Over/Under Shotgun, SKB Model 885 Over/Under Trap, Skeet, Sporting Clays, Stoeger/IGA Condor I O/U Shotgun, Stoeger/IGA ERA 2000 Over/Under Shotgun, Techni-Mec Model 610 Over/Under, Tikka Model 412S Field Grade Over/Under, Weatherby Athena Grade IV O/U Shotguns, Weatherby Athena Grade V Classic Field O/U, Weatherby Orion O/U Shotguns, Weatherby II, III Classic Field O/Us, Weatherby Orion II Classic Sporting Clays O/U, Weatherby Orion II Sporting Clays O/U, Winchester Model 1001 O/U Shotgun, Winchester Model 1001 Sporting Clays O/U, Pietro Zanoletti Model 2000 Field O/U

Shotguns—Side by Sides

American Arms Brittany Shotgun, American Arms Gentry Double Shotgun, American Arms Derby Side-by-Side, American Arms Grulla #2 Double Shotgun, American Arms WS/SS 10, American Arms TS/SS 10 Double Shotgun, American Arms TS/SS 12 Side-by-Side, Arrieta Sidelock Double Shotguns, Armsport 1050 Series Double Shotguns, Arizaga Model 31 Double Shotgun, AYA Boxlock

Shotguns, AYA Sidelock Double Shotguns, Beretta Model 452 Sidelock Shotgun, Beretta Side-by-Side Field Shotguns, Crucelegui Hermanos Model 150 Double, Chapuis Side-by-Side Shotgun, E.A.A./Sabatti Saba-Mon Double Shotgun, Charles Daly Model Dss Double, Ferlib Model F VII Double Shotgun, Auguste Francotte Boxlock Shotgun, Auguste Francotte Sidelock Shotgun, Garbi Model 100 Double, Garbi Model 101 Side-by-Side, Garbi Model 103A, B Side-by-Side, Garbi Model 200 Side-by-Side, Bill Hanus Birdgun Doubles, Hatfield Uplander Shotgun, Merkel Model 8, 47E Side-by-Side Shotguns, Merkel Model 47LSC Sporting Clays Double, Merkel Model 47S, 147S Side-by-Sides, Parker Reproductions Side-by-Side, Piotti King No. 1 Side-by-Side, Piotti Lunik Side-by-Side, Piotti King Extra Side-by-Side, Piotti Piuma Side-by-Side Precision Sports Model 600 Series Doubles, Rizzini Boxlock Side-by-Side, Rizzini Sidelock Side-by-Side, Stoeger/IGA Uplander Side-by-Side Shotgun, Ugartechea 10-Ga. Magnum Shotgun

Shotguns—Bolt Actions and Single Shots

Armsport Single Barrel Shotgun, Browning BT-99 Competition Trap Special, Browning BT-99 Plus Trap Gun, Browning BT-99 Plus Micro, Browning Recoilless Trap Shotgun, Browning Micro Recoilless Trap Shotgun, Desert Industries Big Twenty Shotgun, Harrington & Richardson Topper Model 098, Harrington & Richardson Topper Classic Youth Shotgun, Harrington & Richardson N.W.T.F. Turkey Mag, Harrington & Richardson Topper Deluxe Model 098, Krieghoff KS-5 Trap Gun, Krieghoff KS-5 Special, Krieghoff K-80 Single Barrel Trap Gun, Ljutic Mono Gun Single Barrel, Ljutic LTX Super Deluxe Mono Gun, Ljutic Recoilless Space Gun Shotgun, Marlin Model 55 Goose Gun Bolt Action, New England Firearms Turkey and Goose Gun, New England Firearms N.W.T.F. Shotgun, New England Firearms Tracker Slug Gun, New England Firearms Standard Pardner, New England Firearms Survival Gun, Perazzi TM1 Special Single Trap, Remington 90-T Super Single Shotgun, Snake Charmer II Shotgun, Stoeger/IGA Reuna Single Barrel Shotgun, Thompson/Center TCR '87 Hunter Shotgun

NOTES

    1. Roberti-Roos Assault Weapons Control Act of 1989, Cal. Penal Code §§ 12275–12290.

    2. N.J. Stat. Ann. §§ 2C:39-1 to -15, 43-6 to 7; 58-5 to -14.

    3. Public Act 93-306.

    4. A number of cities and counties have also enacted a ban. E.g., New York City: Local Law 78.

    5. Haw. Rev. Stat. §§ 134-1, 134-4, 134-8.

    6. The one-vote margin in the Senate was on a procedural motion to strip the "assault

weapon" ban from a comprehensive crime bill. Other related Senate votes, such as for adoption of the crime bill containing the gun ban, were passed by a wider margin.

7. Brad O'Leary, "Fire Power," *Campaigns & Elections,* December/January 1995, p. 32.

8. Ibid.

9. Evelyn Theiss, "Clinton Blames Losses on NRA," (Cleveland) *Plain-Dealer,* January 14, 1995, p. A1 ("the fight for the assault-weapons ban cost 20 members their seats in Congress. . . . The NRA is the reason the Republicans control the house.")

10. O'Leary, "Fire Power," pp. 32-34. Of the fifty-five House races and ten Senate races identified, thirty-eight House races and seven Senate races resulted in a progun Republican taking the seat away from Democratic control (by defeating an incumbent or, more typically, winning an open seat from which a Democrat was retiring). Ten Senate races also involved a progun winner winning by less than the number of self-identified NRA members in the state.

11. The list of protected guns, while legally meaningless, was a brilliant move by the gun prohibition advocates. The list of 670 "protected" guns helped point up the contrast between banning "only" nineteen guns and "protecting" 670. Some dubious arithmetic was involved on both sides of the 19/670 figure. As the text points out, the law actually outlaws nearly two hundred guns. Of the 670 guns on the "protected" list, 88 percent are not semi-automatic, and so should not be in need of "protection" from the operation of other parts of the gun ban. The list also counts variants of the same gun numerous times; for example, the Remington 870 pump action shotgun is listed sixteen different times. So when "protecting" guns, the bill's drafters carefully counted each imaginable variant of a gun separately. When banning guns, the bill's drafters lumped dozens of variants into a few "types." Thus, a bill that bans nearly two hundred semi-automatic firearms while exempting about eighty-five semi-automatic firearms, was portrayed as a bill that banned only nineteen guns while "protecting" 670.

12. *Defense Intelligence Agency, Small Arms Identification and Operation Guide— Eurasian Communist Countries* (Washington, D.C.: Government Printing Office, 1988), p. 105.

13. Because the guns are "selective fire," the shooter can flip a selector switch to choose between automatic and semi-automatic fire (with sometimes the additional option of tri-burst fire).

14. National Firearms Act, ch. 757, 48 Stat. 1236 (1934).

15. 26 U.S.C. §§ 5811-5812, 5845.

As of May 1986, production of new automatics (including assault rifles) for the civilian market became completely illegal, although there have been some disputes among the lower federal courts about the constitutionality of the prohibition. Contrast the interpretations given to 18 U.S.C. § 922(o) by *Farmer* v. *Higgins,* 907 F.2d 1041 (11th Cir. 1990), *rev'g* 1:87-CV-440-JOB (1989) *cert. denied,* 112 L.Ed.2d 773 (1991) with *United States* v. *Dalton,* 990 F.2d 1166 (10th Cir. 1992); *United States* v. *Rock Island Armory, Inc.,* 773 F. Supp.. 117 (C.D. Ill.), *app. dism'd* 1991 U.S. App. LEXIS 19505 (7th Cir. 1991).

Some states impose their own bans on automatics.

16. The name "AR-15" is technically applied only to automatics. Semi-automatic look-alikes always include an extension of the name, such as "AR-15 Sporter" or "AR-15A2 H-Bar."

17. A few guns labeled "assault weapons" are revolver-type guns (such as the Striker 12 shotgun), while others are single-shot (being able to fire only a single shot before reloading), such as the Encom CM-55 shotgun, which was banned by California's 1989 "assault weapon" law and by local laws that copied the California ban.

18. Again, there are a few exceptions. The Uzi Pistol is used by the Israeli army.

19. The phrase "assault weapon" is used in quotes because, as will be detailed below, the phrase is not a definition of firearms that are in any meaningful way different from other firearms. In contrast, the phrase "assault rifle" is generally used without quotation marks, because "assault rifle" clearly defines a set of firearms that are distinguishable from other firearms. From a technical, rather than a political, viewpoint, there is no such thing as an

"assault weapon." It is a pejorative, outcome-determinative label applied to guns that are different only in appearance from other guns. As Mark Twain observed, "If ten thousand people call a dog a cow, it's still a dog."

20. Cal. Penal Code § 12275.5. Similarly, Bridgeport, Connecticut, police chief Thomas Sweeney asserted: "World War II-era semi-automatics are not included in the ban [enacted by Connecticut] because they don't fire as fast as modern semi-automatics." "Cop Out," *Shooting Industry,* Shot Show Issue 1994, p. 173.

21. William R. Magrath, "An Open Letter to American Politicians," *Police Marksman,* May/June 1989, p. 19; Edward Ezell (Smithsonian Institution), *The AK-47 Story* (1986). See also Kent Jenkins, Jr., "Calls for Ban Boost Assault Rifle Sales," *Washington Post,* March 6, 1989, p. B1 ("Bureau [of Alcohol, Tobacco and Firearms] experts say that the guns' firing mechanisms are no different from those of other rifles . . .").

According to testimony of the Bureau of Alcohol, Tobacco, and Firearms:

> The AK-47 is a select fire weapon capable of firing 600 rounds per minute on full automatic and 40 rounds per minute on semi-automatic. The AKS and AK-47 are similar in appearance. The AK-47 is an NFA [National Firearms Act of 1934] type weapon, having been manufactured as a machine gun. The AKS is difficult to convert, requiring additional parts and some machinery. . . . The AKS is a semi-automatic that, except for its deadly military appearance, is no different from other semi-automatic rifles. As a matter of fact, the identical firearm with a sport stock is available and, in appearance, no different than other so-called sporting weapons.

"Assault Weapon Import Control Act of 1989," 1989: Hearings on H.R. 1154 before Subcomm. on Trade of the House Comm. on Ways and Means, 101st Cong., 1st Sess. (1989).

22. In a bolt-action gun, after one cartridge is fired, the shooter pulls on the bolt handle to load the next cartridge into the chamber. R. A. Steindler, *The Firearms Dictionary* (1970), p. 15. The bolt-action rifle was the military firearm of the U.S. Army during World War I and of military forces in other parts of the world for decades thereafter.

23. Affidavit of Ron Phillips, State of Colorado exhibit 29, p. 2, in *Robertson* v. *Denver,* no. 90CV603 (Denver District Court, February 26, 1993); Johnson affidavit, Colo. ex. 51, p. 3, in *Robertson* v. *Denver* (Defense Intelligence Agency expert in assault weapons classification).

24. Steindler, *The Firearms Dictionary,* p. 20.

25. Don Feder, "Gun Control Delusions," *Washington Times,* August 30, 1994.

26. Daen Speir, "Media Deception and Fraud on Gun Issues Are Abuse of 1st Amendment," *Guns,* June 1993. To reiterate: all automatics (including automatic Uzis) have been strictly regulated since 1934; "assault weapon" laws impose no further controls on automatics.

27. Cal. Penal Code § 12275.5.

28. For some guns, there is instead a nondetachable tubular magazine.

29. Gary Kleck, *Point Blank: Guns and Violence in America* (1992), p. 79.

30. President Bush proposed a fifteen-round limit; the lobby Handgun Control, Inc., supports a six-round limit.

31. James B. Jacobs, "Assault Rifles Are Bad Targets," *Newsday,* May 28, 1993 ("a spent magazine can be popped out and a new one inserted in an instant").

32. Purdy used not an AK-47 but a Chinese, semi-automatic gun known as the AKM-56S. 135 Cong. Rec. S1870 (February 28, 1989).

33. The effect of the law will occur slowly, since there is still a finite supply of larger magazines which law-abiding gun owners may purchase. Handgun Control, Inc., the main force behind the current magazine limitation, proposes tightening the law by lowering magazine to six, and allowing possession of larger magazines only to persons who pass through a licensing process similar to the current machine gun-licensing process.

34. The robber had recently been released from prison, having served less than three months of a two-year robbery sentence. *The Daily Breeze,* August 17, 1994, summarized in "The Armed Citizen," *American Rifleman,* January/February 1995, p. 8.

35. Tom Jackson, "Keeping the Battle Alive," *Tampa Tribune,* October 21, 1993.

36. Statement of Edward D. Conroy, Deputy Associate Director, Law Enforcement, BATF, before U.S. Senate Subcommittee on the Constitution, February 10, 1989, p. 1; Charles Mohr, "Firearms Market Thrives Despite an Import Ban," *New York Times,* April 3, 1989, p. A14.

37. Senate Hearings on The Antidrug, Assault Weapons Limitation Act of 1989, S. Rep. No. 160, 101st Cong., 1st sess., May 6, 1989, testimony of Detective Jimmy L. Trahin of the Los Angeles Police Department Firearms/Forensics Ballistics Unit, p. 3 [hereinafter, "Senate Report"] ("99 percent of these so-called assault weapons are not easily converted").

A machine gun expert explains the complexity of converting a semi-automatic rifle to automatic:

> If time and effort are of no consequence, any firearm, even a lever-action rifle, can be converted to fully automatic fire. Converting a semiautomatic-only AK to automatic fire requires a great deal of skill and knowledge and no small amount of effort and equipment. Without being too specific, the procedure is more or less as follows:
>
> 1) A portion of the receiver must be modified. A hole through each side of the receiver (larger on one side than the other) must be precisely located (to within 0.0015") and drilled to accept the axis pin for the auto safety sear and its coil spring. This special coil spring also retains the hammer and trigger pins. If not installed correctly, the hammer and trigger axis pins will not be retained, and these components will fall out of the receiver. A slot must also be carefully milled into the rightside bolt-carrier rail to accept the auto safety sear. The three new components required are not easily procured or fabricated.
>
> 2) The hammer must be built up by welding and then with great skill reshaped to provide a notch not present on the semi-automatic-only version.
>
> 3) An extension must be added at the rear of the sear by welding and then reshaped to contact the selector lever.
>
> 4) A portion of the selector-lever stop on the rightside exterior of the receiver must be removed and another detent milled into the receiver for the new semiauto position.
>
> 5) The bolt carrier must be built up by welding and then reshaped to actuate the auto safety sear.
>
> If welded components are not subsequently and properly heat-treated, wear will be accelerated and these parts will fail in a short period of time, often with dangerous consequences. Furthermore, if this conversion is performed on an AKM type with a sheet-metal receiver, failure to install a completely unavailable five-component, anti-bounce mechanical drag device on the hammer (especially if the firing pin is not spring-retracted) will probably result in a disastrous ignition out of battery.

Peter G. Kokalis, "Full Auto," *Soldier of Fortune,* December 1989, p. 16.

38. Michael Hancock, "The Convertible Submachine Gun Boondoggle," *New York Times,* June 15, 1985, p. A22.

39. The author is a technical consultant to the International Wound Ballistics Association.

40. Frank C. Barnes, *Cartridges of the World,* 7th ed. (1993), pp. 59, 92, 110, 231, 249.

41. Malcolm Gladwell, "Irrational Bans on 'Assault Weapons' Draw False and Ignorant Distinction," *Dispatch* (Columbus, Ohio), March 27, 1993, p. 7.

42. Barnes, *Cartridges of the World.*

43. The formula is: $KE=\frac{1}{2}MV^2$ (where KE is Kinetic Energy, M is Mass, and V is Velocity).

If the bullet enters and exits the target's body, only part of the kinetic energy is transferred to the target. If the bullet does not exit, all the kinetic energy will be transferred. Accordingly, bullets designed to deform on impact, and not exit the body, will generally do more damage than will other bullets. Bullets designed not to exit the target's body are available for virtually all types of firearms.

44. Mohr, "Firearms Market Thrives Despite an Import Ban"; Lindsey, "The Idolatry of Velocity, or Lies, Damned Lies, and Ballistics," *Journal of Trauma* 20 (1980): 1068.

45. The videotape produced by Handgun Control, Inc., as a part of the lobbying campaign for prohibition acknowledges that "assault weapon" bullets are nothing special. The tape includes an interview with Dr. Hermann, Director of the Institute for Forensic Sciences. Dr. Hermann explains that the Uzi bullet is "slightly larger and slightly faster than the .38 special [a medium-sized handgun bullet]. It does not produce a large cavitary destructive wound through the body." Handgun Control, Inc., *The Deadly Distinction* (1989).

46. Martin L. Fackler, "Getting Your Guns Straight," *Washington Post,* April 24, 1993, p. A25.

47. *Wall Street Journal,* April 10, 1989, p. A13 (letter to the editor).

48. Fackler, "Getting Your Guns Straight." See also T. Bowen and R. Bellamy, *Emergency War Surgery—NATO Handbook* (Washington, D.C.: Government Printing Office, 1988), ch. 2 ("... many wounds from this weapon resemble those caused by much lower velocity handguns"); M. L. Fackler, "Wounding Patterns of Military Rifle Bullets," *International Defense Review* 59 (1989): 22; M. L. Fackler, et al., "Wounding Effects of the AK-47 Rifle Used by Patrick Purdy in the Stockton Schoolyard Shooting of January 17, 1989," *American Journal of Forensic Medicine and Pathology* 11 (1990): 185; Fackler, "Wound Ballistics: A Review of Common Misconceptions," *JAMA* 259 (1980): 2730.

49. V. DiMaio, *Gunshot Wounds: Practical Aspects of Firearms, Ballistics and Forensic Techniques* (New York: Elsevier, 1985), p. 146 .

50. Peter Alan Kasler, "False Witness," *American Survival Guide,* June 1993.

51. Ibid.

52. The text of the law at the end of this chapter lists the various characteristics.

53. Jack Lewis, *Assault Weapons,* 1st ed. (Northbrook, Ill.: DBI Books, 1986), p. 46,

54. A new muzzle brake, the "Ballistic Optimizing Shooting System" (BOSS), allows the shooter to "tune" the barrel vibrations that are produced by recoil. Different types of ammunition will produce recoil vibration waves; in the 270 Winchester rifle caliber, for example, a 160-grain bullet with 51 grains of gunpowder will produce different vibrations from a 130-grain bullet with 55 grains of gunpowder. The BOSS muzzle brake can be adjusted by the shooter based on different types of ammunition, to optimize the recoil vibration for each particular type. One reviewer described the results of the tuning allowed by the Browning muzzle brake as, "The most significant advancement in rifle accuracy in my lifetime." Jon R. Sundra, "Outdoor Marketplace," *Shooting Industry,* Shot Show Super Issue 1994, p. 36. Other reviewers have been equally positive; they note that the BOSS brake significantly reduces felt recoil to the shooter, and thereby reduces the flinch that causes shooters to jerk the rifle off-target. Peter Maxwell, "Meet the 'BOSS'," *New Zealand Guns,* March/April 1994, pp. 56–57.

BOSS brakes are currently available only for bolt-action guns, but it seems reasonable to expect that they will eventually be manufactured for semi-automatics and other action types.

55. Virginia Governor's Task Force, Meeting on Assault Firearms Definition, July 8, 1993, transcript, reported in Richard E. Gardener (NRA), memorandum of December 20, 1993, to James J. Baker, at 1.

56. While night sights are not listed as a specific "assault weapon" characteristic, some

prohibition advocates argue that many "assault weapons" are configured to allow easy attachment of night sights, even though "it is generally illegal to hunt at night," *Robertson* v. *Denver,* City of Denver's brief in support of motion for summary judgement, p. 17. It should be noted, however, that a mounting attachment that is perfectly configured to attach night sights is also perfectly configured to attach sights that work only during the day.

The night sights issue again raises the issue of what guns are for. If guns are for big game hunting, there is little need for night sights (although predator control on a farm is not illegal at night). On the other hand, it is legal to defend home, person, and property at night. Turning on a light to try to find an attacker's position would reveal one's own position, and thereby give the criminal the first shot.

57. N.J.S.A. § 2C43-7(1).

58. Another useful defensive configuration is the ability to select different types of ammunition "on the fly." Imagine a parent confronted with a violent burglar. Shooting the burglar might be the only way to protect nearby children. But a conventional hunting rifle cartridge would penetrate the criminal, then a wall, and might hit a child. The parent would be better off with a shotgun loaded with light birdshot—to knock the burglar down but not penetrate a wall.

On the other hand, suppose the burglar's entry had transpired a little differently. The whole family might be huddled in one room, while the burglar kicked and banged at the creaking door. Then the optimal self-defense shot would be a slug from a shotgun—to crash through the thick door and into the burglar.

In short, different home family defense situations require different ammunition. An excellent gun for home defense, then, would be a shotgun for which the shooter could rapidly select different loads. There is such a gun. The shotguns which are singled out by name in most "assault weapon" legislation, such as the Striker 12, are the only long guns with such beneficial features. The Striker 12 is so named because it is a shotgun with an external rotating cylinder. The shooter can quickly dial any of twelve different rounds.

59. Crime problem or not, bayonets are taken seriously by BATF. In 1993, some Chinese-made SKS semi-automatic rifles (which are not "assault weapons" by federal definition) were imported into the United States with bayonets illegally attached to them. (Neither bayonets nor SKS rifles are illegal, but the presence of a bayonet violates BATF regulations which implement a 1968 federal statute that only guns suitable for "sporting purposes" may be imported into the United States.) BATF moved swiftly to address the "serious" problem, and asked wholesalers and retailers to remove all the SKS bayonets before the rifles were sold to the public. "ATF Defines Problems with Imported SKS Rifles," October 26, 1993 (BATF Press Release).

60. 18 U.S.C. §§ 841–844.

61. James Bovard, "The Assault on Assault Weapons," *Wall Street Journal,* January 6, 1994. Grenade launchers were used by the FBI in its attack on the Branch Davidian home in Waco, but it is not at this point clear whether the FBI's actions were criminal.

62. There is no reasonable way for a person of common intelligence to know if a particular pistol was originally based on a rifle design or on the design of an automatic weapon. It is irrationally burdensome to require citizens who wish to learn if their pistols are legal to research both how their pistol was designed, and how the ancestors to that pistol were "originally designed."

Under the detailed "assault pistol" definition, a person who has somehow discovered the design history of a pistol must then attempt to discover its design mechanics—if the pistol has "the same" action as the ancestor rifle. In redesigning a rifle into a pistol, the designer will often modify the action (such as by shortening the piston stroke). It is irrational to require ordinary persons to reconstruct the technical development of a complex part of their firearms.

63. To prohibit some object based on the mere fact that that object has some historical relation to the military could be considered to reflect bias against the military.

64. See Steven R. Myers, "The Legitimate Uses of Assault Weapons," *Washington Post,* March 4, 1989 (letter to the editor); Patrick Mott, "In Defense of the AK-47," *Los Angeles Times,* February 24, 1989, p. V1 (the headline is a misnomer; as noted above, the AK-47 is an automatic weapon that is scarcely seen in the United States outside of firearms museums). The statements about reliability in this chapter do not, of course, apply to every single gun that is sometimes denominated an "assault weapon." The TEC-9 pistol, for example, is often criticized for jamming at the wrong moment.

65. Cathy Reynolds, *Headlines,* Summer 1989 (newsletter).

66. The accuracy advantage is maintained only out to distances of about two hundred yards. Above that distance, the tighter chambering of bolt-action rifles, despite the bolt-action's higher recoil, results in greater accuracy.

67. "Council Panel OKs Ban on Assault Weapons," *New York Post,* July 25, 1991. Mayor Dinkins, whose 24 hour-a-day government bodyguards would don tuxedos for the mayor's black-tie evening social functions, did not need to concern himself with the "nonsense" of personally owning a gun for self-defense.

68. State of Florida, Commission on Assault Weapons, *Report* (May 18, 1990), summary of March 18, 1990, meeting, p. 3 (Commission member stating that California "chose those weapons from a book of pictures").

69. California deleted the Encom from the banned list in 1991. The many jurisdictions that copied California's ban have not made similar corrections.

70. S.C. Helsley, Asst. Dir., Invest. & Enforcement Branch, Calif. Dept. of Justice, memorandum to Patrick Kenday, Asst. Atty. Gen. (February 14, 1991), pp. 3–4. Helsley eventually became so unhappy with the government's approach to the issue that he resigned, and is now a lobbyist for the NRA in California.

71. Jacobs, "Assault Rifles Are Bad Targets."

72. Such "protected" "recreational" guns include: Iver Johnson M1 Carbines, Marlin Model 9 Camp Carbine, Cimarron 1860 Henry, Cimarron 1866 Winchester, Cimarron 1873 Sporting Rifle, Cimarron 1873 Express, Dixie Engraved 1873, E.M.F. Model 73 Lever-Action Rifle, Marlin Model 1894CL, Mitchell 1858 Henry, Mitchell 1866 Winchester, Mitchell 1873 Winchester, Navy Arms Iron Frame Henry, Navy Arms Henry Carbine, Navy Arms 1873 Winchester, Navy Arms 1873 Sporting Rifle, Uberti Henry, Uberti 1866, Uberti 1873, Armscor Model 20P, Browning Auto-22, Marlin Model 60 and 60ss, Norinco Model 22 ATD, Remington 552BDL, Browning BL-22, Marlin 39TDS, Marlin 30AS, Remington 572BDL, Rossi Model 62, and Winchester Model 9422.

As the names suggest, many of the "recreational" firearms with large-capacity magazines are modern replicas of nineteenth-century military rifles such as those made by Henry and Winchester. The metamorphosis of the nineteenth century's most deadly infantry rifles into supposedly benign "recreational" firearms in the twentieth century illustrates the perils of making artificial distinctions between "military" and "recreational" firearms.

73. Denver City Council hearing, November 6, 1989, transcript, p. 6, reproduced at Defendants' exhibit B, affidavit of Barbara Romero (Senior Secretary for City Council), in support of Defendants' Motion for Summary Judgement, in *Robertson* v. *Denver.*

74. Police Firearms Data, Colo. ex. 65, in *Robertson* v. *Denver.* I represented the State of Colorado in the trial court. The trial court found the law unconstitutional. That decision was reversed in part by a 6-1 vote of the state Supreme Court.

75. Colo. ex. 64, *Robertson* v. *Denver.*

76. "Few Assault Weapons Seized in Akron Last Year," *Beacon Journal,* January 6, 1993 (quoting police Major Leonard Strawderman).

77. Robert Hiles, "Police Gunning to Boost Odds," *Akron Beacon-Journal,* March 13, 1989, p. A9.

78. Ronald Banks, "Letters to the Editor," *Baltimore Evening Sun,* February 11, 1991.

79. Vincent DeMaio, S. Kalousdian, and J. M. Loeb, "Assault Weapons as a Public Health Hazard," *JAMA* 268 (1992): 3073 (letter to the editor).

80. Torrey D. Johnston, *Report on a Survey of the Use of "Assault Weapons" in California in 1990* (Office of the Attorney General, California Department of Justice, September 26, 1991). The report, prepared in response to a request by a California state senator, was suppressed by the California attorney general's office, which claimed that the report did not exist. A leaked copy was released to the media. David Alan Coia, "Assault Rifles Said to Play a Small Role in Violent Crimes," *Washington Times,* June 27, 1992; Alan W. Bock, "Statistical Overkill on Banned Rifles," *Orange City Register,* June 26, 1992, p. K4; Mike McNulty, "The War on Gun Ownership Still Goes On!" *Guns & Ammo,* December 1992, pp. 30–31, 90.

81. David Freed, "Assault Rifles Are Not Heavily Used in Crimes," *Los Angeles Times,* April 21, 1992.

82. Jay Edward Simkin, "Control Criminals, Not Guns," *Wall Street Journal,* March 25, 1991.

83. Gene O'Shea, "Chicago Police Back Assault Weapon Ban Approved by Senate," *Southtown Economist,* June 12, 1990.

84. J. G. Mericle, "Weapons Seized during Drug Warrant Executions and Arrests," unpublished report of Metropolitan Area Narcotics Squad, Will and Grundy Counties, Illinois (1989), discussed in Kleck, *Point Blank,* p. 130.

85. Major Kenneth H. Kirschner, Commanding Officer, Bureau of Police Support, letter Lt. Col. George H. Moore, Commanding Officer, Off. of Admin. Serv., Hartford, March 11, 1993, p. 1.

86. Trahin, May 6, 1989, Senate testimony.

87. H. Range Hutson, Deirdre Anglin, and Michael J. Pratts, "Adolescents and Children Injured or Killed in Drive-By Shootings in Los Angeles," *New England Journal of Medicine* 330 (1994): 326.

88. Letter of Thomas E. Hickman, State's Attorney for Carroll County, Maryland, submitted to the Maryland Senate Judicial Proceedings Committee, February 14, 1991, pp. 1–3.

89. Trooper M. Arnold, Massachusetts State Police, Firearms Identification Section, "Mass State Police Ballistics Records."

90. M. Arnold, Massachusetts State Police, Firearms Identification Section, "Massachusetts State Police Ballistic Records," March 14, 1990, and April 11, 1991.

91. Jess I. Galan, Criminalist, Crime Laboratory Bureau, letter to Richard Gardiner, National Rifle Association.

92. Sgt. W. Reins, Memorandum to Chief J. Laux, April 3, 1989, p. 1; Minnesota Med. Assoc. Firearm Inj. Prev. Task Force, "Firearm Mortality in Minnesota," *Minnesota Medicine,* March 1994, p. 23.

93. Sgt. Brooks Harris, Crime Analysis Section, Nashville P.D., letter to Sen. Harlan Matthews, June 2, 1993, pp. 1–2.

94. Nicholas Veronis, "Newark Survey Finds Assault Rifle Used in only One Shooting in '80s," (Newark) *Star-Ledger,* May 16, 1990, p. 15.

95. Testimony of Deputy Chief Joseph Constance of the Trenton New Jersey Police Department, before the Maryland Senate Judicial Proceedings Committee, March 7, 1991, p. 3.

96. "Florio Urges Ban on Assault Rifles, Stresses His Support for Abortion," (Newark) *Star-Ledger,* July 18, 1989, p. 15.

97. Iver Peterson, "Both Sides Say Trenton's Ban on Assault Rifles Has Little Effect on Crime," *New York Times,* June 20, 1993.

98. "Handguns, not Assault Rifles, are NYC Weapon of Choice," *White Plains Reporter-Dispatch,* March 27, 1989, pp. A8–A9 (citing Lt. Moran, head of the New York City Police Ballistics Unit).

99. Unpublished data from New York State Division of Criminal Justice Services, discussed in Frederic Dicker, "Real Story on Assault Weapons is Hit & Myth," *New York Post,* January 10, 1994, p. 14.

100. R. Zien, Sergeant, Weapons Homicide Section, Oakland Police Dept., *Year End Report 1990: Homicide Section Weapons Unit* (Oakland Police Dept., 1991).

101. Oakland Police Dept., *Supplementary Homicide Reports* (1991).

102. "Proposed Law Is Misguided," *Orlando Sentinel,* February 8, 1994, p. A-8 (editorial).

103. Michael D. McGonigal et al., "Urban Firearms Deaths: A Five-Year Perspective," *Journal of Trauma* 35, no. 4 (1993): 532–37. For murders perpetrated with a handgun, there was a shift from 1985 to 1990 toward decreased use of revolvers and greater use of semi-automatic pistols. The study did not specify the model of semi-automatic pistol, so it is not known how many, if any, of the pistols used were the type sometimes called "assault pistols."

Consistent with the Philadelphia study, which found an increase in the number of shots fired, a Washington, D.C., study found that the average number of wounds of hospital patients who were the victim of gun assault increased from 1.44 in 1983 to 2.04 in 1990. D. W. Webster et al., "Epidemiologic Changes in Gunshot Wounds in Washington, D.C., 1983–1990," *Archives of Surgery,* 127, no. 6 (1992): 694–98. Since a revolver can fire six shots (and can be reloaded in a few seconds), it is not necessarily evident that even a ban on all semi-automatic firearms would reduce the average number of wounds.

104. Joe Hughes, "Smaller Guns Are 'Big Shots' with the Hoods," *San Diego Union,* August 29, 1991 (report of study by city's firearms examiner).

105. *House Ways & Means Hearings,* p. 68; Eric C. Morgan, "Assault Rifle Legislation: Unwise and Unconstitutional," *American Journal of Criminal Law* 17 (1990): 151.

106. Margaret Edds, "Assault Weapons Rarely Used in Crimes, Gun-Control Panel Told," *Virginia Pilot & Ledger-Star,* August 4, 1993.

107. Kent Jenkins, Jr., "Calls for Ban Boost Assault Rifle Sales: Weapons Not Considered Factor in Killings," *Washington Post,* March 6, 1989, p. B1.

108. G. R. Wilson, Chief, Firearms Section, Metropolitan Police Dept., January 21, 1992, cited in K. Bea, *CRS Report for Congress—"Assault Weapons": Military Style Semi-Automatic Firearms Facts and Issues* (Cong. Res. Svc., May 13, 1992) (rev. ed. June 4, 1992), p. 18, Table 5.

109. In 1990, 3.7 percent of homicides were perpetrated with rifles. FBI, Uniform Crime Reports, *Crime in the United States 1990* (1991), p. 17.

110. The numbers are published annually, and were supplied to the author in a telephone conversation of March 25, 1993, by Ms. L. Behm, an FBI Technical Information Specialist. For data from 1978 to 1992, see Bureau of Justice Statistics, *Sourcebook of Criminal Justice Statistics—1993* (Washington, D.C.: Government Printing Office, 1994), p. 401 (62 in 1992).

111. Alan S. Krug, *The "Assault Weapon" Issue* (National Rifle Assoc., 1993 ed.), pp. 16–17 (using FBI, state, and local police data).

112. More than twice the number of police officers die by suicide than are killed by homicide. "More Police Died in Suicides Than in Line of Duty," *Los Angeles Times,* December 31, 1994, p. A34 (Reuters). Although national statistics are not available, the evidence from individual jurisdictions suggests that a large fraction (well over half) of police suicides are accomplished with the officer's own gun. If the only thing that mattered in society was reducing the number of police firearms deaths, disarming police officers would be far more effective than any other possible "gun control" measure.

It would, however, be a foolish move to attempt to protect police from guns by disarming them all. Disarmament would leave them more vulnerable to armed and unarmed attackers, and render the police less capable of helping other people. Even if confiscating all police guns would produce a net savings of police lives (if the drop in police suicides were larger than the increase in police homicides), the gun confiscation would still be a net negative to society. The same point may be made, much more strongly, about outlawing "assault weapons" as a method of saving police lives; banning guns which are almost never used in police homicides, and which are superb for personal defense may lead to a net increase in the deaths of innocents.

113. George T. Williams and Charles B. Moorman, "A Decade of Peace Officers Murdered in California: The 1980s," *Journal of California Law Enforcement* 46 (February 1991): 1, 6.

114. Kleck, *Point Blank,* pp. 78–79.

115. Jim Stewart and Andrew Alexander, "Assault Guns Muscling in on Front Lines of Crime," *Atlanta Journal-Atlanta Constitution,* May 21, 1989, pp. A1, A8.

116. "Assault weapons" were also involved in 11 percent of traces relating to the Gun Control Act of 1968 (which criminalizes nonviolent behavior such as the sale of a handgun to a person from another state, and imposes various record-keeping requirements on firearms dealers) and in 30 percent of the very small number of organized crime traces conducted by BATF.

117. Daniel M. Hartnett, Bureau of Alcohol, Tobacco and Firearms, Letter to Rep. Richard T. Schulze, March 31, 1992, p. 2.

118. Kleck, *Point Blank,* p. 75. To many people, it may seem surprising that the use of "assault weapons" in Washington, D.C., is so low. It should be noted that since Washington passed its "assault weapon" liability law in 1990 allowing anyone in Washington (even a criminal) injured by an "assault weapon" to sue the manufacturer, not a single suit has been brought.

119. BATF 1990 report, cited in Kleck, *Point Blank,* p. 75.

120. Bea, Congressional Research Service, p. CRS-65.

121. Keith R. Fafarmanm, "State Assault Rifle Bans and the Militia Clauses of the United States Constitution," *Indiana Law Journal* 67 (1991): 187, 189 (1st Winchester semi-automatic in 1903; first Remington in 1906); Harold F. Williamson, *Winchester: The Gun that Won the West* (1952), p. 13 (Volcanic Company was producing carbines that could fire thirty rounds without reloading in 1856).

122. That the guns are rarely used in crime should not be surprising; rifles and shotguns are difficult to conceal, and so-called assault pistols are (for handguns) quite large.

123. Jeff Snyder, "Who's Under Assault in the Assault Weapon Ban?" *Washington Times,* August 25, 1994.

124. "Lock and Load for the Gunfight of '89," *U.S. News & World Report,* March 27, 1989, p. 9. Wright observed, "If criminals can get all the drugs they want, they can get guns, too."

125. James Wright, "Second Thoughts about Gun Control," *The Public Interest* 91 (Spring 1988): 30–31.

126. Bureau of Alcohol, Tobacco, and Firearms, *Analysis of Operation CUE (Concentrated Urban Enforcement),* interim report (Washington D.C.: February 15, 1977), pp. 133–34, cited in Paul Blackman and Richard Gardiner, *Flaws in the Current and Proposed Uniform Crime Reporting Programs Regarding Homicide and Weapons Use in Violent Crime,* paper presented at 38th Annual Meeting of the American Society of Criminology; Atlanta, October 29–November 1, 1986.

127. *Los Angeles Times,* February 8, 1989.

128. David B. Kopel, *The Samurai, the Mountie, and the Cowboy: Should America Adopt the Gun Controls of Other Countries?* (Amherst, N.Y.: Prometheus Books, 1992), pp. 218, 231–32, 393.

129. John Kaplan, "Controlling Firearms," *Cleveland State Law Review* 28 (1979): 8.

130. Testimony before Maryland Senate, March 7, 1991, regarding SB 267.

131. "Court Upholds Conviction for Failing to Register Assault Rifles," Associated Press Wire, December 6, 1994; Raymond Fazzi, "Sportsmen Offer Aid in Weapon Ban Appeal," *Asbury Park Press,* August 18, 1993; Jim O'Neil, "Gun Conviction Seen as Possible Test Case," (Newark) *Star-Ledger,* August 18, 1993; Jim O'Neil, "Collector Guilty of Assault Weapon Charge," (Newark) *Star-Ledger,* June 22, 1993; "A Case for the NRA," *Home News,* June 22, 1993; Rick Malwitz, "Casualty of N.J. Gun Laws," *News Tribune,* June 17, 1993.

The *Elrose* case has not been the only abusive "assault weapon" prosecution. In California in 1993, James Dingman heard a fight going on in front of his motel room. He called the police, who arrived after the combatants had left. The police asked Dingman if he had any guns, and if they could see them. He complied, and was arrested for possessing unregistered "assault weapons." In fact, his guns were not "assault weapons" by California law, but they looked like other guns that were. After forty-seven days in jail, Dingman pleaded guilty in order to be released. Michael McNulty, "Confusing Law on Assault Guns Misses Target," *Sacramento Bee,* August 17, 1993, p. B7. In 1991, the Lake County (California) Drug Task Force executed a search warrant on a businessman. Finding no drugs, they did find two guns which they incorrectly claimed were "assault weapons" under California law. After a prosecution was commenced, a government official blithely remarked, "It doesn't matter; they're just like the ones that are on the list." Charges were finally dismissed, after the businessman had incurred huge legal fees for which he had to sell his home. The legal guns were never returned, and he cannot afford to sue for them. There have been several other cases in California involving abusive prosecutions of guns that are similar to (but are not) the guns outlawed in California. Don B. Kates and Peter Alan Kasler, "Assault-Weapon Fiasco: Prosecutors and Police Can't Decide What Guns are Banned by State Law," *Daily Journal* (San Francisco), May 11, 1993.

132. *Florida Assault Weapon Commission Report* (Tallahassee: Florida Dept. of State, 1990), pp. 156–57.

133. *Wall Street Journal,* April 7, 1989, p. A12.

134. *Washington Post,* March 6, 1989, p. B1.

135. Senate Report, May 6, 1989, p. 18.

136. *New York Times,* February 5, 1989, p. E26.

137. Memorandum to Patrick Kenady, Assistant Attorney General, February 14, 1991, p. 2.

138. The formal pretext for suspending Pyle was that he had appeared (not in uniform) in an NRA video explaining the difference between automatics and semi-automatics, and in that video had stated that he was a San Jose police officer, but had not expressly stated that his views were not the official views of his department. The rather severe discipline meted out to Pyle seemed odd in light of the fact that Chief McNamara himself wrote political fundraising letters for Handgun Control, Inc., on official city stationery.

139. Jim Fotis, "Police Officers Forced to Lobby for Gun Ban," *The LEAA Advocate,* Fall-Winter 1994, pp. 17–22; Andrew Hays, "Former Arlington County Police Officer Speaks Out: Reveals Intimidation, Threats Made by Chief," *The LEAA Advocate,* Fall–Winter 1994: 23–25.

140. "The Law Enforcement Technology Gun Control Survey," *Law Enforcement Technology,* July/August 1991, pp. 14-15. Two thousand police officers participated in the *Law Enforcement Technology* magazine survey.

141. The wording of the question had a progun tinge, which may have inflated the progun responses. At the same time, the question was also worded vaguely enough so that officers could have been responding to whether they thought machine guns should be legal. Thus, the question might have elicited a "no" response from officers who wanted semi-automatic firearms to be legal, but who also wanted automatic machine guns to be illegal. The actual question was "Do you believe that law-abiding citizens should have the right to purchase any type of firearm for sport or self-defense under state laws that now exist?" The survey is reprinted in Timothy Sekerak, ed., *Issue and Answers* (Bellevue, Wash.: Citizens Comm. for the Right to Keep and Bear Arms, 1992), p. 8.

142. Banning the guns that are actually used to kill police officers would mean banning handguns and shotguns (sawed-off shotguns are typical crime guns), and disarming police officers (about 12 percent of police officers killed are killed with their own gun; if suicides were included, the figure would be much higher).

143. Gary A. Mauser and David B. Kopel, "'Sorry, Wrong Number': Why Media Polls on Gun Control Are Often Unreliable" *Political Communication* 9 (1992): 69.

144. Gallup Polls, September 10–11, 1990; February 28–March 2, 1989.

145. The Texas Poll, conducted for Hartke-Hanks Communications, August 4-19, 1990.

146. Franklin Zimring, "The Medium Is the Message: Firearms Caliber as a Determinant of Death from Assault," *Journal of Legal Studies* 1 (1972): 97. Zimring's research was confined to handgun ammunition.

147. *Assault Weapons and Accessories in America* (Washington, D.C.: Educ. Fund to End Handgun Violence and New Right Watch, September 1988), p. 26.

148. Church, "The Other Arms Race," *Time*, February 6, 1989, p. 25.

149. Ibid.

150. 18 U.S.C. § 922(b)(4), (o)(1). Since 1954 the AK-47 has also been subject to the restrictions on importation of goods from Communist countries.

151. Gloria Hammond, *Time* magazine, form letter to persons complaining about the magazine's firearms coverage, August 1, 1989:

> The July 17 cover story is the most recent in a growing number of attempts on the part of TIME editors to keep the gun-availability issue resolutely in view. Such an editorial closing of the ranks represents the exception rather than the rule in the history of the magazine, which has always endeavored to provide a variety of opinions and comment, in addition to straightforward news reporting. . . . But the time for opinions on the dangers of gun availability is long since gone, replaced by overwhelming evidence that it represents a growing threat to public safety . . . our responsibility now is to confront indifference about the escalating violence and the unwillingness to do something about it.

152. Cong. Rec. February 28, 1989, p. S 1868 (Subcommittee on the Constitution).

153. In February 1993, KABC may have falsified a news item in order to promote the station's gun control agenda. In a news segment regarding 9mm handguns, the station showed clips of a person firing a 9mm handgun at an extremely rapid rate (over one shot per second), and of metal targets being knocked down by the shots. The impression created was that 9mm handguns can fire very rapidly and very accurately at the same time. Undisclosed to the television audience (but later admitted by the person doing the shooting) was the fact that KABC had shot two different segments. In the first segment, the shooter fired as rapidly as possible, and his hand jerked extensively since he did not take time to steady his hand or aim before firing. In the second segment, the shooter slowed down his rate of fire considerably, and aimed at the metal silhouette targets which had been positioned a few yards away. KABC, however, put the different segments' shooting events into one film, thereby creating the impression that the targets were being knocked down one after the other by a shooter firing more than a shot per second.

154. "Watchdogs of Liberty," *Alternative News Network*, April 6, 1994.

155. Jamison, ".223, .308, .30-06, .45-70: The U.S. Military's Fearsome Foursome," *Shooting Times*, March 1990, p. 36.

156. Milek, "Shooting Bench," *Guns & Ammo*, November 1989, p. 16.

157. *Los Angeles Times*, February 24, 1989, p. V1.

158. Hearings on H.R. 1154, p. 70.

159. 135 *Cong. Rec.* 1872 (February 23, 1989).

160. S. Helsley, Acting Assistant Director, Investigation and Enforcement Branch, Memorandum to G. Clemons, Director, Division of Law Enforcement, October 31, 1988, p. 4 ("a ban would devastate competitors in California . . . assault weapons cannot be defined in a workable way . . . we should leave the issue alone.")

161. Denver Rev. Mun. Code, § 38-130(a). Similarly, the city of Cleveland's ban was predicated on the finding that "the primary purpose of assault weapons is antipersonnel. . . ." Cleveland Ord. No. 415-89, § 628.01. California's ban included the legislative finding "The leg-

islature has restricted assault weapons . . . based upon the finding . . . that its function as a legitimate sports or recreational firearm is substantially outweighed by the danger that it can also be used to kill or injure human beings." Cal. Penal Code, § 12275.5.

162. Among the guns recommended for the personal defense in the BATF Report are the H&K 91, the H&K 94, and the Fabrique Nationale semi-automatic. Bureau of Alcohol, Tobacco and Firearms, *Report and Recommendation of the ATF Working Group on the Importability of Certain Semi-Automatic Rifles* (1989).

163. Of the semi-automatics evaluated by Lewis, virtually every one was praised for its utility in survival, law enforcement, or other civil defense-type situations. The guns were also touted for day-to-day home defense for reasons outlined above: reliability, simplicity and ruggedness, low recoil, and intimidating appearance. For example, the Steyr AUG-SA has "excellent bio-engineering," a superior and innovative safety, is easy to maneuver for self-defense, and hard for an attacker to take away. Its barrel is so well made that no amount of target practice will wear it out. The gun never needs cleaning, even if thrown in mud or snow. Jack Lewis, *Assault Weapons,* 1st ed. (Northbrook, Ill.: DBI Books, 1986), pp. 46–49.

The SIG SG-551 SP carbine works "like a fine Swiss watch" and does not have "any notable recoil." Its "fast second shot" is useful for defending livestock from coyotes, and is "perfectly suitable" for police and civilian defensive roles. Jack Lewis, *Assault Weapons,* 2d ed. (Northbrook, Ill.: DBI Books, 1989), pp. 201–13.

The M11 pistol finds its "best role as a home defense weapon," in part because its intimidating appearance would force "most burglars and intruders to consider instant surrender." Ibid., p. 71.

164. See, for example, Richard Maxwell Brown, *No Duty to Retreat* (New York: Oxford, 1991).

165. Why is a gun designed to kill an innocent game animal more legitimate than a gun designed to protect an innocent human being against a criminal attack?

166. Because of budget constraints, the DCM program will lose its federal subsidy. That the program must become financially self-sufficient does not prove that it is no longer important. Many important federal programs, such as aviation safety and airport construction, are financed by user fees.

167. *Los Angeles Times,* May 13, 1988, p. II-3.

168. Hearings on H.R. 1154, p. 77.

169. Kopel, *Samurai,* p. 322.

170. Armed resistance to criminal government was seen simply as a larger case of resistance to a lone criminal, a right so generally accepted as not even to be questioned. Don Kates, "The Second Amendment and the Ideology of Self-Protection," *Const. Comm.* 9 (1992): 87.

Among the more recent expositions of the individual right position are William Van Alstyne, "The Second Amendment and the Personal Right to Arms," *Duke Law Journal* 43 (1994): 1236; Akhil Amar, "The Bill of Rights and Fourteenth Amendment," *Yale Law Journal* 101 (1992): 1193; Akhil Amar, "The Bill of Rights as a Constitution," *Yale Law Journal* 100 (1991): 1131, 1164ff; Elaine Scarry, "War and the Social Contract: Nuclear Policy, Distribution, and The Right to Bear Arms," *University of Pennsylvania Law Review* 139 (1991): 1257; Robert J. Cottrol and Raymond T. Diamond, "The Second Amendment: Toward an Afro-Americanist Reconsideration," *Georgetown Law Journal* 80 (1991): 309; Stephen P. Halbrook, "The Right of the People or the Power of the State: Bearing Arms, Arming Militaries, and the Second Amendment," *Valparaiso University Law Review* 26 (1991): 131.

See also Sanford Levinson, "The Embarrassing Second Amendment," *Yale Law Journal* 99 (1989): 637; Stephen Halbrook, *A Right to Bear Arms: State and Federal Bills of Rights and Constitutional Guarantees* (1989); Stephen Halbrook, "Encroachments of the Crown on the Liberty of the Subject: Pre-Revolutionary Origins of the Second Amendment," *Dayton Law Review* 15 (1989): 91; Leonard Levy, *Original Intent and the Framers' Constitution* (1988), p.

341; David Hardy, "The Second Amendment and the Historiography of the Bill of Rights," *Journal of Law and Policy* 4 (1987): 1; Nelson Lund, "The Second Amendment, Political Liberty and the Right to Self-Preservation," *Alabama Law Journal* 39 (1987): 103; Robert Shalhope, "The Armed Citizen in the Early Republic," *Law and Contemporary Problems* 49 (1986): 125; Don B. Kates, "A Dialogue on the Right to Keep and Bear Arms," *Law and Contemporary Problems* 49 (1986): 143; *Encyclopedia of the American Constitution* 4:1639–40 (Karst & Levi eds., 1986); David Hardy, "Armed Citizens, Citizen Armies: Toward a Jurisprudence of the Second Amendment," *Harvard Journal of Law and Public Policy* 9 (1986): 559; William Marina, "Weapons, Technology and Legitimacy: The Second Amendment in Global Perspective" in *Firearms and Violence: Issues of Public Policy* (Don Kates, ed., 1984); Robert Dowlut, "The Current Relevancy of Keeping and Bearing Arms," *University of Baltimore Law Journal* 15 (1984): 32; Don Kates, "Handgun Prohibition and the Original Meaning of the Second Amendment," *Michigan Law Review* 82 (1983): 204, 244–52; Joyce Malcolm, "The Right of the People to Keep and Bear Arms: The Common Law Perspective," *Hastings Const. Law Quarterly* 10 (1983): 285; Robert Dowlut, "The Right to Arms," *Oklahoma Law Journal* 36 (1983): 65; Senate Subcomm. on the Constitution of the Comm. on the Judiciary, 97th Cong., 2d Sess., *The Right To Keep and Bear Arms* (1982); David Caplan, "The Right of the Individual to Bear Arms," 1982 *Detroit Coll. Law Journal* (1982): 789; Richard Gardiner, "To Preserve Liberty—A Look at the Right to Keep and Bear Arms," *Northern Kentucky Law Journal* 10 (1982): 63; Robert Shalhope, "The Ideological Origins of the Second Amendment," *Journal of American History* 69 (1982): 599.

Few articles from the last decade approximate support position that the Second Amendment guarantees a right of states only. Significantly, two of the articles which do argue that the Second Amendment does not prevent gun prohibition acknowledge that the Second Amendment was intended to confer an individual right. David C. Williams, "Civic Republicanism and the Citizen Militia: The Terrifying Second Amendment," *Yale Law Journal* 101 (1991): 551, reasons that since state governments have neglected their duties to promote responsible gun use through drill in a "well-regulated militia," the right to arms is no longer valid. Beschle, "Reconsidering the Second Amendment: Constitutional Protection for a Right of Security," *Hamline Law Journal* 9 (1986): 69, finds that the Amendment guarantees an individual right of personal security, but suggests that the right can be protected by confiscating all guns. The articles asserting that the Second Amendment confers only a right on states, and not on persons, are Samuel Fields, "Guns, Crime and the Negligent Gun Owner," *Northern Kentucky Law Journal* 10 (1982); Warren Spannaus, "State Firearms Regulation and the Second Amendment," *Hamline Law Journal* 6 (1983): 383; Lawrence Cress, "An Armed Community: The Origins and Meaning of the right to Bear Arms," *Journal of American History* 71 (1983): 22; Keith A. Ehrman and Dennis A. Henigan, "The Second Amendment in the Twentieth Century: Have You Seen Your Militia Lately?" *Dayton Law Journal* 15 (1989): 5; Dennis A. Henigan, "Arms, Anarchy and the Second Amendment," *Valparaiso University Law Journal* 26 (1991): 107.

Forty-three state constitutions include their own right to bear arms provision. See generally, Robert Dowlut, "State Constitutional Rights to Bear Arms: Traditional Interpretation and Public Housing," *St. Thomas Law Journal* 5 (1992): 203; Robert Dowlut and Janet Knoop, "State Constitutions and the Right to Keep and Bear Arms," *Oklahoma City Law Journal* 7 (1982): 177.

One interesting article argues that an individual right to own handguns for personal protection can be found in the federal Ninth Amendment. Nicholas J. Johnson, "Beyond the Second Amendment: An Individual Right to Arms Viewed through the Ninth Amendment," *Rutgers Law Journal* 24 (1992): 1.

171. "Statement by Senator Hubert H. Humphrey on Second Amendment to the Constitution of the United States," attachment to Senator Hubert H. Humphrey, Letter to William B. Edwards, Technical Editor, *Guns Magazine,* October 22, 1959, quoted in David

Hardy, "The Second Amendment as a Restraint on State and Federal Firearm Restrictions," in Don B. Kates, ed., *Restricting Handguns: The Liberal Skeptics Speak Out* (Croton-on-Hudson, N.Y.: North River Press, 1979), pp. 184–85.

At "assault weapon" hearings in 1989, Representative William Hughes told witness Neal Knox (the lobbyist for the Firearms Coalition), that it was outrageous that Knox and his supporters did not trust the government. Knox shot back that it was outrageous that Hughes did not trust the people.

172. Even if the conflict between European settlers and Indians is viewed as war between sovereign nations, the war (on both sides) included numerous attacks on noncombatants, and many successful attempts to starve civilian populations into submission.

173. *Lethal Laws,* Jay Simkin, Aaron Zelman, and Alan M. Rice, Jews for the Preservation of Firearms Ownership, Inc., 2872 South Wentworth Avenue, Milwaukee, Wis. 53207, (414) 769-0760, p. 23.

174. Simkin et al., *Lethal Laws,* p. 23.

175. Ibid., p. 24.

176. Ibid.

177. Gallup poll released December 20, 1944, question 2, in *The Gallup Poll: Public Opinion 1935–1971,* 3 vols. (Am. Inst. Pub. Opinion: 1972), 1: 477.

178. Roger Daniels, *Prisoners without Trial: Japanese Americans in World War II* (New York: Hill & Wang, 1993).

179. Ibid.

180. Michael W. Fitzgerald, "'To Give Our Votes to the Party': Black Political Agitation and Agricultural Change in Alabama, 1865–1870," *Journal of American Historty* 76 (1989): 489.

181. Kopel, *Samurai,* pp. 332–40. See also the chapter by Professors Cottrol and Diamond in this book.

182. Debra Nussbaum, "Crown Heights Indictment Raises Hopes," *Intermountain Jewish News,* August 19, 1994, p. 7 (Jewish Telegraph Agency).

183. Michael Barone and Grant Ujifusa, *The Almanac of American Politics 1994* (1993), pp. 531–32 .

184. Ruth E. Gruber, "Italian Leader Blames Jews for Fall of Lira," *Intermountain Jewish News,* August 19, 1994, p. 3.

185. Mao Tse-tung, *Mao-Tse Tung on Guerilla Warfare,* translated by S. Griffith (New York: Praeger, 1961), cited in Raymond Kessler, "Gun Control and Political Power," *Law & Policy Quarterly* 5 (1983): 395.

186. Kates, "Handgun Prohibition and the Original Meaning of the Second Amendment," *Michigan Law Review,* p. 270.

187. Levinson, "The Embarrassing Second Amendment," *Yale Law Journal,* p. 657.

188. Ammunition, if kept dry, has a shelf life of at least several decades.

189. For example, Mormon families are required to store a year's supply worth of food.

190. Simkin et al., *Lethal Laws,* p. 69.

191. Ibid., p. 70.

192. 389 U.S. 347 (1967).

193. Medical technology has greatly outstripped firearms technology in the past two centuries. Because gunshot wounds are much less likely to result in fatality today, a criminal firing a semi-automatic gun for a given period (such as six minutes) now would kill fewer people today than one firing a more primitive gun two hundred years ago.

194. Such an exemption could not be defended on the grounds that these guns can only be used by persons with special training; as noted above, "assault weapon" prohibitionists may complain that the guns are "very easy to use." Cathy Reynolds, *Headlines.*

The attitude that gun laws are something for other people is not confined to some police administrators. West Virginia Senator Jay Rockefeller owns a Colt AR-15 semi-automatic rifle, one of the "assault weapons" that the senator voted to ban. "John D. Rockefeller IV, Gun Nut," *Washington Times,* Sept. 8, 1994.

Senator Diane Feinstein, chief proponent of the federal "assault weapon" ban had, while mayor of San Francisco, signed a handgun ban and urged all citizens to turn their handguns in to the police. Mayor Feinstein herself turned in one handgun—but retained another one.

195. In December 1992, an off-duty Bureau of Indian Affairs police officer opened fire and shot fifty rounds into a bar in Bemidjii, Minnesota. He used the Colt AR-15 type semi-automatic rifle which he had been issued by the government, as well as 9mm handgun he personally owned. Pat Doyle, "For 14 Long Minutes, Sheer Terror Filled Bar Attacked by Gunman," *Minneapolis Tribune,* December 29, 1992.

Massacres do not have to be planned. An inexperienced police officer, under stress and armed with a deadly "assault weapon," could do at least as much damage as an ordinary citizen who went berserk. Of course it would be wrong to deprive all police officers of useful firearms to guard against the unlikely possibility that an officer with no prior record of illegal violence would suddenly lose his bearings and start killing people. The same may be said of ordinary citizens.

196. "Gun-Control Foes' Lawsuit Alleges Warrantless Search," *Washington Times,* July 17, 1990, p. B5; "Pro-Gun Groups Sue for Access to Papers Related to '88 Search," *The Sun* (Baltimore), July 17, 1990.

197. The act which the police said justified the taking of photos was the unfurling of a banner comparing Governor Schaefer to Hitler, but no photograph shows such a banner. None of the photos showed persons engaging or seeming ready to engage in violent conduct. The photographs were mostly of speakers and persons quietly listening to them. The rally was the only 1991 State House demonstration where police photographed the demonstrators. "Police Photos Taken at State House Rally Irk Gun-Control Foes," *Washington Times,* March 28, 1991, p. B4; "Police Photos and Gun Rally Blasted," *The Evening Sun* (Baltimore), March 27, 1991, p. A1; "Gun Advocates Charge Intimidation," *Montgomery Journal,* March 28, 1991, p. A1.

198. "Smile! You're on State Police Camera," *Montgomery Journal,* April 1, 1991, p. A4 (editorial).

5

Bad Medicine: Doctors and Guns

Don B. Kates, Henry E. Schaffer, John K. Lattimer, George B. Murray, and Edwin H. Cassem*

INTRODUCTION

Predictably, gun violence, particularly homicide, is a major study topic for social scientists, particularly criminologists.[1] Less predictably, gun crime, accidents, and suicide are also a topic of study among medical and public health professionals. Our focus is the remarkable difference between the way medical and public health writers, on the one hand, and social scientists, on the other, treat firearms issues.

---

*This chapter incorporates material from the following manuscripts: Henry E. Schaffer, "Serious Flaws in Kellermann et al. ['Gun Ownership as a Risk Factor for Homicide in the Home,' *New England Journal of Medicine* 329 (1993): 1084–91]"; Don B. Kates, "A Controlled Look at Gun Control," a White Paper on Firearms and Crime in connection with the author's oral presentation before the Select Committee of the Pennsylvania Legislature to Investigate the Use of Automatic and Semi-automatic Firearms; and Don B. Kates, John K. Lattimer, and Robert J. Cottrol, "Public Health Literature on Firearms: A Critique of Overt Mendacity," a paper presented at the 1991 annual meeting of the American Society of Criminology.

A different version of this chapter, "Guns and Public Health: Epidemic of Violence or Pandemic of Propaganda," by Don B. Kates, Henry E. Schaffer, Ph. D., John K. Lattimer, M.D., and George B. Murray, M.D., appears in volume 62 of the *Tennessee Law Review* (1995). This article does not reflect any changes that may be made by the editorial staff of the *Tennessee Law Review.*

The authors wish to thank the following for their time and helpful comments and advice: James Boen, Philip Cook, Dan Day, Gary Green, Fran Haga, Steve Holland, C. Kates, Paul Stoufflet. Of course, the authors alone are responsible for any errors.

Immersion in the literature produced by medical and health writers suggests to us that certain anomalies of that literature explain why its conclusions on firearms diverge so radically from those of criminological scholarship. We focus on that literature's anomalies both for their own sake and because such a focus allows us to explore some of the more important policy and legal issues of gun control.

THE PUBLIC HEALTH AGENDA

In 1979 the federal government's public health forces adopted the "objective to reduce the number of handguns in private ownership," the initial target being a 25 percent reduction by the year 2000.[2] Based on studies and leadership from the Centers for Disease Control and Prevention (CDC), the objective has broadened so that it now includes: banning and confiscation of all handguns, and restrictive licensing of owners of other firearms, with the goal of eventually eliminating firearms from American life, excepting (perhaps) only an elite of wealthy collectors, hunters, or target shooters.[3]

In this connection, some clarification is needed of the term "gun control." That term could mean no more than noncontroversial measures to prohibit gun misuse or gun possession by high risk groups. In the literature we are analyzing, however, "guns are not an inanimate object, but in fact are a social ill," and controlling them implies wholesale confiscation from the general public so as to radically reduce gun availability to ordinary people.[4] This goal parallels to an extent those of political lobbying groups such as Handgun Control, Inc., and the National Coalition to Ban Handguns (renamed the Coalition to Stop Gun Violence [CSGV], reflecting its present advocacy of banning many long guns as well as handguns; see endnote 3). In fact, the public health agenda of drastically reducing availability goes beyond that of those groups. Handgun Control apparently seeks only to ban gun ownership for self-defense, but would allow licensed sportsmen to have both handguns and long guns for purely sporting purposes[5]; and the CSGV would allow people to have long guns, and limited access to handguns, for sporting purposes.[6]

Exhortations "to speak out for gun control" are seen as part of an admirable tradition of political advocacy by doctors and other health professionals in support of political measures designed to improve public health.[7] In that spirit, writers in public health journals strongly avow the need for active political advocacy, for concerted action with antigun groups, and for openly supporting their political initiatives.[8] (We shall use the phrase "antigun health advocacy literature" as a shorthand for medical and public health publications having this focus or agenda.[9])

Health advocates see no problem reconciling such an openly political agenda with the demands of scholarship. After all, guns are hateful things for which no decent purpose is imaginable, certainly not self-defense.[10] Society's need to radically reduce gun availability is an unarguable truth to which there can be no legitimate opposition. Arrayed against the beneficent alliance of health advocates and antigun political advocates are only sinister "powerful lobbies that impede constructive exploration of the full range of social options"[11] by nefarious machinations, including racist propaganda cunningly designed to exploit white Americans' irrational fears of crime.[12]

This is a struggle between modern enlightenment and (at best) morally obtuse and intellectually benighted atavism. There is no time for arid, academic discussion; the need for gun control is too urgent to require, or allow, equivocation, doubt, debate, or dissent.[13]

> The continued advocacy of long overdue gun control is a constructive long-term approach to [reducing violence]. . . . We reason that the time has come for government and citizens to begin a reasoned dialogue on the "why not" of gun ownership. If the conduct of youth and the need for harmony of humans with Nature is valuable to health and civilization, the world's most powerful country may not find justification for an armed citizenry.[14]

Moreover, there is no point to discussion, detached reflection or dissent in a struggle between the forces of light and those of darkness. Evidence or perspectives that might induce skepticism or produce delay are *per se* invalid, inventions of the Neanderthal, racist gun lovers.[15]

The foregoing attitudes are central to the anomalies we find in reviewing the health advocacy literature against gun ownership. It exists in a vacuum of lock-step orthodoxy almost hermetically sealed from the existence of contrary data or scholarship. Such data and scholarship routinely go unacknowledged; at best, they are evaded by being misleadingly associated with the sinister forces of the gun lobby.[16] With rare exceptions, reference citations in the antigun health advocacy literature are to other writings in that same literature. If the universe of sources thus circumscribed does not yield appropriately antigun data, editorials are cited as if they were data, even when the editorial is not presenting data.[17] On occasion, publications by antigun groups are cited for purported factual data, sometimes without identification.[18] There's nothing wrong *per se* with citing an article without detailing the author's affiliation, but, in contrast to the citations of antigun lobbyists, when a claim from a gun lobby source is mentioned in the health advocacy literature against firearms, that origin is noted both in the text and in the margin. Antigun bias is never suggested as a reason for ignoring claims made by antigun groups; but anything said by a progun group is *ipso facto* instantly dismissed.[19]

To use Znaniecki's frame of reference, the antigun health advocacy literature is a "sagecraft" literature in which partisan academic "sages" prostitute scholarship, systematically inventing, misinterpreting, selecting, or otherwise manipulating data to validate preordained political conclusions.[20] Consciousness that one represents the forces of light against those of darkness can overwhelm not only the canons of scholarship but even the ordinary demands of personal honesty and integrity: Given the urgent needs of political advocacy, all too often academic health "sages" feel no compunction about asserting falsehoods, fabricating statistics, and falsifying references to counterfeit support.

The speciousness and atavistic, insidious malignancy of all opposition to gun control being presumed, there is no need for health advocacy periodicals to waste space on such views or time in evaluating inconsistent evidence. Typical is the statement by the president of the American College of Epidemiology who declares gun ownership the "primary cause" of murder—and then calls for research on the subject.[21] (Whether guns "cause" violence, rather than being only an instrument, is among the cardinal, and most mooted, issues in the gun control debate. For what it is worth, two decades of research and analysis have led most criminologists to discard the idea of guns as a cause of crime—something that results in crime by previously law-abiding, responsible adults—in favor of noting firearms' role in facilitating crime by criminals, and in worsening or bettering those crimes.[22])

Consider the evaluation an epidemiologist and a sociologist jointly offered in a panel presentation at the 1994 annual meeting of the American Society of Criminology. Having noted methodological and other errors in the *New England Journal of Medicine* paper which is discussed in depth below, they point out that support for severely restrictive gun laws has been expressed by the *New England Journal of Medicine* as well as

> by the American Medical Association in its house organ, *JAMA*; the American Academy of Pediatrics in *Pediatrics*; and the American Trauma Society in *Trauma*.
>
> A review . . . reveals several consistent patterns. First, the literature cited is almost always that published by medical or public health researchers. Little is cited from the criminological or sociological field. Second, reports with findings not supporting the position of the journal are rarely cited. Finally, several assumptions are presented as fact: that there is a causal association between gun ownership and the risk of violence, that this association is consistent across all demographic categories, and that additional legislation will reduce the prevalence of firearms and consequently reduce the incidence of violence.
>
> *Incestuous and selective literature citations may be acceptable for political tracts, but introduce an artificial bias into scientific publications. Stating as fact associations which may be demonstrably false is not just unscientific, it is unprincipled.*
>
> The question of advocacy based on political beliefs rather than scientific fact raises the further questions of the proper scope of medical and public health concern. . . .
>
> It would be strange indeed to expect the medical/ public health system to not advocate for health. In the case of firearms, however, the advocacy seems to have preceded the health related research.[23] (Emphasis added)

In sum, health leaders see violence as a public health crisis and the firearm as something akin to an infectious disease: "Guns are a virus that must be eradicated."[24] Their views receive wide exposure because, unlike criminology and most other social scientific journals, medical and health periodicals announce the appearance of their articles on firearms to the press with releases describing the antigun conclusions. This follows the avowed intention of the health advocate sages to promote the idea that firearms ownership is an evil and its elimination a desirable and efficacious means of reducing violence.[25]

THE VERDICT OF CRIMINOLOGICAL SCHOLARSHIP

Since the 1960s, health advocate sages have churned out a vast, and ever-increasing amount of antigun advocacy literature.[26] But the view thus promulgated is strikingly different from that concurrently emerging from criminological research and scholarship. That was not as clear twenty-five to thirty years ago. In the 1960s criminological opinion was dominated by writers who felt more or less as the antigun health advocacy writers do today.[27] But, as two of the most influential of those writers subsequently admitted:

> In the 1960s, there was literally no scholarship on the relationship between guns and violence and the incidence or consequences of interpersonal violence, and no work in progress.[28]

Serious criminological research began in the 1970s and has been pursued progressively more intensively and extensively ever since. The results of that research may surprise lay persons, given the exposure which the popular press has accorded the antigun health advocacy literature. Consider the leading researcher's description of the effect his (and others') research had on his own attitudes. (From an unpublished presentation to the National Academy of Sciences by Florida State University criminologist Gary Kleck):

> Up until about 1976 or so, there was little reliable scholarly information on the link between violence and weaponry. Consequently, everyone, scholars included, was free to believe whatever they liked about guns and gun control. There was no scientific evidence to interfere with the free play of personal bias. It was easy to be a "true believer" in the advisability of gun control and the uniformly detrimental effects of gun availability (or the opposite positions) because there was so little relevant information to shake one's faith. When I began my research on guns in 1976, like most academics, I was a believer in the "antigun" thesis, i.e., the idea the gun availability has a net positive effect on the frequency and/or seriousness of violent acts. It seemed then like self-evident common sense which hardly needed to be empirically tested. However, as a modest body of reliable evidence (and an enormous body of not-so-reliable evidence) accumulated, many of the most able specialists in this area shifted from the "antigun" position to a more skeptical stance, in which it was negatively argued that the

best available evidence does not convincingly or consistently support the anti-gun position. This is not the same as saying we know the antigun position to be wrong, but rather that there is no strong case for it being correct. The most prominent representatives of the skeptic position would be James Wright and Peter Rossi, authors of the best scholarly review of the literature [citing the 1983 Wright, Rossi and Daly study referenced in endnote 1].

[Subsequent research] . . . has caused me to move beyond even the skeptic position. I now believe that the best currently available evidence, imperfect though it is (and must always be), indicates that general gun availability has no measurable net positive effect on rates of homicide, suicide, robbery, assault, rape, or burglary in the U.S. This is not the same as saying gun availability has no effects on violence—it has many effects on the likelihood of attack, injury, death, and crime completion, but these effects work in both violence-increasing and violence-decreasing directions, with the effects largely canceling out. For example, when aggressors have guns, they are (1) *less* likely to physically attack their victims, (2) *less* likely to injure the victim given an attack, but (3) *more* likely to kill the victim, given an injury. Further, when *victims* have guns, it is less likely aggressors will attack or injure them and less likely they will lose property in a robbery. At the aggregate level, in both the best available time series and cross-sectional studies, the overall net effect of gun availability on total rates of violence is not significantly different from zero. The positive associations often found between aggregate levels of violence and gun ownership appear to be primarily due to violence increasing gun ownership, rather than the reverse. Gun availability does affect the rates of *gun* violence (e.g., the gun homicide rate, gun suicide rate, gun robbery rate) and the fraction of violent acts which involve guns (e.g., the percent of homicides, suicides or robberies committed with guns); it just does not affect total rates of violence (total homicide rate, total suicide rate, total robbery rate, etc.). (Citations omitted; emphasis in original)

Scholars engaged in serious criminological research into "gun control" have found themselves forced—often very reluctantly[29]—into four largely negative propositions: (1) there is no persuasive evidence that owning guns causes ordinary responsible, law-abiding adults to murder or engage in any other criminal behavior—though guns can facilitate crime by those who were independently inclined toward it; (2) the value of firearms in defending victims has been greatly underestimated; (3) gun controls are innately very difficult to enforce.[30]

Difficulty of enforcement crucially undercuts the violence-reductive potential of gun laws. Unfortunately, there is an almost perfect inverse correlation between those who are affected by gun laws (particularly bans) and those whom it is desired to affect. Those easiest to disarm are the responsible and law abiding whose guns represent no meaningful social problem. But the irresponsible and/or criminal owners whose gun possession creates or exacerbates so many social ills are also the ones most difficult to disarm. A leading English analyst's pessimistic view has been summarized as follows, "in any society the number of guns always suffices to arm the few who want to obtain and use them illegally."[31]

So the final conclusion criminological research and analysis forces on scholars is, (4) while controls carefully targeted only at the criminal and/or irresponsible have a place in crime-reduction strategy, the capacity of any type of gun law to reduce dangerous behavior can never be more than marginal. As the Wisconsin State Legislative Reference Bureau concluded in a recent review of both criminological and health advocacy literature:

> It is difficult to make rational decisions in an atmosphere where absolute moral values are assigned to an inanimate object. A gun, while powerful and often destructive, is no more than a tool controlled by the person who uses it. . . .
>
> Gun control legislation focuses on regulating access to firearms, but the availability of guns is only one of many factors contributing to crime. Any measures that attempt to restrict access to firearms without reference to drugs, poverty with its attendant lack of educational and employment opportunities, clogged courts and overcrowded prisons are bound to have only marginal effects on firearm crime.[32]

FEAR AND LOATHING AS SOCIAL SCIENCE

In stark contrast to this nuanced assessment, the spirit animating the health advocacy literature on firearms is illuminated by the frank admission of one outspoken advocate of its political agenda, Dean Deborah Prothrow-Stith of the Harvard School of Public Health:

> My own view on gun control is simple. I hate guns and I cannot imagine why anyone would want to own one. If I had my way, guns for sport would be registered, and all other guns [i.e., those designed for self-defense] would be banned.[33]

Our review of the antigun health advocacy literature suggests that such unconstrained, unabashed emotive bias helps account for many of its anomalies and for its remarkable difference in tone and conclusion from the criminological scholarship on firearms issues.

Antigun health advocates seem blind to or unconcerned about the danger that their emotions may preclude rational evaluation of gun ownership. Psychiatrist Emmanuel Tanay, who admits that he loathes guns to the point of being unable to look upon or touch them with equanimity, asserts that gun ownership betokens sexual immaturity or neuroticism. Dr. Tanay deems it evidence of this: that gun owners actually "handle . . . with obvious pleasure" these horrid objects which so repulse him; that collectors "look after" their collections, "clean, pamper and polish" their guns: "The owner's overvaluation of his gun's worth is an indication of its libidinal value to him."[34]

As further evidence, Dr. Tanay invokes Freud's view of the sexual significance of firearms in the interpretation of dreams. This is particularly ironic because Freud's comments were not directed at gun ownership or owners. Insofar as Freud addressed the matter at all, he seems to have associated *fear and loathing of guns* with sexual immaturity and neuroticism.[35] We are emphatically not endorsing Freud's view as either applicable to Dr. Tanay or explanatory of his views. Our concern is with the effect fear and loathing of guns have on the intellect, not the libido. On Dr. Tanay at least the effect is that he can neither recognize how gun collectors' tastes might differ from his own nor comprehend passages from Freud; in fact, he is unable to read them without imposing a meaning almost opposite to what they actually say.

Dr. Tanay is by no means the only antigun health advocate to exhibit such an emotion-based reading disability (or "gun-aversive dyslexia" as we shall hereinafter call it). Arthur Kellermann, one of the most prolific and influential health advocate sages, cites as *supporting* his view "that limiting access to firearms could prevent many suicides" an article expressly concluding the opposite.[36] An article in *JAMA* attributes increased homicide to increased cocaine use and gun availability among New York City minority teenagers. It cites actual evidence to show increased cocaine use; but its citations supposedly showing increased firearms availability indicated the reverse.[37] Another *JAMA* article alleges, "Research examining the effectiveness of gun control in specific locales suggests that it can reduce violence"—but cites articles whose only relevance was in supporting the opposite conclusion.[38]

We do not suggest these gun-aversive dyslexic errors have any great importance in and of themselves. Their importance lies in what they, and innumerable other errors we document, collectively say about the effect of having advocacy deemed (even hailed as) a norm while scholarship receives only lip service. Error becomes endemic when the corrective effects of dissent and criticism are excluded. Lest our comments seem strident and extreme, recall that medicine is a peer-reviewed literature. Each of the articles cited in the preceding paragraph was refereed, as were almost all of the other articles we cite. How did errors of easily establishable fact (e.g., that a source is cited for something opposite to what it says) slip past three reviewers? The short answer is that intellectual sloppiness prevails when sagecraft displaces scholarship.

Worse yet, peer review, and the general process of criticism, actually exacerbates error, given the atmosphere of intellectual lockstep which prevails among health advocates. For instance, it was not enough for the *JAMA* reviewer of Prothrow-Stith's book that it unreservedly avowed her hatred for guns. He reproached not her emotionalism (that he fervently endorses) but the lack of more space devoted to teaching health advocates how to mobilize support for laws to rid our society of these evil objects.[39] An atmosphere in which criticism in general, and peer review in particular, comes from only one perspective not only allows error but promotes it—intentional error as well as inadvertent error, both minor and serious.

Recall how the CDC's principal researchers on firearms and violence characterized firearms as having a "central role in interpersonal violence."[40] This exemplifies the tendency of grossly inaccurate hyperbole to slip through any kind of editorial review process so long as it supports health advocacy's antigun bias. It could rightly have been said that guns are used in 60-65 percent of the approximately twenty-three thousand murders in this country annually. But, though murder is the gravest form of "interpersonal violence," numerically it is only a small part of that category; and guns are used in less than 13 percent of the 6.7 million rapes, robberies, and assaults.[41]

A NOSOLOGY OF HEALTH SAGE ERROR

The abysmal quality of the antigun health advocacy literature may be explained by six conceptually discrete factors: (1) intellectual and locutional sloppiness; (2) intellectual confusion; (3) ignorance of criminological or other facts; (4) fraudulent omission of material fact, or statement of part of the fact calculated to deceive by the suppression of the whole; (5) overt misrepresentation of facts; and (6) what we call gun-aversive dyslexia, i.e., a reading disability engendered by a fear and loathing of guns so profound that health advocate sages who encounter adverse facts may be honestly unable to comprehend them.

Though these six aspects are conceptually discrete, they often run together in the health advocacy literature, so that it is not always easy to clearly distinguish them from each other and to disentangle their mutually exacerbating effects. Consider Dolins and Christoffel's exhortation for health advocates to "educate" the public to believe there is no constitutional impediment to banning and confiscating guns because

> . . . the Second Amendment does not guarantee the right to personal ownership
> of firearms. Legal decisions, including those of the Supreme Court, have repeat-
> edly ruled in favor of this interpretation, and *none of the existing tens of thou-
> sands of [gun control] laws . . . has ever been ruled unconstitutional.*[42] (Empha-
> sis added)

Particularly since neither author is a lawyer, it is impossible to disentangle how much of this results from overt deception and how much represents gun-aversive dyslexia, confusion, ignorance and/or locutional sloppiness. To give them the benefit of the doubt, it is very possible that Dolins and Christoffel do not understand what is implied by the Supreme Court's allowing ordinary citizens legal standing to raise the Second Amendment without being members of the Army or National Guard[43]; the Court's express recognition that the term "right of the people" used in the First, Second, and Fourth Amendments is to be construed *in pari materia* as denoting the rights of citizens against government; or the Court's several listings of the Second Amendment interchangeably with other Bill of Rights provisions as illustrative of explicitly guaranteed personal rights.[45]

Dolins and Christoffel may also plausibly be assumed not to know of the distinction between dicta and a ruling[46] or that all but eight states have constitutional guarantees of the right to arms which are independent of the Second Amendment and under which gun laws can be and have been invalidated.[47] Likewise, when Christoffel asserted that "Well-informed legal scholars agree that [gun bans] are indeed constitutional" (under the Second Amendment), she may not have known that the verdict of modern Constitutional scholarship is overwhelmingly contrary.[48]

Another passage from Dolins and Christoffel illustrates the difficulty of distinguishing how much a particular health advocacy assertion owes to deception from what may be gun-aversive dyslexia. In the first of two consecutive sentences, Dolins and Christoffel try to discredit the individual right view of the Second Amendment by ascribing it to the sinister forces of "The gun lobby. . . ." The next sentence invokes the same specter to discredit two uncongenial sets of criminological data discussed by social scientists whom Dolins and Christoffel cite, but willfully mischaracterize as follows:

> *Gun supporters* contend that widespread gun ownership has helped to curb the increasing rates of violence and crime although most *epidemiologists* interpret the evidence as unconvincing.[49]

We have added emphasis to this passage to highlight the labels falsely bestowed on both sides in this dispute: On the one hand, the "epidemiologists" whose support Dolins and Christoffel invoke are not "epidemiologists" (i.e., medical scientists who study the incidence, distribution, or control of disease). They are criminologists (i.e., social scientists) just as are the social scientists whose findings they reject. This is important, because as we emphasize below, no health advocate sage has had the intellectual courage even to attempt to come to grips with either of the data sets involved here. Dolins and Christoffel's mendacious reference quoted above is the only mention of one of these data sets in the entire health advocacy literature; the other set is rarely mentioned.[50]

It is no less an overt misrepresentation to label the three scholars (Kleck, Wright, and Rossi) who published those two data sets "gun supporters." None of them urges people to arm themselves. But labeling these sociologists "gun supporters," has the advantage not only of demeaningly misrepresenting their position, but of suppressing two embarrassing, but material, facts. First, each of these "gun supporters" began his research as a believer in the health advocacy indictment of guns, but was reluctantly forced to conclude (as two of them later wrote), "The more deeply we have explored the empirical implications of this indictment, the less plausible it has become."[51]

Second, the contention that widespread gun ownership deters violent crime is not exclusive to Wright and Rossi. The work Dolins and Christoffel cite is Wright and Rossi's report of the results of the survey they conducted for the National Institute of Justice (NIJ) among two thousand felons incarcerated in state prisons across the United States. All Wright and Rossi do is report that 34 percent of the felons said they personally had been "scared off, shot at, wounded, or captured by an armed victim"; that 69 percent said they knew at least one other criminal who had also; that 34 percent said that when thinking about committing a crime they either "often" or "regularly" worried that they "might get shot at by the victim"; and that 57 percent agreed with the statement, "Most criminals are more worried about meeting an armed victim than they are about running into the police."[52]

Dolins and Christoffel do not—because they cannot—deny these results. Though they find the felons' answers highly uncongenial to their own view, to label Wright and Rossi "gun supporters" for honestly reporting the data is misleading, tendentious, and defamatory. To fully comprehend the deceptiveness of the entire passage we have quoted from Dolins and Christoffel on the previous page, it is necessary to recall that the Wright-Rossi research is entirely separate, and separately published, from the Kleck work Dolins and Christoffel link with it. But linking them allows Dolins and Christoffel falsely to claim both studies have been analyzed and rejected. Now one "epidemiologist" (actually a social scientist) whose work Dolins and Christoffel cite does reject Kleck's views. But the "epidemiologist" makes no mention of Wright-Rossi.[53] The other "epidemiologist's" study Dolins and Christoffel cite reviews Kleck respectfully and without any demurral. In reviewing Wright and Rossi's data this latter work seeks to put them in perspective, but does not reject them as "unconvincing."[54] (The same source that Dolins and Christoffel cite, falsely, as condemning Kleck is much more critical of a study Dolins and Christoffel rely on to assert the foolishness of defensive gun ownership. Of course, that critical appraisal is yet another thing Dolins and Christoffel do not bother to mention.[55])

"THE VALOR OF IGNORANCE"[56]

A recent interview with Dr. Robert Tanz of Children's Memorial Hospital in Chicago is as illuminating in its way as Dean Prothrow-Stith's frank avowal of the stark hatred which underlies her antigun advocacy. Dr. Tanz and his colleague at Children's Hospital, Dr. Katherine Christoffel, "plan to do to handguns what their profession has done to cigarettes . . . turn gun ownership from a personal-choice issue to a repulsive, antisocial health hazard."[57]

Because the validity of this goal is severely undercut by Professor Kleck's research on the defensive value of firearms, the interviewer asked Dr. Tanz about that research. It should be noted that there is legitimate controversy—among criminologists—about aspects of Kleck's work in this area. Based on an exhaustive data analysis, Kleck concludes guns are more often used by victims to defend themselves each year than misused by criminals to commit crimes.[58] This conclusion rests on consistent results in ten surveys yielding estimates of the numerical frequency of defensive gun use. Yet inconsistent data are obliquely found in a different survey vehicle which, however, was not specifically designed to address defensive gun use. To the extent that the latter survey does address that issue, it yields figures of less than one hundred thousand defense uses per year, which is far below Kleck and Gertz's figures of two million or more. This disparity is emphasized by Kleck's primary critic, Duke University economist Philip J. Cook. He feels there are

> persuasive reasons for believing that the [other survey vehicle] yields total incident figures that are much too low while Kleck's survey(s) may yield total incident figures that are much too high.[59]

Some criminologists, such as Professor Gary Green of Albany State University, agree with Cook.[60] Others accept Kleck's data,[61] as do we and at least one criminologist who challenges another aspect of Kleck's findings.[62] For the purpose of this chapter, who is "right" does not matter. Even the most scrupulous attention to the canons of scholarship cannot guarantee that every conclusion is noncontroversial and error-free; particularly where relevant data are partial and conflict, even the most painstaking and competent scholars may reach inconsistent conclusions. What the canons of scholarship do demand, in order to minimize the likelihood of error, is what Cook's critique of Kleck did: cite Kleck, describe what Kleck says, and proceed to criticize it. If only the health advocacy literature against firearms were so scrupulous and forthright.

The ultimate goal of scholarly writing is to provide readers with the full information necessary to review the matter and make up their own minds. This brings us back to Dr. Tanz, who has no place in this debate—no basis for forming an opinion, much less for commenting on it: for he "acknowledges that he has never read a single word Kleck has written,"[63] nor does he claim even to have read Kleck's critics. Yet Dr. Tanz unhesitatingly informed the interviewer that Kleck's figures are wildly exaggerated, that the actual number of defensive uses is "only about 80,000" annually. (Note that in the valor of his ignorance Dr. Tanz goes beyond Cook and Green, who agree that Kleck has shown the probability of hundreds of thousands of victim defensive gun uses annually, but reject Kleck's upper figures.)

Dr. Tanz is apparently no less ignorant of the fact that the very survey data (the National Crime Victimization Survey) he embraces against Kleck confirm a different Kleck finding that would equally appall Dr. Tanz, if only he knew of it. These data show that gun-armed victims who resist robbery or rape are injured far less often than either those who resist with other weapons—or those who submit![64] Gun-armed victims are also, of course, much less likely to be robbed or raped than those who take Handgun Control's advice never to resist: "the best defense against injury is to put up no defense—*give them what they want or run* (emphasis added)."[65]

(It bears emphasis that Kleck and others who have discussed these facts add various caveats, the most important of which is that a gun is not a magic wand that renders resistance successful and risk-free regardless of the circumstances.[66] Rather, a handgun is analogous to a fire extinguisher. Both are tools that provide an option for action—an option that may be exercised or not, depending on what the circumstances dictate.)

ISSUES, DATA, AND REFERENCES "MISSING IN ACTION"

Kleck's research findings on the utility of defensive gun ownership first appeared in February 1988 based on the early data then available.[67] That research and Kleck's later elaborations of it is appraised by one of Kleck's sometime critics as "the definitive study in this area. . . ."[68] Health advocates are aware of the importance of the issue of defensive gun use[69] and uniformly oppose it.[70] What then accounts for their never citing and refuting the "definitive study" from 1988 until 1991 (when Cook's critical response became available for counter-citation)? Since 1991, Kleck's work has occasionally been cited—but only within the context of Cook's rebuttal and with the statement that it is discredited by Cook or other critics.[71]

Note also the continued lack of citation, when health sages discount defensive gun ownership, to Kleck's findings that gun-armed victims who resist felons are roughly 50 percent less likely to be injured than those who submit, and 67 percent less likely to be injured than those resisting with some other kind of weapon. What accounts for this failure to cite an aspect of Kleck's findings which are not just unchallenged but actually confirmed by the alternative survey (by the National Crime Victimization Survey)? Could it be that the health advocacy literature will not disclose any data or issue which supports the value of armed self-defense until and unless it can be "balanced" by the appearance of some contrary study that supposedly refutes it?

We are not suggesting that health advocate sages join their allies in the anti-gun lobby in counseling victim submission to rapists and other felons. While anti-gun health advocates freely counsel victims never to keep a firearm to defend themselves, their homes, or their families, what victims should do if attacked is yet another issue missing in action from the health advocacy literature.[73]

Incidentally, to suppress knowledge of Kleck's "definitive study," health sages went beyond mere nondisclosure of its existence in the years before 1991. They misstated the facts: "there are *no studies* . . . there is little scientific evidence to support claims that guns are effective devices for protection (emphasis added),"[74] ". . . there is no evidence to support the [value of guns for] self-defense argument."[75] At the time these falsehoods were uttered, other empirical evidence to the contrary, and numerous other studies, were available, and it was upon these that Kleck's 1988 study was based.[76] A scrupulous regard for the truth (then and now) would have forced the health sages we just quoted to write: "There is little scientific evidence congenial to our position[77]; the best available evidence tends to show that guns are effective devices for protection." This assessment remains fair, incidentally, whether one accepts the Kleck-Gertz findings of about two million defensive gun uses annually or the alternative Cook-Green evaluation of only some hundreds of thousands.

Even now when the health sages have Cook's work to counteract Kleck, those who discuss defensive gun use virtually never cite Kleck's "definitive study in this area. . . ." In 1993 Mercy and Rosenberg admitted the continuing importance of the question "How frequently are guns used to successfully ward off potentially violent attacks?," but did not cite Kleck whose studies directly address that question.[78] Equally dishonest is the following from a 1993 article by Teret and Wintemute which fails to cite Wright and Rossi, Kleck, or the other studies discussed above: Gun lobby or manufacturer "advertisements often portray a handgun as a necessary protection of oneself and one's family. However, data do not support this claim."[79]

Doubtless Mercy and Rosenberg and Teret and Wintemute would seek to excuse their suppression of the existence of Kleck's (and other) contrary findings on the ground that they subscribe to Cook's views. The first difficulty with this is that much of the scholarship in addition to Kleck's, which supports the utility of defensive gun use, has not been controverted. The second is that the fact of Cook's disagreement with Kleck on a particular issue does not repeal the normal standards of scholarly discourse; quite the reverse. Normal scholarly discourse demands that health sages either cite Kleck and explain why they think he is wrong, or, if they do not have the space to address the issue at length, cite Kleck and Cook, declare their agreement with Cook, and let their readers decide for themselves. But the health advocacy political agenda requires that the existence of contrary scholarship or views be suppressed or misrepresented to readers as deriving from the dark forces of the gun lobby.

This leads to a more general point about the *persona non grata* status in the health advocacy literature of the entire corpus of Kleck's work, not just his research on defensive gun use. Over the past fifteen years Kleck has been the most important and prolific social scientific researcher in the area. In 1993 the American Society of Criminology bestowed its highest award on his book *Point Blank*, declaring it the single most important contribution to criminology in the past three years.[80] American and foreign reviewers hail the book as the prerequisite to scholarly research or discussion of the issues; even scholars who disagree with Kleck's views call *Point Blank* the essential reference work, the "indispensable" text "for any serious scholar working in the area."[81] Professor Wright, co-author of 1981 and 1983 studies and reviews that previously held sway as the authoritative work on the criminology of firearms, freely concedes that *Point Blank* eclipses it.[82]

So what does it say about the health sages' integrity or reliability that we can find no citation to *Point Blank* by health advocates writing about firearms issues, and virtually no citation of the rest of the vast corpus of Kleck's scholarly research.[83] Insofar as they do cite Kleck, health advocate sages deem they have refuted him without exposing any actual flaws, simply by stating that Kleck questions the efficacy of gun control and/or by implying (falsely) that Kleck is employed by the NRA or financed thereby.[84] The antigun editors who print these advocates presumably accept such refutations as condemning Kleck's work *per se* and without need for further discussion, much less allowing Kleck or any scholar who agrees with him to argue the merits.

Returning to the example of Dr. Tanz with which we began, we see at least a limited defense for his disinclination to read anything adverse to his emotional bias against firearms. Perhaps his failure to read *Point Blank* is occasioned by the assumption that Kleck would simply shirk the evidence Dr. Tanz prefers to credit. Reasonable though such an assumption is to one whose ideas of scholarship are conditioned by the health advocacy literature, it is inaccurate as regards the criminological literature in general and Kleck in particular. Kleck meticulously analyzes every major article in the health advocacy literature which preceded *Point Blank*'s publication; the book's reference section cites at least twenty-five medical or health publications.

Unnatural Selection

Another "exception" to Kleck's *persona non grata* status in the health advocacy literature is particularly striking because it is the proverbial "exception that proves the rule." Despite Dolins and Christoffel's false characterization of Kleck as a Neanderthal "gun supporter," he is actually a liberal Democrat, a member of the ACLU and Amnesty International, but not of any progun group.[85] In fact, Kleck has annoyed the gun lobby by recommending gun controls it opposes and by characterizing its "tough on crime" legislative policy recommendations as "stupid." Long before the Brady Bill, Kleck supported a much more sweeping background check than the bill provides for.[86] Significantly, of all Kleck has written about firearms, this pro-control recommendation is one of only two positive citations his work has received in the health advocacy literature.[87]

It is noteworthy that this is the sole positive citation of Kleck by health advocates to appear in an entire chapter devoted to firearms issues of a health advocacy book (*Injury Prevention*, a supplemental edition of the *American Journal of Preventive Medicine*). Given the available space it is at once ironic and typical that the chapter's authors found no room for the more major points in Kleck's work as a whole—or even in the one Kleck article they cited. To see why Kleck's major work is avoided it is necessary only to quote from the abstract to the cited article:

All of the following assumptions [of antigun advocacy] were found to be substantially at variance with the evidence: (1) Guns are five times deadlier than the
weapons most likely to be substituted [if a gun ban made guns unavailable to
criminals]; (2) The sight of a gun can elicit aggression . . . ; (3) If guns are made
more expensive, more difficult to obtain, or legally risky to own, people will do
without them; (4) Guns are useless for self-defense . . . and have no deterrent
effect on criminals; (5) Homicides are largely "crimes of passion" committed by
otherwise law-abiding citizens not distinguishable from other people. Therefore,
control must be directed at all gun owners rather than select criminal subgroups.[88]

Since most of these insupportable assumptions are present in the health advocacy chapter on firearms, the failure to mention Kleck's (or any other) counterar-
gument is once again striking, yet all too typical of what passes for scholarship
in the sagecraft literature of antigun health advocacy. The ironic and amusing
effect of ignoring the premier researcher and the definitive work is that inevitably
the health literature will sometimes be as sloppy about noncontroversial matters
as it is intellectually dishonest about controversial ones.[89]

The co-author with Kleck of the article recommending waiting periods was
University of Illinois sociologist David J. Bordua. As discussed at endnote 15,
health sages dismiss Bordua's research as "racist" when they find its results uncongenial. How fortunate it is that Bordua's (alleged) racism is not a bar to their
citing his work when it recommends more gun control. (Indeed, the sincerity of
the health sages' concern with racism may be questioned in light of the health literature's nondiscussion of racism historically as a purpose or effect of antigun
laws and their discriminatory application.[90])

Next, recall how Dolins and Christoffel evaded uncongenial aspects of work
by two other major scholarly contributors to the firearms area, falsely characterizing them as "gun supporters."[91] The fact is that Professors James D. Wright and
Peter H. Rossi, who hold endowed chairs in sociology at Tulane and the
University of Massachusetts, respectively, are both liberal Democrats who neither own guns nor belong to the NRA. Their work has been funded by the U.S.
Department of Justice's National Institute of Justice, not the gun lobby.[92] Their
review of the literature on the criminology of firearms was the basic text in the
area until superseded by *Point Blank* a decade later.[93]

Despite its enormous bulk, the health advocacy literature has no comprehensive summary like that of Wright and Rossi or *Point Blank*. Since to cite *Point
Blank* is inconceivable, health sages (including even Dr. Christoffel!) sometimes
find themselves forced to cite Wright and Rossi for some point that cannot otherwise be documented. It is truly wondrous how such dependency transforms
those discreditable "gun supporters" into credible, reliable scholars.[94] In yet
another example of gun-aversive dyslexia, Sloan et al. (in the famous Seattle-
Vancouver comparative article) even cite Wright and Rossi as supporting their
(the doctors') belief that "restricting access to handguns could substantially

reduce our annual rate of homicide."[95] Wright and Rossi had indeed evaluated that belief, but their appraisal was:

> It is commonly hypothesized that much criminal violence, especially homicide, occurs simply because the means of lethal violence (firearms) are readily at hand, and, thus, that much homicide would not occur were firearms generally less available. *There is no persuasive evidence that supports this view.*[96] (Emphasis added)

Two years later, Wright wrote a letter pointing out flaws in a new gun article by Sloan, who responded that "Wright's long-held views on the subject of gun control are also well-known," and his "criticism was predictable."[97] Yet if those "long-held" views were "well-known" to Sloan et al. two years before, the doctors' attribution of the opposite view to Wright (and Rossi) crossed the line from mere gun-aversive dyslexia to out-and-out misrepresentation.

The quotation from Wright and Rossi given above is the centerpiece of the abstract to the executive summary of their NIJ-funded literature evaluation. Naturally, there is no mention in the health advocacy literature on firearms of Wright and Rossi's general conclusions regarding firearms and levels of violence. Readers who get their information from the health sages will never know of the general conclusions of Wright and Rossi's NIJ literature evaluation; with few exceptions, health advocate sages do not inform readers of specific findings in the evaluation that are adverse to the health advocacy position.

In this connection we note Teret and Wintemute's brief mention, in a 1993 article, of prior reviews of scholarship and literature on the criminology of firearms. The NIJ literature evaluation and *Point Blank* are far and away the most important such reviews. But Teret and Wintemute choose not to share that (or any knowledge of either review) with their readers. Instead of Wright and Rossi, they cite an obscure, generally antigun, 1978 review only ninety pages long that has gone virtually uncited since the 600-page Wright and Rossi review appeared in 1981. Instead of the 500-page *Point Blank* (1991) they mention a nine page review done for the AMA in 1989, again with generally antigun conclusions.[99]

Health advocates are understandably uncomfortable with the criminological scholarship represented by Wright, Rossi, Kleck, Bordua, and others—almost allergic to it in fact. Yet ought they not to have some better response than just concealing this enormous body of contrary evidence from their readers? It is trite, but apparently necessary, to say that if the health advocates have some meaningful answer to the criminologists' conclusions, they ought to forthrightly describe those conclusions and tell their readers what is wrong with them.

"SAGECRAFT" AND SCHOLARSHIP

Though he has not read Kleck, Dr. Tanz has read—and highly recommends—a study the *New England Journal of Medicine* published extolling strict Canadian gun control. The study was a comparison of homicide rates in Vancouver with those in Seattle.[100] Being largely or completely ignorant of the vast body of competent contradicting research, health advocacy journals routinely cite this study as the shibboleth of the health advocacy faith:

> lack of availability of guns can decrease the propensity of people to commit violent acts both toward others and themselves, [resulting in] an absolute reduction in the rate of penetrating trauma.[101]

But Dr. Tanz does at least know that opposite conclusions were reached in one of the few skeptical articles a medical or health journal has published, Brandon Centerwall's exhaustive comparison of nationwide Canadian and U.S. homicide data.[102] But that is yet another uncongenial study Dr. Tanz never bothered to read before closing his mind.[103]

Presumably Dr. Tanz is unaware that the rosy conclusions he has formed about Canadian gun control have also been discredited in other Canada-wide studies.[104] But the fact that Dr. Tanz chooses to rely on conclusions he likes based on data from just two cities in the U.S. and Canada, while having no interest in the contrary conclusions dictated by national data comparisons, speaks for itself. Being intellectually indefensible, such a choice can only be explained, not justified; and the only explanation is that it is "result-oriented," i.e., dictated by Dr. Tanz's emotional bias in favor of reaching antigun results despite the contrary conclusions indicated by the best available evidence. Regrettably, the health advocacy literature against firearms is consistently result-oriented. It is a sagecraft literature in which academic "sages" prostitute scholarship, systematically inventing, misinterpreting, selecting, or otherwise manipulating data to validate preordained conclusions.

Dr. Tanz's preference for two-city data that support his view over two-nation data that refute it is typical. And that same intellectually indefensible choice has been made, first, by the authors of the two-city comparison (who are among the most prominent of the health advocate sages); second, by the *New England Journal of Medicine* which published that inferior data article; and third, by the antigun health advocacy community ever since. Professor Centerwall, author of a comparative study between the U.S. and Canada, has kindly allowed us to quote the following personal communication: One of the authors of the two-city comparison, Dr. John Sloan,

> and I were both affiliated with the University of Washington [School of Public Health, where Centerwall still teaches] at the time that [Sloan] was working on

his study comparing Seattle and Vancouver and I on my study comparing the United States and Canada. We were aware of each other's work. Shortly before he began writing his paper, I gave him a copy of my [article draft], so *he was familiar with it in detail before he prepared his own work.*

We have added emphasis to the foregoing to spotlight the issue of sagecraft. Under normal standards of scholarly integrity, Dr. Sloan would have responded by either not submitting his study for publication or by citing Centerwall and then explaining why the Seattle-Vancouver study's results were meaningful and valid despite their contradiction by a vastly larger data set. But the sagecraft ethics prevailing among health advocates on gun issues allowed Sloan et al. to solve their problem more simply, if not more elegantly. They just published their article and omitted to inform their readers of a far larger and more geographically diverse data-set yielding contrary results.

Centerwall's very different attitude toward scholarship is indicated by the fact that his article expressly called the two-city comparison to his readers' attention and then explained why its defective methodology and inferior data set invalidated its results.[105] We now quote Centerwall's letter:

By coincidence [Sloan] and I independently submitted our respective manuscripts to the *New England Journal of Medicine* at the same time. Therefore, the editors had both manuscripts before them on the table, at least metaphorically, and perhaps literally. Thus both [Sloan] *and* the editors of the *New England Journal* knew that there was another study which flatly contradicted Sloan's findings and conclusions, yet Sloan chose not to acknowledge the existence of that study in his paper and the editors of the *New England Journal* did not require him to make reference to it. I might add that it is common for the *New England Journal* to publish two articles on the same subject back-to-back in the same issue when it seems opportune to do so. They have even published back-to-back articles which have flatly contradicted each other. Therefore, accepting one article in no way precluded accepting the other. (Emphasis in original)

Predictably, the *New England Journal* rejected the Centerwall study, published the Sloan piece, and did not even require that Sloan et al. mention Centerwall's findings. The Centerwall article was eventually published in the *American Journal of Epidemiology,* albeit under the unprecedented condition that an antigun author be invited to comment in response. Of course, none of the literally hundreds of antigun articles and editorials published by health advocacy periodicals over the past thirty years has required or invited commentary by either a progun or a neutral analyst. Indeed, in all that time, only one progun commentary, out of all the hundreds of articles addressing gun issues, has appeared in these health advocacy periodicals.[106]

Remarkably, the antigun commentator on the Centerwall article ended up accepting its conclusions and urging careful attention to them by medical and health professionals interested in the firearms area.[107] Of course, this advice fell on deaf ears: the Centerwall article is almost never cited by health advocates; nor is there ever any citation of the other two-nation studies reaching the same negative conclusion as to strict Canadian gun control; in contrast, Sloan et al.'s meager two-city comparison is among the most frequently cited studies in the health advocacy literature on firearms.[108]

Note that Centerwall is yet another nongun owner, non-"gun supporter," whose research forced him to conclusions he did not desire. His comments on that should have particular interest for any health advocates who can rise above gun-aversive dyslexia:

> If you are surprised by my findings, so am I. I did not begin this research with any intent to "exonerate" handguns, but there it is—a negative finding, to be sure, but a negative finding is nevertheless a positive contribution. *It directs us where not to aim public health resources.*[109] (Emphasis added)

Other research has led Centerwall to link high violence rates to the effects of a generation or more of children watching television. Predictably, health advocate sages, who concur with Centerwall on television's danger, have no difficulty citing his work to that effect—even as they ignore the uncongenial findings of his two-nation handgun homicide study.[110] The June 10, 1992, *JAMA,* which was devoted to the issue of violence, included a piece from Centerwall on television as a cause of violence. Many of the other articles were devoted to firearms. Of course, none cited the Centerwall piece or offered, or even mentioned, any view other than the health advocacy shibboleth that more-guns-mean-more-murder, strict-gun-control-means-less-murder. The remainder of this chapter will contrast the health advocacy literature's deceitful promotion of this shibboleth with the overwhelmingly adverse results of the criminological evidence.

INTERNATIONAL DISINFORMATION

In a book published twenty years ago, antigun activist Robert Sherrill derisively commented that no debate over gun policy would be complete without a plethora of brief, often inaccurate and invariably contradictory, references to foreign gun laws and crime rates.[111] The information necessary to avoid many such errors is available in David Kopel's analysis of foreign gun laws, policies, and crime which was named book of the year by the Society of Criminology's Division of International Criminology in 1992.[112] Predictably, we have been unable to find a citation of Kopel's book in the health advocacy literature.

1. Vancouver-Seattle Comparison

References to foreign gun laws and their supposedly miraculous reductive effect on crime appear endlessly in the health advocacy literature.[114] Their quality ranges from the ignorant and simplistic to half-truths to deliberate misinformation. Lest this assessment seem harsh, compare a Canadian criminologist's evaluation of the Sloan two-city comparison. Lamenting that all too often gun control "studies are an abuse of scholarship, inventing, selecting, or misinterpreting data in order to validate *a priori* conclusions," Professor Gary Mauser of Simon Fraser University adds, "A particularly egregious example is 'Handgun Regulations, Crime, Assaults and Homicide,' by John Sloan and his associates, which appeared in volume 319 of the *New England Journal of Medicine* in 1988."[115]

Note that—entirely independent of the contradictory result from Centerwall's superior data base (or Sloan's failure to mention Centerwall's paper)— Sloan's two-city comparison is methodologically worthless, patently invalid, and insufficient to justify its conclusions. As Professor Kleck commented on National Public Radio's "All Things Considered" (December 16, 1989):

> There were only two cities studied, one Canadian, one U.S. There are literally thousands of differences across cities that could account for violence rates, and these authors just arbitrarily seized on gun levels and gun control levels as being what caused the difference. It's the sort of research that never should have seen the light of day.

Of course, neither Sloan et al. nor any other health advocacy sage has acknowledged criticism from scholars like Mauser and Kleck.

2. Israel and Switzerland: Murder and the Availability of Guns

As Kopel's prize-winning international research shows, there is no consistent correlation between gun laws or gun ownership rates and high murder or suicide or crime rates across a broad spectrum of nations and cultures.[116] No doubt health advocates do believe the coincidence of severe antigun laws and low violence rates in some foreign nations is a matter of cause and effect. Foreign gun laws, crime, and history are arcane matters, not likely to be within health advocates' ken. Moreover, the health advocates' ignorance of the criminological literature and allergy to works that might contain uncongenial facts precludes their discovering a fact that undercuts their simple-minded faith in foreign gun laws: such laws cannot have caused the low European homicide rates because those rates long preceded the laws.[117]

The health advocate sages are, however, at least dimly aware of international data which contradicts their shibboleth that gun availability causes high homicide and suicide rates. It turns out that "low violence rates appear in Switzerland

and Israel which encourage (even require) gun possession by their entire citizenry . . . ."[118] Still, health advocate sages evade those uncongenial facts by including Israel and Switzerland among nations "that have strict handgun laws [and] report negligible deaths by handguns."[119]

This is a classic example of deception by half-truth. It is certainly true that Switzerland and Israel have "negligible deaths by handguns." It is also true that Israel has a license requirement to buy and own a gun (any gun, not just handguns). But by providing only half of the story health sages create a false impression of handgun unavailability thereby counterfeiting support for their shibboleth. Gun licensing does not, as they imply, equate with the gun scarcity they deem the indispensable prerequisite to low homicide rates. Outside of the licensing system, Israel and Switzerland routinely loan guns to millions of civilians; for those desiring to own guns, licensure is available on demand to every law-abiding, responsible adult; and Swiss law often allows, while Israeli law and policy actively promote, widespread carrying of handguns to maximize the likelihood that armed civilians will be present in every crowd spot and public place. As an Israeli criminologist notes, Israeli murder "rates are . . . much *lower* than in the United States . . . despite the *greater availability* of guns to law-abiding [Israeli] civilians (emphasis added)."[120]

(Giving credit where credit is due, we take the opportunity to applaud an article whose lead author is Dr. Kellermann, but which wholly departs from the pattern of the health advocacy literature in general and his work in particular. Kellermann et al. accurately state that "Israel and Switzerland [have] rates of homicide [that] are low despite rates of home firearm ownership that are at least as high as those noted in the U.S."[121] In this connection, let us clarify that our criticism is not directed against academics who entertain political views and express them in articles, whether academic or otherwise, if the canons of scholarly discourse are respected. Our problem is with pseudo-scholarly articles and an entire literature marching in lockstep orthodoxy which countenances and encourages fraudulent suppression of the existence of contrary data and opinion. In the notes we cite the only articles in the health advocacy literature we believe can be recommended as comprehensive and generally scrupulous statements of the antigun viewpoint.)[122]

The reason relatively few Israelis own guns is because any law-abiding, responsible trained adult who needs a submachine gun, or a handgun, just draws it from the local police armory, unlike the U.S. where fully automatic weapons have been severely controlled since the 1930s and the importation of even semi-auto Uzis is now prohibited.[123] Unlike the United States where carrying a concealed handgun is often illegal, in Israel if you legally possess a firearm (by loan or licensure) you

are allowed to carry it on your person (concealed or unconcealed). The police even recommend you carry it because then the gun is protected from thieves or children. The result is that *in any big crowd of citizens, there are some people with their personal handguns on them (usually concealed).*[124] (Emphasis added)

American massacres, in which dozens of unarmed victims are mowed down before police can arrive, astound Israelis,[125] who note what occurred at a Jerusalem crowd spot some weeks before the 1984 California MacDonalds massacre: three terrorists who attempted to machine-gun the throng managed to kill only one victim before being shot down by handgun-carrying Israelis. Interviewed by the press the next day, the surviving terrorist complained that his group had not realized that Israeli civilians were armed. The terrorists had planned to machine-gun a succession of crowd spots, thinking that they would be able to escape before the police or army could arrive to deal with them.[126]

3. No Observable Pattern in International Homicide and Suicide

The health advocate shibboleth posits a simple, simplistic, pattern: More guns means more homicide, suicide, and fatal gun accidents; stricter gun control means fewer such tragedies. As we shall see, this is contradicted by the trend in fatal gun accidents. In 1967, for instance, 2,896 Americans died in gun accidents; but, because the vast increase in guns over the next twenty years was accompanied by a steady decline in such fatalities, in 1986 there were only 1,452 fatal gun accidents.[127] The health sages deal with this by simply not mentioning it in relation to their shibboleth; indeed, they generally avoid mentioning the dramatic downward trend in accidental fatalities at all, using instead a figure for fatal accidents in some particular year or the combined figure for fatal accidents over a series of years so as to obscure the actual trend.

Similar statistical legerdemain is required to counterfeit a case for their shibboleth vis-à-vis suicide and murder. We discuss below its refutation by the decline in homicide which accompanied the increasing gun ownership during the early and mid-1980s. To mask the embarrassing downward trend in murder, the health sages began "massaging" the statistics by combining homicide and suicide in one joint figure. This produced an "Intentional Homicide" rate which, once again, they claimed was caused by widespread gun ownership.[128]

But this approach leads to another embarrassing outcome: Though the U.S. has more suicide than homicide, Europe and many other areas have higher yet suicide rates. Consider what would happen to the homicide rate-only international comparison made, strangely enough, by Professor Susan Baker, who originated the combined homicide-suicide approach to American statistics. Lauding Denmark's strict gun laws, she emphasizes that Denmark's murder rate is lower than America's by about seven deaths per one hundred thousand population. But making the same comparison as to suicide would show the Danish rate to be much higher than the American. If we combine the suicide and murder figures according to Baker's own (supposedly preferable) method, the Danish death rate per one hundred thousand population is almost 50 percent higher than the American![129]

Combining suicide and murder statistics in comparing the U.S. to other countries would not serve the health advocates' political agenda. So, it is only when they discuss U.S. figures that Baker and the other health sages combine murder and suicide figures. In making foreign comparisons they continue to separate out the American murder rate and use it only. Curious about what would happen if Baker's advice were applied consistently, we constructed an International Intentional Homicide Table (Table 5.1 below). Of eighteen nations for which figures were readily available, the U.S. ranks below the median when suicide and homicide rates are combined; the U.S. combined homicide/suicide rate is less than half the combined murder/suicide rate in Hungary (where guns were very severely controlled until the fall of Communism) and less than one-third the suicide rate alone of gun-banning Rumania; such relatively firearm-intensive countries as Australia and New Zealand rank low on the table; and the lowest rate is for Israel, a country that actually encourages widespread gun possession.

Table 5.1

International Intentional Homicide Table[130]

Country	Suicide	Homicide	Total
Rumania	66.2	n.a.	66.2 (1984)
Hungary	39.9	3.1	43.0 (1991)
Finland	28.5(1991)	2.86	31.4
Denmark	28.7	.7	29.4 (1984)
Denmark[131]	24.1	4.8	28.9 (1991)
France	20.9(1991)	4.36	25.3
Austria	23.6	1.6	25.2 (1991)
Switzerland	24.45	1.13	25.58
Belgium	23.15	1.85	25
W. Germany	20.37	1.48	21.85
U.S. (1985–88)[132]	12.5	8.3	20.8
Luxembourg	17.8	2.9	20.7
Norway	15.6(1991)	1.16	16.76
Canada	13.94	2.6	16.54
New Zealand	14.7	1.8	16.5 (1991)
Australia	11.58	1.95	13.53
England/Wales	8.61	.67	9.28
Scotland	10.5	1.7	12.2 (1991)
Israel	8.0	1.0	9.0

(For England/Wales, Scotland, and Israel, homicide rate does not include "political" homicides.)

Reviewing the entire health advocacy literature on guns and suicide, we have been unable to find even one reference to the much greater suicide rates in anti-gun European countries. *A fortiori*, that literature never discusses why antigun nations have so much more suicide if the more-guns-means-more-suicide shibboleth is correct. Sloan et al. followed their ludicrous Seattle-Vancouver homicide comparison with an (unintentionally) hilarious comparison of suicide rates in those two cities.[133] Completely unfazed by the fact that Vancouver had the higher suicide rate, Sloan et al. emphasize that it had a lower suicide rate for one subgroup, adolescents and young men. This, they solemnly intone, is due to the U.S. having lax gun laws and more gun availability.

This brings us to an issue health advocacy articles stressed during the 1980s: the poignant phenomenon of suicide among young males, which was supposed to be increasing because of growing firearm availability.[134] Naturally, no health advocate mentioned that suicide among teenagers and young adults has been increasing in much of the industrialized world. By the same token, readers of health advocacy articles blaming American suicide increases in these groups on guns will never learn: (a) that while suicide among American males aged 15–24 increased 7.4 percent in the period 1980–90, (b) the increase in England for this group was over ten times greater (78 percent), with car exhaust poisoning being used most often.[135]

Despite recent increases in youth suicide, the population subgroup most likely to shoot themselves are elderly men. We take leave to doubt that any health advocate (or anyone else) is wise enough to decide for a 76-year-old man in failing health whether he should live or die. But such philosophical considerations are never mentioned by health sages asserting the more-guns-mean-more-suicide shibboleth—nor is modesty about their own wisdom likely to find favor with sages who are confident enough of it to be willing to promote their policy prescription for American society through a literature of deceit.

Setting aside the philosophical issue, it is pragmatically arguable that, if guns are unavailable, people who are seriously enough interested in killing themselves will find some other way.[136] On the other hand, some suicides may occur impulsively because of the immediate availability of a deadly mechanism to a person who might not have completed the act had time for reflection been required. The intellectual desert inhabited by antigun health advocates is epitomized by their failure (or inability) to cite the strongest empirical showing for gun control as a means of reducing suicide. They do not know of this study because it was done by Gary Kleck, whose work they compulsively avoid.[137] Suicide is a serious issue deserving of serious scholarly discussion, rather than use as a political football by unscrupulous propagandists grasping at any opportunity to make a case for their preordained agenda.

Finally, consider the implications of Table 5.1 for the health advocacy shibboleth, strict gun laws = low homicide. The observable pattern which would exist if that were true simply does not. Denmark, whose strict antigun laws Baker praises, has almost four times more homicide than Switzerland and over four times more homicide than Israel. Switzerland's very gun-restrictive neighbor, Germany, has about 25 percent more homicide (and 50 percent more than Israel). England, with very strict laws, even by Western European standards, has the lowest homicide rate of all. But Scotland, with exactly the same laws, has almost three times as much homicide as England and much more than Israel or Switzerland.

These statistics do not, nor are they intended to, prove that strict gun laws "cause" homicide. What they do reinforce are the conclusions set out in "The Verdict of Criminological Scholarship" section above. Gun ownership by responsible adults is not the cause of the social problems associated with firearms; rather, the problems are caused by gun possession by criminal and irresponsible people. Disarming these people is a highly desirable goal, although it is not reasonable to anticipate any more success than the law has had in preventing or deterring them from violent acts. In every society the number of guns suffices to arm those who desire to misuse them.

GUN AVAILABILITY AND SOCIAL HARMS

Having dealt with the international statistics, we move now to domestic statistics. Here again, to sustain the health advocacy shibboleth, sages routinely suppress facts and truncate, select, or even falsify statistics and data. They must doctor the evidence because a full and accurate rendition would not show the easily observable, consistent, and coherent pattern of more-guns-mean-more-murders, suicides, or accidents.

At this point we need to offer the following qualifier: When we say something is never mentioned or discussed in the health advocacy literature, we are not denying that independently knowledgeable readers might be able to ferret out parts of it. For instance, we can find tucked away in a table in one study the fact that young inner city black males have a homicide rate almost 1,000 percent greater than their counterparts in rural areas.[138] But a correlative fact will not be found, much less discussed, because it casts doubt on the shibboleth; namely, that rural blacks have a far lower murder rate despite having a rate of gun ownership and/or availability comparable to whites, i.e., far exceeding that of urban blacks.[139] A fortiori, there is no discussion of how these correlated facts can be squared with the more-guns-means-more-murder shibboleth.

Suppression of Declining Accidental Gun Fatalities

One fact never mentioned in health advocacy articles on fatal gun accidents is that a vast increase in handgun ownership coincided with a dramatic decrease in accidental gun fatalities. Over the twenty-year period 1967–1986 the number of handguns in the U.S. increased 173 percent (from 27.8 million to 63.9 million) while the fatal gun accident rate decreased by almost two-thirds.[140] This remarkable decrease goes unrecorded in the health advocacy literature for three reasons. First, to acknowledge the decrease would undercut health advocates' use of the danger of gun accidents as a reason for opposing gun ownership. Second, it might lead to a well-justified skepticism about their claim that increasing gun availability causes increasing rates of murder and suicide.

Third, admitting the remarkable decline in fatal gun accidents might prompt inquiry as to linkage with the correlative phenomenon that occurred during the same years: the handgun's replacement of the long gun as the weapon kept for defense in American homes and stores. Handgun prohibition advocates themselves argue that their program would reverse that trend, causing Americans to return to long guns for home and office defense—weapons the advocates (in their abysmal ignorance of firearms) erroneously think "safer" than handguns.[141] Necessarily, the effect of such a large-scale reversal would be to greatly increase accidental fatalities. If kept loaded and ready for rapid defensive deployment, long guns are both more likely to accidentally discharge, and much deadlier when discharged, than loaded handguns.[142] Moreover, a long gun is much more difficult to secure from children.

The comparative dangers are demonstrable from a simple comparison of the available figures breaking down gun type involvement in fatal gun accidents: though 90 percent or more of the firearms kept loaded at any one time are handguns, handguns are involved in approximately 41 percent of the accidental gun fatalities.[143] It is estimated that if the 85.2 percent of loaded guns in American homes in the year 1980 had been long guns instead of handguns, the number of fatal gun accidents would have more than quadrupled, from 1,244 to about 5,346; in other words, around 4,100 additional lives per year would be lost in accidental shootings in the home.[144]

Suppression of Decline in Accidental Child Gun Death

To promote the gun-control agenda, health advocate sages have long harped on the emotionally charged issue of child death by gun accident.[145] Multiple reasons dictate their never acknowledging the steep decline in such tragedies: Admitting that decline would, in and of itself, undercut their political agenda. Worse, it could hoist health sages on their own emotional petard: What if someone were inspired to ask whether their proposal to ban handguns might reverse the decline and cause many hundreds more children to die in gun accidents? Finally, by suppressing any mention of the decline, health advocate sages leave themselves free to continue fabricating statistics to exaggerate the number of child deaths—falsehoods which, but for their tragic subject matter, would be comic in their wild inconsistency.[146]

Fraudulent Suppression of Gun/Homicide Comparison Data

Since the mid-1960s the total American gunstock has massively increased:[147] To some extent this may be no more than evidence of an increase in disposable income which has massively spurred sales of consumer products generally. But the enormous increase in handguns particularly seems to reflect a generalized fear of crime. This is not to say that handgun sales can be correlated with crime rates which, since the mid-1960s, have risen and fallen erratically and inconsistently in various states and cities, and in the nation as a whole. There is no reason to think gun buyers are motivated by, or even aware of, changes in homicide rates as such, much less in rates of rape, robbery, and burglary, which have risen and fallen with little consistent relationship to each other or to homicide statistics. What ordinary people are aware of are the crimes that underlie the statistics. For instance, as of 1980 the burglary rate was such that about one in fourteen houses was burglarized each year.[148] Many people who know nothing about the rate might nevertheless be impelled to buy handguns by the experience of being burglarized themselves and/or knowing others who have been. In addition, of course, fears that impel firearms purchasing may be prompted by media sensationalism in the reporting of individual crimes even in comparatively low-crime areas.

In sum, while the demand for guns for protection is stimulated by generally high crime rates, it does not vary greatly in relation to changes in those rates, or even trends, as such. If crime rates remain generally high, many potential victims will want guns for protection, regardless of whether crime rates are modestly rising, modestly falling, or remaining steady on a year-to-year basis or over a period of years.

Table 5.2
Gunstock Increases over a 20-Year Period

1973[149]

Total Gun Stock		Guns per 1,000 pop.	
Handguns	All Guns	Handguns	All Guns
36,910,819	122,304,980	175.9	610.3

Homicide rate: 9.4 per 100,000 population[150]

1992[151]

Total Gun Stock		Guns per 1,000 pop.	
Handguns	All Guns	Handguns	All Guns
77,626,552	221,851,212	304.3	869.7

Homicide rate: 9.3 per 100,000 population

Table 5.2 (contd.)

1994[152]

Total Gun Stock		Guns per 1,000 pop.	
Handguns	All Guns	Handguns	All Guns
82,350,383	231,243,491	315.9	887.0

[Homicide rate unavailable]

In contrast, if the health advocates' more-guns-means-more-murder shibboleth were true, massive increases in guns should translate into a corresponding increase in murders. There might not be a perfect correlation. The 110.2 percent increase in handgun ownership in the twenty-year period 1973–1992 (see Table 5.2) might not have resulted in a full 110.2 percent increase in murders, or even in a simple doubling of the murder rate. But if guns really were the "primary cause" of murder or "one of the main causes," the 110.2 percent increase in handguns, and the 73.3 percent increase in guns of all types, should have been accompanied by a consistent, marked increase in murders—as was predicted by health advocacy sages who bewailed those increases in gun ownership as they occurred.

At the very least, murder should have increased somewhat. But there was no consistent and marked increase in murder. In 1973, the American firearm stock totalled 128 million, the handgun stock 36.9 million, and the homicide rate was 9.4 per one hundred thousand population. At the end of 1992, the firearm stock had risen to 221.9 million, the handgun stock to 77.6 million, but the homicide rate was 9.3, slightly lower than it had been in 1973.[153] Nor had the percentage of murders committed with firearms increased. In 1973 68.5 percent of murders were committed with guns.[154] Twenty years later, after Americans had purchased almost as many new firearms as they had in the preceding seventy-three years, 68.2 percent of homicides were committed with guns.

Note that we are not suggesting that increased gun ownership caused a reduction in homicide or other violence. Our focus is the health advocacy shibboleth(s) that guns are the primary cause of murder and that more guns, particularly more handguns, mean more murder. The data examined so far do not bear this out. Is it just a coincidence that these gun ownership-murder rate comparative data are never mentioned in the health advocacy literature, nor their implications ever discussed? Or does their nondisclosure reflect those implications; to wit, the criminological conclusion we noted earlier that gun ownership by noncriminals does not cause crime, and is not a source of social harm (though firearms in the hands of criminals do facilitate crime)?

In presenting the 1973 and 1992 data we are not suggesting that the homicide rates steadily declined during that twenty-year period. In the five years 1973–77, the homicide rate first rose to 9.8 (1974) and then dropped to 8.8 (1977). Then it steeply rose to its highest point ever, 10.2 (1980). In 1984 it dropped 22.5 percent to 7.9, then began rising again, in 1986 with some ups and downs, to its 1992 level of 9.3. As to homicides committed with guns, over the twenty-year period they fell as low as 58.7 percent (1985), but then rose to 68.5 percent by 1992.[155]

In sum, over a twenty-year period of unparalleled increase in gun acquisition, homicide rates were erratic and unpatterned—and completely inconsistent with the shibboleth that doubling the number of guns, especially handguns, would increase homicide rates. Geographic and demographic studies of homicide are equally inconsistent with the health advocacy position. For instance studies trying to link gun ownership to violence rates find no correlation or else a negative one, i.e., that cities and counties with high gun ownership suffer less homicide and other violence than demographically comparable areas with lower gun ownership.[156] Once again, these are facts that readers whose information comes from health advocacy literature will never learn; nor will they be exposed to the following which we quote from a criminology article in which a major figure in that field repudiated his previous support for banning handguns:

> when used for protection firearms can seriously inhibit aggression and can provide a psychological buffer against the fear of crime. Furthermore, the fact that *national patterns show little violent crime where guns are most dense* implies that guns do not elicit aggression in any meaningful way. Quite the contrary, these findings suggest that high saturations of guns in places, or something correlated with that condition, inhibit illegal aggression."[157]

Likewise never discussed in the health advocacy literature against firearms is that the white homicide rate has steadily fallen since 1980.[158] (Again, when we say a fact is never discussed, we are not denying that it can sometimes be ferreted out of some article in that literature by a reader independently aware of it. But, if mentioned at all, it will be buried in a table or worded so obscurely that its adverse implications for the health advocacy position is not revealed and dealt with.)

HEALTH SAGES' SHIBBOLETH DIVERTS ATTENTION FROM ACTUAL CAUSES

The apparent increase in American homicide from the mid-1980s on is due to the steady fall in white homicide being offset by a vast increase in homicide in drug-ridden, poverty-stricken inner cities. Inner-city and minority youth homicide is a regular theme in the antigun health literature.[159] Of course, health sages never note that per capita gun ownership is far less among African-Americans than among whites.[160] Mentioning that would undermine the sages' contention that gun availability causes homicide and would support the leading English criminological analyst's pessimistic view, "in any society the number of guns always suffices to arm the few who want to obtain and use them illegally."[161]

In sum, increased firearm availability to honest, responsible people (of any race) does not cause increased violence; neither is lower availability to such people associated with lower violence. Taken together or separately, data on firearm availability for the nation as a whole, and for discrete geographic or demographic subpopulations, discredit the shibboleth that "the possession of guns" is "the primary cause" of murder. The actual cause is hopelessness, poverty, and a lack of substantial employment opportunities other than competing in the murderous drug trade. Studies suggest black rates of homicide and other violence are no greater than those of similarly situated whites.[162] In that connection, consider the following:

> ... measures that attempt to restrict access to firearms without reference to drugs, poverty with its attendant lack of educational and employment opportunities, clogged courts and overcrowded prisons are bound to have only marginal effects on firearm crime.[163]
>
> Moreover, an overemphasis on [gun control] diverts attention from the kinds of conditions that are responsible for much of our crime, such as persisting poverty for the black underclass and some whites and Hispanics; the impact of postindustrial transition on economic opportunity for working-class youths; and the shortage of prison facilities that makes it difficult to keep high risk, repeat offenders off the streets.[164]

In this context we note a Marxist criminologist's suggestion that the function, or at least the effect, of gun control advocacy is to divert attention from urgently needed social and political change.[165]

A CRITIQUE OF OVERT MENDACITY

A 1989 article in *JAMA* approvingly quoted a CDC official's assertion that his work for the Centers for Disease Control and Prevention involved "'systematically building a case that owning firearms causes death.'" The official later claimed *JAMA* had misquoted him and offered the only repudiation of the anti-gun political agenda we have found in a health advocacy publication, characterizing it as "anathema to any unbiased scientific inquiry because it assumes the conclusion at the outset and then attempts to find evidence to support it."[166]

Unfortunately, the evidence is clear that that is precisely what CDC is doing. Indeed, this has subsequently been avowed by the prior official's successor.[167] Even more unfortunately, CDC and some other health advocate sages build that case not only by suppressing facts but by overt fraud, fabricating statistics, and falsifying references to support them. The following are but a few of many examples documented in a paper two of the authors of this chapter co-authored with Robert Cottrol of Rutgers University Law School:

[A] 1989 report to the U.S. Congress by the CDC stated, "Since the early 1970s the year-to-year fluctuations in firearm availability has [*sic*] paralleled the numbers of homicides."[168] We leave it to the readers of this article to judge how a 69 percent increase in handgun ownership over the fifteen-year period 1974–88 could honestly be described as having "paralleled" a small decrease in homicide during that same period.[169]

Understandably, the CDC report offered no supporting reference for its claim of parallelism. But the inventive Dr. Diane Schetky, and two equally enterprising CDC writers, Smith and Falk, in a separate article, actually do provide purportedly supporting citations for her claim "Handguns account for only 20 percent of the nation's firearms yet account for 90 percent of all firearms [mis]use, both criminal and accidental."[170] The problem is that the claim is false in every part.

The purpose of that claim is to exaggerate the comparative risks of handguns vis-à-vis long guns so as to fortify the cause of handgun prohibition and avoid admitting the major problem we have already addressed: because handguns are innately safer than long guns, if a handgun ban caused defensive gun owners to keep loaded long guns instead (as handgun ban advocates and experts concur would be the case), thousands more might die in fatal gun accidents annually.

The only citation given by either Schetky or Smith and Falk to support their claim that handguns comprise only 20 percent of all guns but are involved in 90 percent of gun accidents and crime is the FBI's *Uniform Crime Reports* (UCR). Understandably, no page citations are given because the citations are simply false. As anyone familiar with UCR knows, it provides: (a) no data on gun ownership—and thus, (b) no comparative data on handgun versus long gun ownership; (c) no data on accidents, and thus (d) no data on gun accidents—and thus (e) no comparative data on the incidence of handgun accidents versus long gun accidents. Schetky and Smith and Falk could have found data on these matters in the National Safety Council's *Accident Facts*. But those data would not have suited the purpose since they do not support the point Schetky and Smith and Falk sought to make.

Neither does UCR give any data on the number of persons injured in gun crimes or the number of such injuries in handgun crimes versus long gun crimes. UCRs do give such data for gun murders but even those data do not support Schetky's claim that 90 percent are by handgun.[171] Every one of the other purported statistics given by Schetky and Smith and Falk is not only wrong but wrong in only one particular direction, i.e., each false statistic errs in supporting their point whereas accurate statistics would not have done so. It is, of course, elementary that innocent mistakes tend to be random, and even to balance each other out; they do not all err in favor of the position for which they are presented.

It would be misleading to suggest that, heavily politicized though it is, the antigun health advocacy literature commonly exhibits overt mendacity (as opposed to fraudulent misleading by half-truth and suppression of material facts). Overt mendacity is not infrequent, however. Numerous examples will be documented in the next section and in the balance of this chapter.

THE MYTH THAT MURDERERS ARE ORDINARY GUN OWNERS

The case for reducing firearm availability to ordinary people rests on two inter-related myths endorsed explicitly and implicitly in the health advocacy literature on firearms: (1) "most [murderers] would be considered law-abiding citizens prior to their pulling the trigger . . . ," and (2) "most shootings are not committed by felons or mentally ill people, but are acts of passion that are committed using a handgun that is owned for home protection."[172] From these two myths other falsehoods follow, e.g., that firearms availability to ordinary citizens is the "primary cause" of murder[173]; that murder would radically decrease if ordinary citizens were deprived of those guns; and that it is unnecessary to worry much about the enforceability of gun bans because, even if criminals will not disarm, the law-abiding will—and they are the ones committing most murders.

But it simply is not true that law-abiding citizens commit most murders or many murders or virtually any murders; therefore, it follows that disarming them would not and could not eliminate most, or many, or virtually any murders. Among the facts most clearly established in studies of murder is that murderers tend to be extreme aberrants who cannot realistically be assumed to have much more compunction about flouting gun laws than about brutalizing others. The great majority of murderers have life histories of violence against those around them, felony records, substance abuse, and car and other dangerous accidents.[174] Indeed, so firmly established are these facts that they appear even in medico-health discussions of violence[175]—but are never discussed in connection with the health sages' certitudes about ordinary citizens murdering relatives and acquaintances with guns.

A truly startling example of misunderstanding the nature of murder (because it contradicts his own writings!) is that of the CDC's point man for gun prohibition, Dr. Mark Rosenberg. To lead readers into blaming firearms rather than criminals for crime, Dr. Rosenberg actually goes so far as to claim that

> . . . most of the perpetrators of violence [can he really mean not just murderers, but robbers and rapists as well?] are not criminals by trade or profession. Indeed, in the area of domestic violence, most of the perpetrators are never accused of any crime. The victims and perpetrators are *ourselves—ordinary citizens,* students, professionals, and *even public health workers.*[176] (Emphasis added)

The incorrectness of this is evident by comparing it to Dr. Rosenberg's accurate statements in this and other articles: "Violence is foreign to the lives of most public health professionals," and "Most family homicides involve spouses and occur after a series of prior assaultive incidents."[177]

We do not suggest that all statements promoting ordinary citizen-as-murderer mythology in the health advocacy literature are conscious misrepresentations. Some reflect only a combination of ignorance and intellectual confusion. For instance, J. A. Barondess et al. comment in response to letters to *JAMA* criticizing their article "Firearms Violence and Public Health: Limiting the Availability of Guns":

> In relation to the contention that homicide by firearms is carried out by established felons, the FBI has reported that of the 15,377 reported firearms murders in 1992, a total of 7,505 fell under the category of "other felony type," such as "romantic triangle, arguments over money or property, other arguments"; *thus, many who kill for the first time are not felons until they commit the act.*[178] (Emphasis added)

Hopelessly oblivious as Barondess et al. are in their middle-aged, middle (or upper)-class medical professionals' myopia, it seems to have escaped them that those "arguments" may mean something very different when they occur among young men in areas where the willingness and capacity to employ extreme violence is respected; where young men raised in violent families live in an environment whose most attractive employment opportunity is the violent drug trade—young men who "believe that to survive, one must be tough, be willing to fight, carry a gun, and be willing to shoot it"; "who engage in high-risk activities partly because they believe their chances of living beyond thirty are slim anyway"; and who participate in "often deadly battles over respect" which is of heightened concern to them, because they are "deprived of [any] legitimate opportunities to acquire symbols of status."[179] The same myopia, ignorance, and intellectual confusion characterizes Kahn's claim that "most firearm-related violence is being committed" not by criminals, but "by relatives and friends of victims and in the course of arguments."[180]

Their myopia leads Kahn et al. to the unexamined and absurd assumption that felons don't have friends, relatives, or acquaintances, and/or don't engage in " 'romantic triangle[s], arguments over money or property, other arguments.' " Only by indulging that absurd assumption could they jump from the fact that those were the circumstances of 7,505 murders in 1992, to the false conclusion that the murderers were ordinary citizens "who kill[ed] for the first time [and were] not felons until they commit[ted] the act." Kahn et al. fall into this absurdity only through blissful ignorance of the studies which show what is actually meant by terms like "acquaintance homicide" and/or murder in the course of "'romantic triangle[s], arguments over money or property, other arguments'": not previously law-abiding people killing each other, but abusive men eventually killing women they have savaged on many previous occasions; gang figures or drug dealers killing each other, or killing, or being killed, by addicts and other customers.[181] But for gun-aversive dyslexia, Kahn et al. could have discovered these well-established facts about homicide simply by reviewing studies in their own discipline.[182]

The mythology of murderers as ordinary citizens contrasts starkly with the consistent findings of homicide studies dating back to the 1960s: that about 75 percent of murderers have adult criminal records[183]; that when the murder occurred about 11 percent of murder arrestees were actually on pretrial release, i.e., they were awaiting trial for another offense[184]; and that murderers average a prior adult criminal career of six or more years, including four major adult felony arrests.

We emphasize that these are adult records so that readers will not be misled into accepting the claim of Webster et al. (most murderers "would be considered law-abiding citizens prior to their pulling the trigger") as to the roughly 25 percent of murderers who lack adult records. The reason over half of those 25 percent do not have adult records is that they are juveniles.[186] Juvenile criminal records might show these murderers to have an extensive serious crime history. The research literature on characteristics of those who murder yields a profile of offenders that indicates that many have histories of committing personal violence in childhood against other children, siblings, and small animals.[187] (Likewise, the juvenile crime records of the 87 percent of murderers who are adults might show crime careers averaging far more than six adult years with significantly more than just four major felony priors.)

Though juvenile criminal records are not generally available, they occasionally do become known in connection with some high-profile case. In one recent case which generated nationwide publicity, a five-year-old boy was thrown from a fourteenth-story window by two others because he had refused to steal candy for them. Police revealed to the press that both killers, aged ten and eleven, had prior arrests including theft, aggravated battery, and unlawful use of a weapon. At the time of the murder one of the perpetrators was supposed to be confined to his home on a weapons conviction.[188]

As to child abusers and wife batterers, Dr. Rosenberg correctly observes that far too many are never arrested. That is yet another reason why about 25 percent of murderers don't have a record (though most domestic murderers do have prior records[189]). But Rosenberg is wrong to minimize child abuse and wife beating as essentially typical behavior engaged in by "ordinary citizens, students, professionals, and even public medico-health workers." At least those abusers who go on to murder resemble other murderers in being highly aberrant individuals with life histories of substance abuse and of brutalizing family members or others in often irrational outbursts of violence.

> [T]here are significant differences between men who commit [domestic] partner homicide and men in the general noncriminal population. For instance, men who kill their [domestic] partners are more often drug abusers, are more prone to

abuse alcohol and are intoxicated more often, and are more given to [prior ver-
bal] . . . threats and [physical violence] than are other men.[190]

In 90 percent of domestic homicide cases the police had been called to the same
address at least once within the preceding two years; the median number of prior
police calls to that address was five during that period. A leading analyst of
domestic homicide notes that "The day-to-day reality is that most family murders
are preceded by a long history of assaults. . . ."[191]

It is difficult to avoid the conclusion that health advocacy writings against
guns suppress and misrepresent these facts because they are doubly embarrassing
to the argument for banning guns. First, there already are laws against gun ownership by felons, drug abusers, and juveniles. Sensible though these laws are, in
practice they have proven only marginally effective. To reiterate the obvious,
murderous aberrants see little reason to obey laws against their having weapons.
The failure of those laws suggests that it is senseless, and, indeed, counterproductive, to strain police resources further by committing them to enforcing a gun
ban against the general populace who do not misuse guns anyway. Second, since
owning guns does not cause ordinary people to murder (and certainly does not
cause them to rob, rape, or burgle), what is the basis for confiscating their property and depriving them, in this violent society, of the freedom to choose to own
arms for the defense of self, home, and family?

"GUN OWNERSHIP AS A RISK FACTOR FOR HOMICIDE IN THE HOME"

This is the title of a 1993 article whose authors include several of Sloan's co-
authors on the Vancouver-Seattle comparison discussed above.[192] The 1993 article having, like its predecessor, appeared in the *New England Journal of Medicine,* we shall call it *NEJM*-1993. Because space limitations constrain us only to
briefly summarize the great majority of health advocacy articles, we have
selected *NEJM*-1993 for a detailed critique. This is particularly appropriate since
it has received wide publicity[193] and voluminous citation in the health advocacy
literature.[194] Moreover, *NEJM*-1993 continues a long series of widely publicized
health advocacy studies. Regrettably, *NEJM*-1993 and the previous studies would
be more appropriately cited in a statistics text as a cautionary example of multiple statistical errors. Before addressing these, however, it is necessary to set forth
some basics of statistical analysis.

Statistical analyses are used to reach conclusions in the face of certain types
of uncertainty. Uncertainty results from such factors as inherent variation in the
subjects being studied; the effects of many other influences, both known and
unknown; and limited resources which restrict the amount of data that can be collected and studied. Statistical analyses may result in erroneous conclusions for a
variety of reasons, some acceptable, others not. We shall ignore, in this discus-

sion, errors in recording data and of calculation, because, though unacceptable, they have become less common with the use of computers and statistical analysis programs. But many other types of errors can occur and are of grave concern when the conclusions will be used to make decisions on how to act. In the medical area such decisions may affect the choice of medical treatment, or may affect policy decisions in the public sector. In either case, use of flawed conclusions may lead to literally fatal consequences.

When What You See Isn't Necessarily What You Get

We usually assume that the statistical analysis program on the computer does the calculations of the statistical analysis correctly. This is not always true in the Pentium® chip era. Moreover, data entry errors are sufficiently common to require careful checking by the analyst to catch them. But at least neither calculation errors nor any data entry errors that slip through will be biased in favor of any particular agenda the analyst may have.

More serious concerns involve errors by the analyst which can be related to a conscious or unconscious agenda. The analyst is responsible for choosing the correct type of analysis, for making sure that the assumptions required for the use of a type of statistical analysis are met, and that the results are described correctly. When errors occur in any of these areas, the conclusions reached can be partially or completely wrong even in the absence of any other errors. The presence of these errors in a study does not guarantee that the conclusions are *ipso facto* invalid. But the conclusions are then unsubstantiated, and the scientific impartiality of the analyst is called into question. Errors are of particular concern when they are made in such a way as to facilitate conclusions which confirm the previous stands of the analyst.

It is seldom possible to conduct a scientific study in which only the effects to be tested are operating. The statistical field of "Experimental Design" is concerned with methods that allow the detection of the effects to be studied even when other effects are operating.[195] Failure to separate the effects to be studied from extraneous effects leads to a confusion between them, and the unintentional "confounding"[196] of extraneous effects with those to be studied. The resulting conclusions are not based on tests of the effects being studied; rather, they reflect some unknown combination of those effects and extraneous effects confounded with them. Thus the hypotheses supposedly being studied are not in fact being studied—and what you see is not what you get.

Purpose and Design of NEJM-1993

The hypothesis *NEJM*-1993 was supposedly studying is "whether keeping a firearm in the home confers protection against crime or increases the risk of violent crime in the home."[197] Very simplistically described, the study compares a sample of households in which homicide occurred to a supposedly similar sample in which homicides had not occurred. It finds that the homicide households were more likely to have contained guns. From this it concludes that guns are more of a danger than a protection.

The study used data from three urban counties,[198] consisting in all cases of homicide in the home during the chosen time periods. To compare with these homicide cases, a control was selected for each homicide victim. These control subjects were matched to the homicide victim with respect to sex, race, age-range, and neighborhood of residence. Various kinds of information were then obtained by reading police or other official reports as to the homicide cases, by interviewing another occupant of the homicide case households (a case-proxy), and by interviewing either the control subject or another occupant of his/her household (a control-proxy).

Study Design Exaggerates Risks of Defensive Gun Ownership

The data presented in *NEJM*-1993 does not show that even *one* homicide victim was killed with a gun ordinarily kept in that household. Indeed the indirect evidence presented indicates that most of the home gun homicide victims were killed using guns not kept in the victim's home: 71.1 percent of the homicide victims were killed by people whose relationship to the victim[199] indicates that the killer did not live in the victim's household, and thus presumably used a gun not kept in the victim's household.

We do not, incidentally, mean to deny that it may be relevant that the murder household had a gun even though that gun had no direct involvement in the murder. But the nature of that relevance compromises *NEJM*-1993's conclusions about the supposed risk of home gun ownership. What if it turns out that people at higher risk of being murdered are more likely to own guns than those at lesser risk? That is not only intuitively plausible, it is supported by the finding in some high-density urban areas that victims of homicide and other severe violence tend to be engaged in criminal activity or have criminal records, including involvement in the illicit drug trade.[200] So these higher-risk people may own guns more often. If so, *NEJM*-1993's conclusion that murder victims owned guns at a higher rate than the control group of nonvictims does not at all prove that owning a gun is risky. Far from showing that the murdered victims were at higher risk because they were more likely to own guns, the comparison may only demonstrate that they owned guns because they were at higher risk than the members of the supposedly comparable control group. We take up this point in the next section.

A tacit assumption is made by the consistent use of the word "victim" and by the article abstract's introductory statement that "violent crime in the home" is being considered. This assumption is that the victim of the crime and of the homicide, respectively, are the same person. The deceased may actually have been the attacker and so, in those cases, the homicide should have been considered to be a benefit rather than a risk. The cases in which the "offender" is listed as "police officer" seem likely to fall under this misleading classification, as does even the categorization of police as "offender."

Inadequate Consideration of High-Risk Career Criminality

NEJM-1993's authors were not unaware of the problem that their homicide cases might contain a disproportionate number of high risk people. To attempt to avoid the problem, *NEJM*-1993 tried to compare the homicide cases to the controls to see if there were differences in a variety of risk factors, including drinking and drug problems, histories of domestic violence, whether the home was owned or rented, and especially gun ownership. *NEJM*-1993 then reported differences in the presence of these risk factors as being associated with an increase in the risk of homicide.

In this connection, note that gun ownership, the supposed risk factor *NEJM*-1993 emphasizes, was far from being the one most strongly associated with being murdered. Drinking and drug problems, a history of family violence, living alone, and living in a rented home were all greater individual risk factors for being murdered than gun ownership, based on the *NEJM*-1993 results. Even so, it is clear that still other risk factors were not accounted for, e.g., number of criminal associates or frequency of high-risk or criminal activity. These and other factors ignored in this study, will have their effects lumped in with the effects supposedly being studied and inadvertent statistical "confounding" may result. An "association" due to these ignored confounding factors would be more accurately described as a "spurious association." Proper statistical design requires an effort to identify all the risk factors and to take the relevant ones into account by properly collecting the data and choosing the appropriate statistical analysis. *NEJM*-1993 simply did not do this adequately, and therefore the authors' strongly worded conclusions about the factors which they did include are not warranted.

For instance, though some account was taken of whether any member of either the homicide victim household or the control group had been arrested, none seems to have been taken of the seriousness of the crime for which the arrest was made; of any conviction of crime; of whether the specific murder victim had been arrested or convicted and of the seriousness of the crime; and of how many arrests and convictions the murder victim (or others in that household) had had in comparison to the number of arrests in the control household, or other high-risk activity or gang affiliations of any member of the household.

These issues are particularly important because criminological studies indicate that the overall population may be divided into: (a) the overwhelming majority, who are law-abiding; (b) a minority of people who are criminals because they infrequently commit a crime, often a relatively trivial one; and (c) "career criminals" who, though relatively small in numbers, commit the majority of crimes, especially the more serious ones.[201] It may plausibly be postulated that a group containing more career criminals will have both a higher rate of gun ownership and a greater likelihood of being murdered than a supposedly similar control group of people who commit relatively less frequent and serious crimes. If so, that is a confounding factor which would produce a spurious association between owning a gun and being murdered.

This leads us to a more fundamental problem with the entire *NEJM*-1993 study design. Let us suppose that the data problems with comparability of the murdered group to the control group had all been solved. Still, the cases are high-risk households unrepresentative of the general population. The controls, having been drawn from atypically high-violence geographical areas are unrepresentative, as well, of the general population. Therefore, there is no formal research basis for applying any conclusions from this study about the effects of gun ownership to the general population.[202] Nonetheless, *NEJM*-1993 reached unqualified conclusions and presented them as applying to the general population.

False Minimization of Sampling Bias

Whenever only a portion of a phenomenon is studied, the conclusions reached may be in error if the portion selected for study is not representative of all of the cases. One way to avoid this error (which is called a "bias") is to scrupulously include all of the cases in the study. The authors of *NEJM*-1993 are aware of this, and claim, "To minimize selection bias, we included all cases of homicide in the home. . . . High response rates among case-proxies (94.6 percent) and matching controls (80.6 percent) minimized nonresponse bias."[203]

Unfortunately, a rather different picture emerges from close examination of the numbers (instead of reliance on the percentages given by the authors). There were actually 444 cases of homicide in the home reported in the counties studied during the time period selected. Nineteen of the 444 cases were dropped from consideration because the authors deemed murder-suicides and multiple homicides as a single event each and included only one homicide per event. Five additional homicides were dropped for reasons relating to reporting or death certificate change. The remaining cases account for the 94.6 percent of the total cases the authors state were left in the study. An additional 7 percent were dropped because of failure to interview the proxy, and 1 percent more due to failure to find a control.

This left 388 matched pairs, i.e., only 87.4 percent of the cases. This lower percentage is not mentioned by the authors (though they do give the individual drop percentages), thereby downplaying the cumulative effect and the possible biases which could result. Nor is this the end point in the process of diminishing the number of cases included in the analyses. The authors were unable to obtain complete data on all of the matched pairs, but the multivariate statistical analysis used requires complete data. So seventy-two of the 388 matched pairs had to be excluded in the final multivariate analysis.[204]

The end result is that only 316 matched pairs were used in the final analyses, representing only 71.2 percent of the 444 homicide cases. It is very difficult to accept *NEJM*-1993's claim of having examined "all cases" as a fair description of an analysis that was actually based on 71.2 percent of them. We hasten to add that this does not prove that there was any selection or response bias in this study. It just shows that there was ample room for such biases to act. It also shows that the authors avoided coming to grips with this issue and presented the data in a manner that would mislead the readers into thinking that there could be little or no such bias.

Further analysis of the 28.8 percent of the cases dropped might be able to shed some light on whether, and to what extent, *NEJM*-1993 was compromised by the existence of such biases. But the senior author refused to make these data available to others for reanalysis.[205] This research was supported by grants from the CDC. The CDC does not require that data resulting from their grants be made available to the public. This is in contrast to the policies of NIJ, which requires comparable datasets to be made publicly available.

Control Group Selection Did Not Assure Comparability

The validity of *NEJM*-1993's conclusions depends on the control group matching the homicide cases in every way (except, of course, for the occurrence of a homicide). The importance of proper control selection cannot be overemphasized, especially when medical or policy implications are at stake. Use of an inappropriate control can lead to erroneous conclusions and then to harmful practices:

> It is thus, for want of an adequately controlled test, that various forms of treatment have in the past, become unjustifiably, even sometimes harmfully, established in everyday medical practice. . . .[206]

The need for the controls to differ only with respect to the factor being studied is called an "obviosity" because it is so glaringly obvious.[207] In *NEJM*-1993, however, the controls collected do not match the cases in some important ways. The incomplete matching that was done had another untoward effect. It produced a control group that was not representative of the counties being studied, and therefore further decreased the inference that can be legitimately drawn from the data of this study.

The study did match the control group to the case group using several categorizations (sex, race, age range, and neighborhood of residence). But this matching method selects controls which are not necessarily matched with the case group on other important factors. The control selection involved random selection of households that were at least a "one-block avoidance zone" away from the case homicide. The matching criteria did not include any lifestyle or related indicators. A number of lifestyle indicators (referred to as "behavioral factors") were studied[208]; but the large differences between the cases and the control for these invariably shows more substance abuse and other problems in the cases than in the controls, thus revealing that matching was not done for these lifestyle indicators. Other lifestyle indicators such as single-parent versus two-parent homes were not included in the study or shown in the article.

If the population selected from is composed of subpopulations that differ in homicide rates, the matching control must come from the same subpopulation as the case it is supposed to match. This could happen with the matching method *NEJM*-1993 used, but only if the subpopulations were settled in distinct and different large geographic areas. Because of the avoidance method used, these areas would have to be larger than one block in size. How much larger is hard to tell, since the paper does not say how far outside the zone it was necessary to travel to find a matching control who would agree to cooperate.

In any event, risk subpopulations are not distributed in such a coarse-grain manner. Criminal residences and crime areas which define the homicide risk subgroup factors (drug use and dealing, violent criminal events, violently abusive family relationships, etc.) are often fine-grained in their distribution. There are differences in areas within a city, but there is population heterogeneity within these areas.[209] Choosing a control living one or more blocks away will not assure matching with respect to the subpopulation. For example, the characteristics of people living in a high-rise public housing project may differ significantly from those of persons living in duplexes two blocks away.

Of particular interest here is the small, violent, high-risk subpopulation (violent predators) that may be disproportionately represented in the homicide cases. The chances are good that the "controls" with which they will be matched will come from the much larger nonviolent (or less violent) subpopulation(s). This will produce a "spurious association."

The control group may or may not differ from the homicide cases in another characteristic that is central to *NEJM*-1993. The conclusion that gun ownership is a risk factor for homicide derives from the finding of a gun in 45.4 percent of the homicide case households, but in only 35.8 percent of the control households. Whether that finding is accurate, however, depends on the truthfulness of control group interviewees in admitting the presence of a gun or guns in the home.[210] How much confidence that can be in the veracity of persons asked about gun ownership by a surveyor?

NEJM-1993's authors themselves state, "Underreporting of gun ownership by control respondents could bias our estimate of risk upward."[211] So they realize that this is a critical point, but they conclude that there is no underreporting. Predictably, they do not mention the fact that false denial of gun ownership by survey respondents has long been deemed a major problem with calculating the true size of American gun ownership; nor, of course, do they cite Kleck's exhaustive discussion of this issue.[212]

NEJM-1993 justifies its dismissal of underreporting as a problem, noting that "a pilot study [conducted by four of the *NEJM*-1993 authors plus one other person] of homes listed as the addresses of owners of newly registered handguns confirmed that respondents' answers to questions about gun ownership were *generally* valid (emphasis added)."[213] It is reasonable to ask what "generally" means. In the study referred to, 97.1 percent of the families (thirty-four of thirty-five) listed as being the location of a registered handgun admitted to having guns in the home, either at the time or recently. Superficially this appears to be an impressive record of openness. It becomes less impressive when the numbers are placed in full perspective. Seventy-five homes were chosen from new handgun registration records.[214] Due to false addresses and other difficulties, only fifty-five could be found, and of these only thirty-five consented to the interview. These are the thirty-five families mentioned previously. However, they are unrepresentative in an even more significant respect: they are people who, by definition, have chosen to let others, i.e., the government, know that they own guns and have undergone some governmental approval process. To learn that this sample is willing to admit the same facts to survey interviewers can tell us nothing about gun owners in general, let alone about the lower-income gun owners in *NEJM*-1993.

In comparison with this sample of registered owners, it is likely that owners of unregistered guns would be more reluctant to admit to ownership. Among other things, it may involve admission of a criminal offense.[215] The control group could be further biased if criminals and owners of illicit guns are more likely to refuse to be interviewed for a study such as this, let alone to admit to ownership. With this many discrepancies possible between measures of gun ownership in the homicide case and control homes, it appears that the authors are quoting their own previous work in a way that overstates its strength.

To reiterate, *NEJM*-1993's conclusions depend entirely on there having been no substantial underestimation of the control group's gun ownership. It would take only thirty-five of the 388 controls falsely denying gun possession to make the control ownership percentage exactly equal that of the homicide case households. If indeed the controls actually had gun ownership equal to that of the homicide case households (45.4 percent), then a false denial rate of only 20.1 percent among the gun owning controls would produce the thirty-five false denials and thereby equalize ownership. Such a 20.1 percent false denial rate is smaller than either the "refused consent for interview" category or the "inaccurate registration data" category of the pilot study. Therefore, the results of the pilot study are consistent with a false denial rate sufficiently high to bring the control group gun ownership rate up to a level equal to, or even higher than, the homicide case household rate, although the authors cite the pilot study to the reverse effect. Neglect of the false denial rate can produce a bias large enough, by itself, to account for the entire association between gun ownership and homicide claimed in this study.

Inappropriate Method of Statistical Analysis

NEJM-1993 chose to use the Case Control Method (CCM).[216] This method is accepted in medical research as an investigatory tool with a strength in its ability to generate hypotheses, rather than as a final test of hypotheses.[217] A relevant weakness of the CCM is that it has a susceptibility to bias.[218] In the social sciences it is seldom possible to do the properly blinded, randomized, and otherwise controlled studies that would be used to confirm a hypothesis. This makes it even more important to be sensitive to the possible existence of biases and to attempt to minimize them. *NEJM*-1993 makes claims about the association found between gun ownership and homicide, and presents those claims as a conclusion rather than as a tentative hypothesis. According to the conclusion of the article abstract, ". . . guns kept in the home are associated with an increase in the risk of homicide . . ."[219] and "Our study confirms this association. . . ."[220] The authors' occasional qualification of their results ("People who keep guns in their homes appear to be at greater risk of homicide in the home than people who do not"[221]) indicate that they understand the tentative nature of the results of CCM studies, but this does not appear to have tempered their presentation of their conclusions.

THE *NEW ENGLAND JOURNAL OF MEDICINE*

The *New England Journal*'s editor has actually castigated the NRA for opposing gun laws, claiming that this departs from the NRA's original (1870) purpose of promoting civilian marksmanship. Naturally, the irony of his position is lost on Dr. Kassirer, whose myopia in this respect epitomizes the unself-conscious, unexamined self-righteousness that pervades the health advocacy literature against firearms.

However much Kassirer disagrees with the substance of what the NRA says, it is the NRA's right and duty as a membership organization to advance the goals its members have put forward by electing certain officers and rejecting others. Even Drs. Sloan et al. seem to recognize this in their response (in the *New England Journal*) to NRA criticism,

> Coming from an official spokesman for the National Rifle Association, Blackman's invective is no surprise. . . .
>
> We understand [his] need to attack this paper; *it is what he is paid to do.*[222]
> (Emphasis added)

In contrast, politically motivated advocacy is not what Drs. Kassirer, Sloan, Kellermann, and others are paid to do, at least in theory.[223] Yet the politically fixed editorial policy of the *New England Journal* is to suppress publication of anything dissenting from the orthodox health advocacy position on firearms or meaningfully questioning the methodology of the innumerable articles the journal publishes to buttress that position. The *New England Journal* does claim to be open to contrary opinion.[224] But that claim is falsified by the record. To reiterate, in 1989 the *New England Journal* had the chance to publish an article by Sloan et al. claiming severe antigun policies had reduced Canadian homicide and/or an article by Centerwall showing that such policies had not. The Sloan article was based on simplistic comparisons of just two cities in Canada and the U.S., while Centerwall's was based on comparisons of nationwide data from both countries. Predictably, the *New England Journal* chose the Sloan article, with its far inferior data base but antigun conclusion, over the Centerwall one. Predictably, the journal also chose not to publish both together so that readers could compare the results from the differing data bases for themselves. Even worse, the *New England Journal* abetted the inferior article's authors in violating ordinary standards of scholarship by omitting to tell readers of the adverse findings from a superior data set.

From at least 1968, the *New England Journal*'s editorial view has been "squarely on the side of" gun control, as its editors themselves proudly proclaim; from at least that time it has an unblemished record of publishing articles, as well as editorials, condemning gun ownership as a social menace—without once publishing any other view or contrary scholarship or discordant research or opinion piece (beyond 400 word letters to the editor limited to three references).[225]

The *New England Journal*'s record is not unique, but rather typifies the practice of health advocacy periodicals regarding firearms issues. Predictably, when scholarly periodicals hermetically seal their articles from the corrective force of criticism and adverse scholarship, the result is "junk scholarship." The antigun health advocacy literature is fraught with partisan departures from scholarly inquiry as well as more quotidian errors. These include the making of unsubstantiated assumptions, the use of inadequate data and erroneous or unsuitable analytical methods, the suppression of inconvenient or uncongenial facts, the failure to cite and deal with contrary scholarship (and the substitution of *ad hominem* arguments for reasoned refutation when it is attempted), and a statement of results that is not true to what actually occurred.

Throughout this chapter we have shown all these errors in gun-control articles published in well-respected medical journals. Of course, innocent mistakes can and inevitably will be made, but it is hoped that most of them are weeded out by the peer review process. Survival to publication of reporting, methodological, and other errors in health periodicals—errors consistent with the editorial policy of those periodicals—raise questions as to their scientific status.

A pertinent example is *NEJM*-1993. The errors described above leave its conclusions about the dangers of guns ownership as unsupported conjecture. Rather than being a report of scientific research, it is unsuitable for use as a scientifically based justification for policy decisions. Unfortunately this is concealed. Because it is presented in the guise of a scientific study, with all the trappings of proper experimental design and sophisticated statistical data analysis, *NEJM*-1993 can easily be mistaken for the report of a scientific study. Such a misleading article is hard to publish without the tacit support of the journal's editors.

MORE FEAR AND LOATHING: ADVOCACY VERSUS SCHOLARSHIP

The health advocacy literature's primary focus is compiling factoids (and sometimes inventing them) selected to support arguments against firearms ownership. A secondary purpose is to inform health advocates about gun owners and ownership. The two purposes are easily compatible, the information provided being not in the spirit of scholarly inquiry, but on the order of "know thine enemy."

Naturally, the only facts provided are negative or presented in a negative light. Naturally, in the antigun health advocacy literature guns and their ownership are addressed only as social pathology, never as a value-neutral social phenomenon. Readers would never know that some doctors recommend target shooting to patients as a means of perfecting hand-eye coordination and as recreation for those whose conditions preclude more physically taxing exercise.[226] The only admissible firearms article topics in the health advocacy literature are gun accidents, gun violence, gun suicides, gun ownership among extremist groups, and the like. These ills are implicitly deemed to fairly represent the 50 percent of American households that contain guns. It never seems to have occurred to the gatekeepers of the antigun health advocacy literature that gun ownership could present any issue worthy of neutral or non-problematic study.[227]

Predictably, the *leitmotif* running throughout health advocacy articles is how contemptible gun owners are—how irresponsible and foolish, how silly and educationally and intellectually retarded. This contrasts oddly with sociological studies finding gun owners better educated and more prestigiously and remuneratively employed than nonowners. But then such findings get so little play in the health advocacy literature that its readers are unlikely to recognize any disparity.

Nor does that literature *ever* report even one of the following findings of sociological studies: that gun-owner attitudes are not more sexist[228] or racist than those of nonowners; based on three national surveys, that gun owners do not express more "violent attitudes" (defined as approval of violence against social deviants or dissenters)—though gun owners differ from nonowners in being more likely to approve "defensive" force, i.e., force directed by victims against violent attackers[229]; and that, far from being "paranoid" about crime, gun owners express less fear of it than do nonowners.[230] The lesser fear may be explained by findings of a study of "Good Samaritans" who had arrested criminals or rescued their victims. In contrast to the less than 33 percent of Americans who then owned any kind of gun, almost two and one-half as many of the Samaritans (81 percent) "own guns and some carry them in their cars. They are familiar with violence, feel competent to handle it, and do not believe they will be hurt if they get involved."[231]

As to racism, the result of one local attitude study can be deemed to suggest that gun owners are likely to hold racist views.[232] But the asserted correlation between gun ownership and racism is not borne out by the several state and national studies of gun-owner attitudes that have included questions designed to elicit racist attitudes.[233]

But nonpejorative facts about gun owners, as well as the concept of gun owners as Good Samaritans (or good anything), are inadmissible in the health advocacy literature. Other equally inadmissible facts from sociological studies include: that, though gun ownership is lower among political "liberals," those liberals who do own guns express no less willingness to use them in self-defense than nonliberal owners[234]; that 50 percent of those whose motive for owning guns is only protection (not sport) are women, disproportionately African-American women. These findings must be rigorously excluded from the health advocacy literature lest it evoke reader empathy or undercut the contemptuous attitude that literature encourages its readers to feel toward gun owners. To maximize such reader contempt, health advocates seek to portray gun owners as violent, paranoid white men beset by irrational emotions; fear of crime; or racist, machismo desire to kill minority and disadvantaged people. (It is correct that gun owners are primarily white males, but surveys show their reason for ownership is largely or exclusively for sport not protection—a point reinforced by statistical evidence that male gun ownership does not increase with proximity to black areas. It is only female gun ownership that increases, a finding partially accounted for by the disproportionately large number of African-American women who own firearms.)

But let us take this problematic orientation as a given. It only highlights a more remarkable aspect of the antigun health advocacy literature: the dearth of citations or analysis of any significant part of the truly enormous criminological literature. Criminology, after all, has produced a vast body of data and analysis devoted to a set of social problems (violent crime and especially murder) which form the major theme in the health advocacy literature on firearms—or, more correctly, against firearms. But therein lies the problem. For, as we have seen, even criminologists who personally held antigun preconceptions have been forced by their data to conclusions that are unacceptable to the editors at *JAMA,* the *New England Journal* and to the other gatekeepers of the health advocacy literature.

So, with rare exceptions, references in the health advocacy articles on gun control and firearms issues are only to articles by other medical or health writers. More important, they are only to other writers who share the same viewpoint.

In sum, the health advocacy literature against firearms violates the canons of scholarly discourse. These require that in making assertions scholars inform readers of the existence of contrary data, research, or analysis and refute or distinguish it. Thus, for instance, criminological publications on firearms and violence do exhaustively review research and data in medico-health journals—with special attention to those contrary to the conclusions the criminologist is drawing.

It must be understood that articles in medico-health journals are generally "refereed," i.e., they are printed only after being reviewed by multiple anonymous scholarly reviewers who are supposed to possess expertise in the area under discussion. So the reviewers (and/or the editors) must be either unaware of the gross departures from accepted scholarly practice in the articles on firearms which they approve or they must condone these unscholarly practices. Not being privy to their councils, we cannot determine whether ignorance or condonation is responsible for the abysmal quality of the health advocacy literature against firearms.

CONCLUSION

It is documented above that there is an emotional antigun agenda in the treatment of firearms issues in the medical and public health literature. While the antigun editorials and articles presented have had the superficial form of scientific research, the basic tenets of science and scholarship have too often been lacking. These articles and editorials have been so biased and have committed so many errors of fact, logic, and procedure that we can no longer regard them as having a legitimate claim to be scientific, which is why we have labeled them as "antigun health advocacy literature."

This advocacy literature has generally ignored the large amount of criminological and sociological research dealing with violent crime in its presentation of prior results. It also shows a consistent trend of making misleading international comparisons, mistaking the differences between handguns and long guns, and exaggerating the number of children injured or killed—which builds up the emotional content. Many other distortions are typical, such as presenting gun ownership in a manner that ignores or minimizes its benefits, and measuring defensive benefits purely in terms of attackers killed, rather than considering attacks deterred or attackers repelled. The criminological and sociological research literature has dealt extensively with the existence of high-risk groups and of the career criminals who commit many of the serious crimes in our society. Yet the antigun health advocacy literature consistently overlooks this societal structure and attributes equal propensity to commit violent crime to all people.

The advocacy literature exhibits an emotional reaction to guns which has filtered out all consideration of the research of others, with the resulting elimination of contrary views even when other evidence indicates that these contrary views must have been encountered. The works with contrary views tend to be dismissed with *ad hominem* comments, but without the presentation of evidence or analysis to counter these views. The antigun health advocacy literature can be described with the derogatory term "sagecraft," with the implication that professionals use the superficialities of scientific methodology and presentation to advocate their agendas while ignoring the basics of sound research. This shameful performance can only result from the willing collaboration of the researchers, the journals, and the federal funding agencies. While many medical and public health journals have participated in this, the *New England Journal of Medicine* has been one of the most noticeable. With its strongly and explicitly antigun editorial policy, it has not only published poorly executed antigun articles but excluded articles disagreeing with this editorial policy. By these actions it loses its claim—at least in the area of gun control—to be a research journal.

This indictment of the antigun health advocacy literature is serious, especially in an era in which research information is sought as a basis for public debate and formulation of public policy. When emotionally based antigun pseudoscientific advocacy is presented in the guise of research, ill-founded policy decisions may be based on this supposed research. This can lead to a waste of public resources and direct public harm. The medical and public health journals need to abandon their emotionally based advocacy and reclaim a role of presenting scientific research results.

NOTES

1. See, e.g., Samuel Walker, *Sense and Nonsense about Crime and Drugs: a Policy Guide* (Belmont, Calif.: Wadsworth, 1994), chs. 10 and 13; Gary Kleck, *Point Blank: Guns and Violence in America* (New York: Aldine, 1991); Gerald D. Robin, *Violent Crime and Gun Control* (Academy of Crim. Jus. Sciences, 1991); J. Wright, P. Rossi and K. Daly, *Under the Gun: Weapons, Crime and Violence in the United States* (New York: Aldine, 1983); J. Wright and P. Rossi, *Armed and Dangerous: A Survey of Felons and Their Firearms* (New York: Aldine, 1986); and the lengthy article list cited at note 30 below.

2. Quoting from CDC bulletin "Firearm Mortality among Children and Youth," Advance Data #178, National Center for Health Statistics (November 3, 1989). (The authors, CDC firearms specialists Lois Fingerhut and Joel Kleinman, add, "The data presented in this report underscore these concerns." They could, without substantial exaggeration, have added that CDC publications on firearms can be reviewed, as they will be herein, without ever finding analysis of data leading to any other conclusion.) See also Public Health Service [hereinafter PHS], *Healthy People: The Surgeon General's Report on Health Promotion and Disease Prevention* (Washington, D.C.: Government Printing Office, 1979), pp. 9–21 and PHS, *Healthy People: The Surgeon General's Report on Health Promotion and Disease Prevention, Background Papers* (Washington, D.C.: Government Printing Office, 1979), pp. 18, 64–67, 465.

3. "Guns are a virus that must be eradicated. . . . They are causing an epidemic of death by gunshot, which should be treated like any epidemic—you get rid of the virus. . . . Get rid of the guns, get rid of the bullets, and you get rid of the deaths." Health activist Katherine Christoffel, M.D., profiled by Janice Somerville, "Gun Control as Immunization," *American Medical News,* January 3, 1994, p. 9 (also quoting approving comments by an AMA official and the CDC's Mark Rosenberg). See also: Deane Calhoun, "From Controversy to Prevention: Building Effective Firearm Policies," *Injury Prevention Network Newsletter,* Winter 1989–90, p. 17 (praising National Coalition to Ban Handgun's change of name to indicate broader prohibition reflecting its "belief that guns are not just an inanimate object, but in fact are a social ill"); Deborah Prothrow-Stith, *Deadly Consequences* (New York: Harpers, 1991), 198 (discussed and quoted in the "Fear and Loathing as Social Science" section of this chapter below); Webster et al., "Reducing Firearms Injuries," *Issues in Science and Technology,* Spring 1991, p. 78; National Committee for Injury Prevention and Control, *Injury Prevention: Meeting the Challenge,* a supplemental edition of the *American Journal of Preventive Medicine* (1989), p. 3

(hereinafter cited as *Injury Prevention*); Goldsmith, "Epidemiologists Aim at New Target: Health Risk of Handgun Proliferation," *Journal of the American Medical Association* [hereinafter *JAMA*] 261 (1989): 675; Surgeon General's Workshop on Violence and Public Health, "Report" (Rockville, Md., 1985), p. 53 (need to ban private possession of handguns).

   4. In addition to the sources cited in the preceding note, see e.g.: Karl P. Adler et al., "Firearms Violence and Public Health: Limiting the Availability of Guns," *JAMA* 271 (1994): 1281; William Rasberry, "Sick People With Guns," *Washington Post,* October 19, 1994, p. A23 (quoting Dr. Mark Rosenberg on his, and the CDC's, agenda to create a public perception of firearms as "dirty, deadly—and banned"); Harold Henderson, "Policy: Guns 'n' Poses," *Chicago Reader,* December 16, 1994 (quoting Chicago Doctors Robert Tanz and Katherine Christoffel on the need to change public attitudes toward guns as public attitudes toward smoking have been changed); editorial, "Brady Bill Has Medicine's Support," *American Medical News,* May 20, 1991, p. 25 (firearms "are one of the main causes of intentional and unintentional injury. . . . [T]he real cure for the epidemic [of violence by guns] is to eliminate its cause"); American Academy of Pediatrics, Policy Statement, *AAP News* (January 1992), pp. 20–23 (necessity to ban private possession of handguns); Judith Cohen Dolins and Katherine Christoffel, "Reducing Violent Injuries: Priorities for Pediatrician Advocacy," *Pediatrics* 94 (1994): 638, 645 (defining gun control as a process of progressively removing weapons from home environments); Daniel W. Webster and Modena E. H. Wilson, "Gun Violence among Youth and the Pediatrician's Role in Primary Prevention," *Pediatrics* 94 (1994): 617, 621 ("gun manufacturers are polluting our communities").

   5. Handgun Control's eventual goal appears to be national gun licensing under which self-defense would not be a ground for gun ownership; only sportsmen would be allowed to own guns. Eckholm, "A Little Control, A Lot of Guns," *New York Times,* August 15, 1993, quoting Handgun Control Chair Sarah Brady. Her position is that "the only reason for guns in civilian hands is for sporting purposes." Jackson, "Keeping the Battle Alive," *Tampa Tribune,* October 21, 1993. In a more recent interview her husband emphasized that handgun ownership would be allowed for sport but not self-defense. "[Yes, owning handguns] for target shooting, that's ok. Get a license and go to the range. For defense of the home—that's why we have police departments." "In Step With: James Brady," *Parade,* June 26, 1994, p. 18.

   6. "The position of the National Coalition to Ban Handguns is very clear. . . . [B]an the manufacture, sale, and possession of all handguns, except for police, military, licensed security guards, and pistol clubs." Testimony of Michael K. Beard of the National Coalition to Ban Handguns in Support of 8–132, "Handgun Manufacturing Strict Liability Act of 1989," before the Committee on the Judiciary, District of Columbia City Council, March 22, 1989. See also an article by a then official of the National Coalition to Ban Handguns, Sam Fields, "Handgun Prohibition and Social Necessity," *St. Louis University Law Journal* 23 (1979): 35, 51

   7. Quoting Webster and Wilson, "Gun Violence among Youth," p. 622. See, e.g., Douglas L. Weed, "Ethics, Guidelines, and Advocacy in Epidemiology," *American Epidemiology* 4 (1994): 166; William DeJong, review of L. Wallack et al., "Media Advocacy and Public Health: Power for Prevention," *Health Education Quarterly* 21 (1994): 543. Dr. DeJong, who teaches in the Harvard University School of Public Health, advises that "To advance the cause of public health, we need to move to a new paradigm, one in which health educators focus on galvanizing political action and change." In the same spirit he praises "work by a gun control advocate [which] shows us how researchers can choose projects that will bring attention to public policy," i.e., the need to prohibit firearms ownership. See also editorial, *Epidemiology* 4 (1993): 93–94, and Peter Edelman and David Satcher, "Violence Prevention As a Public Health Policy," *Health Affairs* 12 (1994): 123, 124.

   8. See, e.g., Dolins and Christoffel, "Reducing Violent Injuries," pp. 641, 648–49; Tardiff et al., "Homicide in New York City: Cocaine Use and Firearms," *JAMA* 272 (1994): 43, 46; Jeffrey B. Kahn, "Firearm Violence in California: Information and Ideas for Creating

Change," *Western Journal of Medicine* 161 (1994): 565; M. Denise Dowd et al., "Pediatric Firearm Injuries, Kansas City, 1992: A Population-Based Study," *Pediatrics* 94 (1994): 867, 872; Adler et al., "Firearms Violence and Public Health," p. 1281; Webster and Wilson, "Gun Violence among Youth," pp. 621–22; Lester Adelson, "The Gun and the Sanctity of Human Life; Or the Bullet as Pathogen," *Archives of Surgery* 127 (1992): 659, 663–64; editorial by former Surgeon General Koop and *JAMA* editor George Lundberg, M.D., "Violence in America: A Public Health Emergency," *JAMA* 267 (1992): 3075; Leland Ropp et al., "Death in the City: An American Childhood Tragedy," *JAMA* 267 (1992): 2905, 2909–10; Katherine Christoffel, "Toward Reducing Pediatric Injuries from Firearms: Charting a Legislative and Regulatory Course," *Pediatrics* 88 (1991): 294; Calhoun, "From Controversy to Prevention"; and Katherine Christoffel and Tom Christoffel, "Handguns: Risks Versus Benefits," *Pediatrics* 47 (1986): 781, 782. See also the more popular articles cited in note 3.

9. Thus, as used in this chapter, that phrase does not include the very few articles on firearms topics in medical or health publications which treat the issues neutrally, e.g., Robert L. Ohsfeldt and Michael A. Morrisey, "Firearms, Firearms Injury and Gun Control: A Critical Survey of the Literature," *Advances in Health Economics and Health Services Research* 13 (1992): 65, or even take a stance affirmatively supporting freedom of private choice regarding firearms ownership, e.g., Edgar A. Suter, "Guns in the Medical Literature: A Failure of Peer Review," *Journal of the Medical Association of Georgia* 83 (1994): 133.

10. Prothrow-Stith, *Deadly Consequences,* p. 198. As a University of Chicago health advocate put it, "The only legitimate use of a handgun that I can understand is for target shooting." Testimony of Robert Replogle, M.D., testimony on Handgun Crime Control Hearings, Oversight of the 1968 Gun Control Act 1975–76, before the Senate Judiciary Committee, Subcommittee to Investigate Juvenile Delinquency, 94th Congress, vol. II, p. 1974. See also Karl P. Adler et al., "Firearms Violence and Public Health: Limiting the Availability of Guns," *JAMA* 271 (1994): 1281–83; James A. Mercy et al., "Public Health Policy for Preventing Violence," *Health Affairs* 12 (1993): 7, 28 ; Andrew L. Dannenberg et al., "Intentional and Unintentional Injuries in Women: An Overview," *Annals of Epidemiology* 4 (1994): 133, 137; Susan B. Sorenson and Audrey F. Saftlas, "Violence and Women's Health: The Role of Epidemiology," *Annals of Epidemiology* 4 (1994): 140, 145; Mark L. Rosenberg, James A. Mercy, and Vernon N. Houk, "Guns and Adolescent Suicides," *JAMA* 266 (1991): 3030; Daniel W. Webster et al., "Parents' Beliefs about Preventing Gun Injuries to Children," *Pediatrics* 89 (1992): 908, 914; Daniel W. Webster et al., "Firearm Injury Prevention Counseling: A Study of Pediatricians' Beliefs and Practices," *Pediatrics* 89 (1992): 902, 907.

11. J. Michael McGinnis et al., "Actual Causes of Death in the United States," *JAMA* 270 (1993): 2207, 2211; Diane Schetky, "Children and Handguns: A Public Health Concern," *American Journal of Diseases of Children* 139 (1985): 229, 230.

12. Arlene Eisen, "Guns: In Whose Hands? A Portrait of Gun Owners and Their Culture," *Injury Prevention Network Newsletter,* Winter 1989–90, p. 9 (subsection titled "Fear and Racism among Gun Owners" and characterizing—but without providing any example or supporting citation—"the veiled racism of NRA literature promoting self-defense." Also p. 10: "The gun lobby grows fat . . . on a generalized fear and hostility toward African-American people, especially on the association between African-American men and crime in the white public's mind.") See also (in the same issue) Deane Calhoun, "The NRA: The Myth of Protection, the Marketing of Fear"; and Dolins and Christoffel, "Reducing Violent Injuries."

13. Compare *JAMA*'s disparate treatment of two opposing article submissions: Its April 27, 1994, issue carried an article by nineteen medical professionals, seven of them teachers at medical schools, including Columbia and Cornell, urging the banning and confiscation of all handguns, federal restrictive licensing for gun ownership, and a host of other gun control laws. In response *JAMA* promptly received an article submission arguing the other side from thirty-nine authors, twenty-three of them teachers at medical schools, including Harvard and Penn-

sylvania, and two of them law professors. Suter et al., "Violence in America: Effective Solutions." *JAMA* just as promptly rejected it. The article appears instead in the *Journal of the Medical Association of Georgia* (June 1995). As discussed below, in 1977 *JAMA* did publish a critique from a progun perspective. As far as we have been able to find, it remains the only such article in any health periodical other than the *Journal of the Medical Association of Georgia*.

14. William C. Shoemaker et al., "Urban Violence in Los Angeles in the Aftermath of the Riots: A Perspective From Health Care Professionals, with Implications for Social Reconstruction," *JAMA* 270 (1993): 2833, 2836.

15. See, e.g.: Eisen, "Guns: In Whose Hands?" p. 9, dismissing as "racist" an uncongenial finding in a study co-authored by a senior professor of sociology at the University of Illinois and an assistant professor at the State University of New York's School of Criminal Justice (David J. Bordua and Alan J. Lizotte, "Patterns of Legal Firearms Ownership: A Situational and Cultural Analysis of Illinois Counties," *Law and Policy Quarterly* 2 [1979]): 147; and Dolins and Christoffel, "Reducing Violent Injuries," pp. 648–49, describing similarly uncongenial findings as coming from "gun supporters"—though the authors are in fact distinguished social scientists.

Senturia and Christoffel denounce the NRA as espousing what they call "*conservative family values*" (our emphasis), citing an NRA employee's claim that reducing inner city violence will require education in job skills and "stable and moral" home environments. ("Letters," in *Pediatrics* 94 (1994): 777. Yet the need for stable, moral home environments is such a nonpartisan truism that it is invoked even by vehemently antigun health advocates including the CDC's Mercy and Rosenberg. They devote a full 10 percent of their article "Preventing Violence" to the baleful effects of parental criminality and neglectful, unstable, abusive, violent family environments as "pivotal influence[s]" in turning children into violent adolescents and adults, and the need to promote stable and moral home environments in which children are nurtured, loved and taught nonviolence as a way of life. *Health Affairs* 12 (1993): 19–21. For what it is worth, the authors of this article, none of whom are politically conservative, heartily agree.

16. The health advocacy literature's suppression from its readers of the existence of any contrary scholarship runs as a *leitmotif* throughout this article. Health advocates, many of them not even lawyers much less specialists in constitutional law, declare "that the Second Amendment to the Constitution refers [only] to gun ownership by state militias [and] poses no obstacle to gun control laws because it does not guarantee the individual right to own a gun." Dolins and Christoffel, "Reducing Violent Injuries," p. 640. See also Kahn, "Firearm Violence in California," p. 568; Calhoun, "The NRA: The Myth of Protection," p. 16; editorial, *Pediatrics* 88 (1991): 381; and Christoffel and Christoffel, "Handguns: Risks Versus Benefits," *Pediatrics* 47 (1986): 781 (one of the authors is a lawyer).

Nowhere in the health advocacy literature will there be found mention of even one of the contrary law review and other scholarly articles over the past dozen years by distinguished professors of law, history, or political science, many of whom have never owned a gun and have no desire to. Those professors include three of the great liberal icons of modern American constitutional law, Akhil Amar, Sanford Levinson, and William Van Alstyne. But the health advocacy literature portrays the individual rights view as the lunatic invention of wild-eyed gun nuts supported only by gun lobby propaganda. Dolins and Christoffel, "Reducing Violent Injuries," pp. 648–49 ("*The gun lobby* bolsters its posture by arguing . . .") (emphasis added). Having cited gun lobby publications, the ironically named "Right to Be Armed with Accurate Information about the Second Amendment," *American Journal of Public Health* 83: 1773, 1774, comments that "backed by forceful, well-funded lobbying (but not by evidence), [the constitutional right claim] can act as a deterrent to the design and implementation of effective gun control policy." Compare the acceptance of that claim in standard texts edited, authored, or co-authored by law, history, or philosophy professors: Leonard Levy, *Original Intent and the Framers' Constitution* (New York: Macmillan, 1988), p. 341; E. Foner and J. Garrity, *Reader's Com-*

panion to American History (New York: Houghton Mifflin, 1991), pp. 477–78 (entry on "Guns and Gun Control"); *Oxford Companion to the United States Supreme Court* (Oxford University Press, 1992) (entry on the Second Amendment); Joyce Malcolm, *The Right to Keep and Bear Arms: The Origins of an Anglo-American Right* (Cambridge, Mass.: Harvard University Press, 1994); Cottrol and Diamond, " 'The Fifth Auxiliary Right,' " *Yale Law Journal* 104 (1994): 995; Van Alstyne, "The Second Amendment and the Personal Right to Arms," *Duke Law Journal* 43 (1994): 1236; Vandercoy, "The History of the Second Amendment," *Valparaiso Law Review* 28 (1994): 1006; Reynolds, "The Right to Keep and Bear Arms under the Tennessee Constitution," *Tennessee Law Review* 61 (1994): 647 (extensively discussing the Second Amendment in relation to the Tennessee Constitution); Cottrol and Diamond, "Public Safety and the Right to Bear Arms," in D. Bodenhamer and J. Ely, *After 200 Years; The Bill of Rights in Modern America* (Bloomington: Indiana University Press, 1993); Amar, "The Bill of Rights and the Fourteenth Amendment," *Yale Law Journal* 101 (1992): 1193, 1205–11, 1261–62; Levin, "Grass Roots Voices: Local Action and National Military Policy," *Buffalo Law Review* 40 (1992): 321, 346–47; Levinson, "The Embarrassing Second Amendment," *Yale Law Journal* 99 (1989): 637; Nelson Lund, "The Second Amendment, Political Liberty and the Right to Self-Preservation," *Alabama Law Review* 39 (1987): 103; Malcolm, essay review, *George Washington University Law Review* 54 (1986): 582; Fussner, essay review, *Constitutional Commentary* 3 (1986): 582; Shalhope, "The Armed Citizen in the Early Republic," *Law and Contemporary Problems* 49 (1986): 125; Marina, "Weapons, Technology and Legitimacy: The Second Amendment in Global Perspective," in Don Kates, ed., *Firearms and Violence* (1984); Malcolm, "The Right of the People to Keep and Bear Arms: The Common Law Tradition," *Hastings Constitutional Law Quarterly* 10 (1983): 285. See also Glenn H. Reynolds and Don B. Kates, "The Second Amendment and States' Rights: A Thought Experiment," *William and Mary Law Review* 36 (1995); Scarry, "War and the Social Contract: The Right to Bear Arms," *University of Pennsylvania Law Review* 139 (1991): 1257; Pope, "Republican Moments: The Role of Direct Popular Power in the American Constitutional Order," *University of Pennsylvania Law Review* 139 (1991): 287, 328; Williams, "Civic Republicanism and the Citizen Militia: The Terrifying Second Amendment," *Yale Law Journal* 101 (1991): 551 (individual right intended, but now obsolete); John Schoon Yoo, "Our Declaratory Ninth Amendment," *Emory Law Journal* 42 (1993): 967. See also discussion below.

    17. See, e.g., Linda E. Salzman et al., "Weapon Involvement and Injury Outcomes in Family and Intimate Assaults," *JAMA* 267 (1992): 3043, 3045, asserting that "researchers have found no evidence of compensatory increase in homicide with other weapons if firearm access is restricted."—but citing an editorial whose author gives it as her opinion that if guns are banned other weapons will not be substituted. Baker, "Without Guns Do People Kill People?" *American Journal of Public Health* 75 (1985): 587.

    18. See, e.g., Diane Schetky, "Children and Handguns: A Public Health Concern," *American Journal of Diseases of Children* 139 (1985): 229 (of eleven endnotes, one is to a book by then Handgun Control, Inc., chairman Nelson Shields; three are to other Handgun Control, Inc., publications; and one is to a publication by yet another antigun lobbying group).

    19. Sloan, Rivara, and Kellermann, "Correspondence," *NEJM* 323 (1990): 136.

    20. See, e.g., William Tonso, "Social Science and Sagecraft in the Debate over Gun Control," *Law and Policy Quarterly* 5 (1983): 325, based on the concept set out by Florian Znaniecki, *The Social Role of the Man of Knowledge* (New York: Harpers, 1968), pp. 72–74.

    21. Quoted in Goldsmith, "Epidemiologists Aim at New Target." Compare James A. Mercy et al., "Public Health Policy for Preventing Violence," *Health Affairs* 12 (1993): 7, 11 attributing to firearms a "central role in interpersonal violence."

    22. See generally works noted at note 1 and text and works at note 30 below. Briefly summarizing the complex research and literature on the effect of guns: (1) they facilitate robbery of "harder" targets like stores, where robberies are far more remunerative than ordinary

"muggings"; (2) they allow the felon to dominate the situation so that crimes involving firearms result in a tiny fraction of the injuries in similar nonfirearm crimes in which a victim may have to be stabbed or bludgeoned into submission; (3) in the tiny fraction of gun crimes in which a victim is shot, the likelihood of death is far higher than when injury is with a lesser weapon. Thus, if firearms could be magically removed from the environment, the hypothetically likely results would be: (1) the sheer number of crimes would enormously increase if criminals were to attempt to obtain the same income (albeit the increase would not necessarily all be in confrontation crimes like robbery); (2) the number of injured victims would enormously increase; (3) the number of deaths would decrease. Though other weapons are less lethal, they do kill in some cases and the increased number of woundings with them would produce more deaths, thereby at least partially offsetting the reductive effect of removing gun deaths. In addition, the effect on murderous attacks by people truly determined to kill would be unclear since such people can often (but not always) substitute lesser weapons with equally deadly results.

23. David Cowan and David J. Bordua, notes on "Case-Control Study Design and Violence Research" (italics in original); available from Professor Bordua at the Department of Sociology, University of Illinois.

24. Dr. Christoffel quoted in Somerville, "Gun Control as Immunization" (with approving comment by other health advocates). The health advocacy literature describes firearms as disease "vectors," "toxins," and/or causes of an epidemic. See, e.g., Christopher Durso, "Guns 'n' Doctors," *The New Physician,* December 1994; Paul Cotton, "Gun-Associated Violence Increasingly Viewed as Public Health Challenge," *JAMA* 267 (1992): 1171–74. See also Nikki Meredith, "The Murder Epidemic," *Science,* December 1984; Colburn, "Gunshots as an Epidemic: Some Doctors Call Firearms a 'Toxin' in the Environment," *Washington Post Health,* November 1, 1988; "Guns 'n' Poses."

25. Rasberry, "Sick People with Guns," quoting Rosenberg; *Chicago Reader,* reporting views of Christoffel and Tanz that they "plan to do to handguns what their profession has done to cigarettes . . . turn gun ownership from a personal-choice issue to a repulsive, antisocial health hazard." See also Prothrow-Stith, *Deadly Consequences.*

26. Stephen P. Teret and Garen J. Wintemute, "Policies to Prevent Firearms Injuries" *Health Affairs* 12 (1993): 96, 97, indicate that a search in a medical data base "for articles dealing with firearms, excluding literature on the clinical aspects of treating gun shot wounds," shows that by 1992 the number had swelled to "nearly eighty articles annually." Based on an extensive review, it is estimated that today at least one firearms-related article a week appears in one of the enormous number of medical and public health journals. Personal communication from Professor James Boen, Associate Dean of the School of Public Health, University of Minnesota. Symposia in which entire issues of health periodicals, or major portions thereof, are devoted to espousing the evil of firearms and supporting gun bans are also common. See, e.g., the October 1994 issue of *Pediatrics*; the February 3, 1994, issue of *NEJM*; the Winter 1993 issue of *Health Affairs*; the special supplement to the May-June 1993 issue of the *American Journal of Preventive Medicine*; the June 10, 1992, issue of *JAMA*; and the Winter 1989–90 issue of *Injury Prevention Network Newsletter,* not to mention AMA Council on Scientific Affairs, "Firearm Injuries and Deaths: A Critical Public Health Issue" in *Public Health Reports,* March/April 1989.

27. See, e.g., Franklin Zimring, "Is Gun Control Likely to Reduce Violent Killings," *University of Chicago Law Review* 35 (1968): 721, and Norval Morris and Gordon Hawkins, *The Honest Politician's Guide to Crime Control* (Chicago: University of Chicago Press, 1969), pp. 63–71.

28. Franklin Zimring and Gordon Hawkins, *The Citizen's Guide to Gun Control* (New York: Macmillan, 1987), p. xi.

29. See, e.g., Hans Toch and Alan J. Lizotte, "Research and Policy: The Case of Gun Control," in Peter Sutfeld and Philip Tetlock, eds., *Psychology and Social Policy* (New York: Hemisphere, 1992); James D. Wright, "Second Thoughts about Gun Control," *The Public*

Interest 91 (1988): 23; Ted R. Gurr, ed., *Violence in America* 1 (1989): 17–18; Eskridge, "Zero-Order Inverse Correlations Between Crimes of Violence and Hunting Licenses in the United States," *Sociology and Social Research* 71 (1986): 55.

    30. In addition to the volumes cited at note 1, see, e.g., Bruce Danto, "Firearms and Their Role in Homicide and Suicide," *Life-Threatening Behavior* 1 (1971): 10; Colin Greenwood, *Firearms Control: A Study of Firearms Control and Armed Crime in England and Wales* (1972); John Kaplan, "Controlling Firearms," *Cleveland State Law Review* 28 (1977): 1; David J. Bordua and Alan J. Lizotte, "Patterns of Legal Firearms Ownership: A Situational and Cultural Analysis of Illinois Counties," *Law and Policy Quarterly* 2 (1979): 147; Danto, "Firearms and Violence," *International Journal of Offender Therapy* 5 (1979): 135; Gary Kleck, "Capital Punishment, Gun Ownership and Homicide," *American Journal of Sociology* 84 (1979): 882; Lizotte and Bordua, "Firearms Ownership for Sport and Protection: Two Divergent Models," *American Society Review* 45 (1980); Kessler, "Enforcement Problems of Gun Control: A Victimless Crimes Analysis," *Criminal Law Bulletin* 16 (1980): 131; Kaplan, "The Wisdom of Gun Prohibition," *Annals of the American Academy of Political Science and Social Sciences* 455 (1981): 11; Mark Moore, "The Bird in Hand: A Feasible Strategy for Gun Control," *Journal of Policy Analysis and Management* 2 (1983): 18; Gary Kleck and David J. Bordua, "The Factual Foundation for Certain Key Assumptions of Gun Control," *Law and Policy Quarterly* 5 (1983): 271; Kessler, "Gun Control and Political Power," *Law and Policy Quarterly* 5 (1983): 381; Don Kates, "Handgun Banning in Light of the Prohibition Experience," and Gary Kleck, "Handgun-Only Control: A Policy Disaster in the Making" and "The Relationship between Gun Ownership Levels and Rates of Violence in the United States" in Don Kates, ed., *Firearms and Violence* (1984); Gary Kleck, "Policy Lessons from Recent Gun Control Research," *Law and Contemporary Problems* 49 (1986): 35; Lizotte, "The Costs of Using Gun Control to Reduce Homicide," *Bulletin of the New York Academy of Medicine* 62 (1986): 539; Bordua, "Firearms Ownership and Violent Crime: A Comparison of Illinois Counties," in J. Byrne and R. Sampson, eds., *The Social Ecology of Crime* (1986); Eskridge, "Zero-Order Inverse Correlations"; J. Jacobs, "Exceptions to a General Prohibition on Handgun Possession: Do They Swallow Up the Rule?" *Law and Contemporary Problems* 49 (1986): 5; Jo Dixon and Alan J. Lizotte, "Gun Ownership and the 'Southern Subculture of Violence'," *American Journal of Sociology* 93 (1987): 383, Wright, "Second Thoughts"; Kessler, "Ideology and Gun Control," *Quarterly Journal of Ideology* 12 (1988): 1; Gurr, *Violence in America*; Don Kates, "Firearms and Violence: Old Premises and Current Evidence," in Ted R. Gurr. ed.,*Violence in America* (1989) (hereinafter cited as "Current Evidence"); Robert J. Mundt, "Gun Control and Rates of Firearms Violence in Canada and the United States," *Canadian Journal of Criminology* 32 (1990): 137; Gary Kleck, *Point Blank: Guns and Violence in America* (New York: Aldine, 1991); Kleck and McElrath, "The Effects of Weaponry on Human Violence, *Social Forces* 69 (1991): 1–21; Don Kates, "The Value of Civilian Arms Possession as Deterrent to Crime or Defense Against Crime," *American Journal of Criminal Law* 18 (1991): 113 (hereinafter cited as "Value of Civilian Arms"); David Kopel, *The Samurai, the Mountie, and the Cowboy: Should American Adopt the Gun Control of Other Democracies?* (Amherst, N.Y.: Prometheus Books, 1992); Toch and Lizotte, "Research and Policy"; Kleck and DeLone, "Victim Resistance and Offender Weapon Effects in Robbery," *Journal of Quantitative Criminology* 9 (1993): 55; and Kleck and Patterson, "The Impact of Gun Control and Gun Ownership Levels on City Violence Rates," *Journal of Quantitative Criminology* 9 (1993): 249; Walker, *Sense and Nonsense*.

    See also: Bruce-Briggs, "The Great American Gun War," *The Public Interest* 45 (Fall 1976); Stell, "Guns, Politics and Reason," *Journal of American Culture* 9 (1986): 71; Steven B. Duke and Albert C. Gross, *America's Longest War: Rethinking Our Tragic Crusade against Drugs* (New York: Putnam, 1993), p. 113; and Randy E. Barnett, "Bad Trip: Drug Prohibition and the Weakness of Public Policy," *Yale Law Journal* 103 (1994): 2593, 2617–18.

31. "Current Evidence," p. 201, citing the views of Colin Greenwood, author of the seminal study of English gun control. That study has been eclipsed by Kopel's study (see preceding note) of gun control in England, Canada, Australia, New Zealand, Jamaica, Japan, and Switzerland. But Kopel endorses the same conclusions as Greenwood as to the enforceability and utility of gun laws.

32. State of Wisconsin Legislative Reference Bureau, "The Gun Control Debate—An Update," *Informational Bulletin* 94-3 (October 1994), p. 30. Similarly, Gurr comments that handgun prohibition "would criminalize much of the citizenry but have only marginal effects on criminals," *Violence in America* 1: 17.

33. See note 3.

34. Emmanuel Tanay, M.D., "Neurotic Attachment to Guns," quoted in Don B. Kates and Nicole Varzos, "Aspects of the Priapic Theory of Gun Ownership," in William Tonso, ed., *The Gun Culture and Its Enemies* (Bellevue, Wash.: Second Amendment Foundation, 1989), pp. 93, 95.

35. Sigmund Freud and D. Oppenheim, *Dreams in Folklore* (1958), p. 33; see also *The Major Writings of Sigmund Freud* (Great Books ed., 1952), p. 507.

36. Arthur Kellermann et al., "Suicide in the Home in Relation to Gun Ownership," *NEJM* 327 (1992): 467, citing, *inter alia,* Charles L. Rich, et al., "Guns and Suicide: Possible Effects of Some Specific Legislation," *American Journal of Psychiatry* 147 (1990): 342, which found, based on empirical investigation, that when deprived of guns, suicidal individuals turn to other methods (e.g., leaping from great heights), so that reduction in gun suicides is offset by an increase in suicide by other means.

37. Tardiff et al., "Homicide in New York City," pp. 43, 45, blaming increased homicide among minority teenagers on increased availability of firearms to them, but citing CDC, "Weapon-Carrying among High School Students—U.S. 1990," *Morbidity and Mortality Weekly Report* 40 (1991): 681, which indicated a decline in gun carrying, not an increase. (Of the other two citations the article gave to the same point, citation no. 42 contained no information about firearm availability while citation no. 43 had no trend data.)

38. Runyan and Gerken, "Epidemiology and Prevention of Adolescent Injuries," *JAMA* 262 (1989): 2273, 2275, citing two articles by Colin Loftin and David McDowall which actually said (respectively) ". . . the gun law did *not* significantly alter the numbers or types of serious crimes in Detroit," and "Our current working hypothesis and by far the simplest interpretation of the data is that the Florida gun law did *not* have a measurable deterrent effect on violent crime." Emphasis added to both quotes which are (respectively) from " 'One with a Gun Gets You Two': Mandatory Sentencing and Firearms Violence in Detroit," *Annals of the American Academy of Policy and Social Science* 455 (1981): 150, and Loftin and McDowall, "The Deterrent Effects of the Florida Felony Firearm Law," *Journal of Criminal Law and Criminology* 75 (1984): 250, 258.

39. Abraham B. Bergman, "Review of D. Prothrow-Stith, *Deadly Consequences,*" *JAMA* 267 (1992): 3089.

40. Mercy et al., "Public Health Policy for Preventing Violence," p. 11.

41. Bureau of Justice Statistics, Selected Findings from National Statistical Series, "Firearms and Crimes of Violence" 2 (Washington, D.C.: Dept. of Just, February 1994).

42. Dolins and Christoffel, "Reducing Violent Injuries," p. 647.

43. *United States* v. *Miller,* 307 U.S. 174 (1939) held that an indictment should not have been dismissed on the theory that any law regulating sawed-off shotguns necessarily violated the Second Amendment. Partisans of the states' right-only view which Dolins and Christoffel endorse have misunderstood this as a holding that the only firearms the Amendment protects are those of the National Guard and/or organized state militias. That was what the solicitor general argued—"that the right was a collective one that [only] protected the people when carrying arms as members of the state militia." Robert Cottrol, *Gun Control and the Constitution* (New

York: Garland, 1993), p. xxvii. But the Court evidently did not accept that—even though the argument was unopposed because no brief was filed on the other side.

Had the *Miller* court accepted the collective right argument it would have disposed of the appeal on standing grounds, holding that since gun ownership by ordinary citizens is not protected by the Amendment, Mr. Miller was not in a position to challenge the law under it. Instead *Miller* focused on a substantive issue which implicitly accepts that the Amendment protects individuals in possessing certain kinds of arms. *Miller's* focus was whether a law regulating sawed-off shotguns involves the kind of firearms that the Amendment covers. As to that, the Court held that only possession of military-type and/or militarily useful weapons is protected by the Amendment. 307 U.S. at 178. This was based on the Amendment's reference to a militia, but the Court expressly recognized that the militia included virtually the whole male population: "The signification attributed to the term 'militia' appears from the debates in the Convention, the history and legislation of the colonies and the states, and the writings of approved commentators . . . [:] all males physically capable of acting in concert for the common defense. . . . [O]rdinarily when called for service these men were expected to appear bearing arms *supplied by themselves* and of the kind in common use at the time." 307 U.S. at 179 (emphasis added). Since Mr. Miller had disappeared while free on bail pending appeal, no party before the Court even attempted to show that, as a matter of fact, a sawed-off shotgun is a standard military weapon. For equally obvious reasons, absent such a showing, the Court was not in a position to judicially notice that a sawed-off shotgun is (or is not) a military weapon. 307 U.S. at 178.

In sum, the Court's treatment of the issues in *Miller* accepted that individuals do have standing to invoke the Second Amendment, albeit only in behalf of conventional military-standard handguns and long guns.

44. *United States* v. *Verdugo-Urquidez,* 494 U.S. 259, 108 L.Ed. 2d 222, 232–33 (1990) (expressly mentioning the Second Amendment).

45. See, e.g., *Planned Parenthood* v. *Casey,* 120 L.Ed.2d 674, 696 (1992); *Moore* v. *East Cleveland,* 431 U.S. 494, 502 (1976) (plurality opinion) quoting the second Justice Harlan in listing "the freedom of speech, press, and religion; the right to keep and bear arms; the freedom from unreasonable searches and seizures" as part of the "full scope of liberty" guaranteed by the Constitution, *Poe* v. *Ullman,* 367 U.S. 497, 542–43 (1961) (Harlan, J., dissenting).

In so doing the Court is following the Founders who themselves routinely made the same connection, linking the right to arms with freedom of religion and speech, etc., under such joint descriptions as "private rights," "human rights," "essential and sacred rights" (quoting Madison, Monroe, and Gallatin, respectively). For these and numerous other quotes from the 1787–91 debates see Don Kates, "Handgun Prohibition and the Original Meaning of the Second Amendment," *Michigan Law Review* 82 (1983): 203, 223–24.

46. Compare *Quilici* v. *Village of Morton Grove,* 695 F.2d 261 (7th Cir. 1982) (dictum: Second Amendment is not an individual right; ruling: whatever the Second Amendment means, application against a municipal ordinance is precluded by nineteenth-century Supreme Court holdings that it applies only against the federal government) to *Fresno Rifle and Pistol Club* v. *Lungren,* 965 F.2d 773 (9th Cir., 1992) (if the Second Amendment is an individual right, it is still not applicable to the states until and unless the Supreme Court overturns its nineteenth-century holdings that the Amendment applies only against the federal government).

47. David I. Caplan, "State Constitutional Protections for the Right to Keep and Bear Arms: A Recent Judicial Trend," *Detroit College Law Review* 4 (1982): 78; Robert Dowlut and Janet Knoop, "State Constitutions and the Right to Keep and Bear Arms," *Oklahoma City University Law Review* 7 (1982): 177; Glenn Reynolds, and cases there cited.

48. Christoffel, "Toward Reducing Pediatric Injuries," p. 295, citing Franklin Zimring and Gordon Hawkins, *The Citizen's Guide to Gun Control* (New York: Macmillan, 1986). Had Christoffel reviewed the scholarly literature in the decade preceding her own article, she could

have added to her list of "legal scholarship" six articles: "The Second Amendment: A Study of Recent Judicial Trends," *Richmond Law Review* 25 (1991): 501 (whatever the Amendment's actual purpose, the lower federal courts have refused to enforce it); "The Constitutional Implications of Gun Control and Several Realistic Gun Control Proposals," *American Journal of Criminal Law* 17 (1989): 19, 25ff.; Ehrman and Henigan, "The Second Amendment in the 20th Century: Have You Seen Your Militia Lately," *University of Dayton Law Review* 15 (1989): 5; Henigan, "Arms, Anarchy and the Second Amendment," *Valparaiso University Law Review* 26 (1991): 107; Fields, "Guns, Crime and the Negligent Gun Owner," *North Kentucky Law Review* 10 (1982); Spannaus, "State Firearms Regulation and the Second Amendment," *Hamline Law Review* 6 (1983): 383. On the other side, however, she would have found thirty law review articles, including many in top law reviews. In addition to the works already cited at note 16, see: Kates, *Michigan Law Review* 82 (1983): 203, and "The Second Amendment: A Dialogue," *Law and Contemporary Problems* 149 (1986): 43; Stephen Halbrook, "What the Framers Intended: A Linguistic Interpretation of the Second Amendment," *Law and Contemporary Problems* 49 (1986): 153; Thomas Moncure, "The Second Amendment Ain't about Hunting," *Howard Law Journal* 34 (1991): 589; Halbrook, "The Right of the People or the Power of the State: Bearing Arms, Arming Militias, and the Second Amendment," *Valparaiso Law Review* 26 (1991): 131; Tahmbassi, "Gun Control and Racism," *George Mason Civil Rights Law Journal* 2 (1991): 67; Bordenet, "The Right to Possess Arms: The Intent of the Framers of the Second Amendment," *U.W.L.A. Law Review* 21 (1990): 1; Moncure, "Who is the Militia—The Virginia Ratifying Convention and the Right to Bear Arms," *Lincoln Law Review* 19 (1990): 1; Note, "Assault Rifle Legislation: Unwise and Unconstitutional," *American Journal of Criminal Law* 17 (1990): 143; Dowlut, "Federal and State Constitutional Guarantees to Arms," *University of Dayton Law Review* 15 (1989): 59; Halbrook, "Encroachments of the Crown on the Liberty of the Subject: Pre-Revolutionary Origins of the Second Amendment," *University of Dayton Law Review* 15 (1989): 91; Hardy, "The Second Amendment and the Historiography of the Bill of Rights," *Journal of Law and Politics* 4 (1987): 1; Hardy, "Armed Citizens, Citizen Armies: Toward a Jurisprudence of the Second Amendment," *Harvard Journal of Law and Public Policy* 9 (1986): 559; Dowlut, "The Current Relevancy of Keeping and Bearing Arms," *University of Baltimore Law Forum* 15 (1984): 32; Dowlut, "The Right to Arms," *Oklahoma Law Review* 36 (1983): 65; Caplan, "The Right of the Individual to Keep and Bear Arms," *Detroit College of Law Review* (1982): 789; Halbrook, "To Keep and Bear 'Their Private Arms,' " *Northern Kentucky Law Review* 10 (1982): 13; A. Gottlieb, "Gun Ownership: A Constitutional Right," *Northern Kentucky Law Review* 10 (1982): 138; Gardiner, "To Preserve Liberty—A Look at the Right to Keep and Bear Arms," *Northern Kentucky Law Review* 10 (1982): 63; Note, "Gun Control: Is It a Legal and Effective Means of Controlling Firearms in the United States?" *Washburn Law Journal* 21 (1982): 244; Halbrook, "The Jurisprudence of the Second and Fourteenth Amendments," *George Mason Law Review* 4 (1981): 1.

49. Dolins and Christoffel, "Reducing Violent Injuries," p. 649, citing (as the "gun supporters") Kleck, *Social Problems,* p. 35; Wright and Rossi, *Armed and Dangerous*; and (as the "epidemiologists") David McDowall, Colin Loftin and Brian Wiersema, "Evaluating Effects of Changes in Gun Laws," *American Journal of Preventive Medicine* 9 (1993): 39–43; and "Legislative Reference Bureau, The Gun Control Debate," Madison, Wis.: Legislative Reference Bureau, *Informational Bulletin* 93–3 (1993).

50. See discussion in the next section of this chapter ("The Valor of Ignorance").

51. *Under the Gun,* p. 320. See also the works cited at note 30.

52. *Armed and Considered Dangerous,* pp. 145, 150, 154 and table 7.1.

53. McDowall et al., "Evaluating Effects of Changes in Gun Laws," pp. 39–43.

54. Reference Bureau, State of Wisconsin, pp. 5–6 (re Kleck) and p. 6 (re Wright-Rossi). The latter discussion does note that other surveys of criminals suggest dogs deter burglary more than guns.

55. Ibid., p. 6, discounting the conclusions in Arthur L. Kellermann and Donald T. Reay, "Protection or Peril?: An Analysis of Firearm-Related Deaths in the Home," *NEJM* 314 (1986): 1557–60, which Dolins and Christoffel, "Reducing Violent Injuries," p. 645, rely on.

56. This topic heading is taken from Henry Lea's much-ballyhooed work of historical prediction though, of course, our subject matter has no relation to his.

57. Henderson, "Guns 'n' Poses." The quotations given of Dr. Tanz in this and following paragraphs of the text are from pp. 8, 22, and 24 respectively.

Dr. Tanz's writings on firearms and public health include Robert Tanz, "Review of Epidemiology of Child and Adolescent Gun Injuries and Deaths," *American Academy of Pediatrics: Report of a Forum on Firearms and Children* (1989). Dr. Christoffel is among the most prolific and most admired of the antigun health advocate sages. Somerville, "Gun Control as Immunization," *American Medical News,* January 3, 1994, p. 9. Dr. Christoffel's writings will be found referenced throughout this chapter.

58. Gary Kleck and Marc Gertz, "Armed Resistance to Crime: The Prevalence and Nature of Self-Defense with a Gun," *Journal of Criminal Law and Criminology* 85, no. 2 (1995), and Gary Kleck, *Point Blank: Guns and Violence in America* (Hawthorne, N.Y.: Aldine, 1991), ch. 4 (based on nine surveys).

59. Personal communication from Professor Philip J. Cook. For a full review of the debate see: Philip J. Cook, "The Technology of Personal Violence," in M. Tonry, ed., *Crime and Justice: An Annual Review of Research* 14 (1991), criticizing Gary Kleck, "Crime Control through the Use of Force in the Private Sector," *Social Problems* 35 (1988): 1; the criticism of Kleck in David McDowall, Colin Loftin, and Brian Wiersema, "Evaluating Effects of Changes in Gun Laws," *American Journal of Preventive Medicine* 9 (1993): 39–43; and David Mc-Dowall and Brian Wiersema, "The Incidence of Defensive Firearm Use by US Crime Victims, 1987 through 1990," *American Journal of Public Health* 84 (1994): 1982; and compare Kleck's response in *Point Blank,* ch. 4, and Kleck and Gertz, "Armed Resistance to Crime."

60. Green suggests a defensive use figure in the high hundred thousands which would equal or exceed the incidence of criminal misuse of firearms. Personal communication from Prof. Green.

61. See, e.g., James Q. Wilson, "Just Take Away Their Guns," *New York Times Magazine,* March 20, 1994; Toch and Lizotte, "Research and Policy"; Kates, "Value of Civilian Arms"; Gary A. Mauser, "Gun Control in the United States," *Criminal Law Forum* 3 (1992): 147.

62. Personal communication from Prof. Alan Lizotte of the School of Criminal Justice, State University of New York (Albany); compare Toch and Lizotte, "Research and Policy," accepting Kleck's figures, to the criticism of another aspect of Kleck's work in David McDowall, Alan J. Lizotte and Brian Wiersema, "General Deterrence through Civilian Gun Ownership: An Evaluation of the Quasi-Experimental Evidence," *Criminology* 29 (1989): 541.

63. Henderson, "Guns 'n' Poses," p. 33.

64. Kates, "Value of Civilian Arms," pp. 147–50, and table reproduced at p. 166 depicting Kleck's findings from analysis of 1979–85 national data which shows the following comparative rates of injury: only 12.1–17.4 percent of gun-armed victims resisting robbery or assault were injured; 24.7–27.3 percent of victims who submitted were nevertheless injured; 40.1–48.9 percent of those who screamed were injured as were 24.7–30.7 percent of those who tried to reason with or threaten the attacker and 25.5–34.9 percent of those who resisted passively or sought to evade; 29.5–40.3 percent of those resisting with a knife were injured; 22–25.1 percent of those using some other kind of weapon were injured; 50.8–52.1 percent of those resisting bare-handed were injured. See *Point Blank,* pp. 123–26.

Data from subsequent years have yielded confirming results. "A fifth of the victims defending themselves with a firearm suffered an injury, compared to almost half of those who defended themselves with weapons other than a firearm or who used no weapon." Bureau of Justice Statistics, Crime Data Brief, "Guns and Crime" (Washington, D.C.: U.S. Department of

Justice, April 1994), p. 2 (1992 data); Bureau of Justice Statistics, Selected Findings from National Statistical Series, "Firearms and Crimes of Violence" (Washington, D.C.: U.S. Department of Justice, February 1994), p. 8 (summarizing 1987-91 data): "in nearly 400,000 incidents of violence, the victim had a firearm for self-protection [and] in 35 percent of these incidents, the offender was also armed with a firearm. About *a fifth* of the victims using a gun for self-defense were injured [but] among victims defending themselves with a weapon other than a firearm or having no weapon, about *half* sustained an injury" (emphasis added).

65. *Guns Don't Die, People Do,* by then Handgun Control, Inc., Chairman Nelson "Pete" Shields, pp. 124–25 (1981). Submission, running away, or screaming is also the advice offered by M. Yeager and the Handgun Control staff of the U.S. Conference of Mayors, *How Well Does the Handgun Protect You and Your Family?* (1976). In fact, however, running away or screaming is also far more dangerous and far less effective than resisting with a gun. Ullman and Knight, "Fighting Back: Women's Resistance to Rape," *Journal of Interpersonal Violence* 7 (1992): 31, and Ullman and Knight, "Sequential Analysis of Sexual Assaults," a paper delivered at the 1993 annual meeting of the American Society of Criminology, October 29, 1993.

66. See caveats in "Value of Civilian Handgun Possession," pp. 149–50; Kleck, *Point Blank,* pp. 123–26; Bureau of Justice Statistics: Crime Data Brief: "Guns and Crime," 2 (Washington, D.C.: U.S. Department of Justice, April 1994).

67. Kleck, "Crime Control through the Use of Force." Significantly, as more and better evidence has accumulated since 1988 it has consistently lent further support to Kleck's position; compare the 1988 article to Kleck's later *Point Blank* and Kleck and Gertz, "Armed Resistance to Crime." Significantly, the few health advocacy articles that do cite Kleck (see notes below) cite only the 1988 article.

68. Personal communication from Prof. Alan Lizotte; for his criticism of one aspect of Kleck's work see David McDowall, Alan J. Lizotte, and Brian Wiersema, "General Deterrence through Civilian Gun Ownership: An Evaluation of the Quasi-Experimental Evidence," *Criminology* 29 (1989): 541.

69. Indeed, Tanz says: "If somebody were to turn around and prove that guns save more lives than they kill, then I think we [gun control advocates] would have to turn around and reconsider." Henderson, "Guns 'n' Poses," p. 24. (See also the articles cited at note 8.)

70. Ibid.

71. See, e.g., Jerome P. Kassirer, "Editor's Reply," *NEJM* 326 (1992): 1161.

72. Somerville, "Gun Control as Immunization"; Webster and Modena, "Gun Violence among Youth," p. 621; Douglas S. Weil and David Hemenway, "Loaded Guns in the Home: Analysis of a National Random Survey of Gun Owners," *JAMA* 267 (1992): 3033, 3037; Senturia et al.; Patti J. Patterson and Leigh R. Smith, "Firearms in the Home and Child Safety," *American Journal of Diseases of Children* 141 (1987): 221, 223; Webster et al., "Parents' Beliefs," p. 913; Webster, et al., "Pediatricians' Beliefs," pp. 906–907.

73. It is perhaps possible to imply advice from comments such as those of George Pickett and John J. Hanlon, *Public Health: Administration and Practice* (Los Angeles: Times-Mirror, 1990), p. 496, that in acquaintance killings, e.g., by men of mates or women they desire, the "murder is almost always an act of blind rage or illogical passion," with the victim often being blameworthy for hostile behavior, and "when it happens, the killer as well as the killed is the victim." (For the almost total contrafactuality of the author's beliefs about homicide, see discussion below.)

74. Webster et al., "Reducing Firearms Injuries," *Issues in Science and Technology,* Spring 1991, pp. 75–76. The full quote (with emphasis added) is: "[H]andguns are often advised as necessities for self-protection, and that is why most handgun owners have bought them. Yet there is *little scientific evidence* to support the claims that guns are effective devices for protection. . . , *There are no studies* that examine the results of resisting a robbery with a gun per se [but] a study . . . indicated that attempts to resist [robberies in Chicago] place the victim at

much greater risk of being injured or killed." It bears emphasis that the study in question, like all studies reaching this result, did not differentiate gun defense from defense with less effective weapons. When gun-defense cases are isolated, they turn out to result in 75 percent fewer victim injuries than resistance with any other kind of weapon—and 50 percent fewer injuries than submission, as discussed above.

75. Pickett and Hanlon, *Public Health*, p. 497.

76. "[S]cientific evidence," in the form of nationwide data documenting widespread defensive use of firearms, became available by the late 1970s and was repeatedly corroborated in polls of criminals and victims through the 1980s and beyond. Moreover, by 1991, when the sages quoted in the text were writing, this and other data of defensive gun use had been reviewed in at least six different academic publications preceding Kleck's 1988 *Social Problems* article. The earliest data were reviewed in James D. Wright, Peter Rossi, and Kathleen Daly, *Weapons, Crime and Violence in America: A Literature Review and Research Agenda* (Washington, D.C.: Government Printing Office, 1981), ch. 7; in that book's 1983 edition titled *Under the Gun*; and in Wright, "The Ownership of Firearms for Reasons of Self Defense," in Don Kates, ed., *Firearms and Violence* (1984). The evidence from victims was supported by the NIJ-sponsored survey among 2,000 imprisoned felons discussed above. A summary of these results was published in 1985 by the NIJ, Kleck also summarized them in an article titled "Policy Lessons from Recent Gun Control Research," *Law and Contemporary Problems* 49 (1986): 35, 45; and in 1986 the results of the whole survey were published in *Armed and Dangerous*, pp. 145, 150, 154, and Table 7.1.

77. Health sages and other antigun advocates have published studies decrying defensive gun ownership. Their conclusions cannot sustain scholarly review. See discussion of the most recent below and of older ones in Kleck, *Point Blank*, ch. 4, and "Value of Civilian Arms," pp. 126–27, 134–39, 145–47, and 156.

78. Mercy et al., "Public Health Policy for Preventing Violence," p. 19.

79. Teret and Wintemute, "Policies to Prevent Firearms Injuries," pp. 105–106.

80. Hindelang Award given at the 1993 annual meeting of the American Society of Criminology.

81. ". . . [T]horough scholarship and detailed critiques of the literature. As a comprehensive reference, there is nothing like it. It will stand for years as indispensable reading for anyone concerned about guns and violence." Lawrence W. Sherman, *The Criminologist* 18 (1993): 15; ". . . if only as a resource concerning the gun control literature, this book is a necessary acquisition for [libraries] . . . and for any serious scholar working in the area." H. Laurence Ross, *American Journal of Sociology* 98 (1992): 661. See below for quotations from Cook's review.

82. Personal communication from Prof. James D. Wright, co-author of the 1983 *Under the Gun* (note 1).

83. Two articles in health advocacy periodicals, but written by criminologists, attack Kleck's work of defensive firearms use. One of the very few health advocate articles worth reading does cite Kleck for a particular point that it rejects. AMA Council on Scientific Affairs, "Firearm Injuries and Deaths," *Public Health Reports* (March/April 1989): 111–20.

Several articles on juvenile possession and carrying of firearms by Joseph Sheley, a colleague and co-author of Wright, also cite Kleck. E.g., Joseph F. Sheley and Victoria E. Brewer, "Possession and Carrying of Firearms among Suburban Youth," *Public Health Reports* 110 (1995): 18–26.

A final, highly creditable, exception is that *Point Blank* was reviewed in the *NEJM*. Predictably, the reviewer selected was Philip J. Cook, a critic of Kleck's. Unlike the health advocacy sages, however, Cook is a distinguished methodologist whose contributions to the criminological literature on firearms always repay a thorough reading. (In addition to works otherwise cited herein, see Cook, "The Relationship between Victim Resistance and Injury in Non-

Commercial Robbery," *Journal of Legal Studies* 15 [1986]: 405; "The Role of Firearms in Violent Crime: An Interpretative Review of the Literature," in M. Wolfgang and N. Weiler, eds., *Criminal Violence* [1982]: 269; "The Effect of Gun Availability on Robbery and Robbery-Murder: A Cross-Section Study of 50 Cities," *Pol. Stud. Rev. Ann.* 3 [1979]: 743.)

Far from justifying Kleck's complete exclusion from health literature, Cook's review of *Point Blank* should have promoted the book's use; see *NEJM* 330 (1994): 374, describing *Point Blank* as a "comprehensive assessment of the evidence concerning causal links between firearms and violence. . . . Kleck is encyclopedic in covering the relevant literature, noting the shortcomings of others' research and providing careful explanations of his own original contributions." Regrettably, the review has fallen on politically deaf ears so far as the health advocacy literature is concerned.

84. See discussion above of Dolins and Christoffel, "Reducing Violent Injuries." See also John H. Sloan et al., "Correspondence," *NEJM* 323 (1990): 136, and Arthur L. Kellermann, "Obstacles to Firearm and Violence Research," *Health Affairs* 12 (1993): 142, 150–51. Though nothing in the latter is literally false, its attempt to associate Kleck with the gun lobby is tendentious and highly misleading. Moreover, the language is artfully phrased so that readers who are not aware of the facts might think that Kleck is "the research director for the National Rifle Association."

85. Personal communication. See also Kleck, *Point Blank*, "Author's Voluntary Disclosure Statement" (unpaginated, precedes Table of Contents). Far from his work being underwritten by the NRA, Kleck has been criticized by the organization for supporting gun controls it opposes. Paul H. Blackman, Review, *The Criminologist* 18 (1993): 16.

86. As originally proposed, the Brady Bill was limited to a background check on handgun purchases from dealers. Kleck suggests a background check that would be prerequisite to all firearms purchasing, including long guns as well as handguns and transactions between private persons as well as sales through dealers. Gary Kleck and David J. Bordua, "The Factual Foundation for Certain Key Assumptions of Gun Control," *Law and Policy Quarterly* 5 (1983): 271, 294; Kleck, "Policy Lessons from Recent Gun Control Research," *Law and Contemporary Problems* 49 (1986): 35. For this and Kleck's other gun-control recommendations see *Point Blank*, ch. 11.

87. *Injury Prevention*, p. 265, citing the favorable discussion of background checks in Kleck and Bordua, "The Factual Foundation for Certain Key Assumptions of Gun Control."

The other favorable citation to Kleck occurs in a somewhat more ambiguous context. Greg R. Alexander et al., "Firearm-Related Fatalities: An Epidemiologic Assessment of Violent Death," *American Journal of Public Health* 75 (1985): 165, 168, cite an early article by Kleck which concluded that gun ownership among responsible, law-abiding adults does result in increased homicide—a conclusion Kleck later had to repudiate based on a more extensive and better analyzed dataset. Compare Kleck's "Capital Punishment, Gun Ownership and Homicide," *American Journal of Sociology* 84 (1979): 882, to his "The Relationship between Gun-Ownership Levels and Rates of Violence in the United States," in *Firearms and Violence: Issues of Public Policy*. We note that Alexander et al. scrupulously cited articles finding that gun ownership did not increase homicide as well as Kleck's early article to the contrary. We do not fault them for overlooking Kleck's repudiation of his earlier article, as the later article was in a book to which they may not have had easy access. We do emphasize the failure of the health advocacy literature as a whole to cite Kleck's vast scholarly output.

88. Kleck and Bordua, "The Factual Foundations," *Law and Policy Quarterly* 5 (1983): 271.

89. In a 1994 article, Senturia et al., *Pediatrics* 93: 469, cite a 1991 source as "estimat-[ing] that there are 200 million firearms in U.S. homes," and then a 1984 source to conclude, erroneously, that this "includ[es only] 49 million handguns." As of 1994 this estimate was approximately 31 million low for guns of all kinds and 33.3 million low for handguns. See Table 5.2 below. The 200 million estimate for all guns was only somewhat off; Senturia and Christoffel

could have adopted it and specified that it was accurate as to 1987–88, citing the definitive figures in *Point Blank,* Table 2.1, as the latest available. But, since the proportion of all guns that are handguns is a subject of some importance, for them to give an overall gun figure based on a 1991 estimate and a much lower handgun figure from seven years earlier was misleading.

90. Contrast: Robert J. Cottrol and Raymond T. Diamond, " 'Never Intended to Be Applied to the White Population': Firearms Regulation and Racial Disparity, The Redeemed South's Legacy to a National Jurisprudence?" *Chicago-Kent Law Review* (1995); Don Kates, "The Second Amendment and the Ideology of Self-Protection," *Constitutional Commentary* 9 (1992): 87, 98: Robert J. Cottrol and Raymond T. Diamond, "The Second Amendment: Toward an Afro-Americanist Reconsideration," *Georgetown Law Journal* 80 (1990): 309; Raymond Kessler, "The Ideology of Gun Control," *Quarterly Journal of Ideology* (1988): 381; John Salter, "Civil Rights and Self-Defense," *Against the Current,* July-August, 1988; Don B. Kates, "The Battle over Gun Control," *The Public Interest* 84 (1986): 42; Raymond Kessler, "Gun Control and Political Power," *Law and Policy Quarterly* 5 (1983): 381; Don Kates, "Toward a History of Handgun Prohibition in the United States," in Don B. Kates, ed., *Restricting Handguns: The Liberal Skeptics Speak Out* (1979) and sources there cited.

The obliviousness of American health advocates to this issue is rendered particularly ironic, given awareness of it by a leading British Commonwealth gun-control advocate and analyst. Discussing firearms licensing, a Macquarrie University law professor admonished that, while there is no "reason to presume that Australian police [would] be influenced by political considérations in" their administration of a gun-licensing law, "Still the public ought to be assured— by the presence of laws, not simply by the words of men—that the abuses reported in this field throughout the United States are not reproduced in any Australian jurisdiction." J. David Fine, "Issues in Firearms Control," *Australia-New Zealand Journal of Criminal Law Review* 18 (1986): 257, 264.

91. Dolins and Christoffel, "Reducing Violent Injuries," p. 649.

92. Personal communication from Prof. Wright; see *Under the Gun* and *Armed and Considered Dangerous,* pp. 309ff.

93. See reviews of *Under the Gun* in *Contemporary Sociology, The American Journal of Sociology* (by Peter K. Manning) and *Journal of Criminal Law and Criminology* 75 (1984): 314. *Under the Gun* differs from *Point Blank* in that it is purely a work of literature evaluation and does not itself present original research. Wright and Rossi's major original research contribution is *Armed and Considered Dangerous.*

94. Eisen, "Guns: In Whose Hands?" p. 11 (citing *Under the Gun* for seven different points); Senturia et al., pp. 474, 475 (*Under the Gun* cited for survey research on reasons people own guns); *Injury Prevention,* p. 262; and Teret et al., "The Firearm Fatality Reporting System: A Proposal," pp. 3073–74, each citing the separately published *Executive Summary to Wright and Rossi,* Weapons, *Crime and Violence in America: A Literature Review and Research Agenda* (Washington, D.C.: Government Printing Office, 1981) for different points.

95. Sloan et al., "'Handgun Regulations, Crime, Assaults and Homicide," p. 1256, citing *Under the Gun.* A statement of the authors' personal views (which are wholly at odds with those attributed to them by Sloan and Kellermann) is given in chapter 14.

96. From the Abstract to their *Executive Summary,* p. 2.

97. Sloan, Rivara and Kellermann, "Correspondence," *NEJM* 323 (1990): 136.

98. The limited exceptions are these: (*a*) Dolins and Christoffel do note one point in a later Wright and Rossi book, the NIJ-funded felon survey. As discussed above, Dolins and Christoffel misdescribe Wright and Rossi as "gun supporters" and misstate that the point cited has been found "unconvincing" by epidemiologists; (*b*) Wright and Rossi's NIJ literature evaluation is cited twice for points that might encourage at least some skepticism, in Arthur L. Kellermann et al., "The Epidemiologic Basis for the Prevention of Firearm Injuries," *Annual Review of Public Health* 12 (1991): 17, 28, and 29; (*c*) The *NEJM* and other health advocacy

journals print letters to the editor (limited to 400 words) in response to articles. To the extent possible under these constraints, critical correspondents have been able briefly to cite isolated findings from *Under the Gun* to which the authors of the articles reply.

99. Teret and Wintemute, "Policies to Prevent Firearms Injuries," pp.101–102, citing Comptroller General, *Report to the Congress, Handgun Control, Effectiveness and Costs* (Washington, D.C.: Government Printing Office, 1978), and AMA Council on Scientific Affairs, "Firearm Injuries and Deaths: A Critical Public Health Issue," *Public Health Reports* (March/April 1989): 111–20. In fairness it should be stated that, despite their brevity and obsolescence, each of these literature reviews gives a more comprehensive, competent, and candid statement of the antigun position than anything to be found in the health advocacy literature except the surprisingly fair Kellermann et al., "The Epidemiological Basis for the Prevention of Firearm Injuries."

100. Sloan et al., "Handgun Regulations, Crime, Assaults and Homicide," p. 1256.

101. Charles Mock et al., "Comparison of the Costs of Acute Treatment for Gunshot and Stab Wounds: Further Evidence of the Need for Firearms Control," *Journal of Trauma* 36 (1994): 516, 521. To the same effect see the host of health advocacy articles listed below.

102. Brandon Centerwall, "Homicide and the Prevalence of Handguns: Canada and the United States, 1976 to 1980," *American Journal of Epidemiology* 134 (1991): 1245–65.

103. Three years after its publication, Tanz told an interviewer "he's heard it was coming but didn't know it was out." Henderson, "Guns 'n' Poses," p. 24.

104. See, e.g., Robert Mundt, "Gun Control and Rates of Firearms Violence in Canada and the United States," *Canadian Journal of Criminology* 32 (1990): 137–53, and Mauser and Holmes, "Evaluating the 1977 Canadian Firearms Control Legislation: An Econometric Approach," *Evaluation Research* 16 (1993): 603. See also Brandon Centerwall, "Suicide and the Prevalence of Handguns: Canada and the United States, 1976–1980," *Abstract* in Proceedings of the Second World Conference on Injury Control (1993), paper available from Prof. Centerwall at the University of Washington, School of Public Health, Department of Epidemiology; David B. Kopel, "Canadian Gun Control: Should the United States Look North for a Solution to its Firearms Problem?" *Temple International and Comp. Law Journal* 5 (1991): 1; Rich et al., "Guns and Suicide: Possible Effects of Some Specific Legislation" *American Journal of Psychiatry* 147 (1990): 342.

105. *American Journal of Epidemiology* 134: 1245–46.

106. Drooz, "Handguns and Hokum: A Methodological Problem," *JAMA* 238 (1977): 43. Depending on how one wishes to count, there may be as many as three other (noncommentary) articles in health advocacy periodicals since 1965 which significantly depart from the antigun orthodoxy, in addition to articles in the *Journal of the Georgia Medical Association*: Centerwall's, which is a neutral comparison of handgun and nongun homicide in Canada and the United States; Rich et al., an evaluation of suicide rates which concludes that gun controls did not reduce them; and Joseph F. Sheley et al., "Gun-Related Violence in and around Inner-City Schools," *American Journal of Diseases of Children* 146 (1992): 677, 682, an article by three criminologists. Though it does not discuss gun control *per se*, it contains a statement common among criminologists but almost unheard of in the health advocacy literature: The problems of crime and violence "will not yield to simplistic, unicausal solutions. In this connection, it is useful to point out that everything that leads to gun-related violence is already against the law. What is needed are not new and more stringent gun laws but rather a concerted effort to rebuild the social structure of inner cities."

107. Harold B. Houser, "Invited Commentary: Common Wisdom and Plain Truth," *American Journal of Epidemiology* 134 (1991): 1261. The gravamen of the title and commentary is that, while "common wisdom" supports "recommending the reduction of access to handguns as the primary intervention strategy for reducing homicide," the "plain truth" of Centerwall's empirical finding contradicts and invalidates "common wisdom."

108. We have found no citation of Mundt or Mauser and Holmes. Centerwall's article has been cited adversely by one of the co-authors of the Sloan article. Arthur Kellermann, "Preventing Firearm Injuries: A Review of Epidemiologic Literature," *American Journal of Preventive Medicine* 9 (suppl. 1) (1993): 12. It is also cited in Leland Roop et al., "Death in the City: An American Childhood Tragedy," *JAMA* 267 (1993): 2905, 2910, offsetting Roop's favorable citation of the Sloan article. We could find no other citation of the Centerwall article nor does its author know of any others. Personal communication from Brandon Centerwall, M.D.

Citations to the Sloan article are virtually endless. See, e.g., Roop; Mock; Stefan Z. Wiktor et al., "Firearms in New Mexico," *Western Journal of Medicine* 161 (1994): 137, 139; T. Karlsson et al., "Gunshot Fatalities in Stockholm, Sweden with Special Reference to the Use of Illegal Weapons," *Journal of Forensic Science* (1994): 1409, 1421; Webster and Wilson, "Gun Violence among Youth," p. 622; Dolins and Christoffel, "Reducing Violent Injuries," p. 651; Vernick and Teret, p. 1777; Mercy et al., "Public Health Policy for Preventing Violence," p. 28; Teret and Wintemute, "Policies to Prevent Firearms Injuries," p. 107; Peter M. Marzuk et al., "The Effect of Access to Lethal Methods of Injury on Suicide Rates," *Archives of General Psychiatry* 49 (1992): 451, 458; Charles M. Callahan and Frederick P. Rivara, "Urban High School Youth and Handguns: A School-Based Survey," *JAMA* 267 (1992): 3038, 3042; Webster et al., "Reducing Firearms Injuries," *Issues in Science and Technology*, Spring 1991; Roberta K. Lee et al., "Incidence Rates of Firearm Injuries in Galveston, Texas, 1979–1981," *American Journal of Epidemiology* 134 (1991): 511, 520; Lois A. Fingerhut and Joel C. Kleinman, "International and Interstate Comparisons of Homicides among Young Males," *JAMA* 263 (1990): 3292, 3295; *Injury Prevention*, p. 267; Garen J. Wintemute, "Closing the Gap between Research and Policy: Firearms," *Injury Prevention Network Newsletter,* Winter 1989–90, p. 21; James A. Mercy et al., "Firearm Injuries: A Call for Science," *NEJM* 319 (1988): 1283–84.

109. Centerwall, "Homicide and the Prevalence of Guns," p. 1264.

110. See, e.g., Mercy et al., "Public Health Policy for Preventing Violence," p. 28 (citing Sloan but not Centerwall) and 29 (citing B. Centerwall, "Exposure to Television As a Cause of Violence," in G. Comstock, ed., *Public Communications and Behavior* (Orlando: Academic Press, 1989). See also Brandon Centerwall, "Exposure to Television As a Risk Factor for Violence," *American Journal of Epidemiology* 129 (1989): 643, and idem, "Young Adult Suicide and Exposure to Television," *Soc. Psy. and Psychiatric Epidemiology* 25 (1990): 121.

111. Robert Sherrill, *The Saturday Night Special* (New York: Penguin, 1975), p. 176.

112. Kopel, *Samurai,* providing in-depth coverage of: England, Canada, Australia, New Zealand, Jamaica, Switzerland, and Japan.

113. We can find no citation and the author tells us that he has not found any.

114. See, e.g., Webster et al., p. 76; Cotton, *JAMA* 267: 1171; Baker, "Without Guns Do People Kill People?" *American Journal of Public Health* 75 (1985): 587; Schetky, *American Journal of Diseases of Children* 139: 230; Fingerhut and Kleinman, *JAMA* 263: 3295; Bruce R. Conklin and Richard H. Seiden, "Gun Deaths: Biting the Bullet on Effective Control," *Public Affairs Report* 22 (Berkeley, University-Cal. Inst. Gov. Stud. 1981): 1, 4, 7; Roop; Mock; Webster and Wilson, "Gun Violence among Youth," p. 622; Dolins and Christoffel, "Reducing Violent Injuries," p. 651; Vernick and Teret, *American Journal of Public Health* 83: 1777; Mercy and Rosenberg, *Health Affairs* 12: 28; Stephen P. Teret and Garen J. Wintemute, "Policies to Prevent Firearms Injuries," *Health Affairs* 12 (1993): 96, 107; Peter M. Marzuk et al., "The Effect of Access to Lethal Methods of Injury on Suicide Rates," *Archives of General Psychiatry* 49 (1992): 451, 458; Charles M. Callahan and Frederick P. Rivara, "Urban High School Youth and Handguns: A School-Based Survey," *JAMA* 267 (1992): 3038, 3042; Webster et al., "Reducing Firearms Injuries," *Issues in Science and Technology*, Spring 1991; Roberta K. Lee et al., "Incidence Rates of Firearm Injuries in Galveston, Texas, 1979–1981," *American Journal of Epidemiology* 134 (1991): 511, 520; Lois A. Fingerhut and Joel C. Kleinman, "International and Interstate Comparisons of Homicides among Young Males" (1990); *Injury*

Prevention, p. 267; Wintemute, "Closing the Gap," p. 21; James A. Mercy et al., "Firearm Injuries: A Call for Science," *NEJM* 319 (1988): 1283–84.

115. "Gun Control in the United States," *Criminal Law Forum* 3 (1992): 147 and endnote 2. Indicative of the methodological sophistication of health advocacy sages is that, with a straight face, they actually describe as "elegant" a study drawing profound conclusions from a meager two-city data set. See, e.g., Wintemute, "Closing the Gap," p. 21.

116. See discussion in the text below and Kopel, *Samurai.* See also "Current Evidence," pp. 200ff.; Greenwood, *Firearms Control*; David B. Kopel, *Gun Control in Great Britain* (Chicago: University of Illinois Office of International Criminal Justice, 1992); idem, "Japanese Gun Control," *Asia-Pacific Law Review* 2 (1993): 26; idem, *Temple International and Comp. Law Journal* 5 (1991): 1; Mundt; Mauser and Holmes; and Rich et al.

117. "But these countries' low crime rates seem to have preceded the gun laws that supposedly caused them. Violence was low (and falling) in Western Europe from at least the midnineteenth century, but antigun policies only came in after World War I aimed not at crime but at the political unrest of that tumultuous era." "Current Evidence," p. 200 (endnotes omitted); Eric H. Monkkonen, "Diverging Homicide Rates: England and the United States, 1850–1875," in Ted Gurr, 1 *Violence in America* (Beverly Hills, 1989), pp. 80–81; Greenwood, *Firearms Control,* chs. 1 and 2.

118. "Current Evidence."

119. Schetky, *American Journal of Diseases of Children* 139: 230; see also the virtually identical statement in Lois A. Fingerhut and Joel C. Kleinman, "Correspondence," *JAMA* 264 (1990): 2210.

120. Abraham Tennenbaum, "Israel Has A Successful Gun-Control Policy," in Charles P. Cozic, *Gun Control: Current Controversies* (San Diego: Greenhaven, 1992), p. 250. Prof. Tennenbaum teaches in the Department of Criminology at Bar Ilan University.

121. See also Kellermann et al., "The Epidemiologic Basis for the Prevention of Firearm Injuries," p. 28.

122. In addition to Kellermann et al., a generally fair and accurate antigun treatment is AMA Council on Scientific Affairs, "Firearm Injuries and Deaths: A Critical Public Health Issue," in *Public Health Reports,* March/April 1989. A recent high-quality article which affirmatively supports freedom of private choice regarding firearms ownership is Edgar A. Suter, "Guns in the Medical Literature: A Failure of Peer Review," *Journal of the Medical Association of Georgia* 83 (1994): 133.

123. Ibid. Compare Swiss and Israeli laws and practices cited in Glenn H. Reynolds and Don B. Kates, "The Second Amendment and States' Rights: A Thought Experiment," forthcoming in *William and Mary Law Review* 36 (1995), and Don B. Kates, "Handgun Prohibition and the Original Meaning of the Second Amendment," *Michigan Law Review* 82 (1983): 203, 249, n. 193, to Title 18 U.S.C. § 922(o) and the newly enacted (v) and 26 U.S.C. § 5845.

124. Tennenbaum, p. 248.

125. See Tennenbaum's guest editorial, "Handguns Could Help," *Baltimore Sun,* October 26, 1991.

126. "Current Research," p. 209. Such events are not uncommon in Israel, as illustrated by the following from an April 7, 1994, Associated Press story (which was printed in the *Marin* (Calif.) *Independent Journal,* p. A3):

> JERUSALEM—A Palestinian opened fire with a submachine gun at a bus stop near the port of Ashdod today, killing one Israeli and wounding four before being shot to death by bystanders, officials said. . . .
> National police spokesman Eric Bar-Chen said today's attacker, who was armed with an Uzi submachine gun, was shot and killed by a civilian and a soldier who were at the bus stop and hitchhiking post used by soldiers. . . .

Bar-Chen identified the gunman as a Palestinian from the Shati refugee camp in the Gaza Strip. Six ammunition clips and a knife were found on his body, he added.

127. *Point Blank,* table 7.1; see extended discussion in the next section of this chapter.

128. See, e.g., Teret, "Public Health and the Law," *American Journal of Public Health* 76 (1986): 1027, 1028; S. Baker et al., *The Injury Fact Book* (1984), pp. 90–91; Teret and Wintemute, "Handgun Injuries: The Epidemiologic Evidence for Assessing Legal Responsibility," *Hamline Law Review* 6 (1983): 341.

129. Compare Baker, "Without Guns Do People Kill People?," *American Journal of Public Health* 75 (1985): 587 (comparing U.S. and Danish murder) to International Intentional Homicide Table, below.

130. The Table is based on: 1987 data from *The Statistical Abstract of Israel;* an article by Martin Killias which gives averages for many countries for the years 1983–86 ("Gun Ownership and Violent Crime: The Swiss Experience in International Perspective," *Security Journal* 1 [1990]: 169–74); and data on other nations from the latest year available in the UN Demographic Yearbooks for the following years: *UN Demographic Yearbook—1985* (1987); *UN Demographic Yearbook—1991* (1992).

131. We give both 1991 and 1984 figures for Denmark because the 1984 figure would have been the one available to Baker.

132. We calculated these four year averages based on the suicide rates given in *Point Blank,* Table 6.5 and the homicide rates given in Bureau of Justice Statistics, *Sourcebook of Criminal Justice Statistics—1989,* p. 365, Table 3.118 (Washington, D.C., U.S. Justice Department, 1989). The years were selected because they fall within the range of the years given for the other nations and because they were the latest for which *Point Blank* gives suicide rates.

133. Sloan et al., "Firearms Regulations and Rates of Suicide: A Comparison of Two Metropolitan Areas," *NEJM* 322 (1990): 369.

134. Ibid. See also, for example, Mercy and Rosenberg, *Health Affairs* 12: 17; Webster et al., *Pediatrics* 94: 618ff.; J. H. Boyd, "The Increasing Rate of Suicide by Firearms," *NEJM* 308 (1983): 872–74; J. A. Mercy et al., "Patterns of Youth Suicide in the United States," *Educational Horizons* 62 (1984): 124–27; CDC, "Youth Suicide in the United States, 1970–1980" (Atlanta: CDC, 1986); J. H. Boyd and Eve K. Moscicki, "Firearms and Youth Suicide," *American Journal of Public Health* 76 (1986): 1240; Calhoun, "From Controversy to Prevention," p. 12; D. M. Endy et al., "Estimating the Effectiveness of Interventions to Prevent Youth Suicides," *Medical Care* 25 (1987): S57–S65; and the following CDC Reports by Lois A. Fingerhut and/or Lois A. Fingerhut and Joel C. Kleinman et al., "Firearm Mortality among Children and Youth," Advance Data #178 (Atlanta: CDC National Center for Health Statistics, 1989); "Firearm Mortality among Children, Youth, and Young Adults 1–34 Years of Age, Trends and Current Status: United States 1979–1988," *Monthly Vital Statistics Report,* March 14, 1991 (CDC National Center for Health Statistics); and "Firearm Mortality among Children, Youth, and Young Adults 1–34 Years of Age, Trends and Current Status: United States, 1985–1990," CDC Advance Data No. 231 (March 23, 1993).

135. Keith Hawton, "By Their Own Young Hand," *British Medical Journal* 304, no. 6,833 (April 18, 1992): 1000. See also, G. M. G. McClure, "Suicide in Children and Adolescents in England and Wales 1960–1990," *British Journal of Psychiatry* 165 (1994): 510–14 (148 percent increase in suicide for males aged fifteen to nineteen, from 1973 to 1990).

136. In two presumably gun-scarce environments, Ceylon and Fiji, much higher suicide rates exist than in the U.S. The use of paraquat and other agricultural pesticides which produce agonizing death is widespread. Abstract to Lawrence R. Berger, "Suicides and Pesticides in Sri Lanka [Ceylon]," *American Journal of Public Health* 78 (1988): 826: "Sri Lanka has one of the highest suicide rates in the world (29 per 100,000 population in 1980 [when the U.S. rate was 11.8]"). Suicides are especially frequent among young adults, both male and female. Compared to the U.S., the suicide rate for males in Sri Lanka is nearly four times greater; the female rate

is nearly thirteen times greater. The most common mode of suicide is ingestion of liquid pesti-cides." Compare Ruth H. Haynes, "Suicide in Fiji: A Preliminary Study," *British Journal of Psychiatry* 145 (1984): 433.

137. See Kleck, *Point Blank,* pp. 238–56, discussing Kleck's own study and providing the kind of comprehensive, balanced evaluation of the entire relevant literature which will not be found even in the very best of the health advocacy literature.

138. Fingerhut et al., *JAMA* 267 at Table 1 (p. 3049). Again, this fact is not discussed, nor is the fact of the far greater firearm availability to rural blacks mentioned. The theme of this arti-cle is that guns are causing an epidemic of black inner-city teenage homicide.

139. Kleck, *Point Blank,* p. 23: "Black households in rural areas are just as likely to have a gun as white households in those areas. . . ." See discussion of black and white homicide and gun possession rates below.

140. Kleck, *Point Blank,* pp. 275, 280–81, and 304. Compare Kleck's Table 2.1 to Table 7.1. Post-1986 data show the number of fatal gun accidents remaining at about 1,400–1,450, despite the continued dramatic increases in both U.S. gun ownership and population.

141. See, e.g., an article by Sam Fields of the National Coalition to Ban Handguns, "Handgun Prohibition and Social Necessity," *St. Louis University Law Journal* 23 (1979): 35, 51. Mr. Fields is, of course, correct that (insofar as it were effective) a handgun ban would almost certainly result in increasing reliance on loaded long guns as defensive weapons. See discussion in Kleck, *Point Blank,* p. 281.

142. Kleck, *Point Blank,* pp. 280–81; Kates, "Original Meaning," *Michigan Law Review* 82 (1983): 261–64. *Inter alia,* the dangers are particularly great for small children; toddlers can-not operate a handgun, but can easily discharge a long gun if their parents irresponsibly keep it loaded, unsecured, and accessible to the toddler. Ibid.

143. In a large percentage of accidental gun fatalities, the kind of firearm was not identi-fied. We assume the same proportion of handgun involvement in these fatalities as in those in which the kind of firearm can be identified. That figure is 41 percent, which is less than half of the percentage of guns kept loaded at any one time.

144. We thank Prof. Kleck for his assistance and advice in making this estimate.

145. E.g., Webster et al., *Pediatrics* 94: 618ff.

146. Compare the health advocate figures of 365, 500 and 1,000 children killed per year with the actual figure of 273 (averaged over the ten years period 1980–1989; calculation from figures given in Kleck, *Point Blank,* Table 7.5, and National Safety Council, *Accident Facts— 1993,* p. 23).

The false health advocate figures are, in ascending order of inaccuracy: 365 ("one child under age 15 each day") attested to Congress by Dr. Joseph Greensher, representing the American Academy of Pediatrics, 1985–86 Hearings on Legislation to Modify the 1968 Gun Control Act, House Judiciary Committee, Subcommittee on Crime, vol. I, pp. 164, 170. Dr. Tanz, who is an AAP advisor, puts the figure at "five hundred" per year (quoted by Joan DeClaire, "Kids and Guns," *View,* September-October 1992, pp. 30, 33); and two of the most prolific health sages put it at "almost 1,000 children a year." Teret and Wintemute, "Handgun Injuries: The Epidemiologic Evidence for Assessing Legal Responsibility," *Hamline Law Review* 6 (1983): 341, 346.

147. As many new guns were sold in the period 1970–90 as were owned in 1969; as many new guns were sold in those two decades as had been sold in the preceding six decades. The explosion in handgun sales is particularly marked. As of January 1, 1980, there were twice as many handguns as there had been on January 1, 1968. Though gun sales slackened somewhat in the mid-1980s, by January 1, 1994, there were more than three times as many handguns as there had been on January 1, 1968. In each year since 1966 Americans have added between 4.0 and 6.6 new guns to the existing stock, 1.5 to 2.6 million of them being new handguns. Figures from Kleck, *Point Blank,* Table 2.1.

148. National Crime Victimization Survey Data reported in Bureau of Justice Statistics, *Sourcebook of Criminal Justice Statistics—1993* (Washington, D.C.: Government Printing Office, 1994), p. 281.

149. Kleck, *Point Blank,* p. 50, Table 2.1.

150. Homicide rates are taken from Bureau of Justice Statistics, *Sourcebook of Criminal Justice Statistics—1993,* p. 365, Table 3.111 (Washington, D.C.: U.S. Justice Department, 1993); and Bureau of Justice Statistics, *Sourcebook of Criminal Justice Statistics—1989,* p. 365, Table 3.118 (Washington, D.C.: U.S. Justice Department, 1990).

151. *Point Blank* stops at 1987. But Kleck has provided us with subsequent figures through 1990 derived from Walter Howe, "Firearms Production by U.S. Manufacturers," which appears annually in the magazine *Shooting Industry*'s "SHOT Show" issue (the SHOT show is the shooting industry's national trade show held in January of each year). Howe's figures derive from those which the federal Bureau of Alcohol, Tobacco, and Firearms compiles of domestic manufacture (less export, plus import). Unfortunately, these figures lag well behind the current year and are presently available only through 1991. We have calculated the 1992 figure by extrapolation from averaging the three recent years 1989–91. This follows Kleck's recommended method for calculating the figures through the end of 1994 which are given below.

152. These are Kleck's extrapolated figures. See preceding note.

153. *Sourcebook of Criminal Justice Statistics—1993,* p. 365.

154. Kleck, *Point Blank,* Table 6.5, p. 262.

155. Bureau of Justice Statistics, "Firearms and Crimes of Violence," Selected Findings From National Statistical Series, Table 2, p. 13.

156. See, e.g., Lizotte and Bordua (1979) and Bordua and Lizotte (1980); Kleck, "The Relationship between Gun Ownership Levels and Rates of Violence in the United States," in Don B. Kates, ed., *Firearms and Violence* (1984); David McDowall, "Gun Availability and Robbery Rates: A Panel Study of Large U.S. Cities, 1974–1978," *Law and Policy Quarterly* 8 (1986): 135; Bordua, "Firearms Ownership and Violent Crime: A Comparison of Illinois Counties" (1986); Eskridge, "Zero-Order Inverse Correlations between Crimes of Violence and Hunting Licenses in the United States," *Sociology and Social Research* 71 (1986): 55; Kleck and Patterson, *Journal of Quantitative Criminology* 9 (1993): 249–87.

157. "Research and Policy: The Case of Gun Control," co-authored by Prof. Hans Toch of the School of Criminal Justice of the State University of New York at Albany. See also Kleck, *Point Blank,* pp. 214–15, citing ten studies showing that various cities and counties with high gun ownership suffered equal or less violence than demographically comparable areas with lower gun ownership.

158. See, e.g., Bureau of Justice Statistics, Crime Data Brief, "Young Black Male Victims" (Washington, D.C.: U.S. Department of Justice, December 1994), showing that black males age 12–24 are murdered at a rate of 114.9 per 100,000 population whereas the homicide rate for white males in the same age group is only 11.7. In other words, the black rate is almost ten times greater than that of whites of similar age and almost fourteen times greater than that of the American population as a whole.

159. See, e.g., CDC, "Homicide Surveillance: High-Risk Racial and Ethnic Groups—Blacks and Hispanics 1970 to 1983" (Atlanta: CDC, 1986); "Homicide Surveillance: High-Risk Racial and Ethnic Groups—Blacks and Hispanics, 1970–1983," *Morbidity and Mortality Weekly Report* 38 (October 2, 1987): 634-36; CDC, "Impact of Homicide on Years of Potential Life Lost in Michigan's Black Population," *Morbidity and Mortality Weekly Report* 38 (January 13, 1989): 4–11; J. A. Gulaid et al. (1988); P.W. O'Carroll, "Homicides among Black Males 15–24 Years of Age, 1970–1984," *Morbidity and Mortality Weekly Report* 37 (SS-1)(1988): 53-60; "Differences in Death Rates Due to Injury among Blacks and Whites, 1984," *Morbidity and Mortality Weekly Report* 37 (SS-3): 25–31; Lois A. Fingerhut et al., "Firearm and Nonfirearm Homicide among Persons 15 through 19 Years of Age: Differences

by Level of Urbanization, United States, 1979 through 1989," *JAMA* 267 (1992): 3048; Lois A. Fingerhut et al., "Firearm Homicide among Black Teenage Males in Metropolitan Counties: Comparison of Death Rates in Two Periods, 1983 through 1985 and 1987 through 1989," *JAMA* 267 (1992): 3054.

160. Kleck, *Point Blank*, p. 23: "Whites are much more likely to own guns or handguns than blacks . . . ," a difference Kleck suggests is largely "due to the fact that most blacks live in big cities and that gun ownership is low in big cities." See discussion below.

161. Cited in Kates, "Current Evidence," p. 201.

162. See, e.g., Brandon S. Centerwall, "Race, Socioeconomic Status, and Domestic Homicide, Atlanta, 1971–72," *American Journal of Public Health* 74 (1984): 813, 815 (reporting results of research and discussing prior studies); Mercy et al., "Public Health Policy for Preventing Violence, p. 16; Darnell F. Hawkins, "Inequality, Culture, and Interpersonal Violence," *Health Affairs* 12 (1993): 80.

163. State of Wisconsin Legislative Reference Bureau, "The Gun Control Debate—An Update," Informational Bulletin 94–3 (Madison, Wis.: October 1994), p. 30; Gurr, *Violence in America,* 1: 17.

164. Gurr, *Violence in America,* 1: 17.

165. Raymond Kessler, "Gun Control and Political Power," *Law and Policy Quarterly* 5 (1983): 381, and "The Ideology of Gun Control," *Quarterly Journal of Ideology* (1988): 381. A further effect, he argues, is that once disarmed and rendered dependent on police for protection, the citizenry becomes less able or willing to criticize abuses and more inclined to favor burgeoning police power.

166. O'Carroll, "Correspondence: CDC's Approach to Firearms Injuries," *JAMA* 262: 348.

167. Dr. Mark Rosenberg, who directs the CDC's National Center for Injury Prevention and Control, has been quoted avowing his and the CDC's desire to create a public perception of firearms as "dirty, deadly—and banned." Rasberry, *Washington Post,* October 19, 1994, p. A23. See also approving comments by Dr. Rosenberg quoted in Janice Somerville, "Gun Control as Immunization," *American Medical News,* January 3, 1994, p. 9.

168. D. P. Rice et al. "Cost of Injury in the United States: A Report to Congress" (CDC, 1989), p. 23. A similar misrepresentation was offered by a premier health advocacy sage, Wintemute, "Firearms as a Cause of Death in the United States," *Journal of Trauma* 27 (1987): 532, 534 ("Since the early 1970s year-to-year changes in new firearm availability and firearms homicide have often occurred in parallel.")

169. Kleck, *Point Blank,* Table 2.1, compared to the 1988 figures discussed in Table 3 above show that the accumulated handgun stock increased from 39 million to 65.8 million in that period and the total gun stock from 134.5 million to 198.3 million, an increase from 187.9 to 270.6 handguns per 1,000 Americans and from 627.0 to 815.5 guns generally per 1,000 Americans. In contrast, the homicide rate declined from 9.8 in 1974 to 8.4 in 1988. Bureau of Justice Statistics *Sourcebook of Criminal Justice Statistics—1989,* p. 365, Table 3.118 (Washington, D.C.: U.S. Department of Justice, 1990).

170. See Schetky, *American Journal of Diseases of Children* 139 and her reply to a letter to the editor in "The Pediatric Forum" section of the *Journal*'s January 1986 issue. The Smith and Falk claim is identical except that they blame only handguns for a majority of accidental and criminal gun injuries. Gordon S. Smith and Henry Falk "Unintentional Injuries," in Robert W. Amler and H. Bruce Dull, eds., *Closing the Gap: The Burden of Unnecessary Illness* (New York: Oxford, 1987), p. 157.

171. Using multi-year UCR figures, Wintemute calculates that handguns "are used in 70–75 percent of firearm homicides." Garen J. Wintemute, "Closing the Gap," p. 20.

172. Quoting, respectively: Webster et al., "Reducing Firearms Injuries," *Issues in Science and Technology,* Spring 1991, p. 73, and Christoffel, "Toward Reducing Pediatric Injuries," p. 300. See also Calhoun, *Injury Prevention Network Newsletter,* Winter 1989–90, p.

15 (most murderers "are neither felons nor crazy," but rather "people involved in family fights and fights over jobs and money, and people who are sad or depressed"); and Pickett and Hanlon, *Public Health,* p. 496 ("murder is *almost always* an act of blind rage or illogical passion," with victims often guilty of provocative behavior, and "when it happens.") (Our emphasis)

173. Goldsmith, "Epidemiologists Aim at New Target," p. 675 (quoting, *inter alia,* the president of the American College of Epidemiology). Compare: *American Medical News,* May 20, 1991 ("uncontrolled ownership and use of firearms" is "one of the main causes of intentional and unintentional injury and death"); *American Medical News,* January 3, 1994 ("Guns are a virus that must be eradicated"); Calhoun, "From Controversy to Prevention" ("guns are not just an inanimate object, but in fact are a social ill").

174. In addition to the citations given in the following notes, see, e.g., Bureau of Justice Statistics, Special Report, "Murder in Families" (Washington, D.C.: U.S. Department of Justice, 1994), p. 5, Table 7; Bureau of Justice Statistics, Special Report, "Murder in Large Urban Counties, 1988" (Washington, D.C.: U.S. Department of Justice, 1993); Canadian Centre for Justice Statistics, *Juristat Service Bulletin* (Ottawa: Ministry of Industry, Science and Technology, 1992); A. Swersey and E. Enloe, *Homicide in Harlem* (New York: Rand, 1975), p. 17; R. Narloch, *Criminal Homicide in California,* pp. 53–54 (Sacramento, California Bureau of Criminal Statistics, 1973); D. Mulvihill et al., *Crimes of Violence: Report of the Task Force on Individual Acts of Violence* (Washington, D.C.: Government Printing Office, 1969), p. 532.

175. In addition to the examples cited above, see: *Injury Prevention,* p. 265 (prior criminal and assaultive behavior of murderers supports utility of background checks for firearms purchasers); CDC, "Homicides among 15–19-Year-Old Males—United States 1963–1991," *Morbidity and Mortality Weekly Report* 43 (1994): 725, 726–27 (noting drastically rising homicide among inner-city youth and suggesting that "the immediate and specific causes" may include "the recruitment of juveniles into drug markets"); Dowd et al., *Pediatrics* 94: 871 (in city-level study of pediatric shootings: 75 percent "of the 26 perpetrators for whom criminal status was known had a history of one or more arrests by the Kansas City police department . . ."); Sheilagh Hodgins, "Mental Disorder, Intellectual Deficiency, and Crime," *Archives of General Psychiatry* 49 (1992): 476 (citing numerous studies from the U.S., Canada, and Europe to the effect that persons suffering major mental disorder, those with a below-normal I.Q. and substance abusers were each several times more likely to engage in violent crime than ordinary citizens); Andrew L. Dannenberg et al., "Intentional and Unintentional Injuries in Women: An Overview," *Annals of Epidemiology* 4 (1994): 133, 137 ("Risk factors for [wife-]battering may include prior episodes of physical abuse . . ."); and Eugene D. Wheeler and S. Anthony Baron, *Violence in Our Schools, Hospitals and Public Places: A Prevention and Management Guide* (Ventura, Calif: Pathfinder, 1993) ("A history of violence is the best predictor of [whether persons are likely to murder or commit other] violence. It overshadows all others in the area of prediction").

176. M. L. Rosenberg, "Violence as a Public Health Problem: A New Role for CDC and a New Alliance with Educators," *Educational Horizons* 62 (Summer 1984): 124–27.

177. Ibid. as to the first quote. The second appears in M. L. Rosenberg et al., "Interpersonal Violence: Homicide and Spouse Abuse," pp. 1399–1426 in J. M. Last, ed., *Public Health and Preventive Medicine,* 12th ed. (Norwalk, Conn: Appleton-Century-Crofts, 1986), p. 166, and in Mark L. Rosenberg et al., "Violence: Homicide, Assault, and Suicide," in *Closing the Gap: The Burden of Unnecessary Illness,* pp. 164–78.

178. "Correspondence," *JAMA* 272 (1994): 1409.

179. Ironically, we are quoting the cogent objections raised to a different violence-prevention program by an ardently antigun health advocate who is blind to the adverse implications his own objections have for his preferred program of banning guns. Daniel W. Webster, "The Unconvincing Case for School-Based Conflict Resolution Programs for Adolescents," *Health Affairs* 12 (1994): 126, 132–38.

180. Jeffrey B. Kahn, "Firearm Violence in California: Information and Ideas for Creating Change," *Western Journal of Medicine* 161 (1994): 565, 567.

181. In addition to the citations given above, see: P. Goldstein, "Homicide Related to Drug Traffic," *Bulletin of the New York Academy of Medicine* 62 (1986): 509; Zimring and Zuehl, "Victim Injury and Death in Urban Robbery," *Journal of Legal Studies* 15 (1986): 1, 9–12; Kates,"Current Evidence," p. 203; Tardiff et al., "Homicide In New York City," pp. 43, 46.

182. See, e.g., Michael D. McGonigal et al., "Urban Firearm Deaths: A Five-Year Perspective," *Journal of Trauma* 35: 532–36 ("84 percent of victims in 1990 had antemortem drug use or criminal history"); H. Range Hutson et al., "Adolescents and Children Injured or Killed in Drive-By Shootings in Los Angeles," *NEJM* 330 (1994): 324, 325 (71 percent of children and adolescents injured in drive-by shootings "were documented members of violent street gangs").

Medical studies suggest that a minimum of 2,000 murders annually are drug-related, including one-third to one-half or more of the murders in some major cities. *Injury Prevention,* p. 206; Daniel Webster et al., "Epidemiologic Changes in Gunshot Wounds in Washington, D.C., 1983–1990," *Archives of Surgery* 127 (1992): 694, 698. See also studies in three major trauma care centers finding urban knife and bullet wounds to be "a chronic recurrent disease peculiar to unemployed, uninsured law breakers." R. Stephen Smith et al., "Recidivism in an Urban Trauma Center," *Archives of Surgery* 127 (1992): 668, 670.

183. An FBI data run of murder arrestees nationally over a four-year period in the 1960s found 74.7 percent to have had prior arrest(s) for violent felony or burglary. See table in Mulvihill, p. 532. Out of the "582 [Canadian murders] in which an accused was identified in 1991," 249 had previous records of violent offenses, 103 for property offenses and 10 for drug offenses. *Juristat Service Bulletin,* p. 15.

The annual Chicago Police Department bulletin *Murder Analysis* shows the following figures for the percentage of murderers who had prior crime records: 1991: 77.15 percent; 1990: 74.63; 1989: 74.22; 1988: 73.59; 1987: 73.81 (five-year average, 1987–91: 74.68 percent). See also Swersey and Enloe, p. 17 ("We estimate that the great majority of both perpetrators and victims of assaults and murders had previous arrests, probably over 80 percent or more").

184. John DiIulio, "The Question of Black Crime," *The Public Interest* 117 (1994): 3, 16.

185. FBI, *Uniform Crime Report—1975,* pp. 42ff.

186. For this 1991 figure see Heide, "Weapons Used by Juveniles and Adults to Kill Parents," *Behavioral Science and Law* 11 (1993): 397, 398.

187. R. Holmes and S. Holmes, *Murder in America* (London: Sage, 1994), pp. 8–9.

188. *New York Times,* October 15, 1994: "Boy, 5, Is Killed for Refusing to Steal Candy."

189. "Murder in Families."

190. Holmes and Holmes, *Murder in America,* p. 28.

191. Straus, "Domestic Violence and Homicide Antecedents," *Bulletin of the New York Academy of Medicine* 62 (1986): 446, 454, 457, and Straus, "Medical Care Costs of Intrafamily Assault and Homicide," *New York Academy of Medicine* 62 (1986): 556, 557. For a detailed review of relevant studies see Browne and Flewelling, "Women as Victims or Perpetrators of Homicide," a paper presented at the 1986 annual meeting of the American Society of Criminology (available from the authors at the Family Research Laboratory, University of New Hampshire).

192. Arthur L. Kellermann, M.D., M.P.H., et al., "Gun Ownership as a Risk Factor for Homicide in the Home," *NEJM,* 329, no. 15 (October 7, 1993): 1084–91.

193. Within two months of publication, *NEJM*–1993 "received almost one hundred mentions in publications and broadcast scripts indexed in the Nexis data base," including "prominent coverage" in the *New York Times, Los Angeles Times, Washington Post, Boston Globe,* and *Chicago Tribune.* Daniel D. Polsby, "The False Promise of Gun Control," *The Atlantic,* March 1994, pp. 59–60.

194. In the year following its appearance it was cited in at least the following articles: Jeffrey J. Sacks et al., "Correspondence," *JAMA,* September 21, 1994, pp. 847–48; Adler et al., *JAMA* 271: 1281, 1283; James A. Mercy, et al., "Public Health Policy for Preventing Violence,"

pp. 7, 28; Dolins and Christoffel, "Reducing Violent Injuries"; Andrew L. Dannenberg et al., "Intentional and Unintentional Injuries in Women: An Overview," *Annals of Epidemiology* 4 (1994): 133, 137; Webster and Wilson, "Gun Violence among Youth," pp. 617, 622; Susan B. Sorenson and Audrey F. Saftlas, "Violence and Women's Health: The Role of Epidemiology," *Annals of Epidemiology* 4 (1994): 140, 145; and Yvonne D. Senturia et al., "Reply," *Pediatrics* 94 (1994): 777, 778.

195. William G. Cochran and Gertrude M. Cox, eds., *Experimental Designs*, 2d ed. (New York: John Wiley and Sons, Inc., 1992).

196. Klaus Hinkelmann and Oscar Kempthorne, *Design and Analysis of Experiments*, Volume I, *Introduction to Experimental Design* (New York: John Wiley and Sons, Inc., 1994), p. 361, discuss intentional confounding.

197. *NEJM*-1993, p. 1084.

198. Shelby County, Tennessee, containing Memphis; King County, Washington, containing Seattle; and Cuyahoga County, Ohio, containing Cleveland.

199. *NEJM*-1993 Table 1: relationship of offender to victim breakdown. Spouse, first-degree relative, and roommate add up to 29.1 percent, and are indications of people living in the victim's household. The other categories, intimate acquaintance, other relative, friend or acquaintance, police officer, stranger, unknown, and other add to 71.1 percent, and are indications of people not living in the victim's household. Since the category of "roommate" is given, it is assumed that the "intimate acquaintance" category does not include people living in the victim's household. This category constitutes 13.8 percent of the offenders, and if any of these actually did live in the victim's household, the 71.9 percent should be reduced by this number. If all of these lived in the victim's household, then this would leave 57.2 percent of offenders who appear not to have lived in the victim's household.

Other data in Table 1 on the method of homicide, taken in conjunction with the data in Table 3, and other data discussed in the text, shows that in a substantial percentage of the homicides by gun that the gun was brought in from outside, presumably by the perpetrator. *NEJM*-1993's authors refuse to disclose their study data to scholars who want to evaluate their findings. Without access to the data, it is not possible to determine the actual number of guns brought into the household and used in the homicide.

200. In addition to the citations given above, see, e.g., Cook, "Technology," note 4 ("The Metropolitan [District of Columbia] Police Department classifies most homicides by motive: the fraction classified as drug-related increased from 21 percent to 80 percent between 1985 and 1988"); Swersey and Enloe, p. 17 ("We estimate that the great majority of both perpetrators and victims of assaults and murders had previous arrests, probably over 80 percent or more"). See additional citations in chapter 6 of this volume.

201. Based on a survey of 2,190 felons in California, Michigan, and Texas prisons of the crimes they had committed in the two years prior to their incarceration, Chaiken and Chaiken determined that a small minority were responsible for most crimes, and particularly the serious ones. The average "violent predator" (their term for these career criminals) reported committing eight assaults, 63 robberies, 172 burglaries, 1,252 drug deals and 214 miscellaneous other thefts in a one-year period. J. M and M. R. Chaiken, *Varieties of Criminal Behavior* (Santa Monica, Calif.: Rand, 1982), and "Offender Types and Public Policy," *Delinquency* 30 (1984): 195. Compare Marvin E. Wolfgang, *Delinquency in a Birth Cohort* (Chicago, University of Chicago Press, 1972) (between their tenth and eighteenth years, of 9,945 Philadelphia boys born in 1945: 65.1 percent had no offenses; 16.2 percent had one offense; 12.4 percent had a few offenses; and 6.3 percent committed 51.9 percent of the offenses in the cohort—and these were more serious than the generality of offenses committed by the less active); L. W. Shannon, *Assessing the Relationship of Adult Criminal Careers: A Summary* (Washington, D.C.: U.S. Department of Justice, 1982) (5–7 percent of a birth cohort in Racine, Wisconsin, were involved in over 50 percent of police contacts and 5–14 percent were involved in all felonies in the birth cohort); P. E.

Tracy et al., *Delinquency Careers in Two Birth Cohorts* (Chicago: University of Chicago Press, 1990) (between their tenth and eighteenth years, of 13,160 Philadelphia boys born in 1958: 67.2 percent were never arrested; 25.3 percent were arrested four or fewer times; 7.5 percent were arrested five or more times—and accounted for 60.6 percent of the arrests in the total birth cohort).

202. By way of analogy, suppose a study of people who had had a heart attack and then later died of another showed that more of them had taken up strenuous exercise after their first heart attack than had a control group of heart attack victims who had not taken up strenuous exercise after the first attack. That result would suggest that strenuous exercise was a risk factor for people who are at high risk of having a heart attack. But it would not prove anything about the level of risk strenuous exercise imposes on low- (or ordinary-) risk people who have never had a heart attack.

203. *NEJM*–1993, p. 1088. The effect of excluding cases of homicide of children under thirteen years of age, in addition to all of the other exclusions noted, is not clear, but at p. 1084 the authors note that this was done "at the request of the medical examiners."

204. Table 4 in *NEJM*-1993, p. 1089.

205. Arthur L. Kellermann, personal communication.

206. A. Bradford Hill, *Statistical Methods in Clinical and Preventive Medicine* (1962); J. B. Chassan, *Research Design in Clinical Psychology and Psychiatry,* 2d ed. (New York: Irvington Publishers, Inc., 1979).

207. Hinkelmann and Kempthorne, p. 22.

208. *NEJM*-1993, Table 3, includes excessive alcohol use, illicit drug use, and presence or absence of an arrest record.

209. Patricia L. Brantingham and Paul J. Brantingham, "Notes on the Geometry of Crime," in Paul J. Brantingham and Patricia L. Brantingham, eds., *Environmental Criminology* (Beverly Hills, Calif.: Sage Publications, 1981); Keith D. Harries, *The Geography of Crime and Justice* (New York: McGraw-Hill Book Co., 1974), esp. ch. 4; Christopher S. Dunn, "Crime Area Research," in Daniel E. Georges-Abeyie and Keith D. Harries, eds., *Crime: A Spatial Perspective* (New York: Columbia University Press, 1980).

210. While the problem of unwillingness to admit gun ownership is not entirely absent from the homicide case households, it is much less acute. *NEJM*-1993's authors had police reports on these households. In cases where the murder weapon was left near the body the police report would presumably so indicate; in cases where it was not the report would presumably indicate that the home was searched for guns, other occupants (if any) were asked about gun ownership, and registration records were consulted to see if a gun was registered to a person living in the household. The family of the deceased in the case home also had time between the homicide and the interview to go through the effects of the deceased and to discover a gun, if owned. None of this eliminates the possibility that a gun was kept in the homicide household, but that it was concealed from the police and they did not discover it, and the case proxy did not know of it, or did not admit to it. But that possibility is far better minimized as to the homicide case households than as to the control households. There the accuracy of *NEJM*-1993's gun-ownership finding is entirely dependent on the truthfulness of the interviewees.

211. *NEJM*-1993, p. 1089.

212. Kleck, *Point Blank,* appendix 2. The difference between the bare paragraph they devote to this issue, which is vital to their argument, and the appendix Kleck devotes to it is emblematic of the qualitative difference in scholarship between Kleck and the health advocacy literature.

213. *NEJM*-1993, p. 1089, citing A. L. Kellermann et al., "Validating Survey Responses about Gun Ownership among Owners of Registered Handguns," *American Journal of Epidemiology* 131 (1990): 1080–84.

214. Ibid.

215. The state of Tennessee and the city of Cleveland have various handgun registration or transfer regulations. Owners who have not adhered to these regulations have committed an offense which varies in seriousness depending on place of residence. The state of Washington has a permit system for dealer transfer. Additionally, some handgun owners may have heard of the extremely severe limitations on handgun possession in many large cities, e.g., Washington, D.C.; New York; and Chicago. All these would tend to make the owner reluctant to admit to having an unregistered handgun or one not subjected to the full observance of transfer regulations. *NEJM*-1993 does not mention how many of the guns in either the homicide or the control groups were owned legally.

216. *NEJM*-1993, p. 1084.

217. Thomas B. Newman et al., "Designing a New Study: II, Cross-Sectional and Case-Control Studies," in Stephen B. Hulley and Steven R. Cummings, eds., *Designing Clinical Research* (Williams and Wilkins, 1988), pp. 78–86.

218. Hulley and Cummings, *Designing Clinical Research,* "Case control studies are a cheap and practical way to investigate risk factors for rare diseases, or to generate hypotheses about new diseases or unusual outbreaks. These are great strengths, but they are achieved at a considerable cost. . . . But the biggest weakness of case-control studies is their increased susceptibility to bias."

219. *NEJM*-1993, p. 1084.

220. Ibid., p. 1090.

221. Ibid.

222. Sloan, Rivara, and Kellermann, "Correspondence," *NEJM* 323 (1990): 36.

223. In practice, the major kind of gun research which CDC appears interested in funding is agitprop disguised as science; people who can reliably produce the antigun factoids the CDC loves seem to be those whom CDC prefers to fund.

224. A. S. Relman, "Correspondence," *NEJM* 315 (December 4, 1986): 1484–85.

225. Quoting editorial by Arnold S. Relman, "More Than Sutures and Transfusions," *NEJM* 297 (1977): 552, which in turn cites editorials going back to Franz J. Ingelfinger, "Therapeutic Action for a National Ill," *NEJM* 278 (1968): 1399. See generally, N. R Rushforth et al., "Violent Death in a Metropolitan County," *NEJM* 297 (1977): 531–38; R. W. Hudgens, "Editorial: Preventing Suicide," *NEJM* 308 (1983): 897–98; J. A. Mercy and V. N. Houk, "Firearm Injuries: A Call for Science," *NEJM* 319 (1988): 1283–84; Colin Loftin et al., "Effects of Restrictive Licensing of Handguns on Homicide and Suicide in the District of Columbia," *NEJM* 325 (1991): 1615–20; Gray and LoGerfo, "Handgun Regulations, Crime, Assaults and Homicide," *NEJM* 319 (1990): 1256–62; J. H. Boyd, "The Increasing Rate of Suicide by Firearms," *NEJM* 308 (1983): 872–74; A. L. Kellermann and D. T. Reay, "Protection or Peril?: An Analysis of Firearm-Related Deaths in the Home," *NEJM* 314 (1986): 1557–60; J. H. Sloan et al., "Handgun Regulations, Crime, Assaults, and Homicide: A Tale of Two Cities," *NEJM* 319 (1988): 1256–62; J. H. Sloan et al., "Firearm Regulations and Rates of Suicide: A Comparison of Two Metropolitan Areas," *NEJM* 322 (1990): 369–73; J. P. Kassirer, "Guns in the Household" (editorial), *NEJM* 329 (1993): 1117–19.

226. Personal communication from James R. Boen, Associate Dean and Professor of Biostatistics, University of Minnesota School of Public Health, who is himself a quadriplegic who hunts. Prof. Boen adds that many states have special hunting rules to allow the disabled to participate. He cites those of Minnesota, Montana, and Wyoming, which all allow hunting from a standing vehicle (not on a road). See also Melissa L. Relchley, "Rehab Patients Take Their Best Shot at Riflery," *Advance for Physical Therapists,* November 7, 1994, p. 22.

227. Compare nonproblematic works such as Lizotte and Bordua, "Firearms Ownership for Sport and Protection: Two Divergent Models," *American Soc. Review* 45 (1980): 229; Hummel, "Anatomy of A War Game: Target Shooting in Three Cultures," *Journal of Sport*

Behavior 8 (1985): 131; Olmstead, "Morally Controversial Leisure: The Social World of Gun Collectors," *Symbolic Interaction* 11 (1988): 277; Brian J. Givens, "Zen Handgun: Sports Ritual and Experience," *Journal of Ritual Stud.* 7 (1993): 139.

228. A. Stinchcombe et al., *Crime and Punishment—Changing Attitudes in America* (1980), p. 113 ("we found no evidence that gun culture is macho").

229. Alan J. Lizotte and Jo Dixon, "Gun Ownership and the 'Southern Subculture of Violence,' " *American Journal of Sociology* 93 (1987): 383. Interestingly, the holders of violent attitudes were less likely than the average gun owner to approve of defensive force (perhaps perceiving it would be directed against violent people like themselves).

230. Wright, Rossi, and Daly, NIJ Evaluation, pp. 120ff. It should be noted that the differences in fear level are not overwhelming and that the fear differential in one of the studies may be an artifact of its omitting women gun owners from the comparison. See the critique of DeFronzo, "Fear of Crime and Handgun Ownership," *Criminology* 17 (1979): 331, in Hill, Howell, and Driver, "Gender, Fear, and Protective Gun Ownership," *Criminology* 23 (1985): 541. But see the finding that women gun owners are less afraid than nonowners in Thompson et al., "Single Female Headed Households, Handgun Possession and the Fear of Rape," a paper presented at the 1986 annual meeting of the Southern Sociological Society (available from the authors at the Department of Sociology, Louisiana State University, Baton Rouge).

231. Huston, Geis, and Wright, "The Angry Samaritans," *Psychology Today,* June 1976. The percentage of the general public who owned guns derived from Kleck, *Point Blank,* ch. 2, from separate percentages of black and white gun owners given in Erskine, "The Polls: Gun Control," *Public Opinion Quarterly* 36 (1972): 455, 459, on the assumption that 90 percent of the sample was white and 10 percent black.

232. Young, "Perceptions of Crime, Racial Attitudes and Firearms Ownership," *Social Forces* 64 (1985): 473. Kleck, *Point Blank,* ch. 2, criticizes this conclusion because the data cited did not exclude the alternative possibility that the racist attitudes correlated not with gun ownership *per se* but with the political conservatism of the particular set of gun owners responding to the survey.

233. For state data please see Lizotte, Bordua, and White, "Firearms Ownership for Sport and Protection: Two Not So Divergent Models," *American Soc. Review* 46 (1981): 499, 503. The several national datasets are analyzed in Kleck, *Point Blank,* ch. 2.

234. Whitehead and Langworthy, "Gun Ownership: Another Look," *Justice Quarterly* 6 (1989): 263.

6

Children and Guns

David B. Kopel

INTRODUCTION

The evidence of a national crisis involving children and guns seems overwhelming:

- "One child under fourteen is accidentally shot to death every day in the U.S.A." (Center to Prevent Handgun Violence).[1]
- "In the past decade, more than 138,000 Americans were shot just by children under the age of six." (*Hartford Courant*).[2]
- One hundred thirty-five thousand children carry guns to school each day. (Senators Biden and Chafee).[3]
- "Firearms are responsible for the deaths of 45,000 infants, children and adolescents per year" (American Academy of Pediatrics).[4]
- Eleven percent of children in grades six through twelve have been shot at with a gun; 9 percent have shot a gun at somebody (Lou Harris, Governor Roy Romer).[5]

These statistics are horrifying, and few people who read them can avoid concluding that some kind of gun control—any kind, in fact—is an urgent necessity. Fortunately, every one of the above statistics is false. The correct statistics are presented in the relevant sections of this chapter.

Gun-control strategists recognize that children are their most effective issue, even for controls that would apply to adults. Senator John Chafee (R-Rhode Island), who supported the Brady Bill as a minimal first step, has proposed the confiscation of all American handguns. The most important reason Senator Chafee offered for his drastic proposal was that handguns are "infecting" America's schools. The confiscation legislation won immediate support from America's "pro-child" lobbies such as the Children's Defense Fund and the American Academy of Pediatrics.

America's rising tide of teenage homicide has prompted demands from elected officials and the media for severe gun control, although the connection between the crime and the purported solution is sometimes unclear. When a pair of teenage runaways with a stolen revolver murdered a Colorado state trooper in 1992, then State Senator Regis Groff moved quickly to introduce legislation for a handgun waiting period and an "assault weapon" ban. *The Atlantic* plastered an M-11 handgun on its cover and printed a story about a child in Virginia Beach, Virginia, who used the ugly but low-caliber handgun to murder a teacher; the story intoned that adults should be allowed to own handguns only after receiving official permission and passing government tests.[6]

Gun-control advocates are hammering at the issue of children and guns as never before, in the not unrealistic hope that creating an atmosphere of panic about children will allow the enactment of severe gun controls aimed at adults. As Senator Chafee puts it, America must "do something" about the current "handgun slaughter," in which "our children are being killed and are killing," for "sooner rather than later every family in the U.S. will be touched by handgun violence."

The ploy of insisting that we curtail the rights of adults in order to protect children has at various times in American history brought success to campaigns to outlaw alcohol, marijuana, sexually explicit literature, homosexual behavior, lawn darts, and just about everything else that prohibitionists have wanted to eradicate.

America *does* face a crisis with children and guns. But the true facts of the crisis have very little to do with the politicized fear-mongering of some gun prohibition advocates. If Americans are to respond effectively to the problems associated with children and guns—particularly the extremely high murder rate of inner-city black teenage males—it will be necessary to understand the true scope and history of the problems, and to analyze carefully which solutions will make things better, and which will make things even worse.

ACCIDENTS

How many children die in gun accidents? One of America's leading gun-control advocates, Dr. Stephen Teret, puts the figure at "almost 1,000 children" per year.[7] A lobbyist for Handgun Control, Inc., when asked, "Is it true that many accidents in this country involve children playing with a parent's gun and shooting someone accidentally?" responded, "That is right. Fourteen hundred children die in such tragic accidents each year. . . ."[8]

In 1991, the most recent year for which precise numbers are available, there were twenty-four fatal gun accidents involving children under age five, and 203 involving children aged five to fourteen (for a total of 227 for all children under fifteen).[9] Preliminary estimates put the 1993 figures at forty for children under five, and 180 for children under fifteen.[10]

In recent decades, the American firearms supply has risen, and now stands at over two hundred million guns, a third of them handguns. But as the number of guns has risen, the number of childhood gun accidents has fallen sharply, declining by nearly 50 percent in the last two decades. Table 6.1 illustrates the happy trend.

From 1968 to 1993, the rate of fatal gun accidents for all ages fell from 1.2 per 100,000 population per year to 0.6—a decline of 50 percent. In the same period, the motor vehicle fatal accident rate fell from 27.5 to 16.3—a 41 percent decline.[11] Work deaths declined 58 percent.[12]

While there are enormous bureaucracies devoted to reducing work accidents (the Occupational Safety and Health Administration) and automobile accidents (the Department of Transportation), there is no government body charged with

Table 6.1

Yearly Fatal Gun Accidents for Children 0–14

1970	530
1972	470
1974	532
1975	495
1976	428
1977	392
1978	349
1979	364
1980	316
1981	298
1982	279
1983	243
1984	287
1985	278
1986	230
1987	250
1988	277
1989	273
1990	236
1991	227

Source: National Safety Council, *Accident Facts* (Itacsa, Ill., various years)

reducing firearms accidents. Yet thanks to voluntary, private educational efforts, including programs sponsored by the National Rifle Association (NRA), the Boy Scouts, 4-H, and other groups, the number of firearm accidents has declined at about the same rate as that of other activities over which federal bureaucracies have charge.

The true number of childhood gun accidents might be even lower than the official figures suggest. Some fatalities, involving older teenagers, may in fact be homicides, in which the perpetrator claims that pointing the gun at the victim's head or torso and then pulling the trigger was "an accident." In addition, a number of so-called accidents may be child-abuse homicides perpetrated by adults.[13]

Few causes of childhood death have fallen as steeply as have gun accidents, and the fall has taken place without any government programs. The situation might be considered evidence that private safety programs can be more effective than government regulation, and that there is no persuasive case for restrictive gun controls designed to fight childhood gun accidents.

Many gun-control advocates are not persuaded, however. In the push for restrictive laws to deal with accidents, they attempt, often successfully, to create the impression that gun accidents involving children are extremely common. While the actual numbers are readily available from the National Safety Council (NSC) and while the NSC reports have never been challenged for underestimating true accident numbers, gun-control advocates sometimes claim far higher numbers of childhood accidents, without giving any source for their data.[14]

Another approach of gun-control advocates is to discuss accidents in a way that avoids mentioning the actual number of fatalities, and the sharp downward trend in the number. For example, it may be pointed out, accurately, that firearms are the fourth-leading cause of accidental deaths for children aged five to fourteen (behind auto accidents, drowning, and fires and burns); and the third-leading cause for fifteen- to twenty-four-year-olds.[15] What is omitted by the emphasis on ranking is how small a role firearms actually play in accidental deaths, since the leading causes of accidental deaths (principally motor vehicles) so hugely outnumber the lesser causes. Guns account for only 3 percent of accidental deaths of children fourteen and under.[16] A child fourteen or under is five times more likely to drown than to die in a gun accident, five times more likely to die in a fire, and fourteen times more likely to die in an auto accident.[17]

It is to be expected that accidents and other "man-made" factors would be leading causes of death for young persons. In an era of advanced medical care, young people (other than infants) rarely die of natural causes. Accordingly, any cause of death in the under-fourteen or under-twenty-four age groups—even if it occurs infrequently—may have a relatively high rank.

In any case, showing the particular ranking of a cause of injury is hardly the same as proving that the factor related to that injury should be outlawed or drastically restricted. Among children aged five to nine, the rate of reported dog bites is higher than the *combined* rate of reportable childhood diseases (such as measles).[18]

The fact does not by itself prove that dogs should be outlawed, or that the law should require that dogs always be locked up if children might come nearby.

Some medical researchers have suggested that a firearm in the home of a normal, healthy family poses a grave risk to that family's health. For example, the *Journal of the American Medical Association* (*JAMA*) published a report which concluded that a "firearm in the home" is a risk factor for home firearm accidents.[19] The conclusion was certainly correct, since it was nearly a tautology. Having a swimming pool in the home is a risk factor for swimming pool accidents, having a motorcycle in the home is a risk factor for motorcycle accidents, and having an appendix is a risk factor for appendicitis. The report did not prove that the presence of a gun in the home causes a significant increase in the risk of accidental death; given the very low rate of deaths from childhood gun accidents, it would be impossible to prove such a conclusion.

Although the number of childhood gun accidents is low and getting lower, some gun prohibitionists contend that outlawing or drastically restricting firearms would be appropriate, "if it saves one life."

If any object associated with about 227 accidental childhood deaths a year should be outlawed, then it would be logical to call for the prohibition of bicycles (over 300 child deaths a year).[20] An even larger number of children are killed by motor vehicles (3,087).[21] Four hundred and thirty-two children die annually in fires caused by adults who fall asleep while smoking[22]; these 432 deaths would, by the handgun-banning logic, make a persuasive case for outlawing tobacco.

If the focus is on children under age five, then outlawing swimming pools, bathtubs, and five-gallon buckets (450 home drowning deaths) or cigarette lighters (90 deaths) would save many more children under five from accidental deaths than would a gun ban (24 deaths).[23]

Thus, the "if it saves one life" anti-accident logic applies with much greater force to bicycles, automobiles, bathtubs, swimming pools, tobacco, and cigarette lighters than to guns. Gun-prohibition advocates might reply that swimming pools or cars have legitimate purposes, while guns do not. Whereas banning swimming pools or cars in order to "save one life" would deprive people of necessary or useful items, a ban on guns would cause no such deprivation. But guns, like swimming pools, are commonly used for sport and recreation. And although bicycles, bathtubs, and cigarette lighters make life more convenient, these objects do not save lives or prevent injury.

Guns, however, do save lives and prevent crime every day. Chapter 5 presented various studies which found that guns are used for protection against criminal attack at least several hundred thousand times per year, and perhaps over two million times a year. These data are consistent with the polling of felony convicts in state prison systems conducted for the National Institute of Justice (NIJ). As detailed in chapter 5 of this volume, felons apparently have a high level of fear of armed victims, and try to avoid armed targets.[24]

Even if the criminologists' figures for self-defense are ten times too high, the true number of protective gun uses is still far higher than the number of times—namely none—that bicycles, bathtubs, and cigarette lighters are used for self-defense each year. Few persons who want to save "just one life" by banning handguns to eliminate child handgun accidents would propose saving many more children's lives by banning bicycles, bathtubs, and cigarette lighters. Is it possible that the motivation for banning handguns is something other than saving lives?

PROPOSED SOLUTIONS FOR ACCIDENTS

While safety education has already saved many lives, it is opposed by many gun-control organizations. Instead, these organizations favor a variety of restrictive laws that would impair the rights of all gun owners.

"Loaded" Indicators

Former Senator Howard Metzenbaum (D-Ohio), a leading gun-control advocate, proposed giving the Consumer Product Safety Commission (CPSC) authority over firearms.[25] If the CPSC had jurisdiction for firearms, it would have power to order manufacturers to initiate recalls of any or all privately owned firearms and ammunition that did not meet the commission's criteria for safety. Likewise, the commission could, by unilateral administrative action, ban the future production of any and all firearms and ammunition. Currently the CPSC is forbidden to regulate firearms precisely because Congress is afraid that regulation could become a subterfuge for gun prohibition.

One proposed federal safety criterion that tens of millions of guns would fail (and hence be subject to recall) is for the gun to have a "loaded" indicator. The "loaded" indicator, as the name implies, signals whether a gun is loaded. The General Accounting Office (GAO) reports that 23 percent of accidental firearms deaths could be prevented by having a "loaded" indicator.[26]

Although a "loaded" indicator would prevent some accidents, it might cause others. First of all, unless the requirement for a "loaded" indicator were made retroactive, so that the entire United States gun stock was recalled for retrofitting, some guns would have "loaded" indicators and many would not. Accordingly, persons who had learned to rely on "loaded" indicators might treat a loaded gun without the "loaded" signal as if the gun were unloaded.

In addition, it is foolish to expect that the half of American households that own guns would turn over their firearms for retrofitting. When Sturm, Ruger & Co. did a recall of some old revolvers, offering a free retrofit to prevent accidental discharges, only about 10 percent of the guns that had been sold were returned for the free modification, even though Ruger wrote to all known owners and advertised the free retrofit for many years.[27] A government-ordered retrofit would probably be less successful than Ruger's 10 percent, since government involvement might raise fears about gun confiscation or registration.[28]

Even assuming that most guns could be retrofitted, reliance on a "loaded" indicator is contrary to safe firearms-handling rules. Using a "loaded" indicator legitimizes treating a gun as unloaded, and thus engaging in all sorts of inappropriate behavior, such as pointing the "safe" gun at someone. The more cautious approach, fostered by safety training, is to treat every gun as if it were loaded. Even if a person is certain that a gun is unloaded, that gun should never be pointed at anyone except in self-defense.

Finally, the "loaded" indicator is meaningless except to persons who have taken firearms safety classes and have been taught the indicator's meaning, or who have read an owner's manual for the gun. Anyone who has taken a safety class will have been drilled never to point a gun at a person and to treat every gun as loaded. Anyone who reads the safety manual will have read similar safety instructions. Accordingly, the "loaded" indicator is a superfluity for the only segment of the population that would learn of it. And, of course, those who read safety manuals and take safety classes are the type of people least likely to cause accidents in the first place.

Childproof Devices

Another gun redesign program suggested by GAO is that all firearms include a device, such as a pressure-sensitive grip, which could prevent them from being fired by young children. GAO estimates that 8 percent of gun accidents could be prevented by some kind of childproof device.[29] (The GAO estimate was probably twice as high as it should have been, since the GAO study included twice as high a percentage of young children as the population data mandated.[30])

A childproof device of any type could only reliably be expected to protect children under six (or thereabouts), who would have neither the strength nor the ingenuity to defeat a safety device.[31] Even then, the device might not work if the child pulled the trigger with a thumb rather than a finger (as a child could do if pointing the gun at himself). Design standard modifications would be of little benefit in reducing the more common type of childhood gun accident, that involving preteen and older boys.[32]

During the 1880s, Daniel Baird Wesson, head of the Smith & Wesson gun company, ordered his engineers to produce a childproof gun after he read a newspaper account of a child killed in a gun accident. The new gun, with a safety lever in the grip, and a very hard trigger pull, was marketed as the New Departure Model Safety Hammerless. It is said that one evening Mr. Wesson was entertaining guests in his mansion and, to demonstrate his safety innovation, handed a boy a loaded Safety Hammerless and told him, "Go ahead and pull the trigger." The boy did, and a bullet instantly tore through an expensive Persian carpet, lodging itself in the floor near Mr. Wesson's feet.[33]

Although the GAO report implicitly builds the case for a recall of all hand-guns, child-resistant devices are readily available as after-market items, and can be attached to a gun by a consumer who wants one.

Interestingly a large number of modern handguns already incorporate child-resistant design, but these are the very guns some antigun groups wish to see banned. Most semi-automatic handguns have a safety lever or switch to prevent the gun from being accidentally fired. Only if the safety is turned off can the trigger mechanism be operated. In addition, to load a round into a semi-automatic pistol, a person must pull back on the top part of the gun (the slide) to chamber the round. Pulling the slide requires substantial physical force, more than many young children can muster. And of course many children will be unaware of how to engage the slide at all, and thus be unable to load the gun.[34]

Partly because semi-automatic handguns are so accident-resistant, a loaded, accessible handgun is statistically *less* likely to be involved in a fatal accident than a loaded, accessible long gun.[35]

Locks and Similar Devices

Many gun owners store their gun with a trigger lock, a device that prevents the trigger from being squeezed until the lock is removed with a key. Other gun owners store their guns in safes or in "quick-lock" safety boxes which pop open when a combination of buttons is pressed. Some gun owners store their gun separately from their ammunition, or with an essential component (such as the bolt) removed. Any of these steps may be a sensible way to deal with the presence of guns and children in the same house. NRA safety training strongly urges that any gun kept only for sporting purposes be stored in a condition so that it cannot be readily fired.

Does it makes sense legally to mandate such storage conditions? No. The United States Constitution and most state constitutions guarantee the right to own a gun for defense, and mandatory trigger locks nullify that right. A gun that must be locked up may not be readily available in an emergency. A blanket policy of making guns not easily accessible to people who are under attack will harm, not enhance, public safety.

Moreover, the circumstances of protection in each individual home are too varied to mandate any one policy. The mother of a three-month-old baby, who lives in a dangerous neighborhood, could safely keep a loaded gun in a bedside drawer. When the child grew older, she might store the gun's magazine (the device containing the ammunition) on a high closet shelf, with the hope that she could retrieve and insert the magazine if she heard someone breaking into her home. If an ex-boyfriend started harassing her by phone, and threatened to come over that night and kill her, it would be sensible for her to keep the loaded gun on top of her bedside table while she slept, and even to carry the gun in a holster when she was awake. No single safety rule, written in the crime-free confines of a legislative chamber, can determine what the best practices for gun storage will be in all situations. In addition, safe storage laws are often vague and gun owners have difficulty discerning what kind of storage, short of a safe, will satisfy the requirements.

Interestingly, the advocates of requiring all firearms to be locked up do not propose that parents be forced to lock up, or otherwise render inaccessible to children, substances such as liquor, household cleansers, or automobile keys. Every year children die from the poisonous effects of rapid ingestion of hard liquor and household cleansers, or from attempting to "drive" their parents' car. Certainly no adult has a self-defense "need" for rapid access to unlocked liquor cabinets, cleansers, or car keys.

Owner Liability Laws

Another approach to dealing with childhood gun accidents is to enact laws making the owner of the gun involved in the accident guilty of a crime. For example, California makes the offense a three-year felony. Florida, New Jersey, Illinois, and Connecticut are among those states with similar laws.[36] These laws are generally superfluous gestures. Existing laws against reckless endangerment provide ample authority for prosecution in cases where it is warranted.

Does significant good come from handcuffing the grieving parent of a dead child, and adding even more pain and sorrow to what the grief-stricken family must already bear? Sending the adult involved to prison may satisfy a social desire for revenge, and may generate newspaper stories warning against careless behavior. At the same time, it may be asked whether the brothers and sisters of the deceased child should also lose their parent to a prison term.

While most criminal laws are considered to do good by incapacitating criminals, the beneficial impact of criminal storage laws may come from the publicity that attends them. Florida State Representative Harry Jennings, sponsor of Florida's criminal liability law, suggests that the most important effect of his law is not the number of prosecutions (there are only a few every year) but the change in the accident rate. From 1987 to 1989 (before the law), there were an average of sixteen fatal gun accidents in Florida involving children under fourteen. From 1990 to 1992 (after the new law), the number fell to six per year. "We scared the hell out of people around the state," he observed.[37]

Publicity about the new law was not the only educational program in Florida at the time; besides intense media attention paid to the gun accidents themselves (which often cluster around the end of school, in May and June, so that one accident story follows on the heels of the previous one), the Eddie Eagle gun accident prevention program (discussed below), was also going into effect all over Florida. Although determining the precise safety benefit of any particular educational item is impossible, it is intuitively plausible that each item of public education (including publicity about the law) helped. Still, criminal laws should imprison only people who should be imprisoned, and it is questionable whether criminal storage laws do so.

Harassment Lawsuits

Lawsuits against gun owners, gun stores, and gun manufacturers have become a potent tool of antigun organizations. Such suits have met with limited success to date, since they are based on the theory that the manufacturer knew that the gun would be a crime weapon when, in fact, a very small percentage of handguns of any type are ever used in crime.[38]

Taking a different tack, a Texas plaintiff's attorney sued the Boy Scouts of America, claiming that the Boy Scouts magazine *Boys' Life* had enticed a 12-year-old boy into fatal play with a .22 rifle because the magazine had run a sixteen-page advertising supplement involving firearms.[39]

Yet while the antigun lawsuits are rarely found to have merit, they succeed on another level. Even in cases where the defendant prevails, he must spend huge sums on defense costs, with no hope of recovering the costs after the lawsuit has been thrown out. Although courts legally have the power to sanction attorneys who bring frivolous cases, sanctions are rarely imposed.

Safety Education

When a teenage girl in Colorado found a loaded gun at a friend's house, picked it up, began playing with it, pointed it at her brother, squeezed the trigger, and saw her brother die, the children's parent explained, "We talked to our kids about AIDS, about alcohol, about drugs—but not guns. In our wildest dreams, we never thought they'd pick up a gun at a party."[40] Just as parents who do not drink and keep no alcohol in the house have a responsibility to teach their children about alcohol, all parents have a responsibility to teach their children about the dangers of guns. Similarly, even parents who do not own swimming pools should still drownproof their children.

A third to a half of fatal gun accidents occur outside the child's own home. Thus, parents' removing guns from a home, or never acquiring guns, is not enough to protect a child from gun accidents. Since there are over two hundred million firearms in the United States, it is possible that a child may at some point encounter an unattended gun. "Childproofing" guns is not a safe approach, since any safety device can be defeated. What is more important is to "gunproof" every child. All children, including those from gunless homes, ought to be taught the fundamentals of gun safety.

Only a minority of accidental deaths could be prevented by modifying gun design. In contrast, safety education addresses the vast majority of gun accidents, for about 84 percent of accidental shootings involve the violation of basic safety rules.[41] The owners of guns involved in accidental deaths of children are unlikely to have received safety training.[42]

Groups such as the Boy Scouts of America, 4-H, the American Camping Association, and the NRA have long instructed children in the safe use of sporting arms. Junior target shooting programs and the like have helped millions of children and teenagers learn that guns must always be handled with extreme care, according to a strict set of safety rules from which no deviation is ever permitted.

Sadly, some of the groups that complain the most about childhood gun accidents also complain about programs to prevent such accidents. The Educational Fund to End Handgun Violence bemoans the fact that "nearly 23 percent of the accredited camps in the country offer some kind of shooting program. The affiliation of these programs with the National Rifle Association can run from the camp purchasing badges and certificates from the organization to a much more involved relationship."[43]

Programs that teach the safe sporting use of guns are beneficial, but they can reach only a fraction of the childhood population. Children of parents with no interest in the sporting use of firearms will never hear these safety lessons, and it is these children—ignorant of the actual mechanics of guns and bereft of instruction in gun safety—who may be at risk of causing a gun accident. Accordingly, it is necessary that gun safety programs be expanded to reach the broadest group of children possible.

One successful effort to promote safety training for all children is the NRA's "Eddie Eagle" Elementary Gun Safety Education Program (see photo insert). The Eddie Eagle Program offers curricula for children in grades K–1, 2–3, and 4–6, and uses teacher-tested materials including an animated video, cartoon workbooks, and fun safety activities. The hero, Eddie Eagle, teaches a simple safety lesson: "If you see a gun: Stop! Don't touch. Leave the area. Tell an adult." The Eddie Eagle program is a more elaborate version of the approach taken by the Pennsylvania Division of the American Trauma Society, which offers a free coloring book warning children about various potential dangers; for firearms, the children are warned, "If you find a gun, don't touch it. Tell your parents. Remember—no gun is a toy!"[44]

Eddie Eagle includes no political content, no statements about the Second Amendment, and nothing promoting the sporting use of guns. The program and its creator, Marion Hammer, won the 1993 Outstanding Community Service Award from the National Safety Council.[45] It has been adopted in most Florida counties and endorsed by the Police Athletic League. The Georgia legislature and the Oklahoma City city council (as well as some smaller bodies) have enacted resolutions urging schools under their supervision to adopt the Eddie Eagle program.[46] As of early 1995, Eddie Eagle had reached more than six million children.

Unfortunately, some persons in positions of authority over school safety programs have refused to allow Eddie Eagle to be used in their schools, because they disagree with the NRA's position on policy questions.[47]

While safety education in general would seem to be noncontroversial, some groups actively oppose it. Some antigun advocates warn that safety education may promote interest in firearms.[48] (The argument parallels some of the opposition to teaching sex education in the schools.) While no one has ever studied whether educating children about guns promotes interest in guns, research of adult-oriented safety education has not found evidence that education promotes gun use.[49]

The American Academy of Pediatrics (AAP) dismisses safety education, asserting, "No published research confirms effectiveness of gun-safety training for adolescents. Most preventive gun safety education is directed at hunters and marksmen, but hunting and target-shooting are a small part of the adolescent firearms problem."[50] Thus, claims the AAP, only a complete ban on handguns can deal with the problem of childhood gun accidents.

The AAP's point about published research, while technically true, is meaningless. No formal research has been done on whether gun-safety programs for children or teenagers reduce gun accidents. Research involving adult training has shown that it promotes safer firearms practices for adults.[51] Most parents sensibly believe that education reduces accidents, which is why schools teach young children about staying out of traffic, and instruct teenagers on how to drive safely.

Notably, hunter-safety programs have been proven to reduce hunting accidents. In the last several decades, states have required new hunters (but not those who were already hunters) to pass a safety certification class before being granted a hunting license. Today, the majority of hunters have completed safety training, and this group is involved in disproportionately fewer accidents than hunters without training.[52] Hunting accident fatalities have fallen by 75 percent since the late 1960s.[53] There is no reason to assume that safety education suddenly becomes worthless when removed from the hunting context. The AAP's anti-education reasoning is equivalent to advocating a ban on swimming pools because some people may not pay attention to water safety instruction.

The anti-education attitudes of American gun prohibitionists starkly contrast with strategies elsewhere. In New Zealand, the Mountain Safety Council (the leading outdoor sports organization) has worked with the police to produce a pamphlet which promotes responsible gun use by children. The booklet observes that "airgun ownership can contribute in a positive way to growing up."[54] The Council also publishes, again in conjunction with the police, a gun safety comic series called "Billy Hook" which teaches children gun safety rules. The comic endorses supervised gun use by children.[55] The official police instruction book for gun owners, the *Arms Code*, advises parents: "While children should not handle a firearm except under the supervision of a firearms license holder, it can ease their curiosity to show them your firearm and explain that it must never be touched except when you are there."[56] Over the last half-century, there has been a significant decline in firearms deaths and injuries in New Zealand, even as the number of guns has soared.[57]

While schools and other social institutions have an important role to play in gun safety, the primary responsibility rests with parents. A child who can, under parental supervision, invite a classmate to shoot a .22 rifle at a target range may be considerably less awed by the possibility of surreptitiously playing with a friend's father's old pistol.

Given the benefits of gun-safety education, should it be made mandatory, either in schools or for gun owners? Either form of mandatory education would probably reduce accidents, but other factors should be considered. America's public schools already labor under a huge weight of legislative mandates. Many education reformers suggest that we should be removing, rather than increasing, the mandate burden on local schools. Accordingly, decisions about gun-safety classes might best be left to principals and school boards, rather than legislatures.

In addition, mandatory education regarding any controversial subject (including guns or sex) must be carefully constructed so as not to offend the personal and family values of students. The Eddie Eagle program, which carefully avoids stating that guns are *per se* good or bad, or that any particular gun laws are good or bad, meets the standard of neutrality. Other gun-safety programs may not; for example, the Milwaukee police use a "safety" program which encourages children to call the police if they find out that their parents own a gun.[58]

Requiring prospective handgun owners to pass a safety class before buying a handgun is currently the law in California. Such a law might reduce the gun accident rate, but would impose other, unacceptable, social costs. First, the safety training acts as a *de facto* waiting period. A person may not be able to obtain a gun for months while waiting to take the class. In some cities with safety training laws, the only approved class is one taught by the police, and the class is taught only a few times a year. As was discussed in chapter 2, waiting periods may be a net loss to public safety: persons who need a gun for immediate protection cannot obtain one, whereas those who are capable of murder on one day generally remain capable of murder a few weeks later. The experience of jurisdictions that impose mandatory safety training suggests that some police administrators will attempt to use safety training not to ensure that gun owners are well-trained, but to set up administrative roadblocks to gun ownership.[59] For people who, as a matter of principle, want the government to limit gun ownership, mandatory safety training "for the sake of our children" offers a handy wedge.[60]

From a Constitutional viewpoint, mandatory safety training is dubious. No other Constitutional right is limited by a requirement that persons seeking to exercise that right prove their competence to do so. (Driving is not a right, and no driver's license is needed on private roads or other private property.) Many other nations license journalists, and the number of people harmed by libel and other media mistakes would probably decline if journalists were required to take a government-mandated "safe journalism" class covering the fundamentals of libel law and fact verification. If such a law were proposed, most journalists would not bother to argue that the number of truly reckless journalists is small, or that the number of people killed because of media mistakes is negligible.[61] Instead, journalists would argue, correctly, that because the First Amendment guarantees a right rather than privilege, the government may not impose tests on people who seek to exercise their rights. The same principle is true regarding the Second Amendment, and every other amendment.

Finally, many accidents involving adults (the only people who are old enough to be gun buyers, and hence be required to take mandatory safety classes) are the result of recklessness more than ignorance. Adults and older teenagers who cause firearms accidents are unlike the rest of the population. They are "disproportionately involved in other accidents, violent crime and heavy drinking."[62] Without guns, they would likely find some other way to kill themselves "accidentally," such as by reckless driving. Indeed, they tend to have a record of reckless driving and automobile accidents. Safety education can accomplish little for this group.

While children can be helped by affirmative programs that teach gun responsibility, they can also be harmed by media images that glamorize recklessness.[63] Consider a child whose exposure to firearms consists of television imagery. Studies have shown that even very young children learn skills by watching television demonstrations.[64] Television "teaches" (by example) that the first thing you do when you get a gun is put your finger on the trigger, and then point the gun at someone. These television demonstrations violate two key gun-safety rules: keep your finger off the trigger unless you are ready to shoot; and never point a gun at another person (except in self-defense).

While the media can at least claim to be ignorant of actual gun-safety rules, the antigun organizations have less excuse. No matter how important a lobbying group believes its political goals to be, those goals should not be furthered through advertising which directly endangers children. One of the most famous posters of the antigun movement, dramatizing the suposedly high rate of childhood gun accidents, shows a baby looking down the barrel of a gun.[65] Even presuming that the gun was unloaded (or was an imitation gun), the baby/victim in the poster has been unintentionally taught that looking down the barrel of a gun is permissible and interesting. And so have all the preliterate children who see that poster.

The poster is also extremely misleading in its attempt to create an image of a widespread and frequent problem. About one child under the age of one dies in a gun accident in an average year.[66]

As a nation, the United States has no shortage of social pathologies, including pathologies worsened by heavy-handed government. Despite the claims of some gun-control advocates, the problem of childhood gun accidents is relatively small, and is continuing to decline. Prudence suggests that the safest course is to continue the voluntary educational strategies which appear to be working.

TEENAGERS CARRYING GUNS

Every day 135,000 children carry guns to school, we are informed by the American Bar Association,[67] by *USA Today,*[68] and by Senators Joseph Biden and John

Chafee.[69] Senator Christopher Dodd raises the number to 186,000,[70] and MTV, in an education series for schoolchildren, announces that the true figure is 270,000.[71] Frightening numbers to be sure, but completely untrue.

The 135,000 figure appears to be very loosely extrapolated from Centers for Disease Control and Prevention (CDC) surveys asking teenagers in grades nine through twelve, "During the last thirty days, how many times have you carried a weapon, such as a gun, knife, or club, for self-protection or because you thought you might need it in a fight?" The 135,000 factoid assumes that every respondent who carried a gun at least once carried a gun to school every day. In fact, the data suggested that most of the students did not carry a gun every day, but only occasionally. And the students were not asked if they carried a weapon at school.[72] Thus, the "yes" answers applied to occasional carrying anywhere, such as in an automobile when driving at night in dangerous neighborhoods. Accordingly, Florida State University criminologist Gary Kleck estimates that, realistically, about 16,000 to 17,000 students carry a gun to school on a given day. The figure translates into about one in every eight hundred high school students. Common sense suggests that the one in eight hundred will not be evenly distributed; an inner-city school may have more than one in eight hundred students carrying a handgun on a given day, and a different school may have none at all.[73]

It is sometimes said that there has been a large increase in the number of weapons of all types found on school grounds. What has clearly increased is the number of metal detectors, locker searches, and other searches for student weapons. An increase in searches will inevitably lead to an increase in reports of an object being found. For example, the year before airport passenger screening was established, no explosive devices were found in airports. The next year, with screening in place, there was a large "increase" in the number of explosives found.[74] Were more people carrying explosives? More likely, more people were simply getting caught.

Please understand that I am not saying that it is a good thing that one in every eight hundred students feels a need to take a gun to school on a particular day. It is a terrible thing. But we cannot begin to solve problems unless we understand them, and we cannot understand them if we believe in factoids rather than facts.

Teenagers as Crime Victims

Teenagers are victimized by violent crime at a higher rate than any other age group.[75] In 1992, one out thirteen juveniles was the victim of a violent crime.[76] According to the Office of Juvenile Justice and Delinquency Prevention (part of the federal Department of Justice), "In 1991 a 12-year-old was at greater risk of being a victim of violent crime (i.e., murder, forcible rape, robbery, aggravated assault, or simple assault) than anyone above the age of twenty-three. The risk of violent victimization for a 17-year-old in 1991 was about double that faced by a 29-year-old."[77] There are sixty-two violent victimizations annually per thousand persons aged twelve to fifteen; seventy-two victimizations annually for persons aged sixteen to nineteen, but only twenty-six victimizations for persons twenty and over.[78] A twelve-state study found that more than half of female rape victims are under the age of eighteen.[79]

Schools, sadly, are not safe havens. In a six-month period in 1988–89, more than 400,000 students were victims of violent crimes at school.[80] An Illinois survey found that one in twelve public high school students was the victim of a physical attack at school, or on the way to or from school. About the same number (one-twelfth), sometimes stayed home from school because of fear of physical attack.[81]

Interestingly, although teenagers are more likely to be crime victims, they carry firearms for protection at only about one-third the rate of older, less-victimized population groups.[82]

Next to teenagers, the age group at highest risk of being violently attacked is persons aged twenty to twenty-nine. Some persons in this age group choose to carry firearms for protection. Some are able to obtain permits or live in jurisdictions that do not require permits. Others, knowing they cannot obtain a permit to carry, choose to carry anyway, reasoning that it is better to risk being caught breaking the law than to risk being maimed, raped, robbed, or murdered. A very large number of teenagers who carry guns appear to have the same protective motives as those in older ages groups who carry firearms.

"A lot of parents in my district are telling their children to carry weapons," observed the superintendent of a Brooklyn public school. "They give their children weapons to protect themselves when they leave the tenements."[83] Or as one student wrote to the *Washington Post*:

> To put it bluntly, I think students bring weapons to school to save their own lives. They have a constant fear of being attacked, whether for money, for drugs, or for some other reason. They feel they need to bring a weapon with them to school.
>
> To the outsider, this information may seem all blown out of proportion, or just a plain lie. The truth is that there are drugs in the schools. There are kids robbing other kids of their money and personal belongings. And these kids who are committing these crimes also carry weapons such as knives and handguns and they are not afraid to use them.
>
> There's no doubt that we have a serious problem on our hands. I just hope we can find some way to solve it.[84]

"Good kids have guns," acknowledges John Silva, the safety and security director of the Cambridge, Massachusetts, government schools. "From a district attorney's perspective, a good kid would never carry a gun, but the DAs don't live in the projects. There's so much fear. Good kids who want to go to school and do the right thing—they're afraid of the gangs and the drug dealers; they want to protect themselves and their families."[85]

A large percentage of students who carry guns to school may do it for protection rather than aggression. In 1986, there were about 1,700 armed crimes in which the criminal used a gun in American schools.[86] If it is assumed that each crime was perpetrated by a different armed criminal, and that each armed criminal was a student, then about 1,700 students perpetrated a crime with a firearm at school. In actuality, the number of firearmed criminals is likely lower, since some criminals committed more than one crime, and some of them were not students.

In addition, make the assumption that only 16,000 or 17,000 students ever carry a gun to school. The figure is the realistic estimate of the number of students who carry a gun to school on a given day. Since not every person who carries a gun carries it every day, the figure underestimates the total number of students who carry a gun to school sometime during the year.

Making these two assumptions—which artificially maximize the number of students assumed to be criminals, and artificially minimize the total number of students carrying guns—we find that only about 10 percent of the students carrying guns (1,700 out of 16,000 or 17,000) commit crimes with them.

If we use the figure supplied by gun prohibition advocates—135,000 students carrying a gun to school each day—then the number of students carrying for criminal purposes drops to less than 2 percent of the number of students carrying.

It is hardly a sign of a healthy society that any teenager feels a need to carry a handgun for protection at school. It is a sign of advanced social pathology that teenagers are so often attacked by violent criminals. Yet we are hardly going to make society better if we refuse to attempt to understand its problems. And we are not going to understand the problem of violence and guns at school if we refuse to admit that many of the students with guns are victims, not perpetrators.

The statistical analysis is supported by a recent in-depth study of the weapons-carrying behavior of male students in inner-city schools in California, Illinois, Louisiana, and New Jersey. The study also surveyed incarcerated juvenile males in those states.[87] For both the schoolchildren and the teenagers in jail, the study found that "Carrying a gun has become strictly functional behavior meant to support survival."[88] Self-defense by victims was common. For example, 70 percent of the inmates had been "scared off, shot at, wounded or captured" by an armed victim at least once.[89]

There were important differences between the students and criminal sample. For example, when asked, "Do you carry a gun all/most of the time?" 55 percent of the inmates but only 12 percent of the students answered in the affirmative.

For both groups, obtaining a firearm was seen as easy. Only 13 percent of the inmates and 35 percent of the students said that obtaining a gun on the street is difficult. Asked if they could "get a gun with little/no trouble?" 87 percent of the inmates and 65 percent of the students said yes.[90]

While it is sometimes asserted that the reason so many teenagers have access to firearms is that their parents leave guns unlocked, the study found that parents, gun stores, and other sources subject to law enforcement controls did not appear to be major sources of the firearms. One researcher noted, "They told us with humor how easy it was to steal a gun." Many of the guns were obtained for far less than their retail price, indicating that they were stolen. Cars were considered easy targets for stealing a gun.

Contrary to the hypothesis that small, cheap handguns (so-called Saturday Night Specials) are responsible for modern youth being armed, the researchers found that among the criminals, "The preference, clearly, was for high-powered hand weapons that are well-made, accurate, easy to shoot and not easily traced—guns suitable for serious work against well-armed adversaries."

For both students and inmates, protection was the leading reason for obtaining a gun, "easily outpacing all other motivations."[91] Even for juvenile criminals who used guns in crime, self-protection (rather than peer status) was the dominant reason for carrying a gun. The authors concluded that legal controls were unlikely to deter gun carrying, since persons carrying for protection are much less likely to be deterred than those carrying for less important reasons.[92]

Turning the school violence discussion into nothing more than a dragnet for "guns at school" misdirects our attention. First of all, firearms play a relatively small role in the overall problem of violence in schools. In 1986, for example, there were 41,500 aggravated assaults in schools and 44,000 robberies. Firearms were used in a little under 2 percent of these crimes.[93] Thus, even a program that eradicated all guns from school (and prevented their perpetrators from using alternative weapons) would fail to deal with the 98 percent of violent felonies at school that do not involve firearms.

Second, to focus on "guns in school" is to miss the larger picture of the violent communities that spawn violent teenagers. And to focus only on one instrument of violence—the gun—is to begin the search for gun-control laws which have a superficial appeal but will do nothing to remove the causes of violence. As Dr. Joseph Sheley et al. wrote in the *American Journal of Diseases of Children*, after presenting their findings about violence involving inner-city high school students:

> It is clear that the problem of violence in inner-city schools cannot be isolated from the problems of violence in larger society; violent neighborhoods and violent communities will produce violent schools, whatever measures the schools themselves adopt. It is equally clear that this "larger" problem will not yield to simplistic, unicausal solutions. In this connection, it is useful to point out that everything that leads to gun-related violence is already against the law. What is needed are not new and more stringent gun laws but rather a concerted effort to rebuild the social structure of inner cities.[94]

Another commentator traces school violence to the coercion and regimentation prevalent at many schools today.[95]

Third, and most important, to turn the quest for school safety into a war on every teenager who feels a need to carry gun is to increase, not reduce, the victimization. It is awful that any students in and around American schools feel a need to arm for protection. The first step to a solution is not to disarm the victims who are trying to protect themselves, but to act against both the violent aggressors who threaten the students and the conditions that breed the violent aggressors. If schools were made safe, then students would not feel a need to carry a gun for protection.

Many students carrying weapons to school are not bad kids. A 17-year-old female has just as much moral right to use a firearm to resist a rapist as does a 40-year-old female. A 16-year-old male has the same right to escape crippling assault by a gang of thugs as does a 60-year-old male. The students who carry weapons are simply coping with a terrible situation which they have no other idea how to deal with. If society thinks them too immature to carry a gun under any circumstances, then society has the obligation to protect them.

It is irresponsible—indeed childish—for adults who fixate on guns to say, in effect, "We haven't got any solution for your problems, so we are just going to take away the only solution you could figure out and leave you on your own to figure out some other solution."

It is also hopelessly impractical. A society that cannot protect children from rampant crime is also unlikely to be able to disarm them. Moreover, one result of disarming students while failing to offer alternative means of protection would be to drive some of them into gangs for protection. And the result of that will be not that they eschew guns, but rather that they are exposed by their peers to guns and drugs together. It is unjust for the state to compel a student to attend school, assume no legal liability for injury to the student,[96] fail to provide a safe environment at school or on the way to school, and then prohibit the student from protecting himself or herself.[97] In Lafayette, Illinois, a 14-year-old boy who carried a gun to protect himself from gang members was criminally prosecuted for violating the state's law about guns at school.[98] Rather than using the criminal law to "crack down" on people who are trying to protect themselves, a more humane approach would be to protect them better, so that they no longer need to carry a weapon.

POSSIBLE SOLUTIONS TO SCHOOL VIOLENCE

I want a nation where no child feels a need to carry a gun, a knife, or any other weapon to school for protection. To create such a society, I want to make the schools so safe that no student feels at risk, because violent felonies—and violent felons—cannot thrive on school grounds. As Professor Sheley points out, a complete solution to the problem of violent schools must lie in the solution to the problem of a violent society. But even without solving social problems outside the school, there are major steps which could make schools significantly safer than they are now.

"Gun-Free School Zones"

Deserving no place among the strategies for safer schools is catchy legislation for "Gun-Free School Zones," a descendant of the "Nuclear-Free Zones." In the nuclear-free zones movement, pacifist city councils, as well as trendy colleges and prep schools, voted to declare themselves "nuclear-free zones," and outlaw nuclear missiles and nuclear research within their boundaries. The premise of nuclear-free zones was that by declaring themselves above the cold war, cities or schools could escape its effects. But of course the nuclear-free zones were mostly symbolic gestures, which offered only the appearance of peace without doing anything to remove the causes of nuclear tension, such as the totalitarian system in the former Soviet Union.

Advocates of "gun-free school zones" suffer from a similar myopia. Their premise is that schools and thousand-foot zones around schools can become safer merely by the legislative declaration that they are a gun-free zone. Until legislatures and the rest of the community begin addressing the root causes of why students (and many teachers) feel a need to carry a firearm for protection, the schools will remain as violent as ever.

In some cases, a bill for a "gun-free school zone" may impose a weapons prohibition far more sweeping than its innocuous title suggests. For example, a "gun-free school zone" proposal in Maryland would have outlawed the possession of kitchen knives in private homes within a thousand feet of a school. Maryland enacted a narrower bill, but even that legislation criminalized innocent behavior. One celebrated prosecution involved a well-liked music teacher who inadvertently left a .22 caliber pistol on the floor of her car in her high school's parking lot one day. She was suspended without pay for two months and forced to plead guilty to a misdemeanor in order to avoid felony charges. The students in her school were deprived of one of their best teachers, and the limited resources of the county's criminal justice system were expended to punish a good citizen who was no threat at all to public safety.[99]

"Gun-free school zones" cause others sorts of harm to education. In Maryland, for example, volunteer teachers who create living history programs for students have been forbidden to bring not only antique rifles but also spears, arrows, bows, tomahawks, and even shields. Maryland's official state sport is jousting (using a lance to snag a metal ring while riding a horse), but that, too, was made criminal on school grounds, as were weekend hunter-safety classes, even in rural areas where the local school may be the only place large enough to hold the class.[100]

The tendency to expand "gun-free school zones" beyond school property raises problems of its own. The typical distance for expanded "gun-free school zones" is a thousand-foot radius around school property (including nonacademic investment property or property owned by correspondence schools). The school zone bills never require that signs making citizens aware of the school zone be posted.

On the contrary, if "gun-free school zone" signs are posted at all, they are put up on school buildings, creating the misleading impression that the school zone ends where school property does.[101] In addition, many schools have an "End School Zone" sign (for traffic purposes) quite close to the school, again creating the impression that laws relating to school zones apply only in and around the school.

While purporting to deal only with safety near schools, the thousand-foot bills may radically alter existing law regarding the carrying of firearms. Many states, such as Colorado, allow a loaded firearm to be carried in an automobile for protection.[102] A thousand-foot school zone bill may abolish that right, except in open space areas a thousand feet from any school.

Whether states should outlaw the carrying of firearms in private automobiles for protection is the subject of legitimate debate, but that debate should occur in the context of a bill which directly announces its intention to abolish firearms carrying for self-protection, not in a bill claiming to deal only with school safety. Similarly, while there may be a legitimate policy debate about turning unlicensed firearms carrying into a felony, that debate should stand on its own terms and not be submerged in a bill whose title relates only to school safety. The fiscal impact of felonizing a frequently committed act is likely to be heavy. In times of budgetary constraint, when state governments are having trouble keeping violent felons in state prison, it may be asked whether it is wise to create an entirely new class of nonviolent felons, whose only offense is to carry a firearm for protection hundreds of feet away from any school, in an unmarked "school zone."

School zone laws should not apply to universities, since many university students are over twenty-one, and almost all are over eighteen. While colleges will often want to forbid firearms in dormitories, the policy should be set by each school rather than imposed as an inflexible matter of state law. For example, colleges near rural areas might allow students to store hunting guns with dormitory supervisors. And adult graduate students living in university-owned apartments should certainly not be forced to surrender their right to arms, or turned into felons for owning a gun in their own home.[103]

The federal "gun-free school zones" law, which was declared unconstitutional in April 1994, was supposedly based on the congressional interstate commerce power.[104] Yet the law had a far broader sweep than any realistic commerce theory could allow. For example, if a licensed hunter returned home after a day in the field, parked his car across the street from his house, and carried his unloaded rifle from the car into his home without first putting the rifle in a locked case, he violated a federal criminal law if he happened to live 950 feet as the crow flies from a church kindergarten that was open two days a week, and happened to be closed for the summer. Most state "gun-free school zone" laws are more narrow and sensible, just as most state education policies are more sensible than Washington's education mandates.

Zero Tolerance

Under zero-tolerance laws, any student caught bringing a weapon to school is automatically suspended or expelled. Since not all students who carry weapons carry for the same reason, inflexible mandatory punishments are inappropriate. School principals, if allowed flexibility, can recognize that a 17-year-old who points a gun at a teacher and a 15-year-old who starts carrying a knife after she has been pummeled and robbed by a gang should be dealt with differently.

Even if it is decided that a zero-tolerance policy, applicable to criminals and victims alike, is the best response to the problem of guns and schools, two principles should be applied: local schools should set their own policies and the policies should be applied with common sense. Neither principle is currently being honored.

Compounding the foolishness of the 1990 federal "Gun-Free School Zones" law, a 1994 federal "Gun-Free Schools" statute mandates a cutoff of federal funds to schools that do not expel for at least one year any student who brings a gun to school.[105] Why does the federal government presume that local school districts cannot be trusted to deal appropriately with students carrying weapons?

If local school administrators are making mistakes, they are hardly erring on the side of leniency or common sense. In Boston, 7-year-old Amber Nickoles was suspended from school and ordered to undergo psychological counseling because she brought a three-inch pink squirt gun to school. Boston school officials classified the water pistol as a "mock weapon." A school spokesman said, "It may be a toy gun today, but it could be a real gun tomorrow."[106] A 6-year-old boy in Iowa was suspended for bringing a multicolored squirt gun to class.[107] In Illinois, a 12-year-old girl was walking down the road while wearing her brother's jacket. She saw a round of ammunition lying on the road, picked it up, put in the jacket, and forgot about it. Later, the 9-year-old brother was wearing the jacket, and found the ammunition while he was on the playground. He promptly turned it over to the playground supervisor, who set in motion a response that led to the boy's being brought before a juvenile court, even though no one doubted the family's explanation of the source of the ammunition.[108]

In Georgia, a student was expelled for bringing a cap gun to school.[109] Also in Georgia, an elementary student was suspended because she brought a knife to school to cut cookies for her classmates, and a thirteen-year-old was suspended after being found with a pocketknife in his pocket that he forgot to remove after a hunting trip. In Colorado, there was a similar case, in which a second-grader was suspended after being found in possession of his father's rusty little pocket knife. Another Colorado student, a 9-year-old Cub Scout, won a pocket knife at a Scout award ceremony one night. He accidentally left the three-inch pocket knife in his pants, and brought it to school the next day. When he put the unopened knife on his desk, another student reported him to the teacher. The Scout was given a five-day suspension from school, which the principal charac-

terized as a "light sentence." His attendance record had previously been perfect.[110]

Those students at least got off more easily than a 17-year-old African-
American girl who brought some African artifacts to her show-and-tell class.
Among the items was a ceremonial African knife, which her teacher had given
her permission to bring. This girl was charged with a felony carrying a four-year
prison term.[111]

People of the Sikh religious faith carry four-inch daggers, known as "kir-
pans," as a symbol of their devotion to God. There is no evidence that Sikh students in America have ever threatened any of their classmates with these daggers.
But the San Francisco school administration tried (until stopped by a court) to
forbid the students from wearing their ceremonial daggers.[112] This was an intrusion on freedom of religion, similar to a school trying to forbid students to wear
crosses around their necks.

In a previous era, schoolteachers would give a pocket knife to exemplary students. Now such a gift would often constitute a felony on the part of both the
teacher and the student.

Suspensions, expulsions, and felony charges for squirt guns, pocket knives,
and show and tell. Zero tolerance, it seems, is a euphemism for zero judgment.

Metal Detectors

The effective use of metal detectors requires a large number of security officers,
since a great many students have to be scanned in a short time. A high school of
three thousand to four thousand students needs twenty employees to scan students
and to monitor doors.[113] The detectors cost from $2,500 to $7,000 each for the
walk-through detectors, and $15,000 to $20,000 for an X-ray machine for bags
and purses. Handheld wands, which are much less effective, cost $29 to $200.[114]
Salaries for the personnel to run the detectors will often be the largest expense.

Despite the huge expense, metal detectors cannot catch every weapon going
into a school, because searching every student who set off the beeper would cause
students to wait for hours to get into class.[115] While walk-through traffic for metal
detectors at airports is relatively evenly distributed throughout the day, school
metal detectors must process a huge amount of traffic in the few minutes before
classes begin. Even in the few schools that intensively scan all students every day,
it does not take much imagination to figure out how to pass a weapon past a low-
wage security guard, with trickery or bribery. Once past the guard, weapons can
simply be stored at school. Thus, metal detectors reduce, but definitely do not
eliminate, weapons at school. A survey of students in all 115 New York City public high schools found that students at the schools with metal detectors reported
having at some time or other carried a weapon inside the school building about
half as often (7.8 percent versus 13.6 percent) as students in schools without
metal detectors. Students in schools with metal detectors also reported having

carried at some time or other a weapon to or from school at about half the rate of other students (7.7 percent versus 15.2 percent).[116]

Besides being expensive and far from completely effective, metal detectors may be of questionable Constitutionality. While the U.S. Supreme Court has ruled that students may be searched based on individualized "reasonable suspicion" (in contrast to the "probable cause" standard for adults), there is no Constitutional authorization for mass searches of individuals without any suspicion at all.[117]

Although the courts have upheld the use of metal detectors at airports, the searches have been justified on the grounds that the passenger can avoid the search by checking baggage rather than carrying it in the passenger compartment, or by traveling by some other means.[118] In contrast to air travel, attendance at public school is not voluntary; it is required by government.

Like much of the rest of the Constitution, the Fourth Amendment has been significantly weakened in recent decades by public officials and courts who place the perceived needs of the moment ahead of the literal language and original intent of the Constitution. Thus, California's Attorney General Dan Lungren (who helps raise funds for gun control) has issued an attorney general opinion finding that metal detectors are Constitutional and encouraging their use. Many statist courts would likely agree with General Lungren.

Widespread use of metal detectors in school acts as a kind of social conditioning that poses a serious long-term threat to the Fourth Amendment right to freedom from searches without probable cause. Searching a teenager's purse, or making her walk through a metal detector several times a day, is hardly likely to instill much faith in the importance of civil liberties. Indeed, students conditioned to searches without any suspicion in high school are unlikely to resist such searches when they become adults.

And just as metal detectors have moved from airports into schools, there is already pressure to move them from schools into the streets. The Police Foundation, one of the leading supporters of metal detectors in schools, advocates abolishing citizen handgun ownership (except for the police), and has urged that metal detectors be set up on streets and other public places.

Monitors and Patrols

Instead of relying on technology to solve social problems, a better solution would be to mobilize students, teachers, and the rest of the community inside and outside the school. A first step is to ensure that responsible adults are assigned to monitor playgrounds and other areas where trouble is possible.

Another step would be for school administrations to foster volunteer student patrols, which would change the balance of power in the schoolyard, thus ending the reign of terror of outside intruders and gangs. In Israel, the police operate a volunteer armed citizen patrol called the "Civil Guards," which patrols dangerous neighborhoods at night; many of the volunteers are high school students who, after a short period of training, are issued firearms, like any other volunteer.

If Israel can give its high school students firearms with which to conduct civil patrols, surely it is not asking too much for American high school administrators to allow their own students to form voluntary, supervised, unarmed patrols. The idea of voluntary patrols, while perhaps radical in some eyes, is much more firmly rooted in American traditions of community self-help and responsibility than are metal detectors, a technological fix that will undermine privacy values.

Safe Havens

Students often face the greatest dangers when walking to and from school, rather than at school itself. To improve travel safety, area businesses, churches, and homes should be encouraged to post signs offering themselves as safe havens for students who feel threatened. Volunteer parent patrols can supervise safe corridors of passage, and police can be reassigned to guard safe corridors during the hours before and after school. Such programs are already working in New York City and Baltimore.

Violent Felons in Schools

Public schools being public, they sometimes are forced to deal with students who are on parole after incarceration for a violent crime. Juvenile records involving violent felonies should be disclosed to school administrators when the juvenile enrolls at a school.[119] The privacy interests of the juvenile criminal are outweighed by the right of teachers and other school personnel to know whom they are dealing with.

Too often, juvenile parolees proceed "cold turkey" from a juvenile detention facility to a public school, with little support in making the transition. Special transitional schools should be established for parolees, to help prepare them for the normal school environment, or to continue their education, if they are not able to attend a public school without endangering other students.[120]

Compulsory Attendance

There are many good reasons for compulsory education to be abolished, the foremost being that children are neither slaves nor prisoners of the state. Children and their parents, not the government, are the proper decision makers for how children spend their time. Compulsory attendance, rather than being a timeless principle, in most states dates from the era between the Civil War and the turn of the century. When compulsory attendance laws were being instituted, there was no objection that such laws would endanger the safety and even the lives of teachers and of students who wanted to be in school. Circumstances having changed over the last century, it is reasonable to rethink compulsory attendance. Forcing a teenager who does not want to learn to be present on school premises anyway may do little good for the student, and may cause substantial trouble for the students who do want to learn. If violent students are allowed to leave school, some dropouts who have left because of fear may drop back in.

The most common objection to reexamining truancy laws is that letting teenagers out of school merely transfers the problem from the school to the street. But on the street, the dropout will have no opportunity to disrupt the peaceful education of dozens of other children every day. For at least some dropouts, the experience away from school might prove a sobering one, and awaken an interest in the benefits that school attendance can provide. Other dropouts might pass their days more happily and usefully working at a convenience store or loading dock than passing time in an overcrowded classroom from which they would graduate illiterate.

Of course some teenagers will waste their lives out of school with as much determination as they wasted them while in school.[121] But at least they will not prevent other students from learning.

Some proponents of compulsory attendance argue that schools must educate children to be highly skilled workers in the emerging global economy; a teenager who drops out is unlikely have a high lifetime-income potential. True enough, but teenagers kept in school against their will are unlikely to learn much anyway. And through disruptive or violent behavior, those teenagers may help ruin the education of motivated students.

It is also true that when students drop out, the school receives less money from the state or local government. (The fact that government schools receive funding on the basis of their body count is a major reason why government school employee and administrator organizations are such energetic promoters of compulsory attendance.) There is nothing unfair about reducing school funding when the number of students declines; indeed, if students and families were treated like voluntary education consumers instead of prisoners, some schools might work harder at becoming places more people would choose to attend.

Proponents of the government schools as training centers for global economic competition often point to Japan as a nation that produces highly literate, numerate high school graduates. And so Japan does. American schools should not blindly imitate Japanese schools, for they tend to overemphasize rote memorization and groupthink. But one of the reasons that Japanese high schools are so successful at teaching calculus, science, foreign languages, and other subjects whose mastery eludes so many American high school graduates is that attendance at Japanese high schools is completely voluntary. Nobody has to go to high school in Japan unless he or she wants to. As a result, writes criminologist Jackson Toby:

> Dealing as they do exclusively with voluntary students, Japanese high school teachers are more firmly in control of their high schools, without the help of

security guards or of metal detectors. . . . Japanese teachers are not afraid to admonish students who start to misbehave because the overwhelming majority of students care about their teachers' favorable attitudes.

Because the entire high school student body consists of youngsters who *want* to attend, Japanese teachers are able to require of these voluntary students greater studiousness than it is possible to require of involuntary students. . . . Japanese high school teachers are hardly ever assaulted by their students. . . .[122] (Original italics)

While in the United States school violence is greater in high schools than in junior highs, the reverse is true in Japan. In the junior highs, attendance is compulsory, and virtually all the violence is perpetrated by the 7 percent of junior high students who choose not to continue into senior high.[123] Japanese gun-control laws are draconian, but these laws cannot be the primary reason why there is so much less school violence in Japan than America; as noted above, 98 percent of American school violence does not involve firearms. (And besides, guns are readily available on the Japanese black market; for a variety of cultural reasons, Japanese simply choose not to own them.)[124]

Putting aside other arguments for and against compulsory education, abolishing compulsory attendance beyond the fifth grade would almost certainly have an immediate, dramatic effect in reducing school violence in the United States. (Violence in elementary schools is rare enough that a case for abolishing compulsory attendance in the lower grades cannot be made on the basis of reducing violence.) Accordingly, persons who insist on maintaining the present system of compulsory attendance all the way through the twelfth grade should, at the least, offer evidence that the social good of compulsory education more than compensates for the violence (and the disruption of education) which compulsory education inflicts on teachers and on students who want to learn.

Let Poor People Choose Their Own Schools

What could be more unfair than being forced into a dangerous situation, denied effective protection by the government, and then forbidden by the government to protect oneself? That is the situation many thousands of public school students face every day. Wealthy parents, such as President and Mrs. Clinton, rarely choose to send their children to the dysfunctional, dangerous government schools in cities such as Washington, D.C. Is it fair that poorer families do not have the same choice?

Many inner-city parochial and private schools educate children who are just as disadvantaged as those in the nearby government schools. Yet violence in these schools is rare. Schools that are run by principals, parents, and teachers rather than by distant bureaucracies have proven time and again that even in the most difficult circumstances, children can be provided with a good education within a safe environment.[125]

Wisconsin State Representative Polly Williams, sponsor of a successful choice program for disadvantaged students in Milwaukee,[126] notes that a number of problem children from the Milwaukee government schools have turned into well-behaved students in alternative schools.

Since supply tends to respond to consumer demand, the enactment of broad choice programs would likely result in new schools springing up wherever the potential consumers are, including in core urban areas (which, after all, have the highest density of students). The students who are "left behind" in the government schools (by parents who did not choose an alternative school) will be better off, too. For the first time, the school administration will have to deal with students and parents as clients who must be offered good reasons for choosing the government school, rather than as a captive source of tax revenue subject to being hauled into school by the police.

There are many proposals for choice in education, including charter schools, home schooling, choice plans allowing parents to select any government school in a particular district, and choice plans allowing parents to select government or nongovernment schools. More detailed arguments regarding school choice are available in books and monographs devoted to the subject.[127] For now, it is enough to note that, whatever the other benefits or problems of school choice, it might help many children enjoy a safer learning environment.

As most educators acknowledge, schools can only rarely solve the problems of children who come from dysfunctional homes. Proposals for increased school choice (whether to attend, and where to attend) might help make schools much better, and would very likely create safer schools for many of the current victims of school violence. As a result, the number of students carrying weapons to school for protection would probably plummet. But protecting students from violent predators at school does not solve the problem of the violent predators. If we want the streets—and not just the schools—to become safer, then we must deal directly with America's armed, young predators and with the conditions that help create them.

CRIME: THE INNER-CITY CRISIS

One of the central strategies of the gun prohibition advocates has been to tell Americans that they are all in immediate peril of gun violence. The strategy may involve exaggerating the rate of gun accidents. Or it may attempt to place Americans in fear of gun crime. For example, *Fortune* magazine touts handgun prohibition while warning its wealthy readership that the recent rise in youth homicide puts all Americans at imminent risk, for "this onslaught of childhood violence knows no boundaries of race, geography, or class."[128] *JAMA* insists "It's not limited to the inner city."[129]

On the contrary, the problem of homicide is very heavily concentrated among black males, particularly inner-city black males aged sixteen to nineteen, as will be detailed below. That fact, of course, is no reason to be less concerned about the youth homicide problem. Since many problems, including violence, suffered by the urban black community are the long-term result of governmental and societal racism, the moral obligation for all Americans to respond to the crisis is all the greater. Moreover, as the concluding chapter of this volume will detail, many of the problems that have afflicted the black community for the last three decades are spreading to other segments of society; unless we accurately identify and treat the causes of the homicide epidemic for black inner-city youth, that epidemic will in future decades infect the rest of society. Even if white America were not next in line for the crime wave that has swamped inner-city minorities, for America to ignore the teenage murder problem merely because most murders happen in the inner city would be callous and immoral. To respond effectively to the crisis, we must attempt to understand its nature, and not be misled by the efforts of some gun-prohibition advocates to distract attention from the most important factor in any homicide: the killer.

Following the public health model of "treating violence as a disease," the logical approach is to investigate who is suffering most from the disease, and then to identify what factors distinguish that suffering population from the rest of the population. Unfortunately, this investigation is deliberately impeded by certain segments of the public health community, which attempt to conceal how heavily the youth homicide problem is concentrated in inner-city minorities. For example, a 1994 report on youth homicide by the CDC actually refused to release data specifying white and black homicide rates. The CDC defended its refusal to disclose race-related data by stating that youth homicide "is a national problem with the same trends for whites and blacks and the curve looks the same."[130] If urban blacks suffered from an actual disease (such as AIDS) at a rate nine times greater than whites, it is doubtful that many black leaders would tolerate the suppression of that fact by the CDC. Indeed, the CDC officials responsible for concealing the data would be denounced as racists and their job termination would be demanded. Nor would CDC officials escape censure by claiming that the curve is "the same" for both races. If whites suffered from a disease at the rate of 1 percent, and the infection rate doubled to 2 percent, and if blacks suffered from the same disease at a rate of 9 percent, which then doubled to 18 percent, "the curve" would look the same, but blacks would still be suffering nine times as much. Therefore, any sane epidemiologist would start looking for factors that made blacks so highly vulnerable to the disease. But apparently when the suppression of health data serves the politically correct goal of gun control, suppressing important data is all right. Table 6.2 illustrates what the CDC does not want to discuss: historical homicide rates for teenagers stratified by age, race, and gender.

Moreover, if it is all right to combine black and white statistics because homicide is a "national problem" (so that whites will not ignore it), why not combine male and female statistics, so that females will not think that homicide is

Table 6.2

Historical Homicide Rates for Teenagers

	Age 10–13				Age 14–17			
	Male		Female		Male		Female	
	White	Black	White	Black	White	Black	White	Black
1976	0.6	2.7	0.1	0.9	7.6	47.3	0.9	7.2
1977	0.8	2.5	0.1	0.5	7.8	44.1	0.9	4.3
1978	0.8	2.8	0.1	0.4	7.9	44.3	0.9	5.8
1979	0.7	2.8	0.1	0.9	9.5	47.7	0.9	5.9
1980	0.7	3.2	0.1	0.6	9.4	49.4	0.7	5.1
1981	0.8	1.9	0.1	0.4	8.2	51.2	0.9	5.8
1982	0.6	2.2	0.1	0.6	8.2	44.6	0.9	4.5
1983	0.6	1.8	0.1	0.4	7.9	37.0	1.1	5.3
1984	0.7	1.5	0.1	0.5	7.0	32.0	0.9	4.4
1985	0.8	2.5	0.1	0.8	7.2	43.6	0.7	4.7
1986	0.8	2.0	0.1	0.2	9.3	49.8	0.9	4.3
1987	0.7	2.3	0.1	0.6	7.6	50.4	1.0	4.7
1988	0.7	2.8	0.1	0.7	9.3	65.8	0.7	4.7
1989	1.0	3.5	0.0	0.7	10.9	78.1	0.7	4.9
1990	0.8	2.5	0.1	0.3	13.2	102.5	1.0	5.1
1991	0.5	4.3	0.1	0.8	13.6	111.8	0.8	7.0
1992	0.6	3.3	0.2	0.5	14.0	119.0	1.0	7.3

Rate per 100,000.
Source: Bureau of Justice Statistics, *Sourcebook of Criminal Justice Statistics—1993* (Washington, D.C.: Department of Justice, 1994), p. 386.

someone else's problem? Why not combine homicide statistics for all age groups, so that older people will not ignore a problem that is heavily concentrated in the younger population? The reason not to combine the race, gender, and age statistics is, of course, that combining the data conceals where the problem is worst, thereby impeding research and analysis about how to make the problem better. But the CDC's foremost solution is to take away as many guns as possible from as many people as possible, regardless of whether those people belong to high-risk homicide groups. Thus, the CDC has apparently decided that the American people cannot handle too much knowledge about the details of the homicide problem.

A second, more common tactic in diverting attention from the minority homicide crisis is to report the data accurately but to ignore its implications. For example, the famous comparative study of homicide in Seattle and Vancouver, already discussed in chapter 5, did supply homicide figures broken down by race. The emphasis of the report, as restated before Congress by Dr. Katherine Christoffel of the American Academy of Pediatrics Congress, was that, "A resident of Seattle is five times likelier to be murdered with a handgun than is a resident of Vancouver, just 140 miles to the north."[131] Actually, the report's data show that a white resident of Seattle is at no greater risk of gun violence than a white resident of Vancouver, despite Vancouver's more restrictive gun laws. A black or Hispanic resident of Seattle, however, faces a much higher risk of gun violence.[132] (There are few blacks or Hispanics in Vancouver.) Conflating the information about various racial groups produces the erroneous impression of a widespread serious problem with gun crime rather than of a disastrous problem with gun crime among racial minorities.

Also distracting attention from the inner-city youth crisis are unscientific factoids which create the image of a youth crisis much broader than it actually is. Next to the factoid (discussed above) about 135,000 (or 186,000, or 270,000) children carrying a gun to school every day, the most famous youth crime factoids were created by Lou Harris (LH) Research in a poll released in July 1993. The poll reported that among American schoolchildren in grades six through twelve, 15 percent had carried a gun in the last thirty days, 11 percent had been shot at with a gun in the last year, and 9 percent had shot a gun at someone else. The LH survey became one of the central talking points of politicians leading the gun control crusade, including Colorado Governor Roy Romer.[133]

The survey results were, to put it bluntly, preposterous. The CDC's survey of students in grades nine through twelve (as opposed to Harris's six through twelve) had found only 3 percent of this older group carrying a handgun for protection (anywhere, not just at school) in the last thirty days.[134] The National Crime Victimization Survey (NCVS) (conducted by the Bureau of the Census) provides the most thorough national data regarding victimization for all types of violent crimes. If the NCVS data are accurate—and there is no reason to think they are not—the LH figures exaggerate by at least fifty times the number both of youths who have been shot at and of youths who had shot at someone else.[135] Indeed, given the number of gunshot wounds reported annually, the youth of modern America would have to be by far the worst shooters since the invention of gunpowder if a full 9 percent of them had actually shot a gun at someone.

How could the LH poll be so wrong? Part of the problem was the questions posed. The question "During the past thirty days, have you carried a handgun for any purpose, or not?" could include youths who participated in target shooting or helped their parents clean their guns. As to the crime statistics, the LH report did not specify which schools were surveyed, so the students polled may have been concentrated in high-crime schools, rather than being a true national sample. Most importantly, the questionnaire could hardly have been better designed to produce what pollsters call "response-set bias." Before getting to the questions about personal experience with guns and crime, the student respondents were warmed up with twelve questions which made it clear that the pollsters thought that youth firearms crime was an immense national problem. It is well established that for all types of opinion surveys, respondents often attempt to tell surveyors what the respondents think the surveyors want to hear.[136] The Harris student surveys were administered by teachers in a classroom setting, which could not help but amplify the desire of the respondents (the students) to tell the adults what the adults obviously wanted to hear.[137]

In addition to panic-mongering about the particularities of youths and guns, some gun prohibition advocates attempt to inflate public fears about crime in general. Gun-control advocates sometimes convey the impression that current murder rates are dramatically higher than ever before. The homicide rate has stayed at about eight to ten homicides per 100,000 population for the last twenty-five years. For 1993, the rate was 9.5, a figure slightly lower than the all-time high of 10.2 in 1980.[138] (Roughly 7 to 13 percent of American firearms homicides involve legitimate defense against criminal attack.[139])

What the stability in the overall homicide figures conceals is the changing nature of homicide. From 1985 to 1991, arrests of adults for murder declined, but arrests of 17-year-old males for murder rose 121 percent; arrests of 16-year-old males rose 158 percent; arrests of 15-year-old males rose 217 percent; and arrests of boys twelve and under rose 100 percent.[140] In 1984, one out of every fourteen persons arrested for a homicide was a juvenile; in 1991, one out of seven.[141] In 1992, persons under eighteen killed 3,400 people.[142] One-sixth of all persons arrested for rape, robbery, or assault are under eighteen.[143]

To look simply at the category "youth," however, is to miss the real story. The white youth homicide arrest rate has remained relatively low, while the black rate has skyrocketed. The murder arrest rate of whites aged ten to seventeen was the same in 1989 as in 1980 (having dipped in the middle of the decade, and then risen to its former level). But whereas in 1980 the black arrest rate was four times that of whites, by 1989 the black rate had risen to eight times the white rate.[144]

For inner-city black teenagers, the homicide rate has risen to astronomical levels. The huge increase in homicide perpetrated by older urban teenagers has not been replicated in other areas. In the suburbs, small towns, and rural areas, where legal restrictions on guns are generally less severe, the firearms homicide rate has remained relatively low.[145] Just as there is a sharp geographic division in youth homicide statistics, with inner cities being far worse, so is there a sharp racial division, as Table 6.3 indicates.[146]

In some major cities, the disparity is even worse. For example, a study of New York City homicides for the years 1990 and 1991 found that for black males aged fifteen to twenty-four, the homicide rate was 247 (per 100,000). For Hispanic males in the same age group, the rate was 157. For whites, the rate was 16.[147] Research that evaluated changing patterns in Philadelphia homicides in 1985 and 1990 found, "The increase in the absolute number of homicides from 1985 through 1990 in this study was almost exclusively because of a rise in homicides involving young black males."[148]

Another way to understand the enormity of the black homicide crisis is to consider lifetime homicide risks. As of 1989, a white female faced a lifetime 1 in 496 risk of being murdered. (In other words, about 495 of 496 white females

Table 6.3

Youth Homicide Rates according to Demographic Divisions

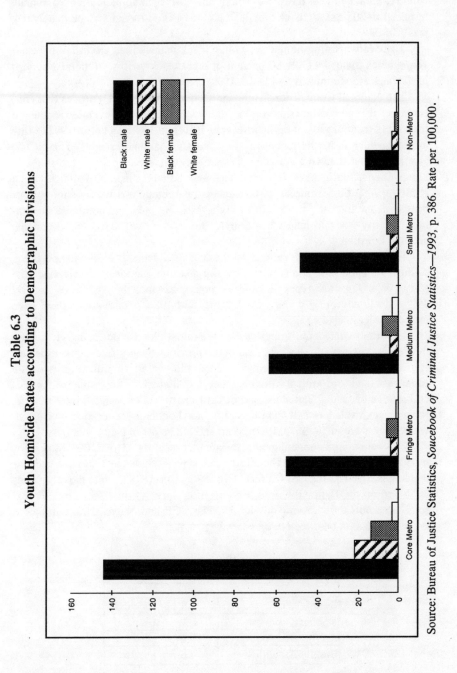

Source: Bureau of Justice Statistics, *Soucebook of Criminal Justice Statistics—1993*, p. 386. Rate per 100,000.

would eventually die as a result of something other than homicide.) A white male faced a 1 in 205 risk. A black female's risk was 1 in 117. And a black male's risk was 1 in 27.[149]

The overwhelming number of young black males killed are killed by other young black males.[150] Over 80 percent of other black youths victimized by violent crimes are victimized by blacks.[151]

The National Council for Crime and Delinquency (NCCD) argues that concern over rising juvenile crime is exaggerated. For example, juveniles accounted for 17.2 percent of violent crime arrests in 1982 and 17.5 percent in 1992, a tiny increase which is hardly evidence of a mounting national crisis.[152] The NCCD also points out that younger offenders are more likely to perpetrate crimes in groups; hence, an increase in arrest rates may be larger than an increase in the crime rates.[153] For example, if six teenagers perpetrate a drive-by shooting, or beat someone to death, there will be six arrests, but only one homicide. In contrast, a thirty-year-old man who strangles his ex-wife will cause one homicide and one arrest.[154]

Exactly how much juvenile crime has changed depends on the period being studied. Juvenile (and adult) crime, by any measure, has risen hugely since the early 1960s. For most types of violent crime, rates since the late 1970s or early 1980s declined for a while (around the mid-1980s), and since then have increased.[155]

All things considered, Americans in the mid-1990s are not being victimized by violent crime at a higher rate than in the previous twenty-five years, especially if they do not live in inner cities. Indeed, the overall victimization rates are somewhat lower for violent offenses other than homicide. According to the federal Bureau of Justice Statistics (part of the Department of Justice), rates of rape, robbery, aggravated assault, simple assault, and homicide are reasonably close to where they were in 1973, some being up and others down (see Table 6.4).

The murder and nonnegligent manslaughter rate was 9.0 per 100,000 persons in 1973, and 9.3 in 1992.[156] (The murder rate is not included in Table 6.4, because that rate is based on the FBI Uniform Crime Reports (UCR), while the other rates are based on the National Crime Victimization Survey, which, for obvious reasons, does not survey homicide victims. The UCR and NCVS data, while both important, cannot be directly compared.[157])

Table 6.4

	1973	1992
Rape	1.0	0.7
Robbery	6.7	5.9
Aggravated Assault	10.1	9.0
Simple Assault	14.8	16.5

The reason that, despite the data, the crime problem might seem suddenly much worse to some people, is that in 1993 the media worked itself into a crime frenzy. According to the Center for Media and Public Affairs, the number of crime stories on the three major networks doubled and the number of murder stories tripled from 1992 to 1993.

Although not necessarily increasing, the violent crime rate remains, as it has been for a quarter century, much too high. Juvenile criminals perpetrate a huge number of violent crimes, and many adult violent criminals started their criminal careers as juveniles. Accordingly, it is appropriate for America to be quite concerned, but not hysterical, about violent juvenile crime. And however one cuts the statistics, there is no denying that teenagers (particularly older black male teenagers in core urban areas) are involved in a shockingly large number of homicides. The crisis of America's rising teenage murder rate is directly linked to the crisis of America's inner-city black youth. Unless the problems of inner cities are addressed, the murder crisis will continue.

Guns and Teenage Homicide

Handguns figure prominently in the rising teenage homicide rate. For example, during the 1980s, the firearms homicide death rate for persons aged fifteen to nineteen rose by 61 percent, while the nonfirearms rate declined 29 percent.[158] In 1987, 64 percent of juvenile homicide perpetrators used a gun, a figure which rose to 78 percent in 1991.[159] Of homicide victims aged fifteen to nineteen, 85 percent were killed with firearms in 1992 (compared to 68 percent of all homicide victims that year).[160] It is true that there are some homicides for which other weapons, or bare hands, could be substituted if guns were not available; the murder of wives by husbands is one example. But for other killings, including those in which teenagers are often perpetrators, if there were no guns, there would be no murder. For example, guns allow the killing to be done at a distance; drive-by homicides are never perpetrated with kitchen knives.

In addition, guns, as "equalizers," overwhelm physical differences between the gun wielder and the target. When a woman defends herself against a male stalker, guns are beneficial equalizers; when a scrawny 16-year-old shoots a larger man during the course of a robbery, guns are harmful equalizers. Thus, if criminal teenagers were deprived of firearms, there would probably be a great deal less homicide.

Firearms are much less of an issue in other violent crimes involving youth. In contrast to youth homicide victims, youth victims of robbery and assault are less likely to have a gun used against them than adults, and most of these crimes do not involve guns anyway.[161]

Most of the "public health" advocates of gun control would agree with the analysis in the paragraphs above. They would conclude that if gun density were reduced, homicide would also be reduced. They do not argue for reducing gun density among (potential) homicide perpetrators; they assert that reducing gun density on a nationwide basis would necessarily lead to a reduction in national homicide. But actually, if there is a statistical relationship between gun density and homicide in the United States, it is often an inverse one. In other words, the regions with the most guns are those with the lowest homicide rates.[162] And while whites have a higher rate of gun ownership than blacks, they have a much lower homicide rate.[163] Time periods in which gun ownership increases heavily are not necessarily periods when homicide rates increase; conversely, periods of increasing homicide are not necessarily times of increasing gun ownership. For example, homicide rates rose in the late 1980s, when firearms purchases were stagnant.[164] Conversely, the homicide rate appeared to level out or decline slightly in 1993–94, a period when the gun industry (thanks to President Clinton's advocacy of gun control and accompanying media histrionics) enjoyed record sales.

The fact that American homicide rates are often lowest among regions and population groups where gun ownership is highest should at least give pause to theorists who insist that gun prohibition or other severe gun controls are the only rational response to rising murder rates. Professor Hans Toch, of the State University of New York's School of Criminology, served in the late 1960s on the Eisenhower Commission, whose purpose was to investigate the causes and cures of American violence. Professor Toch fully endorsed the commission's conclusion that "reducing the availability of the handgun *will* reduce firearms violence" (emphasis in original). But following modern research, Professor Toch has found:

> when used for protection, firearms can seriously inhibit aggression and can provide a psychological buffer against the fear of crime. Furthermore, the fact that national patterns show little violent crime where guns are most dense implies that guns do not elicit aggression in any meaningful way. Quite the contrary, these findings suggest that high saturations of guns in places, or something correlated with that condition, inhibit illegal aggression.[165]

One way in which a high density of guns can, as Toch concludes, be associated with lower levels of violence is that armed citizens successfully resist and deter criminals.[166]

Another, more important factor in the association of high gun ownership rates with low crime rates is that American areas with the highest rate of gun ownership tend to be rural and small-town. In these areas, family structures are relatively strong, and communities are often more stable and unified. Thus, the problem of violence in American inner cities may have less to do with the fact that guns are available there (as they are everywhere else) than with the fact that so many families are dysfunctional, and that so little sense of community can be found.

The public health literature on youth violence endlessly repeats its mantra that rising rates of juvenile gun crime are due to "the increased availability and lethality of firearms."[167] But the assumption that firearms are more available to young people or more lethal is, while intuitively obvious to some people, not necessarily true. American youths have had ready access to deadly weapons from the first day that Indian settlers crossed the Bering Strait. Easy access to firearms has been a constant since white settlers first landed on the Atlantic Coast. Before 1968 (a period when youth gun violence was much lower), there was no federal law (and in most states, no state law) against children buying guns in gun stores. The mid-1990s mark a period when legal restrictions (such as laws banning even parental gifts of handguns to children, and laws requiring that guns in homes with children be secured from the children) related to youth acquisition of guns are at a record high; it is the same period in which youth firearms violence has risen to record highs.

Firearms are hardly more lethal now than in the past. Semi-automatic firearms were invented over a century ago and have been common ever since the introduction of the Colt .45 pistol in 1911. For all the excitement over 9mm semi-automatic pistols (which predate World War I), these pistols remain inferior in stopping power to the venerable Colt. Moreover, as detailed in chapter 5, there has been an important shift in the last fifty years by American gun owners away from rifles and shotguns, and toward handguns, at least for home protection. Rifles and shotguns are much more lethal than handguns, so the most important change in gun-owning patterns has been a trend toward less lethal firearms.

Although legal controls on firearms for adults and juveniles have increased significantly in the last twenty-five years, so has the number of guns, as the previous chapter detailed. Gun density could be said to make guns more available to juveniles, in that more guns owned means more guns available to be stolen. Yet more guns available to be taken surreptitiously by juveniles does not seem like a net increase in "easy access" compared to the pre-1968 ability of juveniles in most states to purchase guns themselves.

Jack McCroskey, a senior fellow at the Independence Institute in Golden, Colorado, points out the one way in which "easy access" to firearms among youths really has increased. Young people today, even those in very poor areas, are much wealthier than their counterparts in previous generations. An average teenager today can probably afford a low-quality handgun (even if he has to buy the handgun on the black market instead of in a gun store), whereas a teenager in the 1930s would have had a harder time finding enough money for a gun, even if he could buy it readily in a hardware store. Although I am not aware of any study of gun price levels, cursory analysis of gun prices compared to wage levels shows that guns (like many other consumer goods) have become much more affordable over the last six decades. In other words, the only meaningful way in which "easy access" to guns by youth has increased is as a byproduct of the growth of the American economy. Rising adolescent affluence also helps explain the increase in low-plot, high-violence movies, as the age of the average moviegoer has shifted downward significantly since the 1930s.[168]

Whatever may be said about rates of gun ownership in America, it is obvious that the United States has more guns, and more gun murders, than other industrial democracies. As a widely reported study by the CDC noted, the American murder rate for teenagers is much higher than that in most industrial countries, where gun-control laws are generally stricter. The CDC researchers therefore concluded that the United States needs tougher gun laws.[169]

While the authors of the study did an excellent job of compiling data (as they have done on other studies), their conclusion that the international data proved that America's gun laws were the cause of its high teenage homicide rate was perhaps overstated. For example, England has harsh gun laws and a lower homicide rate than the U.S., but the historical evidence seems to show no cause and effect between British gun controls and homicide. The lowest rates of violent crime and homicide in England did not occur in the period with the strongest gun laws (the late 1980s and 1990s), but in the era with the weakest gun laws. At the turn of the twentieth century, there was virtually no violent crime in England, and virtually no gun control. Anyone (children included) could buy any type of gun, no questions asked. There were no background checks, no forms to fill out, and no safety training. All that was needed was ready cash. Yet gun homicide and other crime was tiny compared to current British rates. At the turn of the century, Victorian morality was strong; it was a more effective check on British criminal impulses than are the rigid gun laws of today.[170]

Overall, comparative data show little relation between the severity of gun laws and the homicide rate. Scotland has rigorous gun laws, and its murder rate for males aged fifteen to twenty-four is over three times as high as the rate in Switzerland.[171] In Switzerland, the government issues every adult male a fully automatic SIG assault rifle to keep at home and trains him to use it.[172] Switzerland, much more than Scotland, still retains the strong families and shared code of behavior similar to that in Great Britain at the turn of the century.

By looking only at firearms, the CDC study did not consider other factors which might explain why American males aged fifteen to twenty-four are so much more likely to kill each other than their counterparts in other nations. Among possible reasons (some more of which are discussed in the concluding chapter), America is the only country studied that has a three-and-a-half-century history of enslaving and degrading a major part of its population. And America is the Western democracy where demand for drugs is sky-high, and the only such democracy with an all-out drug war.

Drug Policy

The 1986 cocaine overdose death of college basketball star Len Bias and the popularization of crack cocaine in many major cities produced an unprecedented media and political determination to fight a "drug war" in the United States. In the following two years, the young black male homicide rate rose 71 percent.[173]

Some drug policy scholars trace the sudden upsurge in violence to the pharmacological effects of crack cocaine. They note that crack (like PCP and alcohol, but unlike hemp and heroin) often reduces inhibitions against violence and stimulates aggression, paranoia, and irritability, all of which can make cocaine abusers more likely to perpetrate a violent crime, or to provoke someone else to commit a crime against them.

Without denying the destructive effect of crack, other scholars trace the roots of the violence to governmental drug policy. They note that the "war on drugs" has lived up to its name by producing a genuine war in inner-city America. Economist Sam Staley argues that the war on drugs and the criminalization of the drug trade generate levels of violence that make the inner city unlivable, with levels of violence far higher than would occur in a world where drugs were controlled by means other than the criminal law.[174]

Since drug dealers are likely to carry large sums of money, they are at serious risk of robbery. Since they cannot rely on the police for protection, they must, to survive, protect themselves. When drug dealers engage in commercial transactions with each other, there is no Uniform Commercial Code and state district court for resolving disputes about the quality of goods sold. Disgruntled buyers, having no other means of redress, may resort to violence. Similarly, the addicts who sell drugs often consume the drugs that should have been sold; higher-level dealers having no legal means of handling salespersons who steal the merchandise with which they are entrusted, violence again results. Other drug users buy goods on credit but fail to pay their debt. Since the seller has no lawful means of debt collection, violence again may result. In addition, when disputes are settled violently, it is often done in the most vicious manner possible. Acquiring a reputation for being willing to "exert maximum force" may assist the resolution of future disputes.[175]

The surge in violence following the intensification of the drug war is consistent with the hypothesis that conflicts related to the drug trade result in violence. Experienced, older drug dealers with stable territories were removed (and imprisoned); they were replaced by younger, brasher dealers who took advantage of new opportunities for profit, but who lacked stable, reliable organizations for supply and distribution.[176] Professor Paul Goldstein's study of 218 homicides in New York City classified as drug-related found that twenty-one were caused by the pharmacological effect of alcohol and five by the effect of crack; the rest resulted from the turf wars, robberies, and other violence engendered by drug prohibition, just as alcohol prohibition caused violence in a previous era.[177]

While there are many reasons teenagers join gangs, the lure of income from the drug trade is certainly an important factor. If currently illegal drugs were sold in liquor stores, gangs would no longer be able to profit from selling substances at the artificially high prices created by prohibition laws.

On the other hand, even if drug laws may have helped ignite a new cycle of violence, repealing the drug laws would not necessarily end the cycle. Teenagers recruited by crack dealers may have been the first teenagers in their neighborhoods to carry handguns. But the teenage drug operatives have been imitated by many other teenagers. If the teenage drug dealers went out of business as a result of drug relegalization, the practice of carrying weapons might remain, having become an established part of a dysfunctional culture.

Despite the youth violence engendered by drug prohibition, it may be that prohibition yields benefits that outweigh its negative effects. For example, drug laws could (as alcohol prohibition did) result in a net saving of lives, if the reduction in fatalities due to drug abuse were larger than the increase in fatalities due to drug laws.[178] Any realistic analysis of American drug policy should, however, acknowledge the substantial toll of violence that is a, perhaps necessary, price that America is paying for current laws.

Homicide Perpetrators and Victims

Almost any time a young child is murdered with a gun, or dies in a gun accident, the event is widely publicized.[179] But it is not correct to assume that the amount of press coverage devoted to any event correlates with the frequency of that event.[180] Coverage of professional football games saturates many cities' media, but in an average year in most cities, fewer than a dozen professional football games are played.

Homicides account for about 5 percent of the deaths of children ages one to four, and 4 percent of deaths of children ages five to fourteen. The number is about the same as that of children in those age groups who die of heart disease.[181]

The relatively small fraction of homicides perpetrated against children is not likely to be solved through gun control. The most common form of homicide against younger children is child abuse murder by a relative or caretaker.[182] The availability of firearms has little to do with such crimes, since the murderer will generally have limitless opportunity and vastly superior strength.[183] (Reduced availability of firearms might, however, reduce the number of teenagers who shoot parents or stepparents, sometimes in response to abuse.[184])

For older teenagers (fifteen and up), the number of firearms murders is much higher, especially for urban minority teenagers. Of the sharp increase in homicides by teenagers during the last decade, a very large share is due to homicides perpetrated with a handgun; handguns were the weapon in 37 percent of juvenile homicides in 1984 and 61 percent in 1991.[185] Under what circumstances do those teenage handgun murders take place? The American Academy of Pediatrics writes: "A common misperception is that teen homicides are largely related to crime, gang activity, or premeditated assault. The most common event precipitating a shooting is an argument, often over something later seen as trivial. Such shootings are usually impulsive, unplanned, and instantly regretted."[186]

The AAP's assertion about the noncriminal nature of teenage homicide cited only one study as support. That study, however, did not claim that teenage homicides did not involve "crime, gang activity, or premeditated assault." Nor did it claim that teenage shootings were "impulsive, unplanned, and instantly regretted." The cited study only discussed the relationship between murderer and victim, and showed, not surprisingly, that murderers generally target people who have offended them rather than total strangers.[187]

A *Philadelphia Inquirer* investigation of teenage murderers in Philadelphia casts some doubt on the proposition that homicides are "instantly regretted." Of the fifty-seven teenage murders studied, "With few exceptions, the teenagers felt little remorse or regret." More typical were stories such as these:

- Yerodeen Williams, seventeen, killed a man who resisted a robbery at an automatic teller machine. "He brung it on himself," Williams mused, blaming the victim for not submitting. "It must have been his time to go . . . I feel as though it wasn't my fault this thing happened. I ain't seen no blood or nothing."
- Kerry Marshall, seventeen, attempted to rob a woman and her 4-year-old son. When the victim pulled out a gun of her own, he shot her dead. "I know the values," he said, blaming the victim for her death. "If somebody was threatening me, I'd give it up 'cause material things come and go." Marshall complained about his long sentence, because "I don't even think of myself as a criminal. . . . Everybody is vulnerable for mistakes. Mistakes will happen."
- Richard Carabello, seventeen, took a taxi ride, but had no money to pay for it. When the driver grew angry, Carabello killed him. "I'm not a violent person," Carabello explained, "I didn't kill nobody. He killed himself."
- Kenyatta Miles, eighteen, shot a 15-year-old honor student and took his new designer sneakers. "I killed him, but not in cold blood," Miles said. "I didn't shoot him two, three, four times. I shoot him once. . . . I wouldn't call myself no murderer . . . I'm not violent. I'm the easiest person to get along with . . . I'm not really a violent person . . . I look at my right hand 'cause it pulled the trigger. I blame my right hand."
- Daniel Maurice White, sixteen, shot a stranger in a crack house who was resisting a robbery. Again, the victim was to blame: "If somebody see you with a gun, they gonna turn the other way—if not, they must want to get shot. . . . It's not like I'm no serial killer. I didn't kill a lot of people."[188]

It is not implausible that the older teenagers who commit murder share many characteristics with murderers over eighteen. The studies of adult murderers have shown that they are not "nice" people who happened to get too emotional in the presence of a handgun. Rather, murderers are generally people with long records of criminal violence. Two-thirds to four-fifths of homicide offenders have prior arrest records, frequently for violent felonies.[189] A study by the Police Foundation of domestic homicides in Kansas City in 1977 revealed that in 85 percent of homicides among family members, the police had been called in before to break up violence.[190] In half the cases, the police had been called in five or more times. Thus, the average murderer is not a nonviolent solid citizen who reaches for a weapon in a moment of temporary insanity. Instead, he has a past record of criminal violence. Such people on the fringes of society are unlikely to be affected by gun-control laws.

It has long been recognized by criminologists that many murder victims, since they are friends, relatives, and "business" acquaintances of murderers, are themselves unsavory characters and frequently criminals. For example, in a study of the victims of near-fatal domestic shootings and stabbings, 78 percent of the victims volunteered a history of hard-drug use, and 16 percent admitted using heroin the day of the incident.[191] Researchers in Philadelphia determined that 84 percent of murder victims in 1990 (up from 66 percent in 1985) had "engaged in criminal activity or intoxicant use before their deaths."[192] A University of North Carolina study of persons shot in Charlotte found that 64 percent had a criminal conviction (usually a misdemeanor), and 71 percent had an arrest record. The 387 victims with an arrest record had accumulated a collective total of 4,334 arrests and 801 felony convictions.[193]

Studies of trauma center patients with penetrating (bullet or knife) wounds have found that over a third of such patients are repeat users of trauma centers.[194] A study in Detroit followed the histories of persons admitted to a Level I trauma center; over the next five years, 44 percent suffered recurrent trauma, and 20 percent died.[195] Surveys of trauma center physicians show that many have negative feelings toward the practice as a result of the "unsavory" patients who are the victims of most penetrating injuries. Many physicians believe these patients are repeatedly injured because they repeatedly engage in criminal behavior.[196] A Baltimore journalist who investigated his city's emergency rooms concluded that most assault victims "who arrive at a Baltimore hospital are in some way culpable in the violence that has incapacitated them."[197] According to a surgeon at San Francisco General Hospital, eight of ten gunshot victims return for treatment for another gunshot wound within three and a half years.[198]

The pattern for teenage homicides and other violent crimes is similar. The persons most likely to be killed by a teenager with a gun are gang members, gang hangers-on, and other teenage criminals.[199] In many killings of inner-city high school-age persons, the victim is someone who engaged in risky behaviors, such as selling drugs.[200] A study of teenage gunshot victims in New York City found that 40 percent were shot during hours when they legally should have been in school.[201] Of the children and adolescents injured in drive-by shootings in Los Angeles, 71 percent are "documented members of street gangs."[202] An in-depth study of juvenile delinquents in Philadelphia found that juvenile victims of violent crimes were often perpetrators of such crimes as well.[203]

Although one teenage gang member killing another may account for a significant fraction of teenage homicides, there are many other victims of these criminals who have done nothing to put themselves at risk, except to be born in a dangerous neighborhood. And, of course, the mere fact that a murder victim was convicted of a misdemeanor four years ago, or was walking around downtown one night while drunk or under the influence of cocaine, is hardly proof that he deserved to die.

While there are many innocent victims, there are not many innocent murderers. Although the AAP asserts that most teenage murders are "instantly regretted," in reality, the majority of teenage killers seem to have no remorse for actions, and are unhappy only because they were caught.[204] In Harlem, for example, murderous teenagers coldly refer to killing as "getting a body."[205]

If murderers—teenage and adult—are just ordinary people unlucky enough to be near a gun, then the simple solution to homicide is to remove guns from society. In a culture with an appallingly high level of homicide, such a simple solution may sound attractive. But if murderers are indeed different from most other people, then America faces the much more difficult task of dealing with the social pathologies that turn people into murderers in the first place.

Social Decay

The authors of the most extensive study of the gun-carrying habits of modern juvenile felons found them to be

> better armed, more criminally active, and more violent than were the adult felons of a decade ago. Even at that, one is struck less by the armament than by the evident willingness to pull the trigger.
>
> From the viewpoint of public policy, it matters less, perhaps, where these juveniles get their guns than where they get the idea that it is acceptable to kill. It may be convenient to think that the problems of juvenile violence could be magically solved by cracking down or getting tough, but this is unlikely. The problem before us is not so much getting guns out of the hands of juveniles as it is reducing the motivations for juveniles to arm themselves in the first place. Convincing inner-city juveniles, or adults, not to own, carry, and use guns requires convincing them that they can survive in their neighborhoods without being armed . . . that the customary agents of social control can be relied upon to provide for personal security. So long as this is not believed to be the case, gun ownership and carrying in the city will remain widespread.[206]

To the enormous crisis of the inner city, many liberals and conservatives offer the same, seemingly easy solution: use government coercion to remove the evil item that is the cause of violence. Many liberals look to guns as the cause of the inner city's social pathologies; they fail to recognize that the willingness of many criminals to use guns, and the necessity for law-abiding residents of the inner city to carry guns for protection, are symptoms of deeper afflictions. No set of criminal justice approaches focused on gun control is likely to reduce the inner-city problems regarding firearms. Solutions must be found to the lack of hope and economic opportunity, and the decay of cultural values.

At the same time, some conservatives make the same mistake with gangs and drugs that liberals make with guns. Some inner-city youth are attracted to gangs because the gangs "give estranged youth something meaningful to which they can belong, an identity otherwise lacking. Gangs express the pathology of inner-city life and the new urban culture of violence, but are the consequences of these developments, not the cause."[207] The criminal justice system can continue to incarcerate gang members, but gangs will remain attractive until better alternatives for identity appear.

The many youthful lives wasted through drug abuse are tragic. But if there were no narcotics, these lives would be wasted through alcohol abuse or some other method of numbing the mind to the bleakness of ordinary life. A century of sternly enforced drug prohibition has resulted in drugs being more available than ever to inner-city youth. This fact should offer a caution to liberals who imagine that gun laws can succeed where drug laws have failed, and somehow keep a commodity away from a market that demands it.[208] And the fact should suggest to conservatives that a better strategy to reducing drug abuse should be to offer inner-city youth a future brighter than the false consciousness offered by crack dealers.

As long as the debate over the decay of inner-city America focuses only on symptoms—guns, gangs, and drugs—there will never be a solution. As Wright and Sheley put it:

> [U]ntil we rectify the conditions that breed hostility, estrangement, futility and hopelessness, whatever else we do will come to little or nothing. . . . Widespread joblessness and few opportunities for upward mobility are the heart of the problem. Stricter gun-control laws, more aggressive enforcement of existing laws, a crackdown on drug traffic, police task forces aimed at juvenile gangs, metal detectors at the doors of schools, periodic searches of lockers and shakedowns of students, and other similar measures are inconsequential compared to the true need: the economic, social, and moral resurrection of the inner city. Just how this might be accomplished and at what cost can be debated; the urgent need to do so cannot.[209]

Or as Yephet Copeland, a former member of the Hoover Street Crips in Los Angeles, put it, "We need better schools and jobs. That's the way you stop the killing. You have to offer hope. If there's no hope, the killing will go on—gun ban or not."[210]

How to resurrect the inner city? Do we need massive government jobs programs or urban enterprise zones? Should we increase funding for government schools, or should we (as discussed above) end-run the failed government school bureaucracy through charter schools and education vouchers? Are welfare payments insufficiently generous, or is welfare itself a cause of learned helplessness? (The concluding chapter discusses this issue.) All these difficult questions must begin to come to the center of the public debate on the inner city and the disastrous condition of so many of its youth.

Every day that the public allows legislatures to waste their collective breath on symbolic laws that merely address the symptoms of social pathology—such as laws forbidding the wearing of Los Angeles Raiders clothing or gun waiting periods that will supposedly disarm teenagers who are already forbidden to buy guns—is another day lost, another in which the problem grows worse. Gun control is not merely a phony solution to inner-city youth violence. It is a formidable political obstacle to genuine solutions, because gun control offers political officials a high-profile but empty way to tell the public that the legislature is "doing something." Every gun-control bill that is introduced, and every editorial demanding that we "do something about guns," makes it that much harder to force the political system to do something real about the desperate conditions of the inner city, to address the fundamental social pathologies of modern America. Criminologist Gary Kleck summarizes:

> Fixating on guns seems to be, for many people, a fetish which allows them to ignore the more intransigent causes of American violence, including its dying cities, inequality, deteriorating family structure, and the all-pervasive economic and social consequences of a history of slavery and racism. And just as gun control serves this purpose for liberals, equally useless "get tough" proposals, like longer prison terms, mandatory sentencing (e.g., "three strikes and you're out" proposals), and more use of the death penalty serve the purpose for conservatives. All parties to the crime debate would do well to give more concentrated attention to more difficult, but far more relevant, issues like how to generate more good-paying jobs for the underclass, an issue which is at the heart of the violence problem.[211]

There are more than enough guns in the United States to supply a black-market weapon to anyone who wants one, no matter how severely prohibition and confiscation are enforced. William Fox, a former member of the Brawling Street Rolling Crips, observed, "How are you going to get the guns off the street that are already there? No. It ain't going to change. It's not the guns that have to change. It's the people that have to change." It is long past time to stop fixating on the gun supply, and to start dealing with the persons who misuse guns as well as the social conditions under which innocent babies grow in less than two decades into callous murderers.

EFFECTIVE JUVENILE JUSTICE

Improvements in the criminal justice system are sometimes derided as too narrowly focused. Better prevention, not punishment, is said to be what is needed. The prevention-versus-punishment argument is akin to debating which blade of the scissors is more important; punishment and prevention are both necessary.

However important prevention is (and I think it is very important), it cannot replace the need to reduce the current supply of violent teenage criminals. By analogy, if one's basement is flooded, the desirability of building a dam next month does not obviate the necessity to bail the water out of the basement today. Moreover, prisons and other detention facilities are one form of prevention, because they incapacitate criminals and may deter others.

More Funding for Juvenile Justice

America's juvenile courts should be the best-run part of the judicial system, but instead they are among the worst. Juvenile judges too often do not have time to learn about a case in depth. More spending on the juvenile justice system might save public revenue in the long run, through reduced costs in adult criminals courts and reduced need for incarceration. While I would support increased taxes to improve the juvenile justice system, many other people oppose increased taxes under any circumstances. One way to increase juvenile justice funding without raising taxes would be to reprogram other crime spending. If 10 percent of current criminal justice expenditures on drug control (about sixteen billion dollars annually as of 1991[212]) were redirected towards juvenile justice, the taxpaying public might get a much bigger bang for its buck. Losing 10 percent of funding would simply require that drug enforcement target fewer small-scale offenders, while the increased funds would allow a substantial increase in juvenile enforcement.[213]

Open Court Records

Both the states and the federal government already have extremely tough laws for sentencing repeat violent offenders. Unfortunately, many criminals who, in their early twenties, are facing their third or fourth felony conviction are treated as first-time offenders because their previous felonies were committed while they were juveniles. Changing the repeat offender laws so that violent, armed felonies committed by juveniles would be counted toward habitual criminal status for adult offenders is a sensible approach toward concentrating criminal justice resources on the thugs who have shown a repeated willingness to commit violent crimes.[214]

In addition, juvenile records involving violent felonies should be disclosed to school administrators when the juvenile enrolls at a school. The privacy interests of the juvenile criminal are outweighed by the rights of teachers and other school personnel to know whom they are dealing with.

Restitution

One of the most shocking attributes of the new generation of criminals is their lack of human empathy for anyone else, including their victims. While the overcrowded condition of most juvenile facilities makes it impossible to incarcerate all juvenile offenders who should be imprisoned, a minimum step in the resolution of any juvenile criminal case should be mandatory restitution to the victim or the victim's family. Mandatory restitution is becoming increasingly common in juvenile boot camp or probation programs. It is obviously more appropriate for property crimes than for violent crimes; a criminal can pay back the value of a stolen car stereo, but he cannot restore the value of a lost life or a disabling injury.

Intensive Aftercare Probation

Intensive probation programs, increasingly popular for both juveniles and adults, put the probationer under the supervision of a probation officer who has a much smaller caseload than the typical probation officer. While ordinary probation officers usually depend on probationers to attend scheduled meetings, intensive probation officers will leave the office to check on probationers on nights and weekends. Boot camp programs often put their graduates under intensive supervised probation or parole following completion of the camp phase.

Partly because intensive probation participants are watched so much more carefully than ordinary probationers or parolees, detection of violations of probation/parole conditions is common. A Philadelphia study of juveniles placed in an "Intensive Aftercare Probation" (IAP) program found that, while the percentage of juveniles who committed a crime during probation was similar to the rate in standard juvenile probation programs, the total number of offenses was lower. The probation officers believed that because they had a significantly lower caseload than did probation officers in standard programs, the IAP officers could stay on top of juveniles who might otherwise have slipped through the cracks in the system. In addition, the IAP officers, because of their familiarity with their smaller caseload, were able to recommend swift parole revocation in appropriate cases.[215]

In another experiment, the Violent Juvenile Offender Program, close supervision of juveniles after their release from confinement led to a much lower violent crime rate in the period following release. Rutgers University criminologist Jeffrey Fagan, in evaluating the program, pointed out that unless a juvenile is sentenced to life in prison, he will eventually be released into the community. Accordingly, putting more resources into programs which foster successful reintegration might be more effective than extending the length of confinement but then providing few resources to supervise juvenile offenders upon release.[216]

Increased Certainty and Severity of Punishment

In Arizona, the average juvenile offender has nine encounters with the criminal justice system before he finally ends up doing time in a penal facility. A Philadelphia study found that nearly half of juvenile offenders who had been been convicted of four serious crimes had not even received a sanction as severe as probation.[217] A juvenile justice system that lets repeat offenders slip away again and again is worse than useless; by teaching young offenders that there will be no consequences for crime, an ineffective justice system reinforces criminal behavior. Thus, for most juvenile offenses, the issue is not necessarily increasing the severity of punishment but rather making sure that some kind of punishment is imposed.

It is true that deterrence may be of little value for some teenage criminals, since they may have no long-term perspective on their own life. At the same time, the incarceration of violent teenage criminals can still benefit society by incapacitating a person who would likely commit more violent crimes if left to roam at large.

While American prison capacity has more than doubled since 1980, there has not been a corresponding drop in crime. Much of this new prison space has been taken up by prisoners of the war on drugs. As a result, the levels of punishment for violent crimes have fallen to record lows.[218] Multiplying the risk of apprehension by the average sentence served upon conviction, Texas A&M economist Morgan Reynolds finds that the average 1990 murderer served 1.8 years in prison. The expected punishment for murder fell by 20 percent from 1988 to 1990. Similarly the expected punishment for rape (sixty days in prison) fell by 25 percent in just two years; expected punishment for robbery fell by 50 percent (to a mere twenty-three days). Expected punishment for motor vehicle theft is only 1.5 days in prison. From 1950 to 1990, the expected punishment for all serious crimes, taken as a whole, fell by 65 percent. Simply put, crime pays.[219]

Though inner-city teenagers may not have calculated the mathematical risks of arrest, they are well aware of how minimal punishments are for even the most serious armed, violent offenses.[220] They cannot help but infer that society does not really take violent crime seriously.

Politicians tend to look at correctional budgets, for both adults and juveniles, the same way they used to look at defense budgets: conservative hawks want more and liberal doves want less; as each side argues about "how much," they ignore the primary question of "what?" Namely, what kind of incarceration (or military) should we buy? Instead of talking only about the size of the budget, or the number of people incarcerated, we should be thinking more about exactly whom we are incarcerating. In situations where incarceration adds little to public safety (such as jailing small-time drug dealers, who are quickly replaced), we should put fewer resources into such incarceration. The savings should be deployed in ways that will maximize the gain in public safety (such as imprisoning offenders who have been convicted a second time of child sexual abuse, since the recidivism rate for this crime is very high, and since locking up one child abuser does not open up market opportunities for another). Criminologist Richard Kern suggests that one intelligent target for correctional resources is violent offenders aged eighteen to twenty-one. Persons in this group who are incarcerated for three years or more have a significantly lower recidivism rate than do others in the same group who are incarcerated for shorter periods. In contrast, increased severity of punishment appears to have no effect on post-release recidivism for older offenders.[221]

The deinstitutionalization of juvenile offenders is sometimes promoted by a coalition of antipunishment liberals and antispending conservatives, since institutional confinement is so expensive. Some research, however, suggests that deinstitutionalization results in a significantly higher recidivism rate, including for violent offenses.[222] Accordingly, deinstitutionalization should be approached cautiously, unless there are high-quality alternatives available for the deinstitutionalized juveniles. The high-quality alternatives, of course, are usually expensive.

Imposing the death penalty for murders perpetrated by juveniles is a hotly controversial topic. The U.S. Supreme Court has ruled that, at least in some circumstances, inflicting the death penalty for homicides perpetrated by persons under eighteen is not unconstitutional.[223] While the death penalty remains a favorite topic of first-year law school classes, newspaper opinion writers, and legislators, it attracts attention primarily for the moral issues it raises, not its criminological importance. In late twentieth-century America, it is difficult to imagine even the most conservative state executing more than a small handful of juvenile homicide perpetrators every year. At such a low rate of executions per homicide, it seems unlikely that the death penalty for juveniles would have much of a deterrent effect, especially when so many juvenile murderers do not expect to celebrate their twenty-fifth birthday in the first place.

Incarceration options other than traditional prisons have always played a major role in juvenile justice, and should continue to do. Happily, innovative residential programs are constantly being created. While legislators should experiment freely with these new programs, they should also keep an eye on how well the programs actually work. Almost every state legislature has started some kind of boot camp program for young adult offenders (and sometimes for juveniles), although the data suggest that the recidivism rate of boot camp graduates is comparable to that of juvenile offenders not sent to boot camp.[224] Expensive ranch-type residential programs for juvenile delinquents, such as the Arizona Boys Ranch, are used by many states, although there has been little research regarding their effectiveness.[225]

Whatever types of facilities are selected for violent youths, confining a relatively small number of the worst delinquents can have a major impact on public safety. An Orange County report found that 8 percent of juvenile delinquents in the county committed over half of all repeat offenses; a study in Los Angeles County found 16 percent of delinquents perpetrating 67 percent of repeat offenses.[226] Other studies have found that a small percentage of boys perpetrate about half of all juvenile crime, and, when they become adults, a large fraction of adult violent crimes.[227] Although the cost of confining chronic juvenile offenders is high ($44,000 per year in Orange County), the cost may be more than recovered through reduced crime victim suffering and property losses.[228]

Trying Juveniles as Adults

One of the most commonly suggested solutions to juvenile crime is to allow juveniles to be tried in adult courts. This is known as a "waiver," since the juvenile is waived out of the juvenile system.[229] From 1985 to 1989, the number of waivers increased 78 percent.[230] The number of juveniles admitted annually to adult prisons increased thirty percent from 1984 to 1990, reaching 11,782.[231] Even when waived to the adult system, juveniles are generally required to be segregated from adult prisoners.

Apparently not content with current trends, President Clinton's 1994 crime bill allows the adult trial and execution of persons as young as thirteen. Minnesota creates a special category of "extended-jurisdiction juveniles." Certain serious juvenile offenders are given a dual juvenile and adult sentence; if they fail to abide by the terms of the juvenile sentence (such as obeying various probation conditions), the adult sentence (usually jail or prison) is automatically imposed.[232] Georgia imposes ten-year adult mandatory minimums on all persons over the age of thirteen who perpetrate one of seven violent offenses, including robbery with a firearm.[233]

Moving some of the most violent, dangerous juvenile criminals into the adult court system makes sense in certain cases, because it allows the violent criminal to be incarcerated long after he has reached his eighteenth or twenty-first birthday. Under the juvenile system, most offenders are automatically released when they obtain legal (if not emotional) adulthood. An unrepentant, defiant 16-year-old who commits multiple rapes and murders should probably be kept off the streets for decades, rather than until he turns eighteen.[234]

The juvenile court paradigm of *parens patriae* sets up the court as a surrogate parent for the delinquent; in theory, the juvenile court aims to rehabilitate, rather than punish the offender. The rehabilitative approach may make sense for many juveniles, but it may not for some high-rate violent offenders; these offenders have shown themselves to be uniquely resistant to normal rehabilitation programs.[235]

Similar to other facets of the criminal justice system, waiver appears to have made drug law enforcement a higher priority than violent crime enforcement. A survey by the federal Office of Juvenile Justice and Delinquency Prevention found that in 1992, 3.1 percent of juvenile drug cases were waived, compared to 2.4 percent of personal offenses and 1.3 percent of property offenses.[236]

Referral of a juvenile case to adult court should be up to the judge, not the prosecutor. Some juveniles who have perpetrated awful violent crimes can still be reached and rehabilitated through the juvenile system. Even for murder, waiver should not be automatic; a 15-year-old girl who shoots her stepfather to stop his violent sexual abuse is different from a 15-year-old boy who shoots a stranger simply to watch him die.

For any kind of juvenile justice strategy, from incarceration to noncustodial punishment to rehabilitation, one of the most difficult challenges is knowing when to intervene. There are a huge number of juveniles who are arrested for one or two delinquent acts, and who spontaneously end their delinquency careers. Putting such juveniles in expensive rehabilitation programs, assigning them to an already overworked probation officer, or incarcerating them may be a poor allocation of limited resources. Discovering the best time to intervene—to deal with juveniles who will not spontaneously give up crime—remains one of the most difficult questions facing juvenile justice researchers. But some baseline facts are well established. First, the earlier a criminal career begins, the more crimes the offender will be likely to commit; a first offense at age eleven is much more of a danger signal than a first offense at age sixteen.[237] In addition, the odds that a delinquent will, without justice system intervention, end his criminal career are fairly good for first and second offenders, but much worse after a third or subsequent offense.[238]

It is important to remember that juvenile justice programs are end-of-the-line approaches that can often do little more than incarcerate a dangerous person. In the long run, programs which help prevent people from becoming criminals in the first place will pay for themselves many times over in juvenile justice savings, as well as in the savings of young lives.

MEDIA-GENERATED VIOLENCE

Every adult who tries to instill in children responsible attitudes toward firearms must not only teach positive lessons but overcome the many negative lessons taught by America's major television networks and movie industry. Before completing sixth grade, the average American child watches 8,000 homicides and 100,000 acts of violence on television.[239] A look at the movie advertisement pages of any major newspaper shows that cinematic entertainment is no better. A large percentage of movie advertising depicts someone poised to kill.

Even television shows that do not wallow in violence are still violent. Ordinary patrol officers in television "cop shows" often shoot and kill more people than an average real-life SWAT team member does in an entire career.[240]

Over the last two decades, a large body of literature has linked exposure to violent television with increased physical aggressiveness among children and to later violent criminal behavior.[241] One such study was conducted by University of Washington epidemiologist Brandon Centerwall. He found homicide rates in the United States, Canada, and South Africa rose steeply about ten to fifteen years after the introduction of television in each nation. He noted that after television was introduced in Canada, the homicide rate nearly doubled, even though per capita firearms ownership rates remained stable. In the United States, the rise in firearms homicide was paralleled by an equally large rise in homicide committed with the hands and feet. The data, therefore, imply that the underlying cause of the homicide increase was not a sudden surge in availability of firearms, since there was no surge in availability of hands and feet, and hand and foot homicide rose as sharply as firearms homicide. South Africa allowed the introduction of television many years after Canada and the United States (because the apartheid government feared that television would be destabilizing); in South Africa, too, the homicide rate rose sharply after the first generation of television children grew up.[242]

One method by which violent entertainment may promote criminal violence is simple imitation. Two surveys of young American male violent felons found that 22 to 34 percent had imitated crime techniques they had watched on television programs.[243]

Imitation includes more than simply applying a crime technique that the criminal learned through watching television; fictional treatments of crime can inspire and empower potential criminals. John Hinckley drew encouragement from the dozens of times he watched the movie *Taxi Driver,* about an assassin who stalks a presidential candidate and wins a young woman's affection. The man who murdered twenty-two people in Luby's Cafeteria in Killeen, Texas, in October 1991 was found with a ticket to the film *The Fisher King* in his pocket; the film depicts a mass murder in a restaurant. In January 1993, in Grayson, Kentucky, 17-year-old Scott Pennington fatally shot a teacher and a janitor, and held a class hostage; he had recently written a book report on a Stephen King novel in which a student also shoots a teacher and holds a class hostage. The revival of the American Ku Klux Klan (and the countless violent crimes that resulted) was inspired by D. W. Griffith's 1915 film *The Birth of a Nation.* Griffith's twelve-reel film was the first modern motion picture, and the first full-length film to demonstrate the immense commercial potential of cinema (it grossed eighteen million dollars). Based on the Thomas Dixon novel *The Clansman, Birth of a Nation* presented a distorted picture of the South during Reconstruction, and extolled the Ku Klux Klan.[244]

Centerwall's study showing a doubling of the homicide rate after the introduction of television leads him to conclude that "long-term childhood exposure to television is a causal factor behind approximately one half of the homicides committed in the United States, or approximately 10,000 homicides annually." He further estimates that as many as half of American rapes and assaults could be related to television.[245]

Another television researcher pegs the figures far lower. George Comstock, of Syracuse University's Center for Research on Aggression, surveyed 230 studies, and concluded that about 10 percent of American violence is a result of television and cinema violence.[246]

Of course not everyone who watches a *Rambo* movie or its television equivalent becomes a criminal. The harm of violent television is felt most by the already vulnerable segments of the population.[247] Alfred Blumstein, dean of John Heinz School of Public Policy and Management at Carnegie-Mellon, notes, "The glorification of violence on television has little effect on most folks, but it has a powerful effect on kids who are poorly socialized. . . . It dehumanizes them and becomes a self-fulfilling process." Repeated exposure to violence may, through a process of disinhibition, make violence seem ordinary.[248]

Proving cause and effect in the social sciences is never easy, and there is a good number of researchers who believe that the relationship between television and violence may be more complex than is generally acknowledged. For example, while heavy television watching is definitely associated with violence, it may be that it is merely a symptom of other problems, such as neglectful parenting.[249]

Perhaps all sides of the television and violence debate can agree that reducing television violence should be a supplement to, rather than a substitute for, efforts to change the conditions that make the children so vulnerable and dangerous in the first place. As G. K. Chesterton remarked in the 1920s, in response to a furor over a child who murdered his father with a carving knife after watching a movie: "This may possibly have occurred [i.e., the film influencing the child], though if it did, anybody of common sense would prefer to have details of that particular child, rather than about that particular picture."[250]

The Role of Violent Entertainment

The debate over mass media's impact on causing violence among youths has been going on a very long time. In the nineteenth century, novelist George Meredith complained that the "Punch and Judy" puppet show (much more violent then than in its tamer twentieth-century incarnation) "inspires our street-urchins to instant recourse to their fists in a dispute."[251] Similar complaints were offered about mass-market short stories ("penny dreadfuls") sold to adolescent males; one older Victorian recounted the story of a boy who "was so maddened by reading one of the tales provided for his entertainment that he shot dead his father and brother."[252] The recorder of the City of London stated that "There isn't a boy or young lad tried at our Courts of Justice whose position there is not more or less due to the effect of unwholesome literature upon his mind."[253]

Adults who rail against the violent tastes of adolescent males might consider the words of Gershorn Legman, a post-World War II critic of violent comic books: "Comic books do not exist in a vacuum. American parents see nothing wrong with the fictional violence of comic books because they themselves are addicted to precisely the same violence in reality, from the daily accident or atrocity smeared over the front page of their breakfast newspaper to the nightly prize-fight or murder-play in movies, radio, and television coast-to-coast."[254]

Gershorn's observation about the entertainment tastes of adult Americans is at least as true today, with football having displaced baseball as the national sport (in terms of television ratings), with tabloid violence and sensationalism a highly successful format for evening news programs,[255] and the O. J. Simpson murder case apparently (in terms of the volume of coverage) the most important news story of the 1990s.

As University of Florida English professor James B. Twitchell puts it, "All mass media are audience reflectors and magnifiers. . . . Although the critical cant is that the media are manipulated by a few powerful business interests, the reverse is far more accurate. In no other industry are the promulgators manipulated so completely by the seeming whimsy of the many."[256]

Twitchell goes on to suggest that violent entertainment, like dreams, may have the beneficial effect of allowing the imaginary expression of repressed desires.[257] Violent entertainment for young people did not, after all, start with "The A-Team" or even "Punch and Judy." Geoffrey Handley-Taylor's analysis of two hundred traditional Mother Goose nursery rhymes found that over half dealt with the harsher side of life, and in these dark rhymes, there were many cases of murder, torture, and cruelty to humans and animals accomplished through decapitation, drowning, dismemberment, and the like.[258] A content analysis of Grimm's fairy tales found them to be much more violent than prime-time television.[259] Other fairy tales, such as "Hansel and Gretel" (after being abandoned by their parents and captured by a cannibalistic witch, two children save themselves by shoving the witch into an oven), "Little Red Riding Hood" (a malicious stranger, a wolf, procures information from a little girl; the wolf breaks into a grandmother's home, eats her, attempts to devour the girl, and is then shot by a hunter who slices open the wolf's stomach, rescuing the grandmother), and "Jack and the Beanstalk" (a lazy, greedy boy, the hero of the story, steals valuables from a cloud giant, and kills the giant while fleeing the scene of the crime) are sinister and violent. As many parents recognize, these violent stories help children encounter and overcome their fears, and thus play a socially positive role.[260]

It is less important, Twitchell suggests, to count the number of fictional homicides that the average 16-year-old male has watched than to consider why he wants to see so many in the first place.[261] From the eye-gouging wrestling matches of ancient Rome (which Gibbon blamed in part for the fall of the empire); to bull-baiting in the eighteenth century; to "Punch and Judy" and "penny dreadfuls" in the nineteenth; and movies, comic books, professional wrestling, and television in the twentieth, adolescent males have displayed an insatiable appetite for violent entertainment. Twitchell suggests that, far from being antisocial, these entertainments "pantomime what is too traumatic to learn by actual experience. . . . Like fairy tales that prepare the child for the anxieties of separation, sequences of preposterous violence prepare the teenager for the anxieties of action. They are fantastic, ludicrous, crude, vulgar, and important distortions of real life situations, not in the service of repression or incitement (though they certainly have that temporary effect) but of socialization."[262]

Twitchell's analysis does not necessarily conflict with Centerwall's. For the vast majority of adolescent males, media violence may be a beneficial experience, as Twitchell suggests. Perhaps that is why violent entertainment for young men has been such a constant in our culture. At the same time, for a disturbed, vulnerable fringe of adolescent males, violent entertainment may help push them over the edge from thinking about violence to perpetrating violent crimes, according to Centerwall and other researchers. Accordingly, reducing media violence remains a worthwhile component of an anticrime strategy, as long as we recognize that we are only working at the margins. No matter what is done, there will still be large doses of violent entertainment produced for teenage males, because that is what teenage males, in some way, need, just as older people, in some other way, need to fret about it.

Yet even if media violence were entirely eliminated, the criminogenic effect of modern electronic media might not disappear. As *Reason* magazine editor Virginia Postrel points out, the Centerwall studies do not necessarily show a link between television violence and actual violence; rather they demonstrate a link between television itself and actual violence.[263] Pitzer College English professor Barry Sanders, in his book *A is for Ox: Violence, Electronic Media, and the Silencing of the Written Word*, argues that the replacement of reading with electronic entertainment promotes violence.[264] Sanders writes that a sense of the "self," the ability to use abstract categories, and many other core cognitive abilities are dependent on literacy; most of today's young violent criminals are illiterate. If children come from a world of what Sanders calls "orality" (of parents telling them stories, of constant dialogue), then children are eager to master written language. But deprived of orality, children perceive writing as a hostile set of rules which they resist and never master. Sanders identifies a number of reasons for the decline of orality (and hence literacy), including the decreasing number of hours that parents spend with their children and even the practice of bottle-feeding infants rather than breast-feeding. But at the center of Sanders's indictment is electronic entertainment. Although television surrounds children with words, it is a one-way medium which encourages passivity and retards the development of language skills. Modern culture in general, and television in particular, promote instant gratification and do not allow the child a second of boredom; since boredom is the garden from which creativity grows, illiterate, television-oriented children become present-oriented, uninterested in self-restraint, and less capable of human empathy. At the extremes, "a gang kid gets tossed and tumbled around as the daily flow of events washes over him. He lacks the skills that would enable him, like some other youngsters, to sit on the sidelines, contemplatively, and watch those events pass by. . . . They [gang children] enjoy no distance from the events going on around them. . . . They feel victimized, at the mercy of experience, unable to see meaningful choices that would allow them to exercise true agency."[265]

If Sanders is correct, then it is possible that literacy programs for at-risk groups—such as the Family Literacy Program in Middletown, Connecticut—may be important crime prevention tools. At the very least, Sanders offers us reasons to consider that violence may not be all the fault of electronic media, and he reminds us that solving the violence problem (which is partly derived from the literacy problem), cannot be accomplished without strong families, a theme which I discuss in the concluding chapter.

Network Promises

From time to time, the major television networks announce new antiviolence ini-tiatives.[266] Network television programming in the mid-1990s does (apparently in response to viewer preferences) contain a smaller number of violent police and detective shows than in the 1970s. But television still remains violent.[267] The problem with the grand statements about violence control by television execu-tives is that they fly in the face of entertainment economics. University of Penn-sylvania communications professor George Gerbner notes that violent shows require less expensive actors, and can be more readily sold in foreign markets. For example, *Rambo,* as originally written, is the story of an American soldier in Vietnam. As released in the Middle East, *Rambo*'s subtitles change the setting to World War II in the Philippines, and the North Vietnamese enemy becomes Japanese.[268] In Central Africa, English-language versions of the Sylvester Stal-lone movies, without subtitles, are shown to audiences which speak no English; the violence, apparently, works as a *lingua franca.*

The problem is even more serious for children's programming, Gerbner says. It is easier for cartoonists, especially those working on a network assembly line, to depict violence than humor. Many violent cartoon plots are recycled from one show to another, with only the characters being changed.[269] In a 1993 report delivered to the National Cable Television Association, Gerbner noted that cartoons and other children's shows contain more violence than any other form of programming. Children's programs created for the major networks were more violent than equiv-alent cable programming, and averaged thirty-two violent acts per hour.

While television executives promise less violence, they are simultaneously pushing the latest fad in violent entertainment, the misnamed "reality-based tele-vision." Many "reality" shows, while based on case histories of real crimes, are a poor approximation of reality, for while they show numerous shootings, they rarely depict the suffering that accompanies the shooting. Indeed, for all the graphic violence, television and film portrayals of gunfights are highly unrealis-tic. The cameras quickly cut away from dead and dying bodies. The fast break to the commercial teaches no lesson about the permanency of death or injury. Few quadriplegics with shattered spines populate the world of television shootings.[270] Gerbner describes the current style which shows "no pain or tragic conse-quences" as "happy violence."[271]

Accordingly, it is reasonable to consider what steps America can take to reduce the harm caused by violent entertainment, besides trusting the good will of the television networks.

Censorship and the First Amendment

No matter how compelling a person may find the academic case detailing the harm of television, there is no evidence that can justify censorship. The First

Amendment, like the other guarantees in the Bill of Rights, is not subject to revision on the basis of cost/benefit calculations. The amendment sets an absolute bar to certain kinds of government actions precisely because the authors of the Bill of Rights knew that broad freedoms sometimes caused harms, and that cries for "reasonable" restrictions on freedom would arise.[272] Putting aside the First Amendment, it is unjust to censor the entertainment of the huge majority of Americans because a small fraction of them react inappropriately. (And similarly, it is unjust to disarm the populace as a whole because a small fraction commits gun crimes.)

As an empirical matter, it would not be hard to build a case for selective self-censorship of media crime reports. The rapid spread of carjacking from coast to coast, after a publicized incident in Detroit, might suggest that media reports about crime in one area give ideas to criminals in other areas. In Los Angeles, when a man dropped concrete from an overpass onto traffic passing below, the crime was widely publicized in the local papers. A few days later, another man, in a different part of the city, dropped concrete from another overpass. The second man's concrete shattered the windshield of an Iranian student, and the flying glass blinded him for life. In Italy, the press often voluntarily chooses not to report suicides, so as to avoid creating copycat suicides.[273] Would the Iranian student be able to see today if the Los Angeles media had behaved with similar restraint?

The number of assassins and mass murderers who perpetrated their crimes because they knew they would become famous is legion. Arthur Bremer, whose assassination attempt put George Wallace in a wheelchair, was motivated by the publicity that would result. John Lennon's assassin, Mark David Chapman, decided to end his status as "Mr. Nobody" by garnering the fame that would come when he "killed the biggest Somebody on earth."[274] John Hinckley, who nearly killed President Reagan and disabled press secretary James Brady, thought that his act would attract the attention and love of actress Jodie Foster.[275]

James A. Fox and Jack Levin, of Northeastern University, studied mass murders in public places during the last three decades; they concluded that the number of such murders has increased in part because the fame that one murderer achieves as a result of media coverage of the crime inspires other potential murderers to seek similar notoriety.[276]

Suppose there were a policy that prohibited the press from mentioning the name of an assassin or mass murderer. Would Arthur Bremer, Mark David Chapman, and John Hinckley have perpetrated their crimes if such a policy were in effect? Do the media *need* to report the name of every assassin and mass murderer, or would simply reporting all the other facts of the killing satisfy a "reasonable" understanding of the freedom of the press?[277] Would press associations that fought a law against reporting the names of assassins and mass murderers be accused of a "fixation" on the First Amendment?[278]

At least in some cases, government censorship of crime reports or crime entertainment could save lives. That fact, however, is of no consequence against the clear command of the First Amendment. The fact that the First Amendment does not allow the government to compel the media to act responsibly does not, however, preclude the media from choosing to act responsibly. Nor are media stockholders precluded from proposing resolutions at annual stockholders meetings. Nor are consumers precluded from initiating boycotts against media whose irresponsbility promotes violence.

Technological Changes

Certain legal controls on television violence would likely not violate the First Amendment. Dr. Centerwall suggests that all new television sets be required to have built-in time-channel lock circuitry, so that parents could lock out a station or set of viewing times, even when they are not home to supervise television use.[279] In 1990, Congress enacted the Television Decoder Circuitry Act, requiring that most televisions built in 1993 and thereafter have built-in closed-caption circuitry for the hearing impaired. There was no objection that the Act's engineering requirements for television sets violated the First Amendment rights of television makers or viewers. Similarly, requiring a time and channel control to be included in new television sets, as proposed by Representatives Edward Markey (D-Massachusetts) and Jack Fields (R-Texas),[280] would not seem to violate the First Amendment.[281] Newer and more expensive devices employ magnetic cards and card-readers to allow parents to control how many total hours of television can be watched.[282]

Lockout devices are not a perfect solution. Some technologically skillful children will find ways to defeat them. But children with high-level engineering and computer skills are less likely to perpetrate violent crimes in the first place. The more serious weakness of lockout devices involves children who are neglected or ignored by their mother, have no father in the home, and hence have no parent who will use a lockout device. These children are most at risk of becoming violent criminals, as the concluding chapter details. Still, if violent programming declines as a result of other parents using the lockout device, even neglected children will benefit.

Another useful step would be to require the entertainment industry to comply with the same gun laws that law-abiding citizens must obey. The Hollywood moguls who promote pro-death cinema such as the *Terminator* and *Lethal Weapon* movies are a much greater threat to public safety than gun collectors who keep a few wartime souvenirs locked in a case on their wall. At the very least, the entertainment industry ought to live by the same laws it advocates for the rest of the country. Applying California's "assault weapon" ban to Hollywood, just as it applies to everyone else in California, would not violate the First Amendment.[283]

There may be many other steps that could be taken to deal with violence-promoting entertainment. Those steps which do not infringe the freedom of speech deserve serious consideration.

EDUCATION AND SOCIALIZATION

The most important factor affecting how children deal with guns is how they are taught about them. A study of 675 Rochester, New York, ninth and tenth graders contrasted children who had been socialized into gun use by their family with those who had been socialized by peers. The children whose families had taught them about lawful gun use were at no greater risk of becoming involved in crime, gangs, or drugs than those with no exposure to guns. But the children who were taught about guns by their peers were at high risk of all types of crime and improper behavior, including gun crime.[284]

A survey of felony prisoners in Western Australia seems to validate the hypothesis that use of firearms in crime depends less on the availability of guns than on the social conditioning toward them. Rural Aborigines in northwest Australia grow up in a culture where they are surrounded by guns; yet those Aborigines who become criminals are far less likely to perpetrate armed crimes than are their white counterparts. As one Aborigine prisoner put it, "Guns are for shooting tucker [food], not people."[285] Likewise, Aborigine criminals who had been introduced to firearms by authority figures, such as fathers or grandfathers, were less likely to commit armed offenses than were criminals who had been exposed to guns by peers, such as brothers or friends.[286]

The repressive gun laws of cities such as Chicago, Washington, and New York are not merely ineffective; they are themselves a cause of gun violence. By making gun ownership either illegal or possible only for wealthy persons with the clout to move through numerous bureaucratic obstacles, the antigun laws drive most legitimate gun owners underground.

While a man who operates a small grocery store on the Lower East Side of New York City may keep a pistol hidden under the counter in case of a robbery (since he knows that the police cannot protect him), he will likely not take the illegal gun out for practice at a target range. Even if the man acquired a gun license, he could not take his teenage son to a target range to teach him responsible gun use. For the teenager even to hold the gun in his hand under immediate adult supervision at a licensed target range would require the teenager to acquire his own (expensive) handgun license.[287]

An airgun (which uses compressed gas to fire a pellet) can be safely fired inside an apartment, yet New York City makes it illegal for minors to hold an airgun in their hands under direct parental supervision. Thus, the city closes off one more avenue for children to be taught responsible attitudes toward guns.

Having driven responsible gun owners into the suburbs or into hiding, New York; Chicago; and Washington, D.C., are raising a generation of children whose only major role models of gun ownership are criminals and violent television characters. In the city where no child can legally shoot a BB gun with his father, children learn about guns on the street and shoot each other with 9mm pistols.[288]

In a society with over two hundred million firearms, it is childish to imagine that gun-control laws will prevent teenagers from having access to guns. To fail to teach America's young people responsible gun use, under the supervision of responsible adults, is to sow the seeds of a public health disaster, the murder epidemic that too many American cities have created for themselves.

Sports Programs

One place where young people can be exposed to responsible approaches toward firearms is school sports. For the same reasons that schools should not be required to offer gun safety programs, they should not be required to conduct gun sports programs. The decision should be made on a school-by-school basis, but some state laws, such as those in Illinois, make it difficult for high schools or colleges to offer target shooting as an option for student athletes.[289]

At school or in nonschool programs, recreational target shooting can develop character. The sport builds mental discipline and concentration; some parents report that concentration skills developed in target shooting have made their children into better students.[290] Target shooting is nonsexist. Females play on the same teams as males, and regularly defeat them. Many physically challenged students (such as those in wheelchairs) can compete on equal terms with everyone else.

The only facility needed can fit into a 20-by-50-foot room. A student who has been the worst player on the junior high basketball team can take up marksmanship for the first time in high school and win awards. And while high school or college football players do not learn an activity that they can enjoy for the rest of their lives, target shooting, like golf, is a lifetime sport; a number of national champions have been nearly seventy years old.

Target shooting has a lower injury rate than any other sport, and fights between competitors are nonexistent. There has never been an incident of one competitor deliberately harming another in a sanctioned match. In baseball, intentional violence, such as spiking the second baseman and throwing beanballs, are traditional parts of the game. Hockey, boxing, and football all involve the intentional infliction of physical suffering on the opponent.

According to the National Athletic Trainers Association, about 40 percent of American high school football players every year will sustain an injury that will "require the player to suspend activity for at least the remainder of the day on which the injury occurred." Nine thousand three hundred players will require knee surgery.[291] Every year, about twenty-four student football players are killed or catastrophically injured.[292] Thomas Jefferson advised his nephew: "Games played with a bat and ball are too violent, and stamp no character on the mind. . . . [A]s to the species of exercise, I advise the gun."[293]

Other than hatred of guns, there is no strong argument against schools being allowed to offer target shooting as a sport, nor is there an argument against teenagers being encouraged to learn responsible attitudes toward firearms through participation in the shooting sports. Some of the opposition to sports seems to stem from a visceral antipathy toward guns rather than from logic. For example, the Center to Prevent Handgun Violence (an affiliate of Handgun Control, Inc.) and the AAP distribute a brochure warning everyone to "Be extremely cautious about allowing children to participate in shooting activities." The brochure offers no evidence that the shooting sports are dangerous, and, of course, does not disclose that school shooting programs are safer than all other school sports.[294]

Nothing could be more politically incorrect than putting guns into the hands of at-risk youths, but that is precisely what an innovative Orlando program does. Police Lieutenant Angel Rodriguez encourages youths living in Orlando Housing Authority apartments to join him as participants in Civil War reenactments. The teenage boys wear Union uniforms, participate in battle reenactments with thousands of adults, and, like the adults, carry and use the military rifles of the Civil War. Some participants shoot cannons. A younger auxiliary, consisting of boys eleven to thirteen, while not allowed to shoot the rifles, also participates in the program. The program helps the teenagers build relationships with adult males and learn "teamwork, discipline, sensitivity, heartbreak, and concern for one another." Since the program began, only one participant has been arrested or even questioned for illegal activity.[295]

The promotion of responsible gun habits through school sports programs will not turn every hardcore gang member into a law-abiding citizen, any more than the Police Athletic League programs turn all gang members into law-abiding football players. But sports programs can reach the large segment of the teen population that is open to influence from responsible adults.

Classroom Education

Classroom education about responsible firearms attitudes can also be valuable, especially if it does not promote a political agenda. The Eddie Eagle Elementary Gun Safety program (detailed above) teaches young children not to touch an unattended gun. There is no political content. Eddie Eagle, however, is limited, in that it is aimed at young children, and is designed to prevent accidents, not intentional crimes.

While Eddie Eagle has no political content, the Center to Prevent Handgun Violence offers a politicized "safety" program called "KIDS+GUNS: A Deadly Equation." The program has been adopted in Florida's Dade County public schools and elsewhere. The curriculum for younger students uses children's books extolling pacifism. For example, one book is Dr. Seuss's *The Butter Battle Book*, a volume written at the height of the nuclear freeze campaign, which posits moral equivalence between the United States and the former Soviet Union. The book's allegorical message asserts that the conflict between Communist and Western society is as trivial as that over which side of the bread that butter should be placed on. Accordingly, free societies and Communist countries should learn how to settle their trivial disputes without violence. Many Cuban refugees now living in Dade County would likely be disconcerted to learn that their school system teaches that the struggle against Communism was meaningless.

Other programs, fortunately, take a politically neutral approach. Using role-playing and other techniques, the programs explain that walking away from a fight over scuffed sneakers is not dishonorable, and that talking to a friend about a perceived insult is a better response than a deadly attack.[296] Yet despite the impression sometimes conveyed by the media, most adolescents are not shooting each other in arguments over who scuffed whose sneakers. Accordingly, programs that teach conflict resolution skills to the vast nonviolent majority of students are a waste of everyone's time and money. The more successful programs focus intense attention on youths who are at the greatest risk. The Positive Adolescent Choices Training (PACT) program, designed specifically for black teenagers, appears, based on limited evidence, to be effective at engendering attitudinal changes in favor of nonviolent conflict resolution, and in reducing behavior problems at school. The PACT curriculum is much longer than some other nonviolence programs, and works with students in smaller groups.[297] Other programs also report success at short-term attitudinal and behavioral change,[298] although whether a long-term reduction in criminal violence will result is uncertain.

Parenting Skills and other Early Childhood Programs

A large number of little children in America lead miserable lives. Within less than two decades, many of these children will become the core group of high-rate violent criminals. A crime control strategy that relies exclusively on punishing criminals and puts no effort into helping children is shortsighted both practically and morally.

Every day hundreds of children are born to women with inadequate prenatal care, and hundreds more are physically and sexually abused. As the concluding chapter details, many more children, while not directly abused, suffer from "father hunger," growing up in a family where the father has left or was never present to begin with. Violent crime starts early. Child abuse victimization is linked to later criminal behavior, although the link is not as strong as had been previously supposed.[299]

Manifestation of behavioral problems of children as young as five years old is a strong predictor of later arrests for juvenile delinquency.[300] And people most likely to perpetrate violent crimes as adults are those who do so as youths.

One approach to preventing crime is Hawaii's Healthy Start program. The state identifies at-risk parents (alcoholics and victims of child or spouse abuse) and offers them free in-home counseling. The program helps parents learn nonabusive methods of child care, and also assists the parents' application for Medicaid assistance and job training programs. While at-risk parents who are not contacted by the program have a 20 percent risk of perpetrating child abuse, the abuse rate in homes covered by Healthy Start is only 2 percent. Similarly, a visiting nurse program in Rochester, New York, reduced child abuse rates (4 percent for the families served, compared to 19 percent in the control group), and reduced by about three-quarters the number of poor, unmarried, teenager mothers who had a second child within twenty-two months.[301] As the next chapter discusses, the anticrime benefit of preventing illegitimate births is immense.

A fifteen-year study by the Syracuse University Family Research Development Research Program found that when low-income families were visited weekly by child development trainers to help them improve parenting skills, 6 percent of children from those families ended up with a probation record, compared to 22 percent from a control group.[302]

Early-childhood program evaluations generally look at short-term results. One program, which assisted single mothers until the child was thirty months old, found small benefits in the short term, but significant differences ten years later. Children helped by the program were, ten years after, much better behaved, less aggressive, and better liked by their mother than were peers in a control group. All of these factors are predictors of nondelinquency. One other effect, which could not show up in the short term, was that many single mothers did not have another child, and those who did waited a median of nine years after the first child's birth.[303]

Parental skills programs for at-risk parents, beneficial as they can be, raise seriously civil liberties questions. Hawaii's Healthy Start program has already been criticized for being excessively intrusive. Given government's record over past decades, there is every reason to fear that expansion of parental skills programs will lead to government caseworkers telling (and eventually ordering) parents not to smoke, own guns, or do whatever else is politically incorrect. If parental skills programs became more popular, it would be only a matter of time before the federal government began funding such programs in every state, and using regulations to straitjacket the skills programs to suit the needs of Washington bureaucrats and the government "providers" rather than the needs of the parents.

Accordingly, the best strategy for parental skills programs might be for them to be offered by nongovernmental groups, including churches and child welfare organizations.[304] In the concluding chapter, I present a proposal for taxpayers to be given the option of designating some of their tax dollars earmarked for welfare to nongovernmental welfare agencies. Perhaps this proposal would encourage the growth of effective parenting programs, without turning them into a foot in the door for Big Brother.

As an alternative to in-home visitation programs, other programs teach parenting skills at community centers. Parents in these programs report improved skills at explaining appropriate behavior to children, rather than yelling at or hitting them.[305]

A third type of early childhood intervention is subsidizied preschool. Preschool programs, such as Head Start, generally raise a child's IQ, but the the gains are not sustained unless supplementary programs continue beyond preschool.

One preschool program that did show long-lasting results was the Perry Preschool Project, a very high-quality program for 123 low IQ children from low-income black families in the early 1960s. The two-year program cost $6,300 per child per year (in 1986 dollars). The Perry Preschool was a spectacular success. Followup research estimated that the Perry program resulted in criminal justice savings of $2,400 per child in avoided delinquency, and $6,800 per child in avoided adult crime. (Government justice expenditures, as well as financial costs to crime victims were included; pain and suffering of victims were not. All figures are in 1986 dollars.) Perry yielded major financial benefits other than crime; projected welfare expenditures plummeted, while projected tax receipts from the Perry student's increased lifetime earnings soared.[306] The major benefit, of course, was nonmonetary. The Perry children are leading immensely better lives.

Critics of Head Start point out, accurately, that it shows no long-term benefits. The Perry experience suggests that rather than abolishing Head Start, we should massively improve it. Giving at-risk preschoolers the three-year-old's equivalent to an Ivy League education is very, very expensive. High-quality home visitation programs for new welfare mothers are not cheap either.

But prisons are expensive, too, and the suffering caused by violent crime is incalculable. There is so much waste in current educational spending on politically correct noneducational failures (such as DARE, which has been shown *not* to reduce drug use,[307] and nontransitional bilingual programs that keep children in educational ghettos for their entire school career), that every school district ought to be able to transfer funds to at least a few Perry-type programs. Alternatively, legislatures might simply cut fat from the government school budget, and give the money to private groups setting up high-quality early intervention preschools. School voucher plans can create significant long-run savings, since the voucher can be for less than the amount that the government spends on government schools; some of the savings from vouchers could also be redirected toward early intervention. My proposal in the concluding chapter to allow taxpayers to choose how their welfare payments will be spent could also allow for increased funding of many different early intervention programs.

As noted above, preventing severe child abuse is, in the long run, a crime prevention plan; but even if it were not, it ought to be a top priority of any decent society. Yet in New York City, children arrive at city hospitals time and again with broken bones, scars, and bruises symptomatic of child abuse. In one case reported by *Newsday,* "untrained and inexperienced caseworkers ignored blisters and bruises on the boy, failed to talk with his three siblings or his father, failed even to have sufficient command of the English language to write intelligible reports."[308]

Hiring competent child abuse workers is more expensive than New York City's policy of hiring the inept. Yet while local newspapers were exposing the shambles of the New York City child welfare system, former mayor David Dinkins trumpeted a ban on semi-automatic "assault weapons" (used in about 1 percent of New York City gun crime[309]) as the center of his anticrime effort. Thus, children in New York City continue to die at the hands of abusive parents, and many abused children who survive will one day victimize other New Yorkers. By allowing the mayor to pontificate on guns, New Yorkers allowed him to divert attention from how badly New York treats its children.

In one notorious case in Maryland, a 6-year-old boy, whose mother ran a crack house, repeatedly begged his teachers, "Please don't make me go home. I don't want to go back there." When asked why Maryland social services did not even attempt to remove the boy from the crack house and place him in foster care, a state investigator explained that he had twenty similar cases to handle, and he did not have the time to go through the lengthy process of removing a child from his home unless the child was in "imminent danger."[310] Meanwhile, Maryland Governor William Donald Schaefer, every year from 1989 until he left office in early 1995, made stringent gun control the centerpiece of his legislative anticrime agenda. What if the governor had invested a fraction of the energy that he put into "gun control" into increasing the funding for Maryland's child protection services?

There is much that remains uncertain about programs to help young children, but investing social resources in a variety of experimental programs, no matter how expensive they are, is likely to bear much better fruit than proven failures such as "gun control." Incarcerating criminals is not a proven failure, since it at least keeps the particular criminal from harming anyone except fellow prisoners. But doesn't it make sense to help parents and children today, knowing that a child who can enjoy a good childhood is much less likely to be in need of incarceration, at great taxpayer expense, when he becomes a teenager? Conservatives are right when they say that punishing criminals is better than disarming law-abiding citizens, but they are wrong when they dismiss every kind of prevention program as meaningless.

GUN CONTROL LAWS

A large number of gun-control measures have been proffered as solutions to the problems of children and guns. Whatever may be the merits of these proposals in regard to adult gun misuse, the programs will take our society no farther in resolving the real problems of children and guns, but will instead offer legislators a convenient stratagem for avoiding real solutions.

Banning Handguns

In a survey of Washington, D.C., violent criminals confined at the Lorton, Virginia, prison, the criminals (most of them under thirty) did not seem to be influenced by gun-control laws. Seventy-seven percent of them had acquired a handgun in the District, where handgun sales are illegal and handgun possession is almost entirely outlawed. Two out of three agreed that gun control would not reduce D.C.'s violence.[311]

AAP proposes that handguns be outlawed for the entire population, since it is, supposedly, not suitable for children ever to have handguns. The Constitution has long been clear that the rights of adults may not be constricted to what is suitable for children. As Justice Felix Frankfurter put it, allowing adults to possess only what is suitable for children, "is to burn down the house to roast a pig." Or as Justice White wrote, "The government may not reduce the adult population . . . to . . . only what is fit for children."[312]

After all, alcohol and tobacco are not suitable for children, but these products remain legal, even though they are associated with tens of thousands of deaths or crimes annually, and even though these two drugs (unlike guns) have no capacity to save lives by providing protection against crime.

AAP's handgun prohibitionist Katherine Christoffel argues that the Second Amendment is obsolete, for "No one can believe that our Founding Fathers, in crafting the Second Amendment, intended to leave American children as vulnerable to firearms violence as they are today."[313] But guns in the late eighteenth century and early nineteenth centuries were actually more prone to accidental discharge than they are today; guns were owned by a higher percentage of the population, and more likely to be kept loaded than they are today.[314] And then, as now, some persons contrasted the high American murder rate with the much lower British rate.[315]

The eagerness of gun prohibitionists to outlaw handguns is based in part on a determination that handguns are worthless. AAP claims that a ban on handguns would be appropriate "because of their very limited ability to provide personal protection."[316] But in fact, handguns provide an enormous public health benefit, because they are used so often to prevent crime, as chapter 5 details.

Handgun prohibition will also lead to a sharply increased firearms death rate. Some gun misusers would switch to knives (not much less deadly than small handguns), while others would switch to rifles and shotguns (much more likely to kill than handguns).[317] Thus, if at least 44 percent of misusers switched from handguns to long guns, the death toll would increase, even if the other 56 percent gave up crime entirely.[318] The Wright-Rossi NIJ study of felons in state prisons found that 72 percent of "handgun predators" said they would switch to sawed-off shotguns if handguns became unavailable.[319]

Banning Air Guns

AAP calls for outlawing "deadly air guns," although they are involved in only two deaths a year for the entire U.S. population.[320] In terms of child deaths caused, air guns exact a toll about equal to that of baby rattles. Playgrounds, by contrast, are involved in about seventeen fatal accidents every year, and another 170,000 accidents requiring emergency room treatment.[321] Like playgrounds, air guns are used for recreational activities that many children enjoy, and that improve coordination or concentration.

Buy-Back Programs

Government or private programs to buy guns from citizens willing to turn them in do have the advantage of not violating anyone's Constitutional rights. The buy-backs, while well-intentioned, are a waste of taxpayer or corporate money. They give professional gun thieves a market for selling their stolen goods, no questions asked.[322] Honest people turning in firearms are often the widows of hunters, or other older people, rather than teenage gang members who have suddenly decided to abandon a life of violence.[323] Since most persons surrendering their guns are very unlikely to commit a violent gun crime, the public safety benefit, if any, must lie in reducing the supply of guns that can be stolen, or removing a potential suicide instrument. How much disarmament is actually accomplished may be questionable; a study of a 1992 gun buy-back in Seattle found that 66 percent of sellers owned another gun which they did not surrender.[324] The percentage was probably increased by the program's policy of paying only for one gun per participant.[325] Only 5 percent of surrendered guns came from minors.[326]

Sensibly, the authors of the Seattle buy-back study suggested that future buy-backs focus more narrowly on higher-risk gun-owning groups, such as minors.[327] But as long as American cities remain the dangerous places that they are, the need to carry firearms for protection will persist. Thus, even carefully targeted gun buy-backs may not make a significant dent in the numbers of youths carrying guns.

Banning Gun Possession by Minors

Some politicians have proposed laws to more or less outlaw the possession of firearms by persons under eighteen. Oftentimes the laws are badly drafted and outlaw activity that cannot rationally be considered illegitimate. For example, an ordinance was proposed in Aurora, Colorado, which outlawed gun possession by minors in terms so broad that even minors with a state hunting license were forbidden to carry a firearm while hunting. Indeed, the ordinance prevented a 17-year-old licensed hunter from another city from transporting an unloaded rifle in the trunk of his car, while driving along the interstate highway that passes through Aurora to go hunting elsewhere in the state.

As detailed above, it is already illegal nationwide for minors to buy guns in stores. The laws regarding gun possession by minors, then, make it unlawful for adults to give or loan guns to minors, even though being taught about guns by adults is the best way for young people to learn responsible attitudes about guns.

As part of the 1994 federal crime bill, all handgun transfers to minors are now illegal. It is now a federal crime for a father to give a handgun to his 17-year-old daughter, even if she has her own job and her own apartment. Minors may temporarily possess handguns for sporting purposes, but only when carrying written permission from their parents. In other words, if a father takes his son target shooting, and supervises while the son fires the father's handgun at a target range, a federal crime has been committed unless the son is also carrying a written note from the father.

In Tulsa in July 1994 (two months before the federal crime bill became law), four brothers were home alone while their stepfather was running an errand and their mother was at work. An intruder broke into the house, and the oldest boy, thirteen, grabbed his stepfather's .357 Magnum revolver. Although the boy (who had taken gun safety classes) pointed the gun at the intruder, the criminal kept coming. The boy shot him fatally, and the prosecutor determined that the shooting was legally justified self-defense.[328] Sensibly, the federal law, unlike some state or local proposals, includes an exemption for juveniles using firearms against an intruder.[329]

Because minors are not necessarily as responsible as adults, it might be Constitutional for laws to require that minors with guns be subjected to restrictions that could not Constitutionally be applied to adults. For example, a law could require that minors carry guns only if they have permission from their parents, or if they have passed a safety training class.

On the other hand, many antiminor laws strip young people of their right to lawful self-defense. Does it really enhance public safety to enact laws which command that a 16-year-old female driving home from the library at night may not possess a handgun to shoot a rapist, or that a 17-year-old male who works the sales counter at his father's store may not exercise the right to resist a robbery with a shotgun?

While minors generally are not accorded the broadest range of Constitutional rights applicable to adults, the Constitutional rights of minors may not be wholly abridged. For example, while school newspapers may be subject to certain controls not applicable to independently owned newspapers (since school papers are part of the school curriculum), juvenile students have free speech rights, even on school property.[330] Similarly, while lockers of juveniles in public schools can be searched under a "reasonable suspicion" standard rather than the "probable cause" standard that applies to adults, juveniles may not be stripped of Fourth Amendment protections and searched at will.[331] Students suspended from public school have Constitutional due process rights to a fair hearing, albeit not a full-blown adversarial hearing with a right to counsel.[332]

Although a Constitutional argument could be made in favor of some restrictions on juveniles carrying firearms, there can be no such argument for completely abrogating the self-defense rights of minors.

Interdicting the Illegal Gun Market

Virtually every item on the agenda of the antigun lobbies ends up being promoted as something that we must do "for the children," regardless of the presence of a logical connection between the new restriction and juvenile violence. Since the gun-control lobbies' agenda is so intensely focused on regulation of lawful gun purchases and purchasers, insufficient attention has been paid to the black market which supplies firearms to juvenile criminals. David Kennedy, of the John F. Kennedy School of Government at Harvard, suggests that greater attention be paid to disrupting the juvenile gun market. For example, when a violent juvenile is apprehended with a gun, efforts should be made to find out how he obtained the gun, and, if the gun came from a voluntary transaction rather than a theft, to prosecute the person who sold the gun. Black market enforcement efforts are unlikely to completely shut off the gun supply, particularly to juveniles who are highly motivated to obtain guns.[333] At the same time, the manifest failure of most paperwork "gun controls" to impact the juvenile market suggests that black market disruption is at least worth trying on an experimental basis.

CONCLUSION

Improving the juvenile justice system, as discussed above, is a first step toward reducing teenage criminal violence. Taking violent teenagers off the streets is a more effective approach than leaving them on the street and enacting gun-control palliatives. After all, teenagers have ready access to drugs, despite the severe prohibition of drugs for nearly a century. It is foolish, therefore, to pretend that gun control will somehow succeed where drug control has failed. Improving the quality of life of young children is probably the most effective, albeit expensive, long-term strategy.

While Americans must insist that the government begin confronting the real causes of crimes, the problem is ultimately not within the government's sole power to repair. The problem can only be solved one child at a time, as Americans reach out through Big Brother programs, literacy tutoring, the Boy Scouts and Girl Scouts, church programs, and the great range of private endeavors that have worked for America in previous decades.[334] As the African saying puts it, "It takes a whole village to raise a child." Such an approach requires far more effort on the part of every citizen than simply watching the evening news and nodding in agreement as President Clinton promises that enacting the Brady Bill will reduce teenage gun violence. Perhaps that is why so many politicians are so eager to offer voters the placebo of gun control, rather than to challenge voters with the imperative to lead the moral reconstruction of America.

America does indeed have a problem with children and guns; but it is very different from the one invented by the antigun lobbies, which distribute booklets with a cover showing an infant playing with a gun. Yet out of 40,000 infant deaths every year, perhaps one is due to a gun. Gun accidents have declined by 50 percent in the last two decades, and can continue to fall even more unless antigun bureaucrats succeed in quashing safety education programs.

America has a terrible problem of teenage gun crime, both in and out of schools. Despite the sometimes hysterical claims of the national media, the problem is not uniform throughout America but very heavily concentrated among older adolescent males in large metropolitan areas, and within that group heavily concentrated among urban low-income blacks.[335] Within this group, the rate of gun-related death is appallingly large, and calls for immediate action.

Addressing the social pathologies that beset inner-city minorities is the most realistic approach to dealing with this group's very high homicide rate. Since drugs are readily available in the inner city despite extremely severe national prohibition, it is foolish to expect that gun controls will take guns out of urban ghettos. The longer the debate focuses narrowly on one of the symptoms of social decay—the use of guns in homicide—the longer the elected officials and American society will postpone the difficult work of restoring hope to the underclass.

Gun-control advocates, however, attempt to shift the focus away from the despair of the inner city, and to convince America that a children-and-guns epidemic is running rampant throughout the United States. Isolated incidents of firearms homicide are sometimes used as the basis for a claim that teenage firearms homicide is prevalent throughout America.[336] Some medical organizations misinform the public through offering wildly inaccurate claims about children and guns.[337]

At 1966 hearings dealing with the problem of "juvenile delinquents" using guns, Senators Edward Kennedy, Thomas Dodd, and others wrote a report which promised, "By prohibiting the mail-order traffic in concealable firearms entirely and restricting the over-the-counter purchase of concealable firearms by nonresidents, and by regulating the mail-order traffic in shotguns and rifles, the problem will be substantially alleviated."[338] Every one of Senator Kennedy's proposals (and then some) became federal law in the Gun Control Act of 1968. Three decades later, there is no reputable criminological evidence that the restrictions have "substantially alleviated" the problem of juvenile delinquents carrying guns. Yet rather than concede that the 1968 Act is a failure and should be repealed, gun-control advocates call for ever more restrictive legislation, which they promise— this time for sure—will take guns away from juveniles.

The reality of American history is that juveniles have always had ready access to firearms, ever since the first Old World settlers arrived in Massachusetts and Virginia. With so many guns already in private hands, the situation is not likely to change. What has changed in recent decades is not the availability of guns to juveniles, but the way that juveniles have treated those guns.

"Gun control" became a major national issue in modern times thanks to Senator Thomas Dodd's Juvenile Delinquency Subcommittee. Senator Dodd (father of Connecticut's current Senator Christopher Dodd) had been preparing to hold the television and motion picture industries accountable for the surge in teenage violence perpetrated by "juvenile delinquents." The industries persuaded the senator to direct his fire at guns instead, and so Dodd made himself a national celebrity by taking up the "gun-control" cudgel.

The history of the juveniles-and-guns issue in the United States has been

three decades of politicians who dislike the idea of private gun ownership pushing for "one more" repressive gun control that will supposedly disarm youthful
thugs. Even though the laws fail, their sponsors respond by pushing for yet another law that will supposedly succeed where the last one did not.

The gun prohibitions and near prohibitions in cities such as Washington, Chicago, and New York, have not only failed to disarm criminals, they have substantially worsened gun crime by leaving generations of children with no positive
models of responsible civilian gun use. The only gun users whom children in
these cities can regularly see are criminals, police (often perceived as a hostile
presence), and the most irresponsible set of gun users possible: television and
movie characters.

Will elected officials continue to offer the public only the empty promises of
gun control, or will they begin the hard work of combating the true causes of
American violence? The answer may determine whether the Americans of the
1990s bequeath to twenty-first century Americans a society with more violence
and less freedom, or one that in the 1990s finally began to reverse the blight of
its inner cities.

NOTES

1. John Darling, former member of the Board of Directors of the Center to Prevent
Handgun Violence, "You Must Educate Your Children," *USA Today,* June 19, 1989.

2. Marc B. Goldstein, "Guns Don't Kill But They Sure Make it Easier," *Hartford
Courant,* July 5, 1992, p. 14.

3. Sen. Joseph Biden, "Statement of Senator Joseph R. Biden, Jr., Chairman, Senate
Judiciary Committee, 'Children and Guns: Why the Recent Rise?' " Senate Committee on the
Judiciary, October 1, 1992, p. 2 ("135,000 children are carrying guns to school everyday [*sic*]");
Senator John Chafee, "Testimony of Senator John H. Chafee before the Senate Judiciary
Committee during Hearings on 'Kids and Guns,' " October 1, 1992, p. 1 ("An estimated
135,000 boys carry guns to school every day"); Dr. Katherine Christoffel, American Academy
of Pediatrics, testimony on "Children and Guns," House Select Committee on Children, Youth
and Families, June 15, 1989 ("An estimated 135,000 boys carried handguns to school daily in
1987 . . ."). Also, "When Guns Go to School," *USA Today,* February 28, 1992; *Crime Control
Digest,* August 5, 1991, p. 9.

Senator Christopher Dodd pegs the number even higher. "Statement of Senator
Christopher J. Dodd," Hearing on "Children of War: Violence and America's Youth," Senate
Subcommittee on Children, Family, Drugs, and Alcoholism, July 23, 1992, p. 1. ("Each day,
186,000 students bring a gun to school, many out of fear.")

4. American Academy of Pediatrics, reported in "Doctors Worry about Gun Deaths,"
Aurora Beacon News, October 23, 1989 (Associated Press). The 45,000 figure is much larger
than the total number of gun deaths for all ages combined.

5. The Lou Harris poll, released in July 1993, surveyed 2,508 students in grades six
through twelve, at ninety-six schools. Louis Harris Research, Inc., "A Survey of Experiences,
Perceptions, Apprehensions about Guns among Young People in America," conducted for the
Harvard School of Public Health under a grant from the Joyce Foundation, July 1993 (poll conducted April 19–May 21, 1993). The poll is discussed in Gary Kleck, "The Incidence of Gun

Violence among Young People," *The Public Perspective,* September/October 1993, pp. 3–6. See also text at notes 133–37 of this chapter.

No politician has done more to raise the issue of "children and guns" to a level of national hysteria than Colorado Governor Roy Romer. At a special "emergency" session of the Colorado legislature in September 1993, which the governor called to deal with juvenile violence, he quoted the Lou Harris data in his address to the General Assembly.

Other parts of Governor Romer's understanding of the children and guns issue were also disconnected from reality. For example, in his September 1993 speech, at town meetings during the preceding summer, and in a *New York Times* op-ed, Romer said, "If the NRA in Washington is so out of touch with Colorado that it cannot even support the simple proposition that a 14-year-old has no business carrying a loaded gun to school, then the NRA is part of the problem." Roy Romer, "Under 18? Hand Over That Gun," *New York Times,* October 21, 1993, p. 23. Actually, since 1989, Colorado has had a law forbidding anyone (not just 14-year-olds) to bring guns to school. Colorado Revised Statutes, § 18–12–105(1)(d)(enacted by House Bill 89-1245). In 1993, legislation was proposed to strengthen the law; the NRA endorsed the bill, and without the NRA's lobbying, the bill probably would not have passed the Colorado House of Representatives. Governor Romer signed the strengthened law in June 1993; a few weeks later, he was touring the state, fulminating that the NRA was opposing the governor's reasonable, new proposal that 14-year-olds should not carry guns to school.

After the special 1993 legislative session ended, Governor Romer informed politicians and media all over the country how he "beat" the NRA. In fact, the bill that the governor promoted during the weeks preceding the special session—a licensing system for juvenile handgun possession—received so little support that no licensing bill was even introduced. After the special session ended, the governor told the *New York Times* (and anyone else who would listen) that the legislature had enacted a complete ban on juvenile handgun possession, and "The only exceptions to the ban are for licensed hunting, target practice, or shooting competition." "Under 18? . . ." Actually, the stringent ban the governor described was contained in the governor's (modified) flagship bill, introduced on the first day of the special session. The bill was killed that very day by the first committee to hear the bill, on a seven-to-two vote. The juvenile handgun bill that the legislature enacted was neither drafted with nor initially endorsed by Governor Romer. It was written by Republican Jeannie Adkins. After negotiations (and after the Romer bill was killed), Governor Romer and the NRA both endorsed the Adkins bill, which was less restrictive than the governor's initial proposals, but more restrictive than the NRA's initial proposals.

6. Erik Larson, "The Story of a Gun," *The Atlantic,* January 1993, p. 48 (excerpt from Erik Larson, *Lethal Passages: The Journey of a Gun* [New York: Crown, 1994]).

7. Teret and Wintemute, "Handgun Injuries: The Epidemiologic Evidence for Assessing Legal Responsibility," *Hamline Law Review* 6 (1983): 341, 346.

8. "Gun Violence in America: An Interview with Robert J. Walker of Handgun Control, Inc.," *Highlights* (American Association of Retired Persons), January/February 1995, p. 7.

9. National Safety Council, *Accident Facts—1994* (Itacsa, Ill.: National Safety Council, 1994), p. 12.

For children under fifteen, accidental deaths are about 43 percent of total firearms deaths. For persons over fifteen, however, accidents constitute only 5 percent of firearms deaths. For children under fifteen, males are three times as likely to suffer a fatal accident as females, and whites are more likely to suffer an accident than blacks. Patti J. Patterson and Alfonso H. Holguin, study of Texas incidents published in *Texas Medicine,* and discussed in "Survey Says 43 percent of Childhood Firearms Deaths Unintentional," *Crime Victims Digest,* July 1990, p. 9.

There are as many as 105 nonfatal accidental injuries for every accidental fatality. Data from ten cities, reported in United States General Accounting Office, *Accidental Shootings: Many Deaths and Injuries Caused by Firearms Could Be Prevented,* March 1991 (hereinafter "GAO Report"), p. 2.

Including nonfatal accidents, gun accidents cause one billion dollars in lifetime medical costs per year for all age groups. GAO Report, p. 3. Total American medical expenditures in a given year are about four hundred billion dollars.

10. *Accident Facts—1994,* p. 5.

11. Ibid., p. 33.

12. Ibid., p. 37.

13. Gary Kleck, *Point Blank* (Hawthorne, N.Y.: Aldine, 1991), p. 276.

14. For example, an American Academy of Pediatrics advisor claims "five hundred annually." Dr. Robert Tanz, Northwestern University Medical School, quoted in Joan DeClaire, "Kids & Guns," *View,* September/October 1992, pp. 30, 33.

15. GAO Report, p. 2.

16. *Accident Facts—1994,* p. 12 (227 of 7,286 accidental deaths in that age group).

17. Ibid., p. 12 (3,087 motor vehicle; 1,142 drowning; 1,104 fires, burns).

18. Jane Matter Vachon, "Should You Trust a Tail-Wagging Dog?" *Reader's Digest,* November 1992, p. 134.

19. R. K. Lee and J. J. Sacks, "Latchkey Children and Guns at Home," *JAMA* 264 (1990): 3120. The study also asserted, but offered no evidence to prove, that latchkey children were a risk factor for gun accidents.

20. *Accident Facts—1994,* p. 69.

21. Ibid., p. 22.

22. Centers for Disease Control, *Morbidity and Mortality Weekly Report,* March 11, 1988, pp. 144–45.

23. *Accident Facts—1994,* p. 101 (drowning; figure is an estimate for 1993; number of estimated accidental deaths of children under five for 1993 is twenty); John H. Cushman, "Tales from the 104th: Watch Out, or the Regulators Will Get You!" *New York Times,* February 28, 1995, p. A10 (thirty-six child deaths from five-gallon buckets in 1994; 500 in last ten years); *Consumer's Research,* May 1988, p. 34 (cigarette lighters).

The chances that a child between the ages of one and nine will die from a firearms-related injury are about one in 10,000. (Based on Maryland data for 1980–86 contained in the article "Firearms Fatalities: A Leading Cause of Death in Maryland," and prepared by the Johns Hopkins School of Hygiene and Public Health.)

24. James Wright and Peter Rossi, *Armed and Considered Dangerous: A Survey of Felons and Their Firearms* (New York: Aldine, 1986).

25. See GAO Report, p. 4. The senator introduced the bill as S. 892 in the 102d Congress. The laws restricting the CPSC are found at 15 U.S.C. § 2052(a)(1)(E) & § 2080(d)&(e).

26. GAO Report, p. 24 (345 of 1,501 accidental deaths studied). It should be noted that GAO prepared the study at Senator Metzenbaum's request, and it is not impossible that the agency tried to arrive at policy conclusions that would please the powerful senator.

27. Paul Blackman, *Children and Firearms: Lies the CDC Loves,* paper presented at the annual meeting of the American Society of Criminology, New Orleans, November 4–7, 1992, p. 17 n.23.

28. Also, the Ruger refit benefitted any owner who thought that he might accidentally drop the gun one day. The government retrofit would benefit only those owners who expected the gun to one day be handled by a person reckless enough to point a gun at someone else for fun.

29. GAO Report, p. 3.

30. About 3.5 percent of accidents included children under five, but the GAO study made children under five 8 percent of the sample. Conversely, 40 percent of firearms accidents involve persons over thirty, but the GAO sample included only 16 percent from this age group. Office of Policy, Assistant Comptroller General, Letter to Dr. Paul Blackman, National Rifle Association, May 31, 1991. Accordingly, GAO's estimate that a childproof grip would save

$170 million per year in medical costs was likely at least twice as high as it should have been. GAO Report, p. 4.

GAO also likely overestimated the number of handguns involved in gun accidents, since the GAO sample overrepresented urban areas, where the handgun to long-gun ratio is apt to be higher.

The GAO's estimate of the medical costs which arguably could be saved through increased gun regulations may be compared to the two billion dollars annually spent on medical care for persons injured while sliding into base during softball games. There are about 1.7 million sliding injuries per year, which cost an average of $1,223 to treat.

31. GAO Report, p. 3.

32. "Modifications in gun design are unlikely to reduce injury, since those at greatest risk are preteen and teenage boys, both of whom possess adult abilities to circumvent gun safety features." American Academy of Pediatrics, Committee on Adolescence, "Policy Statement: Firearms and Adolescents," *AAP News,* January 1992 (approved by AAP Executive Board in 1991, released in January 1992), p. 21.

33. Massad Ayoob, *Gun Proof Your Children* (Concord, N.H.: Police Bookshelf, 1986), p. 8.

34. In regards to rifles, many so-called assault weapons can use plastic, translucent magazines (ammunition-feeding devices), which make it easier for the user to tell if the gun is loaded.

35. Kleck, *Point Blank,* pp. 280–81.

36. Fla. Stat. §§ 784.05, 791.175.

37. "More Children Using Weapons Frequently in Schools," Associated Press, May 23, 1993.

38. For example, *Farley* v. *Guns Unlimited and S.W. Daniel, Inc.,* Virginia Beach, Virginia Circuit Court, no. 89–2047; *Bengston* v. *Intratec U.S.A.,* Superior Court of Middlesex, Conn., No CV–87–00487025 (case dismissed).

39. The trial court threw out the suit against the Boy Scouts, but allowed the suit against the advertisers to proceed. *Way* v. *Boy Scouts of America,* no. 90–12265–I, discussed in "Boy Scout Gun Suit Rejected," *ABA Journal,* January 1992, p. 21.

40. Kevin Simpson, "While Children Die, Colorado Balks at Firearms Reforms," *Denver Post,* September 26, 1991, p. B1.

41. GAO Report.

42. M. Heins, R. Kahn, and J. Bjordnal, "Gunshot Wounds in Children," *American Journal of Public Health* 64 (1974): 326–30.

43. William W. Treanor and Marjolijn Bijlefeld, *Kids & Guns: A Child Safety Scandal,* 2d ed. (Educational Fund to End Gun Violence), p. 17.

44. American Trauma Society, Pennsylvania Division, *"Ouch!" Anybody Can Get Hurt.* One shortcoming of the Pennsylvania brochure is that it teaches by negative example. Rather than showing a child refusing to touch the gun, the comic shows the child accidentally shooting a friend. In contrast, the fire safety example shows a child leaving a burning house, rather than a child being burned to death after he fails to evacuate.

45. Laurie Cassady, "Shorstein, NRA Aim to Save Kids," *Florida Times-Union,* November 2, 1994, p. B–2.

46. Even the Washington Post calls Eddie Eagle a "must for any parent who keeps a gun in the home." *Washington Post,* January 7, 1992, p. B5.

47. Cheryl Jackson, "Gun Safety Backers Shun NRA Material," (Cleveland) *Plain Dealer,* March 27, 1992. Similar opposition has kept Eddie Eagle out of the Denver public schools.

48. National Committee for Injury Prevention and Control, *Injury Prevention: Meeting the Challenge* (New York: Oxford, 1989), p. 266. Similarly, a government researcher in Western Australia concluded that firearms safety classes in high schools might reduce injuries.

Nevertheless, the researcher opposed the idea because classes might encourage an interest in firearms and because instructors might suggest it was legitimate to own firearms. O. F. Dixon, *Review of Firearms Legislation: Report to the Minister for Police and Traffic* (Perth, Australia: Government Printer, 1981).

49. Ronald E. Vogel and Charles Dean, "The Effectiveness of a Handgun Safety Education Program," *Journal of Police Science and Administration* 14 (1986): 242–49. The program failed to change the reckless habits of the small percent of handgun owners who do not ensure that their gun is unloaded before cleaning it.

50. American Academy of Pediatrics, Committee on Adolescence, *News Release*, p. 21. Authors writing in the AAP's journal express dismay at the "unrealistic expectations" of the half of all gun-owning parents who believe that "active strategies" such as education and supervision are the best method to prevent gun accidents in children over twelve. D. W. Webster et al., "Parents' Beliefs about Preventing Gun Injuries to Children," *Pediatrics* 89, no. 5 (1992): 908–14.

51. In a test program in Charlotte, North Carolina, the city's Police Department made April 1985 "Handgun Safety Month," and blitzed the city with public service announcements, brochures, and speeches. Followup polling showed that the program significantly increased the percentage of handgun owners who kept their gun locked; but it did not increase the number of owners who took additional safety classes or who taught their children about handguns. Vogel and Dean, "The Effectiveness of a Handgun Safety Education Program."

A rather implausible criticism of Eddie Eagle was offered by Diane Sawyer of ABC's "Primetime Live." In a program that described the problems of accidental shootings by children, and also detailed the Eddie Eagle gun safety education program, Ms. Sawyer stated, "In the last year we could find figures available, there was a 25 percent increase in the number of 16-year-old kids committing homicides with guns, So coloring books are not working." "Real Young Guns," ABC News "Primetime Live," February 22, 1990, show #129, transcript p. 2. Ms. Sawyer's conclusion failed to consider that (1) Eddie Eagle is intended to prevent accidents involving preteen children, rather than intentional murders by teenagers, and (2) no person aged sixteen at the time Ms. Sawyer's statistics were compiled could have taken the Eddie Eagle safety class.

52. Kleck, *Point Blank*, pp. 299–300; Hunter Education Association, *Hunting Accident Report with Graphics of 1986–1990 Data* (Seattle: Outdoor Empire Pub., 1991).

53. National Safety Council, *Accident Facts*, 1968 ed. and *Accident Facts, 1994*, p. 92 (139 fatal and 1,132 nonfatal hunting accidents in 1992).

54 New Zealand Police and New Zealand Mountain Safety Council, *Beginning with Airguns* (Wellington, Government Printer, 1986), p. 2.

55. In *Billy Hook Goes to Manuka Lodge*, young Billy learns essential gun safety rules. Home from the lodge, he goes target shooting with his father. See also New Zealand Police and New Zealand Mountain Safety Council, *Gun Safety with Billy Hook* (n.d.).

56. New Zealand Police, *Arms Code: Firearms Safety Manual Issued by the New Zealand Police* (Upper Hutt, New Zealand: Wright and Carman, n.d.), p. 33.

57. Charles I. H. Forsyth, *Firearms in New Zealand* (Thorndon, Wellington: New Zealand Mountain Safety Council, 1985), pp. 2, 121.

58. The Milwaukee police, in conjunction with McDonalds restaurants, produced a cartoon "safety" book featuring talking, animated guns with names like "Sammy Saturday Night Special." The use of talking guns (in contrast to Eddie Eagle's realistic, inanimate guns) obviously detracts from the realism and the effectiveness of the gun-safety message.

Moreover, the comic book tells children to call the police if they find a gun in their parents' home. In the Milwaukee/McDonalds comic, the gun that triggers the phone call happens to be a stolen one, which the father bought without knowing it was hot. But the children didn't know that, nor did the police in the comic, until they had seized the gun and taken it in for tracing.

59. David B. Kopel, *The Samurai, the Mountie, and the Cowboy: Should America Adopt*

the Gun Controls of Other Democracies? (Amherst, N.Y.: Prometheus Books, 1992), pp. 22, 442 (Japan, Detroit).

60. One study found that gun owners who have received training are more likely to store their guns loaded and unlocked, perhaps because they are more confident of their ability to handle the firearm properly without causing an accident. David Hemenway, Sara J. Solnick, and Deborah R. Azrael, "Firearm Training and Storage," *JAMA* 273, no. 1 (January 4, 1995): 46–50. Gun owners who are more interested in personal protection may also be more likely to seek training. Although Hemenway et al. accept the received wisdom of the public health literature that loaded guns in the home are *per se* pernicious, they do not study whether the trained owners' loaded guns were stored where irresponsible children could get hold of them.

61. The number of deaths resulting from misleading, sloppy journalism is not zero. To cite but one example, almost every commercial airplane crash anywhere in the world is covered by media, but car crashes are rarely reported, even in the state where they occur. The media almost never report the data showing that, per passenger mile, commercial air travel is far safer than driving. As a result of the media's unbalanced coverage of air safety, some people choose to drive rather than fly to a distant destination, in the mistaken belief that driving is safer. Statistically speaking, it is a certainty that by indirectly encouraging some people to drive rather than fly, the media cause an increase in transportation fatalities. See generally, Richard B. McKenzie and Dwight R. Lee, *Ending Free Airplane Rides for Infants: A Myopic Method of Saving Lives,* Briefing Paper no. 11 (Washington, D.C.: Cato Institute, August 30, 1990).

62. Philip Cook, "The Role of Firearms in Violent Crime: An Interpretative Review of the Literature," in M. Wolfgang and N. Weiler, eds., *Criminal Violence* (Beverly Hills, Calif.: Sage, 1982), pp. 236, 269. Also, Roger Lane, "On the Social Meaning of Homicide Trends in America," in Ted R. Gurr, ed., *Violence in America* 1 (1989): 59 ("the psychological profile of the accident-prone suggests the same kind of aggressiveness shown by most murderers"); Kleck, *Point Blank,* pp. 282–87.

63. In a highly publicized shooting of a 10-year-old boy by a playmate, the playmate was reportedly watching a movie called *Gotcha.* The playmate asked his friends if they wanted to see a real gun, and went to his father's closet to get a .357 Magnum, which he then loaded and accidentally fired. "Real Young Guns," ABC News "Primetime Live," February 22, 1990, program #129, transcript, p. 1.

64. A.N. Meltzoff, "Imitation of Televised Models by Infants," *Child Development* 59 (1988): 1221. In the Meltzoff study, children aged fourteen and twenty-four months watched an adult manipulate a novel toy in a particular way. Twenty-four hours later, the children were shown the real toy, and they used the toy in imitation of the way the man on television had used it.

65. William W. Treanor and Marjolijn Bijlefeld (Educational Fund to End Gun Violence), *Kids & Guns: A Child Safety Scandal,* 2d ed. The photo is also used by Handgun Control, Inc.'s, tax-exempt affiliate, Center to Prevent Handgun Violence, "Handgun Violence: An American Epidemic" (no date) (fund raising flyer).

66. *Accident Facts,* 1992, 1993, and 1994 editions.

67. L. Stanley Chauvin, "Startling Statistics about Children," *ABA Journal,* February 1990, p. 8.

68. "When Guns Go to School," *USA Today,* February 28, 1992.

69. Sen. Joseph Biden, "Statement of Senator Joseph R. Biden, Jr., Chairman, Senate Judiciary Committee, 'Children and Guns: Why the Recent Rise?' " Senate Committee on the Judiciary, October 1, 1992, p.2 ("135,000 children are carrying guns to school everyday [*sic*]"); Senator John Chafee, "Testimony of Senator John H. Chafee before the Senate Judiciary Committee during Hearings on 'Kids and Guns,' " October 1, 1992, p. 1 ("An estimated 135,000 boys carry guns to school every day").

70. "Statement of Senator Christopher J. Dodd," Hearing on "Children of War: Violence and America's Youth," Senate Subcommittee on Children, Family, Drugs, and Alcoholism, July

23, 1992, p. 1. ("Each day, 186,000 students bring a gun to school, many out of fear.") Since "8" looks something like "3" and since "6" looks something like "5," perhaps the "186,000" was a misreading of a fax or a poor-quality photocopy of a document containing the "135,000" figure.

71. MTV, "Enough is Enough," printed advertisement for MTV series of same name (New York: MTV Networks, 1994).

72. Centers for Disease Control, "Weapon-Carrying among High School Students—United States, 1990" *Morbidity and Mortality Weekly Report* 40, no. 40 (October 11, 1991): 681–84. A survey the next year about various risky behaviors found similar levels of weapons carrying. Again, the survey did not ask about carrying at school. Centers for Disease Control, "Behaviors Related to Unintentional and Intentional Injuries among High School Students—United States, 1991," *Morbidity and Mortality Weekly Report* 41, no. 41 (October 16, 1992): 760–67.

73. A study of students at two inner-city junior high schools found 25 percent of the males reporting having carried a gun. Daniel W. Webster, Patricia S. Gainer, and Howard R. Champion, "Weapon Carrying among Inner-City Junior High School Students: Defensive Behavior v. Aggressive Delinquency," *American Journal of Public Health* 83, no. 11 (1993): 1604–1608.

74. Bureau of Justice of Statistics, U.S. Department of Justice, *Sourcebook of Criminal Justice Statistics—1983* (Washington, D.C.: Government Printing Office, 1984), p. 410.

75. Persons aged twelve to seventeen constitute ten percent of the population, but 23 percent of crime victims. "In U.S., Crime Strikes Youth at High Rate," *New York Times*, July 18, 1994, p. A16.

76. Barbara Allen-Hagen and Melissa Sickmund, *Juveniles and Violence: Juvenile Offending and Victimization,* Fact Sheet #19 (Washington: Office of Juvenile Justice and Delinquency Prevention, Department of Justice, 1994), p. 2.

77. Allen-Hagan and Sickmund, *Juvenile Violence,* p. 2. Parentheses in original.

78. Ibid., p. 1.

79. Ibid.

80. Catherine J. Whitaker and Lisa Bastian, Bureau of Justice Statistics, *Teenage Victims: A National Crime Survey Report,* NCJ–28129 (Washington, D.C.: U.S. Department of Justice, May 1991).

81. 1990 surveys conducted by Illinois Criminal Justice Information Authority.

82. Kleck, *Point Blank,* p. 117 (adult carry rate, citing February 1985 Roper poll).

83. Joanne Wassermann, "Kids on Defense," (New York) *Daily News.*

84. "Students Speak Out: Why Do Some Students Carry Weapons to School?" *Washington Post,* December 1, 1988, p. Md. 15.

85. Wendy Kaminer, "Crime and Community," *The Atlantic,* May 1994, p. 120.

86. Weasel, "Kids and Crime," p. 4. To the extent that crimes were not reported, the number would be higher.

87. James D. Wright, Joseph F. Sheley, and M. Dwayne Smith, "Kids, Guns and Killing Fields," *Society* 30, no. 1 (1992): 84–89.

88. Michael Perlstein, "Guns Are Protection, Teens Explain," (New Orleans) *Times-Picayune,* November 6, 1992, p. 1.

A smaller study of inner-city students found that carrying handguns was statistically associated with aggressive and delinquent behaviors. Webster et al., "Weapon Carrying." Likewise, a study of suburban students found that involvement in violent crime or drugs increased the likelihood of gun carrying. Joseph F. Sheley, "Possession and Carrying of Firearms among Suburban Youth," *Public Health Reports* 110 (1995): 18–26. Webster's and Sheley's results are not inconsistent with the fact that a large number of students who carry firearms do so for protective purposes. Because many delinquents carry guns nearly all the time, while many teenagers carrying for nonaggressive purposes will carry only occasionally, the gun-carrying population will include a large number of delinquents, whose actions will create a statistical association between gun carrying and delinquency. Webster et al. conclude that teenage gun carrying does not appear to be "a purely defensive behavior." Since some students who carry guns are aggressive criminals and some are not, it is correct to conclude that not all gun carrying is purely defensive.

A study of New York City high school students found that students who carried weapons were more likely than other students to believe that carrying or threatening to use a weapon was an effective way to avoid a physical fight. Centers for Disease Control and Prevention, "Violence-Related Attitudes and Behaviors of High Schools Students—New York City, 1992," *JAMA* 270, no. 17 (November 3, 1993): 2032–33. Whether or not the students were right, the findings suggest that at least some weapons carrying may be for defensive, nonaggressive purposes.

89. Wright et al., "Kids, Guns and Killing Fields," p. 88.

90. Other questions: "Have you ever owned a gun?" 86 percent inmates; 30 percent students. "If you've owned a gun recently, was it automatic/semi-automatic?" 57 percent inmates; 49 percent students.

91. Wright, et al., "Kids, Guns and Killing Fields," p. 88.

92. Joseph F. Sheley and James D. Wright, "Motivations for Gun Possession and Carrying among Serious Juvenile Offenders," *Behavioral Sciences and the Law* 11 (1993): 375.

93. Weasel, "Kids and Crime."

94. Joseph F. Sheley, Zina T. McGee, and James D. Wright, "Gun-Related Violence in and around Inner-City Schools," *American Journal of Diseases of Children (AJDC)* 146 (June 1992): 682.

95.

Guns do not make schools dangerous places. Guns are in schools because schools are dangerous places. [Schools focus on regimentation, which leads to rebellion, which leads to violence.] In response, school administrators have emulated police states. Just as in the worst dictatorship, students must have special passes to travel in the halls at the wrong time, they must have picture identifications that must be immediately produced upon the demand of one of the teachers/guards/administrative goons. Doors are locked, sections of the school are blocked off. Anyone voluntarily missing from class is punished. Rebellion against teachers or administrators is the worst crime of all. . . . Those who don't wish to affiliate with gangs often find themselves defenseless unless they drop out, go to private schools or carry arms . . . the liberals' solution to all this is to outlaw guns in schools, so turning those who turn to arms to defend themselves into criminals

"Guns in Schools," *The Nay Sayer,* April 1992, pp. 1–2.

96. E.g., *Johnson* v. *Dallas Independent School District,* 63 United States Law Week 2346 (5th Cir. 1994).

97. A. Mackay-Smith, "Should Schools Permit Searching Students for Weapons, Drugs?" *Wall Street Journal,* May 30, 1984. Mackay-Smith discussed policy in Detroit, where police searches looked for knives and chemical defense sprays carried by girls to protect themselves from rapists.

98. "Around the Nation," *Law Enforcement News,* May 31, 1994, p. 3.

99. Maria E. Odum, "Teacher Arrested with Gun is Back at School: Students Join Celebration of 'One of the Happiest Days of My Life,' " *Washington Post,* January 9, 1993.

Guns do not go off by themselves, so there was no risk that the gun could have accidentally discharged. If the gun on the floor of the car were visible, it could have been stolen. The teacher's carelessness with the gun certainly could have been punished by the school administration, such as by a temporary suspension without pay rather than by felony criminal prosecution.

100. Janet Naylor, "School Rules Deal with Living History," *Washington Times,* February 17, 1994, p. C10; Glenn McMahan, "Aide Charged for Gun in School," *The Frederick Post,* November 17, 1993, p. A–1.

101. "Drug-Free School Zone" postings are similarly misleading.

102. Colorado Revised Statutes, § 18–12–105.

103. Dan Reed, "Berkeley Student Accused over Gun: Law Forbids Firearms on University Proper," *San Francisco Chronicle*, July 2, 1993, p. A25 (prosecution of 26-year-old graduate student who possessed a pistol in an off-campus, university-owned apartment).

104. 18 U.S.C. § 922(q). The law was declared unconstitutional in *United States* v. *Lopez*, 2 F.3d 1342 (5th Cir., 1993), a decision that was upheld by the Supreme Court just before this book went to press. For an excellent analysis of the Commerce Clause issues in *Lopez*, placed in the context of the expansion of the commerce power in the last six decades, see Glenn Harlan Reynolds, *Kids, Guns, and the Commerce Clause: Is the Court Ready for Constitutional Government?* Cato Institute Policy Analysis no. 216 (Washington, D.C.: Cato Inst., October 10, 1994).

105. Kenneth J. Cooper, "President Directs Schools to Bar Students with Guns," *Washington Post*, October 23, 1994, p. A8.

106 "Squirt Gun-packing Pupil, 7, Gets Suspension, Counseling," *The Call*, May 5, 1994 (Associated Press); "Toy Gun or Weapon?" *Grand Junction* (Colo.) *Sentinel*, May 5, 1994.

107. "Around the Nation," *Law Enforcement News*, May 31, 1994, p. 3.

108. Chelsea Irving, "Boy Faces Weapons Charges: 9-Year-Old Turns Over Bullet during Recess," *The Northern Star* (DeKalb, Ill.), April 27, 1994.

109. "Around the Nation," *Law Enforcement News*, October 31, 1994, p. 2.

110. Mark Stevens, "School Suspends Scout for Having Pocket Knife," *Denver Post*, March. 11, 1995, p. 1A.

111. "School Violence," *The Liberator*, Fall 1994, p. 2.

112. After the decision by the Ninth Circuit Court of Appeals, the California legislature enacted legislation guaranteeing the rights of Sikh students. "Iambs and Pentameters," *Liberty*, January/February 1995, p. 5.

113. "Irushalmi Responds to Growing Needs of Security Staff," *School Safety Update*, December 1991, p. 5.

114. Steve Stecklow, "Metal Detectors Find a Growing Market, But Not Many Guns," *Wall Street Journal*, September 7, 1993; Carol Innerst, "'Airline Security' Enters Education," *Washington Times*, August 23, 1992, p. A16.

115. Hamil R. Harris, "D.C. School Officials Eye Tighter Security," *Washington Post*, January 28, 1994, p. A17 (school official: "There are girls wearing those big gold earrings and book bags that must be searched. It would take two hours to search everyone who made the beeper go off.")

116. Centers for Disease Control and Prevention, "Violence-Related Attitudes and Behaviors of High Schools Students—New York City, 1992," *JAMA* 270, no. 17 (November 3, 1993): 2032–33.

117. *New Jersey* v. *T.L.O.*, 469 U.S. 325, 105 S.Ct. 733 (1985).

118. For an excellent survey of the issue, see Stephen P. Halbrook, "Firearms, the Fourth Amendment, and Air Carrier Security," *Journal of Air Law and Commerce* 52 (1987): 585.

119. New laws in Virginia and Utah require that courts inform schools about violent or weapons offenses by juveniles. 1994 Utah Laws, chapter 256; 1994 Virginia Acts, chapters 835, 913.

120. David M. Altschuler and Troy L. Armstrong, *Intensive Aftercare for High-Risk Juveniles: An Assessment*, NCJ 144018 (Washington, D.C.: Department of Justice, Office of Juvenile Justice and Delinquency Prevention, 1994), p. 64.

121. Recent research suggests that once other variables related to the dropout—such as number of prior arrests—are considered, dropping out does not appear to be a strong causal factor in subsequent delinquency. G. Roger Jarjoura, "Does Dropping Out of School Enhance Delinquent Involvement? Results from a Large-Scale National Probability Sample," *Criminology* 31, no. 2 (1993): 149–72.

122. Jackson Toby, "The Politics of School Violence," *The Public Interest,* No. 116 (Summer 1994): 52.

123. Ibid., pp. 52–53.

124. The topic is discussed in much more detail in Kopel, *Samurai,* ch. 2.

125. Anna David, "Disestablishing Public Education," *The Freeman,* February 1993, pp. 68–71.

126. Daniel McGroarty, "School Choice Slandered," *The Public Interest,* No. 117 (Fall 1994): 94–111.

127. Among the books and studies making a case for reducing government control of education and increasing consumer choice are: David Harmer, *School Choice: Will it Work?* (National Book Network: 1994); David Boaz, ed., *Liberating Schools: Education in the Inner City* (Washington, D.C.: Cato Institute, 1990); Sheldon Richman, *Separating School and State: How to Liberate America's Families* (Fairfax, Va.: Future of Freedom Foundation, 1994); Jack D. Douglas, *Only Freedom of Education Can Solve America's Bureaucratic Crisis of Education,* Cato Institute Policy Analysis no. 155 (Washington, D.C.: Cato Institute, 1991); Independence Institute, *Polly Williams Reports on Vouchers in Milwaukee,* Issue Paper no. 19–92 (Golden, Colo.: Ind. Institute, 1992).

128. Ronald Henkoff, "Kids are Killing, Dying, Bleeding," *Fortune,* August 10, 1992.

129. Paul Cotton, "Gun-Associated Violence Increasingly Viewed as Public Health Challenge," *JAMA* 267 (1992): 1171–74.

130. Centers for Disease Control and Prevention, "Homicides among 15-19-Year-Old Males—United States, 1963–1991," *Morbidity and Mortality Weekly Report* 43, no. 40 (1994): 725–27; Fox Butterfield, "Teen-Age Homicide Rate Has Soared," *New York Times,* October 14, 1994, p. A10.

131. Dr. Katherine Christoffel, American Academy of Pediatrics, testimony on "Children and Guns," House Select Committee on Children, Youth and Families, June 15, 1989.

132. J. H. Sloan et al., "Handgun Regulations, Crime, Assaults, and Homicide: A Tale of Two Cities," *New England Journal of Medicine* 319 (November 10, 1988): 1256–62.

133. See note 5.

134. Centers for Disease Control, "Behavior Related to Unintentional and Intentional Injuries among High School Students—United States, 1991," *Morbidity and Mortality Weekly Report,* No. 41 (1992): 760–72.

135. Kleck, "The Incidence of Gun Violence among Young People." The NCVS data are sometimes questioned by researchers, including Kleck; those researchers carry the burden, however, of showing why the NCVS is an inaccurate measure of the particular fact being studied.

136. See, for example, R. M. Groves and L. J. Magilavy, "Estimates of Interviewer Variance in Telephone Surveys," *Proceedings of Survey Research Methods Section, American Statistical Association* (1980): 622. For other citations, as well as a discussion of interviewer effects in the context of gun-control polling, see Gary Mauser and David B. Kopel, " 'Sorry, Wrong Number': Why Media Polls on Gun Control Are Often Unreliable," *Political Communication* 9 (1992): 69.

137. Kleck, "The Incidence of Gun Violence among Young People," p. 6.

138. FBI, *Crime in the United States 1993: Uniform Crime Reports* (*UCR*) (Washington, D.C.: 1994).

139. Kleck, *Point Blank,* pp. 111–15.

140. Fox Butterfield, "Seeds of Murder Epidemic: Teen-Age Boys with Guns," *New York Times,* October 19, 1992, (Reporting study by James A. Fox, dean of Northeastern University's College of Criminal Justice, by National Crime Analysis Project at Northeastern).

141. Kathleen M. Heide, "Weapons Used by Juveniles and Adults to Kill Parents," *Behavioral Sciences and the Law* 11 (1993): 397, 398.

142. Isabel Wilkerson, "2 Boys, A Debt, A Gun, A Victim: The Face of Violence," *New York Times,* May 16, 1994.

143. Ibid.

144. Howard N. Snyder, "Arrests of Youth 1990," OJJDP (Office of Juvenile Justice and Delinquency Programs, Department of Justice) Update on Statistics, January 1992, pp. 9–11.

A recent article claims that "homicide rates for Latinos are almost as high as rates for African Americans in all gender groups." Kenneth Tardiff et al., "Homicide in New York City," *JAMA* 272, no. 1 (July 6, 1994): 43. The article supports this claim with a citation in *Vital Statistics of the United States*. The cited source, however, does not even report homicide rates for Hispanics, let alone those rates in gender groups. Using the raw numbers supplied in *Vital Statistics* shows the Hispanic homicide rate to be less than half the black rate.

145. Lois A. Fingerhut, Deborah D. Ingram, and Jacob J. Feldman, "Firearm and Nonfirearm Homicide among Persons 15 through 19 Years of Age: Differences by Level of Urbanization, United States, 1979 through 1989," *JAMA* 267, no. 22 (June 10, 1992): 3048.

146. "Teenage Victims: A National Crime Survey Report," p. 11.

147. Kenneth Tardiff et al., "Homicide in New York City," *JAMA* 272, no. 1 (July 6, 1994): 44. As is typical in the public health literature relating to guns, the authors present useful statistical information. But having shown that many murder victims in New York City are cocaine users and/or are killed with a firearm, the authors conclude that more controls should be imposed on cocaine and on firearms. After noting that research is divided on whether gun controls would be effective, the authors simply assert, "Strict legislation must be implemented at the national level." In regard to cocaine, the authors announce the need "to decrease cocaine use," but do not consider whether laws criminalizing the sale of cocaine may be responsible for many cocaine-related deaths. Ibid., p. 46.

148. McGonigal et al., p. 535.

149. Stu Cohen and Renée Wilson-Brewer, *Violence Prevention for Young Adolescents: The State of the Art of Program Evaluation,* Carnegie Council on Youth Development, Working Paper (Washington. D.C.: Carnegie Corp., 1991), p. 3, citing unpublished FBI data.

150. In 1976 through 1992, 91.2 percent of black males killed were killed by a black; 85.6 percent were killed by a male. Data supplied by James Alan Fox, National Crime Analysis Program, Northeastern University, in Bureau of Justice Statistics, *Sourcebook of Criminal Justice Statistics—1993* (Washington, D.C.: Government Printing Office, 1994), p. 387.

See also Philip R. Fine et al., "Homicide Among Black Males in Jefferson County, Alabama 1978–1989," *Journal of Forensic Sciences* 39, no. 3 (May 1994): 681; Centers for Disease Control, "Homicide among Young Black Males—United States, 1970–1982," *Morbidity and Mortality Weekly Reports* 34 (1985): 629.

151. Whitaker and Bastian, *Teenage Victims,* p. 6, Table 11 (robbery, aggravated assault, simple assault).

152 Michael A. Jones and Barry Krisberg, *Images and Reality: Juvenile Crime, Youth Violence, and Public Policy* (San Francisco: National Council on Crime and Delinquency, 1994), pp. 11–12.

Were this chapter to follow the argumentative style of much of the "public health" literature (discussed in chapter 5), the only reply necessary to the NCCD's arguments would be to note dismissively that the NCCD is (from the author's viewpoint) ideologically incorrect, since it is an advocacy group which supports rehabilitation and opposes punishment of criminals, and tends to blame only the environment rather than the criminal for the crime. (Compare, for example, the way that some public health authors dismiss criminologists' criticisms of flaws in antigun public health articles; the authors do not refute the criticisms, but simply sneer that the criticizers do not support gun control.)

153. Ibid., p. 14.

154. A Baltimore study of homicides in 1974 through 1984 found that 84 percent of adult homicide perpetrators acted alone, but only 45.7 percent of juvenile perpetrators did. Derral Cheatwood and Kathleen J. Block, "Youth Homicide: An Investigation of the Age Factor in Criminal Homicide," *Justice Quarterly* 7, no. 2 (1990): 277–78.

155. *Sourcebook of Criminal Justice Statistics—1993*, p. 247 (data from National Crime Victimization Survey).

156. Ibid., p. 352.

157. For more on the differences between the UCR and the NCVS, see "Appendix IV: The Nation's Two Crime Measures," in FBI, *Crime in the United States 1991: Uniform Crime Reports* (Washington, D.C.: Government Printing Office, 1992), pp. 388–89.

Briefly stated, the UCR is based on offenses known to the police, while the NCVS is based on Bureau of Census polling. The NCVS is generally a more accurate measure, since it identifies the significant fraction of crimes in which the victim did not report the crime to the police. The NCVS does not survey homicide, since the victim cannot answer questions. Since homicides tend to be reported to the police at a higher rate than other crimes, the effect of underreporting on distorting homicide is much less serious than for other violent crimes.

158. *Myths and Realities: Meeting the Challenge of Serious Violent and Chronic Juvenile Violent Offenders: 1992 Annual Report* (Washington, D.C.: National Coalition of State Juvenile Justice Advisory Groups, 1993). A study of black male homicides in one Alabama county found no change in the proportion of firearms used, from 1978 to 1993. Fine et al., "Homicide among Black Males in Jefferson County," p. 681.

159. Barbara Allen-Hagen and Melissa Sickmund, *Juveniles and Violence: Juvenile Offending and Victimization,* Fact Sheet #19 (Washington, D.C.: Office of Juvenile Justice and Delinquency Prevention, Department of Justice, 1994), p. 1.

160. Ibid., p. 3.

161. Whitaker and Bastian, *Teenage Victims,* p. 4, table 6: Based on data from 1985–88, guns are used in 6 percent of robberies and 16 percent of aggravated assaults against persons aged twelve to fifteen, in 16 percent of robberies and 31 percent of aggravated assaults against persons aged sixteen to nineteen, and 21 percent of robberies and 33 percent of aggravated assaults against persons twenty or more.

162. Kleck, *Point Blank,* pp. 191–201 (study of 170 cities finds that increasing homicide leads to increasing gun density; increasing gun density is associated with lower homicide rates).

163. Ibid., pp. 21–25, 185–203; Yvonne D. Senturia, Katherine Kaufer Christoffel, and Mark Donovan, "Children's Household Exposure to Guns: A Pediatric Practice-Based Survey," *Pediatrics* 93, no. 3 (March 1994): 469–75 (survey of patients at twenty-nine pediatric practices in seven states finds gun ownership higher in households with white parents and lowest in homes of poorly educated minority single mothers in inner cities).

164. Walter J. Howe, "Firearm Production, Imports, and Exports," *Shooting Industry,* January 1992, pp. 91–118.

165. Hans Toch and Alan Lizotte, "Research and Policy: The Case of Gun Control," in P. Suedfeld and P. Tetlock, eds., *Psychology and Social Advocacy* (New York: Hemisphere Press, 1990).

166. Chapter 5 discusses this question in more detail.

167. For an example, Tardiff et al., "Homicide in New York City," p. 43.

168. James B. Twitchell, *Preposterous Violence: Fables of Aggression in Modern Culture* (New York: Oxford University Press, 1989), p. 189.

169. Lois A. Fingerhut and Joel C. Kleinman, "International and Interstate Comparisons of Homicide among Young Males," *JAMA* 263 (June 27, 1990): 3292–95.

170. Kopel, *Samurai,* ch. 3.

171. Fingerhut and Kleinman, "International and Interstate Comparisons of Homicides among Young Males," p. 3923 (the rates were 1.4 in Switzerland and 5.0 in Scotland for 1987).

172. Kopel, *Samurai,* pp. 282–84.

173. Centers for Disease Control, "Compressed Mortality File of the National Center for Health Statistics," 1989 Update.

174. Sam Staley, *Drug Policy and the Decline of American Cities* (New Brunswick, N.J.: Transaction Publishers, 1992).

175. David W. Rasmussen and Bruce L. Benson, *The Economic Anatomy of a Drug War: Criminal Justice in the Commons* (Lanham, Md.: Rowman and Littlefied, 1994), pp. 101-06; Eric Sterling, "Outline of Some Issues Involving Drug Trafficking," address to National Conference on Schools and Communities, Washington, D.C., December 16, 1992; L. Dash, "A Dealer's Creed: Be Willing to Die," *Washington Post,* April 3, 1989. See also Jeffrey Fagan and Ko-lin Chin, "Violence as Regulation and Social Control in the Distribution of Crack," in Mario De La Rosa, Elizabeth Y. Lambert, and Bardnard Gropper, eds., *Drugs and Violence: Causes, Correlates, and Consequences,* NIDA Research Monograph 103 (Washington, D.C.: Department of Health and Human Services, National Institute on Drug Abuse, 1990): 8 (also noting that many crack dealers perpetrate violence unrelated to business needs).

176. Rasmussen and Benson, *The Economic Anatomy of a Drug War.*

177. P. J. Goldstein, H. H. Brownstein, and P. J. Ryan, "Drug-Related Homicide in New York: 1984 and 1988," *Crime and Delinquency* 38 (1992): 459; P. J. Goldstein et al., "Crack and Homicide in New York City, 1988: A Conceptually Based Event Analysis," *Contemporary Drug Problems* 16 (1989): 651.

178. The life-saving effect of the drug laws would obviously be strongest for drugs which are pharmacologically associated with violent behavior or life-threatening addiction (such as cocaine) and weakest for drugs which tend to discourage aggression and which have fewer harmful physical side effects (such as hemp and psychedelics).

179. In 1994 The *Chicago Tribune* put every murder of a person under the age of fifteen on the front page. Thomas Winship, a former *Boston Globe* editor and currently a columnist for the trade magazine *Editor & Publisher,* urged other papers to do the same, in a column in which he also urged papers to "Support all forms of gun licensing; in fact, all the causes the NRA opposes." Thomas Winship, "Step up the War against Guns," *Editor & Publisher,* April 24, 1993, p. 24.

180. Researchers at the University of California at Santa Barbara reported that crime or violence were the subjects of 48 percent of television stories and 40 percent of newspaper stories about children. Laura Sessions Stepp, "The Crackdown on Juvenile Crime," *Washington Post,* October 15, 1994.

181. Select Committee on Children, Youth, and Families, *U.S. Children and Their Families: Current Conditions and Recent Trends, 1989,* 101st Congress, 1st sess., September 1989 (Washington, D.C.: Government Printing Office) (1986 data).

182. J. A. Jason, "Childhood Homicide Spectrum," *American Journal of Diseases of Children* 137 (1983): 578–81.

183. Parents who murder children under the age of twelve use a firearm or a knife in seven percent of all cases. John M. Dawson and Patrick Langan, "Murder in Families," Bureau of Justices Statistics Special Report (Washington, D.C.: Department of Justice, Bureau of Justice Statistics, 1994), p. 5.

184. Eighty-two percent of juvenile patricides and 62 percent of juvenile matricides are perpetrated with firearms. Kathleen M. Heide, "Weapons Used by Juveniles and Adults to Kill Parents," *Behavioral Sciences and the Law* 11 (1993): 397, 404. Children who act violently toward their parents are more likely than other children to have been physically or psychologically abused. Peter C. Kratcoski, "Youth Violence Directed toward Significant Others," *Journal of Adolescence* 8, no. 8 (1985): 145 ("In some cases, the violent youth who struck a parent was acting in self-defense or was trying to protect a parent or a sibling who was being beaten by a spouse, boyfried, or other person in the household." Ibid, p. 155); Peter C. Kratcoski, "Youth Violence Directed toward Significant Others," *J. Adolesc.* 8 (1985): 145–47. See also Paul Mones, "The Relationship between Child Abuse and Parricide: An Overview," in E. Newberger and R. Bourne, eds., *Unhappy Families: Clinical and Research Perspectives on Family Violence* (Mosby, 1989); B. Corder, "Adolescent Parricide: A Comparison with Other Adolescent Murders," *American Journal of Psychiatry* 133 (1976): 957–61; Emanuel Taney, "Reactive Parricide," *Journal of Forensic Sciences* 21 (1976): 76.

185. Dewey G. Cornell, "Juvenile Homicide: A Growing National Problem," *Behavioral Sciences and the Law* 11 (1993): 389–96.

186. American Academy of Pediatrics, "Firearms and Adolescents," pp. 20–21. Also blaming the gun rather than the gun criminal, Richard Kuh, chair of the American Bar Association's Criminal Justice section, called for a broad range of new gun laws to end the "ready access to guns that criminalizes so many young people." "NRA, ABA Debating Gun Control," *Las Vegas Review-Journal,* June 25, 1994, p. 8A.

187. American Academy of Pediatrics, "Firearms and Adolescents," pp. 20–21. The cited study was: Centers for Disease Control, *Homicide Surveillance: High-Risk Racial and Ethnic Groups—Blacks and Hispanics, 1970 to 1983* (Atlanta: Centers for Disease Control, November 1986).

188. Dianna Marder, "A New Generation of Killers: Feeling No Blame and No Shame," *Philadelphia Inquirer,* December 6, 1992, p. 1. It is disturbing to consider how frequently the comments of the killers, blaming the victims for resisting, echo the insistent advice of gun-control organizations and some law enforcement administrators that victims of a criminal attack should never do anything but passively submit. Could the advice, repeated frequently and unquestioningly by the media, have provided the killers with a perceived legitimation of killing victims who resist?

Persons interested in a large volume of stories of youth homicides will enjoy Charles Patrick Ewing, *Kids Who Kill* (New York: Avon, 1990), which collects hundreds of murder stories, almost none of them longer than two pages. As a policy guide to juvenile killings, the book is nearly worthless, since it is founded on sensational and false information such as "in 1987 roughly 135,000 boys carried handguns to school daily," and "the growing number of accidental shootings of children by other children." Ibid., p. 173.

189. Don B. Kates, *Why Handgun Bans Can't Work* (Bellevue, Wash.: Second Amendment Foundation, 1982), pp. 25–26. See also Gary Kleck, "Policy Lessons from Recent Gun-Control Research," *Journal of Law and Contemporary Problems* 49 (Winter 1986): 40–41, stating that 70 to 75 percent of domestic homicide offenders have a previous arrest and about half have a previous conviction.

190. M. Wilt et al., *Domestic Violence and the Police: Studies in Detroit and Kansas City* (Washington, D.C.: Government Printing Office, 1977).

191. Kirkpatrick and Walt, "The High Cost of Gunshot and Stab Wounds," *Journal of Surgical Research* 14 (1973): 261–62.

192. McGonigal et al., p. 534.

193. Richard C. Lumb and Paul C. Friday, City of Charlotte Gunshot Study (n.d.); "Crooks Run Higher Risk of Gunshots," *The News and Observer* (Charlotte), November 26, 1994; Ann Doss Helms, "In Charlotte, Risk of Being Shot Seems Tied to Lifestyle, Study Says," *Charlotte Observer,* November 25, 1994, p. 1A. The study involved only adults, since the criminal records of juvenile shooting victims are not publicly available. Because juvenile records are secret, a large number of the 36 percent of shooting victims without a criminal conviction may actually have had a criminal record contained in closed juvenile court files.

194. M. C. Morrisey, R. C. Byrd, and E. A. Deitch, "The Incidence of Recurrent Penetrating Trauma in an Urban Trauma Center," *Journal of Trauma* 31 (1991): 1536–38; D. W. Sims et al., "Urban Trauma: A Chronic Recurrent Disease," *Journal of Trauma* 29 (1989): 940.

195. J. Cesare et al., "Characteristics of Blunt and Personal Violent Injuries," *Journal of Trauma* 30 (1990): 176–82.

196. J. D. Richardson and F .B. Miller, "Will Future Surgeons Be Interested in a Trauma Call?" *Journal of Trauma* 32 (1992): 229–35.

197. David Simon, "A Journalist's Eye View of the Trauma Physician's Dilemma," *Archives of Otolaryngology* 118 (June 1992): 577, 578.

198. "Eight in 10 Patients Back with Another Gunshot Wound in 3½ Years," *Associated Press,* November 30, 1994.

199. Joseph F. Sheley, Zina T. McGee, and James D. Wright, "Gun-Related Violence in and around Inner-City Schools," *American Journal of Diseases of Children (AJDC)* 146 (June 1992): 677. See also Janet L. Lauritsen, Robert J. Sampson, and John H. Laub, "The Link between Offending and Victimization among Adolescents," *Criminology* 29 (1991): 265.

200. Sheley, McGee, and Wright, "Gun-Related Violence in and around Inner-City Schools."

201 "Around the Nation," *Law Enforcement News,* October 31, 1994, p. 2.

202. H. Range Hutson, Deirdre Anglin, and Michael J. Pratts, "Adolescents and Children Injured or Killed in Drive-By Shootings in Los Angeles," *New England Journal of Medicine* 330 (1994): 325.

203. Simon I. Singer, "Victims in a Birth Cohort," in Marvin E. Wolfgang, Terence P. Thornberry, and Robert M. Figlio, *From Boy to Man, from Delinquency to Crime* (Chicago: University of Chicago Press, 1987): 163.

204. Interviews with young inmates in Lorton prison, which houses Washington, D.C., felons, in Pressley and Harriston, "A Crazed Fascination with Guns," *Washington Post,* February 2, 1992.

205. Eric Pooley, "Kids with Guns," *New York,* August 5, 1991, p. 25.

206. Wright et al., "Kids, Guns and Killing Fields," pp. 88–89.

207. James D. Wright and Joseph Sheley, "Teenage Violence and the Underclass," *Peace Review* (Fall 1992), p. 32, 34.

208. Sociologist James D. Wright observes, "That 'Demand creates its own supply' is sometimes called the First Law of Economics. And it clearly holds true whether the commodity in demand is legal or illegal. In a capitalist economy, it could scarcely be otherwise. So long as people want to own guns, be they criminals or average Joes, guns will be available for them to own." James D. Wright, "Ten Essential Observations on Guns in America," *Society,* March–April 1995, pp. 62–67.

209. Wright and Sheley, "Teenage Violence and the Underclass," p. 35.

210. "Platform: 'The Right to Bear Arms is Outdated,' " *Los Angeles Times,* January 18, 1993.

211. Gary Kleck, "Guns and Violence: An Interpretive Review of the Field," *Social Pathology* 1, no. 1 (January 1995): 34, 37.

212. *Sourcebook of Criminal Justice Statistics—1993,* p. 23. For 1991, the last year reported, state and local drug enforcement spending was $15,907,000,000, a 13 percent increase from the previous year.

213. I am not aware of data estimating total expenditures for juvenile justice, but is seems possible that it may be significantly less than the drug enforcement budget. For example, in 1990, total state government spending for juvenile correctional institutions totaled $1,396,924,000. For drug control in the same year, state correctional expenditures were $4,638,000,000. *Sourcebook of Criminal Justice Statistics–1993,* pp. 12, 23.

214. It is not unconstitutional for a court to consider prior juvenile offenses when setting an adult's sentence. *United States* v. *Johnson,* 28 F.3d 151 (D.C. Cir., 1994); *United States* v. *Holland,* 26 F.3d 26 (5th Cir., 1994); *United States* v. *Booten,* 914 F.2d 1352 (9th Cir., 1990); *United States* v. *Bucare,* 898 F.2d 368 (3d Cir., 1990); *United States* v. *Chanel,* 3 F.3d 372 (11th Cir., 1993), *cert. denied,* 114 S.Ct. 1107 (1994).

215. Henry Sontheimer and Lynne Goodstein, "An Evaluation of Juvenile Intensive Aftercare Probation: Aftercare Versus System Response Effects," *Justice Quarterly* 10, no. 2 (June 1993): 197.

For details of intensive aftercare programs, see David M. Altschuler and Troy L. Armstrong, *Intensive Aftercare for High-Risk Juveniles: Policies and Procedures,* NCJ 147712 (Washington, D.C.: Office of Juvenile Justice and Delinquency Prevention, Department of Justice, September 1994); David M. Altschuler and Troy L. Armstrong, *Intensive Aftercare for High-Risk Juveniles: A Community Care Model,* NCJ 147575 (Washington, D.C.: Office of Juvenile Justice and Delinquency Prevention, Department of Justice, September 1994).

216. Jeffrey A. Fagan, "Treatment and Reintegration of Violent Juvenile Offenders: Experimental Results," *Justice Quarterly* 7, no. 2 (1990): 233–63.

217. Paul E. Tracy, Marvin Wolfgang, and Robert M. Figlio, *Delinquency in Two Birth Cohorts: Executive Summary* (Washington, D.C.: National Institute of Justice, 1985), p. 21.

218. For more, see David B. Kopel, *Prison Blues: How America's Foolish Sentencing Policies Endanger Public Safety*, Cato Institute Policy Analysis no. 212 (Washington, D.C.: Cato Institute, 1994).

219. Morgan Reynolds, "Why Does Crime Pay?" Policy Backgrounder No. 123 (Dallas: National Center for Policy Analysis, December 8, 1992).

220. Ibid.

221. Frank Green, "Put Away Younger Criminals Longer, Panel Told," *Richmond Times-Dispatch*, June 9, 1994.

222. Denise C. Gottfredson and William H. Barton, "Deinstitutionalization of Juvenile Offenders," *Criminology* 31, no. 4 (1993): 591.

223. For an argument that the Supreme Court was wrong, see Mark C. Seis and Kenneth L. Elbe, "The Death Penalty for Juveniles: Bridging the Gap between an Evolving Standard of Decency and Legislative Policy," *Justice Quarterly* 8, no. 4 (1991): 465.

224. Sending convicts to boot camps tends to be cheaper than imprisoning them, but only because boot camp sentences (usually 90 to 120 days, and rarely more than 240 days) are so much shorter than the prison sentence that would have been imposed. On a day-by-day basis, boot camps are more expensive than prisons, because staffing levels must be higher. General Accounting Office, *Prison Boot Camps: Short-Term Prison Costs Reduced, but Long-Term Impact Uncertain* (Washington, D.C.: Government Printing Office, 1993). See also Roberta C. Cronin, *Boot Camps for Adult and Juvenile Offenders: Overview and Update*, NCJ 149175 (National Institute of Justice, August 1994).

225. Joe Hallinan, "Out-of-State Programs a Costly, Short-Term Fix," *Washington Times*, June 27, 1994, p. A10 (Newhouse News Service).

226. Orange County Probation Department, *The "Eight Percent Problem": Chronic Juvenile Offender Recidivism* (Santa Ana, Calif.: OCPD, Program Planning and Research Division, 1994); Los Angeles Probation Department, *Initial Referrals to Juvenile Probation in Los Angeles County January-June 1990: A Cohort Follow-Up* (Downey, Calif.: August 1993) (the study did not include offenses for which perpetrator was charged as an adult, or offenses committed outside Los Angeles County).

227. Paul E. Tracy, Marvin E. Wolfgang, and Robert M. Figlio, *Delinquency Careers in Two Birth Cohorts* (New York: Plenum, 1990). Studying Philadelphia males born in 1945 and 1958, the authors found that in the 1945 cohort, 6 percent of Philadelphia males perpetrated 52 percent of their birth cohort's delinquent acts, 71 percent of homicides, 73 percent of rapes, 82 percent of robberies, and 69 percent of aggravated assaults. For the 1958 birth cohort, violent crime rates increased substantially, but the disproportionate contribution of a violent subgroup did not. Among the 1958 group, 7.5 percent perpetrated 61 percent of all delinquent offenses, 61 percent of homicides, 75 percent of rapes, 73 percent of robberies, and 65 percent of aggravated assaults. Ibid., pp. 279–80. Further research regarding the 1945 birth cohort's adult lives found that 45.2 percent of the juvenile chronic offenders became adult chronic offenders, and that, holding race and socio-economic status constant, juvenile delinquency was the best predictor of adult criminality. Wolfgang, Thornberry, and Figlio, *From Boy to Man*, p. 33. See also Office of Juvenile Justice and Delinquency Prevention, *Comprehensive Strategy*, pp. 34–35, 196 (citing various studies).

228. For an effort to develop a model that identifies which juvenile offenders are most likely to be part of the chronic offender group, and thus merit closer supervision, see Christy A. Visher, Pamela K. Lattimore, and Richard L. Linster, "Predicting the Recidivism of Serious Youthful Offenders Using Survival Models," *Criminology* 29, no. 3 (1991): 329.

229. A "legislative waiver" is a statutory listing of certain offenses for which waiver is automatic. Legislative waivers have traditionally applied only to homicides, but have been expanded in recent years to cover rape, robbery, and other felonies. Another type of waiver is "direct filing" or "concurrent jurisdiction." Under this type, the prosecutor may decide (subject to limits based on the type of crime and the age of the defendant) whether to file in juvenile or adult court. See generally, Melissa Sickmund, *How Juveniles Get to Criminal Court* (Washington, D.C.: Office of Juvenile Justice and Delinquency Prevention, Department of Justice, 1994).

230. Office of Juvenile Justice and Delinquency Prevention, *Comprehensive Strategy for Serious, Violent, and Chronic Juvenile Offenders,* NCJ 143453 (Washington, D.C.: Department of Justice, Office of Juvenile Justice and Delinquency Prevention, 2d printing 1994), p. 5.

231. Ibid.

232. Mandatory probation revocation for any type of probation violation is another idea that sounds better on the floor of the legislature than in practice. Revoking probation for perpetrating a violent crime is obviously a good idea. Automatically revoking probation for what is termed a "technical violation" (such as failing a drug test or not keeping a job) results in overincarceration of less dangerous offenders, and hence reduced incarceration of more dangerous offenders. Generally speaking, probation revocation should be based on the probation officer's analysis of the facts of the particular case. Altschuler and Armstrong, *Intensive Aftercare: An Assessment,* p. 70 (recommending that it is best "to regard technical violations of parole conditions as early warning signals rather than as grounds for revocation.")

Washington State now mandates that imprisonment not be used as a response to technical parole/probation violations; a sixty day jail term should be the maximum punishment. In addition, Washington now requires that parole/probation conditions be set based on the offender's particular offense and past behavior. For example, frequent drug testing would be appropriate for a drug addict who was convicted of burglary, but not for an embezzler with no record of substance abuse. Washington State Sentencing Guidelines Commission, *Preliminary Evaluation of Washington State's Sentencing Reform Act* (Olympia: Wash.: State Sentencing Guidelines Committee, 1983), discussed in Joan Petersilia and Susan Turner, National Institute of Justice, *Evaluating Intensive Supervision Probation/Parole: Results of a Nationwide Experiment* (NIJ Research in Brief) (Washington, D.C.: May 1993) (Rand Corp. study).

233. "Is Waiver to Adult Court the Best Response to Juvenile Crime?" *Juvenile Justice Update,* April/May 1995, p. 13

234. The sponsor of a law that lowered the waiver age in California from sixteen to fourteen years was moved by the case of a killer aged fifteen years, eleven months, who, without known motive, hacked a child to death with a meat cleaver. Because the murderer could not be prosecuted as an adult, he could be released from custody no later than his twenty-fifth birthday. Laura Mansnerus, "Treating Teen-Agers as Adults in Court: A Trend Born of Revulsion," *New York Times,* December 3, 1993, p. B–8.

235. R. B. Coates, "Appropriate Alternatives for the Violent Juvenile Offender," and D. Gadow and J. McKibbon, "Discipline and the Institutionalized Violent Delinquent," both in R. Mathias et al., eds., *Violent Juvenile Offenders: An Anthology* (San Francisco: National Council on Crime and Delinquency, 1984); V. L. Agee, *Treatment of the Violent Incorrigible Adolescent* (Lexington, Mass.: Heath and Company, 1979).

236. Office of Juvenile Justice and Delinquency Prevention, *Juvenile Court Statistics, 1992* (Washington, D.C.: OJJDP, 1994).

237. Wolfgang, Thornberry, and Figlio, *From Boy to Man,* p. 37 (Philadelphia birth cohort study); Rolf Loeber, "The Stability of Antisocial and Delinquent Child Behavior: A Review," *Child Development* 53, no. 6 (1982): 1437–39.

238. Wolfgang, Thornberry, and Figlio, *From Boy to Man,* pp. 65–67.

239. American Psychological Association, *Big World, Small Screen* (1992).

240. Massad Ayoob, *Gun Proof Your Children* (Concord, N.H.: Police Bookshelf, 1986), p. 5.

241. For a good summary of the literature, see Brandon Centerwall, "Television and Violence: The Scale of the Problem and Where to Go from Here," *JAMA* 267 (June 10, 1992): 3059–63.

242. Brandon Centerwall, "Exposure to Television as a Risk Factor for Violence," *American Journal of Epidemiology* 129 (April 1989): 643–52. Centerwall's study was limited to whites in South Africa and the United States.

For a critique suggesting that Centerwall's statistics are overstated, see Victor Strassburger, "Television and Adolescents: Sex, Drugs, Rock 'n' Roll," *Adolescent Medicine* 1, no. 1 (February 1990): 164–94. For a critique of the connection between television and violence, see Marjorie Heins, American Civil Liberties Union, "Media Violence and Free Speech," paper presented at International Conference on Violence in the Media, October 4, 1994, available on ACLU internet site.

243. M. S. Heller and S. Polsky, *Studies in Violence and Television* (New York: American Broadcasting Co., 1986), discussed in Centerwall, "Television and Violence," p. 3059.

In England in 1993, 2-year-old James Bulger was murdered by a pair of 11-year-olds. The last video rented by one murderer was *Child's Play 3*. In the film a baby doll comes alive and its face is splashed with blue paint. The murderers put blue paint on James Bulger's face. The film includes a kidnaping, and Bulger was abducted before being killed. The climax of the film shows two boys mutilating and killing the doll on a train. James Bulger was mutilated and bludgeoned, then left on a railroad track to be run over. "The Video that Caused Murder," *The New York Guardian,* December 1993, p. 3.

In France in 1993, a 17-year-old boy died from an explosion caused by a homemade bomb which he made in imitation of a technique shown on the detective show "MacGyver" (a series which, ironically, sanctimoniously promoted gun control). The year before in France, some boys accidentally set their school on fire, again in imitation of "MacGyver." Marlise Simons, "Blaming TV for Son's Death, Frenchwoman Sues." *New York Times*, August 30, 1993.

In Ohio in 1993, a 5-year-old boy who was watching "Beavis and Butthead" on MTV (a cartoon aimed at teenagers, not 5-year-olds) set a fire that killed his sister after watching a segment in which Beavis and Butthead said that it was fun to pay with matches. A few months before, three girls in Ohio imitated Beavis and Butthead's use of a match to ignite aerosol spray; the girls' fire damaged part of a house but caused no fatalities. "Cartoon on MTV Blamed for Fire," *New York Times*, October 10, 1993, p. 30. MTV moved "Beavis and Butthead" to a later viewing time, thus reducing the chance that young children, whose parents negligently fail to exercise control over television, will see the show. Senator Fritz Hollings (D-South Carolina) found the whole affair so outrageous that he denounced "Beaver and Buffcoat" at congressional hearings.

Some other cases of imitation: Nathan Martinez allegedly fatally shot his stepmother and half sister after watching *Natural Born Killers* six times. While singing "Singing in the Rain," a group of young men in Britain raped a woman, as in a scene from *A Clockwork Orange*. Claiming inspiration from *Magnum Force,* two hold-up men forced their victims to drink Drano, and then shot them, killing three. After seeing *Rambo: First Blood* twenty times, a man shot his former boss; at the trial, a psychologist testified "Rambo gives us permission to kill people," and the man was found not guilty by reason of insanity. Serial murderer Nathanial White said that he did "exactly what he saw in the movie" *Robocop.* After taking a girlfriend to see *Interview with the Vampire*, Donald Sterling stabbed her seven times and then sucked her blood. *Entertainment Weekly,* January 27, 1995.

244. George Brown Tindall and David Shi, *America: A Narrative History*, 3d ed. (New York: W. W. Norton, 1992), p. 1076.

245. Centerwall, "Television and Violence," p. 3061.

246. "The Power of 'Cowabunga,' " *Maclean's,* December 7, 1992, p. 50.

247. Thus, Japan is apparently able to ingest large doses of extremely violent entertainment because its family structures and social cohesion are very strong. Kopel, *Samurai,* p. 413.

248. Explained one former gangster:

You try to get out of the car like Warren Beatty did in *Bonnie and Clyde*. . . . It all becomes scenes from movies—you're doin' James Cagney and Edward G. Robinson, or any of the people you grew up watching as gangsters. . . . I know people who will hum music under their breath. . . .

Quoted in Léon Bing, *Do or Die* (New York: Harper Perennial, 1991), p. 245.

249. Heins, "Media Violence and Free Speech," and sources cited therein.

250. Elizabeth Jensen and Ellen Graham, "Stamping Out TV Violence: A Losing Fight," *Wall Street Journal,* October 26, 1993.

251. George Meredith, *An Essay on Comedy* (New York: Charles Scribner's Sons, 1897; first published 1877), p. 18, quoted in Twitchell, *Preposterous Violence,* p. 86.

252. Edward G. Salmon, "What Boys Read," *Fortnightly Review* 45 (February 1, 1886): 255–56, quoted in Twitchell, *Preposterous Violence,* p. 169.

253. Sir Thomas Chambers, "Comments on Popular Reading," *Boy's Own Paper,* September 5, 1885, p. 783, quoted in Twitchell, *Preposterous Violence,* p. 169.

254. Gershorn Legman, *Love and Death: A Study in Censorship* (New York: Hacker, 1963; first published 1949), p. 50, quoted in Twitchell, *Preposterous Violence,* p. 156.

255. Howard Kurtz, "Murder! Mayhem! Ratings!: Tabloid Sensationalism Is Thriving on Television News," *Washington Post,* July 4, 1993.

256. Twitchell, *Preposterous Violence,* p. 223.

257. Ibid., p. 232.

258. Geoffrey Handley-Taylor, *Nursery Rhyme Reform* (Manchester, England: True Aim Press, 1957), discussed in Twitchell, *Preposterous Violence,* pp. 233–34.

259. Catherine Kirkland, "Fairy Tales in the Age of Television: A Comparative Content Analysis," in Sari Thomas, ed., *Studies in Communication,* vol. 1 (Norwood, N.J.: Ablex Publishers, 1984), discussed in Twitchell, *Preposterous Violence,* p. 305 n. 7.

260. Marie-Louise von Frantz, *An Introduction to the Interpretation of Fairy Tales* (New York: Spring, 1970).

261. Twitchell, *Preposterous Violence,* p. 235.

262. Ibid., p. 262.

263. Virginia Postrel, "TV or Not TV?" *Reason,* August/September 1993, p. 4.

264. Barry Sanders, *A is for Ox: Violence, Electronic Media, and the Silencing of the Written Word* (New York: Pantheon, 1994).

265. Ibid., pp. 68–69. Although social science plays a role in Sanders's book, a very large amount of the text is devoted to his interesting but unproven speculations. Sanders's discussion of guns is limited by the fact that most of what he knows about guns appears to have been learned from the *New York Times* and from *Wall Street Journal* reporter Erik Larson. Sanders is in the same position as someone whose knowledge about Wicca and the New Age Movement has been culled from Religious Right fundraising letters.

Sanders also puts too much emphasis on attacking the electronic screen as a medium; his complaints about the visual qualities of computer screens overshadow an essential difference between computing and watching television: with the computer, the user is active, and the process is interactive.

As part of the denouncement of the computer, Sanders suggests that writing with a word processor is not really writing. Similar complaints were offered (and ignored) when writers switched from Spencerian script to typewriters.

266. Bob Dart, "War against TV Violence," *Denver Post,* December 5, 1992, p. 1 (Cox News Service).

267. Centerwall, "Television and Violence," citing N. Signorielli, L. Gross, and M. Morgan, "Violence in Television Programs: Ten Years Later," in D. Pearl, L. Bouthilet, and J.

Lazar, eds., *Television and Behavior: Ten Years of Scientific Progress and Implications for the Eighties* (Rockville, Md.: National Institute for Mental Health, 1982), pp. 158–73; G. Gerbner et al., *The Violence Profile: Enduring Patterns* (Philadelphia: University of Pennsylvania Annenberg School of Communications, 1989).

In 1993, the four major broadcast networks responded to criticism about violence by running warning announcements just before certain "adult" programs. Edmund L. Andrews, "4 Networks to Offer Warnings of Violence on TV," *New York Times*, June 30, 1993. The warnings will help adults avoid programs they find offensive, and will assist parents who closely monitor their children's viewing, but may accomplish little for poorly supervised or neglected children.

268. Twitchell, *Preposterous Violence,* p. 214.

269. Cultural Indicators Research Team, "Television Violence Profile," (Philadelphia: University of Pennsylvania Annenberg School of Communications, November 1993); "Prime-Time Violence," *Maclean's,* December 7, 1992, pp. 40, 41.

270. Some crime reenactment shows may help reduce crime; for example "America's Most Wanted" has led to the apprehension of numerous felons. "Networks Promise Lawmakers a Harder Line against Violence," *Washington Post,* May 23, 1993 (250 felons).

271. Charles S. Clark, "A Violent Reaction," *Rocky Mountain News* (Denver), June 19, 1993, p. 7C (reprint from *Congressional Quarterly*).

272. In the case of *American Booksellers Assoc.* v. *Hudnut,* 771 F.2d 323, 329–30 (7th Cir. 1985), *aff'd,* 475 U.S. 1001 (1986), the Seventh Circuit Court of Appeals explained that no degree of compelling evidence could overcome the command of the First Amendment:

> [W]e accept the premises of this legislation [against sexualized depictions of women as subordinate]. Depictions of subordination tend to perpetuate subordination. The subordinate status of women in turn leads to affront and lower pay at work, insult and injury at home, battery and rape on the streets. . . . Yet all is protected as speech, however insidious.

Ironically, some civil libertarians who embrace most strongly the courts' First Amendment protection of all free speech, no matter how strong the evidence that the speech causes harm, are willing to ignore the Second Amendment, because they believe that the ownership of guns is harmful. The appropriate response to both the censorship and the gun-control lobbies is to suggest that they seek to amend the Constitution rather than lawlessly ignore the parts with which they disagree.

273. For scholarship suggesting that media reports of suicide do not cause a statistically significant increase in suicide, see Heins, *Media Violence and Free Speech*, n. 33 and sources cited therein.

274. Jack Jones, *Let Me Take You Down: Inside the Mind of Mark David Chapman, the Man Who Killed John Lennon* (New York: Villard Books, 1993).

275. For further discussion of John Hinckley and the Bradys, see chapter 2.

It is true that media are not ultimately responsible for crimes; responsibility lies with the criminal who chooses to imitate the crime he sees on television. The media reports of crime are not intended to cause more crime. Similarly, criminals, and not gun manufacturers, are responsible for gun crime.

276. James A. Fox and Jack Levin, *Mass Murder: America's Growing Menace* (New York: Plenum Press, 1985). See also Clayton E. Cramer, "Ethical Problems of Mass Murder Coverage in the Mass Media," *Journal of Mass Media Ethics* 9 (1994): 26.

277. The assassin's name would not become a state secret. The media could simply choose not to use the assassin's name in stories. After college football bowl games began selling their names to the highest bidder (e.g., "the Federal Express Orange Bowl"), the *New York Times* announced that it would not use the corporate sponsors' names in bowl game stories; thus, a *New York Times* story will discuss "the Orange Bowl," and not "the Federal Express Orange Bowl."

278. Compare President Clinton's assertion that the NRA was excessively "fixated" on the Second Amendment because it opposed bans on so-called assault weapons. The White House, Office of the Press Secretary, "Remarks by the President in Discussion with National Service Volunteerism," March 1, 1993 (New Brunswick, N.J.).

279. Centerwall, "Television and Violence," pp. 3062–63.

280. "Congress Considers Block on Violent TV," *Washington Times,* May 13, 1993 (Associated Press); Edmund L. Andrews, "A Chip that Allows Parents to Censor TV Sex and Violence," *New York Times,* July 18, 1993, p. 13.

281. If, however, Senator Chafee (R-Rhode Island) were calling for the confiscation of all privately owned television sets, if some Washington lobbies insisted that no one needed their own television since they could always watch movies in public theaters, if other lobbies suggested that television viewing should be permissible only when the viewer was watching "legitimate sports," and if antitelevision ideologues claimed that the First Amendment freedom of the press granted no right to ordinary citizens, but instead protected government-sponsored speech from interference, then frightened television owners and manufacturers might resist any new government controls on television. The extremist attitude of many gun-control advocates toward the right to bear arms (insisting that handguns should be confiscated, or that only guns for "legitimate sports" should be permitted, or that the Second Amendment "right of the people" protects only guns owned by the government) poisons the dialogue about gun control, and is an important reason so many gunowners instinctively oppose all forms of control. See generally Don B. Kates, "Bigotry, Symbolism and Ideology in the Battle over Gun-Control," *Public Interest Law Review* 2 (Carolina Academic Press: 1992): 31–46.

282. "Tune Out, Kids," *Newsweek,* April 5, 1993, p. 57.

283. While enacting an "assault weapon" prohibition without a cinematic exemption would seem to pose no First Amendment problem, it is possible that repealing an existing exemption would violate the First Amendment, if the purpose of the repeal were to suppress the content of the kinds of movies in which "assault weapons" are used. See *R.A.V.* v. *City of St. Paul,* 112 S.Ct. 2538, 2543–44 (1992).

284. Alan J. Lizotte et al., "Patterns of Adolescent Firearms Ownership and Use," *Justice Quarterly* 11, no. 1 (1994): 51.

285. Richard W. Harding and Ann Blake, *Weapons Choice by Violent Officers in Western Australia: A Pilot Study,* Research Report no. 1 (Nedlands, Western Australia: Crime Research Centre, University of Western Australia, n.d.), pp. 16–17.

286. Harding and Blake, *Weapons Choice by Violent Officers in Western Australia,* pp. 20–21.

287. At least according to police interpretation of New York City's laws.

288. Commenting on a Maryland law that bans weapons at school in such a sweeping manner that hunter safety classes are felonies, Hap Baker Hampstead, of the Carroll County Sportsmen's Association, noted, "They're teaching them that knives are made for stabbing people and guns are made for shooting people, and what are they [students] doing? By golly, they're shooting and stabbing people." Janet Naylor, "School Rules Duel with Living History," *Washington Times,* February 17, 1994, p. C10.

289. Ill. Stat. Ann. chap. 38, § 87–2 (prohibition on possessing handgun without a license, with no exception for school sports).

290. Woody Anderson, "Aiming at a Scholarship," *Hartford Courant,* March 4, 1994, p. D–9.

291. "The October Almanac," *The Atlantic,* October 1988, p. 16.

292. National Athletic Trainers Association, cited in Stu Durando, "A Disaster Waiting to Happen?" *Las Vegas Sun,* January 22, 1995, p. 4D.

293. John Foley, *The Jefferson Cyclopedia* (New York: Russell and Russell, 1967), p. 318.

294. American Academy of Pediatrics and Center to Prevent Handgun Violence, "Keep Your Family Safe from Firearm Injury" (1994), p. 7.

295. Patricia A. Parker, "In the Heat of the Battle: Orlando Youths Gain Life Skills on a Battlefield," *Police,* March 1995, pp. 17–18.

296. For a catalogue of violence-prevention programs, see Imogne M. Montgomery et al., *What Works: Promising Interventions in Juvenile Justice,* NCJ 150858 (Washington, D.C.: Department of Justice, Office of Juvenile Justice and Delinquency Prevention, 1994).

297. Daniel W. Webster, "The Unconvincing Case for School-Based Conflict Resolution Programs," *Health Affairs* 12, no. 4 (1993): 126–41; Patricia S. Gainer, Daniel W. Webster, and Howard R. Champion, "A Youth Violence Prevention Program: Description and Preliminary Evaluation," *Archives of Surgery* 128, no. 3 (1993): 303 (compared to a control group, inner-city fifth and seventh graders who participated in a violence prevention program appeared to be less supportive of violent resolution of conflicts, according to written attitude tests; the study did not evaluate if actual long-term reductions in violence resulted). The degree to which student's reported attitudinal changes are actually changes, rather than efforts to please the adults who administer classroom attitude evaluations, has yet to be determined.

For an enthusiastic description of several conflict resolution programs, see William DeJong, *Preventing Interpersonal Violence Among Youth: An Introduction to School, Community, and Mass Media Strategies* (Washington, D.C.: National Inst. of Justice, November 1994).

298. For example, see Leihua Sylvester and Karin Frey, Committee for Children, "Summary of Second Step Pilot Studies" (available from Committee for Children, 2203 Airport Way South, Suite 500, Seattle, Wash., 98134, 206–343–1223) (program in western Washington for grades Pre-K through eight).

299. Severe child abuse increases the risk of future juvenile arrest by 53 percent, the risk of adult arrest by 38 percent, and the risk of perpetrating a violent crime by 38 percent. Cathy Spatz Widom, "The Cycle of Violence," *National Institute of Justice: Research in Brief,* NCJ 136607 (Washington, D.C.: Department of Justice, National Inst. of Justice, October 1992), p. 1; Cathy Spatz Widom, "Child Abuse, Neglect, and Violent Criminal Behavior," *Criminology* 27, no. 2 (1989): 251–71. Less intense abuse appears only to have a strong link with status offenses (activities such as buying liquor or carrying handguns, which are legal for adults but generally illegal for juveniles). Matthew T. Zingraff et al., "Child Maltreatment and Youthful Problem Behavior," *Criminology* 31, no. 2 (1993): 173. See generally David N. Sandberg, *The Child Abuse-Delinquency Connection* (Lexington, Mass.: Lexington Books, 1989).

Eighty-four percent of first-time juvenile offenders in Denver reported having been abused before age six. Ronald Henkoff, "Kids are Killing, Dying, Bleeding," *Fortune,* August 10, 1992, p. 68. It is likely, however, that a large number of the criminals who reported abuse were not in fact abused. The consensus of scholarly literature suggests that many, but far from all, juvenile delinquents were abused, that most abused children do not become delinquents, and that the interaction between abuse and delinquency is complex and needs further study. Kevin N. Wright and Karen S. Wright, *Family Life, Delinquency, and Crime: A Policy Maker's Guide—Research Summary,* NCJ 140517 (Washington, D.C.: Office of Juvenile Justice and Delinquency Prevention, Department of Justice, May 1994), pp. 15–17.

300. Jennifer L. White et al., "How Early Can We Tell?: Predictors of Childhood Conduct Disorder and Adolescent Delinquency," *Criminology* 28, no. 4 (1990): 507–33 (New Zealand birth cohort study; authors note that many children with behavioral problems did not become delinquents; accordingly, the "false positive" rate was too high for behavioral problems, as measured by the authors, to be a basis for intensive early intervention; authors suggest further study so that a more accurate predictive model can be refined); Joseph L. Sheline, Betty J. Skipper, and W. Eugene Broadhead, "Risk Factors for Violent Behavior in Elementary School Boys: Have You Hugged Your Child Today?" *American Journal of Public Health* 84, no. 4 (1994): 661, and sources cited therein.

301. Victoria Seitz and Sally Provence, "Caregiver-focused Models of Early Intervention," in Samuel J. Meisels and Jack P. Shonkoff, eds., *Handbook of Early Childhood Intervention* (Cambridge: Cambridge University Press, 1990), pp. 407–408.

302. Stanley Greenspan and Amy Cunningham, "The Kids Who Will Be Killers," *Washington Post,* July 26, 1993, p. C1; Shelley L. Smith, Mary Fairchild, and Scott Groginsky, *Early Childhood Care and Education: An Investment that Works* (Denver: National Conference of State Legislatures, 1995), p. 34.

303. Seitz and Provence, "Caregiver-focused Models," pp. 411–12 (Yale Child Welfare Program).

304. For a catalog of numerous family assistance programs, see Karole L. Kumpfer, *Strengthening America's Families: Promising Parenting Strategies for Delinquency Prevention,* NCJ 140781 (Washington, D.C.: Department of Justice, Office of Juvenile Justice and Delinquency Prevention, 1993).

305. Robert Halpern, "Community-based Early Intervention," in *Handbook,* pp. 474, 484–86.

Excessive, harsh discipline is not by itself a risk factor for turning children into criminals, but becomes one in conjunction with other parental problems such as antisocial orientation. Ronald L. Simons et al., "A Test of Various Perspectives on the Intergenerational Transmission of Domestic Violence," *Criminology* 33, no. 1 (1995): 141.

306. W. Steven Barnett and Colette M. Escobar, "Economic Costs and Benefits of Early Intervention," in *Handbook,* pp. 570–75.

307. James Bovard, *Truth or DARE: The Drug Program That Doesn't Work* (Golden, Colo.: Independence Institute, 1995). There are many well-intentioned, good police officers participating in DARE, but the data suggest that assigning those officers to any other task would be a better use of resources.

308. Mitchell Powell and Rita Giordano, "Parents Who Kill: Crime But Little Punishment," *New York Newsday,* January 8, 1992, p. 1. In 1993, twenty-five New York City children died of abuse, even though the city's Child Welfare Administration knew that homes were abusive. "Around the Nation," *Law Enforcement News,* February 28, 1995, p. 2.

309. See chapter 4.

310. Karl Zinsmeister, "Growing Up Scared," *The Atlantic,* June 1990.

311. Sue Anne Pressley and Keith Harrison, "A Crazed Fascination with Guns," *Washington Post,* February 2, 1992.

312. *Sable Communications* v. *F.C.C.,* 109 S.Ct. 2829 (1989) (unanimous opinion); *Butler* v. *Michigan,* 352 U.S. 380 (1957) (Justice Frankfurter).

313. Dr. Katherine Christoffel, American Academy of Pediatrics, testimony on "Children and Guns," House Select Committee on Children, Youth and Families, June 15, 1989, p. 40.

Dr. Christoffel's response to the practical difficulties of removing handguns from American society is to point to Japan's successful experience in disarming its population, as detailed in Noel Perrin's excellent book *Giving Up the Gun: Japan's Reversion to the Sword, 1543–1879* (Boston: David R. Godine, 1979). Several factors that were crucial to the Japanese disarmament are not present in the modern United States: the gun ban was implemented and enforced by a totalitarian government; people voluntarily surrendered their guns because the government successfully convinced them that the guns would be melted to build a giant temple to the Buddha (the melted guns were actually used to build a monument to the current dictator, Hidéyoshi); there was little gun ownership to begin with by anyone outside the military; guns had only existed in Japan for about half a century and had acquired little popularity outside of military use; there were no elements in Japanese culture with any affection for the symbolic value of firearms; and there was little violent crime, so ordinary persons had little need to consider individual protection. The contrast of all the above factors with the modern United States is stark. See generally Kopel, *Samurai,* chapter 2.

314. The majority of guns today are owned for recreation or for collecting, and thus are kept unloaded almost all the time. Gun ownership in the early American republic was more likely to be for self-protection or for hunting to put food on the table that night—both uses requiring a gun to be loaded almost constantly.

315. Duane B. Davis, *Homicide in American Fiction, 1798–1860* (Ithaca, N.Y.: Cornell University Press, 1957), p. 242 n.1.

316. Dr. Katherine Christoffel, American Academy of Pediatrics, testimony on "Children and Guns," House Select Committee on Children, Youth and Families, June 15, 1989.

317. While handgun wounds are usually survivable, especially if the victim gets medical attention quickly, shotgun blasts at close range are much more likely to be fatal. The shotgun fires a large slug, or from six to more than sixty pellets, with one trigger squeeze. A single shotgun pellet, because it may be of a diameter equal to a small handgun bullet, can inflict nearly as much damage as the latter. At short range, a shotgun is by far the deadliest weapon. Tony Lesce, *The Shotgun in Combat* (Boulder, Colo.: Paladin Press, 1984); Vincent J. M. DiMaio, *Gunshot Wounds: Practical Aspects of Firearms, Ballistics, and Forensic Techniques* (New York: Elsevier, 1985), pp. 182–83 ("At close range, the shotgun is the most formidable and destructive of all arms. . . . Unlike bullets, shotgun pellets rarely exit the body. Therefore, the kinetic energy of wounding in shoguns is usually equal to the striking energy . . . all the kinetic energy is transferred to the body as wounding effects."); Gary Ordog, "Wound Ballistics," in Gary J. Ordog, ed., *Management of Gunshot Wounds* (New York: Elsevier, 1988), p. 45 ("The wound created when the charge of a standard shotgun strikes a victim within a range of 6 meters is characterized by tissue destruction not unlike that caused by high-velocity missiles. Massive soft-tissue loss, bone and vessel disruption, and a high infection rate result"); R. Taylor, "Gunshot Wounds of the Abdomen," *Annals of Surgery* 177 (1973): 174–75 ("Shotgun injuries have not been compared with other bullet wounds of the abdomen as they are a thing apart . . . at close range, they are as deadly as a cannon").

318. Kleck, *Point Blank,* pp. 91-94.

319. James D. Wright and Peter H. Rossi, *Armed and Considered Dangerous: A Survey of Felons and Their Firearms* (Hawthorne, N.Y.: Aldine de Gruyter, 1986), p. 217.

320. AAP Committee on Adolescence, "Firearms and Adolescents," *AAP News,* January 1992, pp. 20–21.

321. Penny Roberts, "Playground Safety: Serious Business," *Dallas Morning News,* August 3, 1994, p. 18C (reprinted from *Chicago Tribune,* with data from U.S. Public Interest Research Group and the Consumer Federation of America).

322. A study of a 1992 gun buy-back in Seattle found that 1.8 percent of the guns had been reported stolen. Charles M. Callahan, Frederick P. Rivara, and Thomas D. Koepsell, "Money for Guns: Evaluation of the Seattle Gun Buy-Back Program," *Public Health Reports* 84, no. 4 (1994): 474. Because many gun owners do not report the theft of a gun, the actual number of stolen weapons may have been higher.

323. Ibid., p. 476.

324. Ibid., p. 474. Three percent of gun sellers said they would use the money to buy another gun, or would donate the proceeds to the NRA. Ibid., p. 475.

325. Ibid., p. 473.

326. Ibid., p. 476.

327. Ibid., p. 477.

328. Ted Bridis, "Teen-Intruder," Associated Press, July 21, 1994.

329. The exception apparently does not apply unless there is an actual intrusion, so leaving an older teenager in charge of the gun while the parents temporarily leave would still, inappropriately, be illegal.

The text of the federal law, as contained in the 1994 Crime Bill, is:

SEC. 110201. PROHIBITION OF THE POSSESSION OF A HANDGUN OR AMMUNITION BY, OR THE PRIVATE TRANSFER OF A HANDGUN OR AMMUNITION TO, A JUVENILE.
(a) OFFENSE.-Section 922 of title 18, United States Code, as amended by section 110103(a), is amended by adding at the end the following new subsection:
(x)(1) It shall be unlawful for a person to sell, deliver, or otherwise transfer to a person who the transferor knows or has reasonable cause to believe is a juvenile—

    (A) a handgun; or

    (B) ammunition that is suitable for use only in a handgun.

(2) It shall be unlawful for any person who is a juvenile to knowingly possess—

    (A) a handgun; or

    (B) ammunition that is suitable for use only in a handgun.

(3) This subsection does not apply to—

    (A) a temporary transfer of a handgun or ammunition to a juvenile or to the possession or use of a handgun or ammunition by a juvenile if the handgun and ammunition are possessed and used by the juvenile—

        (i) in the course of employment, in the course of ranching or farming related to activities at the residence of the juvenile (or on property used for ranching or farming at which the juvenile, with the permission of the property owner or lessee, is performing activities related to the operation of the farm or ranch), target practice, hunting, or a course of instruction in the safe and lawful use of a handgun;

        (ii) with the prior written consent of the juvenile's parent or guardian who is not prohibited by Federal, State, or local law from possessing a firearm, except—

            (I) during transportation by the juvenile of an unloaded handgun in a locked container directly from the place of transfer to a place at which an activity described in clause (i) is to take place and transportation by the juvenile of that handgun, unloaded and in a locked container, directly from the place at which such an activity took place to the transferor; or

            (II) with respect to ranching or farming activities as described in clause (i), a juvenile may possess and use a handgun or ammunition with the prior written approval of the juvenile's parent or legal guardian and at the direction of an adult who is not prohibited by Federal, State or local law from possessing a firearm;

        (iii) the juvenile has the prior written consent in the juvenile's possession at all times when a handgun is in the possession of the juvenile; and

        (iv) in accordance with State and local law;

    (B) a juvenile who is a member of the Armed Forces of the United States or the National Guard who possesses or is armed with a handgun in the line of duty;

    (C) a transfer by inheritance of title (but not possession) of a handgun or ammunition to a juvenile; or

    (D) the possession of a handgun or ammunition by a juvenile taken in defense of the juvenile or other persons against an intruder into the residence of the juvenile or a residence in which the juvenile is an invited guest.

(4) A handgun or ammunition, the possession of which is transferred to a juvenile in circumstances in which the transferor is not in violation of this subsection shall not be subject to permanent confiscation by the Government if its possession by the juvenile subsequently becomes unlawful because of the conduct of the juvenile, but shall be returned to the lawful owner when such handgun or ammunition is no longer required by the Government for the purposes of investigation or prosecution.

(5) For purposes of this subsection, the term 'juvenile' means a person who is less than 18 years of age.

(6)(A) In a prosecution of a violation of this subsection, the court shall require the presence of a juvenile defendant's parent or legal guardian at all proceedings.

    (B) The court may use the contempt power to enforce subparagraph (A).

    (C) The court may excuse attendance of a parent or legal guardian of a juvenile defendant at a proceeding in a prosecution of a violation of this subsection for good cause shown.

(b) PENALTIES.-Section 924(a) of title 18, United States Code, is amended-

(1) in paragraph (1) by striking "paragraph (2) or (3) of"; and

(2) by adding at the end the following new paragraph:
  (5)(A)(i) A juvenile who violates section 922(x) shall be fined under this title, imprisoned not more than 1 year, or both, except that a juvenile described in clause (ii) shall be sentenced to probation on appropriate conditions and shall not be incarcerated unless the juvenile fails to comply with a condition of probation.
  (ii) A juvenile is described in this clause if—
    (I) the offense of which the juvenile is charged is possession of a handgun or ammunition in violation of section 922(x)(2); and
    (II) the juvenile has not been convicted in any court of an offense (including an offense under section 922(x) or a similar State law, but not including any other offense consisting of conduct that if engaged in by an adult would not constitute an offense) or adjudicated as a juvenile delinquent for conduct that if engaged in by an adult would constitute an offense.
  (B) A person other than a juvenile who knowingly violates section 922(x)-
    (i) shall be fined under this title, imprisoned not more than 1 year, or both; and
    (ii) if the person sold, delivered, or otherwise transferred a handgun or ammunition to a juvenile knowing or having reasonable cause to know that the juvenile intended to carry or otherwise possess or discharge or otherwise use the handgun or ammunition in the commission of a crime of violence, shall be fined under this title, imprisoned not more than 10 years, or both.

330. *Tinker* v. *Des Moines School District,* 393 U.S. 503 (1969).

331. *New Jersey* v. *T.L.O.,* 105 S.Ct. 733 (1985).

332. *Goss* v. *Lopez,* 419 U.S. 565 (1975).

333. David M. Kennedy, "Can We Keep Guns Away from Kids?" working paper no. 94-05–12 (Cambridge, Mass.: John F. Kennedy School of Govt., 1994); David M. Kennedy, "Can We Keep Guns Away from Kids," *The American Prospect,* no. 18, Summer 1994): 74.

334. For an excellent description of how scouting programs have helped inner-city teenagers, see Mark Parenti, "Scouts 'n the Hood," *Policy Review* (Spring 1993): 62.

Even the much-maligned midnight basketball programs have their place. These programs have been linked with significant declines in juvenile crime in jurisdictions as diverse as Philadelphia, Phoenix, and Fort Myers. David Alan Coia, "Study Finds Parks Can Cut City Crime," *Washington Times,* June 9, 1994, p. C4. It is, however, totally inappropriate for the federal government to fund such local programs, and preposterous for Congress to attempt to write (as it did in the Clinton crime bill) detailed rules for eligibility in midnight basketball leagues.

335. *Newsweek* magazine's coverage of the children and guns issue is typical of how gun-control advocates may claim insistently that there is a national problem of children committing crimes with guns, although they produce no evidence for the claim. In a March 9, 1992, cover story, "Kids and Guns: A Report from America's Classroom Killing Grounds," the magazine claimed that "gun violence is on the rise in schools all over America," but provides no evidence except for a lurid discussion of particular incidents of violence at a few schools. For a detailed analysis of the *Newsweek* issue, see Lee Nisbet (Medaille College, Buffalo, New York), "How a Media Giant Covers Gun Violence in America's Public Schools," paper presented at the annual meeting of the American Society of Criminology, New Orleans, November 1992.

336. Ellen Graham, "Mainstream America Finds It Isn't Immune to Kids Killing Kids," *Wall Street Journal,* February 7, 1992, p. A1. The article detailed the plight of the mother of a New Jersey shooting victim who "has written to every state legislator seeking a sponsor" of a law to make adults criminally responsible for children's misuse of a gun. Consistent with the article's theme that suburban America was denying a gun problem existed, the article stated that the woman's push for parental liability was "shaping up as a lonely crusade." If the woman's crusade was "lonely," it was because New Jersey already had enacted such a law three weeks before the article appeared. Senator Richard Codey, "Letters to the Editor," *Wall Street Journal,* March 5, 1992.

337. How can medical research bodies, such as the CDC or *JAMA* produce such simplistic "guns are germs" reports, and congratulate themselves on applying "scientific" methods to controlling the "disease" of homicide? How can groups such as AAP make the gross factual errors detailed in this chapter?

What is presently occurring with medicine is a phenomenon typical of intellectual disciplines in the relatively early years of their growth. Today, it seems self-evident that the study of governmental institutions and political behavior is quite dissimilar from the working out of calculus problems. While a calculus equation (usually) has a single correct solution, which can be found through correct application of mathematical rules, politics is far too complex for rigid principles to always lead to a "correct" answer. Any competent calculus student can predict with certainty a future point on a calculus graph, but not even the most brilliant political scholar can predict with certainty the result of the next election.

At most colleges, the political behavior department is generally called the "Political Science Department." The phrase "political science" is a relic of the eighteenth-century Enlightenment, when thinkers such as the French physiocrats believed that all human behavior could be analyzed according to rational rules, and, once these rules were mastered, predicted with as much certainty as the motion of planets. Some scholars actually wrote a "political calculus" which claimed to mathematically quantify all political behavior.

In modern times, scholars of politics have outgrown their predecessors' conceit that the study of politics is a "science."

In the 1870s and 1880s, Harvard Law School Dean Christopher Columbus Langdell and the rest of the Harvard faculty announced the birth of "legal science." Under the premises of "legal science," every legal problem, like every physics problem, had a single, correct solution. (Or so it was thought in the days before quantum mechanics.) Using the "legal science" methodology, a judge need only find the correct rules of decision, apply them to the facts at hand, and reach the inevitable result.

By the early decades of the twentieth century, "legal science" had been largely discredited. While Langdell and his Harvard colleagues had claimed to have found a unitary body of case law which articulated the rules of legal science, the rules of decision actually amounted to a selective reading of Massachusetts, New York, and English cases, with the selectivity generally applied in ways that favored corporate power. Rather than being a single, coherent body of scientific truth, law is a highly complex and often conflicting set of rules of decision. While a Massachusetts court might decide a particular case one way, an Ohio court might decide a similar case the opposite way; the opinions of both courts could find ample support in legal precedent and principles.

While for the simplest legal questions there is a clearly correct answer (e.g., "Can a person not pay his state income taxes simply because he does not want to?"), the most important legal questions do not yield a single correct answer which can be scientifically discovered. That is why truly challenging legal questions—those decided by state supreme courts, federal courts of appeals, and the U.S. Supreme Court—so frequently result in concurring and dissenting opinions.

While the practice of medicine is older than the study of political behavior, the age of competent medicine—in which a physician was more likely to help than to harm a patient—is little more than a century old. The study of disease and of the human body has progressed quite far in the last hundred years, through the application of scientific methods. It should perhaps be understandable, then, given its rapid advances, that a relatively immature discipline such as medicine should fall easy prey to the conceit that its scientific methods can resolve the problems of violence which have thus far eluded the solutions of political scientists, criminologists, legal scholars, and philosophers. And physicians, being highly respected, find that their "scientific" statements on social policy are taken seriously and rarely skeptically analyzed by the media.

Thus, modern America witnesses the spectacle of groups such as Physicians for Social Responsibility, a group of doctors who have ventured outside their area of expertise to promote unilateral American disarmament as the best way to prevent the disease of nuclear war. The group's leader, Dr. Helen Caldicott, predicted in 1984 that nuclear war with the USSR was "a mathematical certainty" if Ronald Reagan were reelected.

Dr. Caldicott's scientific conclusions notwithstanding, the world survived Mr. Reagan's second term. With the threat of nuclear war receding, pacifists are turning their attention away from disarming the American government and toward disarming the American people. Like Physicians for Social Responsibility, which found no moral distinction between a nuclear weapon owned by the American government and one owned by a Communist dictatorship, domestic pacifists consider a firearm owned for protection to be as illegitimate as one used for crime. The pacifist elements of the medical community today promote the disarmament of law-abiding, mentally healthy Americans, wrapping their moral claim in the cloak of "science."

But their methods fall far short of scientific ideals. They make immense quantitative errors. And they unscientifically ignore the vast set of factors that influence human behavior, and instead attribute the problem of human violence to their *idée fixe*—the gun.

Workers in late nineteenth-century America were forced to deal with an intellectual regime of "legal science" which convinced itself (and much of America) that scientific principles proved that legal disputes between workers and employers should be resolved in favor of employers. Americans of the late twentieth century must deal with the "scientific" reality that guns are germs. Since ideas and discourse spread faster in this era than in the nineteenth century, perhaps medicine will outgrow its "scientific" social policy conceits faster than law did.

On the other hand, the CDC is an enormous funder of "public health" research on firearms, and has the financial clout to get the kind of research it wants. A random survey of scientists listed in the Dunhill International listing of scientists reported that, in regard to environmental issues, 68 percent believe that scientists "are under strong pressure to produce politically correct results." "Junk Science," *National Review,* October 24, 1994, p. 22. If medical science is vulnerable to the same pressures as environmental science, then America may be in for a long spell of "scientific" public health proof of the necessity for disarming the law-abiding American public.

338. U.S. Senate Committee on the Judiciary, "Federal Firearms Amendments of 1966," (Report together with Individual Views, to accompany S. 3767), 89th Congress, 2d session, p. 60 (individual views of Senator Kennedy et al.).

7

Conclusion

David B. Kopel

If gun control is not the answer to violent crime, what is? What about a better gun policy? I will begin by summarizing the findings of each chapter, and considering its implications for firearms policy.

WOMEN AND GUNS

Mary Zeiss Stange's chapter explored how women's arming for self-defense has divided much of the feminist community. In one camp, a group that might be called "victim feminists" asks the government to protect women from violence by increasing controls on, and perhaps eventually prohibiting, gun ownership, which is seen as a tool and a symbol of masculine power.

In contrast, "power feminists" are less inclined to rely on the government for protection, and are more interested in acquiring the ability to protect themselves. Professor Stange analyzes how both victim feminists and power feminists have dealt with the gun issues, and concludes that to own a firearm can be a legitimate feminist choice.

Stange puts her finger on an essential point that is frequently overlooked in the gun-control debate: many of the predatory criminals who terrorize women are not strangers, but rather abusive male relatives or acquaintances. Thus, when a woman is forced to use a firearm for protection, the assailant may well be an ex-

boyfriend or someone else the woman knows.[1] According to many gun prohibitionists, the woman's act of lawful self-defense is a "tragic domestic shooting"
that occurred "during an argument." One of Stange's most important contributions is to make the case that women have just as much right to defend themselves
against violent predators whom they know as against predatory strangers.

What policy implications can be drawn from Stange's chapter? Most obviously, the government should not impose special restrictions on female gun owners. Some antigun theoreticians have suggested that firearms advertising aimed at
women be banned by the Federal Communications Commission because it is
inherently deceptive. Unlike men, the theory goes, women are too naive to be
exposed to gun manufacturers' "misleading" claims that owning a firearm can be
part of a personal protection strategy. It seems odd that as the twentieth century
draws to a close, a cadre of supposedly progressive people thinks that women
must be protected from advertising that is commonly and uncontroversially
directed at men.

While women are just as capable as men of making up their own minds about
advertising, Stange's observations about women's self-defense do suggest that
the current legal paradigm of self-defense (a man attacked by a stranger) should
be updated to include the types of self-defense which women, statistically, are
more likely to encounter than men. In my previous book, *The Samurai, the
Mountie, and the Cowboy: Should America Adopt the Gun Controls of Other
Democracies?* I suggested that certain legal standards based on typical male self-
defense should not necessarily be applicable to certain cases of female self-
defense. For example, a person is often required to retreat, if he can do so safely,
rather than use deadly force in self-defense; the retreat rule makes sense in the
context of a barroom confrontation between two men. But it does not make sense
to require a woman to "retreat" from the home that she shares with an abusive
male, especially if leaving the home would mean abandoning children to the
man's abuse.[2]

Self-defense is, appropriately, judged by a standard of "reasonableness,"
based on the facts of the particular case. In recent years, the law has begun to recognize that a determination of the reasonableness of the self-defense actions of a
domestic violence victim must take into account not only the moments of a particular attack, but also the circumstances preceding it. For example, a law enacted in Utah in 1994 specifies that evidence of past abuse may be considered in
determining the reasonableness of the victim's use of force in self-defense.[3]

BACKGROUND CHECKS

In chapter 2, I examined the Brady Bill and other background check proposals.
Despite the vast amount of attention paid to the Brady Bill, it has had at best a
minor impact on violent crime, for the unsurprising reason that violent criminals

rarely purchase guns in gun stores; moreover, the Brady Bill can do nothing do stop criminals from buying handguns on the same black market that supplies drugs and other illegal commodities.

To the extent that background checks on people who purchase firearms in gun stores make a difference, the states using the "instant check" to verify a buyer's legal eligibility are stopping at least as many purchases as those using the Brady five-government-working-day waiting period. Sensibly, the Brady waiting period is scheduled to sunset into a national instant check by 1998.

While the instant check is preferable to the waiting period, both are inferior to driver's license coding, by which all driver's licenses would include a magnetic or other code indicating whether the person is eligible to purchase firearms. Driver's license coding avoids much of the expense associated with an instant check, in that an eligible person does not need to be reverified every time he or she buys an additional gun. Moreover, driver's license coding best avoids the intended cultural conditioning of the Brady Act, which is that gun ownership is not a right, but a privilege which may be exercised only after the government consents.

BLACKS AND GUNS

In chapter 3, legal historians Robert Cottrol and Ray Diamond detailed the racist history of gun control in the United States. Until recent decades, American gun control has been designed, sometimes explicitly, sometimes covertly, to prevent blacks from possessing firearms, while not interfering with white ownership. By disarming blacks, the government has made them more vulnerable to mob violence, and hence more easily controlled. Cottrol and Diamond remind us that as recently as the 1960s in the South, Americans of all races used firearms for precisely the purpose guaranteed by the Second Amendment: collective defense against state-sponsored violence (in this case, racist gangs such as the Ku Klux Klan operating with the approval of local law enforcement).

One lesson that can be inferred from chapter 3 is that new firearms laws should be carefully designed to be racially neutral.[4] It is true that today no legislator would copy the Mississippi Black Codes, and propose a law which directly forbade blacks to own firearms. But the class discrimination inherent in many restrictive gun laws has an obvious disparate impact on blacks. Laws that outlaw "cheap" handguns implicitly state that persons who can afford a $700 Colt pistol should be allowed to have a gun, but that those who can afford only a $65 Davis model should not. Likewise, gun licensing and registration statutes which require hundreds of dollars in fees from gun owners make lawful gun ownership almost impossible by poor people, the very ones who are least likely to receive adequate police protection.

"ASSAULT WEAPONS"

Next to the Brady Bill, "assault weapons" have been the most important item on the gun-control agenda over the last several years. After one examines in detail the physical characteristics of "assault weapons," it becomes apparent that "assault weapons" are not more powerful or more dangerous than other firearms. These guns are simply "cosmetically incorrect" because they have futuristic or military styling, and tend to be black rather than brown. "Assault weapons" are, contrary to the claims of gun prohibition lobbyists, rarely used in crime.

The underlying theory of "assault weapon" prohibition is that citizens may possess only "recreational" firearms, not guns that are suitable for resisting lone criminals, criminal gangs, or criminal governments.

The policy implication of chapter 4, of course, is that "assault weapon" prohibition is built on a factual and theoretical house of sand. Wherever "assault weapon" bans exist, they should be washed away.

DOCTORS AND GUNS

Don Kates, Henry Schaffer, George Murray, John Lattimer, and Edwin Cassem provide a thorough analysis in chapter 5 of the "public health" literature regarding gun control. Over the last decade, the theory that gun control is a public health issue has gained increasing prominence in the media. Kates et al. dissect the public health literature on gun control, and show it to be, in large part, shoddy. The case that severe gun control is a public health necessity can be maintained only by researchers who carefully avoid contrary evidence, or who misunderstand, misstate, and sometimes even fabricate the data that purportedly prove their argument.

There is no law forbidding gun prohibitionists to make claims that cannot withstand careful scrutiny. But there is no reason for the American public to be forced to spend tax dollars subsidizing fear-mongering masquerading as science. Therefore, the public should not be forced to continue to fund the factoid factory at the federal Centers for Disease Control and Prevention (CDC).

The CDC's tactics against gun owners resemble the federal bureaucratic campaign that led to the federal criminalization of marijuana in 1937. The federal "health" advocates of gun criminalization, like those advocating marijuana criminalization, paint lurid, ridiculous images of the evil object they want to ban, meanwhile ignoring the mountain of empirical evidence which contradicts their prohibitionist objective.[5] One reason that the federal Narcotics Bureau fomented national hysteria against marijuana users was that the bureau saw its appropriations and publicity being endangered by the popular Federal Bureau of Investigation.[6]

Without denying the sincerity of the gun prohibitionists at the CDC, we may say that bureaucratic mission creation is much in evidence. The CDC grew out of an agency that was assigned the job of malaria control during World War II. Although the agency had little success at reducing malaria, it managed during the 1940s and 1950s to turn concerns over national security into a charter for the CDC, which has been given authority over every communicable disease.[7]

Except for AIDS (and for temporary issues such as swine flu), communicable disease is not a major issue of American public concern these days. Thus, the CDC has restyled itself as the Centers for Disease Control *and Injury Prevention,* with a new-found mandate to study everything from bicycle accidents to firearms homicides to workplace safety. Not surprisingly, the CDC's gun research diverges from the findings of many social scientists that gun ownership by law-abiding, normal citizens does not endanger, and indeed may enhance, public safety. Rather, the CDC "finds" (through unscrupulous research and data manipulation) that ordinary gun owners are a tremendous "public health" threat. To deal with the public health danger of seventy million American gun owners, the bureaucratically obvious remedy is ever-increasing CDC funding.

Given the chicanery that characterizes so much of the public health propaganda on guns, American taxpayers should not be required to support it. And given the intense antigun sentiment of the CDC staff, there is no reason to expect that any type of reforms could make the agency fair in its judgment. Accordingly, the CDC's National Center for Injury Prevention and Control should be abolished. The federal government already provides generous funding for research on firearms-related topics through the National Institute of Justice (NIJ). Despite the efforts of the public health community to claim expertise in reducing firearms violence, an agency such as the CDC, whose original mission was malaria control, is not the best vehicle for doing research on the reduction of intentional criminal attacks.

As for the nonfirearms agenda of the Center for Injury Prevention and Control, it, too, is duplicative of other federal research. Reducing automobile injuries, for example, is the province of the Department of Transportation. Car fatalities are best studied by government agencies with expertise in cars and not by entities that specialize in germs.

Even if CDC manages to retain its Injury Prevention operation, it should at least be forced to behave according to ordinary standards of government research. NIJ requires that its grantees make their data sets available to other researchers. The CDC does not, but it should be required to. Making data sets available might result in the quick debunking of some of the antigun factoids created by data manipulation in CDC projects. And since the public pays for CDC research, the public ought to be able to examine the data.

CHILDREN AND GUNS

Chapter 6, which deals with children and guns, raises some of the most complex issues. The chapter first studies a relatively simple issue: gun accidents involving children. These have been declining over the last quarter-century, perhaps as a result of firearms safety education programs conducted by various groups, and perhaps also because of the replacement of more deadly long guns with less-lethal handguns as home-defense weapons. Various restrictive legal proposals to reduce childhood gun accidents are discussed, and shown to be ineffective.

From the declining number of gun accidents involving children, chapter 6 turns to the rising problem of intentional criminal misuse of firearms by juveniles. The carrying of guns at school is discussed, and the factoid that 135,000 teens bring a gun to school every day is exposed as a wild exaggeration. A discussion of school violence concludes that the most effective solutions are to set people free: to abolish mandatory attendance laws that keep some violent juvenile felons in school where they endanger others, and to allow students and parents greater school choice, so that they can attend schools that are well-run and orderly. Various authoritarian solutions, such as metal detectors, or "zero tolerance" of students who bring pocketknives to school, are rejected.

Contrary to popular impression, juveniles are not an increasingly large share of the violent criminal population. But they are a significant share, and since the violent crime rate is unacceptably high, a serious, nonhysterical search for juvenile justice solutions is appropriate. Black-on-black teenage male homicides in inner cities have skyrocketed, and are the most urgent juvenile crime problem. The drug economy, the easy availability of firearms, and the social collapse of the inner cities are all discussed as causes of the soaring urban minority homicide rate.

While gun control is unlikely to disarm juvenile criminals any more than drug prohibition has taken away their supplies of cocaine, numerous steps can be taken to reduce juvenile armed violent crime. Chapter 6 suggests a variety of ways to toughen the juvenile justice system without making it draconian or unnecessarily harsh. Ways to reduce media violence, which may incite crime in a small subset of adolescents, are also explored.

The most effective long-term solutions may be better education and socialization. Children need to learn about firearms from older, responsible authority figures, rather than from the streets and the movies. Violence reduction programs in the schools may prove useful, although their long-term benefits are as yet untested. Most importantly, much greater investments in early childhood intervention programs are necessary. Nurse visitation programs for young unwed mothers, and high-quality preschools for at-risk children have been proven to be effective. Expensive as these programs are, they more than pay for themselves in the long run. Is it too much to ask that there be a hundred preschools like the Perry Preschool (described in chapter 6) throughout the United States, with private or public funding? Few expenditures of tax or charitable dollars could be more important.

WHAT NEXT?

"Gun control," in the form of disarming noncriminal citizens, is no part of the solution to the crime problem, this book argues. Each of the preceding chapters discussed an issue that has been at the forefront of the gun control movement's agenda: the Brady Bill, "assault weapons"; gun control as "public health"; and exaggerated fears over various types of generally innocent gun owners, including women, urban blacks, and teenagers. Which of the various items on the gun control lobbies' agenda, when examined carefully, can really be expected to lead to a major reduction in armed violence? Like quack medical treatments that distract patients from looking for efficacious remedies, the gun control agenda is harmful because it takes so much energy away from better ways to reduce violence.

Chapter 6 sketched out several fronts of attack for the problem of juvenile crime. I will now discuss two additional approaches to combat violent crime, namely, prioritizing violent crime enforcement and addressing the problem of illegitimacy. These two approaches, like chapter 6's juvenile violence proposals, are intended to be suggestive rather than definitive. The authors of this book, collectively, know just about everything that any scholarly discipline has had to say about firearms. We certainly have no such collective expertise on the complex issues of juvenile delinquency, media violence, and early childhood intervention—or on the two approaches I will detail next. But having found that gun control—or at least the types of gun control that have dominated the public debate over the last decade—impede our search for violence reduction, we need to point out directions which might lead to better results. Any one of these directions might prove superior to "gun control" in reducing violence; at any rate, they could hardly be worse than what we have now.

PRIORITIZING VIOLENT CRIME ENFORCEMENT

One of the reasons that violent crime flourishes in the United States is that the capture, prosecution, and punishment of violent criminals is not a dominant priority among American law enforcement.

Whether drugs should be legal is a question separate from whether drug enforcement ought to take priority over violent crime enforcement. Without arguing for drug relegalization, I do want to point out that too many law enforcement resources are going into drug crimes at the expense of combating violent crime.

The FBI Uniform Crime Reports classify serious offenses against persons and their property as "Index I" offenses. From 1970 to 1984, on a national average, there were about four Index I arrests for every drug arrest. But with the intensification of the drug war in 1984, criminal justice resources shifted away from serious personal and property crimes and toward drug arrests. By 1989, there were only 2.2 Index I arrests for every drug arrest.[8]

In the courts, drug crimes now account for more felony convictions than violent crimes. In 1992, drug-trafficking offenses accounted for 19 percent of state felony convictions, drug possession offenses for another 12 percent of felonies, and violent offenses for only 18 percent.[9]

The emphasis on drug enforcement at the expense of violence enforcement is especially pronounced in prison sentencing. The number of adults imprisoned for drug offenses more than tripled from 1986 to 1991.[10] Between 1988 and 1993, the average drug sentence also more than tripled, from two years to seven years.[11] Forty-four percent of the state prison population increase from 1986 to 1991 was attributable to drug crimes.[12] In virtually every state, there has been a massive emphasis on imprisoning drug offenders. In Washington state, for example, the number of drug prisoners has risen 966 percent since 1980; they now comprise half of the state's nonviolent prisoners.[13] In New York State, 45 percent of all new prison commitments are for drug charges.[14] Illinois prisons now hold five times as many drug prisoners as they did five years ago.[15] The director of Florida's Department of Corrections described the drug war as "the primary engine fueling the enormous growth experienced by Florida's correctional system."[16]

The states with the largest per capita prison populations are also those with the highest percentages of drug prisoners: California (33 percent), New York (34 percent), Florida (34 percent), Ohio (25 percent), Illinois (28 percent), and Georgia (27 percent).[17] Nevada, the state with the highest percentage of drug prisoners (36 percent), also had the second largest increase in total prison population: 804 percent from 1970 to 1990.[18]

About 70 percent of federal prisoners are drug offenders, according to the Bureau of Prisons, up from 22 percent in 1981.[19] The current federal incarceration percentage for drugs is comparable to the combined figures for drug and alcohol offenses during Prohibition.[20]

Some of the imprisoned drug criminals are major traffickers or are nonspecialist career criminals who perpetrate both drug and violent crime. But many are not. Only 21 percent of drug prisoners sentenced in state systems in 1991 had even a single incident of criminal violence in their background.[21] In the federal system, 70 percent of drug prisoners have no record of violence, while 10 percent have a record of minor violence.[22] Half of all prisoners entering the federal system for drug crime are first-time offenders.[23]

A 1994 report from the Department of Justice, which contains the most detailed analysis conducted of the frequency of the imposition of severe terms on minor offenders in federal prisons, revealed the following: 21.2 percent of the total federal prison population, and 36.1 percent of all federal drug prisoners, are "low-level" drug offenders with no record of violence, whose offense did not involve sophisticated criminal activity, and with no record of serious prior offenses. These 16,316 small-time, nonviolent federal drug prisoners are serving an average of 5.75 years each, about 150 percent more than what they would have served under laws in effect prior to 1986. Of the low-level offenders, 42.3 percent were couriers or had other peripheral roles in the drug offense. They were much less likely to recidivate than the higher-level offenders, and the length of incarceration had no influence on likelihood of recidivism.[24]

Although the federal government has taken the lead in filling up prison space with nonviolent small fry, some states seem to be working to catch up. Richard Lanham, the commissioner of Maryland's Department of Corrections, estimates that "At least 40 percent of those coming into the Maryland prison system are there because of minor drug activity."[25]

In 1990, the number of persons sent to prison for drug crimes (103,800) exceeded that of people incarcerated for violent crimes (87,200) or for property crimes (102,400).[26] About a third of all new commitments to state prisons were for drug crimes.[27] As recently as 1960, only one in twenty-five state inmates was a drug prisoner.[28] If current trends continue, by the year 2000 half of all prison inmates will be drug war prisoners.[29]

Excessive incarceration of petty drug criminals means more violent criminals walking the streets. No matter how much money is spent on prison construction, prison capacity at any given point in time is finite; misallocating that finite resource is a tragically dangerous policy.

"The most extraordinarily violent criminal ever to set foot in Falls County, Texas," was how the district attorney described Kenneth McDuff. McDuff had murdered two teenage boys, then raped a girl and snapped her neck with a broomstick. Every law enforcement official who had encountered McDuff stated that he would kill again if given the opportunity.

Although Texas doubled its prison capacity in the 1980s, the state also quadrupled its incarceration of drug offenders.[30] To cope with space limitations, the Texas parole board lowered its standards for parole eligibility and set McDuff free. Three days later, the naked, strangled body of his first new victim was found. McDuff was apprehended a year later, charged with three murders, and put under investigation for six more.[31]

The McDuff story was repeated, on a less sensational scale, throughout the last several years in Texas. According to Texas A&M professor Morgan Reynolds, the "expected punishment" (average time served, discounted by the probability of conviction) for serious nondrug crime in Texas fell 43 percent in the 1980s. The average time served for violent offenders in Texas dropped from 28.4 months in 1985 to 24.2 months in 1991.[32] Not surprisingly, the Texas crime rate for these offenses rose 29 percent.[33] An Illinois study linked the huge increase in drug law enforcement in that state to a sharp increase in violent crime; one reason was that greater numbers of violent criminals were released from prison early to make room for the surge in drug offenders.[34] In the federal prison system between 1980 and 1990, average sentences imposed for rape, robbery, and kidnaping fell, while the average drug sentence increased sharply.[35]

Resetting Criminal Justice Priorities

Recognizing that drug enforcement consumes too large a fraction of criminal justice resources does not, I want to emphasize, imply that drugs must be relegalized. We should simply recognize that protecting people from violent attack should be the highest priority of the criminal justice system.

In the previous chapter, I suggested that 10 percent of drug war funds be redirected toward juvenile justice programs. Mandatory sentences for low-level drug offenders result in violent criminals being crowded out of prison; accordingly, those mandatory sentences should be repealed. All parts of the criminal justice system should readjust their spending priorities, so that violent crime control receives necessary resources.

Another reform to redirect crime policy should be to change the allocation of forfeiture proceeds. Current forfeiture laws allow government agencies to take a person's property without proving that the person used the property in a crime, or was guilty of any crime at all.[36] Since agencies often get to keep what they seize, forfeiture laws end up encouraging some agencies to engage in a form of legalized piracy. Changes made to the forfeiture laws in 1984 had a direct and immediate effect in setting too many local, state and federal agencies off on treasure hunts for forfeitable property, at the expense of enforcement of laws protecting persons and property from being attacked.[37] Under the 1984 federal law, a local agency can seize the property, in violation of state law, but consistent with federal law. A federal agency will then be called in to "adopt" the forfeiture, and receive a share of the booty. After being passed through the federal "adoption" process, much of the forfeiture proceeds are then returned to the state agency, notwithstanding the state or local agency's violation of state law.

Besides enacting reforms to protect the due process rights of innocent property owners, legislatures should remove the conflict of interest inherent in allowing agencies to generate revenue for themselves by taking property. All forfeiture proceeds should be turned over to the general fund, with proceeds allocated to crime reduction programs such as juvenile justice improvements (discussed in the previous chapter) and reduction of the illegitimate birth rate, which is discussed next.

ILLEGITIMACY

Almost everything that government does to rehabilitate criminals, including juveniles, involves a *post hoc* effort to do what the criminal's family failed to do. The collapse of the American family is not simply a tragedy for the children of broken and never-formed homes. It is an issue central to the problem of reducing violent crime.

Huge numbers of children are being deprived of two-parent families. Over 60 percent of all children will not live with both parents until age eighteen.[38] As few as 6 percent of black children born in 1980 will live with both parents until age eighteen, some researchers project.[39]

Nationally, the white illegitimacy rate rose from 2.3 percent of all births (in 1960) to 21.0 percent (in 1992). Among white high school dropouts, the illegitimacy rate is now 48 percent.[40] For blacks, the rate rose from 23.0 percent to 65.2 percent.[41] In ten major American cities in 1991, over half of all births were illegitimate.[42] In some urban neighborhoods, 80 percent of all births are illegitimate.[43] Unless current trends change, by 2010 over half of all children born in the United States will be born to unmarried women and thus be raised with no father.[44]

To some persons, these trends are meaningless, and should call forth no social response. According to former surgeon general Joycelyn Elders, if a woman wants to have a child without getting married, she should not be criticized simply for making a personal choice. Twenty percent of white teenagers, 30 percent of Hispanic teenagers, and 40 percent of black teenagers agree that unmarried parenthood is just another lifestyle choice.[45] It is not. It is too often a death style. A woman who makes the "personal" decision to have a child with no father dramatically increases virtually every risk of harm that the child will face, and the risk increases all the more if the woman is not employed but instead lives off public assistance.

I want to make several points clear: First, I do not accept the Candice Bergen/Murphy Brown retort to those who raise concerns about the collapse of the family. While working both to ensure that as many children as possible have the benefit of *two* parents and to reduce the illegitimacy rate, we can still acknowledge and honor the many families which for all sorts of reasons are missing one or both parents. These families deserve praise for the hard work they are doing, and for how often they overcome the odds against them. At the same time, helping every child to have the best odds in his or her favor must necessarily mean helping many more children grow up in two-parent homes.

In any case, "Murphy Brown," a highly educated, wealthy woman, is only slightly more representative of the typical single mother than Candice Bergen, the child of a famous movie star and ventriloquist, is herself typical of people who make long-distance phone calls. Women with annual incomes of $75,000 or more account for only 1 percent of illegitimate births.[46]

Let me stress that nothing in this chapter represents any attempt to roll back the social liberation movements of the last thirty years. It is very good that women have many more choices today than they did in the 1950s.

Another change to come along is the raising of some children by gay or lesbian couples. Technically speaking, if "Heather Has Two Mommies," then Heather is fatherless. However, none of my discussion of "fatherless" homes should be taken as also referring to those with two parents of the same sex. While same-sex marriages are controversial, all the data I present regarding pathologies of single-parent homes refer to just that: a home with only one parent. This book does not delve into issues regarding same-sex marriage, and nothing in this chapter should be construed as an argument against it. Notably, David Blankenhorn's book *Fatherless America,* which surveys sociological evidence regarding the damage resulting from the disintegration of the two-parent family, does not present any study which shows that two-parent, single-gender families have inferior outcomes compared to two-parent, two-gender families.

Illegitimacy and broken homes are associated with virtually every problem that a child can face. Children from single-parent families are from 40 to 75 percent more likely to repeat a grade in school, and 70 percent more likely to be expelled from school than children from a two-parent home. A study by the National Association of Elementary School Principals found that 30 percent of children from two-parent homes were high achievers, while only 17 percent of those from one-parent homes were. Conversely, 38 percent of single-parent children were low achievers, compared to 23 percent of two-parent children.[47]

Single-parent families usually are poorer, and poverty is, unsurprisingly, a separate factor related to all sorts of bad outcomes for children. The poverty rate for families headed by a single mother is seven times higher than that for two-parent households.[48]

Being raised in a single-parent family significantly increases the prospects that a girl will have a troubled family life when she grows up. A white woman who grows up in a single-parent family is 164 percent more likely to have an illegitimate child; 111 percent more likely to bear a child while she is still a teenager; and (if she eventually does marry) 92 percent more likely to get divorced.[49]

Girls from intact two-parent families are less likely to engage in early sexual intercourse.[50] A study of black teenagers in Chicago found that, holding other things equal, a girl from a two-parent family was 50 percent more likely to use a contraceptive during her first sexual encounter than a girl from a one-parent family. The odds of eventually becoming pregnant while still a teenager are 3.9 times greater for girls who do not use contraceptives for their first sexual experience.[51]

Illegitimate children, compared to those from two-parent homes, are 25 to 50 percent more likely to suffer from anxiety, depression, hyperactivity, or excessive dependence. They are twice as likely to engage in antisocial behavior.[52] They are two to three times more likely to need psychiatric care.[53]

Illegitimacy and Crime

The repeated commission of violent crimes by juveniles is rarely an isolated problem, but rather an indication of an intense antisocial orientation.[54] While most people from dysfunctional homes do not become criminals, most criminals come from dysfunctional homes. Chronic or serious juvenile delinquents tend to come from disorganized homes with little supervision.[55] Teenage mothers are more likely to have children with conduct disorders, not because all teenagers are inherently unfit to become mothers but because so many current teenage mothers suffer from "Antisocial Personality Disorder" (APD) and low socio-economic status, both of which are associated with serious child personality and behavior disorders.[56]

Early onset of juvenile delinquency (the best predictor of chronic, violent delinquency) is tied to early disruption of parent-child relations.[57] "Insecure attachment" by children to parents often predicts future social problems, including aggression, impulsiveness, poor social skills, and low self-control, all of which are associated with criminality.[58] Many children who display multiple anti-social behaviors progress from being discipline problems in school to chronic juvenile delinquents.[59] As noted in the previous chapter, chronic juvenile delinquency is the strongest predictor of adult criminality. Rehabilitation, once the severely troubled juvenile has become so dangerous that society needs to incarcerate him, is sometimes possible, but almost always difficult and expensive.[60]

A large majority of young violent criminals come from fatherless homes. A Detroit study found that about 70 percent of juvenile homicide perpetrators did not live with both parents.[61] Another study examined girls who were committed to the California Youth Authority (for serious juvenile delinquents); 93 percent came from non-intact homes.[62] Seventy percent of youths incarcerated in state reform institutions come from single-parent or no-parent homes.[63] A survey of juvenile delinquents in state custody in Wisconsin found that fewer than one-sixth came from intact families; over two-fifths were illegitimate.[64] Said one counselor in a juvenile detention facility in California, "You find a gang member who comes from a complete nuclear family, a kid who has never been exposed to any kind of abuse, I'd like to meet him . . . a *real* gangbanger who comes from a happy, balanced home, who's got a good opinion of himself. I don't think that kid exists" (original italics).[65] Sixty percent of rapists come from single-parent/no-parent homes.[66]

One of the most thorough recent studies, by M. Anne Hill and June O'Neill, of Baruch College, carefully held constant variables (such as poor maternal education) that are often associated with female-headed households. Holding other factors constant, for men "the father's absence is associated with a 4 percentage point increase in the probability of a jail sentence; and among black men this probability rises by 10 percentage points." The study found that young black males from single-parent families are twice as likely to engage in crime as young black males from two-parent families. If the single-parent family is in a neighborhood with a large number of other single-parent families, the odds of the young man becoming involved in crime are tripled.[67]

Other neighborhood studies report consistent results. One found that increased male unemployment was associated with a greater percentage of households headed by women. The increased number of female-headed households was in turn associated with higher murder and robbery rates, particularly among juveniles; increased adult violent crime was also statistically significant.[68]

The single best predictor of the violent crime level in a neighborhood is the percentage of one-parent families.[69] This finding is consistent with another study finding that on a neighborhood-by-neighborhood basis, a 1 percent increase in births to single mothers was linked to 1.7 percent higher crime.[70] A state-level analysis found nearly identical results: as the rate of single-parent homes rose, the juvenile crime rate rose even faster.[71]

While illegitimate babies may one day grow into criminals, why should a particular year's illegitimate birth rate in a neighborhood correlate with the crime rate in that neighborhood in the same year? The fatherless babies are obviously not escaping from their cribs to perpetrate robberies. One hypothesis is that marital disruption is an indicator of general instability and conflict in various types of adult relationships. The instability and conflict may reflect, or help cause, a higher rate of adult criminality, and also result in higher crime rates among unsupervised juveniles.

Exactly how illegitimacy leads to crime is not fully understood. Some researchers suggest that the absence of an adult male to teach boys how to be men leads to boys becoming overly aggressive to demonstrate their masculinity. Others say that without a provider mate, the single parent has to work more, and is unable to supervise the children appropriately. Still another theory is that abandonment damages the child's self-esteem.

Different studies, however, suggest that there may be no link between delinquency and broken homes.[72] For example, sociologist Roy Austin's study of national juvenile crime rates from 1971 to 1986 found no relationship between female headship of households (which was rapidly increasing) and the juvenile violent crime (which was not). Austin suggested that his findings, based on national data, might not be inconsistent with previous research finding a connection between female headship and juvenile crime in large cities.[73] Perhaps female headship only becomes associated with crime when a particular area reaches a "tipping point" of family disintegration.

Notably, Austin did not differentiate among the reasons that a household was female-headed. If the father was absent because of divorce, the effect might be different from that of a father being absent because he was killed in Vietnam; this in turn would differ from a situation in which the father never married the mother and refused to take any role in the child's life. Thus, Austin's findings about female headship do not necessarily negate other research finding a connection between illegitimacy (which is only one of several possible reasons for female headship) and crime.[74]

While, generally speaking, most people consider a two-parent family to be best, there are situations in which it is not. A household which has one parent because an abusive spouse was removed is better off. A good one-parent home is better than an abusive or dysfunctional two-parent home.[75]

In the last chapter, I discussed the crime-reductive benefits (among many others) of the Perry Preschool program, a high-quality, expensive program for poor black children. One of the followup studies of the Perry children found that, within the Perry group, illegitimacy was not associated with juvenile delinquency. While the study claims to be proof that there is, in general, no connection between illegitimacy and delinquency, what the study actually shows is that high-quality interventions are capable of breaking the chain that leads from illegitimacy to crime.[76]

Another study which is cited as proving the lack of relationship between illegitimacy and crime compared thirty black male felony prisoners who had grown up in religious homes with thirty black male noncriminals who had been raised in religious homes. The study did not find a difference between the two groups regarding how long the natural father was in the home. Both groups grew up in mostly intact families, which suggests the unsurprising conclusion that families with strong religious values are less likely to separate.[77] Like the study of the Perry Preschool children, the study of the highly religious families may simply show that there are intervening actions (such as strong attachment to religious values) that can break the link between illegitimacy and crime.

Social science research is often conflicting, but the weight of the evidence appears to suggest that two-parent families are better. A meta-analysis of fifty studies concluded that one-parent homes had a 10 to 15 percent higher delinquency rate than two-parent homes.[78] Criminologist James Q. Wilson reports that, contrary to his expectation, the scholarship that had been published as of 1982 did not confirm a link between juvenile delinquency and fatherlessness, but in the last decade, a large body of persuasive evidence has accumulated.[79]

Crime has often been thought of as a problem of race or poverty, since poor people and racial minorities comprise a larger portion of the violent criminal population than of the population as a whole. But in fact, the relationship between fatherlessness and crime is so strong that, once one considers household structure, race and poverty disappear as predictors of crime in a neighborhood. In other words, minority and poor neighborhoods are disproportionately involved in crime only to the extent that they are disproportionately fatherless.[80]

William Niskanen, chairman of the Cato Institute, notes that most of the typical variables that are sometimes said to determine the crime rate have not changed since 1960; thus, reliance on these variables fails to explain the huge surge in crime since 1960. Male unemployment, the poverty rate, and the percentage of church members have stayed approximately the same. Urbanization has increased slightly, but hardly enough to explain the crime surge. Since 1960, real personal income per capita has doubled, and so has the number of police per capita. "The one condition that has changed substantially," Niskanen writes, "is the percentage of births to single mothers, increasing from 5 percent in 1960 to 28 percent in 1991."[81]

There is also a second association between illegitimacy and crime: unwed fathers are more likely to commit crimes than are married fathers.[82]

Thus, illegitimacy creates concentric circles of victims. Illegitimate children are the first set of victims; the last set is persons murdered, robbed, and raped by some of these children when they grow older.

Three decades ago, a report by Daniel Patrick Moynihan for the Department of Labor noted with alarm the rising black illegitimacy rate. It has risen greatly since then, while the white rate is now as high as the black rate was in 1965, and is also on a long-term upward trend. The Moynihan report was denounced furiously as being the essence of political incorrectness, and Moynihan himself was condemned as a patriarchal racist misogynist. Other scholars stepped in to explain how Moynihan had gotten everything wrong; for example, if Moynihan's evidence showed that single-parent children had worse outcomes, it was only because the absence of the father reduced family income. The government, through a high-benefit welfare system, could easily make up for the loss of the father, since his importance was purely economic. The intensity of the reaction against the Moynihan report silenced for many years serious academic discussion of the harms of illegitimacy and fatherlessness.

But thirty years later, there are far fewer people who think that Moynihan was wrong. America has seen the consequences of a social policy that does not consider illegitimacy and broken homes to be a real problem, let alone a crisis. As the Moynihan report put it:

> From the wild Irish slums of the nineteenth century Eastern seaboard to the riot-torn suburbs of Los Angeles, there is one unmistakable lesson in American history: A community that allows a large number of young men to grow up in broken families, dominated by women, never acquiring any stable relationship to male authority, never acquiring any rational expectations about the future—that community asks for and gets chaos. . . . [In such a society] crime, violence, unrest, unrestrained lashing out at the whole social structure—these are not only to be expected, they are virtually inevitable.[83]

Having failed to heed Moynihan's warning, America is reaping the consequences of so many boys growing up without a father. Some parts of American cities have turned into a *Lord of the Flies* writ large. In this new Hobbesian world, teenagers go to each other's baby showers and funerals, but never to each other's weddings. The rising rate of homicides perpetrated by teenagers that has taken place in the last ten years is merely the foretaste of the bitter harvest that American society is beginning to reap as a result of the breakdown of the family, as illegitimacy continues its cancerous growth.[84]

A brochure from the Center to Prevent Handgun Violence (CPHV) almost perfectly sums up the misdirected attention of the gun prohibition organizations. "Every two hours someone's child is killed with a loaded gun," the brochure intones, with its pictures of young, happy children and warnings to be "extremely cautious about allowing children to participate in shooting activities." The brochure talks only about accidents and suicides, and ignores the fact that over half of the gun deaths of children (defined by the brochure as "under the age of 20") are homicides, many of them perpetrated by other "children." And the "children"[85] who are killing and being killed are, tragically, often not "someone's child." The very reason that these 19-year-old "children" joined gangs is that they were never anyone's child. They were abandoned by their father before they were born. And quite often, they were "raised" by a physically abusive, substance abusing, unsupportive, unemployed, illiterate mother or other surrogate. These children never had much of a real family.

At congressional hearings on juvenile violence, congressmen carefully refer to the "parents" of juvenile delinquents, although it is plain to everyone that gang members and other juvenile criminals almost never have "parents" because the father is usually absent, or indeed was never present after the the child was conceived.[86] David Blankenhorn, of the Institute for American Values, summarizes: "Put simply, we have too many boys with guns primarily because we have too few fathers. If we want fewer of the former, we must have more of the latter."[87] While Blankenhorn's message about the crisis of fatherless families has been well-received among conservatives, he points out that the traditional conservative response to crime—more prisons—is inadequate by itself: "[O]ur capacity to build new prisons is being far outstripped by our capacity to produce violent young men. We are generating male violence much faster than we can incarcerate it."[88]

Until we create a better world in which all children have real childhoods with real parents, then the killing will continue, whether or not gun prohibition groups succeed in wiping out sports programs, and whether or not conservatives funnel even more money into prison construction.

WELFARE, ILLEGITIMACY, AND CRIME

If fatherlessness is the essential problem, what is the solution? Blankenhorn offers a twelve-point plan based on jawboning, on putting forth a cultural message that fatherhood is important, and often essential, for the well-being of children.[89] This is a good start, and as we revalidate fatherhood, we should restigmatize illegitimacy (without stigmatizing illegitimate children, who are not at fault for the circumstances of their birth). Having a child out of wedlock is usually not a legitimate choice. True, there are exceptions; maybe "Murphy Brown" will be able to provide a good life for her child. But in the overwhelming majority of cases, choosing to conceive and bear a child without two parents is a harmful, and therefore an immoral, choice.

There is no single magic solution to reverse the cancerous growth of illegitimacy. But as a first step, the government ought to get out of the business of promoting and subsidizing it. Since "you get what you pay for," America has, through its welfare system, been paying for and getting more and more illegitimacy.

If we change the welfare system so that it no longer promotes illegitimacy, then we will have taken a step forward. Of course illegitimate births encouraged by the welfare system comprise far less than half of all illegitimate births, so reforming welfare is hardly a complete answer. But any reduction in illegitimacy, including reductions resulting from welfare reform, is an important first step; moreover, the illegitimate births promoted by the welfare system are often the ones which create the greatest risk to the child, since they are often associated with other factors—such as maternal unemployment, low maternal education, poor prenatal care even when it is free, and (obviously) poverty—all of which magnify the risk of bad outcomes for the child.

Just as not all female-headed households are the same, not all welfare recipients are the same. One large group of welfare recipients is the disabled and the elderly. While this group remains on welfare for long periods, few people object to welfare payments for those who are genuinely unable to work.

A second, large group of welfare recipients are those who use welfare precisely as it was intended: as a temporary safety net. *Thirty percent* of *the people who go on Aid to Families with Dependent Children (AFDC) go off it within two years.* Half have left within four years.[90]

One of the myths about welfare is that it is primarily a black problem. It is true that black women remain on welfare about twice as long as white women. But most of the difference is due to the age of the welfare recipient, the number of children she has, and her educational level.[91] The number of whites on AFDC is about the same as the number of blacks.[92]

Although the largest number of welfare clients are elderly, disabled, or short-termers, there is also a large fraction of the welfare population, of all races, which has the characteristics that many in the public associate with "welfare": long-term dependence on government payments. Overall, about 65 percent of the families receiving AFDC at any given point remain on welfare for more than eight years. More than education, work history, race, fecundity, or any other variable, the bearing of children outside of marriage is the trait most strongly associated with long-term AFDC dependence.[93]

Unfortunately, the welfare population is increasingly composed of the population group least likely to use welfare as a temporary safety net: unwed mothers. Among single women receiving welfare, the percentage who are never-married mothers rose from 21 percent in 1976 to 52 percent in 1992. Interestingly, the proportion of unwed teenage mothers on AFDC has stayed constant; women in their twenties have been the main source of the increasing numbers. Unwed mothers on AFDC are about twice as likely to have four or more children as other nonmarried women.[94]

During the New Deal, President Roosevelt's Secretary of Labor, Frances Perkins, argued against extending federal benefits to unwed mothers because she believed that subsidizing illegitimacy would lead to the breakdown of the family.[95] Ms. Perkins was right.

There is a correlation between the size of welfare benefits and the number of children born out of wedlock. This correlation does not exist because most potential welfare recipients think "I want more money to buy lottery tickets, so I'll have another baby to get welfare money." The reasons why the girls and women who compose the chronic welfare population choose to bear children have more to do with seeing childbearing as a way to cope with feelings of worthlessness and low self-esteem; having a baby may be the only thing she feels she can accomplish. (Many of these feelings of inadequacy can be traced to the absence of a father during the potential mother's childhood.[96]) Welfare does not "cause" the girl or woman to want to have a child, but it does facilitate her choice. The potential mother might also want to travel to Europe, but unless somebody gave her the money to do so, she could not. The knowledge that the welfare check will be available makes it more likely that the potential mother will choose to have and keep a baby, since she knows that the government will give her the money to set up a household for herself and the child.

There are several studies which found that welfare benefits have a major, direct impact on illegitimacy rates. A study by M. Anne Hill and June O'Neill of Baruch College found that a 50 percent increase in the value of food stamps and AFDC led to a 43 percent increase in the number of out-of-wedlock births. A 50 percent increase in AFDC and food stamp benefits also led to a 75 percent increase of the number of women enrolling in these programs, and a similarly large increase in the number of years spent on AFDC. This finding is consistent with a Canadian study, which showed that an increase of only $100 to $200 in annual welfare benefits increased by 5 percent the odds that a poor woman would become a single parent.[97] Another study offered evidence that a 3 percent increase in welfare benefits leads to a 1 percent increase in the number of women on welfare.[98] Researchers from the University of Washington found that a difference in welfare benefits of $228 per month per family more than doubled a white teenager's probability of bearing an illegitimate child.[99]

Roughly half the increase in black illegitimacy since the mid-1960s can be attributed to increased welfare benefits and easier eligibility standards.[100] These were also found to have led to higher illegitimacy rates by both black and white teenagers.[101] Welfare almost always implies fatherlessness; 89 percent of AFDC families have no father present.[102]

Besides promoting illegitimacy, welfare may also discourage marriage. A Cornell University researcher found that a 10 percent increase in AFDC benefits led to an 8 percent decrease in marriages by single mothers.[103] Discouraging marriage tends to perpetuate poverty, since marriage is one of the two major ways in which women move off welfare. (The other way is increased earnings; researchers disagree about which of the two is more important.)[104] As Christopher Jencks and Kathryn Edin point out, though, the number of men who have a stable enough work history to provide for a family, and who are not abusive, may be smaller than the number of women who want to bear children.[105]

Women from long-term welfare families are more likely to enter and remain on welfare than are socio-economically similar women not raised in welfare families.[106] Overall, about 20 percent of women raised in families that were "highly dependent" on welfare also become "highly dependent." Only 3 percent of women not raised on welfare become highly dependent.[107]

Skeptics of the connection between welfare and illegitimacy point out, correctly, that illegitimacy rates rose in the 1970s and 1980s, even though most jurisdictions did not raise maximum welfare benefits; maximum benefits generally rose more slowly than the rate of inflation, and were thereby lowered. Sociologist Charles Murray suggests that reducing welfare maximums may reduce the number of additional children whom women on welfare have; but the most important figure for whether a woman decides to go on welfare in the first place is the minimum benefit—a figure that has continued to rise, even as welfare maximums have been reduced.[108]

Even many of the researchers who are skeptical about claims that welfare is the primary cause of increasing female-headed households find that increased welfare benefits have at least a marginal impact.[109] More fundamentally, studies which find little or no effect from differences in AFDC benefit schedules tell us nothing about whether AFDC *per se* promotes illegitimacy. The fact that illegitimacy may not change much if welfare benefits are increased from $350 to $365 does not disprove the hypothesis that the availability of welfare (whether at $350, $365, or $950) plays a major role in promoting illegitimacy.

Certainly not all of the changes in work and marriage patterns among welfare recipients are due to welfare. William Julius Wilson observes that, with the decline of the manufacturing economy, the earning potential of poorly educated males, including many black males, has fallen significantly.[110] Taking steps to reduce welfare's role in preventing the formation of two-parent families does not preclude taking other steps (such as the massive jobs program advocated by Gary Kleck) to increase employment and wage levels in inner cities. The fact of the decline in low-skill, high-wage jobs is also the starting point for an argument in favor of helping working families whose earnings may leave them below the poverty line; such help could include relaxed standards for Medicaid or food stamp eligibility, although policy makers have found it difficult to assist the working poor without providing disincentives to work.

But the fact that work may not pay very well for most entry-level jobs does not justify having children without a father, or spending a lifetime living off income derived from other people's work. The absence of steady employment, and not low wages, is the main cause of poverty.[111]

Under a properly functioning welfare system, people on welfare would be provided with a special opportunity to lift themselves out of poverty. But one study using 1987 data found that only 18.3 percent of welfare recipients escaped poverty that year, while 45 percent of poor people who had never received welfare escaped poverty that same year.[112] In other words, welfare may make it more likely that the recipient will stay poor.

And what does all this have to do with crime? The Hill and O'Neill study concluded that a 50 percent increase in AFDC and food stamp benefits led, over time, to a 117 percent increase in crimes perpetrated by young black males, mainly as a result of increased illegitimacy.[113]

In some cases, welfare creates more poverty than it relieves. The waste of trillions of tax dollars is the least of the sins of welfare. By paying people to engage in destructive behaviors, welfare encourages poverty and unemployment; it harms the children who are brought into dysfunctional homes without fathers; and it impacts on society at large, from schools that are disrupted by uncontrollable children to crime victims who are violently attacked. From infants who die because of the unhealthy lifestyle choices of their teenage mothers, to adults murdered by gangsters raised by chronic welfare mothers, welfare can promote death.

The word "benefit" is derived from the Latin *bene facere,* meaning "to do well." The word *welfare* comes from the Old English *wel faran,* which means "to fare well."[114] Many recipients of "welfare benefits" are not provided with something that helps them "to do well" or "to fare well." On the contrary, "welfare benefits" pay women to bear children whom they will have difficulty raising properly.

TOWARD A REAL WELFARE SYSTEM

Welfare is broke, and there is no shortage of ideas about how to fix it. In chapter 6, visiting nurse programs for unwed mothers were detailed. These programs have a major impact in convincing unwed mothers to postpone bearing additional children. Interstitial reforms are good, but reconstruction is better.

Work Requirements

Welfare benefits for able-bodied people might be considered an extension of unemployment insurance, available for two years after unemployment benefits run out. People who were not workforce participants would be ineligible. (However, spouses and dependents of workforce participants would be eligible.)

Ending the government welfare program for able-bodied, never-employed recipients (and for able-bodied recipients who stay on welfare for more than two years) does not mean that these people will starve. On the contrary, persons removed from the government's counterproductive system will be helped by the genuine welfare systems run by churches and other charitable institutions. The government check is given anonymously with no sense of reciprocal obligation; in contrast, the charitable civic welfare system ties the donor much more closely to the donee. Donees understand that their benefits are coming out of someone else's pocket, and that they are expected to work toward lifting themselves up to self-sufficiency. Whereas the government system harms its long-term dependent recipient, the charitable welfare system assists donees, in part by helping them progress toward independence.

Opponents of major changes in the government system are wrong to wrap themselves in a mantle of self-righteous compassion. True compassion for the poor means giving them real "welfare benefits," something which private charities do provide, and which, in many cases, the government does not. Marvin Olasky's *Tragedy of American Compassion* provides a historical analysis of how governmental charity (with no strings attached) crowds out private charity which requires behavioral change on the part of the recipient.[115]

Job Training

Job training is only a minimal step toward welfare reform. Just as prisons are a *post hoc* solution to crime, so is job training a *post hoc* solution to welfare. It is true that for persons who are currently violent career criminals, prison may be the only alternative; likewise, for those who are currently long-term welfare dependents, job training may be the only answer.

But in the long term, it is more efficient, as well as more compassionate, to prevent people from becoming criminals or long-term welfare dependents in the first place.

It is virtually impossible to design a welfare system that, in the short run, provides economic incentives for people to leave welfare. Employees can, ultimately, not earn more than the economic benefit that they provide their employer. Most people getting off welfare are unlikely to add enough value to their employer to be able to command a wage that puts them much above the poverty line. Thus, the only way that work can pay much better than welfare is for welfare benefits to be slashed far below the poverty line, an unacceptable option that would harm the large numbers of welfare recipients using welfare as a reasonable safety net.

Job training programs can rarely make their clients ready for a first job that improves the standard of living much better than welfare. Thus, up to two-thirds of long-term welfare recipients quit their jobs within six months and return to welfare.[116] Given the fact that welfare pays about as well as a low-paying job (and sometimes better), the decision to quit work is not entirely irrational. The only real solution would be to make the person ineligible for welfare. Rather than trying to convince people to leave welfare voluntarily, the better solution is to make it clear that no able-bodied person can stay on welfare more than two years. After that, the person must get a job, even if the job pays less than welfare.

There are ways to tinker with the welfare/work transition, such as by allowing people who leave welfare to continue to be eligible for Medicaid. But it is simply not possible to design a humane welfare system that makes it significantly economically beneficial for most recipients to get off welfare and get a job.

Eligibility

Especially in terms of reducing the illegitimacy rate, getting people off welfare is less important than keeping them from going on it in the first place. Thus, the best "workfare" programs are those that require work *immediately* of welfare recipients, rather than allow a period of several months or even years of inactivity. These immediate work programs are effective both at discouraging able-bodied persons from going on welfare, and in encouraging welfare recipients to get off welfare as soon as possible. Because such programs significantly reduce the welfare caseload, it ought to be possible to fund such programs without increasing the total welfare budget.

Workfare is much more expensive for mothers with children under the age of five, since it must also provide day care for those children. Accordingly, workfare should be phased to apply first to all able-bodied recipients other than mothers of small children. To avoid promoting the bearing of children as a way to avoid workfare, a mother on welfare who has another baby should not be allowed to use the new child as an excuse to avoid workfare.

A pilot program in Ohio, in which recipients were required to work at least twenty hours a week performing community service, has had great success in using workfare to reduce welfare dependence. Unlike in most workfare programs, the work requirement was not something that lasted a few months and then expired; as long as the person was receiving welfare, work was mandatory. About 45 percent of single mothers placed in the mandatory work program soon left AFDC. For fathers in two-parent welfare families who were placed in work programs, about 42 percent soon left AFDC. These success rates are much higher than most other job-training or workfare programs.[117]

More to the point of reducing illegitimacy, a good welfare system should stipulate that women under eighteen may not receive welfare unless they are living at home with a parent or other guardian. Exceptions should be made for cases where the teenager has left the home because of abuse, or was living independently for at least a year before applying for welfare.

More radically, the government should simply stop taking on new welfare clients who are unmarried, never-employed, illegitimate mothers. The funds should be reprogrammed to group homes for unwed mothers and to adoption programs, discussed below.

Holding Men Accountable

A study of teenage pregnancies in Ohio found that the number of girls impregnated by adult men was ten times that impregnated by teenagers.[118] In inner cities, many of the pregnant 14- or 16-year-old girls were impregnated by men aged twenty-five or more. In such exploitive circumstances, enforcing statutory rape laws is not a bad idea.

A common proposal for holding absent fathers accountable has been increased child support enforcement. Since the mid-1970s, all levels of government have put much more effort into enforcing child support. More can still be done.

Tracking down nonsupportive fathers of welfare children is not, however, always a cost-effective exercise. About half of young men in some inner cities have not worked a single day in legal employment in a typical year.[119] Thus, if the father claims to be unable to find employment, the government must be ready to put him to work in community service, with his wages garnished for child support. Even if child support enforcement does not raise much money, it can still alter behavior. The more that word spreads that fathering an illegitimate child on welfare will result in an 18-year financial obligation, the fewer the young men who may be tempted to prove their masculinity by "fathering" progeny whom they have no intention to support. In the long run, even a small drop in illegitimate births will result in major governmental and social savings.

As with all the policy recommendations regarding illegitimacy, laws should be drawn so as to allow for appropriate exceptions. For example, if a woman has deliberately misled a man into believing that she was using birth control, he should not be held responsible for her pregnancy.

No AFDC Increases for Additional Births While on Welfare

One of the most successful experiments to reduce illegitimacy has been conducted in New Jersey. There, an experimental "Family Cap" program does not raise AFDC payments for women who have additional illegitimate children while on welfare. These children, however, still qualify the family for more food stamps, and all children remain eligible for Medicaid.

No other American family gets a raise when they have more children. It is a perverse policy to make the only family getting a monthly financial award for giving birth to more babies that very family that should not be having more children in the first place.

New Jersey's experiment was an immediate success. According to a report by the New Jersey state government, natality of welfare mothers subject to the family cap fell by nearly a third compared to a control group.[120] New Jersey lawmakers were happy about the immediate savings in welfare costs, but all New Jersey residents will be safer fifteen to twenty years from now, as there will be fewer hopeless young men born into families that could not raise them properly.

Private Welfare Options

A decent society should have a reliable safety net and a strong welfare system, not the current disastrous system. Not every good thing in a society, including good welfare, necessarily must come from the government. As Alexis de Tocqueville observed in *Democracy in America,* one of the great strengths of American civilization has been the large number of private, voluntary, civic organizations. As government in the last half century has usurped the role of these private charitable organizations, the bonds of civil society have weakened, and government has rarely performed charitable functions as well as those charities which the government supplanted.

The most important welfare reforms do not involve fine-tuning the government benefits system. Instead, welfare should eventually be removed from government control and placed in the hands of better welfare administrators, private charities. The National Center for Policy Analysis proposes that taxpayers be allowed to reallocate the fraction of their tax dollars currently being used by the government welfare system; taxpayers would be allowed to designate private welfare organizations (certified by the government) which could receive the funds instead.

One innovative program which taxpayers could choose to fund is the National Institute for Responsible Fatherhood and Family Development. This Cleveland program has had great success in working with fathers of illegitimate children to convince them to legitimate the child, to support the child financially, to complete their own education, and to work full-time.

Maternity homes are medium-term group residential homes for unwed mothers, which teach the mothers parenting skills, and also help them get their lives organized so that they do not become permanently dependent. These homes have had great success, and they too could flourish under a private-option welfare system.[121]

Among the most promising welfare alternatives is church adoption of people in need of welfare. Such a program is already in effect in Michigan. Each outreach recipient is assigned a church mentor who not only assesses the recipient's physical needs, but also helps the recipient set up a plan to progress toward self-sufficiency. Observes Loren Snippe, director of the welfare department in Ottawa County, Michigan, "Welfare systems can only treat the symptoms of need; they can give food and money, but they can never share the living skills and the values required to change lives. That is the role of the church."[122]

If we divide the number of new unwed mothers applying for welfare in a given year (about three hundred thousand[123]) by the number of churches, each church would need to take only one or two "adoptions" per year. Of course welfare clients are not equally distributed geographically, and many resource-poor inner city churches would be overwhelmed. Thus, there is a need to forge links between more affluent suburban churches and inner-city churches.[124]

Allowing church organizations that help the poor to be eligible for reprogrammed tax dollars would not violate the First Amendment separation of church and state. Many churches currently operate day care programs for poor children which receive government funding. Any nongovernmental welfare organization would, of course, have to use taxpayer dollars exclusively for welfare programs and not for unrelated activities.

Adoption

Any reasonable policy would encourage adoption as the best choice for women bearing children whom they lack the personal resources, including a stable marriage, to raise properly. Young unmarried women who choose adoption are, compared to peers who keep the child, more likely to complete high school, to be employed, not to live in poverty, not to end up on welfare, to marry eventually, and less likely to have a second illegitimate child. Yet only 6 percent of single teenage mothers, and only 1 percent of black single mothers, choose adoption. One reason for the low adoption rate is that 40 percent of pregnancy counselors never even mention adoption, let alone point out its numerous benefits, even when teenage mothers indicate that they are highly ambivalent about the child.[125] Longitudinal research shows that adoption can dramatically reduce the problems which illegitimate children suffer.[126]

In Philadelphia, a baby girl named Michaela Robinson was born addicted to cocaine; her mother had obtained no prenatal care during pregnancy. While undergoing cocaine withdrawal, baby Michaela stayed at Temple University Hospital. While the baby was undergoing drug treatment at the hospital, social workers found it difficult to contact the mother, whom they described as "unaccommodating." The mother had previously been under investigation for neglecting her other three children.

Rather than encouraging the mother to put baby Michaela up for adoption after the baby's months-long stay in the hospital, social workers *persuaded* the mother to take baby Michaela home. In subsequent months, the mother continued to refuse to cooperate with social workers who were trying to help the family. When social workers could see the baby, they found her to be very small, unclean, and neglected. After six months of life, baby Michaela died, the cause of death probably being crack smoke blown into her mouth in an attempt to pacify her. Her body was emaciated.[127] The current policy of discouraging adoption is grossly inhumane.

A pro-adoption policy should first of all remove artificial barriers to adoption. Every jurisdiction should, like Colorado, prohibit race from being used as a barrier to adoption.[128] If there are two equally qualified sets of parents, placing an orphan in a same-race home is reasonable, but keeping a child in an orphanage or foster home simply because some social workers believe that only black parents can raise a black child is outrageous.

In addition, tax credits should be offered for adoption expenses, including court costs. Given how much money adoptive parents save the government, by caring for children who would otherwise be, one way or another, supported by the state, help with adoption expenses is hardly too much for the government to offer parents.

Proposals for changing welfare eligibility rules are controversial and arouse determined political opposition, accompanied by the unfair charge that persons who want to change dramatically the current destructive system are "anti-child." Adoption, however, may be much less controversial. Other than the inertia of social service providers, there is no reason why a much larger number of unwed pregnant girls and women could not be offered a real choice of adoption. If the adoption rate for unwed mothers rose only 5 or 10 percent, more progress in reducing long-term crime would have been made than in all the tens of thousands of hours that legislators have wasted over the last decade debating gun control.

THE SEARCH FOR SOLUTIONS

If you do not think that the illegitimacy-reduction solutions which I have just proposed will work, then propose your own. Or help enact somebody else's proposals. Observes the Heritage Foundation's Patrick Fagan, "the real work of reducing violent crime is the work of rebuilding the family."[129] Unless trends in illegitimacy change drastically, a dystopian future of massive violent crime increases is inevitable, no matter what kinds of firearms laws are adopted. Conversely, as Travis Hirschi (a past president of the American Society of Criminology) and Michael R. Gottfredson put it, "Delaying pregnancy among unmarried girls would probably do more to affect long-term crime rates than all the criminal justice programs combined."[130]

Decentralization

Putting together everything in this book, one final policy recommendation stands above all the rest: decentralize. The Cato Institute's William Niskanen explains:

> The most important policy advice, given the surprising paucity of evidence about what works, is to *decentralize* decisions on the public safety system and on crime prevention programs. Our federal system provides a continuous natural policy experiment if the federal government stays out of the way. If you don't know where the fish are, cast the net broadly. If you don't know what works, don't do the same thing everywhere. Experiment with a variety of policies and be prepared to learn from the experiments in other jurisdictions. Most important, local government should experiment with different ways of deploying police and state governments with different types of sanctions for nonviolent crimes. Moreover, for those who still care, that approach would be more consistent with the letter and spirit of the Constitution. That is why the next step on crime should be to repeal the Violent Crime and Control and Law Enforcement Act of 1994.[131] (Original italics)

Americans could hardly do better than to heed the advice of America's greatest liberal jurist, Louis Brandeis, who in 1922 presciently warned reformers not to "believe that you can find a universal remedy for evil conditions or immoral practices." Rather than imposing rigid solutions from Washington, Americans should, Brandeis said, take advantage of the states as social laboratories with a variety of approaches, as we remember "that remedies are necessarily tentative; that, because of varying conditions, there must be constant inquiry into tactics . . . and much experimentation." And improving the lives of the poor means not just material improvement (as in the modern nostrums of higher welfare checks and fewer guns), but more importantly "the moral and spiritual development of those concerned."

Devolving crime and social policy from Washington makes sense on Constitutional as well as practical grounds. The Constitution specifically authorizes federal enforcement of only two types of laws, both of which involve uniquely federal concerns. The first authorized federal criminal power is based on the Congressional power "To provide for the Punishment of counterfeiting the Securities and current Coin of the United States." The second Congressional criminal authority is "To define and punish Piracies and Felonies committed on the high Seas, and Offences against the Law of Nations."

Besides the specifically granted criminal powers, Congress also has implicit criminal authority over other subjects for which Congress is granted power. For example, Congress may operate a post office and regulate interstate commerce. Thus, Congress may punish attacks on postal workers or may regulate interstate gun sales. But Congress has strayed from the Constitutional text by enacting laws which purport to control the simple possession of firearms by persons not traveling between states.[132]

Fidelity to the Constitution is consistent with common sense. On guns, crime, and many other issues, Congressional micromanagement lacks a solid intellectual base. Many congresspersons are enthusiastic about violence prevention programs for teenagers (and so am I). Yet we have virtually no data about which types of programs work.[133] We do not know with certainty the best ways to reduce illegitimacy, or to run a beneficial, nondestructive welfare system, or to reduce gun crime. State, local, and private experimentation should be encouraged, rather than constricted by federal mandate or steered by federal grants.

There are few domestic issues which genuinely require a uniform federal response. Although marijuana and cocaine are used in large quantities all over America, most other drugs, such as heroin, amphetamines, or PCP, tend to be localized in a few urban areas. This fact suggests that state and local governments should be free to devise their own drug strategies, rather than be shoved into a federal straitjacket.[134] Especially in light of the gigantic budget deficit, congressional control over local law enforcement, through law or federal grants, should be eliminated.

The more all forms of social and criminal law—including welfare, drug, and firearms laws—are under the control of people who pay for them directly (rather than contributing to the national debt, with future generations stuck with the bill), the more likely that sensible, effective policies will be implemented. When experimentation is paid for by state and local taxpayers, experiments that work are more likely to continue and those that fail, to be discarded. Conversely, imposing policy from Washington separates control from consequences, and tends to lead to laws which emphasize appearance rather than reality.

There are exceptions, to be sure. Under section five of the Fourteenth Amendment, Congress is given the power and duty to prevent state and local governments from abridging the Constitutional rights of United States citizens. Thus, Congress could Constitutionally overturn the complete handgun prohibitions that exist in a few cities, or restrict local forfeiture operations that are even more abusive than federal ones.[135]

But the number of cases where state and local governments will make worse decisions than Washington is relatively small. Left to themselves, the people of the fifty states would not have set up welfare systems that aggressively subsidize illegitimacy. Left to themselves, they succeeded in making their law enforcement agencies strike an appropriate balance between violent crime control and drug control, until a 1984 federal law allowed state and local agencies to cash in on forfeitures that violated state laws. It was no accident that the most illogical of all gun controls, the prohibition of cosmetically incorrect "assault weapons," achieved almost no success at the state level, but was imposed as a national policy by Washington.

As part of the devolution of power away from the place—Washington, D.C.— where social policy decisions are more likely to be made wrongly, all federal gun laws, starting with the National Firearms Act of 1934, should be repealed. The only laws retained should be those that deal with genuinely federal issues, such as gun imports, or gun use on federal lands, or interstate gun-running. Likewise, federal drug laws relating to nonfederal issues (such as simple possession) should be repealed.[136] This does not mean that all states should repeal their own antidrug laws, nor does it mean that states should not enact reasonable gun controls (such as setting the standards for gun dealer licensing). The point is that everything that the federal government is doing so badly these days—trying to run a national, uniform welfare system; a national, uniform crime policy, and a national, uniform gun policy—ought to be abandoned. State and local governments may do better. Common sense and our Constitution suggest that it is time to give them a chance.

NOTES

1. This is consistent with a study of homicides perpetrated by females in Detroit, which found that many involved defensive killings of male batterers. Ann Goetting, "Patterns of Homicide Among Women," *Journal of Interpersonal Violence* 3, no. 1 (1988): 3.

2. David B. Kopel, *The Samurai, the Mountie, and the Cowboy: Should America Adopt the Gun Controls of Other Democracies?* (Amherst, N.Y.: Prometheus Books, 1992), pp. 417, 437.

3. 1994 Utah Laws, chapter 26.

4. One author suggests that, given the racist history of gun control, courts should "use the same demanding standards when reviewing the constitutionality of a gun control law that they use with respect to a law that discriminates based on race." Clayton E. Cramer, "The Racist Roots of Gun Control," *Kansas Journal of Law and Public Policy* 30 (Winter 1995): 17.

5. David W. Rasmussen and Bruce L. Benson, *The Economic Anatomy of a Drug War* (Lanham, Md.: Rowman & Littlefield, 1994), p. 129 (discussing marijuana prohibition campaign).

6. Ibid., p. 129.

7. Elizabeth W. Etheridge, *Sentinel for Health: A History of the Centers for Disease Control* (Berkeley and Los Angeles: University of California Press, 1992).

8. Rasmussen and Benson, *The Economic Anatomy of a Drug War,* p. 119.

9. Patrick A. Langan and Helen A. Graziadei, *Felony Sentences in State Courts,* NCJ 151167 (Washington, D.C.: Dept. of Justice, Bureau of Justice Statistics, 1995), p. 1.

10. ABA Criminal Justice Section, Midwinter meeting, 1993; quoted in "Drug Cases Swamping CJ System," *Law Enforcement News,* February 28, 1993, p. 3.

11. "Reno Orders Review of Sentencing Rules for Low-Level Drug Offenders," *Justice Bulletin,* May 1993, p. 2.

12. Allen Beck et al., *Survey of State Prison Inmates, 1991,* NCJ-136949 (Washington, D.C.: Bureau of Justice Statistics, 1993), p. 4.

13. David Foster, "Prisons Feel Squeeze on Drugs, Crime," *Seattle Times,* April 12, 1993.

14. "Tough Sentencing for Low-Level Drug Felons." Ninety percent of New York drug offenders are sentenced under mandatory minimum laws. Correctional Association of New York, *Mandatory Sentencing Laws and Drug Offenders in New York State* (February 1993), cited in Campaign for an Effective Crime Policy, *Evaluating Mandatory Minimum Sentences* (Washington, D.C.: October 1993), p. 5.

15. Stephen Chapman, "Many a Draconian Sentence Just Doesn't Fit the Crime," (Colo. Springs) *Gazette-Telegraph,* March 23, 1993, p. B5 (syndicated from *Chicago Tribune*).

16. Harry K. Singletary, "State Corrections Approach to Treatment," in United States Sentencing Commission, *Drugs and Violence in America* (Washington, D.C.: U.S. Sentencing Commission, 1993), p. 226.

17. Assemblyman Daniel J. Feldman, "Behind Bars," *The New Democrat,* October 1992, p. 24

18. Ibid.

19. John Hanchette and Paul Barton, "Criminals Freed Early, Even as More Cells Being Built," *Courier-Post,* June 6, 1993, p. 6B.

20. Margaret Werner Cahalan, *Historical Corrections Statistics in the United States, 1850–1984,* NCJ-102529 (Washington, D.C.: Bureau of Justice Statistics, 1986), pp. 152-55; Bureau of Justice Statistics, *Drugs, Crime, and the Justice System,* NCJ-133652 (Washington, D.C.: Department of Justice, Bureau of Justice Statistics, 1992), p. 195.

21. Stuart Taylor, Jr., "How a Racist Drug War Swells Violent Crime," *American Lawyer,* April 1993, p. 31. The percentage with "violent" offenses would be higher if burglary were counted as violent crime. It should be noted, though, that the burglaries themselves may be the result of drug laws. One reason that cocaine and heroin addicts commit burglaries to feed their habits, while nicotine and alcohol addicts do not, is that the price of illegal drugs is artificially inflated by their illegality and the consequent risk premium charged by sellers.

22. William Booth, "Drug War Locks up Prisons," *Washington Post,* July 7, 1993, p. A14.

23. "Mandatory Minimums Undermine Sentencing Guidelines, Studies Show," *Justice Bulletin,* August 1993, p. 5.

24. United States Department of Justice, *An Analysis of Non-Violent Drug Offenders*

with Minimal Criminal Histories (Washington, D.C., February 4, 1994). Persons with no criminal history points (under U.S. Sentencing Commission guidelines) amounted to 12,727 low-level drug offenders, constituting 28.2 percent of federal drug prisoners and 16.6 percent of total federal prisoners. Ibid., pp. 2–3. The figures are based on the federal prison population as of June 1993.

25. Michael James, "Prison Boss Prefers Alternatives," *Baltimore Sun,* August 3, 1993, p. 2B.

26. Darrell K. Gilliard, *Prisoners in 1992* (Washington, D.C.: Department of Justice, Bureau of Justice Statistics, 1993), p. 10, appendix table 2.

27. Ibid., p. 10, appendix table 1 (32.1 percent). The figure is for new court commitments to state prisons, and thus does not include commitments for parole/probation violations.

28. "Kicking the Prison Habit," *Newsweek,* June 14, 1993.

29. Stephanie Mencimer, "Righting Sentences," *Washington Monthly,* April 1993, p. 28.

30. Carl Reynolds, "Texas Commission Proposes Corrections Overhaul," *Overcrowded Times,* April 1993, p. 16.

31. Mencimer, "Righting Sentences," p. 26.

32. Morgan Reynolds, *Crime in Texas,* report no. 102 (Dallas: National Center for Policy Analysis, 1991); Morgan Reynolds, *Why Does Crime Pay?* backgrounder no. 123 (Dallas: National Center for Policy Analysis, 1992).

33. Federal Bureau of Investigation, *Crime in the United States, 1980,* p. 57; Federal Bureau of Investigation, *Crime in the United States, 1989* (Washington, D.C.: Government Printing Office, 1990).

34. Bruce L. Benson and David W. Rasmussen, *Illinois' War on Drugs: Some Unintended Consequences,* Policy Study no. 48 (Chicago: Heartland Institute, 1992).

35. Bureau of Justice Statistics, *Federal Criminal Case Processing, 1989–90,* NCJ-136945 (Washington, D.C.: Department of Justice, Bureau of Justice Statistics, 1992), p. 17, Table 17.

36. Henry Hyde, *Forfeiting Our Property Rights* (Washington, D.C.: Cato Institute, 1995).

37. Rasmussen and Benson, *The Economic Anatomy of a Drug War,* pp. 135–39.

38. Karl Zinsmeister, "Growing Up Scared," *The Atlantic,* June 1990.

39. William J. Bennett, "Reflections on the Moynihan Report," *The American Enterprise,* January/February 1995, p. 31.

40. John C. Goodman, Gerald W. Reed, and Peter S. Ferrara, *Why Not Abolish the Welfare State?* Policy Report no. 187 (Dallas: National Center for Policy Analysis, 1994), p. 11.

41. National Center for Health Statistics, cited in William J. Bennett, *The Index of Leading Cultural Indicators,* vol. I (Washington, D.C.: Heritage Foundation, 1993), p. 10.

42. National Center for Policy Analysis, *Welfare Reform That Really Works* (Dallas: National Center for Policy Analysis, 1995).

43. Patrick Fagan, *The Real Root Cause of Violent Crime: The Breakdown of Marriage, Family and Community* (Washington, D.C.: Heritage Foundation, 1995), pp. 23–24, citing National Center for Health Statistics, *Vital Statistics of the United States 1990,* vol. 1: Natality, pp. 194–236, tables 185 and 186.

44. Patrick Fagan, *America's Fatherless Families* (Washington, D.C.: Heritage Foundation, 1994), p. 1.

45. Ibid., p. 3.

46. White women with a college education account for 4 percent of illegitimate births. Charles Murray, "The Coming White Underclass," *Wall Street Journal,* October 29, 1993.

47. Zinsmeister, "Growing Up Scared."

48. James Bock, "Study of Children Paints Mixed Picture," *Baltimore Sun,* February 2, 1994, p. 1B (discussing report from Maryland Kids Count Partnership: "A Baltimore toddler

who lives with only his mother is seven times as likely to be poor than a city child who lives with both parents"). Similar results were found in a 1989 Piton Foundation study of Denver.

49. Irwin Garfinkel and Sara S. McLanahan, *Single Mothers and their Children: A New American Dilemma* (Washington, D.C.: Urban Institute, 1986), pp. 30–31.

50. "Family Structure Predicts Substance Use and Early Sexual Intercourse," *Brown University Child Behavior and Development Letter* 6, no. 5 (May 1990): 2.

51. Dennis Hogan, Marie Astone, and Evelyn Kitagawa, "Social and Environmental Factors Influencing Contraceptive Use among Black Adolescents," *Family Planning Perspectives,* July/August 1985, pp. 165–69; discussed in Robert Rector, *Facts about Families, Poverty, and Welfare* (Washington, D.C.: Heritage Foundation, 1993) (hereinafter, Rector, *Facts*).

52. Deborah Dawson, *Family Structure and Children's Health: United States 1988, Data from the National Health Survey,* Series 10: No. 178 (Hyattsville, Md.: U.S. Department of Health and Human Services, Centers for Disease Control, National Center for Health Statistics, June 1991); discussed in Robert Rector, *Combating Family Disintegration, Crime, and Dependence: Welfare Reform and Beyond,* Backgrounder no. 983 (Washington, D.C.: Heritage Foundation, 1994) (hereinafter Rector, *Combating*).

53. Deborah A. Dawson, "Family Structure and Children's Health and Well-Being: Data from the 1988 National Health Interview Survey on Child Health," paper presented at the Annual Meeting of the Population Association of America, Toronto, May 1990, Table 5, discussed in Rector, *Combating*.

54. R. Bleich, "Toward an Effective Policy for Handling Dangerous Juvenile Offenders," in F. Hartman, ed., *From Children to Citizens,* vol. 2: *The Role of the Juvenile Court* (New York: Springer-Verlag, 1987).

55. David P. Farrington, "Parenting and Delinquency: Parent Training and Delinquency Prevention," *Today's Delinquent,* No. 5 (1986): 55 (Pittsburgh: National Center for Juvenile Justice).

56. Mary Anne G. Christ et al., "Serious Conduct Problems in the Children of Adolescent Mothers: Disentangling Confounded Correlations," *Journal of Consulting and Clinical Psychology* 58, no. 6 (1990): 840–44.

57. Rolf Loeber, "The Stability of Antisocial and Delinquent Child Behavior: A Review," *Child Development* 53, no. 6 (1982): 1431; Michael Rutter and Norman Garmezy, "Developmental Psychopathology," in E. Mavis Hetherington, ed., *Handbook of Child Psychology,* vol. 4: *Socialization, Personality, and Social Development* (New York: John Wiley & Sons, 1983), p. 775.

Incompetent parenting, like poverty, can in some studies be disaggregated, so that bad parenting (or poverty) becomes a more important variable than illegitimacy in predicting criminality. Similarly, one might compare premature deaths in a city (such as Dresden or Tokyo during World War Two) which was firebombed, to premature deaths in a city that had a normal number of accidental household fires. The variable "proximity to an uncontrolled fire coupled with absence of an escape route" would be a much better predictor of death than the variable "residence in a city that was firebombed" (since many people in the firebombed city would survive, while almost all persons—including those in the city that had only the accidental fires—who were trapped near an uncontrolled fire would die). Therefore, some commentators could argue, society should stop getting so worried about firebombing and instead work on policies that improve escape routes for all people.

The disaggregation, whether of firebombing or illegitimacy, masks the underlying truth: if Y (incompetent parenting or inescapable fires) is the proximate cause of death, then X (illegitimacy or firebombing) is still worth reducing if X creates an environment in which Y can flourish (since more illegitimacy means more parenting by less capable, less assisted mothers, and since more firebombing means more fires).

Reducing illegitimacy, which is equal in long-term destructive power to firebombing, does not prevent society from also working to make escape routes available for the victim children.

58. Rolf Loeber and Magda Stouthamer-Loeber, "Family Factors as Correlates and Predictors of Juvenile Conduct Problems and Delinquency," in Michael Tonry and Norval Morris, eds., *Crime and Justice: An Annual Review of Research*, vol. 7 (Chicago: University of Chicago Press, 1986); M. Ainsworth, "Attachment: Retrospect and Prospect," in C. Parkes and J. Stevenson-Hinde, eds., *The Place of Attachment in Human Behavior* (New York: Basic Books, 1982). See also G. R. Patterson, B. D. DeBaryshe, and E. Ramsey, "A Development Perspective on Antisocial Behavior," *American Psychologist* 44 (1989): 329.

Similarly, insecure attachment is associated with adolescent psychopathology. "Insecure Attachment Can Predict Psychopathology in Adolescents," *Brown University Child and Adolescent Behavior Letter* 10, no. 6 (June 1994): 4.

59. David P. Farrington, Rolf Loeber, and Welmoet B. Van Kammen, "Long-Term Criminal Outcomes of Hyperactivity-Impulsivity-Attention Deficit and Conduct Problems in Childhood," in Lee N. Robins and Michael Rutter, eds., *Straight and Devious Pathways from Childhood to Adulthood* (Cambridge: Cambridge University Press, 1991), p. 62 (study of lower-class English children); Loeber, "The Stability of Antisocial and Delinquent Child Behavior: A Review," p. 1431. Four-fifths of future criminals can be categorized as "antisocial" by age eleven; two-thirds of "antisocial" five-year-olds commit delinquent acts by age fifteen. Jennifer L. White et al., "How Nearly Can We Tell?: Predictors of Childhood Conduct Disorder and Adolescent Delinquency," *Criminology* 28, no. 4 (1990): 507–33.

60. David M. Altschuler and Troy L. Armstrong, *Intensive Aftercare for High-Risk Juveniles: An Assessment*, NCJ 144018 (Washington, D.C.: Department of Justice, Office of Juvenile Justice and Delinquency Prevention, 1994), pp. 67–68.

61. Ann Goetting, "Patterns of Homicide among Children," *Criminal Justice and Behavior* 16, no. 1 (1989): 63–80.

62. Jill Leslie Rosenbaum, "Family Dysfunction and Female Delinquency," *Crime and Delinquency* 35, no. 1 (1989): 31–44 (study of 240 committals during 1960s).

63. Allen J. Beck et al., *Survey of Youth in Custody 1987*, NCJ 113365 (Washington, D.C.: Department of Justice, Bureau of Justice Statistics, 1988), p. 2.

64. Fagan, *The Real Root Causes*, p. 26, citing Wisconsin Department of Health and Social Services, Division of Youth Services, *Family Status of Delinquents in Juvenile Correction Facilities in Wisconsin* (April 1994).

65. Quoted in Léon Bing, *Do or Die* (New York: Harper Perennial, 1991), pp. 14–15.

66. Nicholas Davidson, "Life without Father," *Policy Review* (Winter 1990): 41–42.

67. M. Anne Hill and June O'Neill, *Underclass Behaviors in the United States: Measurement and Analysis of Determinants*, City University of New York, Baruch College, Center for the Study of Business and Government (New York: Baruch College, August 1993) (Research funded by grant no. 88ASPE201A from the U.S. Dept. of Health and Human Services).

68. Robert J. Sampson, "Urban Black Violence: The Effect of Male Joblessness and Family Disruption," *American Journal of Sociology* 93, no. 2 (1987): 348. Despite the title of the first article, Sampson also found female-heading of households to be associated with increased violent crime among whites.

See also Ross L. Matsueda and Karen Heimer, "Race, Family Structure, and Delinquency: A Test of Differential Association in Social Control Theories," *American Sociological Review* 52, no. 6 (1987): 826 ("broken homes influence delinquency by impeding the transmission of antidelinquent definitions and increasing the transmission of prodelinquent patterns").

69. Paul J. McNulty, "Natural Born Killers: Preventing the Coming Explosion of Teenage Crime," *Policy Review* (Winter 1995).

Compare M. Denise Dowd, Jane F. Knapp, Laura S. Fitzmaurice, "Pediatric Firearms Injuries, Kansas City, 1992: A Population-Based Study," *Pediatrics* 94, no. 6 (1994): 868, which found that 63 percent of persons under the age of sixteen who were victims of firearms discharges lived in census tracts where the percentage of families living in poverty was approximately double the rate for the Kansas City as a whole. Since neighborhoods at the high end of the poverty scale are almost always at the high end of the illegitimacy scale, the Kansas City study may offer more evidence of the link between illegitimacy and violent armed crime.

Households headed by a single parent are about twice as likely to be victimized by violent crime as those headed by a married couple. Barbara Allen-Hagen and Melissa Sickmund, *Juveniles and Violence: Juvenile Offending and Victimization,* Fact Sheet #19 (Washington, D.C.: Department of Justice, Office of Juvenile Justice and Delinquency Prevention, 1994), p. 3, table 3.

70. William A. Niskanen, "Crime, Police, and Root Causes," Cato Institute Policy Analysis no. 218 (Washington, D.C.: Cato Institute, November 14, 1994), p. 15. Niskanen points out that, since illegitimate children are not crime perpetrators shortly after birth, the effect of illegitimacy appears to be "a proxy for more general patterns of social behavior." Ibid.

71. Patrick Fagan, *The Real Root Cause of Violent Crime: The Breakdown of Marriage, Family and Community* (Washington, D.C.: Heritage Foundation, 1995). The Fagan study is an excellent synthesis and summary of social science research regarding the connection between dysfunctional parenting and virtually every type of future social disorder.

72. Helene Raskin White, Robert J. Pandina, and Randy L. LaGrange, "Longitudinal Predictors of Serious Substance Use and Delinquency," *Criminology* 25, no. 3 (1987): 715; Lawrence Rosen and Kathleen Nielson, "Broken Homes and Delinquency," in Leonard Savitz and Norman Johnson, eds., *Contemporary Criminology* (New York: John Wiley and Sons, 1982).

73. Roy L. Austin, "Race, Female Headship, and Delinquency: A Longitudinal Analysis," *Justice Quarterly* 9, no. 4 (1992): 585–607.

74. Similarly, another study of black teenagers in various cities did not find a connection between family structure and delinquency, but did not distinguish why the family was female-headed. Phyllis Gray-Ray and Melvin C. Ray, "Juvenile Delinquency in the Black Community," *Youth and Society* 22, no. 1 (1990): 67.

75. Joan A. McCord, "Long-Term Perspectives on Parental Absence," in *Straight and Devious Pathways,* p. 1116.

76. Margaret Farnworth, "Family Structure, Family Attributes, and Delinquency in a Sample of Low-Income, Minority Males and Females," *Journal of Youth and Adolescence* 13, no. 4 (1984): 349.

77. Naida M. Parson and James K. Mikawa, "Incarceration and Nonincarceration of African-American Men Raised in Black Christian Churches," *Journal of Psychology* 125, no. 2 (1991): 163.

78. L. Edward Wells and Joseph H. Rankin, "Families and Delinquency: A Meta-Analysis of the Impact of Broken Homes," *Social Problems* 38, no. 1 (1991): 71.

79. James Q. Wilson, "The Family-Values Debate," *Commentary,* April 1993, p. 26.

80. Douglas Smith and G. Roger Jarjoura, "Social Structure and Criminal Victimization," *Journal of Research in Crime and Delinquency* 25, no. 1 (1988): 27–52.

81. Niskanen, "Crime, Police, and Root Causes," p. 16.

82. Robert Lerman, "Unwed Fathers: Who Are They?" *The American Enterprise,* September/October 1993, p. 33.

83. Daniel Patrick Moynihan, "The Negro Family: The Case for National Action," (Washington, D.C.: Govt. Printing Office; Dept. of Labor, Office of Policy Planning and Research, March 1965).

84. I recognize that illegitimacy may fluctuate up or down within a period of a few years. The long-term trend for all races is sharply up.

85. American Academy of Pediatrics and Center to Prevent Handgun Violence, "Keep Your Family Safe" (AAP, 1994). If we use the CPHV/AAP figure of "every two hours" for firearms deaths for "children" (all persons nineteen and under by the CPHV/AAP brochure's

usage), then there are about a dozen such deaths every day. About half of these would be homicides, since the Office of Juvenile Justice and Delinquency Prevention (OJJDP) reports that there are about seven youth (defined as by OJJDP as under eighteen) homicides per day. Including eighteen- and nineteen-year-olds (the CPHV/AAP "children") would of course raise the percentage of deaths among youth caused by firearms. As discussed in the previous chapter, most youth homicides are perpetrated with firearms and by other youth. Barbara Allen-Hagen and Melissa Sickmund, *Juveniles and Violence: Juvenile Offending and Victimization,* Fact Sheet #19 (Washington, D.C.: Office of Juvenile Justice and Delinquency Prevention, Department of Justice, 1994).

86. David Blankenhorn, *Fatherless America: Confronting Our Most Urgent Social Problem* (New York: Basic Books, 1995), p. 242.

87. Ibid., p. 31.

88. Ibid., p. 32.

89. Ibid., pp. 225–33.

90. U.S. House of Representatives, Committee on Ways and Means, *1994 Green Book* (Washington, D.C.: Government Printing Office, 1994, Table 10-42 and accompanying text).

91. Mark R. Rank, "Racial Differences in Length of Welfare Use," *Social Forces* 66, no. 4 (1988.): 1080 (Wisconsin data).

92. *1994 Green Book,* Table 10-44.

93. *1994 Green Book: Overview of Entitlement Programs* WMCP: 103–27 (Washington, D.C.: Government Printing Office, 1994); *1994 Green Book,* Tables 10-42, 10-44, and accompanying text.

94. General Accounting Office, *Families on Welfare: Sharp Rise in Never-Married Women Reflects Societal Trend,* GAO/HEHS-94-92 (May 31, 1994).

95. Jennifer Marshall, "Sanctioning Illegitimacy: Our National Character is at Stake" (Washington, D.C.: Family Research Council).

96. Blankenhorn, *Fatherless America,* pp. 45–48.

97. Hill and O'Neill, *Underclass Behaviors in the United States*; Douglas W. Allen, "Welfare and the Family: The Canadian Experience," *Journal of Labor Economics* 11 (1993): 201–23, discussed in Rector, *Combating.*

98. Anne E. Winkler, "The Incentive Effects of Medicaid on Women's Labor Supply," *Journal of Human Resources* 36 (1990), discussed in Rector, *Facts.*

99. Shelly Lundberg and Robert D. Plotnick, "Effects of State Welfare, Abortion and Family-Planning Policies on Premarital Childbearing among White Adolescents," *Family Planning Perspectives* 22 (1990): 246, 250.

100. C. R. Winegarden, "AFDC and Illegitimacy Ratios: A Vector-Auto Regressive Model," *Applied Economics,* No. 20 (March 1988): 1589–1601; discussed in Rector, *Facts.*

101. Robert D. Plotnick "Welfare and Out-of-Wedlock Childbearing: Evidence from the 1980's," *Journal of Marriage and the Family,* August 1990.

102. *1994 Green Book,* Table 10-27.

103. Robert Hutchins, "Welfare, Remarriage and Marital Search," *American Economic Review,* June 1989. See also Robert D. Plotnick, "The Effect of Social Policies on Teenage Pregnancy and Childbearing," *Families in Society* 74, no. 6 (1993): 326–27 (reviewing prior research and concluding that high welfare benefit levels discourage marriage). Lundberg and Plotnick, "Effects of State Welfare," p. 250 (a $228 increase in monthly welfare benefits nearly triples the probability that a pregnant white teenager will not marry).

104. *Green Book 1994,* Table 10-50 and accompanying text.

105. As Jencks and Edin also observe, staying in high school does not improve a woman's earning potential much, unless she is also motivated to learn something while in school; "not dropping out" is by itself insufficient. Jencks and Edin point out that the great divide on welfare between liberals and conservatives is whether poverty is worse than illegitimacy. Liberals think poverty worse, and will accept increased illegitimacy as the price of reducing poverty.

Conservatives think illegitimacy worse, and will accept increased poverty to reduce illegitimacy. Christopher Jencks and Kathryn Edin, "Do Poor Women Have a Right to Bear Children?" *The American Prospect* (Winter 1995): 43–52.

106. S. Kimenyi, "Rational Choice, Culture of Poverty and Intergenerational Transmission of Welfare Dependence," *Southern Economic Journal*, April 1991; in Rector, *Facts.*

107. Greg Duncan and Martha Hill, "Welfare Dependence within and across Generations," *Science*, January 29, 1988, pp. 466; *1994 Green Book*, Table 10-48 and accompanying text.

108. Charles Murray, "Welfare and the Family: The U.S. Experience," *Journal of Labor Economics* 11 (1993): 5224.

109. William Julius Wilson, *The Truly Disadvantaged: The Inner City, the Underclass, and Public Policy* (Chicago: University of Chicago Press, 1987), and researchers cited in discussion on pages 184–86.

110. Ibid.

111. Lawrence W. Mead, "Poverty: How Little We Know," *Social Service Review* 68, no. 3 (1994): 322. Wilson's response to Mead and like-minded critics is that even low-paying jobs are not available in the hyperghetto. Wilson, *The Truly Disadvantaged*, pp. 160–62.

112. Richard Vedder and Lowell Galloway, *The War on the Poor*, IPI Policy Report no. 117 (Lewisville, Tex.: Institute for Policy Innovation, June 1992), p. 23.

113. Hill and O'Neill, *Underclass Behaviors in the United States*, p. 14.

114. *The American Heritage Dictionary of the English Language* (Boston: Houghton Mifflin, 1981).

115. Marvin Olasky, *The Tragedy of American Compassion* (Washington, D.C.: Regnery, 1992).

116. Anthony Flint and Gloria Negri, "Clashing Blueprints Offered for Road from Welfare to Work," *Boston Globe*, May 15, 1994, p. 1.

117. Bradley R. Schiller and C. Nelson Brasher, "Effects of Workfare Saturation on AFDC Caseloads" *Contemporary Policy Issues* (1993), discussed in Robert Rector, "Welfare Reform, Dependency Reduction, and Labor Market Entry," *Journal of Labor Research* 14, no. 3 (1993): 291.

118. "Teens Having Babies with Adult Men More Often than with Peers," (Denver) *Rocky Mountain News*, February 22, 1995, p. 26A.

119. Zinsmeister, "Growing Up Scared."

120. In the ten months following the program's effective date (which was delayed so as not to penalize women who were pregnant when the law was enacted), 6.75 percent of unwed welfare mothers in a control group had additional children, compared, to 5.46 percent in the group subject to the family cap, meaning that the latter group at about a 19 percent lower natality rate. After adjusting for differences between the control group and the group subject to the cap (such as factoring in maternal educational levels), the state of New Jersey estimated that the cap cut natality by 29 percent. Robert Rector, "New Jersey Experiment Sharply Cuts Illegitimate Births among Welfare Mothers" (Washington, D.C.: Heritage Foundation, 1995)(available on CompuServe in Town Hall Forum).

121. George Liebmann, "Back to the Maternity Home," *The American Enterprise*, January/February 1995, pp. 49–55.

122. Virgil Gulker, Executive Director of Kids/Hope/USA (Spring Lake, Mich.), in Verne Barry et al., "What Will Happen to the Children: Who Will Step In When Welfare Is Abolished?" *Policy Review*, Winter 1995.

123. Marvin Olasky, "A Welfare Fantasy," *The American Enterprise*, January/February 1995, p. 43.

124. John M. Perkins, "What Will Happen to the Children?"

125. J. Musick, A. Handler, and K. Waddill, "Teens and Adoption: A Pregnancy Reso-

lution Alternative?" *Children Today* 13 (1984): 24–29; Gracie Hsu, "Adopting Adoption Reform" (Washington, D.C.: Family Research Council).

126. Barbara Maughan and Andrew Pickles, "Adopted and Illegitimate Children Growing Up," in *Straight and Devious Pathways,* pp. 36–61.

127. Zinsmeister, "Growing Up Scared."

128. 1994 Colo. Session Laws, chapter 127.

129. Fagan, *The Real Root Causes,* p. 31.

130. Michael R. Gottfredson and Travis Hirschi, "National Crime Control Policies," *Society* 32, no. 2 (January/February 1995): 36.

131. Niskanen, "Crime, Police, and Root Causes," p. 20.

132. For an excellent discussion of how Congress has used its authority over interstate commerce to delve into issues that are neither interstate nor commercial, see Glenn Harlan Reynolds, *Kids, Guns, and the Commerce Clause: Is the Court Ready for Constitutional Government?* Cato Institute Policy Analysis no. 216 (Washington, D.C.: Cato Inst., October 10, 1994).

133. Stu Cohen and Renée Wilson-Brewer, *Violence Prevention for Young Adolescents: The State of the Art of Program Evaluation,* Carnegie Council on Youth Development, Working Paper (Washington, D.C.: Carnegie Corp., 1991).

134. John G. Haaga and Peter Reuter, "The Limits of the Czar's Ukase: Drug Policy at the Local Level," *Yale Law and Policy Journal* 8 (1990): 36–74.

135. Under an aggressive Fourteenth Amendment enforcement policy, Congress could choose to roll back all local gun bans which outlaw firearms not prohibited by the federal government, or could choose to eliminate state firearm permit procedures that are more onerous than those in the Brady Act.

136. Daniel K. Benjamin and Roger Leroy Miller, *Undoing Drugs: Beyond Legalization* (New York: Basic Books, 1991).

List of Contributors

Edwin H. Cassem, M.D., who is also an ordained Catholic priest, has taught at Harvard Medical School (of which he is a graduate) since 1967 and is Chief of Psychiatry at Massachusetts General Hospital. He has taught and lectured all over the world, including visiting professorships at Stanford Medical Center, the University of Pennsylvania School of Medicine, the Mayo Clinic, Johns Hopkins Hospital, and Sloan-Kettering Cancer Center. Professor Cassem is an editor of the *Harvard Review of Psychiatry*.

Robert J. Cottrol is a Professor of Law at Rutgers University (Camden). Professor Cottrol earned an undergraduate degree and a doctoral degree in American Studies from Yale University, and a law degree from the Georgetown University Law Center. He is the editor of *Gun Control and the Constitution,* and the author of *The Afro-Yankees: Providence's Black Community in the Antebellum Era,* as well as numerous articles in legal and historical journals on race, constitutional law, and legal history.

Raymond T. Diamond is a Professor of Law at Tulane University. A scholar of antitrust law and of constitutional law, he has authored articles that have appeared in the *Tulane Law Review,* the *Vanderbilt Law Review,* the *Georgetown Law Journal,* the *Yale Law Journal,* and the *American Journal of Legal History,* among other publications. Professor Diamond is a graduate of Yale College and Yale Law School.

Don B. Kates, a San Francisco criminologist and constitutional lawyer, attended Reed College and Yale Law School, and has taught constitutional law, criminal law, and criminology courses at St. Louis University School of Law and Stanford University. He is the author of numerous law review and other scholarly articles on constitutional law, criminal law, and criminology, and he is the editor of several books and symposia on the law and criminology of firearms.

David B. Kopel is research director of the Independence Institute, a free-market think tank in Golden, Colorado, and is also an associate policy analyst with the Cato Institute in Washington, D.C. He graduated from the University of Michigan Law School and from Brown University. Mr. Kopel is the author of numerous scholarly articles and several books on crime policy and on environmental law, including *The Samurai, the Mountie and the Cowboy: Should America Adopt the Gun Controls of Other Democracies?* (Prometheus Books, 1992), which was named Book of the Year by the American Society of Criminology's Division of International Criminology.

John K. Lattimer, M.D., Professor Emeritus, Columbia Medical School, and an experienced battle surgeon, is an internationally renowned medical authority. He is the author of several books and several hundred scholarly and medical journal articles, including articles in the *Journal of the American Medical Association* and the *New England Journal of Medicine.*

George B. Murray, M.D., who is also an ordained Catholic priest, teaches at Harvard Medical School and is Chief of the Psychiatric Consultation Service, Massachusetts General Hospital. He has authored over fifty articles in medical and psychiatric journals, including articles in the *Journal of the American Medical Association* and the *New England Journal of Medicine.* Professor Murray is also a referee for the *New England Journal of Medicine.*

Henry E. Schaffer's doctorate is in Genetics and Statistics. He has been on the faculty at North Carolina State University since 1966, has also served as Associate Provost for Academic Computing, and is now Professor of Genetics and Biomathematics. He has also taught at Brandeis University, done post-doctoral study at Cornell University, and has been a Visiting Scholar in Computer Science at Duke University. He has published one book and numerous articles in genetics literature.

Mary Zeiss Stange is Director of the Women's Studies Program and Associate Professor of Religion and Women's Studies at Skidmore College, where she teaches and writes about feminist theory as it relates to a broad range of contemporary social and cultural issues. Her articles have appeared in such publications as the *Journal of the American Academy of Religion,* the *Journal of Feminist Studies and Religion, Women's Studies Quarterly,* and *Commonweal.*

Index

sault and homicide cases, 180; and saving police lives, 225; and self-defense, 176, 193–94; and semi-automatic weapons, 163; sporting use of, 193–94; summary of federal law on, 161; and threaded muzzles, 171; use of quotes around in this book, 218–19; Washington, D.C., lawsuits against manufacturers of, 226

"Assault weapons" bans: as achievement of the gun control lobby, 160; applied to the movie industry, 366; banned and "protected" classes in, 218; in California, 366; in Denver, 179; in New Jersey, 172; 1994 federal, 11; text of, 204–17

Assize of Arms of 1181, 128–29

Atlantic, The, 310

Atwood, Margaret, 15

Aurora, Colorado, and gun possession by minors, 375

Austin, Roy, on link between juvenile crime and female headship of families, 420

Austin, Texas, denial of right to buy a gun in, 82

Australia, 295; suicide and homicide rates in, 256 (table)

Austria, suicide and homicide rates in, 256 (table)

Authority, in gun debate, 13–14

Automobile theft. *See* Motor vehicle theft

Automatic weapons, 162. *See also* Assault rifles, Machine guns

Background checks, 53–126; analysis of by Treasury Department, 80, 119; Blose and Cook on, 86; and Bush administration, 86; cost of, in New Jersey, 79, 119; and court rulings, 55; Gary Kleck on, 294; and Hinckley assassination attempt, 59; in Illinois, 78; and *Law Enforcement Technology Magazine* read-

ers support for, 69, 70; in New Jersey, 79; and quality of criminal records, 92

Baker, Susan, critique of study of American homicides and suicides by, 255

"Ballistic Optimizing Shooting System," 221

Baltimore: "assault weapons" confiscated in, 179–80; background of teenage crime victims in, 350; homicides in, 389; and safe havens for school children, 333

Barondess. J. A., and background of murderers, 266

Barr, William, 94, 176

Bates, Daisy, 144

Bates, Edward, on black citizenship, 152

Bayonet mounts, and "assault weapons," 173

Bayonets, 222

BB guns, 181

"Beavis and Butthead," 396

Belgium, suicide and homicide rates in, 256 (table)

Bentsen, Sec. Lloyd, lobbying for "assault weapons" ban, 189

Beretta pistol, 170

Bergen, Candice, 417

Bermuda, and gun confiscation, 122

Bexar County, Texas, "assault weapons" confiscated in, 179–80

Bias, Len, 346

Biden, Sen. Joseph, and number of children carrying guns to school, 322

Bill of Rights, English, 129, 130

Bill of Rights, U.S.: framers intent behind, 201; and incorporation, 141; national enforcement of, 140–42; police attitude toward, 70; theory of, 128

"Billy Hook," 320

Bingham, Jonathan, 141

Birth of a Nation, The, 360

Black codes, 140–41

Black Panther Party for Self-Defense, 157